Also by Duane Elgin

Voluntary Simplicity

Awakening Earth

PROMISE

AHEAD

PROMISE AHEAD

A VISION OF HOPE
AND ACTION FOR
HUMANITY'S FUTURE

DUANE ELGIN

WILLIAM MORROW

An Imprint of HarperCollins*Publishers*

HarperCollins books may be purchased for educational, business, or sales promotional use. For information please write: Special Markets Department, HarperCollins Publishers Inc., 10 East 53rd Street, New York, NY 10022.

FIRST EDITION

Designed by Jam Design

Printed on acid-free paper

Library of Congress Cataloging-in-Publication Data

Elgin, Duane.
　　Promise ahead : a vision of hope and action for humanity's future / by Duane
　　Elgin.
　　　p. cm.
　　Includes bibliographical references (p.) and index.
　　ISBN 0-688-17191-5
　　1. Philosophical anthropology.　　2. Social evolution.　　I. Title.
　　BD450.E397 2000
　　128—dc21　　　　　　　　　　　　　　　　　　　　　　　　99-087191

00　01　02　03　04　　BP　　10　9　8　7　6　5　4　3　2　1

DEDICATED TO MY MOTHER AND FATHER,

MARY AND CLIFFORD ELGIN,

WITH LOVE AND APPRECIATION FOR

THE KINDNESS AND CREATIVITY

THEY DEMONSTRATED IN THEIR LIVES

CONTENTS

INTRODUCTION

—

by *Vicki Robin*

SOME books require no introduction. Within pages a good novel has you in the grip of its plot and characters. How-to books assume that you suffer from the complaint of the day and quickly lure you in with the promise of material salvation through their particular plan. Even many of the recent spate of spiritual books fit into this category. Contemporary nonfiction books, from the political to the prurient, require only that you have followed the news to draw you in.

All of these books, though, tell pretty much the same familiar story. We live short and unpredictable lives, struggling in a world that is often senseless and cruel. Islands of goodness, from romance to family to business success, can take the edge off this reality. So can the millions of consumer products touted from every television screen and billboard. The steady stream of scandals that greets us at the checkout counter of the supermarket week in and week out keeps us equally mesmerized. People who find themselves anchored in some haven of security may tithe a token of their time or money to ease the burden of "those less fortunate." But the story remains—poverty of every sort will always be with us. Politics—from family to national—is the art of making do.

Isn't this true? Isn't the very repetitiveness of this story, however dreary, somehow comforting? How many of us want to be disturbed by the kind of idealism that rises up in human groups from time to time, hinting that life itself might promise much, much more than thin thighs and fat wallets?

This book, *Promise Ahead,* invites you into that arena of grounded idealism, into the world of dreaming a new dream not just for your personal life, but for a multifaceted, rich and finely detailed unfolding story of our whole species. While this might not seem to matter to your day-to-day life, the promise of such a future can rearrange your personal world in quite remarkable ways.

Not too long ago, when John Lennon and the Beatles invited us to "imagine" a sweet, gracious, and peaceful world, we had the audacity to allow ourselves to dream. Now we have to wade through layers of distraction and demands to gain the ease that imagining requires. So let me invite you to briefly remove your twenty-first-century so-phistication and indulge in some very pleasant fantasies.

Imagine that your boss likes your work. Imagine that your responsibilities are such that you can truly clear your desk and close up shop at the end of the day. Imagine that your house is truly a home, a haven of peace, that your commute is short and that you've just paid off your last debt (yes, even your house and car). Imagine that your kids like each other/school/what you fix for dinner and get decent grades. Imag-ine you have enough time to follow the thread of their curiosity about why things are the way they are. Imagine that every day something happens that makes you smile. It could happen, admit it.

Imagine trusting the media and the government again.

The news informs. People care. Politicians are public servants and make a median wage. Imagine . . .

We've arrived, now, at a very special place. The world of possibility. The unknown. Out of the unknown will come everything of real value in your life, because the future is, in reality, unknown. Your children and grandchildren, your next jobs and eventual retirement, your vacations and new friends are all waiting for you—in the unknown. Imagination is like a steering wheel for this world of infinite possibility. If you start to shed the quiet despair about the possibility of your life and our collective life ever making sense again, you might just find yourself with childlike eagerness, peering expectantly into the unknown.

Entering the space of imagination will help you enter the magnificent world that Duane Elgin shares in *Promise Ahead*—not because it's a book of fantasy, but rather because it's a book based in years of research and contemplation about achingly beautiful possibilities embedded in hard reality. He surveys much of what's known about the universe and our place in it, then invites us to peer into the unknown with him and imagine an evolutionary journey that's better than any Hollywood pyrotechnics could evoke.

In *Promise Ahead* Elgin invites us to think in several new ways: First, we are invited to approach living as a member of the human species. Sure, we have our personal story, abundant with friends, family, activities, and significance. But we are also part of a larger identity, the "body" of humanity. As a species, as humanity, we have a history much longer than a few measly decades. You and I are actually thirty-five thousand years old. We've invented tools, language, cities, and civilization. We've puzzled over the

mysteries of life and created stories and religions to link us
to the unseen world. We've mastered fire, directing it to
warm our homes, power our cars, and send us into space.
At the same time, our bombs and guns, designed to subdue
our enemies, are returning to haunt us as children shoot
children and terrorists reduce buildings to rubble. All of us,
with all the achievements and contradictions of our species,
are part of this human journey. While thinking of oneself as
part of humanity is no shocking revelation, thinking that
humanity itself can, as a single creature, think—that's the
stretch you're being invited to take. What if "humanity" is
more than just a designation that distinguishes our species
from other creatures? What if "humanity," like an individual, is on a journey—and is at a crossroads? Elgin asks us to
contemplate with awe the beauty and terror of our collective
pilgrimage through time and space, take stock and choose,
both consciously and collectively, our future.

Second, we are invited to see this mighty task in a unique
way. Our collective history of social, cultural, and political
change has been traditionally presented as an ongoing struggle and clash of ideas and people, all vying for power over
the resources of the present and the directions of the future.
Elgin, though, sees where we are and where we are headed
through a different lens. For him, our historical power dynamics can be seen as kid's stuff—the "terrible two's," the
skinned knees of grade school, the teenage recklessness that
is the stuff of parental nightmares. As a species, we've just
been kids in the cosmos—making mistakes, making mis-
chief, making friends, and making more of us at an astound-
ing rate. Now we are at that turning point called "growing
up." Will we, like Peter Pan, refuse to mature? Or will we,

as a species, have the will, good sense and courage to move on to adulthood?

"Growing up" for many teens has about as much appeal as a bath does for a dog. Don't you know a lot of teenagers running around in adult bodies, defying limits everywhere—overspending, speeding, playing around on their mates, and using various drugs to mute their consciences? But consider traditional cultures (and our own a few short generations ago). Achieving adulthood was more like winning an Olympic gold medal. We endured many trials to prove to our elders we were worthy to be counted as one of them. This is the opportunity humanity now faces, according to Elgin. Growing up, in the best sense of the phrase.

While optional, this choice to mature is by no means window dressing. It is very consequential. Adults, by their very nature, *want* to understand and nurture the world beyond the boundaries of their own self-centered playpen. With all the social and environmental challenges ahead, we need a wisdom crew on Spaceship Earth, not a bunch of unattended children amusing themselves with expensive and dangerous toys.

Third, with the nature of change itself changing, Elgin says our hope lies in the simple power of conscious communication, not in traditional forms of analysis and organizing. As humanity bonds with itself and together faces the future, we'll need to do what all marriage counselors recommend: talk with one another. Talking, though, doesn't mean just chatter. It means purposefully bringing up those tough subjects we'd all rather ignore, listening to opinions that don't match our own, thinking clearly, speaking accurately, and—most amazing—acting on new information or insights. Just because we started to talk at age two doesn't mean we know how to communicate. This learned art, hard enough by itself, is getting harder by the day as we pour the oatmeal of junk-information all over the wiring of the global brain—the media. Elgin singles out the imperative to communicate intelligently via this collective voice as one of humanity's essential next steps. Enriching the menu of options on traditional media is certainly essential to upping our collective IQ, but the intoxicating wild card is the internet. How we use this precious gift of connectivity can steer our species out of the shallows of mediocrity and into our true brilliance. Our news must broaden again out of the constraints of infotainment, our discussions must foster respect and insight, and our democracy, drowning now in cynicism and consumerism, must actually start to work. We need good information, great conversations, and a sense that our voices can be heard. Our collective brain must hum with the aliveness of millions of bits of accurate data shuttling around, resonate with the pure drumbeat of feelings, crackle with enlightening insights, and be bathed in the water of compassion. To put it simply, we need a good head on our shoulders. So it will be from the stuff of dialogue, not ideology, that the future will be made.

Finally, Elgin invites our imagination (but not our incredulity) to expand into the vast reaches of space and time. He doesn't ask us to take any leaps of faith that have no basis in science. Rather, he lays before us what science has unearthed about our more-than-earthly reality. He explores recent findings in physics that point to the possibility that our universe is a single, living system and may not be all that exists "out there." Taken together, these insights reverberate with meaning. Our lives—including our most mundane decisions—are part of a coherent, purposeful unfolding. Yet nothing is assured. *We* must wake up to our personal and social wholeness and act like . . . well . . . grown-ups!

We seem to be on the brink of as big a shift in our collective understanding of the cosmos as people faced back in the "flat earth" days. Those flat-earthers, though, had several centuries to make the shift, whereas all of us alive are headed into this new reality at breakneck speed. We are walking—no, racing—into the unknown together. With courage, imagination, and knowledge, we can embrace this mysterious wind that is blowing in from the future. We can enjoy the journey and thrill at the *Promise Ahead*. Whaddya say? Are you on board?

Vicki Robin is the coauthor with Joe Dominguez of *Your Money or Your Life*.

Chapter One

—

IS HUMANITY GROWING UP?

Life is occupied both in perpetuating itself
and in surpassing itself;
if all it does is maintain itself,
then living is only not dying.
—*Simone de Beauvoir*

HUMANITY'S AGE

HOW grown up do you think humanity is? When you look
at human behavior around the world and then imagine our
species as one individual, how old would that person be? A
toddler? A teenager? A young adult? An elder?

As I've traveled in different parts of the world, speaking
to diverse audiences, I've begun many of my presentations
by asking this question. Initially, I didn't know whether people would be able to relate to or even understand my question, much less agree on an answer. To my surprise, nearly
everyone I've asked has understood this question immediately and has had an intuitive sense of the human family's
level of maturity. Whether I've asked this question in the
United States, England, India, Japan, or Brazil, within seconds people have responded in the same way: *at least two-
thirds say that humanity is in its teenage years.*

The speed and consistency with which different groups around the world have come to this intuitive conclusion were so striking that I began to explore adolescent psychology. I quickly discovered that there are many parallels between humanity's current behavior and that of teenagers:

· Teenagers are *rebellious* and want to prove their independence. Humanity has been rebelling against nature for thousands of years, trying to prove that we are independent from it.

· Teenagers are *reckless* and tend to live without regard for the consequences of their behavior. The human family has been acting recklessly in consuming natural resources as if they would last forever; polluting the air, water, and land of the planet; and exterminating a significant part of animal and plant life on the Earth.

· Teenagers are concerned with *appearance* and with fitting in. Similarly, many humans seem focused on expressing their identity and status through material possessions.

· Teenagers are drawn toward instant *gratification.* As a species, we are seeking our own pleasures and largely ignoring the needs of other species and future generations.

· Teenagers tend to gather in groups or *cliques,* and often express "us versus them" and "in versus out" thinking and behavior. We are often clustered into ethnic, racial, religious, and other groupings that separate us from one another, making an "us versus them" mentality widespread in today's world.

Other authors have noted that we are acting like teenagers. Al Gore wrote in his book, *Earth in the Balance,* "The metaphor is irresistible: a civilization that has, like an adolescent, acquired new powers but not the maturity to use them wisely also runs the risk of an unrealistic sense of immortality and a dulled perception of serious danger. . . ."[1] In a similar vein, Allen Hammond, senior scientist at the World Resources Institute, who has been exploring the world of 2050, has written, "Just as parents struggle to teach their children to think ahead, to choose a future and not just drift through life, it is high time that human society as a whole learns to do the same."[2]

If people around the world are accurate in their assessment that the human family has entered its adolescence, that could explain much about humanity's current behavior, and could give us hope for the future. It is promising to consider the possibility that human beings may not be far from a new level of maturity. If we do develop beyond our adolescence, our species could begin to behave as teenagers around the world do when they move into early adulthood: we could begin to settle down, think about building a family, look for meaningful work, and make longer-range plans for the future.

Adolescence is a time when others—such as parents, schools, churches, and so on—are generally in control. As we step into adulthood, we enjoy a new freedom from control, and a new responsibility to take charge of our lives. In a similar way, during our adolescence as citizens of the Earth, most humans have felt controlled by someone else—especially by big institutions of business, government, religion, and the media. As we grow into our early adulthood as a species, we will discover that maturity requires taking more responsibility and recognizing that we are in charge. Instead of waiting for "Mom or Dad to fix things," an adult pays attention to the larger situation and then acts, recognizing

that our personal and collective success are deeply intertwined.

Is it plausible that humanity is truly on the verge of moving beyond our adolescence? Not only do I consider it plausible, I would like to offer a rough timetable for the
maturing of humanity. I estimate that we awoke in the *infancy* of our potentials roughly thirty-five thousand years ago.
Archeologists have found that, at that time, there was a virtual explosion of sophisticated stone tools, elaborate burials,
personal ornaments, and cave paintings. Then, with the end
of the ice ages roughly ten thousand years ago, we began to
settle down in small farming villages. I believe this period
marks the transition to humanity's *childhood*. The food surplus that peasants produced made possible the eventual rise
of small cities. I estimate we humans then moved into our
late childhood with the rise of city-state civilizations roughly
five thousand years ago in Iraq, Egypt, India, China, and the
Americas. At that time, all the basic arts of civilization were
developed, such as writing, mathematics, astronomy, civil
codes, and central government. Still, the vast majority of
people lived as impoverished and illiterate peasants who had
no expectation of material progress. With the scientific-
industrial revolution roughly three hundred years ago, humanity began to move into our *adolescence*. Beginning in
Europe and the United States, industrialization has spread
around the world, particularly in the last half-century. Now,
with the industrial revolution devastating the whole planet
and challenging humanity to a new level of stewardship, it
seems plausible that we are on the verge of moving into the
communications era and our *early adulthood*.

This timetable gives only a rough estimate of the average
level of maturity of our species, but it does make an im-

portant point: that human beings are growing up, becoming more seasoned and wiser through hard-earned experience. Despite humanity's seeming immaturity in the past, I believe we could be close—within a few decades—of taking a major step forward in our evolution as a species.

Humanity's Heroic Journey of Awakening

IF we look beneath the complexity of human history and culture, there seems to be a story that humanity shares regarding the purpose of life. Joseph Campbell, a world-renowned scholar who spent a lifetime exploring the stories that have brought meaning to people throughout history, described the common story at the heart of all the world's cultures as the "hero's journey." Although the details vary depending on where and when it has been told, it is essentially the story of an individual who grows up by going through a series of tests that teach him or her about the nature of life. The person then brings this precious knowledge back to his or her personal life and life of the community.

If we assume that the overall human family is on an heroic journey of development, then the pivotal question becomes: "Where are we on the hero's journey?" To explore that key question, it is important to know that the hero's journey usually consists of three stages: separation, initiation, and return.[3] It begins with the hero (or heroine) leaving home to search for the deeper meaning and purpose of life. This is the stage of separation. There eventually comes a time when the hero undergoes a supreme test, whereby he is initiated into the nature and ways of the universe and no longer feels separate. With initiation, he experiences the deep unity and aliveness at the foundation of the universe and his sense of life purpose in relation to it. He returns from his adventure with that hard-won knowledge and the capacity for personal renewal or even, says Campbell, "the means for the regeneration of society."[4] The core purpose of that sacred knowledge, according to Campbell, is to "waken and maintain in the individual a sense of wonder and participation in the mystery of this finally inscrutable universe."

Just as all major cultures share the story of the hero's journey, all have customs of initiation as well. Initiatory rites of passage around the world have at least two things in common.[5] First, for the individual, the initiation marks a decisive transition from one stage or kind of life to another (such as from adolescence to adulthood). Second, initiation rites are also stressful social situations in which new ways of relating to other people are learned and established. The experience of initiation forges bonds of connection among those who have gone through it, bonds that transcend previous distinctions based on status, age, or kinship. Long after the rites are concluded, these links and emotional bonds persist and provide much of the social glue that holds the community together.[6]

Let's look at humanity's journey in terms of this simple model of separation, initiation, and return.

· **Separation**—By my reckoning, a complex phase of progressively divorcing ourselves from nature has extended over the last thirty-five thousand years—from the time of our initial awakening as gatherers and hunters up to the present. During these millennia, humanity has increasingly pulled away from nature in order to develop our unique capacities and talents as a species. The last half-century seems to mark our final severance from nature as we cause, for example, the mass extinction of other species and the disruption of the global climate.

· **Initiation**—To undergo initiation is to make a major transition to a new and larger life, and it often involves going through a powerful experience. As we confront challenges such as climate change and species extinction, humanity seems poised to undergo an initiation that will give us the opportunity of becoming an authentic human family—in feeling and experience as well as in name.

· **Return**—To pass successfully through our initiation, we will have to forge new bonds both within our species and with nature as a whole. This phase marks our passage into our early adulthood and the beginning of a long process of reconnecting with nature. A promising future lies ahead as we begin a task for grown-ups—building a sustainable planetary civilization.

Figure 1 illustrates this description of our evolutionary journey as separating from and then reconnecting with nature. It is important to note that there is no negative implication in the downward direction of the first arrow. Its purpose is simply to show that we pulled away from nature. We shall soon enter a period of initiation, in which we see that we have a choice of connecting consciously with nature and the universe. Making the transition from separation to integration, without losing the scientific understanding and technical sophistication we have gained, is perhaps the most important evolutionary turn that humanity will ever have to accomplish.

When we view humanity's evolution this way, our times take on new significance. Humanity is about to move into

Two Major Phases in the Human Journey

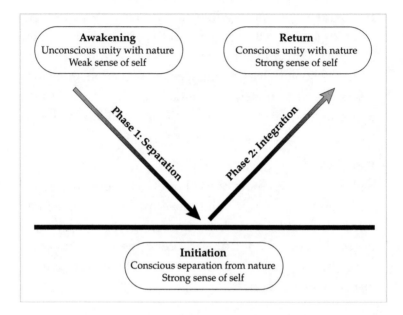

a stage of initiation—a period of stress and testing in which we will be challenged to discover ourselves as a single family with responsibilities to one another, the Earth, and future generations. Although the challenges we face may seem to be evidence of humanity's failures, reaching this stage is actually an expression of our great success over the past thirty-five thousand years. I believe that the apparent crises we face are, in reality, part of our initiation into a new relationship with one another and the Earth. The rapidly approaching initiation represents a time of birth—a stressful but entirely natural process.[7]

When we began our journey of awakening roughly thirty-five thousand years ago, we had only an indistinct sense of ourselves and a strong but largely unconscious feeling of connection with nature.[8] Over the millennia, we have acquired a strong sense of ourselves, but at the cost of separating ourselves from nature. Looking ahead, we have the opportunity to reconnect consciously with nature and the larger human family. As in the hero's journey, our challenge is to return to where we started, but with a new level of insight, compassion, and creativity. T. S. Eliot foretold of this return when he wrote: "And the end of all our exploring/Will be to arrive where we started/And know the place for the first time."[9]

INITIATION: HITTING THE EVOLUTIONARY WALL

HERE is how William D. Ruckelshaus, the former director of the Environmental Protection Agency, describes the evolutionary task that we are facing:

> Can we move nations and people in the direction of sustainability? Such a move would be a modification of society comparable in scale to only two other changes: the Agricultural Revolution and the Industrial Revolution of the past two centuries. Those revolutions were gradual, spontaneous, and largely unconscious. This one will have to be a fully conscious operation . . . If we actually do it, the undertaking will be absolutely unique in humanity's stay on the Earth.[10]

What would motivate us to attempt such an undertaking? I believe it will take both the push of environmental necessity and the pull of evolutionary opportunity for humanity to attempt to overcome thirty-five thousand years of pro-

gressive separation from nature and discover how to live in
conscious harmony with one another and the Earth. Like
adolescents pressing to find the limits of their parents' authority, we are pushing up against the limits of nature, as
though seeking to discover just how much abuse our planet
will tolerate. But we face much more than physical problems; we face equally great challenges in our own consciousness and character. The historic path of development is being
confronted not only with an environmental wall but by an
even more formidable evolutionary wall. It would be useful
to distinguish here between the two:

· An **environmental wall** refers to the physical limits of the
  global ecosystem to support our species. We are fast approaching these limits because we are rapidly consuming
  more resources than the Earth can renew and polluting the
  environment with more toxins than it can absorb. Given
  an abundance of resources, nearly every organism exploits
  its environmental niche to the fullest extent; thus, overshoot and collapse are a common occurrence in natural
  systems. Human beings learn through experience, and we
  have no experience exercising restraint as a species and
  being mindful of the overall biosphere. Since we have
  never encountered this situation before, it seems only natural that humanity would reach, and then extend beyond,
  the limits of the Earth's ecosystem.

· An **evolutionary wall** refers not only to the physical limits
  of the Earth's ability to sustain humanity, but also to our
  own social and spiritual limits to sustain dysfunctional and
  destructive behaviors. Modern, industrial civilization is
  breeding pathological behavior—alienation from others

and from nature, extreme competitiveness and greed, cynicism in politics, and despair for the future. How much poverty, alienation, and misery can humanity experience before we eventually damage our collective psyche and soul? An evolutionary wall presents humanity with an identity crisis at least as great as our environmental crisis: Who are we as a species? What is our larger story? Are we going to allow "overshoot and collapse" to happen to us? Do we see ourselves as separate, isolated beings or part of the larger web of life?

In seeing the initiation that awaits us, it is clear that we have come to a great choice-point in our journey. Although human beings have been faced with challenges throughout history, we have never before been confronted with a challenge to our entire planet and species. *Our time is unique in one crucial respect: the circle has closed—there is nowhere to escape.* For the first time in our history, the entire human population is confronted with a common predicament whose solution will require us to work together.

This book looks beyond the possibility of a destructive evolutionary crash to the possibility of an evolutionary bounce. I believe that in the coming decades, there is the distinct possibility that we may surpass ourselves and evolve to a level of maturity that we could not attain without confronting these trials that I am calling "initiation." How might an evolutionary bounce look? I see it as a leap forward in our collective maturity to build a life together that would be harmonious in three ways. It would be:

· **Sustainable**—in harmony with the Earth's biosphere (the *physical* ecosystem)

· **Satisfying**—in harmony with others (the *social-cultural* ecosystem)

· **Soulful**—in harmony with the "life force" (the *spiritual* ecosystem)

There are two compelling reasons for making this evolutionary turn. First, it is eminently desirable and will lead to a higher quality of life for all. Second, it is necessary if we are to avoid creating a planet that is hotter, hungrier, poorer, and more polluted, diseased, and biologically impoverished than it already is.[11]

HUMANITY'S PROMISING FUTURE

IF we do get through these difficult times and grow into our early adulthood as a species, how long might we then survive? We can gain some perspective by looking at the longevity of early humans and other animal species. The typical life span of a species is estimated to be between one and 10 million years.[12] For example, our early ancestor *Homo erectus* survived more than a million years before becoming extinct. Some species live far longer. Dinosaurs survived roughly 140 million years before a natural catastrophe wiped them out. If humanity is as capable of survival as the dinosaurs were, our species would be able to endure for more than twenty-five thousand times the span of recorded human history. *If we can make it through this evolutionary initiation and begin building a sustainable, satisfying, and soulful planetary civilization, we have the prospect of a long and promising future.*

Just as every child makes missteps on the path to adulthood, humanity has made and will continue to make painful mistakes as we evolve. We learn through our mistakes, however, and we keep moving ahead step by step. We are ever more experienced, ever more seasoned, and ever more mature. Although our future is uncertain, we already have the resources and capacities we need for success. The biologist Lewis Thomas describes the promise of our species beautifully:

> We may all be going through a kind of childhood in the evolution of our kind of animal . . . If we can stay alive, my guess is that we will someday amaze ourselves by what we can become as a species. Looked at as larvae, even as juveniles, for all our folly, we are a splendid, promising form of life and I am on our side.[13]

I too believe that humanity has a promising future. The word *promise* has its origin in the Latin word "to send forth." A promise, then, is a sending forth of a declaration, vow, pledge, or commitment. I believe we are reaching a unique point in our evolution where we can make a promise to future generations. It is a declaration that we will not forget them in the rush and busyness of our day-to-day lives. The promise is our marriage with the larger flow of life—both past and future—and our recognition that we are now a critical link in maintaining the integrity of that flow. It is our sacred covenant with the future whereby we send ahead not only our good intentions, but also our commitment of active engagement to turn the direction of our evolution in favor of a promising future. It is our vow to future generations that we shall hold them in our hearts and minds as

we make decisions, recognizing that we all share the same
Earth and a common journey through eternity.

LOOKING AHEAD

THE remainder of this book explores humanity's journey
toward our young adulthood. We begin in chapter two by
taking a hard look at the world and at the key adversity
trends that we face. Then in chapters three through six, we
explore four equally powerful opportunity trends. Next, we
look at the convergence of these trends and consider two
basic outcomes—either an evolutionary crash or an evolutionary bounce. In chapter eight, we step back to consider
the big picture of the human journey. An evolutionary
bounce means the human family will pull together for a
common purpose. But what purpose is so compelling that
it overcomes historic divisions and differences? Sustainability
alone promises little more than "only not dying." Is there a
higher purpose that describes our journey? Finally, with perspective for the journey ahead, we return in chapter nine to
where we started, to consider how we can collectively
awaken and mobilize ourselves to realize the promise ahead.

Chapter Two

—

ADVERSITY TRENDS:

HITTING AN EVOLUTIONARY WALL

What is difficult is to imagine how to get out of the
situation we're in right now in a time frame that is in line
with the rate of deterioration that we're seeing.
—*Paul Hawken*

If we do not change our direction,
we are likely to end up where we are headed.
—*Ancient Chinese Proverb*

ARE WE ON A COLLISION COURSE WITH NATURE?

ASSUMING that our species is in its teenage years, I don't
think we will easily turn away from our rebellious, reckless,
and shortsighted behavior. In fact, we seem determined to
run headlong into the consequences of our adolescent actions before deciding whether to make the turn toward a
higher maturity. Like many teenagers, we will likely face a
time of testing and initiation before moving into our early
adulthood.

The question is whether we will pull together as a human
family under the extreme pressures of approaching the time
of initiation. To answer this question, we need a much

clearer sense of the driving trends that will intersect in the next few decades. We begin by considering the problematic trends that promise great misfortune for humanity if we do not face up to them squarely. I call them adversity trends. Two questions seem paramount: How difficult might our situation become? And how soon might we encounter an unyielding evolutionary wall?

After studying driving trends for more than thirty years, I am all too aware that no one can predict the future with certainty. I also know that we can make educated guesses about how the major trends—population, resources, and environment—will unfold in the decades just ahead. Where disagreements emerge is in interpreting the overall meaning of the combined trends. On the one hand, there are some who believe that, with engineering, biotechnology, and human ingenuity, we can solve the problems we face and realize an ever-improving future. On the other hand, there are those who conclude from these same trends that we have already overreached our relationship with life on our planet and, to secure a sustainable future, we will need a profound change in human culture and consciousness as much as a change in technology.

Writing about the "coming age of abundance," Stephen Moore is an economist who epitomizes the perspective of technological optimism: "Every measurable trend of the past century suggests that humanity will soon be entering an age of increasing and unprecedented natural resource abundance."[1] Fred Smith, president of the Competitive Enterprise Institute, writes that while "doomsayers" think there are too many people consuming too much for the planet to sustain, "cornucopians, in contrast, argue that humanity faces no real problems; technological and institutional advances have and will continue to make it possible to address any shortages."[2] The late Julian Simon, a former professor of business, is another optimist: "The standard of living has risen along with the size of the world's population since the beginning of recorded time. There is no convincing economic reason why these trends toward a better life should not continue indefinitely."[3] His rationale for this optimism is that, historically, the opportunity for people to make a profit has spurred human ingenuity and problem-solving—and we end up better off.[4]

The rosy views of the future portrayed by these economists benefit from the fact that, over the last few decades, various predictions of calamity have not materialized. For example, the global "population bomb" was projected to result in massive famines by the turn of the century. As dates for eco-catastrophe and global famine have come and gone without the disastrous events occurring, people's patience for ominous predictions has worn thin.

But can even the most optimistic among us afford to brush off the warnings of the world's leading scientists? In 1992, more than sixteen hundred of the world's senior scientists, including a majority of the living Nobel laureates in the sciences, signed an unprecedented "Warning to Humanity." In this historic statement, they declared that "human beings and the natural world are on a collision course . . . that may so alter the living world that it will be unable to sustain life in the manner that we know." This is their conclusion:

> We, the undersigned senior members of the world's scientific community, hereby warn all humanity of what lies ahead. *A*

great change in our stewardship of the earth and the life on it is
required, if vast human misery is to be avoided and our global home
on this planet is not to be irretrievably mutilated[5] [emphasis added].

Is this a valid warning? Are we on a collision course with
nature and perhaps our own human nature? As a way to
explore this vital question, let us look one generation into
the future—roughly the next twenty to thirty years—and
picture the world that a child born at the turn of the millennium will likely inhabit as a young adult. What kind of
legacy are those of us who are alive today leaving for the
next generation?

There are dozens of trends that we could consider, such
as ozone depletion, rain forest destruction, topsoil erosion,
and the overfishing of the world's oceans. To keep the inquiry manageable, however, let's consider only five key
driving trends: climate change, population growth, species
extinction, resource depletion, and global poverty. These
five adversity trends will be sufficient to reveal whether the
warning from our leading scientists is valid and, if so, the
time frame within which we risk "irretrievable mutilation"
of the biosphere.

GLOBAL CLIMATE CHANGE

IT is no accident that, of the ten warmest years on record,
all have occurred in the last fifteen years. In 1995, the In-
tergovernmental Panel on Climate Change (IPCC)—the international body charged by the United Nations to study
global climate change—reached the conclusion that "there
is a discernible human influence on global climate."[6] They

found that the primary cause for these climate changes is the increase in greenhouse gases that trap heat in the atmosphere. The principal greenhouse gas is carbon dioxide, which comes from burning gasoline, coal, and natural gas. Figure 2 shows how accumulations of carbon dioxide have recently skyrocketed compared to levels during the last hundred thousand years. It also shows how, over the millennia, the rise and fall of global temperatures have corresponded closely with the rise and fall of concentrations of carbon dioxide in the atmosphere. Lastly, this figure suggests that we should expect a major disturbance in the generally favorable weather the world has experienced over the last ten thousand years (since the beginnings of agriculture and a settled way of life).

The several thousand scientists involved in the IPCC study have determined that preindustrial levels of carbon dioxide will at least double by the middle of the next century.[7] This is very bad news, because there is a growing scientific consensus that anything more than a doubling of greenhouse gas concentrations beyond preindustrial levels poses an unacceptable risk.[8] If the levels of atmospheric carbon dioxide should double as the IPCC scientists predict, here are some of the impacts that we could expect:

· Widespread disruption and dislocation of agricultural growing regions
· More rain in some areas, more drought in others
· Stronger storms, more floods, stronger hurricanes
· Stronger effects from El Niño
· Heat waves that kill people, animals, and crops
· Expansion of the Earth's deserts

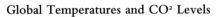

FIGURE   2

Global Temperatures and CO² Levels

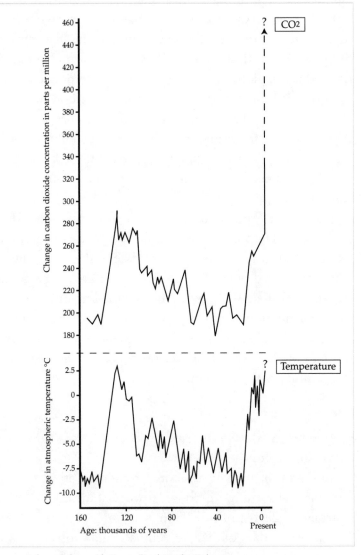

Source: Adapted from Al Gore, *Earth in the Balance*

· Melting of the polar ice caps, with a destructive rise in the sea level
· The spread of infectious diseases that endanger human and animal health
· Stress on the rest of the ecosystem (forests, wetlands, natural habitats)
· Enormous financial burdens placed on individuals, communities, insurance companies, other public and private financial institutions, and nations

The increase in greenhouse gases is already affecting our climate in two distinct ways: it is producing greater variability in weather patterns and increasing the average global temperature. Even now, we are experiencing greater variability in weather patterns. This instability, which is expected to increase considerably, is particularly harmful for agriculture. An early frost in the fall can kill some crops and freeze others in the ground. Heavy rains in the spring can delay planting. A shift in rainfall patterns can change the kind of crops that can be grown in a given area. Because an erratic and unstable climate jeopardizes the productivity of global agriculture, the melting of the global ice caps is not required for the greenhouse effect to have a disastrous impact on the human family.

Here are just a few examples of how global warming might affect agriculture. Canada's climate could improve the area as a wheat-growing region, although its soils are not as productive as the prairie soil in the United States that was built up over millions of years.[9] More frequent droughts in the "breadbasket" of the American Midwest would make it difficult to maintain current levels of productivity in growing wheat and corn. Agricultural productivity will also likely fall in sub-Saharan Africa, parts of Asia, and tropical Latin America—the regions where many of the world's poorest people live. With these kinds of impacts occurring around the world, climate change could cause a dramatic restructuring of the economy at all levels, from local to global.

How rapidly might major changes in the world's climate occur? Scientists are reaching the stunning conclusion that the increase in greenhouse gases is producing a warmer world much faster than expected—so fast that even present generations could feel the dire impacts of global warming. The last great ice age began roughly 120,000 years ago, with a period of abrupt global warming that was followed by rapid cooling. Evidence now indicates that, within a hundred-year span, there was a period of global warming that caused oceans to rise as much as twenty feet, followed by a period of rapid cooling in which the oceans fell by nearly fifty feet. If the human family were to be taken on such a breathtaking roller-coaster ride of massive and sudden climate fluctuations, the consequences would be disastrous.

Instead of there being a gradual warming trend over decades—one to which we could adapt—the world's climate could change abruptly, becoming suddenly much warmer or cooler. For example, dramatic cooling could occur in Europe if the North Atlantic Current—the enormous flow of warm water from the southern hemisphere to the north— were disrupted. Roughly the equivalent of a hundred Amazon Rivers, this current is a conveyor belt of warm water that slowly flows from the equatorial region up to the North Atlantic, giving Europe an unusually warm and favorable climate. Were it not for this flow of warm water, Europe would have the climate of Canada, and its now bountiful agriculture would be reduced to a fraction of current levels. Global warming could bring bring the North Atlantic Current to a halt, with catastrophic consequences for Europe. Professor William Calvin has researched this possibility and has concluded that "the abrupt cooling promoted by man-made warming looks like a particularly efficient means of committing mass suicide."[10]

This first adversity trend—global climate change—is so powerful that it could, by itself, constitute an environmental wall that forces humanity to change directions. Climate change promises to be a persistent force in our collective future as we will run up against its consequences for centuries to come. Although we cannot predict the degree of fluctuation and disruption that will occur in the next several decades, a growing body of research indicates that the changes could be far more rapid and substantial than anyone previously thought.

WORLD POPULATION GROWTH

CURRENT trends in world population growth give reason for both optimism and concern.[11] There is cause for optimism because we are moving toward global population stability. There is cause for concern because there remains so much momentum in population growth (with so many young people now reaching child-bearing age) that the human family will increase by several billion more people in the decades ahead before we reach stability. Mid-range estimates are that population will grow for another fifty years before it peaks at around 10 billion—four billion more peo-

Trends and Projections in World Population Growth:

1750–2150 (in billions of people)

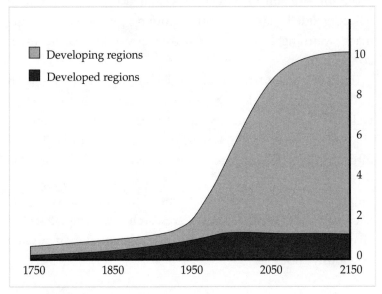

Source: World Resources Institute, 1996–97

ple than the number alive at the year 2000. The predicted range in global population in 2050 is between 8 and 12 billion people, with 10 billion being the mid-range estimate.[12]

Figure 3 shows world population growth in both developed and developing regions from 1750 (the beginning of the Industrial Revolution), with projections to 2150 (this is assuming, of course, that there will be no great die-off in the human population).

Within the time frame covered by this book (roughly until the end of the 2020s), middle-range estimates are that two to three billion people will be added to the Earth's population.[13] This is roughly the equivalent of adding the population of a city the size of New York or Los Angeles to the Earth *each month*. Moreover, 95 percent of this population growth is expected to occur in the poorest countries, which can least afford it, putting enormous pressures on natural resources and already overburdened cities.

It appears that cities, particularly those in developing countries, will bear much of the burden of increasing population. This is because of migration as well as population growth. The movement of people from rural to urban areas is changing the complexion of human culture. A half-century ago, the world was overwhelmingly rural. At the turn of the millennium, the world is half rural and half urban. It is estimated that, by 2050, two-thirds of the world's population will be urban. The shift to a predominantly urban world will produce a radical change in humanity's cultural consciousness.

In the twenty-five years between 1990 and 2015, increasing births and migration will cause the cities in the world's poorest countries to grow by an estimated two billion people.[14] These impoverished cities will then hold three-quarters of the urban population of the world. Poor countries are not ready for this flood of humanity; they are still trying to cope with the one billion people who arrived during the last forty years. The United Nations estimates that by 2015 there will be twenty-seven mega-cities in the world, each with a population of 10 million or more; twenty-three of these cities will be in developing countries. The Worldwatch Institute estimates that, if recent trends continue, 6.5 billion people will live in cities by 2050, more than the world's total population at the turn of the millennium.[15] Yet, even today, urban areas in developing countries contain massive shantytowns that lack adequate housing, paved roads, sewers,

clean water, public transportation, schools, health care, fire
and police protection, and space to grow food. Because of
overcrowding and a lack of sanitation, epidemics of the
past—such as cholera, dysentery, and typhoid—are returning. If the U.N. estimates prove to be correct, we will see
an enormous burgeoning of these places of misery, pollution,
and disease within the next few decades.

It appears that we may be approaching a Malthusian solution to the world population problem. Either by choice
(people consciously shifting to smaller families) or by consequence (increasing deaths from starvation, disease, or conflicts over resources), the world population may stabilize by
mid-century at around 8 billion people instead of the 10
billion currently predicted. However many people join the
human population in the next fifty years, it is clear that humanity is already pushing against the ability of the Earth to
carry the burden of our current forms of development. Population growth constitutes a powerful dimension of the evolutionary wall—one that could turn humanity either
toward a more sustainable path of development or toward
chaos.

MASS EXTINCTION OF SPECIES

PERHAPS the most direct measure of the health of the biosphere is the status of its biological diversity. Instead of
supporting a flourishing and robust biosphere, humans are
busy cutting down forests, overfishing the oceans, paving
over the land, and pouring toxins into the water, soil, and
air. The net result is decimation of the community of plant
and animal life on the Earth. The health of the planet is in

jeopardy as industrial activity is causing mass extinction of animal and plant species.

In a 1998 survey of four hundred scientists by the American Museum of Natural History in New York City, nearly 70 percent of the biologists polled said they believed that a *"mass extinction" is under way, and predicted that up to one-fifth of all living species could disappear within 30 years"*[16] [emphasis added]. They attribute nearly all the loss of plant and animal species to human activity. Another estimate—this one appearing in *National Geographic* magazine—concludes that 50 percent of the world's plant and animal species (fish, birds, insects, and mammals) could be on a path to extinction within a hundred years.[17]

Such massive extinctions have occurred only five times before, and each of these was due to natural causes such as the impact of an asteroid and sudden climate change. The sixth great extinction is now under way, and we are the cause. Because of the ruthless way in which humans are destroying other living organisms and their habitats, we have been called an exterminator species.

While it is true that mass extinctions have occurred before and life on the planet has recovered, it is also true that recovery was very slow—generally over millions of years. The mass extinction that is now under way is progressively degrading the resilience and integrity of the biosphere. As plants and animals disappear, their absence affects the entire ecosystem, particularly with regard to natural services such as pollination, seed dispersal, insect control, and nutrient cycling.[18] In addition, with a smaller pool of species, there are fewer candidates to take the place of those species that cannot weather catastrophic droughts, freezes, pest invasions, and diseases.[19] Diminishing biodiversity also affects health care; roughly 25 percent of the drugs prescribed in the United States include chemical compounds from wild organisms.[20] Illustrative of these natural medicines are digitalis, which is derived from foxglove and used to treat heart failure; taxol, a cancer drug that is derived from the bark of the yew tree; and an important blood-clotting agent found in the horseshoe crab. We have no idea how many natural medicines are being eliminated as we clear-cut forests, pollute rivers and oceans, and pave over natural habitats to make room for our enormous cities.

Our extermination of other species has been compared to popping rivets out of the wings of an airplane in flight. How many rivets can the plane lose before it begins to fall apart catastrophically? How many species can our planet lose before we cross a critical threshold where the integrity of the web of life is so compromised that it begins to come apart, like an airplane that loses too many rivets and disintegrates? Loss of biodiversity is another adversity trend that, by itself, could create an unyielding evolutionary wall.

Depletion of Natural Resources

THERE are many natural resources that we are rapidly depleting with no regard for future generations. Two of these vital resources—water and oil—illustrate how we are approaching limits to traditional forms of growth.

Growing water scarcity. Studies by the World Bank have found that worldwide demand for water is soaring and that supply cannot keep pace with demand.[21] In 1995, eighty countries were found to have water shortages that threatened both public health and economic health. More than 40 percent of the world—more than 2 billion people—did not have access to clean water at that time. Northern China, western and southern India, South America, sub-Saharan Africa, and much of Mexico all face water scarcity. In the twenty-first century, the most ferocious competition for resources may not be for oil but for fresh water.

Sandra Postel, who does research on international water and sustainability issues, estimates that, *"by 2025, nearly 40 percent of the world's population will be living in countries whose water supplies are too limited for food self-sufficiency"*[22] (emphasis added). Reasons for the scarcity include overpumping of ground water and the redirection of water from agriculture to cities.

Hundreds of Chinese cities already face acute water shortages—in some, residents are allocated only a meager trickle of water for a few hours each day. Another ominous indicator is the condition of China's famed Yellow River, which supports the breadbasket of China's agriculture. In 1972, it ran dry for the first time in history; since 1985, it has run dry each year until 1997, when it failed to reach the sea for more than half of the year.

Because China depends on irrigation to produce 70 percent of its grain, water shortages translate into food shortages and the need to import grain.[23] Importing a ton of grain is the equivalent of importing a thousand tons of water used to grow that grain elsewhere. China has such an enormous population that its imports of grain could absorb all of the world's available exports, thereby pushing up sharply the world price of grain. For the 1.3 billion people around the world who live at the edge of survival—on the equivalent of $1 or less per day—these price increases could be

life threatening. Food shortages could quickly translate into
profound social and economic instability around the world.

Former U.S. Senator Paul Simon estimates that by the
year 2050, 4 billion people will live in regions of severe
water shortages. He writes that "no nation's leaders would
hesitate to battle for adequate water supplies," the lack of
which "could result in the most devastating natural disaster
since history has been recorded . . ."[24]

The end of cheap oil. Much of the growth of the industrial
era has been fueled by a one-time gift from nature: the fossil
fuels that accumulated over millions of years. Petroleum has
fueled not only our transportation but also a revolution in
agriculture with petroleum-based pesticides and fertilizers.
Although oil prices at the turn of the millennium are quite
low, fossil fuel resources are running out more quickly than
most people realize.

Colin Campbell and Jean Laherrere have each worked in
the oil industry for more than forty years. They predict that
conventional oil production will begin to decline by around
2010. "There is only so much crude oil in the world, and
the industry has found about 90 percent of it."[25] They conclude that "barring a global recession, it seems most likely
that world production of conventional oil will peak during
the first decade of the 21st century."[26] Even optimistic projections of remaining reserves suggest that conventional oil
will top out by 2020.[27] The respected oil geologist L. F.
Ivanhoe agrees with this estimate and recently wrote, "Most
of the world's large, economically viable oil fields have already been found, so a permanent oil shock is inevitable
early in the next century."[28] The permanent oil shortage will
begin, he says, when the world's demand for oil exceeds

global production—a condition he expects to emerge around 2010.

There are alternatives to petroleum such as natural gas, solar energy, geothermal energy, wind power, and fuel cells. The widespread use of fuel-cell technology will be particularly important. Nonpolluting and highly efficient, fuel cells create electricity through a chemical reaction that uses gasoline or hydrogen gas and produces no emissions but water. Fuel cells will transform the power systems for automobiles and could be in widespread use by 2015.[29]

If we make the transition to a variety of alternative approaches to energy, there need be no long-term scarcity. It will take decades, however, for us to convert to renewable energy systems, or to develop fuel cell technologies to serve 6 billion people, or to build pipelines for a natural-gas-based economy. We now have several, precious decades in which to make this transition, but little is being done to implement a sustainable energy system globally. Thus, it seems likely that the end of cheap oil will result in serious economic and social dislocations by the 2020s.

An often overlooked consequence of the end of cheap oil will be that the cost of maintaining a high level of agricultural productivity will rise as petroleum-based pesticides, herbicides, and fertilizers become more expensive. At the very time the Earth will contain an added 2 to 3 billion people, the skyrocketing cost of petroleum could undermine the ability of the poorest countries to feed those additional billions. Although high-yield agriculture is possible without heavy reliance on petroleum-based products, it would be a different kind of agricultural system than the one in place today. It would be smaller in scale, decentralized, attentive to local conditions, and operated by well-trained organic farmers. The key question is whether we can make a smooth transition to another agricultural system as the cheap oil runs out in the next decade or two.[30]

Overall, the world water crisis and oil crisis seem to be reaching a critical threshold in roughly the same time frame of the next several decades. While we could respond with foresight—for example, by investing in renewable energy alternatives for oil and desalinization plants for water—we are not yet displaying a high level (or even a modest level) of collective initiative. Therefore, the depletion of critical natural resources such as oil and water constitutes another powerful factor in defining the evolutionary wall.

POVERTY AND DIMINISHED OPPORTUNITY

THE late prime minister of Canada, Lester Pearson, observed: "No planet can survive half slave, half free; half engulfed in misery, half careening along toward the supposed joys of an almost unlimited consumption . . . Neither ecology nor our morality could survive such contrasts."[31] If history is any guide, as the world becomes increasingly divided into the rich and the desperately impoverished, it will produce revolutionary movements in search of fairness and justice. Figure 4 vividly illustrates how far we are from an equitable distribution of material wealth. It shows the percent of global income distributed among five equal segments of the world's population.

If the poverty line is set at $1 a day, at the turn of the millennium it includes 1.3 billion people or roughly 20 percent of humanity. If the poverty line is set at $3 a day, it includes roughly 3.6 billion people or some 60 percent of

F I G U R E   4

Global Income Distribution[32]

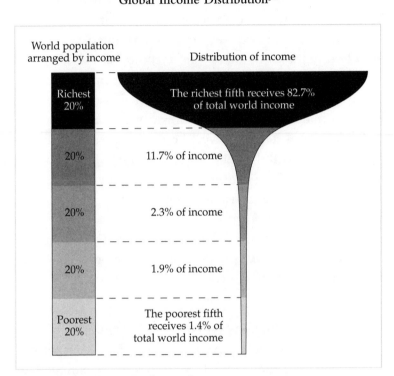

Source: UNDP, *Human Development Report* 1992

humanity. By comparison, the official poverty level in the United States is approximately $11 a day or $4,000 per year, per person—almost four times more than what most people in the world subsist on. What this means is that grinding poverty and the absence of opportunity are the way of life for a majority of human beings today.

Another way to consider global income distribution is by looking at the shape of Figure 4. The long, thin portion of the outline (akin to the stem of a champagne glass) represents

the annual income of a majority—approximately 60 percent
of the people in the world. The portion where the stem
begins to widen out appreciably represents the income of
the next 20 percent—the emerging global middle class. The
broadest portion illustrates the income received by the
world's wealthiest 20 percent. It is apparent that the human
family is made up of a huge impoverished class, a small but
growing middle class, and a small and very wealthy elite.

While global statistics reveal how widespread poverty is,
they do not reveal the depth of that poverty. The following
statistics, taken from the press in the late 1990s, give us a
hint of how deep and crushing poverty is:

· In Russia, one-third of the population now lives in dire
  poverty. More than 44 million people live below the poverty line, which in Moscow is roughly $1 per day.[33]

· The Asian economic crisis in the mid 1990s suddenly doubled—from 20 million to 40 million—the number of people living in absolute poverty (on less than a $1 per day
  per person) in Indonesia. The poverty is so extreme that
  doctors at two clinics said the number of patients had fallen
  by half because people could no longer afford to pay the
  consultation fee, the equivalent of five cents in U.S. currency.[34]

· Although China's economy is growing rapidly, the World
  Bank estimates that "more than one-quarter of all Chinese—about 350 million—are in substantial deprivation,
  subsisting on less than $1 a day. Of these, 60 to 100 million
  are on the edge of starvation with less than 60 cents a
  day."[35]

- India continues to be the world's poorest nation. More than 500 million Indians earn less than $1 a day (many of them earn less than 10 cents a day) in terms of real purchasing power.[36] Another indication of deprivation: 78 percent of Indian homes do not have access to electricity.[37]

- Worldwide, almost 3 billion people (50 percent of the world's population) use wood as their primary source of energy.

Nothing reveals the vulnerability of the world's poor more than the prospect of widespread food scarcity. As long as global food production grows faster than population, the poor can be relatively patient, hoping that their share of the world's resources will rise eventually.[38] When food production falls behind population growth, however, then how food is allocated becomes an intense and immediate political issue. As Lester Brown has said, while there are substitutes for oil, there are no substitutes for food. He uses the case of China—which contains one-fifth of humanity and has recently become a net food-importing nation—to illustrate the coming food challenge:

> If China's rapid industrialization continues . . . its import demand will soon overwhelm the export capacity of the United States and all other grain-exporting countries. China's rising grain prices are now becoming the world's rising grain prices, China's land scarcity will become everyone's land scarcity, and China's water scarcity will become the world's water scarcity.[39]

Compounding this situation, by the 2020s, billions of people will be living in urban slums without clean water, sanitation, telephones, transportation, health care, or a place to grow food—yet most will have access to television that shows them in vivid detail the high-consumption lifestyles that will never be theirs. This is a recipe for resentment and revolution. For these billions, even a small rise in the price of food can be a serious threat to survival. To have a majority of humanity struggle all day to make a meager living and then view on television a flood of advertisements from the affluent world is to create a schizophrenic planet that is divided against itself. A world in which a majority of people are both wired and poor is a highly unstable world. Fueled by hopelessness and desperation, the potential for terrorism will be enormous.

Although a core concern of this book is the prospect of a whole-systems or planetary-wide crisis, it is important to acknowledge that, for the greater part of the human family, a systems breakdown is a daily reality. A majority of the human family already lives on less than $3 a day in real income, with an impoverished diet, without access to health care, in urban shantytowns and rural villages without electricity, clean water, or fire and police protection. In this sea of poverty and diminished opportunity claiming billions of people, a systems crisis is a current fact.

The human family is in a real quandary. On the one hand, if poverty and famine grow, our collective future will be in doubt as we descend into resource wars and civil breakdown. On the other hand, if consumption grows unrestrained, our collective future will be in doubt as we overtax the Earth's limits.

A World Bank report released in 1997 projects that five

developing countries—Brazil, China, India, Indonesia, and Russia—will become economic superpowers by 2020.[40] Projections are that the economies of China and Indonesia will each grow to more than five times their present size, that of India will grow four times, and that of Brazil will grow three times. Because the Earth is already showing signs of ecological stress from current levels of economic activity, Lester Brown poses the obvious question: "If the global economy is already overrunning its natural capacities, what happens as China, India, and other fast-developing countries strive to emulate the American lifestyle?"[41] For example, if car ownership and oil consumption per person in China were to reach U.S. levels, then China would consume roughly 80 million barrels of oil per day. Yet, in 1996, the entire world produced only 64 million barrels of oil per day. This is a stark example of how the industrial model of development "is not viable for China or for the world as a whole, simply because there are not enough resources."[42]

Our planet does not have the resources to sustain the consumerist culture that is rapidly spreading from developed nations to the rest of the world. The only path through the dilemma of increasing poverty on the one hand and natural limits to unrestrained consumption on the other hand seems to be a middle way of conscious balance and mutually assured development.

THE COMING WORLD-SYSTEM CHALLENGE

WHEN we look a generation ahead to the decade of the 2020s, it is clear that the five adversity trends that we have just considered could dramatically alter the experience of living on the Earth. We have a tendency to compartmentalize these powerful trends and think that we can deal with them one by one when, in reality, they are increasingly interacting and amplifying each other's impact. Here are some of the interconnections that I see. The success of our global industrial economy is destabilizing the climate and supporting an unprecedented increase in world population. A dramatically larger population together with expanding industrialization are consuming an increasing proportion of the Earth's biosphere and destroying ecosystems, causing the most massive extinction of species in the last 65 million years. As industrialization continues, water is becoming scarce and cheap oil is being depleted—and both these resources are vital to agricultural production. Another result of expanding population and industrialization is that several billion human beings now live in impoverished urban slums without access to land and water for growing their own food. At the very time that worldwide agriculture will have increased demands placed on it, it will be taxed by climatic changes, shortages of water and cheap oil (which is needed for fertilizer and pesticides), and possibly even the loss of many of the pollinating insects that are crucial to agricultural production. The result could be waves of famine in regions that do not have enough water and arable land to be self-sufficient. Another result could be resource wars and massive civil unrest.

We do not have to go down this path and hit the wall of absolute limits to growth. We have the time and opportunity to design ways of living that are adapted to the unique ecology, culture, and resources of each bioregion of the planet. But instead of progress, we see continued deterioration and delay. This is described in the 1997 United Nations progress report issued five years after the first Earth Summit in Rio:

> Progress towards a global sustainable future is just too slow. Internationally and nationally, the funds and political will are insufficient . . . even though the technology and knowledge are available to do so. The gap between what has been done thus far and what is realistically needed is widening.[43]

It seems as though our situation is not yet sufficiently critical to mobilize the collective attention of people around the world. It seems likely, however, that we will soon encounter enough pressure from adversity trends to force us to wake up to our time of choice: Will we or will we not collectively take responsibility for the health of the human family and our planet? How we respond to that wake-up call will be a direct measure of our maturity as an evolving species.

WILL WE LEARN THE LESSONS OF HISTORY?

IF the adage is true that those who do not remember the lessons of history are destined to repeat them, then it would be wise for us to recall the civilizations throughout history that have overtaxed their environmental base and collapsed.[44] One was Sumer—one of the earliest known civilizations— that emerged in Mesopotamia, which is in present-day Iraq. Sumerian civilization blossomed in cities in the region around 3,000 B.C. and flourished for more than a thousand years before disintegrating. All that remains today is a desolate and largely treeless landscape. To understand the growth and decline of Sumerian civilization, it is important to examine how the productivity of its agricultural base changed over the centuries.

Despite its hot and dry climate, Sumer achieved a high level of agricultural productivity and a food surplus through extensive irrigation. Irrigation was a stimulus for civilization; it required cooperative efforts and large-scale organization to dig and repair the canals and divide the water. Irrigation also increased the salt content in the soil, a process which eventually undermined the productivity of the land. Crop yields remained high for roughly six hundred years until salinization finally reached critical thresholds and crop yields fell dramatically. From 2000 B.C. onward there are reports that "the earth turned white"—a clear reference to the layer of salt on top of the soil.[45] By 1800 B.C. crop yields had fallen to a third of their initial levels and the agricultural base for Sumerian society effectively collapsed. This contributed to destructive wars between the city-states and exposed Sumer to external attacks that finally overwhelmed it.[46] The Sumerian region then "declined into insignificance as an underpopulated, impoverished backwater of empire."[47]

Other examples of ecological destruction impairing civilizational growth can be found in the Mediterranean region. Vegetation in the Mediterranean is now characterized by low bushes, vines, and olive trees. Before human settlement, however, the natural vegetation of the region was a forest with a diverse mixture of trees. As the land became populated, trees were cleared for agriculture, for building homes and boats, and for cooking and heating. Overgrazing of the cleared land by goats, cattle, and sheep insured that the original forests could not grow back. The signs of widespread environmental destruction were clearly evident in Greece by 650 B.C. Plato left this description of deforestation and soil erosion in his *Critias:* "What now remains compared with what then existed is like the skeleton of a sick man, all the fat and soft earth having wasted away and only the bare framework of the land being left."[48]

The Roman empire was another civilization in which environmental deterioration became an important contributing factor in its decline. As Rome expanded its empire, it placed increasing pressures on the Mediterranean to provide food to support its large urban population as well as its standing armies. These pressures eventually led to widespread deforestation and soil erosion in the lands around the Mediterranean, including northern Africa. The decline in the quality of the soils and the encroachment of the deserts in Africa helped weaken Roman civilization and eventually contributed to the collapse of the empire between A.D. 400 and 500.

In the Americas we see a similar pattern at work. The Mayan civilization flourished in what is now the southern part of Mexico and northern Central America. Although Mayan society and population grew slowly beginning around 1200 B.C., by A.D. 800, the major city of Tikal had fifty thousand inhabitants. Cities in the region had similar architecture and contained ceremonial centers with steep pyramid temples that were over one hundred feet high. The Mayans also developed a complex and highly accurate calendar. Despite this sophistication, within a few decades after A.D. 800, the society began to disintegrate. Today, only a small number of peasants live in the area.

The primary cause of the collapse of Mayan civilization was a lack of food, which resulted from unsustainable demands that were placed on the land. Fragile soils of the tropical rain forest are easily eroded once exposed. Once the land was cleared for agriculture, soil erosion increased and crop yields eventually declined. When the land became exhausted, the surplus food disappeared, which led to conflict between the peasants who grew the food and the ruling elite and their armies in the cities. The outcome was a catastrophic fall in population. The Mayans were unable to maintain the elaborate culture they had built on their fragile environmental base. Civilization collapsed rapidly.[49] Within a few decades the great cities were abandoned, to be reclaimed by the jungles, where they remained hidden from the larger world for the next thousand years.

The main lesson that I draw from these stories is that we need to take modern-day adversity trends seriously. History is filled with too many examples of civilizations that made excessive demands on the environment and then disintegrated. In each case, the pattern is similar. The rise of a civilization begins with the development of intensive agriculture, which generates a food surplus. Unsustainable agricultural practices eventually produce deforestation and soil erosion, with a subsequent loss in agricultural productivity and the collapse of the civilization. Does the human family need to learn lessons at a global level that we have already learned many times before at a smaller scale? Or will we wake up together to the lessons of history and choose a sustainable pathway into the future?

———

Chapter Three

A New Perceptual Paradigm: We Live in a Living Universe

In the history of the collective as in the history
of the individual, everything depends on the
development of consciousness.
—*Carl Jung*

The whole of life lies in the verb *seeing*.
—*Teilhard de Chardin*

Humanity's Fourth Awakening

IN the previous chapter, we considered powerful adversity trends that are pushing humanity toward an evolutionary crash. In the next four chapters, we turn to consider equally powerful opportunity trends that are pulling us toward a positive future—an evolutionary bounce.

The first opportunity trend that could transform our impending crash into a spectacular bounce is a shift in our shared view of the universe—from thinking of it as dead to experiencing it as alive. In regarding the universe as alive and ourselves as continuously sustained within that aliveness, we see that we are intimately related to everything that exists. This startling insight—that we are cousins to everything that exists in a living, continuously regenerated universe—represents a new way of looking at and relating to the world and overcomes the profound separation that has marked our past. From the combined wisdom of science and spirituality is emerging an understanding that could provide the perceptual foundation for the diverse people of the world to come together in the shared enterprise of building a sustainable and meaningful future.

For some, a shift in perception may seem so subtle as to be inconsequential. Yet, all of the deep and lasting revolutions in human development have been generated from just such shifts. Only three times before in human experience has our view of reality been so thoroughly transformed that it has created a revolution in our sense of ourselves, our relationships with others, and our view of the universe. I want to mention these briefly here and then explore them more fully later (in chapter eight, "Humanity's Central Project").

The first transformation in our view of reality and identity occurred when humanity "awakened" roughly thirty-five thousand years ago. The archeological record shows that the beginnings of a reflective consciousness emerged decisively at this time as numerous developments were occurring in stone tools, burial sites, cave art, and migration patterns. Because we were just awakening to our capacity for "knowing that we know," we were surrounded by mystery at every turn. Nonetheless, human culture was born in these first glimmerings of personal and shared awareness.

The second time our view of reality and human identity changed dramatically was roughly ten thousand years ago, when humanity shifted from a nomadic life to a more settled existence in villages and farms. It was midway during the agrarian period, roughly five thousand years ago, that we see the rise of city-states and the beginnings of civilization.

The third time that our perceptual paradigm was transformed was roughly three hundred years ago, when the stability of agrarian society gave way to the radical dynamism and materialism of the scientific-industrial era. Each time that humanity's prevailing paradigm has changed, all aspects of life have changed with it, including the work that people do, the ways they live together, how they relate to one another, and how they see their role in society and place in the universe.

A paradigm is our way of looking at and thinking about ourselves and everything around us. It is the frame of mind out of which we operate. Our paradigm sets the limits on what thoughts we can think, what emotions we can feel, and what reality we can perceive. Willis Harman, renowned futurist, described a paradigm as "the basic way of perceiving, thinking, valuing, and doing associated with a particular vision of reality."[1] A paradigm tells most people, most of the time, what's real and what's not, what's important and what's not, and how things are related to one another. A paradigm is more than a dry mental map—it is our window onto the world that shapes how we see and understand the nature of reality, our sense of self, and our feelings of social connection and purpose.

We are now living at a time when humanity's perceptual paradigm is undergoing one of its rare shifts, and that shift has the potential to dramatically transform life for each of us. A paradigm shift therefore goes to the core of people's lives. It is much more than a change in ideas and how we think. It is a change in our view of reality, identity, social relationships, and human purpose. A paradigm shift can be felt in the body, heart, mind, and soul.

How do paradigm shifts occur? Paradigms operate beneath the surface of popular culture, largely unnoticed until the old way of perceiving begins to generate more problems than it solves. These problems then become the catalyst for triggering the shift to the next paradigm, which opens up new opportunities. When we first enter a new civilizational paradigm (such as during the shift from the agricultural era to the industrial era), we experience new freedoms and creative potentials. As we fulfill the potentials of that paradigm, however, it eventually becomes a constricting framework. Its partial or incomplete nature leads to a crisis, which in turn leads to a breakthrough into the next, more spacious paradigm, in which a new level of learning and creative expression can unfold.

The paradigm of the scientific-industrial era, while it has afforded great benefits, is now generating far more problems than it is solving. These problems are catalysts for a paradigm shift. They are forcing us to expand our perceptual horizons to a higher and more inclusive level. Albert Einstein described a paradigm shift by saying that we cannot solve problems at the same level at which they are created.

The emerging paradigm represents a convergence of insights from modern science and the world's spiritual traditions. At the heart of the new paradigm is a startling idea—that our cosmos is not a fragmented and lifeless machine (as we have believed for centuries) but is instead a unified and living organism. Although it is new for our times, the idea that the universe is alive is an ancient one. More than two thousand years ago, Plato described the uni-

verse as "one Whole of wholes" and "a single Living Creature which encompasses all of the living creatures that are
within it."[2] What is unprecedented is how this notion is
being informed today by both modern science and the
world's diverse spiritual traditions. Let us look at the evidence from both these sources, beginning with recent scientific discoveries. We shall explore then the implications of
this paradigm shift, and the opportunity it presents for imagining and building a sustainable future.

Scientific Evidence of a Living Universe

LESS than a hundred years ago, when Einstein was developing his theory of relativity, he considered the universe a
static, unchanging system no larger than the cloud of stars
that we now know to be our galaxy. Today, we know that
the universe is expanding rapidly and contains at least 50
billion galaxies, each with a 100 billion or more stars. What
is more, we now know that our cosmos embodies an exquisitely precise design. Researchers have calculated that if
the universe had expanded ever so slightly faster or slower
than it did (even by as little as a trillionth of a percent), the
matter in our cosmos would have either quickly collapsed
back into a black hole or spread out so rapidly that it would
have evaporated. Such amazing precision implies a living
intelligence is at work. Beyond these surprising findings are
even more extraordinary conclusions that, taken together,
suggest our universe is a living system.

Although there is no clear agreement among scientists as
to what constitutes a living system, it seems reasonable that
if our cosmos is alive, it would exhibit specific properties

that are characteristic of all life—such as being a unified entity, having some form of consciousness, and being able to reproduce itself. As we shall explore, these are among the properties of our universe that are emerging from modern science.

The cosmos is a unified system. Physicists used to view our universe as being composed of separate fragments. Today, however, despite its unimaginably vast size, the universe is increasingly regarded as a single functioning system. Because other galaxies are millions of light-years away, they appear so remote in space and time as to be separate from our own. Yet, scientific experiments show that things that seem to be separate are actually connected in fundamental ways that transcend the limitations of ordinary space and time.[3] Described as "nonlocality," this is one of the most stunning insights from modern science. Even though we live in a world of apparent separation, the new physics describes the more fundamental reality as that of seamless interconnection. Physicist David Bohm says that ultimately we have to understand the entire universe as "a single undivided whole."[4] Instead of separating the universe into living and nonliving things, Bohm sees animate and inanimate matter as inseparably interwoven with the life-force that is present throughout the universe and includes not only matter but also energy and seemingly empty space. For Bohm, then, even a rock has its unique form of aliveness. Life is dynamically flowing through the fabric of the entire universe.[5]

Our home galaxy—the Milky Way—is a swirling, disk-shaped cloud containing 100 billion or so stars. It is part of a local group of nineteen galaxies (each with 100 billion stars), which in turn is part of a larger Local Supercluster of thousands of galaxies. This supercluster resembles a giant, many-petaled flower. Beyond this, astronomers estimate that there are perhaps 100 billion galaxies in the observable universe (each with 100 billion or so stars). Scientists and spiritual seekers alike ask the question: If this is a unified system, then could all this be but a single cell within a much greater organism?[6]

It contains immense amounts of background energy. In the new view of reality, an extraordinary amount of energy permeates the cosmos. Empty space is not actually empty. Even in a complete vacuum, there exist phenomenal levels of background energy called "zero point energy." Bohm calculated that a single cubic centimeter of "empty space" contained the energy equivalent of millions of atomic bombs.[7] This is not simply a theoretical abstraction. A number of people are working to create energy devices that can tap into this background energy. Our universe is permeated by and exists within a vast ocean of flowing life energy.

The cosmos is continuously regenerated. For decades, the dominant cosmology in contemporary physics has held that creation ended with the Big Bang some 12 billion years ago and that since then nothing more has happened than a rearranging of the cosmic furniture. Because traditional physicists think of creation as a one-time miracle from "nothing," they regard the contents of the universe—such as trees, rocks, and people—as being constituted from ancient matter. In sum, the dead-universe theory assumes creation occurred billions of years ago, when a massive explosion spewed out lifeless material debris into equally lifeless space and has, by random processes, organized itself into life-forms on the remote planet-island called Earth.

In striking contrast, the living-universe theory describes the cosmos as a unified system that is completely re-created at each moment. Unlike traditional physicists who believe that creation ended with the miraculous birth of the cosmos billions of years ago, living-universe theorists hold that the cosmos continues to be maintained, moment by moment, by an unbroken flow-through of energy. They compare the cosmos to the vortex of a tornado or a whirlpool—as a completely dynamic structure. David Bohm calls the universe an "undivided wholeness in flowing movement."[8] In this view, our universe has no freestanding material existence of its own. The notion of continuous creation is even more remarkable when we consider that it includes not only matter but also the fabric of seemingly "empty" space. Space is not a simple emptiness waiting to be filled, but is itself a dynamically constructed transparency. Therefore, the entire cosmos is being regenerated at each instant in a single symphony of expression that unfolds from the most minute aspects of the subatomic realm to the vast reaches of thousands of billions of galactic systems. The whole cosmos, all at once, is the basic unit of creation.

It utterly overwhelms the imagination to consider the size and complexity of our cosmos with its billions of galaxies and trillions of planetary systems, all partaking in a continuous flow of creation. How can it be so vast, so subtle, so precise, and so powerful? Metaphorically, we inhabit a cosmos whose visible body is billions of light years across, whose organs include billions of galaxies, whose cells include trillions of suns and planetary systems, and whose molecules include an unutterably vast number and diversity of life-forms. The entirety of this great body of being, including the fabric of space-time, is being continuously regenerated at each instant. Scientists sound like poets as they attempt to describe our cosmos in its process of becoming. The mathematician Norbert Wiener expresses it this way: "We are not stuff that abides, but patterns that perpetuate themselves; whirlpools of water in an ever-flowing river."[9] Physicist Max Born writes, "We have sought for firm ground and found none. The deeper we penetrate, the more restless becomes the universe; all is rushing about and vibrating in a wild dance."[10] Physicist Brian Swimme tells us, "The universe emerges out of an all-nourishing abyss not only 12 billion years ago but in every moment."[11]

The new physics allows us to see everything in the cosmos as a flowing movement that co-arises along with everything else, moment-by-moment, in a process of continuous regeneration. If all is in motion at every level, and all motion presents itself as a coherent and stable pattern, then all that exists is profoundly orchestrated. All flows comprise one grand symphony in which we are all players, a single creative expression—a uni-verse.

Freedom is at its foundations. Another shift in the scientific view of the universe has to do with views about the existence of freedom. Whereas traditional physicists have seen the cosmos as being like a clockwork mechanism that is locked into predetermined patterns of development, the new physics sees it as a living organism that has the freedom and spontaneity to grow in unexpected ways. Freedom is at the very foundation of our cosmos. Uncertainty (and thus freedom) is so fundamental that quantum physics describes reality in terms of probabilities, not certainties. No one part of the cosmos determines the functioning of the whole; rather, everything seems to be connected with everything else, weaving the cosmos into one vast interacting system. Everything that exists contributes to the cosmic web of life at each moment, whether it is conscious of its contribution or not. In turn, it is the consistency of interrelations of all the parts of the universe that determines the condition of the whole. We therefore have great freedom to act within the limits established by the larger web of life within which we are immersed.

A living universe is a learning system in which we are free to make mistakes and to change our minds. In other words, if the universe is being continuously re-created, then each moment provides an opportunity for a fresh start. This is how the philosopher Renée Weber describes the creative and experimental nature of the universe: "Through us, the universe questions itself and tries out various answers on itself in an effort—parallel to our own—to decipher its own being."[12] Every moment, the universe re-creates itself and provides us with an opportunity to exercise our basic freedom to do the same.

Consciousness is present throughout. Consciousness, or a capacity for self-organizing reflection or knowing, is basic to life. If the universe is alive, we should therefore find evidence of some form of consciousness operating at every level—and that is exactly what we find. The respected physicist Freeman Dyson writes this about consciousness at the quantum level: "Matter in quantum mechanics is not an inert substance but an active agent, constantly making choices between alternative possibilities . . . It appears that mind, as manifested by the capacity to make choices, is to some extent inherent in every electron."[13] This does *not* mean that an atom has the same consciousness as a human being, but rather that an atom has a reflective capacity appropriate to its form and function.

Consciousness is present even at the primitive level of molecules consisting of no more than a few simple proteins. Researchers have found that such molecules have the capacity for complex interaction that is the signature of living systems. As one of the researchers who made this discovery stated, "We were surprised that such simple proteins can act as if they had a mind of their own."[14]

At a somewhat higher level, we find consciousness operating in the remarkable behavior of a forest slime mold in search of a new feeding area. For most of its life, slime mold exists as a single-cell amoeba. When it needs food, however, it can transform itself into a much larger entity with new capacities. Individual amoebas send out signals to others nearby until thousands assemble. When they reach a critical mass, they organize themselves, without the aid of any apparent leader, into an organism that can move across the forest floor. Upon reaching a better feeding area, they release spores from which new amoebas are formed.[15] Thus, under conditions of great stress, the forest slime mold is able to mobilize a capacity for collective consciousness and action so as to ensure its own survival.

If some form of consciousness is operating at the level of atoms, molecules, and single-cell organisms, we should not be surprised to find that consciousness is a basic property of the universe that is manifest at every level. Scientific investigation of intuitive or psychic abilities in humans provides further insight into the nature and ecology of consciousness. Dean

Radin, director of the Consciousness Research Laboratory at the University of Nevada, did an exhaustive analysis of parapsychological or psi research involving more than eight hundred studies and sixty investigators over nearly three decades. Based on this research, he concluded that consciousness includes both "receiving" and "sending" potentials.

Evidence of the receiving potentials of consciousness comes from experiments concerned with perception at a distance, which is sometimes called "remote viewing." This is the ability to receive meaningful information by nonphysical means about a remote person or location simply by opening our knowing faculty to that possibility. In remote viewing, the receiver does not acquire exact information but rather intuitive impressions regarding, for example, where a person might be located or his state of well-being. Radin found that remote viewing has "been repeatedly observed by dozens of investigators using different methods."[16] He concluded that a capacity for conscious knowing "operates between minds and through space."

Evidence of the sending potentials of consciousness comes from experiments dealing with mind-matter interactions, such as influencing the swing of a pendulum clock. Radin concluded that "after sixty years of experiments . . . researchers have produced persuasive, consistent, replicated evidence that mental intention is associated with the behavior of physical systems."[17]

I would have been reluctant to write about consciousness being a basic property of the universe—and in particular about parapsychology—had I not had an unusual opportunity to learn about it firsthand. During the early 1970s, I worked as a senior social scientist at the Stanford Research Institute, a large think-tank south of San Francisco now called SRI International. There I did studies of the long-range future, primarily for government agencies such as the President's Science Advisor and the Environmental Protection Agency. While doing this work, I was invited to participate in parapsychological experiments being conducted at SRI by two senior physicists, Dr. Hal Puthoff and Dr. Russell Targ. Several days a week for three years I went to their laboratory to take part in both formal and informal experiments.

One series of formal experiments involved remote viewing. The procedure was simple. I would be locked in a bare room with a pad of paper, a pencil, and a tape recorder and asked to describe where in the Bay Area one of the experimenters would be. After my door was locked, his destination was selected from a pool of more than a hundred possible locations by drawing an envelope at random from a locked safe. My task, after waiting a half hour for him to travel to his destination, was to describe in words or drawings the location of this outbound person. Was he in a boat on the bay? In a car on the freeway? In a grove of redwood trees? In a movie theater? In the room next door? My only instructions were, "Take a deep breath, close your eyes, and tell us what you see." Although my impressions were subtle and fleeting, I gradually learned that we all have an intuitive ability to "see" at a distance. Through our intuition, each of us can acquire useful impressions, images, and insights about a person or place that is distant from us. In my experience and that of the other subjects, the drawings and descriptions were often sufficiently accurate to allow independent judges to differentiate significantly among the various targets and, at levels far beyond chance, to match many of those descriptions closely with the actual locations.[18]

Another series of experiments involved working with a

computer that would randomly select one of four buttons prominently displayed on top of it. My task was to intuitively discover which of the four had been selected and to press the correct button. More than seven thousand selections were tallied under controlled conditions—an exhausting process requiring intense concentration over dozens of test sessions. The overall results were significantly above chance.[19]

These grueling experiments convinced me that we do have an intuitive connection with the universe; they also demonstrated that our capacity to use our intuition is still in its infancy given our early stage of learning. The most important insight that I take away from these and other experiments is that we *all* have an intuitive faculty. An empathic connection with the universe is nothing special; it is built into the workings of the cosmos. Participating in these experiments showed me that our being does not stop at the edge of our skin but extends into and is inseparable from the universe.

If consciousness is found at every level of the cosmos and, further, is not confined within the brain, but extends beyond the body and can meaningfully interact with the rest of the universe in both sending and receiving communications, then this is striking evidence that our cosmos is subtly sentient, responsive, conscious—and alive. The physicist Freeman Dyson thinks it is reasonable to believe in the existence of a "mental component of the universe." He says, "If we believe in this mental component of the universe, then we can say that we are small pieces of God's mental apparatus."[20] While it is stunning to consider that every level of the cosmos has some degree of consciousness, that seems no more extraordinary than the widely accepted view among scientists that the cosmos emerged as a pinpoint some 12 billion years ago as a "vacuum fluctuation" where nothing pushed on nothing to create everything.

The cosmos seems able to reproduce itself. A key attribute of any living system is its ability to reproduce itself. A startling finding from the new physics is that our cosmos may very well be able to reproduce itself through the functioning of black holes. In his book, *In the Beginning: The Birth of the Living Universe,* astrophysicist John Gribbin explains that the explosion of our universe in the Big Bang is the time-reversed mirror image of the collapse of a massive object into a black hole. Many of the black holes that form in our universe, he reasons, may thus represent the seeds of new universes: "Instead of a black hole representing a one-way journey to nowhere, many researchers now believe that it is a one-way journey to somewhere—to a new expanding universe in its own set of dimensions."[21] Gribbin's dramatic conclusion is that "our own universe may have been born in this way out of a black hole in another universe." He explains it in this way:

> If one universe exists, then it seems that there must be many—very many, perhaps even an infinite number of universes. Our universe has to be seen as just one component of a vast array of universes, a self-reproducing system connected only by the "tunnels" through spacetime (perhaps better regarded as cosmic umbilical cords) that join a "baby" universe to its "parent."[22]

Gribbin suggests not only that universes are alive, but also that they evolve as other living systems do: "Universes that are 'successful' are the ones that leave the most offspring."[23]

The idea of many universes evolving through time is not new. David Hume noted in 1779 that many prior universes "might have been botched and bungled throughout an eternity ere this system."[24]

Is the cosmos a living system? It certainly appears so in the light of recent scientific findings. Our universe is revealing itself to be a profoundly unified system in which the interrelations of all the parts, moment-by-moment, determine the condition of the whole. Our universe is infused with an immense amount of energy, and is being continuously regenerated in its entirety, while making use of a reflective capacity or consciousness throughout. As an evolving, growing, and learning system, it is natural that freedom exists at the quantum foundations of the universe. It even appears that the universe has the ability to reproduce itself through the vehicle of black holes. When we put all of these properties together, it suggests an even more spacious view of our cosmic system. Our universe is a living system of elegant design that was born from and is continuously regenerated within an even larger universe. *We are living within a "daughter universe" that, for 12 billion years, has been living and growing within the spaciousness of a Mother Universe.* The Mother Universe has existed forever, holding countless daughter universes in its grand embrace while they grow and mature through an eternity of time.

THE MOTHER UNIVERSE

WHEN our cosmos blossomed into existence from an area smaller than a pinpoint some 12 billion years ago, it emerged out of "somewhere." Modern physics is beginning to speculate on the nature of this generative ground. The distinguished Princeton astrophysicist John Wheeler describes space as the basic building block of reality. He explains that material things are "composed of nothing but space itself, pure fluctuating space . . . that is changing, dynamic, altering from moment to moment." Wheeler goes on to say that "of course, what space itself is built out of is the next question . . . The stage on which the space of the universe moves is certainly not space itself . . . The arena must be larger: *superspace* . . . [which is endowed] with an infinite number of dimensions."[25] What Wheeler calls "superspace," I am calling the Mother Universe.

The idea of a "superspace" or Mother Universe is not simply a creation of theoretical physics. It is a reality that can be directly experienced and has ancient roots in the world's meditative traditions. For example, more than twenty centuries ago, the Taoist sage Lao-tzu, described it this way:

> There was something formless and perfect
> before the universe was born.
> It is serene. Empty.
> Solitary. Unchanging.
> Infinite. Eternally present.
> It is the mother of the universe.
> For lack of a better name,
> I call it the Tao.[26]

Regardless of what the Mother Universe is called, all wisdom traditions agree that it is ultimately beyond description. Nevertheless, many attempts have been made to describe her paradoxical qualities. Here are six of the key attributes of the Mother Universe as seen by both East and West:

· **Present everywhere**—The clear, unbounded life-energy of the Mother Universe is present in all material forms as well as in seemingly empty space. The Mother Universe is not separate from us, nor is it other than the "ordinary" reality that is continuously present around us. The Mother Universe is also not limited to containing only our universe; there likely are a vast number of other universes growing in other dimensions of her unimaginable spaciousness.

· **Nonobstructing**—The Mother Universe is a living presence out of which all things emerge, but it is not itself filled or limited by these things. Not only are all things in it; it is in all things. There is mutual interpenetration without obstruction.

· **Utterly impartial**—The Mother Universe allows all things to be exactly what they are without interference. We have immense freedom to create either suffering or joy.

· **Ultimately ungraspable**—The power and reach of the Mother Universe is so vast that it cannot be grasped by our thinking mind. As the source of our existence, the Mother Universe is forever beyond the ability of our limited mental faculties to capture conceptually.

· **Compassionate**—Boundless compassion is its essence. To experience the subtle and refined resonance of the Mother Universe is to experience unconditional love.

· **Profoundly creative**—Because we humans do not know how to create a single flower or cubic inch of space, the creative power of the Mother Universe to bring into existence and sustain entire cosmic systems is utterly incomprehensible.

It is useful to contemplate these extraordinary characteristics of the Mother Universe so as to awaken ourselves to the profound miracle in which we are immersed. In that spirit, here is an evocative portion of what the Chinese monk Shao has written in describing what I call the Mother Universe:

> If you say that It is small,
> It embraces the entire universe.
> If you say It is large,
> It penetrates the realm of atoms.
> Call It one; It bears all qualities.
> Call It many; Its body is all void.
> Say It arises; It has no body and no form.
> Say It becomes extinct; It glows for all eternity.
> Call It empty; It has thousands of functions.
> Say It exists; It is silent without shape.
> Call It high; It is level without form.
> Call It low; nothing is equal to It.[27]

In looking across the world's spiritual traditions, the insight emerges again and again: although we live in a world of seeming separation and division, our universe is a unified whole brimming with life and infused with a divine presence. Here are a few examples:

"Earth's crammed with Heaven, and every common bush afire with God."
>   —*Elizabeth Barrett Browning,* poet

The Tao is the sustaining life-force and the mother of all things; from it, all "things rise and fall without cease."[28]
>   —Taoist tradition

"Heaven and earth and I are of the same root . . . are of one substance."[29]
>   —*Sojo,* a Zen monk

Jesus was asked, "When will the kingdom come?" He replied, "It will not come by waiting for it. . . . Rather, the Kingdom of the Father is spread out upon the earth, and men do not see it."[30]
>   —*Gospel of Thomas,* Gnostic Gospels

"For those who are awake the cosmos is one."[31]
>   —*Heraclitus,* ancient Greek philosopher

"My solemn proclamation is that a new universe is created every moment."[32]
>   —*D. T. Suzuki,* Zen scholar and teacher

"I am in some sense boundless, my being encompassing the farthest limits of the universe, touching and moving every atom of existence. The same is true of everything else . . . It is not just that 'we are all in it' together. We all *are* it, rising and falling as one living body."[33]
>   —*Francis Cook,* Buddhist scholar,
>   describing Hua-yen Buddhism

"All Hindu religious thought denies that the world of nature stands on its own feet. It is grounded in God; if he were removed it would collapse into nothingness."[34]

>—*Huston Smith,*
>scholar of the world's sacred traditions

"There is a life pouring into the world, and it pours from an inexhaustible source."[35]

>—*Joseph Campbell,*
>scholar of world's creation stories

"Creation, then, is an ongoing story of new beginnings, opportunities to begin again and again. God began to create, is still creating; nothing is finished."[36]

>—*Wayne Muller,* ordained minister

"God is creating the entire universe, fully and totally, in this present now. Everything God created . . . God creates now all at once."[37]

>—*Meister Eckhart,* Christian mystic

"The entire cosmos comes forth moment by moment from this one fundamental innate mind of clear light."[38]

>—*Lex Hixon,*
>scholar of the world's sacred traditions

Christians, Buddhists, Hindus, Jews, Muslims, Taoists, mystics, tribal cultures, and Greek philosophers have all given remarkably similar descriptions of the universe and the life-force that pervades it. These are more than poetic and metaphorical descriptions. Because we find the notion of a living universe emerging across cultures and millennia as well as from modern science, there is compelling evidence that it forms the basis of a powerful perceptual paradigm—one that will open up enormous opportunities for the human family as we are pressed to create a sustainable future for ourselves.

IMPLICATIONS OF THE LIVING UNIVERSE PARADIGM

LIKE any paradigm shift, the shift to a living universe paradigm is transformative. In addition to changing our view of the universe, it can alter our sense of identity, our sense of life purpose, how we relate with others, and much more. Let's consider a few of its many implications.

A rebirth of connectedness in all aspects of life. To explore how our experience of the world might change with a shift to a living universe paradigm, let's look at how American Indians perceived and experienced the world. Their culture provides a clear window into the experience of living with an infusing aliveness that is an intimate part of everyday life.

Author Luther Standing Bear expresses the wisdom of indigenous peoples around the world when he says that for the Lakota Sioux, "there was no such thing as emptiness in the world. Even in the sky there were no vacant places. Everywhere there was life, visible and invisible, and every object gave us a great interest in life. The world teemed with life and wisdom; there was no complete solitude for the Lakota."[39] For the Lakota, who inhabited the upper Midwest of the United States, religion was based on a direct experience of an all-pervading spirit throughout the world. Since a life-force was felt to be in and through everything, all things were seen as being connected and related. Because everything is an expression of the Great Spirit, everything deserves to be treated with respect.

This paradigm was not unique to the Lakota. One of the most dense concentrations of Indian populations in North America—the Ohlones—lived along the fertile region that is now San Francisco, Oakland, San Jose, and Monterey in California.[40] The Ohlones lived sustainably on this land for four thousand to five thousand years. Like the Lakota, their religion was without dogma, churches, or priests because it was so pervasive, like the air. Malcolm Margolin describes their experience of the world in his book, *The Ohlone Way*:

> The Ohlones, then, lived in a world perhaps somewhat like a Van Gogh painting, shimmering and alive with movement and energy in ever-changing patterns. It was a world in which thousands of living, feeling, magical things, all operating on dream-logic, carried out their individual actions . . . Power was everywhere, in everything, and therefore every act was religious. Hunting a deer, walking on a trail, making a basket, or pounding acorns were all done with continual reference to the world of power.[41]

In shifting to the living universe paradigm, we rediscover the aliveness that is at the foundation of the universe, and we realize that we are not disconnected from the larger universe, and never have been. An Ojibwe Indian poem expresses this realization beautifully:

> Sometimes I go about pitying myself,
> and all the while I am being carried
>   on great winds across the sky.

With a cosmology of a living universe, a shining miracle exists everywhere. There are no empty places in the world.

Everywhere there is life, both visible and invisible. All of reality is infused with wisdom and a powerful presence.

The awakening of cosmic identity. In the industrial era paradigm, we are no more than biological beings, ultimately separate from others and the rest of the universe. The new findings from physics, however, reveal that we are intimately connected with the entire cosmos. Our actual identity or experience of who we are is vastly bigger than we thought— we are moving from a strictly personal consciousness to a conscious appreciation of ourselves as integral to the cosmos. Physicist Brian Swimme explains that the intimate sense of self-awareness we experience bubbling up at each moment "is rooted in the originating activity of the universe. We are all of us arising together at the center of the cosmos."[42] We thought that we were no bigger than our physical bodies, but we are discovering that we are beings of cosmic dimension, part of the flow of continuous re-creation of the cosmos. By becoming aware of that stream of life in our direct experience, we become conscious of our connection with the living universe.

Technically, we humans are more than *Homo sapiens* or "wise"—we are *Homo sapiens sapiens* or "doubly wise."[43] In other words, whereas animals "know," humans have the capacity to "know that we know." In the new paradigm, our sense of identity takes on a paradoxical and mysterious quality: we are both observer and observed, knower and that which is known. We are each completely unique yet completely connected with the entire universe. There will never be another person like any one of us in all eternity, so we are absolutely original beings. At the same time, since our existence arises from and is woven into the deep ecology of the universe, we are completely integrated with all that exists. Awakening to the miraculous nature of our identity as simultaneously unique and interconnected with a living universe can help us overcome the species arrogance and sense of separation that threaten our future.

Living lightly in a living universe. In a dead universe, materialism makes sense; in a living universe, simplicity makes sense. Let's consider these two alternatives.

If the universe is unconscious and dead at its foundations, then each of us is the product of blind chance among materialistic forces. It is only fitting that we the living exploit on our own behalf that which is not alive. If the universe is lifeless, it has no larger purpose or meaning, and neither does human existence. If we are separate beings in a lifeless universe, there are no deeper ethical or moral consequences to our actions beyond their immediate, physical impacts. It is only natural, therefore, that we focus on consuming material things to minimize life's pains and maximize its comforts.

On the other hand, if the universe is conscious and alive, then we are the product of a deep-design intelligence that infuses the entire cosmos. We shift from feelings of existential isolation in a lifeless universe to a sense of intimate communion within a living universe. If life is nested within life, then it is only fitting that we treat everything that exists as alive and worthy of respect. Our sense of meaningful connection expands to the entire community of life, including past, present, and future generations. Every action in a living universe is felt to have ethical consequences as it reverberates throughout the ecosystem of the living cosmos. The focus of life shifts from a desire for high-consumption lifestyles (intended to provide both material pleasures and protection from an indifferent universe) toward sustainable and simple ways of living (intended to connect us with a purposeful universe of which we are an integral part). In a living universe, it is only natural that people would choose simpler ways of living that afford greater time and opportunity for meaningful relationships, creative expression, and rewarding experiences. As we consciously explore our connection with a living universe, concern with material consumption will naturally tend to shift into the background of our lives.

Living with purpose in a living universe. The shift to a new paradigm also brings a shift in our sense of evolutionary purpose. We are shifting from seeing our journey as a secular adventure in a fragmented and lifeless cosmos without apparent meaning or purpose, to seeing it as a sacred journey through a living and unified cosmos. Our primary purpose is to embrace and learn from both the pleasure and the pain of the world. If there were no freedom to make mistakes, there would be no pain. If there were no freedom for authentic discovery, there would be no ecstasy. In freedom, we experience both pleasure and pain in the process of discovering our identity as beings of both earthly and cosmic dimensions. In the words of the Australian aborigines, we are learning how to survive in infinity.

Living ethically in a living universe. A form of natural ethics accompanies our intuitive connection with a living universe. When we are truly centered in the life current flowing through us, we tend to act in ways that promote the well-being and harmony of the whole. Our connection with the Mother Universe provides us with a sort of moral tuning fork that makes it possible for individuals to come into collective alignment. An underlying field of consciousness weaves humanity together, making it possible for us to understand intuitively what is healthy and what is not, what works and what doesn't. We can each tune into this living field and sense what is in harmony with the well-being of the whole. When we are in alignment, we experience—as a sort of kinesthetic sense—a positive hum of well-being.[44] In a similar way, we also experience the hum of discordance.

The new paradigm will usher us into an era in which people will be inclined to live ethically because they understand that everything they do is woven into the infinite depths of the Mother Universe. In his *Book of Mirdad,* Mikhail Nimay describes this insight beautifully:

> So think as if your every thought were to be etched in fire
>   upon the sky for all and everything to see. For so, in
>   truth, it is.
> So speak as if the world entire were but a single ear intent
>   on hearing what you say. And so, in truth, it is.
> So do as if your every deed were to recoil upon your head.
>   And so, in truth, it is.
> So wish as if you were the wish. And so, in truth, you
>   are.[45]

When we discover that all beings are part of the seamless fabric of creation, it naturally awakens in us a sense of connection with and compassion for the rest of life. We automatically broaden our scope of empathy and concern when we realize that we are inseparable from all that exists. We no longer see ourselves as isolated entities whose being stops at the edge of our skin, and whose empathy stops with our family, or our race, or our nation. We see that, because we all arise simultaneously from a deep ocean of life-energy, a vital connection exists among all beings.

The emergence of a living universe paradigm is not simply a lateral shift from one set of values to another; it is a contextual shift, from one cultural atmosphere to another, from one perceptual environment to another. It transforms the human story. After 12 billion years of evolution, we stand upon the Earth as agents of self-reflective and creative action on behalf of the universe. We see that we are participants in an unceasing miracle of creation. This recognition brings a new confidence that our potentials are as exalted, magnificent, and mysterious as the living universe that surrounds and sustains us.

—

Chapter Four

CHOOSING A NEW LIFEWAY:

VOLUNTARY SIMPLICITY

The price of anything is
the amount of life that you have to pay for it.
—*Henry Thoreau*

Too many people spend money they haven't earned,
to buy things they don't want,
to impress people they don't like.
—*Will Rogers*

A QUIET REVOLUTION

THE second opportunity trend that can make an enormous contribution to an evolutionary bounce is a voluntary shift toward more sustainable and satisfying ways of living. This is a promising development for, in order to meet the coming evolutionary challenges successfully, I believe that we will need to make major changes in every aspect of our lives—including the transportation we use, the food that we eat, the homes and communities that we live in, the work that we do, and the education that we provide. Although it is appealing to think that marginal measures such as intensified recycling and more fuel-efficient cars will take care of things, they will not. We need to make sweeping changes—both externally and within ourselves. A sustainable future will demand far more than a surface change to a different *style* of life—it requires a deep change to a new *way* of life.

Is it realistic to think that a new way of life could emerge? The American Dream is founded on the premise that the more you consume, the happier and more satisfied you will be. But decades of social science research reveal that, except for the very poor, our level of income has no significant effect on our level of satisfaction with life. As soon as we reach a comfortable level of income, the correlation between income and happiness diminishes dramatically.[1] Studies of entire nations reveal a similar pattern. For example, in the United States, while per-capita disposable income (adjusted for inflation) doubled between 1960 and 1990, the percentage of Americans reporting they were "very happy" remained essentially the same (35 percent in 1957 and 32 percent in 1993).[2]

In an article in *The New York Times* on the high price of the pursuit of affluence, Alfie Kohn says that researchers have amassed significant evidence that "satisfaction simply is not for sale."[3] In fact, Kohn says that "people for whom affluence is a priority in life tend to experience an unusual degree of anxiety and depression as well as a lower overall level of well-being." The single-minded pursuit of affluence actually reduces people's sense of well-being and satisfaction. This is the dark side of the dream of getting rich, and it seems to hold true regardless of age, level of income, or culture. Researchers have also found that "pursuing goals that reflect genuine human needs, like wanting to feel connected to others, turns out to be more psychologically beneficial than spending one's life trying to impress others." Lily Tomlin seems to be right when she says, "the trouble with being in the rat race is that even if you win, you're still a rat."

Are people waking up to another way of life, focused not on the pursuit of affluence, but on close and caring relationships, a rich inner life, and creative contributions to the world? Is there a new way of life emerging that pulls back from materialism not out of sacrifice but in an attempt to find authentic and lasting sources of satisfaction and meaning?

Amid a frenzy of conspicuous consumption, an inconspicuous revolution has been stirring. A growing number of people are seeking a way of life that is more satisfying and sustainable. This quiet revolution is being called by many names; including voluntary simplicity, soulful simplicity, and compassionate living. But whatever its name, its hallmark is a new common sense—namely, that life is too deep and consumerism is too shallow to provide soulful satisfaction. As a result, more and more people, particularly in the United States and Europe, have been exploring life beyond advertising's lure. These people have experienced the good life that consumerism has to offer and found it flat and unsatisfying compared to the rewards of the simple life. Their choice of a lifeway of conscious simplicity is driven not by sacrifice but by a growing understanding of the real sources of satisfaction and meaning—gratifying friendships, a fulfilling family life, spiritual growth, and opportunities for creative learning and expression.

This is a leaderless revolution—a self-organizing movement where people are consciously taking charge of their lives. It is a clear and promising example of people growing up and taking responsibility for how their lives connect with the Earth and the future. Many of these lifeway pioneers have been working at the grassroots level for several decades, often feeling alone, not realizing that scattered through society are others like themselves numbering in the millions.

What Is Voluntary Simplicity?

THERE has been a tendency in the mainstream media to equate a simple way of life with a lifestyle of material frugality and then to focus on the material changes people are making, such as recycling, buying used clothing, and planting gardens. While these are a few of the visible expressions of the simple life, this portrayal misses much of the juice, joy, and purpose of simple living. The overwhelming majority of those choosing a life of simplicity are not seeking to fulfill some romantic notion of returning to nature. Instead, they are seeking greater sanity and soulfulness in a society in which separation from nature is rampant. For the most part, these lifeway pioneers are not moving back to the land; they are making the most of wherever they are by crafting a way of life that is more satisfying and sustainable.

Richard Gregg, my mentor on the subject of simplicity, wrote in 1936 that the purpose of life was, fundamentally, to create a life of purpose. He saw simplicity, when it is voluntarily chosen, as a vital ally in achieving our life purpose because it enables us to cut through the complexity and busyness of the world. Gregg asked us to consider: What is the unique and true gift that only you can bring to the world? Realizing your life-purpose—or using your true gift—will determine how you structure your life. For example, if your true gift is to adopt and raise a bunch of kids, then you may need to own a large house and car. If your true gift is creating art, then you may choose to forego the house and car and instead travel the world and develop your art. Simplicity is the razor's edge that cuts through the trivial and finds the essential. Simplicity is not about a life of poverty, but about a life of purpose. Here is a key passage from Gregg's writing that describes the essence of voluntary simplicity:

> Voluntary simplicity involves both inner and outer condition. It means singleness of purpose, sincerity and honesty within, as well as avoidance of exterior clutter, of many possessions irrelevant to the chief purpose of life. It means an ordering and guiding of our energy and our desires, a partial restraint in some directions in order to secure greater abundance of life in other directions. It involves a deliberate organization of life for a purpose. Of course, as different people have different purposes in life, what is relevant to the purpose of one person might not be relevant to the purpose of another . . . The degree of simplification is a matter for each individual to settle for himself.[4]

The more I thought about the phrase "voluntary simplicity," the more I appreciated its power. To live more *voluntarily* is to live more consciously, deliberately, and purposefully. We cannot be deliberate when we are distracted and unaware. We cannot be intentional when we are not paying attention. We cannot be purposeful when we are not being present. Therefore, to act in a voluntary manner is not only to pay attention to the actions we take in the outer world, but also to pay attention to the one who is acting—to our inner world.

To live more *simply* is to live more lightly, cleanly, aerodynamically—in the things that we consume, in the work we do, in our relationships with others, and in our connections with nature. We each know the unique distractions, clutter, and pretense that weigh upon our lives and make our passage through life needlessly difficult. In living more simply, we make our journey more easeful and rewarding.

Voluntary simplicity means living in such a way that we consciously bring our most authentic and alive self into direct connection with life. This is not a static condition, but an ever-changing balance. Simplicity in this sense is not simple. To live out of our deepest sense of purpose—integrating and balancing the inner and outer aspects of our lives—is an enormously challenging and continuously evolving process. The objective of the simple life is not to live dogmatically with less, but rather to live with balance so as to have a life of greater fulfillment and satisfaction.

There is no instruction manual or set of criteria that defines a life of conscious simplicity. Gregg was insistent that "simplicity is a relative matter depending on climate, customs, culture, and the character of the individual."[5] Henry Thoreau was equally clear that there is no easy formula defining the worldly expression of a simpler life. "I would not have anyone adopt my mode of living on my account . . . I would have each one be very careful to find out and pursue his own way."[6] Because simplicity has as much to do with our purpose in living as it does with our standard of living and because we each have a unique purpose in living, it follows that there is no single right and true way to live more ecologically and compassionately.

Drawn from my book *Voluntary Simplicity,* here are a few firsthand descriptions of this way of life, offered by people who are pioneers of living simply by choice:

"Voluntary simplicity has more to do with the state of mind than a person's physical surroundings and possessions."

"As my spiritual growth expanded and developed, voluntary simplicity was a natural outgrowth. I came to realize the cost of material accumulation was too high and offered fewer and fewer real rewards, psychological and spiritual."

"It seems to me that inner growth is the whole moving force behind voluntary simplicity."

"We are intensely family oriented—we measure happiness by the degree of growth, not by the amount of dollars earned."

"I feel this way of life has made my marriage stronger, as it puts more accent on personal relationships and inner growth."

"I consciously started to live simply when I started to become conscious."

"The main motivation for me is inner spiritual growth and to give my children an idea of the truly valuable and higher things in this world."

"I feel more voluntary about my pleasures and pains than the average American who has his needs dictated by Madison Avenue (my projection, of course). I feel sustained, excited, and constantly growing in my spiritual and intellectual pursuits."

"To me, voluntary simplicity means integration and awareness in my life."

What emerges from these descriptions is the sense that something intangible is essential to these people's lives. Perhaps it is living with a feeling of reverence for the Earth and all life, or cultivating a sense of gratitude rather than greed, or focusing on the quality and integrity of relationships of all kinds. At the heart of a life of conscious simplicity is some form of experiential spirituality. In contrast to the larger society where cynicism is rampant, this is a community of people who are tapping into, valuing, and trusting their felt experience of the sacred, although they describe that experience in many different ways.

VOLUNTARY SIMPLICITY AND SOULFUL LIVING

WRITING in 1845, Henry Thoreau set the soulful tone for the simple life in *Walden,* in which he wrote these famous lines:

I went to the woods because I wished to live deliberately, to confront all of the essential facts of life, and see if I could learn what it had to teach, and not, when I came to die, to discover that I had not lived. . . . I wanted to live deep and suck out all the marrow of life . . .[7]

The Hindu poet Tagore wrote, "I have spent my days stringing and unstringing my instrument while the song I came to sing remains unsung." Those choosing a life of simplicity are not leaving the song of their soul unsung. Instead, they are living "deep," diving into life with engagement and enthusiasm. And, in living that way, they are no doubt experiencing what Thoreau discovered—that "it is life near the bone where it is sweetest." To live simply is to approach life and each moment as inherently worthy of our attention and respect, consciously attending to the small details of life. In attending to these details, we nurture the soul. Thomas Moore explains in *Care of the Soul*:

> Care of the soul requires craft, skill, attention, and art. To live with a high degree of artfulness means to attend to the small things that keep the soul engaged . . . to the soul, the most minute details and the most ordinary activities, carried out with mindfulness and art, have an effect far beyond their apparent insignificance.[8]

For many, the American dream has become the soul's nightmare. Often, the price of affluence is inner alienation and emptiness. Not surprisingly, polls show that a growing number of Americans are seeking lives of greater simplicity as a way to rediscover the life of the soul.

Although the mass media may focus on the external trappings of a simple life, if we look below the surface, we find a powerful new form of personal spirituality motivating the vast majority of these lifeway innovators. For many, their spirituality is an individualized form of faith that minimizes rules and absolutes, and bears little resemblance to the pure form of any of the world's religions.[9] Their experience with the soulful dimensions of life and relationships is so rich and meaningful that a consumerist lifestyle appears pale by comparison.

I have had a quarter century of experience writing about,

speaking about, and living a life of voluntary simplicity. Based on that, here are other priorities (beyond material frugality) that I have found that characterize this way of living:

· **Relationships**—Those choosing the simple life tend to place a high priority on the quality and integrity of their relationships with every aspect of life—with themselves, other people, other creatures, the Earth, and the universe.

· **True gifts**—This way of living supports discovering and expressing the true gifts that are unique to each of us, as opposed to waiting until we die to discover that we have not authentically lived out our true potentials.

· **Balance**—The simple life is not narrowly focused on living with less; instead, it is a continuously changing process of consciously balancing the inner and outer aspects of our lives.

· **Meditation**—Living simply enables us to approach life as a meditation. By consciously organizing our lives to minimize distractions and needless busyness, we can pay attention to life's small details and deepen our soulful relationship with life.

All of the world's spiritual traditions have advocated an inner-directed way of life that does not place undue emphasis on material things. The Bible speaks frequently about the need to find a balance between the material and the spiritual sides of life, such as in this passage: "Give me neither poverty nor wealth" (Proverbs 30:8). From China and the Taoist tradition, Lao-tzu said that "he who knows he has enough is rich." In Buddhism, there is a conscious emphasis on discovering a middle way through life that seeks balance and material sufficiency.

The soulful value of the simple life has been recognized for thousands of years. What is new is that world circumstances are changing so that this way of life now has unprecedented relevance for our times.

THE SPRINGTIME OF SIMPLICITY

IN the 1960s, voluntary simplicity was a lifeway adopted by a handful of social mavericks; today, a little more more than thirty years later, it is a mainstream wave of cultural invention involving millions of people. Gerald Celente, president of the Trends Research Institute, reported in 1997 on how the voluntary simplicity trend is growing throughout the industrialized world: "Never before in the Institute's seventeen years of tracking has a societal trend grown so quickly, spread so broadly and been embraced so eagerly."[10] In the United States, a conservative estimate is that in the late 1990s, 10 percent of the adult population—or more than 20 million people—are opting out of the rat race of consumerism and into soulful simplicity.[11]

The following surveys provide further evidence that a lifeway of soulful simplicity, with its new pattern of values, is emerging as a significant trend in the world.

Yearning for Balance—A 1995 survey of Americans commissioned by the Merck Family Fund found that respondents' deepest aspirations are nonmaterial.[12] For example, when asked what would make them much more satisfied with their lives, 66 percent said, "if I were able to spend more time with my family and friends," and only 19 percent said, "if I had a bigger house or apartment." Twenty-eight percent of the survey respondents said that in the last five years, they had voluntarily made changes in their lives that resulted in making less money, such as reducing work hours, changing to a lower-paying job, or even quitting work. The most frequent reasons given for voluntarily downshifting were:

- Wanting a more balanced life (68 percent)
- Wanting more time (66 percent)
- Wanting a less stressful life (63 percent)

Had it been worth it? Eighty-seven percent of the down-shifters described themselves as happy with the change. In summing up the survey's findings, the report states, "People express a strong desire for a greater sense of balance in their lives—not to repudiate material gain, but to bring it more into proportion with the nonmaterial rewards of life."

The Rise of Integral Culture—A random national survey conducted by Paul Ray in 1995 found that about 10 percent of the U.S. population (roughly 20 million adults) are choosing to live in a way that integrates a strong interest in their inner or spiritual life with an equally strong concern for living more in harmony with nature.[13] Ray calls these people "cultural creatives." As a group, they live more simply, work for ecological sustainability, honor nature as sacred, affirm the need to rebuild communities, and are willing to pay the costs for cleaning up the environment. As individuals, they are largely unaware of one another and feel relatively isolated.

World Values Survey—This massive survey was conducted in 1990–1991 in forty-three nations representing nearly 70 percent of the world's population and covering the full range of economic and political variation.[14] Ronald Inglehart, global coordinator of the survey, concluded that over the last twenty-five years, a major shift in values has been occurring in a cluster of a dozen or so nations, primarily in the United States, Canada, and Northern Europe. He calls this change the "postmodern shift."[15] In these societies, emphasis is shifting from economic achievement to postmaterialist values that emphasize individual self-expression, subjective well-being, and quality of life. At the same time, people in these nations are placing less emphasis on organized religion, and more on discovering their inner sense of meaning and purpose in life.[16]

Health of the Planet Survey—In 1993, the Gallup organization conducted in twenty-four nations a landmark global survey of attitudes toward the environment.[17] In writing about the survey, its director Dr. Riley E. Dunlap concluded that there is "virtually worldwide citizen awareness that our planet is indeed in poor health, and great concern for its future well-being." The survey found that residents of poorer and wealthier nations express nearly equal concern about the health of the planet. Majorities in most of the nations surveyed gave environmental protection a higher priority than economic growth, and said that they were willing to pay higher prices for that protection. There was little evidence of the poor blaming the rich for environmental problems, or vice versa. Instead, there seems to be a mature and widespread acceptance of mutual responsibility. When asked who is "more responsible for today's environmental problems in the world," the most frequent response was that industrialized and developing countries are "both equally responsible."

World Environmental Law Survey—The largest environmental survey ever conducted was done in the spring of 1998 for the International Environmental Monitor. Involving more than thirty-five thousand respondents in thirty countries, the survey found that "majorities of people in the world's most populous countries want sharper teeth put into laws to protect the environment."[18] Majorities in twenty-eight of the thirty countries surveyed (ranging from 91 percent in Greece to 54 percent in India) said that environmental laws as currently applied in their country "don't go far enough." The survey report concludes, "Overall, these findings will serve as a wake-up call to national governments and private corporations to get moving on environmental issues or get bitten by their citizens and consumers who will not stand for inaction on what they see as key survival issues."

Could a shift to postmaterialist values occur rapidly if this reservoir of sympathy and support were encouraged? Could these social entrepreneurs be planting seeds of innovation for an evolutionary bounce several decades hence?

Although these global surveys show promising evidence of a shift from consumerism toward sustainability, it is not clear whether this shift will influence the newly modernizing economies of Africa and Asia. For example, in a Gallup survey conducted in China in October 1994, people were asked which attitudes toward life came closest to describing their own. Sixty-eight percent said that to "work hard and get rich" came closest to describing their approach to life, while only 10 percent selected "don't think about money or fame, just live a life that suits your own taste."[19] Clearly, consumerist attitudes are flourishing in Asia and are likely to come into conflict with the need to develop more ecological ways of living. Indeed, the trends toward sustainability in a number of postmodern nations could be overwhelmed by the impact of rapid industrialization in just two nations, China and India, with their combined population of roughly 2 billion people.

Implications for the Future

IF a new way of life does emerge that values simplicity and satisfaction over consumerism, the implications will be enormous. I believe they will include sustainable economic development, greater economic justice, new forms of community, greater participation in the political system, the development of human potentials, and the advancement of our civilizational purpose.

Sustainable Economic Development. Consumer purchases account for nearly two-thirds of the economic activity in the United States. If a significant percent of Americans were to change their consumption levels and patterns, the effects would be dramatic. Over the years, I have noticed that people choosing a simple life tend to make these kinds of changes in their consumption:

· They tend to buy products that are durable, easy to repair, nonpolluting in their manufacture and use, energy-efficient, not tested on animals, functional, and aesthetic.

In addition, they are more inclined to make their own furniture, clothing, and other products as a form of self-expression.

· Regarding transportation, people choosing a life of simplicity tend to use public transit, car-pooling, bicycles, and smaller and more fuel-efficient cars; they may walk rather than ride; they often live closer to work; and they tend to make more extensive use of electronic communication and telecommuting as a substitute for physical travel.

· They often pursue livelihoods that contribute to others and enable them to use their creative capacities in ways that are fulfilling.

· They tend to shift their diets from highly processed food, meat, and sugar toward foods that are more natural, healthful, simple, locally grown, and appropriate for sustaining the inhabitants of a small planet.

· They recycle metal, glass, plastic, and paper and cut back on their use of things that waste nonrenewable resources.

· They reduce undue clutter and complexity in their lives by giving away or selling things that they seldom use, such as clothing, books, furniture, and tools.

· They tend to buy less clothing, jewelry, and cosmetics; they tend to focus on what is functional, durable, and aesthetic rather than on passing fads, fashions, and seasonal styles.

· They usually observe holidays in a less commercialized manner.

Bit by bit, these and other small changes by individuals and families could coalesce into a tremendous wave of economic change in support of a sustainable future. Professor Stuart Hart, writing in the *Harvard Business Review* about strategies for a sustainable world, says that "over the next decade or so, sustainable development will constitute one of the biggest opportunities in the history of commerce."[20]

How would a sustainable economy differ from a consumer economy? For one thing, it would be much more differentiated: some sectors would contract (especially those that waste energy and are oriented toward conspicuous consumption), while other sectors would expand (such as information processing, interactive communications, intensive agriculture, retrofitting homes for energy efficiency, and education for lifelong learning). To minimize the costs of transportation and distribution, markets would be more decentralized than they are today. People would buy more goods and services from local producers; in turn, there would be a rebirth of entrepreneurial activity at the local level. Small businesses well adapted to local conditions and needs would flourish. New types of markets and marketplaces would proliferate, such as flea markets, community markets, and extensive bartering networks (whose efficiency will be greatly enhanced by new generations of computers that match goods and services with potential consumers or traders). The economy would also be more democratized as workers take a larger role in decision making. All types of products—such as cars, refrigerators, and carpeting—would be designed to be easily disassembled and then recycled into new products, minimizing waste. Less money would be spent on material goods and more on entertainment, education, and communication.

One criticism of the simple life is that it would undermine economic growth and produce high unemployment. This criticism is based on the erroneous assumption that high-consumption lifestyles are necessary to maintain a vigorous economy and full employment. However, in modern consumer societies such as the United States, there are an enormous number of unmet needs—for example, restoring the natural environment, retrofitting our homes for sustainable living, rebuilding our decaying cities, caring for the elderly, and educating the young. For the foreseeable future, there will be no shortage of real work and meaningful employment if we are committed to meeting the real needs of people.

Likewise, in developing nations, there is enormous economic opportunity if approached from the mind-set of sustainability. Sixty percent of the world's population lives on the equivalent of $3 or less a day, mostly in the developing world, in urban shantytowns without adequate shelter, clean water, sanitation, schools, health care, fire and police protection, access to communications technology, dependable energy, paved roads, public transportation, or space to grow food. These enormous needs represent equally great economic opportunities for meaningful work.

Economic justice. The Universal Declaration of Human Rights affirmed by the United Nations in 1948 states in part that "everyone has the right to a standard of living adequate for the health and well-being of himself and of his family, including food, clothing, housing and medical care and necessary social services." A significant part of humanity has no way to exercise that right, and I see little possibility of that changing under the trickle-down economic system we have today.

Given the new perceptual paradigm that is emerging—

whose core expression is a shift in experience from existential separation in a dead universe to empathic connection in a living universe—it is not surprising that those who choose a simpler life tend to feel connected with and a compassionate concern for the world's poor. This sense of kinship with people around the world fosters a concern for social justice and greater fairness in the use of the world's resources. Because economic inequality is increasing rapidly in the world, a conscious cultural shift toward more sustainable levels and patterns of consumption seems essential if there is to be greater equity in how people live. Indeed, I see a lifeway of choiceful simplicity and graceful moderation as the only realistic foundation for achieving a meaningful degree of economic fairness and thereby building a foundation for pulling together as a human family.

We need to learn to use resources more fairly if we are to live peacefully. Armies and military weapons are enormously expensive and represent a huge drain on resources that could otherwise be used for sustainable development. If we are able to narrow the gap between the rich and the poor of the world, the prospect of conflict over scarce resources will diminish. This, in turn, could free up people and resources for building a future that benefits us all.

New forms of community. Community provides the foundation for a civilization of simplicity. To encourage self-reliance at the most local scale feasible, community design would likely involve a nested set of living arrangements. For example, a family would live in an "eco-home" (designed for considerations such as energy efficiency, telecommuting, and gardening), nested within an "eco-neighborhood," within an "eco-village," within an "eco-city," within an "eco-region," and so on. Each eco-village could contain a telecommuting center, child-care home, community garden, and recycling area. Urban land that was formerly used for lawns and flower gardens could be used for supplemental food sources such as vegetable gardens, and fruit and nut trees. These micro-communities or neighborhood-size villages could have the flavor and cohesiveness of a small town combined with the urban flavor of a larger city. Each eco-village might specialize in a particular kind of work—such as crafts, health care, child care, gardening, or education—providing fulfilling work for many of its inhabitants. People could earn time-share hours that could be bartered for the products or services of neighbors—such as gardening, food, music lessons, carpentry, or plumbing. People could balance their work between serving their local community and serving the world.

Because the populations of eco-villages (five hundred or so people) would approximate the scale of a tribe, many people could feel quite comfortable in this design for living. With an architecture sensitive to the psychology of these modern tribes, a new sense of community could begin to replace the alienation of today's massive cities. To support these innovations in housing and community, there could be accompanying changes in zoning laws, building codes, financing methods, and ownership arrangements. Overall, these smaller-scale, human-size living and working environments could foster a rebirth of community; we could again have face-to-face contact in the process of daily living in local neighborhoods.

Greater participation in politics. Many of those choosing a simpler way of life have pulled back from traditional politics, unable to identify with either conservatives (who tend to trust in the workings of business and the marketplace) or liberals (who tend to trust in the workings of government and bureaucracy). They are turning instead to their own resources as well as to their friends and local community. The politics of simplicity are neither left nor right, but represent a new combination of self-reliance, community spirit, and cooperation.

We can use the analogy of humanity's adolescence to get a better sense of how politics may change in the future as we mature into our young adulthood. It seems to me that humans have been acting like political adolescents; on the whole, we have been waiting for "Mom and Dad" (our big institutions of business and government) to take care of things for us and we blame them when they don't. As we move into our early adulthood, however, we are beginning to face our challenges head on, recognizing that we are in charge, and that no one is going to save us. To create a sustainable future for ourselves on this planet, particularly given the speed, cooperation, and creativity that our situation demands—will require the voluntary actions of millions, even billions, of free individuals acting responsibly and in concert with one another. Never before in human history have so many people been called upon to make such sweeping changes voluntarily and in so little time. The new politics are grounded in the unflinching recognition that we are being challenged to grow up and take charge of our lives, both locally and globally.

Our indispensable ally in this process is the communications revolution. When the politics of sustainability are combined with the power of television and the internet, the combination could be transformative. As we shall explore in the next chapter, the communications revolution will support a dramatic increase in the public's ability to hold corporations and governments accountable for their actions. Internet campaigns will flourish that blow the whistle on government and corporate abuses and encourage people to boycott the products of firms and nations whose policies are unethical environmentally, economically, or socially.

Finally, a new era of volunteerism could blossom. For instance, young people could be encouraged to contribute a year or more of local or national service, perhaps restoring the environment, working with youth, or building community centers.

The development of human potentials. A life that is outwardly simple and inwardly rich naturally celebrates the development of our many potentials. As the simple life makes time available, areas for learning and growth blossom. These include the physical (such as running, biking, and yoga); the emotional (such as learning the skills of emotional intelligence and interpersonal intimacy); the intellectual (such as developing skills in the arts and crafts as well as basic skills such as carpentry, plumbing, appliance repair, and gardening); and the spiritual (such as various forms of meditation and relaxation, and exploring the mind-body connection with biofeedback).

The advancement of our civilizational purpose. Choosing to live more simply does not mean turning away from progress; quite the opposite. A life-way of voluntary simplicity is a direct expression of our growth as a maturing civilization. After a lifetime of studying the rise and fall of more than twenty of the world's civilizations, the highly esteemed historian, Arnold Toynbee, concluded that the conquest of land or people was not the true measure of a civilization's growth. The true measure, he said, was expressed in a civilization's ability to transfer an increasing proportion of energy and attention from the material to the nonmaterial side of life to develop its culture (such as music, art, drama, and literature), sense of community, and strength of democracy. Toynbee called this the "Law of Progressive Simplification."[21] He said that authentic growth consists of a "progressive and cumulative increase both in outward mastery of the environment and in inward self-determination or self-articulation on the part of the individual or society."[22] I believe that Toynbee is correct, and that our outward mastery will be evident by living ever more lightly upon the Earth, and our inward mastery will be evident by living ever more lightly with gratitude and joy in our hearts.

Choosing a way of life that is simpler, more satisfying, and more sustainable could help us transform an evolutionary crash into a bounce. Obviously, the simple life offers no magical solutions. It will take millions and even billions of people tending to the small details of their lives to craft a more soulful and satisfying existence for themselves and for us all. It is, nonetheless, empowering to know that each of us can make a meaningful difference by taking responsibility for changes in our own lives. Most of us have seen the limits of bureaucracy and understand that, if creative action is required, it will likely come through the conscious actions of countless individuals working in cooperation with one another. A lifeway of conscious simplicity is made to order for self-organizing action at the local scale. Small changes that seem insignificant in isolation can have an enormous impact when undertaken together by millions.

Seeds growing in the garden of simplicity for the past generation are now blossoming into the springtime of their planetary relevance and could provide a crucial ingredient for an evolutionary bounce.

Chapter Five

COMMUNICATING OUR WAY INTO

A PROMISING FUTURE

The communications industry is the only instrument
that has the capacity to educate on a scale that is needed
and in the time available.
—*Lester Brown, President of Worldwatch Institute*

AWAKENING AS A PLANETARY SPECIES

OUR ability to communicate has enabled humans to progress
from nomadic bands of gatherers and hunters to the edge of
a planetary civilization. Thus it should come as no surprise
that our ability to communicate will determine whether we
are successful in achieving a promising future. Anything that
dramatically enhances human communication will have an
equally dramatic influence on our evolution. Because we are
in the midst of an unprecedented revolution in the scope,
depth, and richness of global communications, the impact of
this revolution on our future will be equally unprecedented.
The global communications revolution is such an extraordinary force for change in the world that I consider it one
of the key factors that could transform an evolutionary catastrophe into an exhilarating leap forward for humanity.

Prior to the era of electronic communications, the world

was a vast place where oceans and continents insulated people from one another. Events in one part of the world might
be utterly unknown elsewhere for months or years, if they
were ever known at all. Over the last few decades, the
change in our ability to communicate has been extraordinary. To illustrate just how much things have changed, I'll
use my own experience as an example.

In the 1950s, I was in my early teens, living on a family
farm in Idaho, several miles from a town of five hundred
people. I felt disconnected from the larger world, as a couple
of radio stations were my primary contact with life beyond
our small town. Television was just arriving and consisted
of three channels broadcasting snowy, black-and-white images during the afternoons and evenings. The weekly paper
was a scant few pages covering the news of a small town, so
I looked forward to the weekly edition of the *Saturday Evening Post* and the monthly *National Geographic*. To a great
extent, the events occurring around the world were largely
unknown, and unknowable to me.

One of the most exciting events during those years occurred one winter when I built my first shortwave radio
from a kit. For several days, I soldered together resistors,
capacitors, tubes, and transformers. Then I went outside and
hooked an antenna wire from the roof of our house to a
telephone pole some thirty yards away. On a cold and clear
winter night, I turned on my shortwave receiver to listen in
on the world. After a few minutes of turning the dial, a
voice came in distinct and strong—from Australia! I was
completely amazed to be listening to someone speaking from
the other side of the world. Hearing that voice suddenly
made the Earth feel much smaller and more approachable.

What was miraculous to me then is now commonplace

given the explosive growth in communications technologies. Whereas I was able to listen to a random voice by accident, people can now interact purposefully and inexpensively with countless other people around the planet. The internet is collapsing the world into an electronic village where we are all neighbors, while television is providing a common world-language through its visual images.

The spectacular growth in global communications offers humanity the possibility of communicating our way through this time of planetary challenge. All of the adversity trends that were discussed in chapter two—such as climate change, population growth, poverty, the extinction of species, and the depletion of fresh water—are, at their core, communications challenges. For example, coping with climate change is not primarily a technical issue concerning carbon dioxide in the atmosphere; more fundamentally, it is about our ability to communicate together as a global family and respond in concert in ways that will reduce emissions. Over-population is, in many ways, a more fundamental problem of illiteracy and lack of educational opportunity for women—again, a communications challenge. Responding to global poverty represents an enormous communications challenge as we try to reach a working understanding of how to live fairly in a communications-rich world where inequities have become glaringly obvious. Ensuring that there is enough food, water, and fuel for humanity's future is not simply a material concern, it is also a matter of planning ahead on a planetary scale, and this is a communications challenge. Which energy future we take—relying on decentralized sources of renewable energy such as solar and wind, or relying on centralized sources such as nuclear power—is also a communications issue. It seems very hopeful to me that we are fast acquiring the communication tools needed to talk through all of these challenges.

The two most powerful expressions of the communications revolution are television and the internet. Let's look at each of these media briefly.

TELEVISION: THE PATHWAY TO COLLECTIVE VISUALIZATION

TELEVISION has been called "the boob tube," "a vast wasteland," and "a golden goose that lays scrambled eggs," yet it is an incredibly powerful medium. It is powerful because it makes use of visual communication, and we are a visually oriented species. (We don't say things like "seeing is believing" and "one picture is worth a thousand words" for no reason.) The visual imagery of television creates a common language that makes it humanity's primary source of shared information and understanding. Television is the window through which we see the world, and the mirror in which we see ourselves.

A key measure of the power of television in today's world can be seen when there is a military challenge to the authority of a national leader. In decades past, during a military coup, the army would seek to take over the train stations and airports, as these were the main conduits of power. No longer. In a showdown of power today, the focus of military attention as well as civilian attention are the television stations. In the recent era, when there has been the threat of civil war—whether in Russia, the Philippines, or Eastern Europe—the armies and civilians have gathered primarily around the television stations and towers, recognizing these are the real seats of power as they provide the all-important, visual connection with the collective consciousness of the society.

In the United States, 98 percent of all homes have a TV set, which the average person watches more than four hours per day. Taken together, this means that Americans watch approximately one billion person-hours of television daily. A majority of Americans get a majority of their news about the world from this medium. There are more homes in the United States with a TV set than with indoor toilets, stoves, or refrigerators. A similar emphasis on televised communication exists elsewhere around the world. In China, for example, just 2 percent of homes in major cities had hot running water in 1997, but 89 percent had televisions.[1] In India, South America, and other developing regions, many people who lack indoor plumbing, refrigerators, and other basics nonetheless have a TV set connecting them with the world. Despite enormous disparities in material wealth, people in developing nations are already part of the global communications culture.

The closeness and intimacy of television's window onto the world can give people a feeling of connection with the fate of the Earth. At the speed of light, television can unite the entire planet. Through the eyes of television, we can see a starving child in Africa, the destruction of rain forests in Brazil, urban decay in New York City, and the effects of acid rain in Germany. Television makes every viewer an active witness—a knowing and feeling participant in what is being shown. Professor of communications George Gerbner recognized the power of television as the primary storytelling machine of civilizations. He said that to control a nation you don't have to control its laws or its military, but rather control who tells its stories. Television tells most of the people most of their stories most of the time. And the people who now control television are advertisers despite the fact that it is the public who "own the airwaves."

Whether used for good or ill, the influence of television often overwhelms the power of religious institutions, its capacity to shape public opinion surpasses that of many political institutions, and its ability to program the minds of children is stronger than that of our schools. Television is our social witness, our vehicle for "knowing that we know" as communities, nations, and as a human family. If issues and concerns do not appear regularly on television, then for all practical purposes they do not exist in mass social consciousness. Television is now an integral part of the social brain of our species.

THE INTERNET: PATHWAY TO THE GLOBAL BRAIN

WHERE television has overcome language barriers with the power of visual communication, the internet has overcome distance barriers with the power of its planetary reach. The internet—with its billions of cross-cultural communications and connections flowing daily around the world—has transformed political and social boundaries into permeable membranes. Individuals are gaining instant access to one another, and are communicating in ways formerly reserved only for the very wealthy. A communications-rich future holds the promise of the radical empowerment of humanity at the grassroots level. Web observer Mark Pesce has written that "it is not an overstatement to frame the World Wide Web as an innovation as important as the printing press—it may be as important as the birth of language itself . . . in its ability to completely refigure the structure of civilization."[2]

The raw power of internet technologies is like nothing we have known before. According to Joseph Pelton, who has written extensively about the globalization of telecommunications, a single advanced satellite or fiber-optic cable currently has the capability of sending the entire *Encyclopedia Britannica* with all its illustrations every three seconds.[3] Future prospects are even more breathtaking: "In another quarter of a century these are likely to be . . . systems that could send the equivalent of the entire U.S. Library of Congress in less than 10 seconds."[4] Another observer of the internet is John Midwinter, who has written that the computing and communications industry "shows every sign of continuing its breathtaking pace for at least one or two decades more (e.g., doubling performance every one or two years), implying a revolution in capability every five to ten years."[5] Growth of the internet supports this claim. Worldwide, an estimated 40 million people used the internet in 1996. This number is expected to jump to 500 million by 2001.[6] By 2010, there will be an estimated one billion people continuously connected to the World Wide Web.[7]

When this planetary scope of human connection is combined with the functional intelligence of computers, a new level of human awareness and communication—a "global brain"—could potentially emerge. What this means is that we could soon achieve a quantum increase in the functional intelligence of our species.[8] Billions of messages are swirling around the globe each day, weaving the human family into an ever-tighter web of communication and consciousness. With the connection of billions of people into a single system, a rudimentary global brain is emerging.[9] When a billion

people or more are connected into an integrated communication network twenty-four hours a day, seven days a
week, a new level of collective consciousness with unexpected potentials will awaken in the world.

THE QUICKENING PACE OF GLOBAL AWAKENING

HOW soon might the emerging global brain reach a critical
threshold and turn on with a rudimentary collective consciousness? Research by the Institute for Information Studies
states that the physical infrastructure of the global communications network that will serve as the conduit for widespread economic, social, cultural, and political exchange will
"start to come into place around the second decade of the
twenty-first century."[10] This is same time frame in which
the adversity trends discussed in chapter two are expected to
converge into a whole-systems crisis for the people of the
Earth.

Because fiber-optic cable will likely be the medium of
choice for high-density routes in developed countries, the
rate of its use is one meaningful indicator of the rate at which
the global brain is being wired. Projections by Bell Northern
Research for the growth and deployment of optic fiber in
developed countries indicate that by the mid-2020s, the basic
communications infrastructure will be in place to support a
major leap forward in our ability to communicate.[11]

Expanding the reach of the internet, hundreds of satellites
will be launched over the next few years to form the infrastructure for a wireless communications system. Writing in
Scientific American, Joseph Pelton predicts that by 2003, there
will likely be one thousand commercial communications sat-

ellites in service, up from about two hundred twenty in 1998.[12] This new generation of satellites, placed in low Earth orbit, will revolutionize global communications. For better or worse, many people will soon be continuously connected with the world no matter where they are.

Combined with satellites, cellular phones will enable developing countries to bypass the need to build a vast network of telephone lines strung along poles. There is an enormous advantage to this—it enables developing countries to literally leapfrog into the future, by avoiding investment in traditional forms of equipment and communication networks.[13] The internet could also have a very positive impact on developing countries.[14] For some people, it offers the opportunity of global telecommuting. There are now software programmers in India, for example, who telecommute daily to work in the Silicon Valley. For others, the internet offers tele-medicine—low-cost, online, medical assistance—even in remote areas of the world. The internet can also help isolated groups find markets for goods and services, and empower local activists by linking them with supporters across the globe.

Given all these communication trends, it seems likely that *within ten to twenty years, we will have in place the communications infrastructure that could support a quantum increase in the collective communication—and the collective consciousness— of our species.*

I do not assume that electronic communication can or should carry the entire burden of human communication. It is vital that we combine the power of global communication with study circles and other forms of grassroots dialogue. With the combination of the two, a local-to-global conversation could emerge to shape the outlines of a sustainable

future. Individuals could engage in face-to-face conversations locally—in homes, schools, churches, civic organizations, and workplaces—and then connect with local groups
around the world via the internet. If we could generate this
kind of worldwide dialogue, it seems plausible that the human family could mobilize itself to begin building a future
that we scarcely could have imagined a decade or two earlier.

THE ABUSE OF POWER—PERCEPTUAL
TOTALITARIANISM

LIKE all powerful technologies, the tools of global communication present humanity with a double-edged sword.
On the one hand, these are the tools that we need to build
a sustainable future. On the other hand, these are also the
tools that are now being used to promote mindless consumerism around the planet—which may be the primary threat
to a sustainable future.

In the course of a year, the average American will view
approximately twenty-five thousand commercials. A commercial represents far more than a pitch for a particular product; it is also an advertisement for the attitudes, values, and
lifestyle that surround the consumption of that product. The
unrelenting consumerist bias of television distorts our view
of reality and social priorities, leaving us entertainment rich
and knowledge poor. Television may be our window onto
the world, but the view it now provides is cramped and
narrow. Television may be the mirror in which we see ourselves as a society, but the reflection it gives is distorted and
unbalanced.

The mirror that mainstream television holds up to the world as the realistic norm of consumption is far removed from the lives of a majority of people on the Earth. The use of television to promote primarily materialistic values has become a severe, although largely unacknowledged, mental health and public health problem for the United States and the world. We are in a double bind: while the mass media that dominate our consciousness tell us to consume more, our ecological concerns tell us to consume less. Carl Jung defined schizophrenia as a condition where "the dream becomes the reality." The American dream of a consumerist way of life has become a dangerous illusion that no longer fits the reality of the world and our human potentials. By allowing a commercialized view of the world to become our primary way of defining reality, we are becoming a schizophrenic society. As commercial television spreads throughout the world, with it grows a deep conflict within our collective psyche.

A major survey of American college freshmen over a period of thirty years gives us striking evidence of the powerful impact of television on values. This study, by the American Council on Education and UCLA, found that there has been a dramatic shift in the values of college freshmen since the 1960s.[15] In 1966, "developing a meaningful philosophy of life" was the top value, being endorsed as a "very important" or "essential" goal by more than 80 percent of the entering freshmen. "Being well-off financially" lagged far behind, ranking fifth on the list, with less than 45 percent of freshmen endorsing it as a very important or essential goal in life. Since then, these two very different values have essentially traded rankings, as Figure 5 shows. In 1996, being well-off financially was the top value (74 percent of freshmen iden-

FIGURE 5

Contrasting Value Trends of U.S. College Freshmen

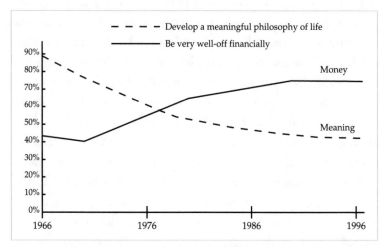

Source: American Council on Education and UCLA

tified it as very important or essential) and developing a
meaningful philosophy of life fell to sixth place (only 42
percent named it as very important or essential).

According to the researchers who conducted this study, a
major reason for this profound shift is the impact of television viewing on values. They found that "the more television watched, the stronger the endorsement of the goal of
being very well off financially, and the weaker the endorsement of the goal of developing a meaningful philosophy of
life."[16] Freshmen entering college in the late 1960s had been
exposed to much less television while they were young than
had freshmen entering college in the late 1980s. Given how
ubiquitous the mass media have become since the 1960s, all
generations henceforth will be swimming in increasingly

sophisticated forms of television and thoroughly influenced by it.

I believe there may be no more dangerous challenge to our future than the cultural hypnosis that is generated daily by commercial television, which trivializes the human experience and distracts humanity from our larger potentials. *By programming television for commercial success, we are programming the mind-set of entire civilizations—indeed, the species-civilization—for evolutionary stagnation and ecological failure.* If television is our social brain, then American television currently provides the highest level of intelligence that beer and car commercials can buy. This dumbing down of our collective intelligence is happening at the very time that we face unprecedented upheaval and change. Our evolutionary maturity is being tested. Our future as a species may well depend on whether we take self-organizing action to ensure that our tools of collective communication support the social conversation required to build a sustainable future.

More than twenty years ago, author Gene Youngblood warned that the mass media could hold back human evolution simply by controlling the perception of alternatives. He said that in order to perpetuate the status quo, it is not necessary that the mass media create a genuine desire for a consumerist way of life; all they have to do is prevent genuine desire for any other way of life from being publicly expressed and collectively affirmed:

Desire is learned. Desire is cultivated. It's a habit formed through continuous repetition . . . But we cannot cultivate that which isn't available. We don't order a dish that isn't on the menu. We don't vote for a candidate who isn't on the

ballot . . . What could be a more radical example of totalitarianism than the power of the mass media to synthesize the
only politically relevant reality, specifying for most people
most of the time what's real and what's not, what's important
and what's not . . . ? This, I submit, is the very essence of
totalitarianism: the control of desire through the control of
perception.[17]

By excluding visions of more sustainable ways of living
and consuming, the mass media perpetuate the status quo
while simultaneously crippling society's capacity for envisioning more promising alternatives. The experience of the
Soviet Union provides a powerful example of what happens
when people cannot consider alternatives via the public media. Historically, even though a majority of Soviet citizens
were opposed to party-boss Communism, this opposition
did not lead to radical reform of the social system because
citizens were denied the opportunity to publicly consider
alternatives to Communism. They knew what they were
against, but they did not know what they were for. As one
observer of the Soviet experience explains, "there was no
'model' of such reformation in the social consciousness."[18]
Just as the Soviets have suffered in their transition because
they lacked publicly considered alternatives to communism,
Americans are suffering—and so is the world—because of an
absence of publicly considered alternatives to consumerism.

As citizens of maturing societies, it is time to pay attention
to how we pay attention collectively. It is time to break
through the perceptual totalitarianism of the consumerist
mind-set that undermines our future, and give ourselves
alternative images of a sustainable future as vivid and compelling as the consumer messages that dominate our col-

lective consciousness day after day. Only with sustained communication about alternative visions of the future can citizens consciously visualize, discuss, reflect, select, and build the future we want.

A closely related concern is the degree to which communications technologies become available in developing countries. If communications technologies continue to be another factor that separates the "haves" from the "have-nots," humanity will become increasingly divided into the "communications rich" and "communications poor," and this could foster further division and breakdown. Paradoxically, the fast developing, global communications network is making these economic divisions transparent to the rest of the world. For example, in the early 1990s, villagers in India could receive four channels of television, largely government controlled. By the late 1990s, the number of channels that could be received jumped to fifty-two and included a flood of U.S. and European programming. With that increase in channels has come a continuous stream of TV programs concerned with the lifestyle problems of middle-class people in developed countries. Because a majority of people in developing countries are seeing ways of living that are completely out of their reach for the foreseeable future, it would not be surprising if they were to feel resentment that comparable opportunities are not available to them and their children.

If only a minuscule fraction of people living in abject poverty in developing nations were to choose violence as the weapon of last resort, the impacts could be enormous in our interdependent world. To be heard, some among the disenfranchised may forgo physical violence only to embrace other forms of destruction. Warfare could shift to an electronic battleground, where terrorists could scramble or damage data critical to vital computer systems in government and business. Conflicts could range from minor skirmishes to all-out assaults on the electronic integrity of corporations, nations, or the entire planet. A recent estimate by information warfare specialists at the Pentagon reveals how vulnerable developed nations are to disruption. They estimated that a properly prepared and well-coordinated attack by fewer than thirty computer virtuosos, strategically located around the world, with a budget of less than $10 million, could bring the United States to its knees, shutting down everything from electric power grids to air traffic control centers.[19]

POWER IN A TRANSPARENT WORLD

IN describing democracy in America in the early 1800s, Alexis de Tocqueville said that newspapers were a vital force, as they could put a single idea into ten thousand minds all on the same day. Less than two hundred years later, we have tools of communication that can put a single idea into several billion minds all at the same instant. The question is: What mixture of ideas and stories are we going to put into our collective consciousness?

How we use our tools of mass communication is not just another issue, it is the basis for understanding and responding to all issues. Through the internet, for example, we can quickly harness the expertise of the world to re-create our lives for sustainability. We can learn about solar technology for heating, photovoltaic technology for generating electricity, intensive urban gardening for supplemental sources of food, and so much more. New forms of business will emerge, providing services and products ranging from renewable energy systems to organic agriculture, from telemedicine to clothing and crafts from around the world. Nearly frictionless markets will facilitate barter networks, and will give people in developing countries much easier entry into global commerce.

The mass media and the internet are creating a transparent world where injustices are increasingly difficult to hide. This transparency is bringing a new level of accountability and ethicality into institutional conduct. There is no longer a rug under which corporations can sweep unjust labor practices, or governments can hide human rights abuses. Just as a rising tide lifts all boats, so too will a rising level of global communication lift all injustices into the healing light of public awareness.

What we see and hear through the new media may challenge the emotional intelligence and maturity of the species. As our social consciousness awakens, deep psychic wounds will emerge that have festered through history. We will begin to hear the voices that we have ignored and the pain that we have not acknowledged. Awakening may bring with it "the psychic sludge of history" in the form of racism, ethnic conflict, and religious discord.[20] It may seem unwise to bring the dark side of our past into the light of day, but, unless we do, this unresolved pain will forever pull at the underside of our consciousness and diminish our future potentials.

For the first time in human history, we are acquiring a way to listen to and talk with one another as members of one family. For the first time, all the cousins in the human clan can communicate with one another. In awakening to ourselves as a planetary species and seeing ourselves directly and whole for the first time, we will see that we have the potential for an evolutionary bounce. The question is whether we will have the collective maturity to seize this precious opportunity.

Chapter Six

—

Reconciliation and the

Transformation

of Human Relations

Love is mankind's most potent weapon
for personal and social transformation.
—*Martin Luther King, Jr.*

To him in whom love dwells,
the whole world is but one family.
—*The Buddha*

The Power of Love

IN the preceding chapters, we explored three trends that
have the power to fuel an evolutionary bounce. One is the
power of perception and the emergence of a perceptual paradigm that allows us to see the universe as alive rather than
dead. Another is the power of choice and our ability to shift
voluntarily toward a simpler way of life. A third is the power
of communication and the opportunity to use the internet
and the mass media to support a quantum increase in conversation about our common future. This chapter is about
the fourth trend that has the capacity to transform a crash
into a bounce—the power of love. By this I mean not romantic love, but a mature and soulful compassion that looks

beneath surface differences and sees our common connection with the community of life.

Compassionate love is a transformative power that we cannot quantify or measure, yet it brings incomparable strength and resilience into human relationships. "Love," said Teilhard de Chardin, "is the fundamental impulse of Life . . . the one natural medium in which the rising course of evolution can proceed."[1] Without love, he said, "there is truly nothing ahead of us except the forbidding prospect of standardisation and enslavement—the doom of ants and termites."

A compassionate love can provide a vital "social glue" to hold us together as we face the challenges ahead. If we pull apart, an evolutionary crash seems assured. If we come together authentically, however, we have the real potential to achieve an evolutionary bounce. And to pull together, we need to reconcile the many differences that now divide us. We need to discover harmony where there is now discord. We need to cultivate the respect and regard for others that ultimately come from a foundation of love.[2]

Love is the deepest connecting force in the universe, and thus a vital ingredient in our evolutionary journey toward wholeness. The unfolding of love is not different from the unfolding of awareness. Jack Kornfield, esteemed meditation teacher, put it this way: "I will tell you a secret, what is really important . . . true love is really the same as awareness. They are identical."[3] If we can learn the lesson that love will further our evolution and that the greater our love the greater our awareness, then we are aligned for success in our journey home. With love—or a maturing awareness—as a foundation, the hallmark of the emerging era could be the healing of our many fragmented relationships. If that were to occur, it truly is possible to imagine a future that works for everyone. With reconciliation, there is little doubt that an evolutionary bounce could happen.

A compassionate or loving consciousness has ancient roots, but it is taking on a new importance as our world becomes integrated ecologically, economically, and culturally. Because we now share one another's fate, it is increasingly clear that promoting the well-being of others directly promotes our own. We have reached the point where the Golden Rule is becoming essential to humanity's survival. This ancient ethic, which is found in all of the world's spiritual traditions, advises that the way to know how to treat others is to treat them as you would want to be treated. Here are some of the ways the Golden Rule has been expressed:

"As you wish that men would do to you, do so to them."
—Christianity (Luke 6:31)

"No one of you is a believer until he desires for his brother that which he desires for himself."
—Islam (Sunan)

"Hurt not others in ways that you yourself would find hurtful."
—Buddhism (Udanavarga)

"Do naught unto others that which would cause you pain if done to you."
—Hinduism (Mahabharata 5:1517)

"Do not unto others what you would not have them do unto you."
—Confucianism (Analects 15:23)

As diverse and divisive as we are, the human family recognizes this common ethic of compassion at the core of life. This indicates to me that there is a basis for reconciliation within humanity.

Love and compassion not only have ancient roots; history also attests to their impact and enduring power. Compassionate teachers through the ages such as Jesus, Buddha, Mohammed, and Lao-tzu have all lacked wealth, armies, and political position. Yet as the late Harvard professor Pitirim Sorokin explains in his classic book, *The Ways and Power of Love,* they were warriors of the heart, and have reoriented the thinking and behavior of billions of people, transformed cultures, and changed the course of history: "None of the greatest conquerors and revolutionary leaders can even remotely compete with these apostles of love in the magnitude and durability of the change brought about by their activities."[4] In contrast, most empires built rapidly through war and violence—such as those of Alexander the Great, Caesar, Genghis Khan, Napoleon, and Hitler—have crumbled within years or decades after their establishment.

The ruler Ashoka, who lived in India three hundred years before Jesus was born, is an example of the power of love in human affairs.[5] Prince Ashoka was born into a great dynasty of warriors and inherited an empire that extended from central India to central Asia. Nine years into his reign, he launched a massive campaign to win the rest of the Indian subcontinent. Finally, after a fierce battle in which more than a hundred thousand soldiers were slain, the land was conquered. Ashoka walked the battlefield that day, looking at the dead and maimed bodies, and felt profound sorrow and regret for the slaughter and for the deportation of people he had conquered. He immediately ceased his military campaign, converted to Buddhism, and devoted the rest of his life to serving the happiness and welfare of all.

Ashoka's thirty-seven years of benevolent rule left a legacy of concern not only for human beings but for animals and plants as well. His decrees creating sanctuaries for wild animals and protecting certain species of trees may be the earliest example of environmental action by a government.[6] Ashoka's works of charity included planting shade trees and orchards along roads, building rest houses for travelers and watering sheds for animals, and giving money to the poor, aged, and helpless. His political administration was marked by the end of war and an emphasis on peace. All his political officers were encouraged to extend goodwill, sympathy, and love to their own people as well as to others. One of their main duties was to be peacemakers, building mutual goodwill among races, sects, and parties. His cultural activities promoted education and the arts of the stage, including the construction of amphitheaters. Sorokin sums up Ashoka's legacy as "a striking example of a peaceful, love-motivated, social, mental, moral and aesthetic reconstruction of an empire."[7]

Ashoka's compassionate rule established the largest kingdom in India until the arrival of the British more than two thousand years later. The lion pillar—a statue that is the symbol of Ashoka—survives to this day as the official emblem of the Republic of India, and is found on nearly every Indian coin and currency note. "Amidst the tens of thousands of names of monarchs that crowd the columns of history," wrote historian H. G. Wells, "the name of Ashoka shines, and shines almost alone, a star."[8]

Based on examples such as these, Sorokin concluded that love-inspired reconstructions of society carried out in peace

are far more successful and yield much more lasting results
than reconstructions inspired by hate and carried out with
violence. Again and again, he found that "hate produces
hate, physical force and war beget counterforce and coun-
terwar, and that rarely, if ever, do these factors lead to peace
and social well-being."[9]

RECONCILING OUR MANY DIVISIONS

IN the industrial era, extended relationships and traditional
communities have been torn apart. We have become a species marked by rootless, mobile societies, in which temporary relationships and friendships predominate. Friends come
and go. Marriages break up. People move away from their
parents and siblings, sometimes geographically, sometimes
emotionally.

On the larger scale, we divide ourselves from one another
in all kinds of ways, on the basis of any trait that distinguishes
one human being from the next. Here are the main areas to
which I believe humanity could choose to bring a spirit of
reconciliation:

· **Economic reconciliation**—Disparities between the rich
and the poor are enormous, and they keep growing. Reconciliation would require narrowing these differences and
establishing a minimum standard of economic well-being
for all people. Economic reconciliation also suggests that
wealthier individuals and nations would begin to voluntarily simplify the material side of life and shift increasing
attention into psychological, cultural, and spiritual growth
and to assist those living in extreme poverty.

- **Racial, ethnic, and gender reconciliation**—Discrimination on the basis of race, ethnicity, gender, and sexual orientation profoundly divides humanity. How can we create a common future unless we can develop mutual respect? The healing of relations between different groups will transform the psychic wounds of humanity's history.

- **Spiritual reconciliation**—Religious intolerance has produced some of the bloodiest wars in history. Reconciliation among the world's spiritual traditions is vital to humanity's future. It is possible for us to learn to appreciate the core insights of each tradition and to see each as a different facet of the larger jewel of human spiritual wisdom.

- **Generational reconciliation**—Sustainable development has been described as development that meets our needs in the present without compromising the ability of future generations to meet their needs.[10] At present, industrial nations are consuming nonrenewable resources at a rate that will handicap future generations. We have the opportunity to reconcile ourselves with generations yet unborn. We would be wise to use as our example the Iroquois, who, in making major decisions look at the expected impact seven generations ahead.

- **Species reconciliation**—Living in sacred harmony with the Earth is essential if we are to survive and evolve as a species. Our future depends on the integrity of our ecological system, whose strength depends on a broad diversity of plants and animals. We have the opportunity to reconcile ourselves with the larger community of life on

Earth. To do so would be to move from indifference and exploitation to reverential stewardship.

Although there is continuing conflict in each of these areas, there is also new hope for reconciliation. Let's look briefly at changes happening in just one area—the relationship between women and men, which is shifting from patriarchy to partnership. Global surveys show that the status of women is improving and that their acceptance in a partnership role in society is increasing. In 1995, the Gallup organization conducted the *Gender and Society* survey in twenty-two countries in Asia, Europe, North America, and Latin America.[11] The survey found that in most countries, large majorities said that job opportunities should be equal for men and women. In all countries but one, majorities believed that their country would be governed better if more women were involved in politics.

Because the relationship between men and women is so basic, a shift in gender relations from domination to partnership dramatically increases the possibility that we will live more cooperatively and sustainably. Susan Davis, an activist who has worked internationally for both gender equality and sustainability, concludes that equality is not a luxury but is a prerequisite for sustainable development: "We're talking not just about ending oppression. We're talking about unleashing leadership, creativity, and real wisdom. We will not get there without achieving gender equality."[12]

We could say much the same thing about any group that has been oppressed. To have a sustainable future, we need the creativity and talents of the whole human family. Without reconciliation, that will not be possible.

It is important to emphasize that reconciliation does not mean homogeneity. Quite the contrary, our diversity is fundamental to our success. According to the historian Arnold Toynbee, homogeneity appears to weaken societies, while diversity appears to strengthen them. After surveying the growth and decline of the world's major civilizations, he found that a "tendency toward standardization and uniformity" marked their disintegration while the opposite, a "tendency toward differentiation and diversity," marked their growth.[13] As we seek reconciliation, it is important for us to preserve and learn about the unique gifts of culture and history of different people and groups.

THE PROCESS OF RECONCILIATION

RECONCILIATION does not mean forgetting the suffering and injustices of the past; rather, it means not letting the past stand in the way of opportunities for the future. When historic injustices are publicly acknowledged and realistic remedies are found, hurts from the past no longer stand in the way of collective progress. Freed from the need to continue blaming and feeling resentful, people can shift their focus from past grievances to mutual opportunities in the present and the future.

The process of reconciliation is complex and involves at least three steps: the injured need to be heard publicly, the wrongdoers need to apologize publicly, and if appropriate, they need to provide restitution or reparations.

Being heard is the first step in being healed. By listening to and acknowledging the stories of those who have suffered, we begin the process of healing. Our collective listening to the wounds of humanity's psyche and soul is vital to our collective healing.

In *An Ethic for Enemies,* his book on the politics of forgiveness, Donald Shriver, Jr., explains that in popular usage, the phrase "to forgive" is thought to mean "to forget." But, he says, that is not what forgiveness means: "Instead, 'remember and forgive' would be a more accurate slogan."[14] Forgiveness requires that we surrender revenge as a basis for justice. We need to call forth mercy and forbearance in order to break through the cycle of violence and counterviolence. Forgiveness also requires that the injured seek to understand the actions of the wrongdoer so as to restore the wrongdoer's humanity. As a final step in reconciliation, both parties need to create a new relationship so that they can live together in peace and mutual respect.

Archbishop Desmond Tutu knows more about the process of reconciliation than most of us do. He was the chairman of the Truth and Reconciliation Commission (TRC), which was established to investigate crimes committed during the apartheid era in South Africa from 1960 to 1994. He describes the logic of reconciliation in his country in this way. When apartheid ended, South Africa's black majority had to choose among three ways to seek justice and continue to live together with the country's white minority. They could have chosen justice based on *retribution*—an eye for an eye; on *forgetting*—don't think about the past, just move forward into the future; or on *restoration*—granting amnesty in exchange for truth. This is how Tutu explains their choice:

> We believe in restorative justice. In South Africa, we are trying to find our way toward healing and the restoration of

harmony within our communities. If retributive justice is all you seek through the letter of the law, you are history. You will never know stability. You need something beyond reprisal. You need forgiveness.[15]

The commission received over seven thousand applications for amnesty in exchange for truthful accounts of violations of human rights. Before the commission finished its work in 1998, nearly two thousand people testified before it, and it received roughly twenty thousand statements of rights abuses. In concluding the work of the TRC, Tutu said that although he was "devastated by the depths of depravity that the process has revealed," he also had "been amazed, indeed exhilarated by the magnanimity and nobility of spirit of those who, instead of being embittered and vengeful, have been willing to forgive those who treated them so horribly badly."[16] The deputy chairman, Dr. Alex Boraine, said that perhaps the greatest contribution of the TRC toward social reconciliation was the recognition that "reconciliation is not easy, is never cheap and is a constant challenge." Although the process of bringing closure to the era of apartheid was messy and agonizing, it was effective in creating the foundation for a new beginning. Boraine explained that many people testified that appearing before the commission finally put an end to their "nightmares of isolation" and that, for the first time since losing their loved ones, they could sleep at night. Yet others told of a "broken heart which had been healed."[17]

The strong sense of community found in South African culture helped to inspire this approach to reconciliation. In the African view, the community defines the person. The word for this is *ubuntu,* which, translated roughly, means

"each individual's humanity is ideally expressed in relationship with others" or "a person depends on other people to
be a person."[18] From this feeling for community emerged
the nonviolent means to move South Africa from racial separation and minority rule to integration and democracy.

A second step in the process of reconciliation is for the
wrongdoer to offer a sincere public apology. Here are examples of important public apologies offered in recent years:[19]

· In 1988, an act of Congress apologized "on behalf of the
people of the United States" for the internment of Japanese
Americans during World War II.

· In 1996, German officials apologized for the invasion of
Czechoslovakia in 1938 and established a fund for the reparation of Czech victims of Nazi abuses.

· In 1998, the Japanese prime minister expressed "deep re-
morse" for Japan's treatment of British prisoners during
World War II.

A powerful example of a public apology and social healing
is provided by the relationship between the Aboriginal people and the European settlers in Australia. On May 26, 1998,
Australia commemorated its first "Sorry Day" to express
people's regret and shared grief about a tragic episode in
Australian history—the organized removal of Aboriginal
children from their families on the basis of race. Through
much of this century, Aboriginal children were forcibly removed from their families with the aim of assimilating them
into Western culture.[20] According to an indigenous council
member, Patricia Thompson, Sorry Day provides a way for
Australians to come to terms with their history and to come

together to build a future on a foundation of mutual respect. Said Thompson, "What we want is recognition, understanding, respect and tolerance—of each other, by each other, for each other." In cities, towns, and rural centers, in schools and churches, people stopped their everyday activities to acknowledge this injustice. In addition, hundreds of thousands of Australians have signed the "Sorry Books."

The third step in reconciliation is restitution or the payment of reparations. Archbishop Desmond Tutu gives a good explanation of the role of restitution when he says that completing the process of reconciliation involves more than the recognition and remembering of injustice: "If you steal my pen and say 'I'm sorry' without returning the pen, your apology means nothing."[21] In cases like this, what is needed is restitution. Apologies create a truthful record. Restitution creates a new record. The purpose of reparation is to repair the material conditions of a group so as to restore some balance or equality of power and material opportunity.[22]

Beyond reconciliation is the day-to-day reality of former antagonists living together. One of the most notable examples of successful reconciliation within the recent past is the shift in the relationship between the United States and Germany and Japan. World War II began in the age of total warfare, when massive civilian casualties were the norm; and it could have taken many generations to heal the psychological wounds from that war. Yet, within a few decades, the United States and its bitter enemies from the war, Germany and Japan, became peaceful allies—clear examples of successful reconciliation culminating in renewed relationships and mutual respect. Other important examples of reconciliation include the ongoing peace process in the Middle East, certainly one of the most volatile regions in the world, and in Northern Ireland, where the process of reconciliation seems poised to overcome centuries of separation and conflict.

As these examples make clear, with authentic reconciliation—with listening, apologizing, and restoring—the suffering of the past does not need to stand in the way of future progress.

THE COST OF KINDNESS

THE cost of compassion is far less than we might think. The world does have the material resources for all of us to live together sustainably. We could begin by eliminating the worst aspects of poverty—a fundamental requirement, I believe, for an evolutionary bounce to occur. As the *United Nations 1998 Human Development Report* concludes, we have "more than enough" resources to accomplish this.[23] To make this point, the report presents these stark contrasts:

- To achieve universal access to water and sanitation, the estimated additional annual cost is $12 billion, which is what is spent on perfumes in Europe and the United States each year.

- To achieve universal basic health and nutrition, the estimated additional annual cost is $13 billion, which is $4 billion less than annual expenditures on pet foods in Europe and the United States.

- The world's spending priorities are further reflected in these figures: Annual expenditures on business entertainment in Japan amount to $35 billion; on cigarettes in Europe, $50 billion; on alcoholic drinks in Europe, $105 billion; and on military spending in the world, $780 billion.

The *Human Development Report* concludes that "advancing human development is not an exorbitant undertaking." The added bill to provide universal access to basic services— education, health, nutrition, reproductive health, family planning, safe water, and sanitation—is estimated to be an additional $40 billion per year.[24] This is less than one-tenth of one percent of world income. As the report notes, this is "barely more than a rounding error."

Given that we can easily afford to eliminate the worst forms of poverty, what are we doing about it? The report states that development aid is now at its lowest level since the U.N. started keeping statistics. Donor countries allocate an average of only 0.25 percent (one-quarter of one percent) of their total GNP to development assistance for poorer nations. The United States is the stingiest developed nation in terms of the proportion of total wealth that it donates.[25]

The resources exist to make a dramatic improvement in the quality of life for a majority of humanity and to begin a process of reconciliation between the rich and the poor. Instead of trickle-down development from the wealthy to the poor, we could launch a bottom-up approach that directly targets the poor and the voiceless.[26] If we use equity, simplicity, and cooperation as our guideposts, we have the resources to sustain all of humanity into the foreseeable future. As Gandhi said, "We have enough for everyone's need, but not for everyone's greed."

We cannot achieve our maturity if we remain divided into a minority that has great wealth and a majority that is consigned to absolute poverty. We need to create a future of

mutually assured development—where progress leaves no
one behind and also strengthens the ecosystems on which
our common future depends. We could create something
akin to the Marshall Plan, which restored Europe after
World War II. The entire world could be united in establishing a foundation of sustainability. Given intelligent designs for living lightly and simply, a decent standard and
manner of living could vary depending on local customs,
ecology, resources, and climate. Within this diversity, if the
human family saw its collective development as its central
enterprise, the world would have a strong foundation for an
evolutionary bounce.

Archbishop Desmond Tutu said that you can immediately
tell when you enter a happy home: "You don't have to be
told; you don't have to see the happy people who live there.
You can feel it in the fabric, the air."[27] In a similar way, he
says, we have it in our power to create a cultural atmosphere
on Earth that is infused with kindness, joy, laughter, truth,
and love. If we can bear witness to the reservoir of unresolved pain that has accumulated through history, we will
release an enormous store of pent-up creativity and energy.
Instead of mobilizing around enemies, we could release our
collective energy in building a future that is worthy of our
name as doubly wise humans.

Chapter Seven

Evolutionary Crash or Evolutionary Bounce: Adversity Meets Opportunity

The future enters into us,
in order to transform itself in us,
long before it happens.
—*Rainer Maria Rilke*

Even if you are on the right track,
you'll get run over if you just sit there.
—*Will Rogers*

The Dynamics of Initiation

THE preceding chapters explored the titanic forces converging at this time in human history. Powerful adversity trends—global climate change, the rapid extinction of species, the depletion of key resources such as water and cheap oil, a burgeoning population, and a growing gap between the rich and poor—are converging into a whole-systems crisis, creating the possibility of an evolutionary crash. At the same time, four equally powerful trends are converging into a whole-systems opportunity, creating the possibility of an evolutionary bounce. The first opportunity trend is the emergence of a new perceptual paradigm that invites us to see the aliveness and unity of the universe. In seeing through the deadness of materialism and into the subtle aliveness that infuses the world around us, we transform the human experience from a secular to a sacred journey. The second trend is the shift toward simpler ways of living. With the ability to voluntarily simplify our lives, we can choose ways of life that are more satisfying and more sustainable. The third trend is the global communications revolution, which gives us the tools to communicate our way into a positive future. We can now engage in conversations about our common future both locally (such as across the kitchen table) and globally (such as via the internet), recognizing that the very act of doing so has the power to ripple out into a world hungry for visions of hope. These three trends make possible the fourth trend, that of reconciliation—between men and women, black and white, rich and poor, humans and other species, current and future generations, and many more. Reconciliation gives us the ability to heal old wounds that keep human beings from unleashing our potentials.

From the meeting of adversity trends and opportunity trends comes our time of initiation into our adulthood as a human family. There is a profound irony in all this: we are initiating ourselves. By our own actions, we are creating the circumstances that are now challenging us to reach new heights of maturity and community.

As you may recall from chapter one, the purpose of an initiation is to enable a person or community to cross a threshold from one life into another, and to mark the transition into a new level of social membership. Historically, the process of initiation is characterized by shared ordeals, adventures, and discoveries that produce bonding and a sense of a new beginning that overcomes old differences. That is precisely the opportunity I see for humanity—to cross the threshold from our adolescence into our adulthood with a sense of authentic membership in the human family.

Another way of looking at our coming time of initiation is to see it as an important experience in the awakening of our species as *Homo sapiens sapiens*. Recall that humans are regarded as more than *sapient* or "wise"; we are *sapient sapient* or "doubly wise."[1] Whereas animals "know," humans "know that we know." In that subtle circling back of consciousness upon itself, a revolutionary potential is born. In his book *The Phenomenon of Man*, Teilhard de Chardin says that when the first living creature consciously "perceived itself in its own mirror, the whole world took a pace forward."[2] The capacity for self-observation or double wisdom is not a trivial enhancement of evolutionary potential. It is an explosively powerful capacity that has given a supercharged boost to the evolutionary process. As Teilhard de Chardin says, "The being who is the object of his own reflection, in consequence of that very doubling back upon himself, becomes in a flash able to raise himself into a new sphere."[3]

When a group—a tribe, a nation, or an entire species—"knows that it knows," it has the ability to be self-observing and to take responsibility for its actions. For the first time in our history, humanity is acquiring the means to "know that we know" as a species and, just as this capacity is explosively powerful for individuals, so too can it give a supercharged boost to humanity's evolution. When humanity consciously recognizes itself as a single community with responsibilities to the rest of life, both present and future, we will cross the threshold to a new level of maturity and a new culture and consciousness will begin to grow in the world.

How soon might the human family move into a time of initiation? In my view, although many of the adversity trends are already quite serious at the turn of the millennium, they are still not sufficiently compelling to awaken humanity's collective attention and galvanize us into concerted action. There seems to be enough resilience left in the world system to absorb further economic, environmental, and social shocks without being pushed to the breaking point. But while the problems that I am calling "adversity trends" may seem manageable and relatively independent of one another at the turn of the millennium, I believe they will soon coalesce into a tight and unyielding web, most likely by the decade of the 2020s. My guess is that, when this happens, our planetary system will be like a rubber band stretched to its limits: it will lose much of its elasticity and ability to cope with further disruptions. This is a condition ripe for either breakdown or breakthrough.

Our coming initiation will be a defining period in human history. The choices we make at this decisive time will reverberate far into the future. After traveling a path of separation and division for the past thirty-five thousand years, humanity will be challenged in a brief moment of time to make a conscious turn toward a new life of connection and cooperation. Will we make a successful turn toward our higher maturity? As we rush headlong toward the answer to that question, let us look briefly at the major stages through which we seem likely to move in the next few decades:

Stage I: Denial—Many insist that things will not become so chaotic and turbulent as to require major change. Others say that great changes have happened through history, so there is nothing unique about this time, and no particular reason to be concerned. Others consider the situation far too complex and feel powerless to get involved. Still others recognize the urgency of change but procrastinate, not wanting to upset a comfortable (or at least predictable) way of life.

Stage II: Innovation—Without public fanfare, a growing number of people are crossing a threshold of awakening and launching innumerable social and technological innovations. While the larger society may be relatively unaware of what is occurring, there is intense grassroots activity under way to design ourselves into a workable and meaningful future. Diverse networks of communication—ranging from small local groups to internet-based global dialogues—are vital to this burst of innovation.

Stage III: Initiation—By the time the adversity trends and the opportunity trends reach a critical point of convergence, only one outcome seems certain: humanity will enter the fire of initiation. We will move into a time of intense, planetary compression. A circle will have closed. All frontiers will be gone. There will be nowhere to escape. It will be obvious that the Earth is an integrated system—environmentally, economically, and socially. The forces of adversity will intensify one another and become so unyielding, and the forces of opportunity will become so promising, that humanity will be pushed to make an unprecedented choice. Do we hold on to the past and descend into chaos, or liberate ourselves from historical limitations so that we can consciously create our future? I believe that we will not be able to stop the process leading to initiation any more than a pregnant woman can stop the birth of her baby. With no way back, our success lies in consciously moving forward.

Stage IV: Bounce or Crash—The outcome of our journey is yet to be determined. Will we reconcile ourselves around building a future worthy of our potentials? Or will humanity be torn apart by adolescent conflicts as we squander our abundant resources and mutilate our home?

Figure 6 presents a highly simplified view of the dynamics likely to be involved if humanity moves successfully through our evolutionary initiation in the coming decades.

Stages of Evolutionary Initiation and Transition

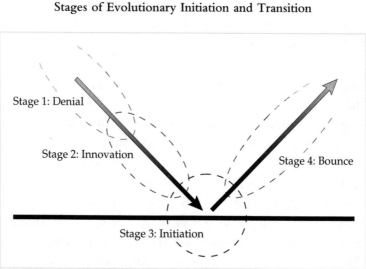

If this sequence of stages is roughly accurate, then the time of greatest opportunity for social reflection and creative invention is prior to our entry into the stage of initiation with its demands for immediate action. Stated more bluntly, it takes little collective intelligence to crash blindly into an evolutionary wall and then decide it would be wise to take corrective measures. If that is the best we can muster, then our future is in great peril. By my reckoning, we have two precious decades between the turn of the millennium and the 2020s before a global systems challenge seems likely to emerge full force. A fundamental test of our maturity as a species will be how well we use this brief window of opportunity for genuine social dialogue and innovation in support of a sustainable and meaningful future.

Ultimately, I believe that whether we experience an evolutionary bounce or an evolutionary crash will be determined by whether the human family chooses to pull together and cooperate, or to pull apart and compete. To pull together implies that we are on a shared journey, and that we have a common story and a common purpose. It means that our social and cultural fabric is resilient, flexible, and able to stretch without tearing. If we pull together, we can conserve the evolutionary momentum of the past and use it to carry us into a promising future. If, instead of pulling together, we struggle and separate—rich against poor, men against women, black against white, nation against nation—we may do lasting harm to the fabric of human connection, and veer off on an evolutionary detour.

A crash or a bounce may seem like a stark set of choices, so let's pause to consider other outcomes. Are these the only two scenarios that are possible? Not necessarily. It is possible that, with a combination of high technology and good luck, the human family could find a way to mature without undue hardship. Although this is a happy prospect, it is one that I find highly unlikely for all of the reasons outlined in chapter two. Because adversity trends seem to be unyielding, I think a more likely outcome is one that combines elements of both the crash and the bounce—a condition described by historian Arnold Toynbee as dynamic stagnation or "arrested growth."[4] Arrested growth occurs when a civilization is unable to advance and yet has gone too far to turn back, when all of the society's energy is being used just to stay where it is. A future of dynamic stagnation would mean that we would have to run as fast as we could simply to maintain a stalemate between the forces of advance and the forces of collapse. By intensifying efforts that worked well in the past, we may be able to hold on, maintaining ourselves but unable to muster the energy and creativity to surpass ourselves, while becoming progressively weaker. This is a delaying tactic, not a long-term solution and the eventual outcome is still likely to be either an evolutionary crash or a bounce. Therefore, I want to focus on the heart of the evolutionary choice: Do we strive for a new level of maturity and wholeness as a human family (an evolutionary bounce), or do we pull apart in conflict (an evolutionary crash)? This chapter explores these two possible outcomes.

An Evolutionary Crash

I do not view the extinction of humanity as the likely outcome of an evolutionary crash. Because I expect humans to have an enduring presence on the Earth, my concern is not with our extinction but with our evolution. An "evolutionary crash" refers to a breakdown in our capacity to unfold our potentials, both personal and collective. It means that when the human family confronts monumental adversity (primarily of our own making), we will not able to move beyond our adolescent consciousness and behaviors. Instead of pulling together for our common future, we may pull even further apart. If this happens, the result could be a deep wounding of the biosphere as well as of humanity's collective psyche. We may find our collective psyche so wounded and crippled by the experience of initiation that our ability to evolve to a higher maturity would be diminished for generations to come. Instead of surpassing ourselves, we would be struggling just to hold on—to maintain ourselves. Living would become little more than "only not dying," to use Simone de Beauvoir's phrase. While I am confident that humanity will survive, I am apprehensive about the kind of life that we may create for ourselves together.

Even if we should experience some form of evolutionary crash, we may have more chances to evolve and grow in the future. What we would miss is an unusually favorable opportunity to advance—one that may not reappear for generations, if it at all.

Although history has seen the rise and fall of more than twenty major civilizations, what happened on Easter Island provides the most vivid—and chilling—example of how devastating an evolutionary breakdown can be. It illustrates what could lie in humanity's future if we do not rise to a higher level of maturity and halt the "irretrievable mutilation" of the natural environment.

The story of Easter Island. Located in one of the most remote places on Earth—in the Pacific Ocean, roughly two thousand miles off the coast of South America—Easter Island is only one hundred fifty square miles in area. A person can walk around it in about a day. The first Europeans to visit the island were the crew of a Dutch ship that arrived on

Easter Sunday in 1722—hence the name Easter Island. They found a primitive society of approximately three thousand people, living in wretched reed huts and caves, engaged in almost perpetual warfare, and resorting to cannibalism in a desperate attempt to supplement the meager food supplies available on the treeless island.[5] What was most amazing to the Dutch were the massive stone statues that covered the island. There were more than six hundred, each averaging over twenty feet in height, with some as tall as forty feet. The Europeans could scarcely believe that the primitive and impoverished islanders were capable of carving, transporting, and erecting so many enormous statues, whose presence indicated that an advanced society had once flourished there.

Archeological evidence reveals that when Easter Island was first settled by a few dozen Polynesian colonists in approximately A.D. 500, it had a mild climate and volcanic soil, was covered by forests, and teemed with animal and plant life (although, given the island's remoteness, there were relatively few species). Among the foods that the settlers brought with them, yams and chickens were particularly suited to the climate and soil. Although the diet was monotonous, the islanders prospered, and their numbers grew to an estimated seven thousand when the population peaked around 1550.[6]

Because food production was so easy, the islanders had abundant free time. Families coalesced into clans that competed with one another in creating elaborate rituals and erecting the massive statues. Over a thousand years, they developed one of the most advanced and complex societies in the world, despite their limited resources and technologies.[7] From early on, however, they used the resources of the island beyond their regenerative capacity. Archeological evidence shows that the destruction of the island's forests was well under way by the year 800—only three hundred years after settlers first arrived. By the 1500s, the forests and palm trees had disappeared as people cleared land for agriculture and used the surviving trees to build homes and oceangoing canoes, burn as firewood, and transport statues. The islanders apparently used logs to move and raise the statues in a competitive rivalry to see which clans could build the most. At the end, the remaining forests disappeared quickly. It is astonishing to note that given Easter Island's small size, everyone would have been able to see when the last tree was being cut down, thereby sealing their fate as prisoners on the tiny island. The loss of tree cover increased soil erosion and reduced soil quality, and thus crop yields declined.

The ecological destruction was not confined to the forests. Jared Diamond, professor of medicine at UCLA, describes how the animal life was also eradicated:

> The destruction of the island's animals was as extreme as that of the forests: without exception, every species of native land bird became extinct. Even shellfish were overexploited, until people had to settle for small sea snails . . . Porpoise bones disappeared abruptly from the garbage heaps around 1500; no one could harpoon porpoises anymore, since the trees used for constructing the big seagoing canoes no longer existed . . .[8]

By the mid 1500s, the biosphere was so devastated that it was beyond short-term recovery. With no trees to build boats, ocean fishing was impossible. With animals hunted to extinction, the people turned on one another. Centralized authority broke down, and the island descended into chaos. Rival clans lived in caves and competed with one another for survival. Eventually, according to Diamond, the islanders "turned to the largest remaining meat source available: humans, whose bones became common in late Easter Island garbage heaps. Oral traditions of the islanders are rife with cannibalism."[9] Warfare continued after the Europeans left and, by the late 1700s, the population had crashed to between one-quarter and one-tenth of its peak level. Here is how author Clive Ponting summarizes the rise and fall of civilization on Easter Island:

> Against great odds the islanders painstakingly constructed, over many centuries, one of the most advanced societies of its type in the world. For a thousand years they sustained a way of life in accordance with an elaborate set of social and religious customs that enabled them not only to survive but to flourish . . . But in the end the increasing numbers and cultural ambitions of the islanders proved too great for the limited resources available to them. When the environment was ruined by the pressure, the society very quickly collapsed with it, leading to a state of near barbarism.[10]

The parallels between Easter Island and the Earth are strong. Professor Diamond concludes, "Easter Island is Earth writ small. Today, again, a rising population confronts shrinking resources . . . we can no more escape into space than the Easter Islanders could flee into the ocean."[11] As Easter Island reveals, we humans have already demonstrated our ability, on a small scale, to descend from greatness into collective madness and devastate an entire biosphere and culture irreparably.

Humanity's potential for collective madness. A concern for the sanity of nations is not new. In 1841, Charles Mackay wrote of the madness of crowds and nations: "in reading the history of nations, we find that, like individuals, they have their whims and their peculiarities; their seasons of excitement and recklessness, when they care not what they do."[12] Nearly a century later, in 1930, Sigmund Freud expressed his concern for the neuroses of civilizations in his book *Civilization and Its Discontents*:

> If the development of civilization has such a far-reaching similarity to the development of the individual and if it employs the same methods, may we not be justified in reaching the diagnosis that, under the influence of cultural urges, some civilizations or some epochs of civilization—possibly the whole of mankind—have become "neurotic"?[13]

I do not think that Freud goes far enough in his assessment of collective madness. He speaks of neuroses—which are relatively mild forms of dysfunctionality—to describe civilizational behavior. This is far too gentle a term for some of the examples of collective madness that have emerged in recent centuries. Let us look at just one of these examples— the witch hunts in Europe during the Middle Ages—as they are a dramatic illustration of humanity's capacity for collective madness.

The witch hunts can be described as nothing less than a period of collective psychosis. During these dark centuries, the idea persisted in Europe that disembodied spirits inhabited the Earth, and that some people—witches—had the power to summon evil spirits so as to bring misfortune to others. As a result, an epidemic of terror seized Europe. Few thought themselves secure from the powers of evil spirits. A witch was suspected as the cause of every calamity. If a storm blew down a barn—it was witchcraft. If cattle died unexpectedly—it was witchcraft. If a loved one suddenly became ill—it was witchcraft. Spurred by invisible terror, people hunted down, tortured, and killed those they thought to be witches.

The witch hunting craze began in earnest in the 1400s with the encouragement of the Catholic Church. A declaration issued in 1484 by Pope Innocent VIII provided the moral authority and official encouragement for the witch hunts. It reads in part:

> . . . many persons of both sexes, heedless of their own salvation and forsaking the catholic faith, give themselves over to devils male and female, and by their incantations, charms, and conjurings, and by other abominable superstitions and sortileges, offences, crimes, and misdeeds, ruin and cause to perish the offspring of women, the foal of animals, the products of the earth, the grapes of vines, and the fruits of trees . . . We therefore . . . remove all impediments by which in any way the said inquisitors are hindered in the exercise of their office . . . it shall be permitted to the said inquisitors . . . to proceed to the correction, imprisonment, and punishment of the aforesaid persons . . .[14]

This was religious madness. The witch hunts resulted in the public torture and cruel deaths of at least several hundred thousand women (as well as many men and children) over a period of two and a half centuries. "Witch mania" generated so many trials for witchcraft in France, Italy, Germany, Scotland, and other countries that for years other crimes were seldom considered. One bishop (in Geneva) burned five hundred "witches" within three months, another bishop six hundred, and another nine hundred.[15] After two hundred and fifty years, this wave of cultural madness began to subside, gradually giving way to the rationalism of science and the Industrial Revolution.

The examples of Easter Island and the witch hunts in Europe show how vulnerable we have been to collective madness. Are we still? I and many others believe that we are. Consciousness researcher Dean Radin conjectures that ". . . there may be a mental analogy to environmental ecology—something like an ecology of thought that invisibly interweaves through the fabric of our society. This suggests that disruptive, scattered, or violent thoughts may pollute the social fabric . . . Perhaps periods of widespread madness, such as wars, are indicators of mass-mind infections."[16]

In the coming planetary initiation, it seems very plausible that the world could go mad with such divergent views and paradigms that we would be unable to come together in meaningful dialogue or to build a working consensus for the future. The conversation of the planet could collapse to the lowest common denominator consistent with security and survival. In the face of monumental stress, and with no overarching and trusted source of perspective, humanity's collective psyche could fragment, and the people of the Earth could descend into perpetual conflict. The conviction could grow that humanity is an ill-fated species that never had a chance to succeed. A further generation could reconfirm the suspicion that we live in a hostile universe, that we do not share a coherent view of reality, that humanity cannot work together, and that we are a doomed species. Particularly in developed nations, people could feel enormous guilt and responsibility for the devastation of the planet and the wasting away of opportunities for future generations. Many could feel that after tens of thousands of years of slow development, we ruined our chance at evolutionary success within the span of a generation or two—and that a new Dark Age now looms ahead for the people of the Earth.

If humanity misses this chance for an evolutionary leap forward, we may have other opportunities. But what we will have allowed to pass by is a moment unique in its promise for realizing our collective maturity. If we do not rise to the opportunity this time, it seems very likely that we will so devastate the biosphere and so burden ourselves with hatreds and resentments that it could take infinitely more effort to realize our evolutionary potentials in the future. We may pay a heavy price if we forgo this evolutionary opportunity.

AN EVOLUTIONARY BOUNCE

AN evolutionary bounce represents a period of rapid acceleration in the evolution of the species. However, a leap forward will not happen automatically. The most essential ingredient for creating a bounce will be conscious choice. Instead of flying off in all directions, we can choose to focus our energies and conserve the historical momentum of human development.

The difference between a crash and a bounce will be not so much in the circumstances that we encounter, but rather in how we respond to those circumstances. In a crash scenario, there will be destructive conflict, paralyzing chaos, and deep separation. In a bounce scenario, there will also be conflict, chaos, and separation—but the conflict will be constructive, the chaos will be creative, and separation will be balanced with integration. Barring an environmental catastrophe, all the forces that would be present in a crash would be present in a bounce scenario, but in the latter we would respond to those forces in a more reflective, mature, and productive way.

Although adversity trends are providing humanity with a wake-up call, I see no advantage in allowing them to grow into an irreversible calamity. The destruction of our biosphere is not likely to bring us to collective sanity. On the contrary, if we allow an environmental crash to devastate the Earth, it could be infinitely more difficult to regain our evolutionary direction and momentum. There is already sufficient suffering in the world to motivate change. What is needed is the unflinching maturity to face the coming challenges head on. We need to start acting like adults. When we do, when we consciously recognize ourselves as a single community of life with responsibilities to future generations, we will be taking a leap forward in our evolution.

Given the separation and conflict that have marked our species in the past, it might be difficult to imagine humanity pulling together to create a sustainable and meaningful future. But our pulling together is not a far-fetched idea. There are already many examples of successful, planetary-wide cooperation:

· The world weather system merges information from more than one hundred countries every day to provide weather information globally.

· Nations around the globe have cooperated to eradicate diseases such as smallpox, polio, and diphtheria.

- International civil aviation agreements assure the smooth functioning of global air transport.

- The International Telecommunications Union (ITU) allocates the planetary electromagnetic spectrum so that television signals, cellular phones, and radio signals are not overwhelmed with noise.

- In 1990, the world's nations agreed to ban CFCs—a chemical used in refrigerators and cooling systems that damages the ozone layer.

There is no reason why we cannot expand on these areas of cooperation in the future. We have already begun building the foundation for an evolutionary jump.

I believe that we have all the material resources and technologies we need for an evolutionary bounce. All that we need is the social will to make it happen. Just how great an evolutionary jump we could achieve is vividly demonstrated by the following story of a village that has risen from a grassy desert in South America—Gaviotas.

The story of Gaviotas. The village of Gaviotas is located on the vast, desolate plains of eastern Colombia where nothing but a few nutrient-poor grasses grow. It is surely one of our planet's least desirable places in which to live. Paolo Lugari, who founded the village in 1971, explained why the villagers chose this site: "They always put social experiments in the easiest, most fertile places. We wanted the hardest place. We figured if we could do it here, we could do it anywhere."[17] When people would tell him that the area was "just a big, wet desert," Lugari would reply, "The only deserts are deserts of the imagination."[18] In the space of a single generation—less than thirty years—Gaviotans have transformed one of the most resource-starved regions in the country into a sustainable economy, a nurturing community, and a flourishing ecosystem. In doing so, they have given us a brilliant example of just how rich and fertile the human imagination can be.

In the early 1970s, Lugari brought scientists, engineers, doctors, university students, and other advisors to this remote and inhospitable site to explore how it could be transformed into a thriving community. They produced a dazzling array of low-cost but highly efficient technologies. To pump water, they created a lightweight windmill with blades contoured like the wings of an airplane, able to trap the soft equatorial breezes. They attached highly efficient water pumps to seesaws, so that as children play, they pump water for the community. They erected solar water heaters that could catch the diffuse energy of the sun even on the many cloudy days. They placed underground ducts in hillsides to provide natural air conditioning for their hospital. To provide electricity, they put photovoltaic cells on rooftops. And they developed hydroponic gardens to grow some of the village's food.

The transformation of the local ecosystem has been as remarkable as the development of innovative technologies. Since the early 1980s, the Gaviotans have planted roughly two million Caribbean pine trees, the only tree that would grow in the nearly toxic soil. As a result, the village is now home to more than twenty thousand acres of forest. From the trees, the villagers harvest and sell pine resin, which is used in the manufacture of paint, turpentine, and paper. In addition to providing a source of income for the community, the pine forest has brought fresh nutrients to the soil, cooled the ground, and raised the humidity.[19] In turn, these changes have allowed dormant seeds of native trees to sprout and grow. The sheltering pine trees are enabling a diverse, indigenous forest to regenerate itself with surprising speed. As a result, the local populations of deer, anteater, and other animals are growing. The villagers have decided to allow the indigenous forest to choke out the pine forest over the next century, enabling the area to return to its original state as an extension of the Amazon.

The Gaviotans have been equally inventive socially.[20] Everyone earns the same salary, which is above minimum wage. Many of the basics of life are free, including housing, health care, food, and schooling for the children. With no poverty, there has been no need for police or a jail. Government is by consensus and unwritten rules of common sense. Dogs, pesticides, and guns are not allowed. Alcohol use is confined to homes. Laziness is not tolerated. In this community of social invention, people exude happiness. The people of Gaviotas have a sustainable future, a strong community, meaningful work, and a peaceful life.[21]

As the village grows, its creator envisions new satellite villages. "I see enclaves of maybe twenty families, little satellites surrounding Gaviotas, no more than twenty minutes away by bicycle."[22] He envisions "little island communities where people live in productive harmony with nature and technology. And with each other."[23]

In his book *Gaviotas: A Village to Reinvent the World,* Alan Weisman beautifully summarizes the net result of the Gaviotans' efforts:

> Surrounded by a land seen either as empty or plagued with misery, they had forged a way and a peace they believed

could prosper long after the last drop of the earth's petroleum was burned away. They were so small, but their hope was great enough to brighten the planet turning beneath them no matter how much their fellow humans seemed bent on wrecking it. Against all skeptics and odds, Gaviotas had lighted a path through a magnificent but darkened land, whose sorrows mirrored a beautiful, embattled world.[24]

With the rapid growth of the internet, information about how to create communities such as Gaviotas will soon be accessible to people around the world. The entire planet will become everyone's backyard as we use the internet to scan for social inventions, farming techniques, and energy-production technologies that make sustainable living possible. The Earth will be alive with inventions—both physical and social—that are exquisitely suited to each particular ecosystem, climate, and culture. Gaviotas demonstrates that even in the harshest conditions, we have the ingenuity and cooperative capacity to create a sustainable and meaningful life for ourselves. This small village is a testament that the human imagination is fertile enough to transform virtually any desert.

The potential for collective awakening. Just as we have a potential for collective madness, I believe that humanity has a corresponding potential for collective awakening—and to a much greater degree than we may imagine. In this section, we shall briefly explore the idea of collective consciousness or a group mind, which is the vehicle or context through which our collective awakening could occur.

The idea of collective consciousness has emerged perhaps most clearly in the work of the Catholic priest and mystic

Pierre Teilhard de Chardin, who wrote about the awakening of a collective field that he termed the "noosphere." The noosphere can be thought of as the planetary mind-field or collective consciousness; it is the product of humanity's entire evolutionary experience and expression. This mind-field is enriched as we develop, whether the development is in language, art, music, technologies, society, or any other area of endeavor. In his book *The Future of Man,* Teilhard de Chardin describes the noosphere this way:

> In the passage of time a state of collective human consciousness has been progressively evolved which is inherited by each succeeding generation of conscious individuals, and to which each generation adds something. Sustained, certainly, by the individual person, but at the same time embracing and shaping the successive multitude of individuals, a sort of generalised human superpersonality is visibly in the process of formation on the earth.[25]

In recent years, many different voices have been telling us that humanity's most basic challenge is to awaken our collective consciousness so that we can respond successfully to the social and ecological problems that confront us. Psychiatrist Roger Walsh writes that "the state of the world reflects our state of mind; our collective crises mirror our collective consciousness."[26] Václav Havel, president of Czechoslovakia, stated in a 1990 address to a joint session of the U.S. Congress, "Without a global revolution in the sphere of human consciousness, nothing will change for the better . . . and the catastrophe toward which this world is headed—the ecological, social, demographic, or general breakdown of civilization—will be unavoidable."[27] Philosopher of consciousness Ken Wilber offers a similar view of our Earth's situation: "Gaia's main problems are not industrialization, ozone depletion, overpopulation, or resource depletion. Gaia's main problem is the lack of mutual understanding and mutual agreement in the noosphere about how to proceed with these problems."[28] Author Marianne Williamson describes the contemporary challenge this way: "There is within every person a veiled, oceanic awareness that we are all much bigger than the small-minded personas we normally display. The expansion into this larger self, for the individual and the species, is the meaning of human evolution and the dramatic challenge of this historic time."[29]

Our evolutionary success depends not only on awakening our collective consciousness but also on promoting its health and healing. The tools that will enable this awakening are the internet and related technologies. The internet will soon connect a billion or more people, twenty-four hours a day, seven days a week. My belief is that, with this level of continuous communication—which is unprecedented in human history—humanity will begin the process of collectively "waking up." A new intelligence and awareness could infuse the human family, providing a powerful lift to our evolutionary efforts.

Would our collective awakening enable us to respond at a higher level to the crises of our time? To get a better understanding of what this may mean, let's look at some of what we know about collective consciousness.

Robert Kenny is a management consultant who has explored group consciousness for many years. He has found considerable evidence that group consciousness can foster a high level of synergy among people. Settings where a group consciousness emerges most naturally include highly skilled sports teams; orchestras and jazz ensembles; teams engaged in risky activities requiring a high degree of physical coordination; semi-autonomous, high-performance teams in organizational settings; organizations with a high degree of commitment to a mission; and intentional communities with actively engaged members and a clear sense of spiritual purpose.[30] In these kinds of groups, members feel strongly connected and view themselves as interdependent parts of a larger team or effort. They develop a genuine concern for the well-being of other members and for the productive functioning of the group as a whole. According to Kenny, groups that develop a shared consciousness can perform tasks fluidly, efficiently, cooperatively and in coordination, with minimal communication. He says that an intuitive connection or empathy gives people the ability to anticipate the actions, thoughts, or words of others in the group; as a result, teammates work as a unit rather than as an aggregate of individuals.[31]

Another person who has explored the group mind is Brian Muldoon, who has many years of experience in the area of conflict resolution, and observing what promotes cooperation in groups and organizations. The group mind can emerge, says Muldoon, when people engaged in a common project let go of their personal frame of reference and begin to think on behalf of the whole—which, he says, is not so different from being in love.[32] What draws out the group mind is work on something larger than one's self—a compelling image of collective possibility, a higher potential that can only be realized together.[33] Muldoon's observations lead me to wonder whether humanity can create an evolutionary project compelling enough to draw out and mobilize our group mind.

The importance of the collective mood and atmosphere of a nation has long been appreciated by leaders. Abraham

Lincoln is an example. He said, "With public sentiment nothing can fail; without it, nothing can succeed."

In the United States, in recent decades, there are several powerful examples of collective awakening made possible by the mass media. Television brought the Vietnam war into America's living rooms and gradually awakened the collective consciousness—and aroused the conscience—of the nation. It also brought the nonviolent marches of the civil rights movement into America's collective consciousness and helped to awaken broad recognition of racial oppression. Finally, in airing the voices and views of women calling for liberation, the mass media helped to catalyze the women's movement and its explicit call for consciousness raising.

We have even experienced group consciousness at the planetary level. One example was in 1969 when the human family experienced a few hours of collective self-observation and shared recognition as several billion people around the world paused to watch the first humans walk on the moon. The power of this event was not only in seeing one of our own species on the moon for the first time, but also in the shared awareness that a significant portion of humanity was watching the live telecast and that we were participants in a singular experience.

As these examples illustrate, there is a faculty of knowing at work in our collective lives. Although subtle and easy to overlook, collective consciousness is a natural part of life and presents itself in practical ways.

However we describe it, I believe the co-evolution of culture and consciousness is the core task in our collective future. The question is, in which direction will our collective consciousness develop—toward collective awakening or collective madness?

Chapter Eight

━

HUMANITY'S CENTRAL PROJECT:

BECOMING DOUBLY WISE HUMANS

Once the journey to God is finished,
the infinite journey in God begins.
—*Annamarie Schimmel*

All things arise and pass away,
but the awakened awake forever.
—*The Buddha*

BECOMING FULLY HUMAN

TO achieve an evolutionary bounce, we will all need to pull together for a common purpose. But what purpose is so compelling? Sustainability alone does not present a very compelling purpose—it offers little more than "only not dying." Is there a higher purpose that could energize and draw the human family together in a common project?

I believe our core purpose as a species lies largely unexplored in the scientific name that we have given to ourselves. As *Homo sapiens sapiens* or "doubly wise humans," we have the capacity to know that we know. *If we use our scientific name as a guide, then our core purpose as a species is to realize— both individually and collectively—our potential for double wisdom.*

We turn, then, to explore our evolutionary purpose as it relates to the development of our capacity for double wisdom. Portions of this chapter draw from my book *Awakening Earth* (which is available in electronic form at www. awakeningearth.org).

What is the nature of "double wisdom?" Human beings not only have the ability "to know" but we also have the ability to turn the mirror of knowing around and to reflect on the miracle of knowing itself. In other words, we can pay attention to how we are paying attention—a process at the heart of meditation. By consciously choosing to live more consciously, we can make a leap forward in our maturity as well as reconnect with the stream of life and the Mother Universe.

VISUALIZING THE UNIVERSE'S EVOLUTIONARY INTENTION

HOW does humanity's journey of awakening fit within the larger pattern of evolution in the universe? I believe that we need to draw from the depths of nature's wisdom to discover our aligning purpose for moving into the deep future. Our challenge is to discover the evolutionary pathway most in accord with the universe's preexisting intentions. If we fight against nature, we will be fighting against ourselves—and our evolutionary journey will be one of frustration, stalemate, and alienation. If we cooperate with nature, we will be serving our deepest essence—and our journey will be one of satisfaction and learning.

One way to learn about nature's evolutionary direction is by examining the designs expressed in the physical systems of the universe. Wherever we look in the natural world, we see a recurring organizing pattern at work. The basic physical structure of that pattern is the torus, which has the shape of a donut. At every level of the cosmos, we find the characteristic structure and geometry of toroidal forms. *The torus is significant because it is the simplest geometry of a dynamically self-referencing and self-organizing system which has the capacity to keep pulling itself together, to keep itself in existence.* The torus is nature's most common signature of self-organizing systems. Figure 7 shows six different expressions of this easily recognizable form—from the minute topology around a black hole, to the scale of everyday human experience, and then to the scope of a magnetic field around a galaxy.

It is not by chance that at every level of the universe we find self-referencing and self-organizing systems. I believe there is an evolutionary direction and intention being expressed by nature's designs. Self-organizing systems have a number of unique properties that can help us discern the direction of evolution occurring throughout the cosmos:

· **Identity**—A self-organizing system requires a center around which and through which life-energy can flow.

· **Consciousness**—A self-organizing system is self-creating and therefore must be able to reflect upon itself in order to "get hold of itself."

· **Freedom**—To be self-creating, systems must exist within a context of great freedom.

· **Paradoxical nature**—Self-organizing systems are both *static and dynamic* (they are flowing systems that manifest as stable structures). They are both *open and closed* (they are

F I G U R E   7

Different Expressions of the Torus—
the Signature of Self-Referencing and Self-Organizing Systems

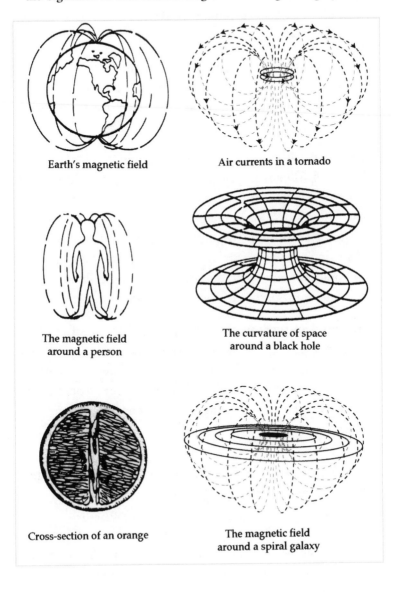

Earth's magnetic field

Air currents in a tornado

The magnetic field
around a person

The curvature of space
around a black hole

Cross-section of an orange

The magnetic field
around a spiral galaxy

continuously opening to the flow-through of energy and continuously closing into an identifiable entity). And they are both *unique and unified* (they are uniquely manifesting themselves at each moment while being completely immersed within and connected to the whole universe).

· **Community**—Self-organizing systems grow in concert with other systems in a mutually supportive process of co-evolution. Communities of free systems are the building blocks of existence.

· **Emergence**—Surprising potentials emerge as communities of self-organizing systems grow to higher levels of integration. We cannot predict the nature and capacities of new systems that may emerge from combinations of smaller systems. For example, we could not have guessed the nature of molecules by looking only at the properties of atoms, and we could not anticipate the nature of living cells by looking only at the properties of molecules, and so on.

· **Enlarged experiences**—An expanded scope of community, attained by combining smaller systems, supports new levels of learning and experience for members of that community. Members broaden and deepen their life-experience by co-evolving new orders of systems with others.

These properties suggest the universe does have a central project; namely to support the development of self-referencing systems that are able to live sustainably at the local scale while joining into communities at larger scales that offer the opportunity for learning and expression in a context of ever-broadening freedom. Of course, this is no more than an evolutionary orientation. The universe does not provide a cookbook and recipes for unfolding this orientation—and that is the point. Nature is filled with *self-organizing* systems. Evolution is truly a do-it-yourself project.

How does humanity's development into doubly-wise beings fit with the universe's central project of developing self-organizing systems? They are one and the same. If we want to choose an evolutionary direction that is congruent with nature's evolutionary intentions, it will involve developing our species-potential to become fully self-reflective. To the degree that we cultivate this capacity we will, I believe, be successful in our evolution. Becoming fully self-reflective means nothing less than becoming full members of the species *Homo sapiens sapiens.*

As humanity develops its capacity for reflective consciousness, the universe is simultaneously acquiring the ability to look back and reflect upon itself. We are the culmination of 12 billion years of evolution. It has taken the universe these billions of years to grow organisms on the Earth that have a sufficiently developed consciousness to be able to reflect on and appreciate the simple fact of being here, and to be able to look out consciously at the universe in wonder and awe. After billions of years of evolution, a life-form has emerged on the Earth that is literally the Mother Universe looking at her creations through the unique perspective and experience of each person. A gardener appreciating a flower or an astronomer peering out at the night sky represents the closing of a loop of awareness that began with the birth of our cosmos some 12 billion years ago. A Mother Universe gave birth to and sustains a daughter universe, which gave birth to living planets, which, in turn have given rise to life-forms that are now able to know that they know and look back at the universe with wonder and awe. We are returning to where we started and are awakening as doubly wise beings who can consciously reflect on the miracle of the universe and the gift of our existence. In the words of theologian Thomas Berry, humanity enables the universe "to reflect on and to celebrate itself and its deepest mystery in a special mode of conscious self-awareness."[1] The evolution of human consciousness enables the universe to know itself and to experiment consciously in its own evolution. Thus we are partners with the universe in the unfolding story of cosmic evolution.

THE SOUL'S BODY

WHY is knowing that we know so central to our life journey? What is so important about this specific capacity that evolution would be centered around it? To me, there is a compelling answer—one that reaches to the limits of human knowledge and language, and then disappears into the great mystery of life and existence.

The world of science and the world of spirituality converge in agreeing that there is a powerful stream of life at the very center of our moment-to-moment experience. *I believe that in developing our capacity for double wisdom, we are directly entering the life-stream and consciously cultivating a body of knowing that is our vehicle through the deep ecology of the Mother Universe—through eternity.* With double wisdom, that stream becomes directly aware of its unfolding existence. From this perspective, a soul is not a static "thing" but a flow of becoming. Each person's life-stream or soul has a unique quality of resonance and texture that is built up through our distinctive experiences and is expressed in our singular personality. In the words of the spiritual teacher Thomas Merton, "Every moment and every event of every man's life on earth plants something in his soul." We live in a world that is exquisitely designed for soul-growing, both for individuals and for entire civilizations. Neither individuals nor civilizations emerge fully evolved. We learn our way into succeeding stages of our maturity. A farmer becomes a farmer by farming season after season; a nurse becomes a nurse by nursing year after year. In a similar way, during the course of our lives we develop the character and texture of our lifestream or soul. In the words of ninety-year-old Florida Scott-Maxwell, "You need only claim the events of your life to make yourself yours. When you possess all you have been and done, you are fierce with reality."

Cultivating the ordinary miracle of our soulful presence in the world is supremely challenging—and uniquely satisfying. A soulful life embraces the full range of living. Just as soul music cuts beneath the surface to deep feelings that are authentic and true, soulful living likewise cuts through to the marrow and truth of life, whether it is heavy with suffering or light on wings of joy.

When we leave this world, none of us will take away a single penny or diploma or title. All of the world's spiritual traditions tell us that, no matter who we are, when we pass on from this world, we take with us only the knowing-resonance or love at the core of our being. That is our true identity. If, during our lives, we have nurtured qualities such as aggressiveness and unrelenting competition, then that is the residue of knowing-resonance that we will take from our brief passage through this world. On the other hand, if the soulful resonance at the center of our being has been nurtured with kindness and enthusiasm for living, then those are the qualities that we will take when we leave this world.

This is not only our learning. Everything we do and learn is woven into the living ecology that is the Mother Universe. We each learn and act on behalf of the totality. In the long sweep of cosmic evolution, everything material will eventually vanish; however, the intensity, character, and texture of knowing-resonance that we experience and nurture within ourselves lives in eternity.

Here are four characteristics of our soulful experience that we can cultivate in everyday life:

- **The soul is a body of love**—Spiritual traditions throughout history have affirmed that we are created from life-energy whose essential nature is love. It is our core essence, at the very heart and center of our experience. Because love is at the center of all, we are able to make friends with ourselves and others. Teilhard de Chardin wrote that the only way for billions of diverse individuals to love one another is "by knowing themselves all to be centered upon a single 'super-center' common to all." The love that is the life-energy of the Mother Universe provides that common center for us all.

- **The soul is a body of light**—The new physics describes light as the basic building block of material reality. In this sense, matter can be viewed as "frozen light."[2] Because we live in a universe of light, it seems fitting to consider the soul as a more subtle body of light that has the potential to evolve into more subtle ecologies of light after the physical body dies. It is interesting that, according to the Gospel of Thomas, when Jesus was asked by a disciple to describe where he came from, he replied "We came from the light, the place where the light came into being on its own accord and established itself."[3] Elsewhere in this same gospel, Jesus says, "Whoever has ears, let him hear. There is light within a man of light, and it lights up the whole world."[4] In Eastern traditions, we find similar descriptions that we are beings of light. In Buddhism, the awakened consciousness is described with phrases such as "self-luminous recognition." It is with good reason that awakening experiences are often described with phrases such as "enlightenment," "seeing the light," and "becoming illumined."

· **The soul is a body of music**—Quantum physics describes all that exists in terms of wave-forms or patterns of resonance. Not surprisingly, we each have a complex hum or resonance that is instantly evident to others as they encounter us and experience our feeling-tone. We are each literally a body of music. Given different temperaments and personalities, each individual is a unique symphony of knowing-resonance.

· **The soul is a body of knowing**—When we allow our ordinary experience of knowing to relax into itself, we find a self-confirming presence. When we know that we know without the need for thoughts to confirm our knowing, we are entering our life-stream directly. As we cultivate our capacity for mindful living or self-referencing knowing, we lessen the need for a material world and physical body to awaken the knowing process to itself. Ultimately, the body that provided the aligning structure to awaken self-referencing knowing can die, and we will endure as a body of light and knowing with the freedom to develop in more subtle ecologies beyond this realm. Once grounded in our capacity for double wisdom, we can be self-remembering in these subtle ecologies without fear of forgetting ourselves. There is no more elevated task than to learn, of our own free will, the skills of living in eternity.

In the view of many spiritual traditions, the soul is a body of love, light, music, and knowing. The qualities we cultivate during our brief stay on Earth infuse the soul, and when our physical body dies, these qualities remain with the soul or life-stream, which is our vehicle through eternity.

If we do not recognize ourselves as a body of love, light, music, and knowing while we live in a physical body, we can overlook ourselves when our physical body dies. Jesus said, "Take heed of the Living One while you are alive, lest you die and seek to see Him and be unable to do so."[5] In Buddhist terms, it is precisely while we have a physical body that we need to recognize our core nature as pure awareness or as the "ground luminosity."[6] In the words of the fifteenth-century Hindu and Sufi master, Kabir:

The idea that the soul will join with the ecstatic
just because the body is rotten—
that is all fantasy.
What is found now is found then.
If you find nothing now,
you will simply end up with an apartment in the City of Death.
If you make love with the divine now,
in the next life you will have the face of satisfied desire.[7]

If we do not use our physical body and world to discover that we already embody the gift of immortality, then when we die we may look out from our subtle body of light and awareness and not recognize our refined existence. If we use our time on Earth to come to self-referencing awareness, we will have anchored the gift of eternity in direct knowing. We can then evolve through the ever more subtle realms of the Mother Universe.[8]

At the beginning of this chapter I questioned what purpose could be so compelling that it could draw the human family together into a common project. What could be more compelling than discovering the priceless gift of eternity? And because life is so interdependent, it is a journey that we are taking together.

THE UNFOLDING OF DOUBLE WISDOM

ALTHOUGH there have surely been awakened individuals throughout history and in every major culture of the world, my concern is with the changing consciousness of the majority of humans beings—the changing "social average." How has the complex capacity for double wisdom awakened and developed for the overall human family?

Just as there are relatively distinct stages that characterize the development of an individual from infancy to early adulthood, there are also discernible stages in the development of our species. However, to discover those stages, we need to look beneath the people and events that make headlines and that tend to float on the surface of the stream of life. It is the deeper changes, working below the surface of popular culture, that ultimately make history.

In this section I shall explore seven stages of growth that I believe are vital for developing humanity's full potential

for double wisdom or reflective consciousness. I recognize
that a stages-of-growth description of human evolution can
give the impression that evolution is linear—a march from
one stage to the next in a smooth and direct flow. Of course,
it is not. Human evolution is an untidy process that seldom
conforms to orderly progressions and clear boundaries. Our
path through the various stages will surely be filled with
many surprises, accidents, and confusing twists and turns that
will make it uniquely human and characteristically unpredictable. With these qualifications, I do think that there is a
general direction to evolution that leads toward our initial
maturity as a planetary civilization.

Reflective consciousness is a rich and multifaceted faculty
whose full range of potentials develops through a series of
stages or learning environments. At each stage, a different
set of observing or reflective potentials is awakened, developed, and integrated. Our evolutionary challenge is to consciously retain the lessons of each era while moving on to
the next. Our consciousness and culture are maturing
through a nested series of experiences, and the complete
spectrum is vital in order for us to become fully human.

Stage 1: The era of archaic humans—contracted consciousness.
For several million years, our archaic ancestors lived in the
faint dawn of reflective consciousness. Their capacity for
knowing that we know was almost entirely undeveloped;
consequently, our earliest human ancestors functioned primarily on instinct and habit. As a result, their way of life
remained virtually unchanged over thousands of generations.
Stone tools, for example, show a monotonous sameness over
an immense span of time—for roughly ten thousand gen-

erations there is no evidence of invention.[9] Some degree of reflective consciousness must have begun to awaken more than a million years ago, when *Homo erectus* migrated out of Africa and, to cope with the harsh Ice Age climate, learned to use animal skins for warm clothing, construct shelters, and use fire. Nonetheless, it is only with the earliest evidence of burials, approximately sixty thousand years ago, that we find a clear recognition of death and evidence of conscious reflection on the "self" that lives and then dies.

Stage 2: The era of awakening gatherers and hunters—sensing consciousness. Although the glowing ember of double wisdom was passed along by our ancestors for several million years, it did not emerge as a distinct flame of self-observation and reflective knowing until roughly thirty-five thousand years ago. At this time, the glacially slow development of culture and consciousness finally achieved a critical mass, and a flow of development began that leads directly to the modern era. Humans made a dramatic leap in their capacity for self-observation, and this is vividly expressed in tremendous changes in toolmaking, painting, and carving as well as in evidence of expanding social and trading networks.

The capacity for fleeting self-recognition that emerged at this time, however, should not be confused with the stabilized "I-sense" that emerges later. There is enormous evolutionary distance between the capacity for momentary self-observation and a steady mirroring capacity that we can consciously mobilize as we move through life. For awakening gatherers and hunters, life was so immediate that, for the most part, it was not contemplated with reflective detachment; instead, things just happened.[10] Much of the time, people operated on automatic—moving through the repetition and routine of a simple, nomadic life. The world was experienced as up close and immediate—a magical place filled with unknown and uncontrollable forces, unexpected miracles, and strange happenings. Nature was a living field without clear boundaries between the natural and supernatural. Daily life was a mixture of unseen forces and unexplained events, for people had neither the concepts nor the perceptual framework to describe rationally how the world worked.

Social organization was on a tribal scale, and individuals felt themselves to be inseparable from the empathic field of their family and tribal group. People's sense of identity came from affiliation with a tribe and from a sense of intimate connection with nature. With few possessions, there was little basis for material differences, or material conflict. Meaning was found in the direct sensing of and engagement with life. A sensing consciousness was bodily based, directly felt, implicit, and tacit. Without an objectified sense of time—without being able to name it or describe its workings—there was little sense of the future; instead, most things happened in the simple, passing present.[11] Every recurring season and event was a unique miracle: the return of springtime after a long winter, the annual migration of animals, the waxing and waning of the moon—all were mysterious wonders.

Stage 3: The era of farming-based civilizations—feeling consciousness. Roughly ten thousand years ago human perception again expanded. People were able to step back even further from unconscious immersion in nature to see how they could tame nature through farming. Combining the gathering of wild grains with seasonal hunting, they made a gradual transition to a settled way of life. Humans made small, incremental improvements in food-raising that, over time, amounted to a revolution in living. Over thousands of years, people learned to pull weeds from wild fields of wheat to increase their yield, to plant seeds around the margins of wild fields to extend the size of the crop, and to protect the fields from grazing animals. From such modest beginnings came one of the most fundamental transformations the world has ever known. The surplus of food that farming produced made possible the eventual rise of large-scale, urban civilizations.

The mind-set of the agricultural era was cyclical, governed by nature—the seasons go round, but the world remains essentially the same. Life was not perceived to be "going anywhere." The vast majority of people lived in small villages and found meaning through belonging to an extended community. No longer were blood and tribal ties the primary cultural glue. In an increasingly differentiated society, it was the power of fellowship, emotional bonds, social status, and shared symbols of meaning that provided the connective tissue. In this stage, the power of consciousness is used to reflect on feelings of affiliation with others who had certain commonalities—such as living in the same geographic area, sharing ethnic origins, and having a common religion. In a largely preliterate and prerational society, feeling-based communications were the dominant currency of culture. Despite its growing depth, reflective consciousness in the agrarian culture tended to be limited by rigid customs, irrational superstitions, social immobility, widespread illiteracy, a patriarchal society, and the authoritarian character of the church and state. Although all of the basic arts of civilization (such as writing, organized government, architecture, mathematics, and the division of labor) arose during this stage, most people lived as impoverished peasants with no expectation of material change or progress. For the majority, life was brutal, bleak, and short.

While this era represented a dramatic change from the hunter-gatherer and small-village way of life, it also contained many primitive elements—a lack of social mobility, arranged marriages, the oppression of women, restricted access to formal education, and rule by political and spiritual elites.[12] In addition, the range of occupations was quite narrow, as people were expected to pursue the same craft or trade as their family. Although the agrarian era represented a great advance in reflective consciousness and the building of large-scale cultures, it was still only an early stage in the journey to develop the full expression of humanity's capacity for double wisdom.

Stage 4: The era of scientific-industrial civilizations—thinking consciousness. The next great change in consciousness arrived in full force by the 1700s as a number of powerful revolutions blossomed in England, Europe, and the United States. These include a scientific revolution that challenged the belief in the supernatural and the authority of the church; a religious reformation that questioned the role and function of religious institutions; the Renaissance, which brought a new perspective to the arts; an industrial revolution, which brought unprecedented material progress; an urban revolution, which brought masses of people together in new ways, breaking apart the feudal pattern of living; and a democratic revolution, which fostered a new level of individual empowerment and involvement. These powerful revolutions, which still affect us today, were expressions of a new perceptual paradigm and mark a dramatic break with the agrarian era.

When the industrial revolution began in earnest in the late 1700s, more than 90 percent of the population in Europe and the United States lived and worked on farms. Two hundred years later, more than 90 percent of the population in these countries lived and worked in cities and suburbs. In this single statistic is the story of an extraordinary transformation of these societies—a transformation that is now being repeated in countries around the world.

The flat wheel of time that oriented perception in the agricultural era opens up to become a dynamic, three-dimensional spiral in the industrial era. In experiencing that time is "going somewhere," people perceive the potential for material progression or progress. As the mystery of nature gives way to science and an analyzing intellect, material achievements became a primary measure of success.

All of life on Earth has paid a very high price for the learning realized during this era. Although people in industrialized societies are more intellectually sophisticated and psychologically differentiated, they are also more isolated— often feeling separated from nature, others, and themselves. Feelings of companionship and community have been stripped away; many people live nearly alone in vast urban regions of alienating scale and complexity. Unprecedented economic and political freedom have been won, but at great cost when life seems to have little meaning or sense of purpose beyond ever more consumption. The perceptual paradigm of the scientific-industrial era has immense drive but virtually no sense of direction beyond the acquisition of power and things. Despite these limitations, reflective consciousness has advanced considerably in this era, fostering greater citizenship in government, entrepreneurship in economics, and self-authority in spiritual matters.

Stage 5: The era of communication—observing consciousness. Because the communications revolution has enabled humanity to begin observing itself consciously as a species, the capacity for double wisdom is now taking another quantum leap forward. No longer operating largely on automatic, entire societies are increasingly conscious of the simple fact of consciousness—and that changes everything. With reflection comes the ability to witness what is happening in the world and the freedom to choose our pathway into the future.

Reflective consciousness provides the practical basis for building a sustainable future. We cannot afford to run on automatic given the scope and urgency of challenges converging around us. Because of the severity of the combined adversity trends, we are being challenged to pay attention to how we are paying attention collectively. With reflective consciousness we can objectively witness environmental pollution, religious intolerance, poverty, overconsumption, racial injustice, sexual discrimination, and other conditions that have divided us in the past. With a more objective perspective combined with the skills of conflict resolution and the tools of mass communication, we can achieve a new level of human understanding and discover an authentic vision of a future that serves the well-being of all.

Reflective consciousness provides the glue that can bond the human family into a mutually appreciative whole while simultaneously honoring our differences. As we cultivate our capacity for knowing that we know, we begin to heal our sense of disconnection from the larger universe. We catch glimpses of the unity of the cosmos and our intimate participation within the living web of existence. No longer is reality broken into relativistic islands or pieces. If only for a few moments at a time, we see and experience existence as a seamless, living totality. These few moments can have a transformational impact. As the Sufi poet Kabir wrote, he saw the universe as a living and growing body "for fifteen seconds, and it made him a servant for life."[13]

Stage 6: The era of bonding—compassionate consciousness. In the next stage in the unfolding of double wisdom, I believe that an observing consciousness will mature into a compassionate consciousness, and love will genuinely infuse our civilizing activities. The same energy of compassion that binds a family is the unifying force that will make global reconciliation and commitment possible. It is love that will enable us to join in a purposeful union of global scope so as to ensure a sustainable home for all life.

We will not enter this stage with our capacity for compassion fully developed; instead, it will be through working together day after day over generations that we shall evolve our capacity for loving engagement with the world. In turn, it will be the strength of this union that will enable us to withstand the enormous stresses that will be unleashed during the next stage of growth. Where the dispassionate consciousness of the communications era was sufficient to enable us to achieve embryonic reconciliation, it is the compassionate consciousness of the bonding era that will enable us to move ahead to build a creative, global civilization.

A compassionate consciousness would foster a new cultural atmosphere where people feel that they are among friends no matter where they are in the world. During the agrarian era, universal literacy seemed almost impossible, yet we are working to achieve it in industrial societies today. In the same way, a compassionate consciousness as a cultural norm may seem unimaginable today, but it could become a reality within a few generations.

In this era, humanity could take on the restoration and renewal of the biosphere as a common project, which could promote a deep sense of community and bonding. A global culture of kindness could foster world projects that include transforming massive cities into decentralized eco-villages, hosting global celebrations and concerts, and developing ongoing world games as an alternative to warfare.

Stage 7: The era of surpassing ourselves—flow consciousness. With flow consciousness, we experience existence as fresh, alive, and arising anew. The observer no longer stands apart from any aspect of reality, but participates fully. We return consciously to the center of our ordinary lives, and bring the power of our wakefulness to our creative expression. We know, moment by moment, through the subtle hum of knowing-resonance at the core of our being, whether we are living in a way that serves the well-being of the whole.

In this stage, humanity will move beyond maintaining ourselves to surpassing ourselves. In this "surpassing era," compassionate consciousness coalesces into self-organizing action and becomes a force for focused, creative expression in the world. A primary challenge of this era will be to liberate the creative potentials of the species without destroying the foundation of global unity and sustainability developed in the previous stages. To meet this challenge, it will be important to develop and integrate all aspects of reflective consciousness into a balanced whole:

- **Sensing consciousness** of the era of awakening hunter-gatherers

- **Feeling consciousness** of the agrarian era

- **Thinking consciousness** of the scientific-industrial era

- **Observing consciousness** of the communications era

- **Compassionate consciousness** of the bonding era

- **Flow consciousness** of the surpassing era

Figure 8 illustrates these stages in the unfolding of reflective consciousness. When we have fulfilled and integrated the potentials of all these stages, humanity will have become a consciously self-organizing planetary family with the perspective, compassion, and creativity to sustain ourselves into the deep future. We will have consciously developed a rich sensory existence, a textured emotional life, a complex intellectual world, the capacity for reflection and reconciliation, a deep love for the Earth and compassion for all its inhabitants, and the subtle freedom of flow consciousness.

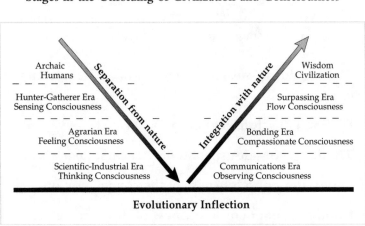

FIGURE   8

Stages in the Unfolding of Civilization and Consciousness

I want to emphasize that *these stages represent a pathway, not a prediction.* What is important is that we begin to see, however dimly, the story of humanity's journey of awakening to the potentials of our self-given name as a species—*Homo sapiens sapiens.*

If my informal surveys of people around the world are correct and humanity is in its adolescent years of development, then we have long-term opportunities in front of us and a long way to go before reaching our full potentials, individually and collectively. The widely shared intuition that we are in our teenage years also suggests that if we are asked, we recognize that we have already traveled a considerable evolutionary distance since our awakening as gatherers and hunters some thirty-five thousand years ago.

While moving toward a globalized world, it is vital that we remember the living wisdom that is at the core of each of the major stages of human experience—as gatherers and hunters, as farmers of land, as dwellers in cities and, increasingly, as dwellers in cyberspace. Each stage represents an invaluable building block in the nested process of developing a sustainable species-civilization that honors both human diversity and global unity.

It is also important to emphasize that this description of the stages in the unfolding of culture and consciousness should not be interpreted to mean that one stage is better than another. As someone who grew up on a farm and now lives in a city, I do not believe that the mind-set of the urban-industrial era is "better" than that of the agrarian era. At the same time, it is important not to romanticize the past. In my view, while all of humanity's past modes of thinking and living will be invaluable for solving the challenges of the future, none of them will be sufficient. We have further learning to do, both as individuals and cultures, in our ways of thinking, living, communicating, and relating.

To portray humans as participants in an experimental and creative universe is not to elevate our stature unduly. Our subordinate status is clear—we do not know how to create a single cubic inch of empty space or matter, let alone the elegance of a flower. The status of the Mother Universe is not threatened by our participation in life on an island called Earth in an immense cosmos with billions of other planets that are likely nurturing life. Rather, we are fulfilling the purpose for which the cosmos was created. We are the agents of evolution, enabling the Mother Universe to reflect upon, and then to surpass herself creatively.

In my view, completing these stages will not represent the end of humanity's journey. It will be our beginning at a new level of possibility. Humans will not become angels or saints; we will simply be awake to the fullness of who and what we already are. Just as reaching adulthood marks the beginning of creative work in the world for individuals, attaining our early adulthood as a planetary civilization will mark the beginning of a new phase in humanity's exploration and learning.

I want to return one last time to the question I asked at the beginning of this chapter: Is there a purpose that is so compelling that it could draw the human family together in common enterprise? My answer is that the highest and most compelling purpose we could possibly imagine is beckoning us—namely, to continue unfolding our capacity for reflective consciousness, both individually and culturally, so that we might learn how to live consciously and compassionately within the Mother Universe. That is the challenge—and the promise—of our journey.

Chapter Nine

⌐

ENGAGED REFLECTION

IN THE TURNING ZONE

Mindfulness must be engaged.
Once there is seeing, there must be acting.
Otherwise, what is the use of seeing?
—*Thich Nhat Hanh*

It is not the answer that enlightens,
but the question.
—*Eugene Ionesco*

THE POWER OF CONSCIOUS EVOLUTION

WE have looked at the big picture, now what? Responses are clearly called for, but which responses? There are many specific actions that we could take to turn toward a positive future, but where do we begin? These are the kinds of questions that I want to explore in this chapter.

If we human beings are to succeed in our evolutionary journey and mature into our adulthood, I believe that all four of the opportunity trends discussed in chapters three through six need to flourish if we are to succeed. None will be sufficient without the others. All four will be necessary if humanity is to turn the corner and realize an evolutionary bounce. Seeing the universe as alive and a sacred field of evolution will not be sufficient if it does not translate into practical, worldly expressions. Choosing a simpler way of life will not, by itself, be sufficient to secure a sustainable future, although it is surely necessary. Awakening the global brain will not be sufficient if this communication system remains disengaged from the reality of the human situation. Working toward genuine reconciliation across the many barriers that divide humanity will not be sufficient to heal ancient wounds if the process is not supported by change in other spheres of life. In short, achieving an evolutionary bounce will require nothing less than a combined transformation in how we think, live, communicate, and relate.

Despite the great importance of these four factors, there is another that I believe is even more fundamental to our success at this pivotal stage in our evolutionary journey. That factor is the development of the powerful tool of conscious reflection in our personal and collective lives. A basic theme of this book is that evolution is fostering the development of self-organizing systems that have the ability to reflect upon themselves and thereby provide themselves with self-orienting feedback. Building upon this theme, I conclude that the most direct, powerful, and natural way to support ourselves in maturing as individuals and as a species is by increasing opportunities for conscious reflection from the personal to the planetary scale.

Personal reflection refers to seeing ourselves in the mirror of consciousness as individuals and to observing the unfolding of our lives. By analogy, social reflection refers to seeing ourselves in the mirror of collective consciousness as social groupings using tools such as the mass media and the internet. With authentic social reflection, we can achieve a shared understanding and a working consensus regarding appropriate actions. Actions can then come quickly and voluntarily. We can mobilize ourselves purposefully, and each person can contribute their unique talents to the creation of a life-affirming future.

Voluntary or self-organized action will be vital to our success. Our swiftly developing world situation is far too complex for any one individual or group to figure out and propose remedies that will work for everyone. Nonetheless, the world has become so interdependent that our consciousness as citizens needs to match the actual nature of the world of which we are an inseparable part. Thus, this will be a time for rapid learning and experimentation locally while being mindful of how we connect globally.

With sustained reflection and dialogue, we could choose a new pathway into the future. We could look a generation or two into the future and see that we have a choice: we can ignore our situation now and put ourselves through enormous suffering in the future, or we can respond to our situation now and take a higher path. Without reflection, the human agenda seems likely to sink to the lowest common denominator that greed and fear can create.

If we are going to grow up as a species and move the social average of our behavior from adolescence to early adulthood, then the challenge we face is not so much in the world "out there" as it is in our own inner maturity. For example, if in response to adversity trends we focus primarily on making technological and economic changes, we will be missing the heart of the human story—which is making a leap forward to a new level of maturity. No material change is as essential as our collective willingness to look squarely at ourselves and our impact on the Earth—and then to focus our efforts appropriately.

Engaged reflection is the foundation for concerted, voluntary action in democratic societies. In order for social reflection to lead to effective actions, it is important to recognize the creative tension between two pulls toward engagement. On the one hand, there is the pull to have social reflection occur locally where it is tangible, and grounded in face-to-face conversation with others such as family, friends, neighbors, and co-workers. On the other hand, there is a pull to have the scope of social reflection match the scope of the challenges—many of which are at the more impersonal scale of community, country, and planet. Therefore, effective social reflection needs to foster both face-to-face conversations as well as conversations of national and global scale, recognizing there is a creative tension in this polarity.

SMALL-GROUP REFLECTION TO DISCOVER A NEW "COMMON SENSE"

PERHAPS the most important action we can take is to talk with one another, both personally and professionally, about the challenges we face, as well as our visions for a positive future. In living rooms, classrooms, meeting rooms, and boardrooms, we can strike up fresh conversations about humanity's future. Face-to-face conversations can have unexpected power: they can be a vehicle for shared learning that clarifies what we care about, strengthens our commitment to constructive change, and informs what actions are most appropriate for building a sustainable future.[1]

Because the entire world is caught up in a process of globalization, much of humanity is in transition—"between stories" regarding who we are, where we have come from, and where we are going. The human family is just beginning to discover and give voice to our common story that includes, but goes beyond, the stories of our past. It is understandable that we do not have a common story for orienting and organizing ourselves. Humanity has yet to develop a sense of common purpose that mobilizes our collective efforts and elicits our enthusiastic participation in creating a new life together. Because we are all learners together, a core challenge will be to discover our compelling evolutionary story together—a new "common sense," a sense of reality, identity, and social purpose that we can hold in common and that respects our radically changing circumstances. How can we discover such a story in the course of our everyday lives? Let us look at some possible ways.

Study circles. These are typically small groups of a half-dozen to a dozen people who gather together regularly to speak from the heart, tell their stories, and learn from the collective wisdom of the group. Study circles provide a feeling of community around the concerns being explored. Members generally agree to listen respectfully to others without interruption, although they engage in spirited conversations so as to understand the perspectives of those with whom they disagree. Study circles on the theme of voluntary simplicity, for example, have been flourishing in the United States in recent years.[2]

There are innumerable topics to discuss. Here are a few questions drawn from themes in this book: What are people's views regarding the "age" of the human family? What are the circle's views on the major adversity trends? What are views on the major opportunity trends? What do people think is the likelihood that these trends will converge into an evolutionary wall within the coming generation? What might our time of planetary initiation be like? What might an evolutionary crash look like? An evolutionary bounce? Is humanity involved in a larger journey beyond simply maintaining ourselves in ever greater comfort? If so, what is the nature and purpose of that journey? What actions can we take now to live more sustainably and compassionately?

Churches, synagogues, temples, mosques, and meditation halls. Houses of worship could intensify their inquiry into humanity's soulful direction at this critical juncture in history. These spiritual centers could also collaborate with one another in discovering a higher vision that responds to questions such as: What are the guiding spiritual insights for this time of historic transition? What actions could be taken to promote justice and reconciliation in a world divided by gender, wealth, race, religion, geography, and more? What is the role of faith communities as growing numbers of people seek a more experiential or first-hand spirituality? What ways of living are appropriate in this new era?

Classrooms. What is education for if not to learn and think creatively about humanity's future? Educators could develop curricula relevant to the emerging future with its many challenges. For example, reconciliation could become a core area of study; students could learn skills of conflict resolution in the classroom. We could also explore opportunities for lifelong learning to enable people to acquire needed knowledge and skills. From practical skills (such as gardening and health care) to entrepreneurial skills (such as creating a values-based business), schools could make it a priority to educate people to be a self-organizing force for sustainability.

Community and professional groups. Many organizations have local chapters that meet as discussion groups. Conversations about sustainability and the prospects of hitting an evolutionary wall could be integrated into these ongoing groups. Professional groups (such as doctors, lawyers, teachers, and engineers) could explore the nature of a sustainable future in the context of their professions and could encourage their members to take actions appropriate to their professions. For example, engineers may be encouraged to focus on sustainable energy technologies, and lawyers on the legal rights of future generations and other species.

Corporate boardrooms. It is difficult to have a healthy business in a sick world—economic health and environmental health go hand in hand. Instead of focusing exclusively on profits in the short run, corporations could focus on the interests of stakeholders in the longer run. In the past, businesses were able to optimize their performance without worrying about the environmental consequences. Now, with climate change, resource depletion, and other forms of global stress apparent, companies could reframe their approach to business by shifting to triple-bottom-line accounting—and publicly assessing the economic viability, social impact, and environmental consequences of their operations.

There are many places in which to establish the process of social reflection in small group conversations happening daily throughout our lives. In the next section, we turn to consider the other end of this polarity—social reflection at the mass scale of communities, nations, and the Earth.

SOCIAL REFLECTION AND CONSCIOUS DEMOCRACY

WHEN it comes to social transformation, small group conversations and mass communication are two sides of the same coin. Both are essential. Although the foundation for a reflective society is in individual, face-to-face conversations, it is important that these conversations unite at larger scales of social reflection—at the regional, national, and global levels. *Ultimately, the scale of social reflection must match the scale of evolutionary concern—and that is now the entire Earth.*

Communication at these larger scales necessarily involves television and the internet. So, let's look at the circulatory system of effective communication in our modern democracies. In particular, three ingredients are essential to sustain a reflective democracy and learning society: Citizens need to be adequately *informed* through the mass media, they need the opportunity to engage in electronically supported *dialogue* with others in order to build a working consensus, and they need the opportunity to *petition* leaders for making positive changes.

Consider what would happen if any of these three ingredients are missing. If citizens are deprived of essential information, they cannot make sound judgments, so the democratic process will be ill-informed, which is dangerous and counterproductive. If they are adequately informed but cannot peacefully assemble, then they cannot discuss what they know and build a working consensus. The result would be informed individuals with no ability to form the critical mass of consensus necessary for change to occur. Finally, if citizens have the ability to be informed and to gather in electronic dialogue, but are deprived of the ability to convey their shared sentiments to their leaders, then participation is meaningless. The result would be the proverbial "all talk and no action." It is the mutually reinforcing support of these three rights working as a system that provides the foundation for a reflective democracy and learning society.

Currently, around the world, all three ingredients of a conscious democracy are woefully inadequate for meeting the challenge of the combined adversity trends. For the most part, the media treat their viewers as consumers who want to be entertained and distracted, not as citizens who seek to be informed and involved. In addition, we have scarcely begun to exercise the rights of mature citizenship by developing electronic town meetings and other forums where citizens can assemble for sustained dialogue and petition for change. Conscious democracy, with a healthy circulation of communication, is still in its infancy—waiting to be invented by citizen-entrepreneurs facing a time of momentous change.

I recognize that television and the internet are converging into a new medium of global communication, but I find it is useful to focus on television to illustrate three fundamental ingredients of a conscious democracy in the communications era: that it be informed, conversant, and responsive. Let's look at each of these.

An informed citizenry. Many people are ill-informed through no fault of their own. The vast majority of commercial television time is devoted to entertainment, not relevant in-

formation. Even news programming is becoming "infotainment." Our situation is like that of a long-distance
runner who prepares for a marathon by eating a steady diet
of junk food. We are trying to run modern democracies on
a diet of televised entertainment just when we are confronting challenges of marathon proportions.

To build a workable tomorrow, we need a quantum increase in the depth and quality of information about our common future. We need a hearty, robust diet of socially relevant
media programming about the critical trends and choices facing communities, nations, and humanity as a whole. We need
far more documentaries and investigative reports that give us
an in-depth understanding of the challenges we face. We
need programs that vividly portray what life will be like
within a generation if nothing is done to alter current trends,
and we need programs that suggest what life could be like if
we begin designing ourselves into a sustainable future. Lester
Brown, president of the Worldwatch Institute, has written
that "while heads of the world's major news organizations
may not have sought this responsibility, only they have the
tools to disseminate the information needed to fuel change
on the scale required and in the time available."[3]

We cannot consciously build a future that we have not
first imagined. We are a visual species. When we can see it,
we can do it. The power of positive visualization is widely
recognized in the realm of individual mind-body medicine,
but we have been slow to apply this wisdom to the healing
of our social mind-body. Positive visions can be a catalyst
for positive actions, which reinforce the power of creative
visioning, which can set into motion a self-fulfilling spiral of
constructive development.

Here is just one example of the kind of television programming that I believe could stir the public consciousness into authentic reflection. To balance the onslaught of aggressive consumer commercials, alternative commercials, which I call *"Earthvisions,"* could be developed. Produced by nonprofit organizations and community groups working in partnership with local television stations, *Earthvisions* could be thirty-second ministories portraying some aspect of a sustainable and meaningful future. They could be low in cost and high in creativity, and done with playfulness, compassion, and humor. They could focus on humankind's connection with the web of life, or on positive visions of the future from the perspective of future generations, or on awakening an appreciation of nature and sustainability. My guess is that the public would be delighted with these refreshing perspectives. Once under way, a virtual avalanche of *Earthvisions* could emerge from communities around the world and be shared over the internet. Other media— such as public access TV, newspapers, radio, and specialty publications—could be used to enrich the dialogue.

We could also develop a rich array of programming beyond thirty-second spots. For instance, television comedies could offer a humorous look at everyday life in a sustainable society (such as the challenges of living in an eco-village). Television news-magazine shows could be developed that focus in-depth on themes pertaining to a sustainable future and our evolutionary success. Dramas could explore the deeper tensions and larger opportunities that families and communities may encounter as we begin designing ourselves into this new future. Because inspiring and hopeful visions for the future are largely absent from our money-obsessed media culture, the opportunities for envisioning creative alternatives are enormous.

A conversing citizenry. Democracy has been called the "art of the possible." However, unless we understand what the majority thinks and feels, we cannot know what's possible. Only when we the public know together what we think as a whole can we confidently communicate a working consensus back to our elected representatives. Therefore, a major step in empowering the citizenry in modern societies is to support communication among citizens so that a working consensus can emerge. A conscious democracy talks to itself and knows its own mind. A conscious democracy is vigilant, watchful, and wide awake. An informed public that knows its own mind can be trusted. After reviewing half a century of polling public opinion in the United States, George Gallup, Jr., found "the collective judgment of the people to be extraordinarily sound."[4] Often, he said, "people are actually ahead of their elected leaders in accepting innovations and radical changes."[5]

Only full and open communication will empower people to act with the level of energy, creativity, and cooperation that our circumstances demand. Initially, people will need to express their anger that the Earth has been so devastated, their disappointments that their material dreams have not been fulfilled, and their unwillingness to make sacrifices unless there is greater fairness. As people work through their anger, sorrow, and fear, they can develop an authentic working consensus. When people can tell their leaders, with confidence, where they want to go and how fast they want to get there, then leaders can do their jobs.

It is time to explore our common future, recognizing that

we are a powerful, contentious, and extraordinary species that has ascended to the verge of a planetary civilization. It is time to begin telling the stories of our long adventure of awakening and to celebrate the sacred nature of our journey.

A feedback citizenry. A conscious democracy requires the active consent of the governed, not simply their passive acquiescence. Of course, citizen involvement is no guarantee that people's choices will always be "right." What involvement does assure is that citizens will be invested in the choices they make. Rather than feeling cynical or powerless, they will feel engaged in and responsible for society and its future.

Once a citizenry knows its own mind and has confidence in its views and values, it can use electronic forums to give feedback to its elected leaders. In a conscious democracy, a working consensus among citizens would presumably guide but not compel elected representatives. Assuming citizen feedback is advisory or nonbinding, it would respect the responsibility of representatives to make decisions and the responsibility of the citizenry to make their views known to those who govern.

My own work to revitalize the conversation of democracy is relevant here. During the 1980s, I launched and directed two nonprofit and nonpartisan organizations—one national called Choosing Our Future and the other local to the San Francisco area called Bay Voice. The purpose of both organizations was to give all people a voice in how the most powerful instrument in our modern society and democracy—television—is being used. Among our many actions, Choosing Our Future worked in partnership with the ABC-TV affiliate in San Francisco to develop a pilot electronic town meeting (ETM) that was seen by over 300,000 people. The hour-long pilot, which aired in 1987, featured feedback from a preselected, random sample of citizens throughout the Bay Area who watched the program from their homes. The program began with an informative mini-documentary to place the issue in context and then moved to an in-studio dialogue with experts and a diverse audience. As questions became better formulated in the studio discussion, the preselected members of the scientific sample were asked to respond. They did so by dialing in numbers on their telephone to register simple votes, which were then tallied by a computer and shown to both in-studio participants and viewers at home. Six votes were taken during the hour-long, prime-time ETM, enabling far more than a one-time "knee-jerk" response from the public. This just begins to suggest the untapped potential for interactivity and dialogue—particularly as these tools are combined with the internet, radio, newspapers, and other forums such as study circles.

Electronic town meetings are an ideal forum for citizen dialogue and feedback. A core issue in building a more reflective society and democracy will be: Who should sponsor these? If ETMs are initiated by commercial television stations and internet sites, they will likely have a bias toward commerce and entertainment. If they are sponsored by a local government body, they will likely be reluctant to deal with concerns of a national and global nature. If they are sponsored by an issue-oriented organization or an institution representing a particular ethnic, racial, or gender group, then there will be a tendency to focus around their concerns. Because of these difficulties, I believe that a new social institution is needed to act on behalf of all citizens as the nonpartisan sponsor of electronic town meetings. Metropolitan areas

could develop nonpartisan, nonprofit "community voice" organizations that would perform two key functions: conducting research to determine the issues that are important to the
community, and working with television stations, internet
providers, and a range of other media to broadcast ETMs. The
community voice organization would not promote or advocate any particular outcome; rather, its goal would be to support community learning, dialogue, and consensus building—
and then to let the chips fall where they may.

A more specialized form of electronic town meeting also
could be developed—a viewer feedback forum. The idea is
simple. Television almost never turns its cameras around to
look at itself directly. To bring balance, television broadcasters could be held accountable for their programming and
advertising in the court of public opinion, perhaps on a
weekly basis. A community voice organization could sponsor regular viewer feedback forums. These forums could employ live polling of a random sample of citizens to get an
accurate sense of public sentiment. Beyond traditional issues
such as TV violence, viewer feedback forums could raise
questions vital to a sustainable future for the Earth: Is television creating a level of desire for consumption that cannot
be sustained globally? If media-generated desires cannot be
sustained, then how will those people who are left out respond? Does the mirror of television accurately reflect the
reality of our world? Is the consumerist bias of current programming diverting our cultural attention from critical concerns, dumbing-down our potential, and holding back our
evolution? By programming television for commercial success, is the television industry simultaneously programming
the mind-set of civilizations for ecological failure? How
might the mass media nourish and strengthen our culture

and enable us to cope with ecological, social, and spiritual challenges? The working consensus of the community could be presented to representatives of television stations at the end of each program, holding them publicly accountable for their legal responsibility to present a balanced diet of relevant programming that serves the public interest.[6]

THE POWER OF SOCIAL REFLECTION

WHAT difference would it make to have a more conscious society in which there is a healthy circulation of information, conversation, and feedback? Could the process of social reflection be so powerful that it could act as the catalyst for an evolutionary bounce? I believe that it could. Here are five examples to illustrate the kinds of difference that social reflection could make.

Visualizing more sustainable ways of living. I want to repeat what I consider to be a staggering statistic: the average American watches roughly twenty-five thousand television commercials a year. Most are advertisements for a consumerist way of life as much as they are pitches for particular products. What difference would it make to our collective psyche if there were counterbalancing messages in favor of a more sustainable and compassionate world? What if the culture of consumption found itself side-by-side on television with a culture of consciousness that valued simplicity and sustainability? My sense is that high-quality alternative programming such as thirty-second *Earthvisions* and weekly, hour-long viewer feedback forums would awaken public interest in seeing alternative approaches to living and consuming. This highly public feedback process, involving local viewers, would be far more effective in bringing about meaningful change than the cumbersome process of passing laws or involving remote regulatory agencies. Without passing a law, and with breathtaking speed, an entire nation—and ultimately the entire world—could begin reconsidering the levels and patterns of consumption that we value.

Transforming injustice. Martin Luther King, Jr., said that to realize justice in human affairs, "injustice must be exposed, with all of the tension its exposure creates, to the light of human conscience and the air of national opinion before it can be cured."[7] Injustice and inequities flourish in the darkness of inattention and ignorance. But when public awareness is focused on them, it functions as a healing light and creates a new consciousness among all involved. When people know that the rest of the world is watching, a powerful corrective influence is brought into human relations. When economic, ethnic, ideological, and religious violence is brought before the court of world public opinion through the mass media, it encourages people, corporations, and nations to discover more mature and nonviolent ways of relating to others. The global media will soon have the ability to broadcast information about virtually any place, person, issue, or event on the planet within seconds. In a communications-rich world, old forms of political repression, human rights violations, and warfare will be extremely difficult to perpetrate without an avalanche of world opinion descending on the oppressors.[8]

Redefining business success. What is the purpose of business? To serve stockholders by making money? To serve custom-

ers by making products they need? To serve the evolution
of life on Earth? With the communications revolution, these
kinds of concerns are being brought into public consciousness and scrutiny. Business operations are becoming transparent in the new information society. A growing number
of advocacy organizations are bringing previously hidden or
obscure areas of corporate life into the spotlight of public
scrutiny. With no place to hide, firms know that if they are
to be viewed and trusted as good citizens of the world community, then they have to behave accordingly. In a
communications-rich society, corporations are being pushed
to look beyond the interests of shareholders and short-term
profits to the well-being of the stakeholders—such as local
communities, the environment, and future generations.

Investing in a healthy future. Social reflection could also produce a dramatic increase in investments in a positive future.
It is average working-class individuals who own a majority
of the massive assets of pension funds and insurance companies. These institutions are currently investing primarily
for shorter-term profits in firms (such as tobacco companies)
whose products will produce a lower quality of life for re-
tirees in the future (as money will have to be spent to care
for more people with lung cancer). We could use study circles at the local level and electronically supported dialogues
at the regional, national, and global levels to hold pension
funds and insurance companies publicly accountable for investing their funds in companies that will produce a higher
quality of life when people retire.[9] Bringing these choices
into collective awareness could create a groundswell of public support to encourage some of the largest financial institutions in the world to invest in a healthier future.

Rezoning cities for eco-villages and sustainable neighborhoods.
Zoning laws are notoriously difficult to change; yet our
changing times call for experiments in different forms of
neighborhoods and communities that are designed for sustainability. From community dialogues, a public consensus
could emerge to create special zoning districts that would
allow new urban forms to grow. If these experimental communities can prosper while serving sustainability and local
needs, larger projects could be undertaken, leading to an
organic rebuilding of the urban infrastructure. Economic and
social life could become more decentralized, creating numerous local anchors of security and sustainability during a
time of sweeping global change. Once again, the starting
point for this cascade of change is public dialogue and a new
social consensus.

These five examples illustrate the rapid and profound impact
that authentic social reflection could have in many areas of
life—in how we consume, respond to injustice, define business success, invest for the future, and live in our cities. *Social
reflection has enormous power for transforming every aspect of life.*
  If the power of local dialogues (in study circles, church
groups, boardrooms, and classrooms) were combined with
the power of electronically supported dialogues across cities,
nations, and the Earth, the result would be transformative.
No matter what our other differences may be, we all have
a common stake in a world that communicates with itself
effectively. Whether liberal or conservative, rich or poor,
women or men—our future depends on a conscious public
that communicates with itself about questions that matter.
  As we enter the time of planetary initiation and find our
historic moorings gone, social reflection may exude us to

reach beneath the surface chaos and discover potentials for collective knowing and communication that were always present but required demanding circumstances to draw them forth. Trusting this sense of shared recognition and knowing, we could simply get it into our collective mind to do things differently. Without an immensity of suffering, we could reflect together on our situation and choose a path of sanity and maturity. As reflection turns to action, our capacity for shared knowing would make possible voluntary actions at the local level that have integrity and coherence at the global level. Trusting in the subtle atmosphere of shared consciousness, people could liberate their creativity locally, mindful of how their actions would contribute to building a sustainable future at the regional, national, and planetary level. A new "spirit of the age"—electric with possibility and invention—could permeate the Earth. People could feel a sense of collective purpose, recognizing they are pioneers of an awakening Earth and stewards for the tender beginnings of a new phase in humanity's future.

There Is Promise Ahead

SOMETIMES when I am looking at the many challenges involved in humanity's evolution, I try to gain perspective by considering what might be happening elsewhere in the universe. Has intelligent life emerged on any of the billions of planets circling around stars like our sun? Has intelligent life successfully evolved through its adolescence to build a sustainable planetary civilization on any of these planets? Astronomer Carl Sagan estimated that there are between fifty thousand and one million civilizations in advance of Earth

in our galaxy alone.[10] If there are mature planetary civilizations scattered throughout our cosmos, then the daunting
challenge of awakening to early adulthood and achieving a
sustainable future must have been met successfully by other
civilizations many times before.

Although the awakening of global civilization may be
commonplace when viewed from a cosmic scale, the experience of awakening in each world is surely unique. For
better or worse, we find our species waking up together on
a small planet circling a relatively young star located at the
outer edge of a swirling cloud of a hundred billion stars—
an average-size galaxy in a universe of billions of galaxies.
Will we become one of the unfortunate cosmic seeds that
has taken root but is so crippled by fear and self-destructive
behavior that we never flower into the fullness of our potential? Or will we become one of the gems of the galaxy,
the Earth a place of great beauty and humanity notable for
its conscious and compassionate planetary civilization? These
are pivotal times for our species and the Earth.

Our coming time of initiation is not a sign of evolutionary
failure but of our tremendous success. We are entering a
time of great opportunity—and great peril. Although the test
of our evolutionary intelligence has already begun, I believe
it will be another decade or two before a momentous initiation and great turning will manifest with full force and
produce consequences that will reverberate into the deep
future. Future generations will look back on the actions we
take in these years before the initiation, and will reflect on
how we rise to meet the challenge of living through one of
the most stressful, pivotal, exciting, and important times in
human history.

Because we have the means and the opportunity to

achieve an evolutionary bounce, being alive at this time confers on us all a unique responsibility as well as a unique
opportunity. Because we are here now, we are "on duty"
and responsible for preserving the evolutionary integrity of
the human experiment. *We* are the leaders we have been
waiting for. *We* are the social innovators and entrepreneurs
we have been seeking. *We* are the ones who are challenged
to self-organize and pull ourselves up by our own bootstraps.

We have already traveled far. We are beginning to make
the turn back to the Mother Universe and our soulful nature. By my reckoning, we are halfway home and our young
adulthood as a species is much closer than we may think.
We can get there together. Let's not stop now. There is
promise ahead.

For regularly updated information, resources, and links
concerning the themes of this book,
please see my web page:

www.awakeningearth.org

ACKNOWLEDGMENTS

———

THIS book synthesizes thirty years of research and work. Along the way, a diverse community of individuals has made important contributions to my life and to this book. I would like to acknowledge and thank these treasured souls here: Sherry Anderson, Cecile Andrews, Alan AtKisson, Ted Becker, Barbara Bernstein, Fr. Daniel Berrigan, Juanita Brown, Tom Callanan, Joseph Campbell, Pat Clough, Ram Dass, Dee Dickinson, Dave Ellis, Scott Elrod, Georg Feuerstein, Ellen Furnari, Foster Gamble, Joseph Goldstein, Deborah Gouge, Willis Harman, Barbara Marx Hubbard, Tom Hurley, Jean Houston, David Isaacs, Bob Johansen, Peter and Trudy Johnson-Lenz, Brooks Jordan, Sam Keen, Will Keepin, Marilyn King, Jack Kornfield, Dave and Fran Korten, Roxanne Lanier, Sidney Lanier, Gary Lapid, Ervin Laszlo, Coleen LeDrew, Rob Lehman, Stephen Levine, John Levy, Mike Marien, Robert McDermott, Lester Milbrath, Arnold Mitchell, Brian Muldoon, Michael Murphy, Annie Niehaus, Wendy Parker, Hal Puthoff, Richard Rathbun, Paul Ray, Vicki Robin, Laurance Rockefeller, Rob Shapera, Scott Sherman, David Sibbet, Anne Stadler, John Steiner, Tara Strand-Brown, Brian Swimme, the System Sisters of Perpetual Responsibility, Russell Targ, Mary and Tom Thomas, Sylvia Timbers, Justine and Michael Toms,

Allen Tough, Rinpoche Tarthang Tulku, Sarah van Gelder, Frances Vaughan, Kathy Vian, Roger Walsh, John White, and Tom Yeomans. I have treasured my friendship with Vicki Robins for nearly two decades and I greatly appreciate the enthusiasm and insight that she brought to her introduction of this book. I want to thank Toni Sciarra, my editor at William Morrow, for her talented work as an editor and as a seasoned advocate in guiding this book through the publishing process. I want to acknowledge Deborah Gouge for the skillful and sensitive editing that she has brought to a number of my writing projects in recent years, including this book. Her assistance has been immensely appreciated throughout. I want to thank Coleen LeDrew for being such a supportive partner in the completion of this book as well as for her feedback on the manuscripts. Thanks to Linda Larsen who developed the graphics. Huge appreciation goes to my three sons—Cliff, Ben, and Matt—who brought precious gifts of perspective, balance, humor, and love into my life over the decades in which this book developed. A portion of this book was developed in 1998 as the report "The 2020 Challenge" for a project hosted by the Union Theological Seminary of New York and under the guidance of Deborah Stern and Holland Hendrix.

References

CHAPTER ONE: IS HUMANITY GROWING UP?

1. Al Gore, *Earth in the Balance,* NY: Houghton Mifflin Co., 1992, p. 213.
2. Allen Hammond, "Three Global Scenarios: Choosing the World We Want," *The Futurist,* Bethesda, MD, April 1999, p. 43.
3. Joseph Campbell, *The Hero with a Thousand Faces,* New York: Meridian Book Edition, 1956, p. 30.
4. Ibid, p. 37.
5. Peter Farb, *Humankind,* Boston: Houghton Mifflin Co., 1978, p. 431.
6. Ibid, p. 432.
7. Barbara Hubbard, *Conscious Evolution,* Novato, CA: New World Library, 1998.
8. See chapter two of my book *Awakening Earth,* New York: William Morrow, 1993.
9. T. S. Eliot, *Four Quartets,* New York: Harcourt & Brace, 1943.
10. William D. Ruckelshaus, "Toward a Sustainable World," *Scientific American,* September 1989, p. 167.
11. Elizabeth Dowdeswell, "Lessons Learned in Sustainable Development," from a speech, 1998.
12. Kevin Kelly, "Deep Evolution: The Emergence of Postdarwinism," *Whole Earth Review,* Sausalito, CA, Fall 1992, p. 15.
13. Lewis Thomas, *The Fragile Species,* New York: Macmillan, 1992.

CHAPTER TWO: ADVERSITY TRENDS: HITTING AN
EVOLUTIONARY WALL

1. Stephen Moore, "The Coming Age of Abundance," *The True State of the Planet,* NY: The Free Press, 1995, p. 110.
2. Fred Smith, "Reappraising Humanity's Challenges, Humanity's Opportunities," in *The True State of the Planet,* p. 379.
3. Julian Simon, *The Ultimate Resource 2,* NJ: Princeton University Press, 1996, p. 12.
4. Ibid.
5. The "Warning to Humanity" was sponsored by the Union of Concerned Scientists, 26 Church St., Cambridge, MA 02238.
6. *Climate Change 1995: The IPCC Second Assessment Report,* Cambridge University Press, 1995.
7. Molly O'Meara, "The Risks of Disrupting Climate," *World Watch,* Nov–Dec 1997, p. 12.
8. Simon Retallack, "Kyoto: Our Last Chance," *The Ecologist,* Nov–Dec, 1997.
9. Personal communication, Donella Meadows, July 1998.
10. William Calvin, "The Great Climate Flip-Flop," *Atlantic Monthly,* January 1998, p. 47.
11. *World Resources: A Guide to the Global Environment: 1996–97,* A publication by The World Resources Institute, The United Nations Environment Programme, The United Nations Development Programme, and the World Bank, NY: Oxford University Press, 1996, p. xi.
12. Ibid., p. 173.
13. The World Bank's mid-range projections are that global population will reach 8.4 billion in 2025 and slightly more than 10 billion by 2050 (Paul Raskin, Michael Chadwick, Tim Jackson, and Gerald Leach, *The Sustainability Transition: Beyond Conventional Development,* Stockholm, Sweden: Stockholm Environment Institute, SEI/UNEP, 1996, p. 21). Recently revised (1996) world population estimates by the United Nations give mid-range projections of 8.04 billion people by 2025 and 9.37 billion by 2050 (reference: *World Population Prospects: The 1996 Revision,* United Nations, forthcoming; presented in the *United Nations Report on the World Social Situation 1997,* New York: United Nations, 1997, p. 14). The Population Reference Bureau's World Population Data Sheet for 1998 projects a world population of 8.08 billion in 2025 (reference: *World Population Prospects: The 1996*

Revision, United Nations, forthcoming; presented in the *United Nations Report on the World Social Situation 1997,* NY: United Nations, 1997, p. 14).

14. Gerard Piel, "The Urbanization of Poverty Worldwide," *Challenge,* Jan–Feb, 1997.
15. Lester Brown, Gary Gardner, and Brian Halwell, "16 Impacts of Population Growth," *The Futurist,* February 1999, p. 40.
16. Joby Warrick, "A Warning of Mass Extinction," *Washington Post,* April 21, 1998.
17. Virginia Morell, "The Sixth Extinction," *National Geographic,* February 1999, p. 46.
18. Lester Brown, "The Future of Growth," in *State of the World 1998,* NY: W. W. Norton, p. 11.
19. Bob Holmes, "Life Support," *New Scientist,* England, August 15, 1998.
20. John Tuxill and Chris Bright, "Losing Strands in the Web of Life," in *State of the World 1998,* p. 42.
21. John Vidal, "Is an Era of Water Wars Looming?" in the *San Francisco Sunday Examiner and Chronicle,* August 20, 1995.
22. Sandra Postel, "Water for Food Production: Will There Be Enough in 2025?" *BioScience,* vol. 48, no. 8, August 1998.
23. Lester Brown and Brian Halwell, "China's Water Shortage Could Shake World Food Security," *World Watch,* Jul–Aug 1998.
24. Paul Simon, *Tapped Out,* Welcome Rain Publishers, 1998 (quoted in *Parade Magazine,* August 23, 1998).
25. Colin Campbell and Jean Laherrere, "The End of Cheap Oil," *Scientific American,* March 1998, p. 81.
26. Ibid.
27. Ibid., p. 82.
28. L. F. Ivanhoe, "Get Ready for Another Oil Shock!" *The Futurist,* Jan–Feb 1997.
29. Anthony DePalma, "The Great Green Hope: Are Fuel Cells the Key to Cleaner Energy?" *The New York Times,* October 8, 1997, D1.
30. Personal communication with Dana Meadows, who is an organic farmer as well as a global researcher.
31. Lester Pearson, quoted in *Changing Images of Man,* O. W. Markley and Willis Harman, eds., NY: Pergamon Press, 1982, p. 13.
32. Source: UNDP, *Human Development Report 1992,* NY: Oxford University Press, 1992.
33. Leslie Shepherd, "44 Million Russians in Dire Poverty," *San Francisco Chronicle,* October 20, 1998.

34. Nicholas Kristof, "Human Costs of Asian Meltdown," *San Francisco Chronicle,* June 9, 1998.

35. Patrick Tyler, "In China's Outlands, Poorest Grow Poorer," *The New York Times,* October 26, 1996, p. 1.

36. Quoted in *World Watch,* Jul–Aug 1998, p. 37.

37. Pacific News Service, "78% of Indian homes without electricity," in *San Francisco Examiner,* March 16, 1997, A14.

38. Lester Brown, *Who Will Feed China,* NY: W. W. Norton, 1995, p. 132.

39. Lester Brown, "Who Will Feed China," *The Futurist,* Jan–Feb 1996, p. 14.

40. Lester Brown, "The Future of Growth," in *State of the World 1998,* NY: W. W. Norton: 1998, p. 12.

41. Ibid.

42. Ibid., p. 13.

43. United Nations Progress Report (5 years after the Earth Summit in Rio de Janeiro), June 1997.

44. For this section I am indebted to historian Clive Ponting who describes how the rise and decline of great civilizations have often been powerfully influenced by environmental factors. Clive Ponting, *A Green History of the World,* NY: Penguin Books, 1993.

45. Ibid, p. 72.

46. Samuel Kramer, *The Sumerians: Their History, Culture, and Character,* Chicago: University of Chicago Press, 1963, p. 268.

47. Ponting, *A Green History,* p. 72.

48. Ibid., p. 76.

49. Ibid., p. 83.

CHAPTER THREE: A NEW PERCEPTUAL PARADIGM: WE LIVE IN A
LIVING UNIVERSE

1. Willis Harman, *An Incomplete Guide to the Future,* Stanford, CA: Stanford Alumni Association, 1976.

2. Quoted in David Fideler, "What Is a Cosmos?" from a lecture presented at the Great Lakes Planetarium Association, Grand Rapids, Michigan, October 1995.

3. Lee Smolin, *The Life of the Cosmos,* NY: Oxford University Press, 1997, pp. 252–253.

4. David Bohm, *Wholeness and the Implicate Order,* London: Routledge & Kegan Paul, 1980, p. 175.

5. Michael Talbot, *The Holographic Universe*, NY: HarperCollins, 1991.
6. Louise B. Young, *The Unfinished Universe*, NY: Simon & Schuster, 1986, p. 205.
7. Bohm, *Wholeness*, p. 191.
8. Ibid.
9. Norbert Wiener, *The Human Use of Human Beings*, NY: Avon Books, 1954, p. 130.
10. Max Born, *The Restless Universe*, NY: Harper & Brothers, 1936, p. 277.
11. Brian Swimme, *The Hidden Heart of the Cosmos*, NY: Orbis Books, 1996, p. 100.
12. Renée Weber, *Dialogues with Scientists and Sages*, NY: Routledge & Kegan Paul, 1986, p. 19.
13. Freeman Dyson, *Infinite in All Directions*, NY: Harper & Row, 1988, p. 297.
14. Philip Cohen, "Can Protein Spring into Life?" in *New Scientist*, April 26, 1997, p. 18.
15. Mitchell Resnick, "Changing the Centralized Mind," *Technology Review*, July 1994.
16. Dean Radin, *The Conscious Universe*, San Francisco: Harper Edge, 1997, p. 109. See also Harold Puthoff and Russell Targ, "A Perceptual Channel for Information Transfer Over Kilometer Distances," published in the proceedings of the *I.E.E.E.*, vol. 64, no. 3, March 1976.
17. Radin, *Conscious Universe*, p. 144.
18. Puthoff and Targ, "Perceptual Channel," pp. 338–340. See also R. Targ and H. Puthoff, *Mind-Reach: Scientists Look at Psychic Ability*, NY: Delacorte Press/Eleanor Friede, 1977, pp. 79–83.
19. In the first series of 2,800 trials, the probability of obtaining these results by chance was less than one in three million. In the second series of 1,700 trials (with a more complex configuration of technology), the probability was near chance. In the third series of 2,500 trials (with only the computer but being observed constantly), the probability of obtaining these results by chance was less than one in two thousand. Russell Targ, Phyllis Cole, and Harold Puthoff, *Development of Techniques to Enhance Man/Machine Communication*, report prepared for NASA project 2613, Stanford Research Institute, Menlo Park, California, June 1974. Also see Targ and Puthoff, *Mind-Reach*, pp. 124–129.
20. Freeman Dyson, *Infinite in All Directions*, NY: Harper & Row, 1988, p. 297.

21. John Gribbin, *In the Beginning: The Birth of the Living Universe,* NY: Little, Brown and Co., 1993, pp. 244–245.

22. Ibid., p. 245.

23. Ibid., p. 252.

24. Gregg Easterbrook, "What Came Before Creation?" *U.S. News & World Report,* July 20, 1998, p. 48.

25. Wheeler, quoted in Renée Weber, "The Good, The True, The Beautiful," in *Main Currents,* New Rochelle, NY: Center for Integrated Education, 1975, p. 139.

26. Stephen Mitchell, trans., *Tao Te Ching: A New English Version,* NY: Harper & Row, 1988, chapter 25.

27. The quotation by Shao is taken from Garma Chang, *The Buddhist Teaching of Totality: The Philosophy of Hwa Yen Buddhism,* University Park: The Pennsylvania State University Press, 1971, p. 111.

28. Lao-Tzu, *Tao Te Ching,* trans. Gia-Fu Feng and Jane English, NY: Vintage Books, 1972.

29. A saying of Sojo, quoted in D. T. Suzuki, *Zen and Japanese Culture,* NJ: Princeton University Press, 1970, p. 353.

30. Gospel of Thomas, *Nag Hammadi Library,* James M. Robinson, general editor, San Francisco: Harper & Row, 1977, pp. 129–130.

31. Quoted in Timothy Ferris, *Galaxies,* NY: Stewart, Tabori & Chang, 1982, p. 87.

32. Suzuki, *Zen and Japanese Culture,* p. 364.

33. Francis H. Cook, *Hua-yen Buddhism: the Jewel Net of Indra,* University Park, PA: The Pennsylvania State University Press, 1977, p. 122.

34. Smith, *The Religions of Man,* p. 73.

35. Joseph Campbell, *The Power of Myth,* with Bill Moyers, NY: Doubleday, 1988, p. 217.

36. Wayne Muller, *Sabbath,* NY: Bantam Books, 1998, p. 36.

37. Matthew Fox, *Meditations with Meister Eckhart,* Santa Fe, NM: Bear & Co., 1983, p. 24.

38. Lex Hixon, "The Morning Star of Enlightenment," in Georg and Trisha Feuerstein, eds., *Voices on the Threshold of Tomorrow,* Wheaton, IL: Quest Books, 1993, p. 388.

39. Luther Standing Bear, quoted in Joseph Epes Brown, "Modes of Contemplation Through Actions: North American Indians," *Main Currents in Modern Thought,* NY: Center for Integrative Studies, Nov–Dec 1973, p. 194.

40. Malcolm Margolin, *The Ohlone Way: Indian Life in the San Francisco–Monterey Bay Area,* Berkeley, CA: Heyday Books, 1978.

41. Ibid., pp. 142–143.

42. Ibid., p. 112.

43. The designation of modern humans as *Homo sapiens sapiens* is wide-spread; see, for example: Joseph Campbell, *Historical Atlas of World Mythology, vol I: The Way of the Animal Powers, Part 1: Mythologies of the Primitive Hunters and Gatherers,* NY: Harper & Row, Perennial Library, 1988, p. 22; Richard Leakey, *The Making of Mankind,* NY: E. P. Dutton, 1981, p. 18; Mary Maxwell, *Human Evolution: A Philosophical Anthropology,* NY: Columbia University Press, 1984, p. 294; John Pfeiffer, *The Creative Explosion: An Inquiry into the Origins of Art and Religion,* Ithaca, NY: Cornell University Press, 1982, p. 13; Clive Ponting, *A Green History of the World,* NY: Penguin Books, 1993, p. 28.

44. Maxwell, *Human Evolution,* p. 111.

45. Mikhail Nimay, *Book of Mirdad,* Baltimore: Penguin Books, 1971, p. 57.

CHAPTER FOUR: CHOOSING A NEW LIFEWAY: VOLUNTARY SIMPLICITY

1. Amitai Etzioni, "Voluntary Simplicity: Characterization, select psychological implications, and societal consequences," *Journal of Economic Psychology,* Elsevier Science, 19 (1998), p. 629.

2. Ibid.

3. Alfie Kohn, "In Pursuit of Affluence, at a High Price," *The New York Times,* February 2, 1999.

4. Richard Gregg, "Voluntary Simplicity," reprinted in *Co-Evolution Quarterly,* Sausalito, CA, Summer 1977 (originally published in the Indian journal, *Visva-Bharati Quarterly,* August 1936).

5. Ibid., p. 20.

6. David Shi, *The Simple Life,* NY: Oxford University Press, 1985, p. 149.

7. Henry David Thoreau, *Walden,* Boston, 1854, p. 168.

8. Thomas Moore, *Care of the Soul,* NY: HarperCollins, 1998, p. 285.

9. George Barna, *The Index of Leading Spiritual Indicators,* Dallas, TX: Word Publishing, 1996, p. 129.

10. Richard Celente, *Trends Journal,* Winter 1997.

11. Paul Ray, "The Rise of Integral Culture," *Noetic Sciences Review,* Sausalito, CA: Institute of Noetic Sciences, Spring 1996.

12. *Yearning for Balance: Views of Americans on Consumption, Materialism, and the Environment,* A report by the Harwood Group about a survey conducted for the Merck Family Fund, 6930 Carroll Ave., Takoma Park, MD (July 1995).

13. Ray, "The Rise of Integral Culture."

14. Ronald Inglehart, *Modernization and Postmodernization: Cultural, Economic, and Political Change in 43 Societies,* NJ: Princeton University Press, 1997.

15. Ibid.

16. Ibid., p. 328.

17. Riley E. Dunlap, "International Attitudes Towards Environment and Development," in Green Globe Yearbook 1994, an independent publication from the Fritjof Nansen Institute, Norway, NY: Oxford University Press, 1994, p. 125.

18. Environics International, news release, Washington, D.C., June 5, 1998, "Citizens Worldwide Want Teeth Added to Environmental Laws."

19. Don Clifton, Chairman of the Gallup Organization, personal correspondence, November 1996.

20. Stuart Hart, "Strategies for a Sustainable World," *Harvard Business Review,* Jan–Feb 1997, p. 71. Another perspective is provided by David Korten, *The Post-Corporate World: Life After Capitalism,* San Francisco: Berrett-Koehler, 1999.

21. Arnold Toynbee, *A Study of History* (Abridgement of vols. I–VI, by D. C. Somerville), NY: Oxford University Press, 1947, p. 198.

22. Ibid, p. 208.

CHAPTER FIVE: COMMUNICATING OUR WAY INTO
A PROMISING FUTURE

1. "TV, No Hot Water in Typical Chinese Home," Gallup Poll reported in the *San Francisco Chronicle,* October 27, 1997.

2. Mark Pesce, *Proximal and Distal Unity* (San Francisco, May 1996). From a paper taken from the internet: http://www.hyperreal.com/~mpesce/pdu.html.

3. Joseph N. Pelton, "The Globalization of Universal Telecommunications Services," in *Universal Telephone Service: Ready for the 21st Century?* (Institute for Information Studies, A Joint Program of Northern Telecom and the Aspen Institute, Queenstown, MD, 1991), p. 145.

4. Ibid, p. 156.

5. John Midwinter, "Convergence of Telecommunications, Cable and Computers in the 21st Century: A Personal View of the Technology," in *Crossroads on the Information Highway* (Annual review of the Institute for Information Studies, Aspen Institute, and Northern Telecom, 1995), p. 62.

6. *U.S. News & World Report,* January 6, 1997, p. 60; International Data Group, *MacWorld Magazine,* January 1997, p. 169; Paul Taylor, "Internet Users Likely to Reach 500m by 2000," *Financial Times,* May 13, 1996.

7. Leslie Helm, "A Computer Engineer Shares His Thoughts on the Web of the Future," *Los Angeles Times,* 1998.

8. Robert M. Entman, "The Future of Universal Service in Telecommunications," in *Universal Telephone Service,* p. ix.

9. Peter Russell, *The Global Brain Awakens,* Palo Alto, CA: Global Brain, Inc., 1995, p. 140.

10. Pelton, "Globalization," p. 171.

11. "Fiber to Subscriber," Bell Northern Research, quoted in Pelton, "Globalization," p. 154.

12. Joseph Pelton, "Telecommunications for the 21st Century," in *Scientific American,* April 1998.

13. Lester Brown, et al., *Vital Signs 1998,* NY: W. W. Norton, 1998, p. 22.

14. Payal Sampat, "Internet Use Grows Exponentially," in *Vital Signs,* Lester Brown, et al., Worldwatch Institute, Washington, 1998, p. 98.

15. Alexander Astin, et al., *The American Freshman: Thirty Year Trends, 1966–1996* (Higher Education Research Institute, Graduate School of Education and Information Studies, University of California, Los Angeles, February 1997).

16. Ibid., p. 14.

17. Gene Youngblood, "The Mass Media and the Future of Desire," *CoEvolution Quarterly,* Sausalito, CA, Winter 1977–78, pp. 12–15.

18. G. Diligenskii, "The Masses and Politics in Modern Russia," *Russia,* no. 1, 1995, p. 73.

19. Quotation from *Future Survey* review on Averting an Electronic Waterloo. CSIS Global Organized Crime Project (Task Force Director and Editor: Frank Cilluffo). Washington, DC: Center for Strategic and International Studies, December 1998.

20. Christopher Bache, *Dark Night, Early Dawn: Steps to a Deep Ecology of Mind,* Albany: State University of New York Press, 2000.

CHAPTER SIX: RECONCILIATION AND THE TRANSFORMATION OF
HUMAN RELATIONS

1. Pierre Teilhard de Chardin, *The Future of Man,* NY: Harper & Row, 1964, p. 57.
2. Pitirim Sorokin, *The Ways and Power of Love,* Chicago: Henry Regnery Co., 1967.
3. Jack Kornfield, "The Path of Compassion: Spiritual Practice and Social Action," in *The Path of Compassion,* Fred Eppsteiner, ed., Berkeley, CA: Parallax Press, 1988, p. 29.
4. Sorokin, *Ways and Power of Love,* p. 71.
5. This description is drawn primarily from: Sorokin, *Ways and Power of Love,* p. 67, and Eknath Easwaran, *The Compassionate Universe,* Petaluma, CA: Nilgiri Press, 1989.
6. Gitanjali Kolanad, *Culture Shock! India,* Portland, OR: Graphic Arts Center Publishing, 1994, p. 23.
7. Sorokin, *Ways and Power of Love,* p. 68.
8. Ibid., p. 110.
9. Ibid., p. 69.
10. See, for example, Donella Meadows, et al., *Beyond the Limits,* Post Mills, VT: Chelsea Green Publishing Co., 1992.
11. *Gender and Society: Status and Stereotypes.* An International Gallup Poll Report, The Gallup Organization, Princeton, NJ, March 1996.
12. Susan Davis, quoted in "Women Leaders Review Earth Charter," *Boston Research Center for the 21st Century Newsletter,* Fall 1997, p. 6. See also her article "Principle-Centered Evolution: A Feminist Environmentalist Perspective," in *Women's Views on the Earth Charter,* Boston Research Center, November 1997.
13. Arnold Toynbee, *A Study of History* (Abridgement of vols. I–VI, by D. C. Somerville), NY: Oxford University Press, 1947, p. 555.
14. Donald Shriver, Jr., *Forgiveness in Politics,* NY: Oxford University Press, 1995, p. 7.
15. Desmond Tutu quoted in Terry Tempest Williams, "Two Words," *Orion,* Great Barrington, MA, Winter 1999, p. 52.
16. Archbishop Desmond Tutu, "A Message from the Chairperson," *Truth Talk: The Official Newsletter of the Truth and Reconciliation Commission,* South Africa, July 1998.
17. Dr. Alex Boraine, "A message from the Deputy Chairperson of the TRC," *Truth Talk: The Official Newsletter of the Truth and Reconciliation Commission,* South Africa, July 1998.

18. Michael Battle, *Reconciliation: The Ubuntu Theology of Desmond Tutu,* Ohio: The Pilgrim Press, 1997, p. 39.

19. These examples were drawn in part from Emily Mitchell, "The Decade of Atonement," *Index on Censorship,* May–Jun 1998, London (reprinted in the *Utne Reader,* Mar–Apr 1999, pp. 58–59).

20. John Bond, "Aussie Apology," *Yes! A Journal of Positive Futures,* Bainbridge Island, WA, Fall 1998, p. 22.

21. Ibid., p. 224.

22. Eric Yamamoto, *Interracial Justice: Conflict and Reconciliation in Post-Civil Rights America,* NY: New York University Press, 1999.

23. *Human Development Report 1998,* United Nations Development Programme, NY: Oxford University Press, 1998, p. 37.

24. Ibid.

25. Slobodan Lekic, "Rich Nations Grow More Stingy With Poor Nations," *San Francisco Chronicle,* October 17, 1997, World Section, A14.

26. Glenys Kinnock, "One World," in E. and D. Shapiro, eds., *Voices from the Heart,* NY: Tarcher/Putnam, 1998, p. 122.

27. Desmond Tutu, "Becoming More Fully Human," in Shapiro, *Voices from the Heart,* p. 277.

CHAPTER SEVEN: EVOLUTIONARY CRASH OR EVOLUTIONARY
BOUNCE: ADVERSITY MEETS OPPORTUNITY

1. For the designation of modern humans as *Homo sapiens sapiens,* see footnote 43 to chapter 3.

2. Pierre Teilhard de Chardin, *The Phenomenon of Man,* NY: Harper & Row, 1959, p. 181.

3. Ibid., p. 165.

4. Arnold Toynbee, *A Study of History,* NY: Weathervane Books, 1972, p. 132.

5. Clive Ponting, "The Lessons of Easter Island," in *A Green History of the World,* NY: Penguin Books, 1993, p. 168.

6. Ibid., p. 169.

7. Ibid.

8. Jared Diamond, "Easter's End," *Discover Magazine,* August 1995, p. 68.

9. Ibid.

10. Ponting, "Lessons of Easter Island," pp. 6–7.

11. Jared Diamond, "Easter Island Tells Tale of Warning," *San Diego Union-Tribune,* October 25, 1995.

12. Charles Mackay, *Extraordinary Popular Delusions and the Madness of Crowds* (1841; reprint NY: Harmony Books, 1980).

13. Sigmund Freud, *Civilization and Its Discontents,* James Strachey, trans., NY: W. W. Norton & Co., 1961, p. 102.

14. Innocent VIII: BULL *Summis Desiderantes,* December 5, 1484.

15. Kenneth Cameron, *Humanity and Society: A World History,* Bloomington: Indiana University Press, 1973, p. 264.

16. Dean Radin, *The Conscious Universe,* San Francisco: Harper Edge, 1997, p. 293.

17. Alan Weisman, "Gaviotas: Oasis of the Imagination," in *Yes! A Journal of Positive Futures,* Bainbridge Island, WA, Summer 1998, p. 36.

18. Ibid.

19. Donella Meadows, "Village Thrives on Sun, Ingenuity and Spirit," The Global Citizen Column, *Valley News,* March 14, 1998.

20. Adapted from an article by Alan Weisman in the *Los Angeles Times Sunday Magazine,* September 25, 1994. See *In Context,* #42, Context Institute, Fall 1995.

21. Alan Weisman, *Gaviotas: A Village to Reinvent the World,* VT: Chelsea Green Publishing, 1998, p. 8.

22. Ibid., p. 218.

23. Ibid., p. 219.

24. Ibid., p. 222.

25. Pierre Teilhard de Chardin, *The Future of Man,* NY: Harper & Row, 1964, p. 33.

26. Roger Walsh, *Staying Alive,* Boulder, CO: Shambhala, 1984.

27. Václav Havel, President of Czechoslovakia, in an address to a joint session of the U.S. Congress, Washington, DC, February 21, 1990.

28. Ken Wilber, taken from his Website, January 8, 1997.

29. Marianne Williamson, *The Healing of America,* NY: Simon & Schuster, 1997, p. 41.

30. Robert Kenny, "Some Reflections on Group Consciousness and Synergy," NY: International Center for Integrative Studies Forum, April, 1992, p. 4.

31. Ibid.

32. Brian Muldoon, *The Heart of Conflict,* NY: G. P. Putnam's Sons, 1996, p. 167.

33. Ibid.

CHAPTER EIGHT: HUMANITY'S CENTRAL PROJECT: BECOMING
DOUBLY WISE HUMANS

1. Thomas Berry and Brian Swimme, *The Universe Story,* San Francisco:
Harper & Row, 1992, p. 264.

2. David Bohm has described matter as "condensed or frozen light"
and has said that light is the fundamental building block of our cosmos.
See also Renée Weber, *Dialogues with Scientists and Sages,* NY: Routledge & Kegan Paul, 1986, p. 45.

3. James Robinson, ed., *Nag Hammadi Library,* 1st edition, San Francisco: Harper & Row, 1977, p. 123. Elsewhere in the Gnostic sources
Jesus is quoted by the disciple James as saying: "Search ever and cease
not till ye find the mysteries of the Light, which will lead you into
the Light-kingdom."

4. Ibid., p. 121.

5. Jesus quoted in The Gospel of Thomas, *Nag Hammadi Library,*
p. 124.

6. See, for example, Tsele Natsok Rangdrol, *The Mirror of Mindfulness:
The Cycle of the Four Bardos,* E. Kunsang, trans., Boston: Shambhala
Press, 1989.

7. Robert Bly, trans., *The Kabir Book,* Boston: Beacon Press, 1977, p. 24.

8. Govinda, *Creative Meditation and Multi-Dimensional Consciousness,*
Wheaton, IL: Theosophical Publishing House, 1976, p. 200.

9. John Pfeiffer, *The Creative Explosion,* Ithaca, NY: Cornell University
Press, 1982, p. 11.

10. Erich Neumann, *The Origins and History of Consciousness,* Princeton,
NJ: Bollingen, 1970, p. 275.

11. For background on the topic of time, see, for example, Marie-Louise
von Franz, *Time: Rhythm and Repose,* NY: Thames and Hudson, 1978;
Joseph Campbell, ed., *Man and Time,* NJ: Princeton University Press:
Bollingen Series, 1957; and J. T. Fraser, ed., *The Voices of Time,* NY:
George Braziller, 1966.

12. Ibid., pp. 225–226.

13. Bly, *The Kabir Book,* p. 11.

CHAPTER NINE: ENGAGED REFLECTION IN THE TURNING ZONE

1. Juanita Brown and David Isaacs, "Conversation as a Core Business
Practice," *The Systems Thinker,* vol. 7, no. 10, December 1996, Pegasus
Communications, Inc., Cambridge, MA.

2. In particular, see the work of Cecile Andrews and her book: *Circles of Simplicity: Return to the Good Life,* NY: HarperCollins, 1997.
3. Lester Brown and Jennifer Mitchell, "Building a New Economy," in *State of the World 1998,* Washington, DC: Worldwatch Institute, 1998, p. 187.
4. George Gallup, Jr., "50 Years of American Opinion," *San Francisco Chronicle,* October 21, 1985.
5. Ibid.
6. How do Earthvisions, Viewer Feedback Forums, Electronic Town Meetings and the rest fit into U.S. communications law (which often provides an important indication of which way the winds of freedom are blowing for the rest of the world)? Does this represent an inappropriate intrusion of the public into the affairs of broadcast TV stations or do these activities represent a fully legitimate exercise of the public's rights and duties in a modern democracy? Because most U.S. citizens are reluctant to act when not given the authority to do so, it is important to know that Earthvisions, Electronic Town Meetings, etc. are fully legitimate expressions of our democratic processes and are strongly supported across a broad spectrum of Constitutional law, Congressional legislation, and FCC regulation.

The legal cornerstone for an electronically supported democracy is found in the First Amendment to the U.S. Constitution, which states that "Congress shall make no law . . . abridging the freedom of speech . . . or the right of people to peaceably assemble, and to petition the Government for a redress of grievances." An electronic town meeting is the fulfillment of this constitutional guarantee. It is a forum where citizens can assemble peacefully and communicate freely with the intention of petitioning appropriate government bodies for changes they think are in the public interest.

Turning from Constitutional to communications law, the public has been given very strong communication rights from the earliest stages in the development of broadcasting law. The predecessor to the Federal Communications Commission—the Federal Radio Commission—in 1928 set down the basic requirement that continues today; namely that broadcasters must give first priority to serving the "public interest, convenience, and necessity." The Commission stated that: ". . . broadcast stations are not given these great privileges by the United States Government for the primary benefit of advertisers. Such benefit as is derived by advertisers must be incidental and entirely secondary to the interest of the public." The Commission further stated that: "The emphasis must be first and foremost on the interest, convenience, and necessity of the listening public, and not on the interest, convenience, or necessity of the individual broadcaster or advertiser."

This high standard of obligation to the public has remained in effect since the inception of broadcasting and is reflected, for example, in the 1969 Supreme Court decision that clarified the responsibilities of broadcasters. The court ruled that: "It is the right of the viewers and listeners, not the right of the broadcasters, which is paramount." In addition: "It is the purpose of the First Amendment to preserve an uninhibited marketplace of ideas in which truth will ultimately prevail, rather than to countenance monopolization of that market, whether it be by the Government itself or a private licensee."

The public has responsibilities just as do the broadcasters. The expressed duty of the public to intervene in broadcasting issues was clearly stated in a major 1966 U.S. Court of Appeals decision: "Under our system, the interests of the public are dominant . . . Hence, individual citizens and the communities they compose owe a duty to themselves and their peers to take an active interest in the scope and quality of television service which stations and networks provide . . . Nor need the public feel that in taking a hand in broadcasting they are unduly interfering in the private business affairs of others. On the contrary, their interest in television programming is direct and their responsibilities important. They are the owners of the channels of television—indeed, of all broadcasting."

It has been thought by some that the sweeping deregulation of television in the 1980s negates this half-century of communications law affirming a duty to serve the public interest. This is not the case. The FCC's 1984 ruling states that "[deregulation] . . . does not constitute a retreat from our concern with the programming performance of television station licensees." Instead, what the FCC has done is to drop specific programming standards and enforcement mechanisms (for example, the FCC dropped minimum requirements for news and public affairs programming, eliminated the requirement that stations keep public logs that show how stations are using air time, and dropped any requirement that the stations poll the community to learn of its needs and wants).

Despite this hands-off approach of the FCC, the broadcasting community continues to recognize it has strong (though now largely unenforced) obligations to serve community interests. For example, in 1985, the President of the National Association of Broadcasters stated: "Broadcasting is indeed a unique industry . . . much different from other corporate citizens in America. . . . We have never advocated removal of the public interest standard. In fact, our obligation is to serve the public interest first and stockholder interest second . . . not the other way around."

7. Quoted in Stephen B. Oates, *Let the Trumpets Sound: The Life of Martin Luther King, Jr.,* NY: New American Library, 1982, p. 226.

8. Joseph N. Pelton, "The Globalization of Universal Telecommunications Services," *Universal Telephone Service: Ready for the 21st Century?* Institute for Information Studies, A Joint Program of Northern Telecom and the Aspen Institute, Queenstown, MD, 1991, p. 146.

9. I appreciate this suggestion given by Nicholas Parker.

10. See the calculations of Carl Sagan and I. S. Shklovskii, *Intelligent Life in the Universe,* San Francisco: Holden-Day, 1966, pp. 409–418.

INDEX

INTERCULTURAL
ALLIANCES

INTERNATIONAL AND
INTERCULTURAL COMMUNICATION ANNUAL

Volume XXV   2002

Editor
Mary Jane Collier
University of Denver

Editorial Assistant
Katia Campbell
University of Denver

INTERNATIONAL AND INTERCULTURAL COMMUNICATION ANNUAL
VOLUME XXV   2002

INTERCULTURAL ALLIANCES

Critical Transformation

editor
Mary Jane Collier
University of Denver

Published in Cooperation with
National Communication Association
International and Intercultural Division

SAGE Publications
International Educational and Professional Publisher
Thousand Oaks ■ London ■ New Delhi

Copyright © 2003 by Sage Publications, Inc.

For information:

Sage Publications, Inc.
2455 Teller Road
Thousand Oaks, California 91320
E-mail: order@sagepub.com

Sage Publications Ltd.
6 Bonhill Street
London EC2A 4PU
United Kingdom

Sage Publications India Pvt. Ltd.
M-32 Market
Greater Kailash I
New Delhi 110 048 India

Printed in the United States of America

Library of Congress Cataloging-in-Publication Data

Intercultural alliances / Mary Jane Collier, editor.
    p. cm.
Includes bibliographical references and index.
ISBN 0-7619-2589-9 (cloth) — ISBN 0-7619-2590-2 (pbk.)
  1. Intercultural communication. 2. Intercultural communication-United States. 3. Ethnic relations-Cross-cultural studies. 4. Race relations-Case studies. I. Collier, Mary Jane.
HM1211 .I56 2003
303.48´2—dc21

                                2002009417

02   03   04   05   10 9 8 7   6   5   4 3   2   1

Acquiring Editor:	Margaret H. Seawell
Editorial Assistant:	Alicia Carter
Production Editor:	Claudia A. Hoffman
Copy Editor:	Jamie Robinson
Indexer:	Molly Hall
Cover Designer:	Janet Foulger

Contents

Acknowledgments

I wish to thank several people without whom the publication of this volume would not have been possible. First, my editorial assistant, Katia Campbell, doctoral candidate in the department of Human Communication Studies at the University of Denver, functioned as a trusted liaison with authors, copy editor for manuscripts, and an informed resource for discussing possible content areas for revision in manuscripts. I am also grateful to Teresa McPhee, M.A., International and Intercultural Communication at the University of Denver, who also served as copy editor. In addition, I wish to acknowledge Gregg Kvistad, Dean of Arts, Humanities and Social Sciences at the University of Denver, for continuing to provide funding for a graduate student editorial assistant. Margaret Seawell, Executive Editor at Sage, was an advocate for this last volume under my editorship to be published as a site of outstanding scholarship in international and intercultural communication.

The reviewers for this volume ensured that each essay submitted received detailed and supportive commentary. My sincere appreciation goes to Brenda J. Allen, Deborah Atwater, Benjamin Broome, Guo-Ming Chen, Victoria Chen, Leda Cooks, Robbin Crabtree, Fernando Delgado, Natalie Dollar, Lisa Flores, Lawrence Frey, Marouf Hasian, Radha Hegde, Fern Johnson, Tricia S. Jones, Robert Krizek, Judith Martin, Dreama Moon, Sujata Moorti, Thomas Nakayama, Kent Ono, Mark Orbe, Diana Rios, Philippe Salazar, William Starosta, Stella Ting-Toomey, Richard Wiseman, and Gust Yep. Finally, I thank all of the scholars who submitted their work to a volume that will, I trust, make a noteworthy contribution to programs of research related to culture, communication, and intercultural relationships and alliances, in multiple disciplines. My sincere hope is that Volumes 23 to 25 of the *International and*

Intercultural Annual not only serve as valued resources of exemplary research but also stimulate dialogue among scholars, students, and practitioners across contexts and theoretical perspectives and inspire diverse discourses about informed social change.

1

Negotiating Intercultural Alliance Relationships

Toward Transformation

MARY JANE COLLIER • *University of Denver*

Terrorism. Death counts. Globalization. Dialogue. Violence. Settlements. Refugee camps. Closed borders. Ethnic cleansing. Imperialism. Multiculturalism. Cease-fires. Common ground. Fear. Capitalist expansion. Modernity. Women's rights. Human rights. Rewriting histories. Poststructuralism. Postcolonialism. Antigovernment. Antimedia. Antiracism. Rhetoric.

In 2002, the context in which we live is complex, paradoxical, and filled with violence and injustice, as well as with glimmers of hope. The theme of Volume 25 of the *International and Intercultural Communication Annual* reflects our need as humans to make sense of our international communities and relationships, which are economically, politically, and socially interdependent and inextricably bound together. The authors in this volume are wrestling with questions about cultural identifications, representations, and the quality of intercultural relationships at all levels. The chapters reflect the struggle in which we are all occupied to comprehend our world, the events that are occurring, and how we might improve the ways in which we engage each other.

If we are to understand the ubiquitous presence of conflicts across the globe and in our own homelands, cities, and local communities, we must do more than analyze the interests of each party. We cannot ignore the complexity of culture, and we must understand how relationships emerge in historical contexts, within institutional and political forces and social norms that are often invisible to some groups. Building knowledge about the conditions that are barriers or deterrents is important, as is coming to understand alliances that are persisting. From description in context, informed critique, and analysis of histories and structural influences, and from

experiences of situated practices, can emerge the means for discussing potential and relevant transformation.

The theme of this volume of the annual addresses what intercultural alliances are and potentially can be, as well as situations in which they have not emerged. Authors in this volume recognize the power of context and orient their work regarding alliances to include the broader relationships that occur between groups and individuals; those that are constrained and enabled by institutions, ideologies, and histories; and those that occur in situated contexts. These authors give attention to barriers that must be overcome, delineate conditions that may be essential in order to construct alliances, and describe examples of failed attempts and exemplars of allies who are doing bridgework and translation. In addition, the authors outline directions that we—as researchers, teachers, and practitioners—might take in the future.

Although references to intercultural alliances are not common in everyday discourses in any location, I have found during the last 10 years that very different individuals—Palestinian, Israeli, and U.S. American young women; adolescents in Great Britain; young adults in South Africa; and participants in workshops and seminars in the United States—talk in some similar ways about cultural and intercultural alliances. *Ally* connotes partner, advocate, collaborator, and supporter, and *alliance* most often means to be associated, connected, and joined in a united front; an alliance is a relationship in which parties are interdependent and responsible for and to each other. Intercultural allies recognize their cultural differences as well as their interdependence, and often seek similar goals, but they are not necessarily friends.

Rosenfield and Tardieu (2000) define allies in the context of the Fourth World movement as "women and men from all walks of life who decide to become the allies of the poorest of the poor within society . . . they take stands against injustice, open doors, give weight and credibility to the voice of the poorest and to the struggle against poverty in all spheres of society" (p. 257). Anzaldúa (1990) speaks to women of color about alliances, saying, "To be part of an alliance or coalition is to be active, an activist. . . . We are searching for powerful, meaning-making experiences. To make our lives relevant, to gain political knowledge, to give our lives a sense of involvement, to respond to social oppression and its debilitating effects" (p. 217).

The theme of intercultural alliances and my editorial perspective in this volume also reflect a feminist orientation that I continue to struggle to make

transnational, intercultural, and reflexive. Feminisms, as I incorporate them, encompass work toward overcoming oppression of all kinds, with recognition that women bear the brunt of discriminatory institutions and practices throughout the world. As Grewal and Kaplan (1994) posit, "In calling for transnational alliances, our purpose is to acknowledge the different forms that feminisms take and the different practices that can be seen as feminist movements" (p. 20). They note as well that

> in debates within the United States, for example, it is important to examine the ways in which race, class, and gender are fast becoming the holy trinity that every feminist feels compelled to address even as this trinity delimits the range of discussion around women's lives. What is often left out of these U.S.-focused debates are other complex categories of identity and affiliation that apply to non-U.S. cultures and situations. (p. 19)

Notions such as *global feminism* have been opened to critique. Acknowledging differences in women's lives as well as links between transnational power structures is called for. For instance, Kaplan (1994) articulates the importance of giving attention to a politics of location in feminist scholarship and praxis: "As a practice of affiliation, a politics of location identifies the grounds for historically specific differences and similarities between women in diverse and asymmetrical relations, creating alternative histories, identities, and possibilities for alliance" (p. 139).

It is important for me to acknowledge that I bring my own cultural itineraries, location, and positionality with me into my editorial practices and decisions. As a white U.S American whose ancestors are European, as a middle-aged, middle-class, heterosexual professor teaching at a private university, I have a number of sources of privilege and status that I am socialized to take completely for granted. I am committed to learning how to uncover such privileges and take seriously the challenge to collaborate in the creation of alternative modes of intercultural dialogue. The theme and content of this volume illustrate that intention.

The chapters in this volume reflect my beliefs in the value of multiple trajectories and levels of intellectual and theoretical discourse, which includes deconstruction and critique, interpretive and engaged inquiry, and reconstruction and praxis. The authors whose work is featured here select a variety of cultural identifications, representations, and issues to discuss and orient their research, using diverse theoretical approaches and methodologies.

OVERVIEW OF CHAPTERS

This volume is organized based on my reading of common or complementary issues that emerged from the chapters. The issues that I used to sort the chapters are by no means the only nor the primary issues raised by the authors, but illustrate one way to frame the broader ideas and draw meaning from the chapters.

The first three chapters relate to the power of whiteness ideology in affecting relationships and potential alliances among different cultural groups in the United States. In the second chapter, Kathryn Sorrells describes her collaboration, through participant observation and in-depth interviews, with women artists who are Navajo weavers and Pueblo potters residing in the Southwestern United States. Sorrells gives attention to the relationships between the artists and others, such as elders from within their various communities, and between the artists and the consumers who purchase the art, in order to detail how the artists negotiate multiple cultural identifications and representations. She shares the artists' struggles as their art becomes commodified by the tourist industry, and how the artists manage contradictory tensions between such dialectic forces as history and present social forces, tradition and innovation, and authenticity and uniqueness.

In Chapter 3, Aimee Carrillo Rowe points the reader to the possibilities and failed moments experienced by academic women in their discussions of transracial feminist alliances. She describes the role of institutional structures and norms of relating that serve to foreclose affective connections that could go beyond racial boundaries. She also problematizes categories of race, national origin, ethnicity, class, sexuality, gender, and institutional status, and illustrates how such categories not only have disparate meanings as lived experiences but also are reinforced through whiteness to keep the experiences of women of color at a distance.

In Chapter 4, Sean Tierney and Ronald Jackson II deconstruct whiteness ideology and point to three rhetorical fantasy themes that constrain interracial alliance building between blacks and whites in the United States. Through an examination of academic literature and popular discourse the authors uncover three common, publicly understood, and socially manufactured ideas. They are that whiteness equals humanity, that color-blindness is beneficial for the group in power, and that race is used by the group in power to recycle notions of otherness.

The next two chapters broaden the geopolitical focus to sites outside of the United States by addressing whiteness ideology in relation to experiences and barriers to alliance relationships in South Africa and in

Panama and Iceland. Melissa Steyn, in Chapter 5, provides us with an analysis of radio talk-show caller discussions of two controversial questions in the new South Africa: Can white South Africans be regarded as African? and Do white South Africans owe black South Africans financial restitution (due to the apartheid era)? She found that black callers express a range of opinions, from rejection to skepticism to conditional acceptance of whites considered to be African, with general resistance to the idea. In contrast, the demotic discourses of white callers are very much in favor of whites being considered African and are based in broad definitions of what constitutes "African" and in power evasive discourses of color-blindness. With regard to the issue of restitution, Steyn shows that black callers use such demotic discourses, making a case for dismantling the economic, political, and historically established support bases for whites, and point to white denial. The discourses of white callers about this issue reflect positions advocating for the status quo and claims that restitution would be a threat to the current economy. She concludes that there are two nations of discourse among the callers and that the image of the new South Africa as "the rainbow nation" and a place in which alliances between blacks and whites are common are, at present, unrealized ideals.

In Chapter 6, Leda Cooks and Elizabeth Fullon examine their respective experiences as sojourners. They incorporate attention to multiple whitenesses in their discussions of the ways bodies (white, nonwhite, male, female, other) are positioned and privileged. Their analysis occurs in the form of critical autoethnographic and narrative accounts of their sojourns. As a white woman in Panama and a Filipino American woman in Iceland, each describes the ways in which her cultural identifications are marked and made visible and the politics of her position negotiated.

Chapters 7 and 8 deal with alliance relationships developed through and influenced by technological forms and media portrayals. Radhika Gajjala showcases how South Asian diaspora women connect though the Internet on a sa-cyborg list. Her analysis of postings demonstrates that new technologies do offer the opportunity for relationship development, but that the role of technology as any sort of "great equalizer" must be addressed in the context of political and economic globalization. The postings reflect varied voices and formats; reveal conflicted subject positions, creativity, poetry, and academic arguments; and deal with the negotiation of gendered and diaspora identifications, changing cultural practices, and intersecting histories, hierarchies, and situated experiences.

Jolanta Drzewiecka addresses the intersections of collective memory, media representations, interpretations and identifications, and the resulting

dialogue among various Polish groups in response to the documentary film *Shtetl*. The film documents memories of events in 1942 when Nazis ordered Polish farmers near Bransk to transport a large group of Jews to a nearby train station from which they were taken to gas chambers at Treblinka. The film also includes interviews with Bransk farmers as well as descendants of Bransk Jews in the United States and Jewish Israeli high school students. Drzewiecka uses conjunctural analysis to pinpoint audience interpretations and analyzes the responses of an interpretive community of viewers who contributed in Polish and English to online discussion groups about the documentary. She provides evidence of how collective memories selectively appropriate the past, shape cultural identifications, and serve political goals in ambivalent and contradictory ways.

Chapters 9 and 10 discuss the politics, contested boundaries, and conditions affecting the relationships between cultural identity groups who reside in a "homeland" and related groups who have resettled in the United States, and the relationships between advocates of indigeneity movements and advocates for critical and/or poststructural movements. Providing evidence from extended interviews, in Chapter 9 Rona Halualani makes the case that the members of the heterogeneous community of Hawaiians living in the United States have recreated a new and authentic but nonetheless hybrid Hawaiian diasporic identification. She shows that this identification is historically situated, has emerged in response to colonial forces causing displacement, is fluid, and is unstable. She provides discursive examples of three themes of identification that emerge from such signifiers as government documents, interviews, and community gatherings. The first theme, a search for home, is enacted by a few people who maintain homesteads in Hawaii, and by others who resettle in the United States and create new spaces that preserve their cultural spirit. The second theme is the act of *pi'koi*, claiming links to royal ancestry, which functions to authenticate claims of racial purity and identification. The third theme is the use of blood authority, which reinforces the idea that where one lives is not as important as who one is.

S. Lily Mendoza summarizes in Chapter 10 the issues pertaining to lived cultural politics and debates among academics with regard to identifications of Filipinos and Filipino Americans. She points out that there is a need for contextualization of claims as well as translation across the positions being advanced. Her goal is to function as a bridging voice in order to describe what is needed for a space ultimately to be opened for dialogue. Such bridgework requires the recognition of the interdependence between signifier and signified and between structures and agency. The focus

of engagement is shifted to the intersection of forces, identifications and representations, and positions that are in dynamic flux. Both the indigeneity and poststructural movements can inform the study of identity politics in a broader context, which includes globalization and Westernization, as well as embodied experiences in situated communities.

The last chapter in this volume is a relatively uncommon form of intellectual engagement and discourse, a forum of scholarly dialogue similar to that in Volume 24. In this chapter, I invited four scholar-practitioners to participate in a dialogue about their experiences and/or facilitation of intercultural alliances. The goals of the cyberdialogue are for participants to connect with the ideas expressed, to listen with critical intelligence, and to become vehicles for generating new possibilities to transform difficulties in conversation. Because of the relevance of the cyberdialogue to the negotiation of alliance relationships, I provide an overview of central discussion points below.

There are three participants and two cofacilitators, Victoria Chen and myself. The three scholar-practitioners, Brenda J. Allen, Benjamin J. Broome, and Tricia S. Jones, begin the chapter by detailing their firsthand experiences with a particular intercultural alliance, and then move through discussions of conditions and visions for their own and then each other's intercultural alliances. Next they overview concerns that could affect (or affected) the creation of their alliances, and finally, they offer thoughts about actions that can be (or were) taken to develop alliances. Brenda Allen addresses her experiences with interpersonal intercultural alliances formed in her academic department; Benjamin Broome focuses on his continuing role facilitating Greek and Turkish Cypriot intergroup dialogue; and Tricia Jones describes her experiences with a project bringing educators and NGO (nongovernmental organization) representatives together with a U.S. team, in both South Africa and the United States.

The participants in the cyberdialogue show that in the contexts of their projects and experiences, intercultural contact includes what occurs between individuals with varied social group identifications, such as race, sex, sexual orientation, age, nationality, ethnicity, socioeconomic class, political standpoint, access to resources, and region. A general definition of *intercultural allies* as those in a relationship working to achieve a goal, who have an association to further the common interests of group members, is proposed contingent upon each of their complex descriptions of their situated experiences and observations. Tricia Jones, for instance, describes the very different orientations to intercultural alliances that emerged in her project; alliances were instruments through which needed resources could be

obtained, were the means through which funders could see evidence of a successful project outcome, and/or were lasting relationships that could withstand social pressures and historical inequities. She further notes that *alliance* was defined by some as an internal state and attitudinal orientation and by others as a reaction to outside forces or antagonisms. Brenda Allen remarks that while her intercultural alliances were formed in a rather serendipitous way, they resulted from an invitation for her to respond or react to situations that somehow challenged and/or troubled different parties.

When discussing the conditions and characteristics that comprise intercultural alliances, Tricia Jones points to the importance of paradox and delineates that to ally with one group or individual is to distance oneself from others; "movement toward is also movement away and/or against in some larger social context." She also describes some of the multiple ways that culture impacted their project, the cultural framing of interests as collective and individual, orientations of "power-with" and "power-over," and differences in what was perceived to be appropriate conduct with each other. In addition, she proffers that development of alliances may require that allies are open to and cognizant of differences in communication styles, have the willingness and ability to metacommunicate and make their styles explicit and/or change them, and have a "willingness to embrace explicit differences or work together to negotiate new patterns that are novel to both to some extent." Finally, she offers that important factors in development and maintenance of intercultural alliances may be the extent to which group members have the respect and support of various cultural constituencies, the nature of general expectations by the groups in the broader society about the alliance, and sufficient time to develop intercultural relationships.

Brenda Allen adds further characteristics of buy-in by appropriate stakeholders at the local level and higher, and the availability of a variety of resources. Benjamin Broome also extends the list by saying that allies must realize that the goal they hold cannot be reached without the other. In addition, in his experience, *relational empathy*, which he defines as a collective interpretation of the situation and relative consensus about actions to be taken, is a key condition among Turkish and Greek Cypriots. Brenda Allen remarks that the popular group problem-solving steps and techniques used in the United States are not appropriate for all groups. Benjamin Broome agrees by describing examples of how methods of group facilitation are culture bound, saying that "imposing outside methods and products in a selfish or arrogant way is destructive," but also sharing how he adapted these methods to his work in Cyprus. He also gives examples of the power of

strong interpersonal relationships to withstand disagreements and assaults from outside the working group.

The conditions necessary for alliance development become concerns that need to be acknowledged and addressed. Concerns in this context deal with what is problematic, difficult, or needs attention, and the three participants bring up issues of power, equality, and trust. They describe that dialectic tensions of inclusion and exclusion, and individualism and collectivism, among others, must be managed in an ongoing way and, as the participants illustrate, that levels of trust that ebb and flow and alliances within a larger group change and affect alliances with outsiders. In the case of Cyprus, two groups' different perceptions of history made it essential for them to move toward an understanding of each other's point of view about historical events so that they could build a shared vision of the island's future. In Cyprus two different orientations to action became evident—one was more proactive and risk-taking and the other was more reactive and careful. Tricia Jones offers that in the South African project, it may not have been necessary that parties frame history in exactly a common way but that there needed to be a common understanding of where historical frames differed.

Actions recommended by the participants from their own experiences include a range of specific to more general recommendations such as celebrating and acknowledging victories. Participants talk about the ways in which they expanded or worked with limited agency and used relational empathy. They also point out the need to take time to reflect and rejuvenate, and the need to know when to move on without abandoning the relationships established. Finally, they each comment about the need for long-term commitments to intercultural alliances, and the ways in which they personally have been changed for the better because of their involvement.

THEMES RELATED TO CULTURE
AND COMMUNICATION ACROSS THE CHAPTERS

The chapters in this volume reflect several interrelated themes and issues that are noteworthy ones in contemporary research about culture and communication. Each of the themes is described briefly below.

Expanding and Complex Notions of Culture

The multiple ways that authors in this volume approach culture illustrate how far intercultural scholarship has advanced since the days of culture

being equated with a group of people whose ancestors come from the land of X or who look like Y. *Culture* is defined and approached in a variety of ways, such as national identification, racial representation, ethnic identification, diaspora, resettled community, "residents of the mainland (or homeland)," academic voices, poststructuralist locations, indigeneity movements, hybridity, "pure blood," royal ancestry, liminal space, memory, what is traditional, women, artists, feminists, whiteness ideologies, the "other," media images, consumer interpretation, and Internet list member. Equally important to note is that none of the authors in this volume focuses on one cultural identification or representation in isolation; all of the authors give attention to multiple and intersecting group identifications.

While national cultural identifications such as South African, Filipino, and U.S. American are discussed, the authors show the difficulty of discussing national identifications alone and give attention to other identifications, including ethnic, gender, and class identifications. For instance, Mendoza's chapter on the indigenization and poststructuralism debates among Filipinos and Filipino Americans involves multiple representatives of groups with diverse political orientations, all of whom are affected by globalization. In Steyn's analysis, although South Africans share a nationality as South African, racial identifications among them cannot be understood without giving attention to concomitant representations, ideological structures and hierarchies, and different views of the importance of the past and history. The public discourse of blacks and whites in South Africa reflects quite different views about who is African and whether black Africans deserve restitution from the apartheid era.

The Power of Acknowledging Historical Contexts

Many of the authors note that histories are powerful constraints that should be acknowledged by scholars and practitioners who wish to understand not only diverse and contested identifications but also the conditions that constrain relationships. Drzewiecka outlines collective memories that not only are socially constructed by Poles and Polish Americans about events in 1942 but also are impacted by cultural events such as the Holocaust, politics such as Westernization and anti-Semitism, and economic status and mobility for Poles and Jews. In the discursive examples from South African radio talk-show callers, a difference in views about history emerges between black and white South African callers. For black callers, the history that is most salient is their experience during the recent apartheid years as well as their ancestry as part of indigenous peoples prior

to white exploration. The comments from the white South African callers tend to orient their history as starting when their ancestors landed on the shores of South Africa. It is notable that their arguments against financial reparations reflect an orientation toward the future, a desire to keep what they earn for the present well-being of their families, and a tendency to blame blacks for the inequities that have arisen from the past.

Sorrells clearly shows the importance of understanding the history of the Southwest region in the United States and events that shaped Navajo and Pueblo art becoming a tourist industry. She describes the way "quality" becomes what the curio market determines is profitable and what consumers decide looks "traditional." Finally, Benjamin Broome articulates the importance of understanding the multiple versions and histories held by the Greek and Turkish Cypriots in order to appreciate their own complicated identifications and ascriptions about the "other" in their bicommunal dialogues.

Recognizing Whiteness Ideology as Omnipresent

Acknowledging the ways that whiteness ideology is a transnational and an intranational condition pervading general experiences of and scholarship about intercultural alliances is illustrated in a number of chapters in this volume. To feature a few examples, Steyn's discussion of South African discourse of white callers shows invisible privilege, an individualistic orientation to hard work as an account of their higher economic status, and a color evasive view about who benefits from the apartheid system. Cooks and Fullon uncover the ways whiteness became a constraint in how Panamanians objectified the first author in multiple contexts, and how whiteness ideology, exemplified by some Icelanders, contributed to racism and questions about the second author's legitimacy as a scholar. Tierney and Jackson articulate three rhetorical fantasy myths related to whiteness that have become naturalized and unquestioned frameworks about the way the world is and should be. They also show how such themes diffuse attention from structural inequities, objectify nonwhites, and reinforce the status quo.

Viewing Alliances as Identity and Representation Politics

Because most of the authors in this volume choose to orient their work by employing, at least in part, a critical theoretical perspective, it should come as no surprise that in addition to uncovering dominant ideologies, the authors focus on identity and representation politics. For example,

Drzewiecka analyzes the conflict between representations in a mediated text (a film documentary) and avowed identifications of cultural groups such as Poles and Jews. Sorrells also notes the conflict between consumers' representations and expectations of traditional art and the Navajo and Pueblo Indian artist identifications. This struggle reflects the dialectic tension between being more contemporary and heterogeneous and/or honoring past traditions.

Identifications are also constrained by institutions such as education and politics, among other forces, as Mendoza's discussion of Filipino and Filipino American movements of indigeneity and poststructuralist critique exemplify. The consequences of identity politics and the emotionality of identification issues are also expressed by the South Asian women who contribute to the online dialogue described by Gajjala. Additionally, all three participants in the cyberdialogue argue that broader societal views, views of leaders in key institutions such as the church or majority government, are key conditions in which identity politics and relationships are encouraged or prohibited.

Questioning Authenticity and Agency in Intercultural Alliances

Authenticity is obviously a key construct in Halualani's discussion of the Hawaiian diaspora. Having royal ancestry, using blood authority, and living in identifiably traditional ways are criteria used to determine who is an authentic Hawaiian. In the South African discourse, the discussion of who is African is a debate about authenticity, as well as a discussion about who should decide. Authenticity is linked to indigeneity in Mendoza's description of Filipino and Filipino American identity politics and academic debate, but she also notes that binaries of authentic/inauthentic should be open to deconstruction and critique.

In the cyberdialogue there is an unfolding discussion of authenticity. Brenda Allen is the first to mention authenticity, which she defines as occurring when allies have a "feeling of comfort being and expressing who they are, to be authentic selves, free to exhibit any of their multiple facets," and Tricia Jones adds that authenticity occurs in sites that are felt to be "safe places." She also adds that power (related to "power over" and "power with") and authenticity are interrelated. Benjamin Broome extends the discussion by saying that authenticity in Cyprus was evident when individuals listened to and learned about each other's perspectives, appreciated the suffering that both sides have experienced, and acknowledged that their own community had contributed to the suffering of the other.

Agency is also addressed throughout this volume, and many authors note that the dualistic or binary view of agency as either high or low is not consistent with the lived experiences of subjects. The Navajo and Pueblo women in Sorrell's study exercise the agency to incorporate some of their own designs in their pots, but they use clay gathered in a traditional manner. Women with racialized identifications in Carrillo Rowe's chapter show how the formalized discourse of the academy, the ease with which white women are able to say "we can't change the institution or the system," and patriarchal departmental governing systems with authoritarian chairs, all collude to constrain the agency of nonwhite and racialized women academics while at the same time placing the burden upon them to initiate alliances. The agency of the Hawaiian diaspora community members is evidenced in their efforts to construct new communities and create rituals while at the same time retelling their history and practicing *pi-koi*.

Positionality and Engaged
Scholarship About Intercultural Alliances

The authors in these chapters recognize that who they are as cultural beings and cultural objects affects every step of the knowledge-building process. For example, Carrillo Rowe acknowledges her intimate engagement and how her lived experience affects her writing about transracial alliances by making her positionality and varied identifications explicit. She describes her creation of moments of vulnerability as she places herself within the text as an "embodied, complicated, and invested author" attempting to speak from a place of connection and "positionality in process that strives-toward-bridge." Tierney and Jackson bring their different racially embodied experiences into their analysis of dominant rhetorical themes of whiteness and discussion of the implications of the themes for interracial alliance building. Cooks and Fullon recognize that their multiple identifications as raced, sexed, and educated are contested and reframed through sometimes consistent but mostly contradictory ascriptions by those with whom they worked in Panama and Iceland.

Toward Transformation of Intercultural Alliances

Several noteworthy interpretations can be drawn from the chapters in this volume with regard to the potential for transforming intercultural relationships. Rather than attempting to paraphrase what the authors so eloquently argue, below I highlight three conclusions that I think have important

implications for scholars and practitioners of international and intercultural communication.

First, there are more ideological forces, institutional policies and practices, and social norms that reinforce hierarchy and elites keeping their privileges in place than there are ideologies, policies, practices and norms encouraging and rewarding intercultural alliances. The authors demonstrate that whiteness ideology, histories, political policies, media portrayals, academic institutions, and other forces act to constrain alliance relationships. As scholars and practitioners, how we experience, research, and teach about alliances emerges from this context.

It is evident that a first step toward transformation is therefore to begin with a critical analysis of how dominance is being enacted and reinforced, and how those processes preclude intercultural alliance connections. It is also clear from the chapters in this volume that such reflexive acknowledgement of privilege by those who benefit from whiteness ideology, patriarchy, and dominance does not often occur. It will not occur without systematic and sustained dialogue with individuals who have different identifications, locations, and experiences.

A second conclusion is that intercultural alliances are much more complex and dynamic than popular ideas of allies in armed conflict, the corporate boardroom, or the culturally diverse classroom. Cultures are multiple, overlapping, contradictory, and contexted, as well as formed through identifications enacted and representations produced. Collier, Hegde, Lee, Nakayama, and Yep (2001) propose that an approach to culture as identification and representation, as a political location that comes with histories and itineraries, may allow us to recognize the complexity and layered nature of cultures. The importance of broadening our focus and our scholarship about alliances, from a relationship between members of "group X and group Y" to views of alliances as based on multiple identifications and representations that occur in particular contexts, has been unquestionably demonstrated by the authors in this volume.

A third conclusion from the work in this volume is that alliances as transformative praxis require risk and vulnerability and are worth the effort. Several authors, including Carrillo Rowe and Sorrells, among others, point out that the responsibility should not be placed solely on those with marginalized locations to initiate the alliance or the dialogue. Brenda Allen in the cyberdialogue describes the rewards she has experienced from intercultural alliances, including personal growth and development, knowledge about social identities that she has incorporated into

her teaching, ideas and experiences that have extended her research program, and the motivation to work to heighten awareness and as a change agent for social justice.

Anzaldúa (1990) offers several powerful metaphors to represent the ways women of color can approach alliances with white women in the struggle to transform unequal relationships and resources. Her images are an apt closing for this chapter. First she describes that bridgework is enormously challenging and that at times "the you that is the mediator gets lost in the dichotomies, dualities, or contradictions you're mediating. You have to be flexible yet maintain your ground, or the pull in different directions will dismember you" (p. 223). Then she continues that sometimes being a bridge means "risking being 'walked' on, being 'used'" (p. 223). Anzaldúa explains that it can become necessary to pull up the drawbridge and gather with insiders to regain energy and regroup, or to retire to an island. She advises however, "consider making some decisions and setting goals to work on yourself, with another, with others of your race, or with a multi-racial group as a bridge, drawbridge, sandbar, island, or in a way that works for you" (p. 229).

The authors in Volume 25 are exemplars of scholars who are engaged in not only the study but also the practice of building intercultural alliances. Their work provides us with knowledge about the complexities of the struggle and the moments of connection. How we develop intercultural alliances to transform the world in which we live is up to us; our future depends upon it.

REFERENCES

Anzaldúa, G. (1990). Bridge, drawbridge, sandbar or island: Lesbians of color Hacienda Alianzas. In L. Albrecht & R. M. Brewer (Eds.), *Bridges of power: Women's multicultural alliances* (pp. 216-233). Philadelphia: New Society.

Collier, M. J., Hedge, R. S., Lee, W., Nakayama, T. K., & Yep, G. A. (2001). Dialogue on the edges: Ferment in communication and culture. In M. J. Collier (Ed.), *International and intercultural communication annual: Vol. 24. Transforming communication about culture: Critical new directions* (pp. 234-262). Thousand Oaks, CA: Sage.

Grewal, I., & Kaplan, C. (1994). Transnational feminist practices and questions of postmodernity. In I. Grewal & C. Kaplan (Eds.), *Scattered hegemonies: Postmodernity and transnational feminist practices* (pp. 1-36). Minneapolis: University of Minnesota Press.

Kaplan, C. (1994). The politics of location as transnational feminist practice. In I. Grewal & C. Kaplan (Eds.), *Scattered hegemonies: Postmodernity and transnational feminist practices* (pp. 137-152). Minneapolis: University of Minnesota Press.

Rosenfeld, J. M., & Tardieu, B. (2000). *Artisans of democracy: How ordinary people, families in extreme poverty, and social institutions become allies to overcome social exclusion.* Lanham, MD: University Press of America.

2

Embodied Negotiation

Commodification and Cultural Representation in the U.S. Southwest

KATHRYN SORRELLS • *California State University, Northridge*

INTRODUCTION

In the highly commodified world in which we live, culture has become a product that can be invented, packaged, and consumed. The marketability of a culture frequently depends upon the ways in which the cultural forms of representation embody difference—difference from the dominant culture. This "difference" between the culture that is commodified and those who consume it must be constructed as "real," which depends heavily upon rhetoric of "authenticity." When the dynamics of commodification are in motion, cultural representation often is "fixed" or "frozen" in the past, perpetuating stereotypical and limiting images of the dominant culture's notion of the "other."

In this chapter, I examine the impact of commodification on cultural representations of particular groups, explore how the dynamics of commodification shape intercultural encounters, and discuss how the commodification of the cultural "other" operates as a continuation of colonialism. Within this contested space, I am primarily interested in highlighting the ways that women use their cultural forms as sites to negotiate representation, tradition, and identity. Furthermore, I illustrate how women transform themselves, their culture, and the world around them through their resistive and creative efforts. The study discussed in this chapter focuses on cultural forms of representation created by Pueblo and Navajo[1] women in New Mexico, grounding the research in a specific geographic, historical, political, and cultural context. As my goal is to understand how women artists relate to their cultural forms of representation within a commodifying system of unequal power, I use both interpretive and critical methods of analysis.

17

For generations and generations, Pueblo and Navajo women have been re-presenting themselves and their cultures through creative forms of expression. As they shape their creative forms, women convey meaning about their lives, the collective experience of their cultures, and their relationships with other cultures. Pueblo women gather the earth around them, and mold vessels that hold their culture. Pottery made by Pueblo women also represents the complex confluence and conflictual interaction of cultures that characterize the history of the Southwest region of the United States. Similarly, and yet in distinct ways, Navajo women collect the material from their environment and transform it into weavings that tell the cultural stories of the Navajo people. As they weave, Navajo women also visually depict the dynamics of power and the history of colonial imposition that have forged intercultural interactions in New Mexico.

The forms of cultural representation created by contemporary Pueblo and Navajo women in New Mexico extend from deeply rooted and intertwined cultural and intercultural histories. The history of interaction among these groups and with the Hispano and dominant Anglo cultures form a context for making sense of the complex processes of commodification and representation that take place today. What follows is an overview of the historical context of intercultural interactions in New Mexico, and a review of theoretical issues relevant to understanding the commodifying of indigenous cultures and the resulting negotiation of representation.

HISTORICAL CONTEXT
AND THEORETICAL FOUNDATIONS

New Mexico has a rich and complex history. It is, as Limerick (1987) reminds us, a history marked by conquest where the dynamics of domination and subordination continue to shape both land and people. New Mexico's history is also one of contradictions where multiple and conflictual worldviews have collided, where resistance to dominating forces (while not often recorded) has been strong, and where transformation has occurred through these processes of contestation.

Colonization

The indigenous people of New Mexico, the Pueblo and later arrivals, the Navajo, have experienced two waves of conquest, first by the Spanish and then by Anglo-Americans. Without question, the indigenous cultures have

been significantly altered by this contact as well as through interaction with each other. Along with death, disease, and destruction, the Spanish Conquistadors brought with them religious, social, and economic systems, imposing these upon the indigenous people of New Mexico. In the mid-1800s when Anglo-Americans representing the U.S. government annexed the geographic territory that is now called New Mexico, they, in turn, super-imposed their legal, educational, religious, and economic systems upon the Spanish-speaking population and upon Indian people alike.

Within this colonial context, theories of racial superiority and interracial relations were invented, were imposed, and continue to be transformed in New Mexico. During the period of Spanish colonization, racist notions translated into a hierarchical system that equated social class with racial ancestry (Gutiérrez, 1991; Wilson, 1997). Later, along with trade and economic development, Anglo-Americans imposed an ideology of racial superiority, fueled by the rhetoric of manifest destiny, on the people of New Mexico (Simmons, 1977). By the middle of the 1800s, assimilationist practices aimed at "mainstreaming" both Native American and Hispanic people were in full swing. Boarding schools, designed to "Americanize" the indigenous population, removed children from their homes and placed them in contact with Anglo-American Protestants. These, along with other dramatic and devastating efforts to control and pacify "hostile Indians," such as the incarceration of Navajo people at Bosque Redondo in the 1860s, resulted in the physical, economic, and cultural disruption and dislocation of indigenous people.

In the late 1800s, demands for racial "purity" that would advance the prospects of statehood gave rise to New Mexico's rhetoric of "tri-culturalism." Despite the 1875 census in Santa Fe, which reported that 75% of the population were of mixed racial background, the rhetoric of tri-culturalism, the notion of three separate, distinct, and "pure" cultures in New Mexico, was fashioned and still prevails today (Wilson, 1997). Three centuries of genocide, incarceration, forced assimilation, and racist ideology mark the geographic terrain, physical bodies, and mental space of New Mexico. While more subtle, the history of colonization continued into the 20th century through the commodification of cultures.

Commodification and Colonization

With the arrival of the railroad in the 1880s, the economic base for Pueblo and Navajo people shifted from a barter economy to a cash-based economy. Manufactured goods were only part of the cargo traveling

westward at the turn of the century. The railroad also brought tourists and market interests that would radically shape New Mexico's indigenous cultures into consumable "native" products. Tourists, with their curio-market preferences, dramatically influenced the size, shape, and designs of Pueblo pottery (Dillingham, 1992). Pottery became smaller to allow for ease and safety in transport. Designs and shapes borrowed from European and Anglo-American crafts such as glassware were introduced by Anglo traders. Trinkets and ashtrays were made with native designs to meet the tourists' desires. "Traditional" pueblo pottery and Navajo weaving filled shops, railway stations, hotels, and restaurants across New Mexico.

Navajo weaving was, perhaps, more drastically affected by the changes ushered in with the railroad than was Pueblo pottery. As Dillingham (1992) suggests, the primary material of the potter, the earth, remained consistent even as designs and shapes changed to respond to the desires and demands of Anglo tourists, buyers, and collectors. Navajo weaving was impacted, however, by the influx of new materials, designs created by traders and East Coast buyers, and traders who dictated the styles, colors, and materials used in the weavings. Anthropologist Hatcher (1967) observed that by the early 1900s Navajo weavings show "the Indian's idea of the trader's idea of what the white man thought was Indian design" (p. 174).

The Indian Building at the Alvarado Hotel in Albuquerque, erected in 1902, illustrates how the ambivalence toward cultural difference—a combination of fear and fascination, aversion and attraction—was neutralized and palatably packaged in order to be consumed (Root, 1996). Based on the World's Fair model, the Indian Building, touting "the most extensive ethnographical museum in the country" (*Albuquerque Journal-Democrat,* March 7, 1902, as cited in Howard & Pardue, 1996, p. 57), incorporated an extensive collection of Native American art forms along with "live" demonstrations by "Native" artists (Howard & Pardue, 1996). Despite the fact that the Fred Harvey Company[2] had a difficult time enticing Native artists to participate in their "living museum" (a downplayed yet active form of resistance by Native people), it became the main attraction for hundreds of tourists who passed through Albuquerque daily. The trains stopped for 30 minutes to allow the Eastern tourist a brief glimpse at the exotic, "a step into another world" (Howard & Pardue, 1996, p. 57), and the opportunity to consume Natives and their art. The successful commodification of New Mexico's cultures depended upon creating an image of an exotic and unusual, yet safe, place to consume the "other."

In addition to the representation of New Mexico's cultures as exotic yet consumable, the process of commodification of indigenous cultures further

reenacts colonial relationships through dynamics of appropriation. With the arrival of the transcontinental railroad, many private entrepreneurs, along with major museums and institutions such as the Smithsonian, became involved in the acquisition of Pueblo pottery and Navajo weaving. Batkin (1987) notes that the traditional knowledge base, or the "library" as he calls it, was depleted significantly as the better pieces were bought or removed from New Mexico (p. 46). This void left potters little other than potsherds, memories, and their imaginations from which to continue creating their work. The appropriation of cultural forms enacts a colonial attitude that values the objects of a culture while dismissing the artists and the cultures that have created them. In fact, it is the denigration and destruction of the culture that supports the sense of entitlement necessary for appropriation (hooks, 1992; Root, 1996).

In addition, the epitome of the romanticized, noble savage, evoking both pity and nostalgia, was that of the Indians fading at the hands of civilization. Romanticizing the destruction of a race of people creates a nostalgia for that which is being destroyed and also enables the redefinition of the "dying race" according to the conquerors', colonizers', or consumers' own terms (Berkhofer, 1978; Root, 1996). The Anglo romanticization of the soon-to-be-extinct native people in the early decades of the 20th century served to both legitimize the appropriation of Native American material culture and advance the subsequent commodification of the cultures. These colonial dynamics support practices and policies that attempted to "preserve" the cultures in the past. As Wilson (1997) notes, the "fixed," "frozen," and "preserved" representation is fundamental to the industry of tourism and the resulting commodification of the cultural "other."

New Mexico was also reimagined and reconstructed to present a "romantic" image with a distinctive regional and cultural identity through the influences of the Museum of New Mexico, antimodernists, and the expatriate artist community. This trend, following the Romantic traditions of Europe, glorified and idealized the "picturesque," the "authentic," and the "spiritual," aspects of traditional cultures, which provided aesthetic, moral, and spiritual salvation from the depravity of industrialization. Berkhofer (1978) argues that the primitivist tradition, the notion that a paradise exists on earth as an alternative to current conditions, has shaped the imagery and descriptions of North American Indians since Columbus. The nonindustrialized Indian cultures, and, by extension, their architecture and crafts were touted as antidotes to the ills and evils of industrial society. As Dillingham (1992) suggests, the "fascination with the Indian way of life and the mystique of

the Wild West translated into the desire to own an 'authentic' piece of Indian craftsmanship [sic]" (p. 158).

Yet, as articulated by anthropologist McCannell (1976), the commodification of cultural symbols "represents an end to the dialogue, a final freezing of ethnic imagery which is both artificial and deterministic" (p. 375). Native American artists are constrained in their artistic expression by the stereotypical expectations and limitations placed upon them by the market. In a reciprocal manner, the form as a representation of the culture fixes or freezes the identity of native people in the past. The tourist and modern consumer come to New Mexico nostalgic for a "traditional" past. Ironically, the modern world, from which the tourist seeks to escape, has played a significant role in destroying the indigenous cultures in the Southwest.

The historical and political intersection between the dominant Anglo culture and Pueblo and Navajo cultures can be characterized in multiple ways. The literal appropriation of material culture in the form of museum acquisitions and commodification could be understood as violent penetration within an inequitable system of power: cultural rape. A somewhat more moderate characterization of the interaction is that Anglo culture has been patronizing and intrusive (Dillingham, 1992). Some might characterize the interaction as supportive and sustaining. The opening of markets revived and sustained dying forms that were rapidly being replaced by manufactured products. To varying degrees, all of the interpretations can be supported. However, operating within a framework of commodification, pottery made today by Pueblo women and weavings created by Navajo women continue to manifest the dynamics of power that characterize colonial relations. The art created by women from the two cultures is a contested site where issues of representation and identity, and notions of tradition, are negotiated.

Representation, Commodification, and Colonization

Pueblo pottery and Navajo weavings have been constructed through commodification and representation as signifiers of their respective cultures and cultural identities. Yet, both forms have been influenced in fundamental ways by interactions with other cultural groups in the Southwest, and each has been greatly affected by the dominant European-American culture in the United States that consumes, sells, and trades the creative forms. In fact, the creative forms are as much a representation of the dominant culture's notion of the "other" as they are representations of the native culture as marketed. Hall (1997) suggests it is difference that carries meaning. More

precisely, the difference or "otherness" from the dominant group or privileged group that signifies. "'Difference' has been marked. How it is then interpreted is a constant and recurring preoccupation in the representation of people who are racially and ethnically different from the majority population. Difference signifies. It 'speaks' " (Hall, 1997, p. 230).

Marking difference defines boundaries and creates classification systems that allow for the establishment of binary dichotomies such as insider/outsider, us/them, civilized/primitive and traditional/contemporary (Douglas, 1966; Kristeva, 1982). Signifying practices function to "fix" or assign qualities or characteristics to a group of people as inherent or "natural." The stereotypes promoted through visual representation and verbal tropes that portray Indian people as "quaint" or "primitive" are representational practices that reduce the complexity of individuals and groups to easily identifiable and often denigrating characteristics. These representational practices also attempt to fix "difference" and make the stereotypical characteristics permanent (Hall, 1997, p. 258). The practice of verbal or visual stereotyping, working within systems of power, reduces groups of people to essentialized categories and classifies people according to the norms of the dominant group (Lidchi, 1997). Those who are not constructed as part of the norm are relegated to the category of "other."

Orientalism, as articulated by Said (1978), describes the discourse by which European culture constructed the "Orient," and justified colonization of the East. The Orient, as the mystical and backward "other," offered a new object of knowledge, which was "suitable for study in the academy, for display in museum, for reconstruction in the colonial offices, for theoretical illustration in anthropological, biological, linguistic, racial and historical theses" (p. 8). Through a century-long process of appropriation and representation, the Southwest has become the American Orient (Babcock, 1997). While the marking of difference defines the "other" in opposition to the normalized, dominant group, and tends towards exclusion and distinction, it also works to make difference attractive and alluring, reflecting the desires and projections of the dominant group (Babcock, 1978; Hall, 1997; Said, 1978). As hooks (1992) describes in "Eating the Other," difference is marketed as exotic, and delicious for the consumption of the dominant culture. Through the appropriation of cultural forms, such as Pueblo pottery and Navajo weaving, and the re-presentation of them as the fetishized and essentialized "other," the commodification process operates as a continuation of colonization.

Nevertheless, while representational practices attempt to fix meanings, the production of meaning cannot be controlled and does not remain stable over long periods of time, as Hall (1997) suggests:

Ultimately, meaning begins to slip and slide; it begins to drift, or be wrenched, or inflected into new directions. New meanings are grafted on to old ones. Words and images carry connotations over which no one has complete control, and these marginal or submerged meanings come to the surface, allowing different meanings to be constructed, different things to be shown and said. (p. 270)

Through alternative readings, the trans-coding of negative images into positive ones, and other strategies, the dominant regime of representation is resisted (Hall, 1997). Viewers, readers, and creators of "texts" are active in the process of making meaning and have the potential to negotiate and contest representation (Fiske, 1987). In this way, cultural forms of representation, such as pottery made by Pueblo women and rugs woven by Navajo women, become sites where representation, notions of tradition, and identity are negotiated and transformed. Through resistive and creative efforts, women artists exert agency as they challenge the restrictive stereotypes and the essentializing categories of the "other" (Anzaldúa, 1990; Aptheker, 1989; hooks, 1995). Before exploring these representational processes in more depth, I briefly describe the methods of inquiry used in the study.

METHODOLOGY

Dialectic Orientation to Critical and Interpretive Approaches

The study discussed in this chapter is part of a larger body of research examining intercultural communication processes manifest in creative forms of expression. As my purpose is to highlight the artists' relationship to their cultural forms of representation within a commodifying system of unequal power relations, I use both critical and interpretive theoretical and methodological approaches.

Both the interpretive and critical approaches provide assumptions that establish a foundation for this research, offer perspectives that inform the process of inquiry, and propose methods for interpreting the experiences of the women considered in this study. As Martin and Nakayama (1999) suggest, working between and across paradigms in a dialectic fashion enables engagement in a critical process of questioning the assumptions, methods, and ways of interpretation used in each approach. Scholars working from interpretive and critical positions have criticized research emerging from the traditional ethnographic paradigm and have developed alternative approaches based on different assumptions (Anzaldúa, 1990; Clifford, 1983;

Ellis

Ellis & Bochner, 1996; Tanno & Jandt, 1998; Trinh, 1991). Others (e.g., Martin & Nakayama, 1999) have articulated the limitations of critical research, which primarily has focused attention on mediated communication.

Critical approaches provide theories for understanding the political dimensions of communication processes and illustrate how the artists and their work must be understood within their political, historical, and cultural contexts. Although the interpretive approach shares assumptions of the social construction of reality and the subjective nature of research with the critical approach (Lindlof, 1995), the primary goal of research from an interpretative perspective is to describe and understand human communication (Collier, 1998; Martin & Nakayama, 1999). An interpretive approach is useful in providing methods for engaging in, interpreting, and writing about the interactive experiences with women artists in the research. In this study, the two approaches complement each other; each approach provides a partial but necessary way of understanding the negotiation of meanings and representation process.

Methods

For this research project, I utilized a variety of methods, including participant observation, interviews, and photographs of the women's creative work as means to understand the processes of representation embodied in creative forms of expression. Prior to the formal interviewing process, I had the opportunity to talk with and observe approximately 20 Pueblo women potters and 20 Navajo women weavers. Informal interviews and conversations took place for several years before the more structured interviews with the particular women who participated in the study.

I conducted in-depth interviews with 3 Pueblo potters and 3 Navajo women about their work over a time period of a year and a half. I made contact with these women in various ways. Some were introduced to me through a network of friends. Others I met at events, markets, or fairs where Native American artists are featured. The women involved in the study primarily live in northern New Mexico within a half-day drive from Albuquerque, New Mexico. Some of the women live near their tribal homes on the Navajo Reservation or one of many Pueblos in the area. Other women participating in the study live in or near Albuquerque, Santa Fe, or Taos, New Mexico.[3]

My approach to the research process was based on a commitment to relationship building and the feminist notion that research can be "the collective critical reconstitution of the meaning of women's social experience

as women live through it" (MacKinnon, 1983, p. 255). I assumed that information about the women's lives and their relationship to their work would emerge gradually over time. Fostering relationships with the women who participated in the study was critical to the research process. During the initial meetings, my questions focused on how, when, and from whom they had learned their particular art form. What was their learning process? What did it mean to them to work in this form? I learned a great deal about them personally, their families, and how their artwork was situated in a cultural and intercultural context.

After two to three visits to each participant's home, where I spent anywhere from 3 hours to a full day developing a relationship with the woman and learning about her artwork, I conducted more formal, tape-recorded interviews of 1 to 2 hours in length. During these interviews, I asked each participant to describe her work and to talk about what it represents to her. We discussed particular pieces as well as each woman's work as a whole. I asked the women in greater detail what it means to them to work in the art form they chose and why they do this work. In addition, we discussed their experience selling their work, their interactions with retail buyers, gallery owners, and tourists. I asked the women involved in the study how they felt about selling their work and what they thought their work meant or represented to those who purchased it.

Taped interviews were repeated at approximately 3-month intervals to gain more in-depth understanding of the artists' work and to gather feedback from them on what I had written about each of them. This process allowed the women involved to play an integral role in the research process. In addition, I used the photographs I took of the artists, their work, and the process of creating their forms as a way to further discuss their work and issues of representation with each of the artists.

In addition to the in-depth interviews with the creators of the forms, I conducted approximately 25 interviews with people who were buying either Pueblo pottery or Navajo rugs. The purpose of these interviews was to understand more fully the reasons why people were interested in the forms and to discuss with them what the forms represented to them. Most of these interviews took place informally at public events such as markets and fairs where people gather to view and buy artwork.[4] The data gathered from artists and consumers for the larger research project were rich and varied. For the purposes of this chapter, I have used only data relating to the theme of commodification. I turn now to a more thorough exploration of the ways Pueblo and Navajo women are negotiating and transforming representation, tradition, and identity through their creative forms of expression.

EMBODIED NEGOTIATION

In the process of creating their artistic forms, Pueblo and Navajo women work through tensions that reflect varied and opposing perspectives. As women create their art for a consumer market, questions of representation arise, are acknowledged, and are challenged. Increasingly, women from both cultures are shaping forms and images that reflect the confluence and intersection of cultures rather than cultures in isolation. Images that come from their personal experiences outside their cultural tradition and from contemporary culture are appearing in their artwork. The increasingly hybrid nature of the creative forms embodies several processes of negotiation active in their lives. Through their artistic forms of expression, many women are addressing questions of representation, challenging notions of tradition, and redefining their identities. Their artwork is a site of embodied negotiation.

Negotiating Representation

At Indian Market in the summer of 1998, I stood in front of the display and sales booth of a potter from Zia Pueblo. Her pottery was beautiful, and as I admired it, we began talking about the pieces she had on display. Several tourists came along, looked at a few pieces, smiled and left. Shortly after, an Anglo woman, whom I later discovered was a tourist visiting from the East Coast of the United States, came along and started asking questions about the designs. Her first question was "Is this traditional? Is this a traditional design?" Receiving the affirmative answer she wanted, she continued asking questions about specific designs. When she pointed to one design, the potter from Zia Pueblo responded by saying: "Yes, those are the *kiva*[5] steps. They are the steps to the *kiva*. Or you could think of them as the steps to the church." To this, the customer responded, "No, no, I want them to be *kiva* steps." This is only one example of many exchanges that I witnessed or overheard that point to the need of the consumer culture to control or determine the representation of Pueblo and Navajo artists. The Zia potter was suggesting a hybrid image that layered or combined the symbols of *kiva* steps and church steps. Yet, the consumer did not want to hear about the mixed or overlapping meanings in the image. She would rather maintain an invented notion of the "pure" or "authentic" native person and culture. After the tourist left, I asked the Zia potter if I could take her picture. Her response fit the scenario perfectly. She said, "Do you want me to act traditional?"

Figure 2.1   "Do you want me to act traditional?"[6]

Several Pueblo potters at Indian Market in Santa Fe in the summer of 1997 and 1998 shared with me their frustration that their pottery was not selling. I was initially drawn to their work because it departed significantly from what I had considered Pueblo pottery. Separately, each told me she felt the reason for the lack of sales was because her work did not look "Indian" or "native" enough. Somehow, their work was not "Indian enough" to sell. I admitted that their artwork did not look like what I expected. Our discussion evolved toward the question: What is Indian art? Does a piece of pottery, a weaving, or any other art form have to follow a prescribed form or appear like other images to be considered Indian art? To what degree must a piece reference what has been defined as "traditional" by the market for it to be considered Indian art? Nada Currier, a Navajo weaver, articulates the dilemma: "A lot of times I don't do the old style rugs . . . the 'traditional' ones. When I do that, I know I can't sell them" (N. Currier, personal interview, May 21, 1999).

During the spring of 1999, I had the opportunity to sit behind the booth with Jemez potter Emma Yepa at the Jemez Red Rocks Arts Fair. Emma, now in her late 20s and the mother of four, learned pottery from her mother who learned from her mother at an early age. At 95, her grandmother still makes pots occasionally. The view and conversation from the other side of the table, the sellers' and artists' side, was intriguing and informing. The most frequently asked questions during the 6 hours were: "Did you make these?"; "Are they made by hand?"; and "Are they traditional?" Emma told me that sometimes when she makes her more contemporary designs, customers who are buying her work ask her to make them more traditional. They say, "We want more tradition. And I say, 'This is traditional.' You know? Especially with all the ceramics[7] being done you're telling me what to do. You're telling me what is tradition and what is not" (E. Yepa, personal interview, April 23, 1999). Emma, recognizing how strongly the consumer market influences (and oftentimes narrows the range of) representations of Native American culture, laughed as she told this story:

> My mom would tell me when they were young, my grandma would make 50 of the same kind of pots, miniatures of the same kind that she would sell in a store in Albuquerque. They'd paint them with these fluorescent colors. . . . And the store-owners, they called that traditional Pueblo pottery!

With the appropriation of Pueblo pottery and Navajo weaving over the last century, the notion of what these forms should look like and what they represent has been frozen in the past and controlled by the image

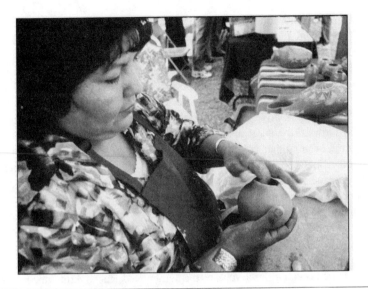

Figure 2.2   Emma Yepa Shaping a Pot at the Jemez Pueblo Red Rock
Art Fair

non-Indian people have of people from native cultures. In order to serve the market needs, Pueblo pottery and Navajo weaving have been labeled, packaged, and sold as "traditional." In interviews with over 25 consumers during Indian art markets and fairs, I consistently received a version of three basic responses. "I think it's beautiful because it's handmade and traditional," "I like that it's all natural and that it's made by native people," and "I really like Indian culture because it's so traditional and spiritual" (Consumer interviews, August 21-23, 1998). When queried further, consumers responded that Pueblo pottery and Navajo weaving represent nonindustrialized, land-based, "native," and therefore, spiritual cultures. For most of the respondents, owning a piece of pottery or a weaving and displaying it in their home brought a piece of that world, the natural, the pure, the authentic, and the spiritual, to what can be described as their highly mechanized, technological, and disenchanted postmodern lives. The motivation for consuming the cultural artifacts often was nostalgia for a world, lifestyle, and way of being that has all but disappeared.

Multiple ironies are embedded in this interpretation. The dominant consumer culture is nostalgic for a time and place long gone, the "native way" or "the land of enchantment." The people who embodied that way of life

have, in fact, nearly been destroyed or assimilated by those who now want to reinvent them. So, the consumer culture has reimagined these characteristics of natives and reinscribed them to a people who may once have had this type of life and worldview, but who are now trying their best to negotiate multiple and often contradictory cultural worldviews. As Roseann Willink, professor of Navajo language and culture at the University of New Mexico, states, "for the money, they (Navajo women) will weave a certain way. There used to be more older rugs that showed they were closer to the earth, closer to the spiritual world . . . now the dominant culture has come in with all this stuff and now the weaving is different . . . it's changed" (R. Willink, personal interview, April 16, 1999). According to my interviews, the Pueblo and Navajo artists would like to present themselves as multifaceted human beings influenced by the complexities of the postmodern world. Yet, their own representations of themselves and their culture are fixed and defined. While subtler and less direct than forms of colonization in earlier centuries, the fixing of cultural symbols through the process of commodification is a form of colonialism.

On several occasions, friends or colleagues with a less avid interest in Pueblo pottery accompanied me to one of the summer fairs. After a short while, many remarked how all the pottery looks the same. Of course, I would argue that it doesn't, but their observation points to the homogeneity imposed by the consumer market expectations. What are the implications of this market-imposed homogeneity? Does it result in a kind of visual stereotyping and essentializing? During a visit to one of the museums in Santa Fe, several students in the group of 20 that were with me had a very interesting response to the artwork displayed in the gift shop. Their response to the shelves of Pueblo pottery was, "Oh, no. Not this again." They turned away and did not look further at the pieces. The pottery was a visual stereotype, easily recognized and easily dismissed.

The notion of tradition—how it is defined, how it operates to control images, and how it is understood differently by creator and consumer—is a central issue in the negotiation of representation. The manipulation of the notion of tradition by the commodifying market is a further sign of continued colonization.

Negotiating Tradition

The ways in which the artists negotiate "tradition" are discussed in this section. Buyers and collectors in the contemporary market have significantly controlled and altered the notion of "traditional." Dillingham

(1992, p. 193) argues that the word "traditional" most accurately applies to pottery made for domestic and ceremonial functions, of which very little is produced today. He suggests that the term "old style" may be more appropriate for much of the work created today. Additionally, many of the forms and styles considered "traditional" in the current market, such as the blackware made by Maria Martinez of San Ildefonso, were developed in the early decades of the 20th century (Peterson, 1997) in response to interests outside the culture. The notion of "traditional" is greatly influenced by the trends and fads of an ever-changing market.

As Dillingham (1992) poignantly states, contemporary Native American artists "must try to balance the pressures, constraints, and opportunities of two worlds" (p. 187). They are challenged by a variety of conflicting ideas and orientations stemming from two very different cultural worldviews. A balance must be found between their own cultural notions of "traditional" and the Anglo notion of "traditional" as dictated by the market.

Pueblo pottery and Navajo weaving are rooted in the past. They are connected to forms made in earlier times, techniques passed on from generation to generation, and unique designs specific to a particular geographic area and cultural group. Yet, the forms have evolved over time, changing as a result of influences from other cultures and innovations from within the culture. As Tammy Garcia expressed in an interview with Pueblo journalist Rosemary Diaz (1997), the tension or dichotomy between traditional and contemporary is imposed and artificial:

> Some people say they want something traditional, but I'm not sure they even know what that means. We have to do today what we need to, to improve things. We can't be expected to live or work in the Stone Age so that we can be considered traditionalists. I want my work to document what's happening today, to reflect what is occurring now. I look to the past for inspiration, and I'm sure other artists do, too. We take ideas from what's been done in the past and incorporate that into what we're doing and experiencing today. (p. 68)

The notion of traditional as it operates in the consumer market often dismisses the contemporary experiences of many artists. By requiring artists to reproduce the images, techniques, and styles of the past, the unique mixing of cultural influences that describes and defines their lives is silenced.

The tension between traditional versus contemporary and traditional versus innovative may have been initiated by the influences of the market and commodification, which came from outside the culture, but the issue is also fervently debated within the cultures as well. Autumn Borts, a potter

originally from Santa Clara Pueblo, now living in Taos where I spent many hours discussing her work, articulates the dilemma:

> It's an interesting head game when you want to express your creativity. You get put down. But at the same time you wouldn't be an artist if you didn't do it. My work is different. I try to incorporate tribal, and traditional designs into the contemporary. It's not the average traditional piece. There's a fine line between traditional and innovative. I have a great deal of respect for the way we were taught and it's important not to disappoint the elders. But we do have to pay the rent and feed our families. You do need money so sometimes you have to do what you have to do. There's a huge animosity about this issue on the Pueblo. When we fire our pots, we get a metal milk crate and put the crate up on a stand and build a cedar fire underneath. Well, I'm sure our ancestors 200 years ago didn't have a metal milk crate. But somebody along the line said well instead of building a big pit, let's put it in a can. Somebody modified that somewhere along the way. (A. Borts, personal interview, March, 1997)

The idea of tradition is also negotiated in Navajo weaving. In an interview, Roseann Willink noted that the ideas of the traders, collectors, and consumers have had a tremendous impact on Navajo weaving over the last century. What the consumer market considers "traditional" has been significantly altered from the traditions of Navajo culture:

> Well, they [traders, buyers, and collectors] did influence the rugs. They asked the women to weave. The idea that everything is perfect or should be perfect comes from the ideas of the traders. For the Navajo women, you are not supposed to weave something that is perfect. The world is not perfect. The female and male is in each rug . . . some are smaller, some are bigger. There are symbols for male and female that are put in there. Sometimes the dealers can't see that. They don't understand it, so they would tell them to do things that they thought would bring a bigger price. And to this day, they still want to control it. I have heard that from the weavers. So then when they weave in the imperfection, the trader says it is a mistake and tries to give them a lower price. It's their [the weavers'] tradition to do that. (R. Willink, personal interview, April 16, 1999)

The notion of tradition is also negotiated within Navajo culture as some people follow taboos that determine what images should and should not appear on Navajo rugs. Nada Currier lives with her family in a modern *hogan*[8] she and her husband built 16 years ago. The structure maintains the round, open feeling of a traditional *hogan*, but light flooding in from skylights, and private bedrooms added on behind, give the house a modern feel.

Figure 2.3   Nada Currier in her Kitchen Discussing Weaving

As a young adult, Nada worked outside of the home and found herself too busy to weave. When she was 34, she met her husband, Robert Currier, a psychiatrist at the local hospital in Zuni, New Mexico. It was Robert's interest in and knowledge of weaving that motivated her to return to her weaving. He knew how to weave and he knew how to set up the loom, so with the tools her mom and grandmother had given her, she started weaving again. Nada throws back her head and laughs hard as she recalls how she surprised the television journalists from *Good Morning America*. When they came to interview her, she told them that she, a Navajo, was learning weaving from her husband, an Anglo.

The two worlds Nada inhabits, Navajo and Anglo, come together in curious and creative ways. Her dream as a child was to leave Ramah (a small town situated in the western region of the Navajo Nation, which was founded by Mormon settlers in the 1880s) and everything Navajo behind. She laughs about her fate of having married an Anglo man who loves the land and Navajo culture: "And here I am still, living in a *hogan!*"

Nada Currier discussed the question of tradition in Navajo weaving:

> Yeah, my Mom is more traditional. She's more into the old ways and the tradition. I notice that as the years progress, people change things. They say, "You're not supposed to do this." And then later, they say, "No, it's okay, as long as you do this or that." The tradition changes. But my mom says, "No it's not supposed to change. It's supposed to stay this way forever." (N. Currier, personal interview, May 21, 1999)

In the past, when Nada was weaving rugs, both her mother and father told her not to weave certain designs into the rug. The way she negotiated and resolved the dilemma was to weave the rugs according to her designs but not show them to her parents. For Nada and other weavers, Navajo rugs are sites where tensions about tradition are negotiated and where change is manifested.

Roseann Willink discusses how the impact of the market and the dominant culture has shaped Navajo weaving:

> For the money, many of the women will weave a certain way. The older rugs used to show how they were closer to the earth and closer to the spiritual world. Now the dominant culture has come in with all this stuff and now the weaving is different. It changes it all. (R. Willink, personal interview, April 16, 1999)

What constitutes tradition is addressed, embodied, and transformed in the creative work of Navajo and Pueblo women. Notions of tradition, those reinvented ideals imposed from outside the culture in the commodification process, and notions of tradition passed along from generation to generation within the culture, are negotiated and contested in the process of creating these forms. All of the artists I interviewed challenge the false dichotomy between tradition and innovation. For them, the infusion of change and innovation is what allows traditions to sustain and flourish. Without the incorporation of new techniques, designs, and ideas, traditions die. Notions of tradition and what is considered traditional are closely linked to questions of identity. The following section explores how issues of identity are expressed and negotiated in the two creative forms.

Negotiating Identity

For the women I interviewed, their creative forms provide a way to reflect upon, understand, and express their multiple and often contradictory identities. Each one shared with me an understanding of herself as a

Figure 2.4   Esther José Concentrates on Weaving

member of a cultural group. Esther José, now a grandmother, has been weaving off and on since childhood. She works her weaving in and around her work with the Navajo Nation District Court in Pine Hill, her family, and community responsibilities. "The reason why I like to keep it up is because of the culture and traditions. That's what I was told and taught. The culture and the traditions, we have to carry them on. I didn't want to let go of all that" (E. José, personal interview, May 22, 1999).

Along with this sense of group identity, the artists expressed a deep desire to be seen as unique individuals. Their creative work, which combines forms grounded in their culture with personal stories and experiences, embodies multiple aspects of their identities. If a selection of each woman's work were assembled or a series of photographs taken, the collection would reflect an evolving understanding of multiple and intersecting identities. The work not only mirrors the changes in the women's lives but also serves as a place to work on and develop the complex, fluid, and multifaceted nature of their identities.

Autumn Borts shared how her sense of self is shaped by her environment and reflected in her pottery. She has chosen to live in Taos, relatively close to home at Santa Clara Pueblo, but not on the Pueblo itself. Her life choices in relation to her multiple identities are mirrored in her work:

My pottery would be different if I lived on the Pueblo. My design is what is in me right now. I take what I see around me and incorporate it in my work. It's intentional for me to get off the beaten path. Everything my grandmother does is traditional—the shapes and designs. This generation has the choice. Are we going to keep this traditional style? Are we going to keep this way of doing the artwork? Or are we going to go off and do something different? I think it is important to always have respect for the tradition that you know. But what I want to do is take it to a new kind of level. I want to add a twist to the original forms that we know. Some people will stick to the traditional; others will go and do what they want to do. There is some balance. (A. Borts, personal interview, March, 1997)

Autumn Borts wrestles with the tensions between creating what her elders have defined as traditional work and what she wants to create as representations of her own experience and identity. She continued stressing her desire to express her own individual creativity:

I want to put something that is me into the piece. I mean no disrespect for what I have been taught. That's totally embedded in my mind and heart. My technique is traditional but the designs are different. I want to express my creativity. (A. Borts, personal interview, March, 1997)

Like Autumn Borts, Emma Yepa also likes to incorporate contemporary designs that express her individuality in her work. In addition to shaping her pottery as a way to express her creativity, Emma wants people to appreciate her work and to be known personally for her work. She shares how she began combining traditional Jemez forms and designs with her own more contemporary designs:

I was thinking I wanted to do something different when I work on my clay. I look at it, and then I talk to my clay, and I say, "You know, I want you to look beautiful." My mom's work is more traditional, all the way. But mine is more contemporary. I like to do different things with it. I don't really want to copy anyone else or repeat another potter's work. I want to have my own style. (E. Yepa, personal interview, January 23, 1999)

Each of the other potters emphasized the desire to have her work recognized as hers. They all struggle with the tension between creating work that is uniquely theirs and that is representative of their group. Autumn Borts wants her name on the bottom of the piece to reflect the clean perfection for which she is striving, and she feels that the flower motif inspired by Georgia O'Keefe is becoming her personal signature (A. Borts, personal interview, March, 1997).

Figure 2.5   Dora Tse Pe Working on her Pottery at San Ildefonso
Pueblo

Dora Tse Pe also spoke to the issue of representing herself:

> There are some Indian artists who are hiring other people or having people help them with certain pots. I just don't believe that I want to do that. The only thing that my children help me with is gathering and cleaning the clay. Nobody polishes my pot, nobody makes my pot, and nobody carves my pot. If my name is going to go on that pot, then I did it. Besides, I'm very picky. Nobody's going to do it the way I do it. (D. Tse Pe, personal interview, May 10, 1999)

Recognition as individual artists is clearly important to the women with whom I spoke. Shaping Pueblo pottery and weaving Navajo rugs are means to construct and represent their personal identities. Their work does reflect their cultural or tribal identity; however, the strong emphasis placed on individual identities in the interviews suggests that they are using their artwork as sites to negotiate and bridge their collective and individual identities. In addition to the interests of their mothers and grandmothers before them to have their pottery represent their cultural traditions and tribal identity, the younger, contemporary potters also want to express their identities as individuals.

Historically, Pueblo culture and Navajo cultures have been defined as collectivistic cultures. The dominant commodifying culture has fetishized their group identity to the exclusion of personal or individual identities. In resistance to the ways they have been framed from outside the culture, the Pueblo and Navajo women interviewed feel a need to assert their individuality and personal identities in their work. Their livelihood, sense of self, and careers depend upon negotiating difficult dialectical tensions. They must navigate that ambiguous terrain between their personal visions as artists and what consumers will buy, between notions of tradition learned from their elders and those prescribed by the commodifying market, and between the realities of their complex postmodern lives and the performance of the cultural "other" expected by consumers.

As the women artists work in these contradictory and contested spaces, they develop a deep sense of personal and economic agency. As Emma Yepa suggests, pottery making is a site of empowerment:

> I'm really proud of my work. I am proud for my Pueblo and I also want to incorporate my own designs. I'm really pushing myself. I want to work hard and make a name for myself. My goals and my dreams are to be a well-known potter. It makes me feel good about myself when people appreciate my work. Like when I go to art shows and people see my work, and say, "Isn't that beautiful work?" I

like to know that it is nice. It makes me feel good. (E. Yepa, personal interview, January 23, 1999)

For Dora Tse Pe, making pottery has given her the strength and economic ability to support her family throughout the years. After her marriage ended, pottery was her means of survival. She explains how pottery is a source of strength and agency:

> Pottery was my way out. I was on my way. I never, at any time, have felt like I'm on my way to getting rich, because that is not how I was raised. I felt, I was on my way to raising these children by myself if I have to. I'll do the best I can with what I've been given. As long as we're healthy, and we have a roof over our heads and we have food, we'll be fine. And that's how I still feel. And that's how it is. I'm not going to be rich. But I will be able to provide. (Tse Pe, personal interview, May 10, 1999)

Navajo weaver Esther José also speaks of the sense of economic agency weaving allows. Her grandmother told her long ago, "I want you to learn how to do this and learn how to make rugs. In the future even if you have kids or even if you're by yourself, if you need money, then you can trade them [rugs] for groceries or for money" (E. José, personal interview, May 22, 1999). Roseann Willink also articulates a strong connection between weaving for Navajo women, economic independence, and cultural sustainability:

> The main thing about weaving is that it was given to us by the Holy People to help us through life. But now, you weave rugs to feed your children, or provide for your family. Everything they make with their hands helps them provide for their family. And also because it keeps our culture going. People need to be reminded about their unique abilities. This was mandated by the Holy People. I think that's what it is. It's being Navajo. Another thing is that it is a way of combating poverty and hunger and a way of working against the bad part and what we are trying to overcome. These are some of the things we have to learn. (R. Willink, personal interview, April 16, 1999)

Aspects of group identities and individual identities are reflected in the creative forms of expression examined in this study. The forms serve as sites for negotiating identity, tradition, and representation. Sometimes, these negotiations are between artist and consumer. Representations are imposed, conformed to, and disrupted in the creative forms of expression. At other times, the question of how an individual understands herself in relation to her

own group is negotiated. The meaning of group identity and the meaning of tradition evolve as the creative forms are manifest. In other contexts, the forms embody negotiation between the multiple worldviews and perspectives that influence and inform the artists' lives. Regardless of the issue at hand, pottery and weaving offer women tangible forms for creating and negotiating representation, tradition, and identity. As women shape pottery and weave rugs, they bring themselves forward as active, creative, and resourceful agents in the world. Through the processes of negotiation embodied in their creative work, women bring forth new forms, traditions, and identities that transform their lives and the world around them.

CONCLUSIONS

Through processes of appropriation and commodification imposed by the dominant consumer market, Pueblo pottery and Navajo weaving have become contested sites where cultural representation is negotiated. Women produce their artistic forms of expression in a context where culture is a product that can be fabricated, packaged, and consumed. The marketability of the forms often depends on the ways in which they embody difference from the dominant commodifying culture. When culture is commodified in forms like Pueblo pottery and Navajo weaving, the resulting image or form is often stereotypic. The stereotype freezes or fixes representations in the past as a means to exaggerate difference from the dominant culture and to present a product that is desirable because it is exotic and "other." Boundaries imposed from outside the culture, in part, determine representation in limiting ways. Commodification, then, functions as a continuation of colonization by essentializing and selectively narrowing representation.

In this study, I incorporated theories and methods from both the interpretive and critical approaches. Combining the two paradigms in a dialectical manner enables a more complete understanding of the complex and intersecting issues of cultural representation. The interpretive approach provides assumptions and methods for gaining an in-depth understanding of the lives and experiences of Pueblo and Navajo women artists from their perspective. Participant observation and interviews with the women in the study reveal the ways in which culture and identity are constructed through their artistic forms of communication. The critical approach, where culture is viewed as a dynamic site of struggle, complements the interpretive approach by offering a way of understanding cultural forms of representation within a broader historic and political context.

While an interaction between a Pueblo potter and an Anglo tourist may transpire in a fleeting moment of the present, generations of interactions between these two cultures shape a context of unequal power relations in which the present intercultural communication occurs. As demonstrated in this study, approaching the work of contemporary Navajo weavers and Pueblo potters from a critical perspective exposes how the commodification of culture is a continuation of colonization, and how forms of cultural representation are sites of resistance, negotiation, and transformation. The limitations of the interpretive and critical approaches are avoided by using a dialectical approach that integrates the two. Combining the approaches brings to light how Pueblo and Navajo artists are negotiating representation, tradition, and identity within the context of commodification by the dominant culture.

The concept of "traditional" has been attached to Pueblos and Navajos and the artistic forms produced by individuals from these cultural groups. Consumers want to buy products that reflect their notion of traditional, which is something "pure," "authentic," and "untainted" by outside influences. The manipulation of the concept of tradition by the commodifying markets fetishizes Pueblo and Navajo cultures. In effect, the identities of the cultures and of individuals within the cultures have been relegated to a static, "pure" moment in the past. This results in a process of containment.

While the artistic forms represent the ways the cultures in New Mexico have been reinvented by the dominant culture through commodification, the strong assertions by the women with whom I spoke indicate that their artistic forms are sites where representation is negotiated. Their desire to incorporate their personal experiences in their work, to develop personal signatures, and to use techniques appropriate to the modern world in which we live all suggest tensions between how they represent themselves and how the consumer market attempts to confine or contain their representation. For the women I interviewed, their creative forms are forms that embody cultural identity. However, the cultures that the forms represent are changing. The women in the study want to use their forms as a way of understanding and expressing these changes. A greater emphasis on personal identity is an aspect of this change. The degree to which cultural and individual identity is referenced in the work reflects processes of negotiation between the creator and her culture and between the creator, her culture, and the consumer market. Women living in the borderlands between cultures use their creativity to navigate, negotiate, and create their own identities. Speaking of women and their creative work, Anzaldúa (1987) suggests:

Art is about identity, among other things, and her creativity is political. Creative acts are forms of political activism employing definite aesthetic strategies for resisting dominant cultural norms and are not merely aesthetic exercises. We build culture as we inscribe in these various forms. (p. xxiv)

Women creating these forms are also negotiating the concept of tradition with members of their own cultural groups. Does tradition mean that a form, an image, or a style remains exactly the same? Or is it the infusion of change that allows tradition to be sustained and to flourish over time? How much change or what type of change is acceptable and what is not? These are questions the women I interviewed are negotiating with themselves, with members of their cultural groups, and with the dominant, commodifying culture.

The commodification of cultures creates barriers to intercultural relations and alliances. When consumers from non-Native cultures demand that cultural forms of representation fit their notions of what Indian art is, a superficial level of engagement is established that often precludes intercultural exchange. The relationship is defined by and often limited to the consumption of one group by another within a system of inequitable power. The freezing of images of Native people in the past, and the containment of their identities as the "other," detour the potential for intercultural dialogue. What could be a moment, a space for connection and alliance—the shared appreciation of beauty between consumer and artist, the recognition of struggle and survival in a changing world, and the textured layering of cultural influences manifest in creative forms—frequently dissolves into a reinscription of colonial patterns. Intercultural alliances require that each party or group attend to the needs and desires of the other. While Pueblo and Navajo women artists have responded out of necessity to the demands of the consumer, a much greater level of interest in and appreciation for the complex and multidimensional messages embodied in their lives and creative work is required from the non-Native consumer.

In the creation of Pueblo pottery and Navajo weaving, women are grappling with issues of representation. The fixed and stereotypical representation of cultural identity imposed by the process of commodification is being challenged. Women creating these artistic forms are working on ways to represent themselves and their cultures as they create their work. As women create hybrid forms that reflect the confluence of traditional and contemporary imagery, and of their personal visions and group affiliations, their creative work is a site for negotiating and transforming representation. They are using their creativity as a strategy to forge new ways of understanding

themselves, their culture, and the complex interplay of cultural influences in their lives. The artistic forms are embodied sites where women negotiate representation, tradition, and identity. As they reclaim and redefine themselves and their cultures through their work, women create new possibilities and invoke transformation in their lives and the world around them.

NOTES

1. One of the challenges of this study was finding the appropriate name to use to refer to the cultural groups studied. The process of naming can be highly sensitive and problematic. The names used to refer to groups of people in New Mexico have changed over time in response to shifting historical, political, and social circumstances. For groups of people who have experienced repeated cycles of colonization, as is the case for the indigenous people in New Mexico, names reflect the layers of power imposed by one group over another. The names used here reflect the most commonly used terms in northern New Mexico in the late 1990s.

2. The Fred Harvey Company was one of the most successful promoters of the Southwest as a consumer destination. The "Harvey girls," white women from the East and Midwest, were hired as waitresses on the trains to provide an image of "safety" to passengers who were traveling to the "wild" and "exotic" West (Peterson, 1997).

3. The names used here are the artists' real names, used with permission of the artists who participated in the study.

4. The Santa Fe Indian Market, an annual competitive event first organized in 1922 to recover the quality of work produced prior to the impact of tourism, is the largest and most widely known market for the consumption and exchange of Native American artwork in the world. The artwork is juried for admission and judged for prizes. Each artist must have proof of tribal enrollment or documentation of at least one-quarter-Indian blood. The work submitted cannot be mass-produced (Cline, 1998). Other fairs include the Eight Northern Pueblo Art Fair, as well as ones sponsored by particular pueblos such as the Jemez Red Rock Festival.

5. A *kiva* is a ceremonial site at a Pueblo that is used for religious purposes.

6. The photograph that appears here was taken on July 30, 2002, almost 4 years after the original interaction on August 22, 1998. The quality of the original photo was such that it could not be reprinted in this volume. Through a network of Pueblo friends, I found the artist, Eusebia Shije, at her home at Zia Pueblo when I returned on a trip to New Mexico. After I explained the context and content of our first meeting four years earlier, she agreed to retake the picture. As she did not have the type of pot that was "traditional" to carry on one's head, she substituted another pot instead. Interesting, that through this act another level of irony is added to the original incident. Perhaps, in her own subtle way, she is also poking fun at me, the ethnographer who seeks to duplicate the "traditional" pose.

7. Ceramics refers to high production, slip cast pottery made in molds.
8. A *hogan* is a one-room home traditional to Navajo culture. The structure, made of logs, approximates a round shape.

REFERENCES

Anzaldúa, G. (1987). *Borderlands/La frontera: The new mestiza.* San Francisco: Aunt Lute.

Anzaldúa, G. (1990). *Making face, making soul/Haciendo caras: Creative and critical perspectives by feminist women of color.* San Francisco: Aunt Lute.

Aptheker, B. (1989). *Tapestries of life: Women's work, women's consciousness, and the meaning of daily experience.* Amherst: University of Massachusetts Press.

Babcock, B. (1978). *The reversible world: Symbolic inversion in art and society.* Ithaca, NY: Cornell University Press.

Babcock, B. (1997). Mudwomen and whitemen: A meditation on Pueblo potteries. In L. Lamphere, H. Ragoné, & P. Zavella (Eds.), *Situated lives: Gender and culture in everyday life* (pp. 420-439). New York: Routledge.

Batkin, J. (1987). *Pottery of the pueblos of New Mexico, 1700-1940.* Colorado Springs, CO: Taylor Museum of the Colorado Springs Fine Arts Center.

Berkhofer, R. F., Jr. (1978). *The white man's Indian: Images of the American Indian from Columbus to the present.* New York: Knopf.

Borts, A. (1997, March). Personal interview with Autumn Borts (of Santa Clara Pueblo), Taos, NM.

Clifford, J. (1983). On ethnographic authority. *Representation, 1,* 118-146.

Cline, L. (1998, August 19). The critical art of judging Indian Market. *Indian Market: 1998 SWAIA Official Guide, 12.*

Collier, M. J. (1998). Researching cultural identity: Reconciling interpretive and postcolonial perspectives. In D.V. Tanno & A. Gonzáles (Eds.), *Communication and identity across cultures* (pp. 122-147). Thousand Oaks, CA: Sage.

Consumer Interviews. (1998, August 21-23). Personal interviews with anonymous consumers at Indian Market, Santa Fe, NM.

Currier, N. (1999, May 21). Personal interview with Nada Currier, Ramah, NM.

Diaz, R. (1997). Potter Tammy Garcia: Conversation with Rosemary Diaz. *Indian Artist,* Spring, 67-70.

Dillingham, R. (1992). *Acoma and Laguna pottery.* Santa Fe, NM: School of American Research.

Douglas, M. (1966). *Purity and danger.* London: Routledge & Kegan Paul.

Ellis, C., & Bochner, A. P. (Eds.). (1996). *Composing ethnography.* Walnut Creek, CA: AltaMira.

Fiske, J. (1987). *Television culture.* London: Methuen.

Fiske, J. (1993). *Power plays, power works.* London: Methuen.

Gutiérrez, R. A. (1991). *When Jesus came, the corn mothers went away: Marriage, sexuality, and power in New Mexico*, 1500-1846. Stanford, CA: Stanford University Press.

Hall, S. (1997). The work of representation. In S. Hall (Ed.), *Representation: Cultural representation and signifying practices* (pp. 1-74). London: Sage.

Hall, S. (1997). The spectacle of the "other." In S. Hall (Ed.), *Representation: Cultural representation and signifying practices* (pp. 225-279). London: Sage.

Hatcher, E. P. (1967). *Visual metaphors: A methodological study in visual communication*. Albuquerque: University of New Mexico.

hooks, b. (1992). *Black looks: Race and representation*. Boston: South End.

hooks, b. (1992). Eating the other. In *Black looks: Race and representation* (pp. 21-39). Boston: South End.

hooks, b. (1995). *Art on my mind: Visual politics*. New York: New Press.

Howard, K. H., & Pardue, D. F. (1996). *Inventing the Southwest: The Fred Harvey Company and Native American Art*. Flagstaff, AZ: Northland.

José, E. (1999, May 22). Personal interview with Esther José, Ramah, NM.

Kristeva, J. (1982). *Powers of horror*. New York: Columbia University Press.

Lidchi, H. (1997). The poetics and politics of exhibiting other cultures. In S. Hall (Ed.), *Representation: Cultural representation and signifying practices* (pp. 151-222). London: Sage.

Limerick, P. N. (1987). *The legacy of conquest: The unbroken past of the American West*. New York: Norton.

Lindlof, T. R. (1995). *Qualitative communication research methods*. Thousand Oaks, CA: Sage.

MacKinnon, C. A. (1983). Feminism, Marxism, method, and the state: An agenda for theory. In E. Abel & E. K. Abel (Eds.), *The signs reader: Women, gender, and scholarship* (pp. 227-256). Chicago: University of Chicago Press.

Martin, J. N., & Nakayama, T. K. (1997). *Intercultural communication in context*. Mountain View, CA: Mayfield.

Martin, J. N., & Nakayama, T. K. (1999). Thinking dialectically about culture and communication. *Communication Theory, 9*(1), 1-25.

McCannell, D. (1976). *A new theory of the leisure class*. New York: Schocken.

Peterson, S. (1997). *Pottery by American Indian women: The legacy of generations*. New York: Abbeville.

Root, D. (1996). *Cannibal culture: Art, appropriation, and the commodification of difference*. Boulder, CO: Westview.

Said, E. (1978). *Orientalism*. Harmondsworth, UK: Penguin.

Simmons, M. (1977). *New Mexico: An interpretive history*. Albuquerque: University of New Mexico Press.

Tanno, D. V., & Jandt, F. E. (1998). Redefining the "other" in multicultural research. In J. N. Martin, T. K. Nakayama, & L. A. Flores (Eds.), *Readings in cultural contexts* (pp. 447-484). Mountain View, CA: Mayfield.

Trinh, T. M. (1991). *When the moon waxes red: Representation, gender and cultural politics.* New York: Routledge.

Tse Pe, D. (1999, May 10). Personal interview with Dora Tse Pe, San Ildefonso Pueblo, NM.

Willink, R. (1999, April 16). Personal interview with Roseann Willink, Albuquerque, NM.

Wilson, C. (1997). *The myth of Santa Fe.* Albuquerque: University of New Mexico Press.

Yepa, E. (1999, January 23). Personal interview with Emma Yepa, Jemez Pueblo, NM.

Yepa, E. (1999, April 23). Personal interview with Emma Yepa, Jemez Pueblo, NM.

3

Bridge Inscriptions

Transracial Feminist Alliances, Possibilities, and Foreclosures

AIMEE M. CARRILLO ROWE • *University of Iowa*

Racial difference exists as a conundrum for *transracial*[1] feminist alliance formation. While it has long presented a fault line for sisterhood that spans the bounds of race and class, feminist alliances that bridge such boundaries of difference offer a viable routing to higher and more livable ground. The work of bridging—of straddling difference, of striving for empathy, of struggling for social justice—cobbles together radical new meanings of racial difference that hold out the promise of movement. The influential *This Bridge Called My Back: Writings By Radical Women of Color*, written over 20 years ago now, is a collection of poems, prose, stories, and embodied theorization in which radical women of color articulate the position of serving as a "bridge" between various groups. As Rushin (1981) writes in "The Bridge Poem," doing so involves paving the way for understanding, empathy, and even political solidarity among a variety of disparate cultural groups:

> I explain my mother to my father my father to my little sister
> My little sister to my brother my brother to the white feminists
> The white feminists to the Black church folks the Black church folks
> To the ex-hippies the ex-hippies to the Black separatists the
> Black separatists to the artists the artists to my friends' parents (p. xxi)

AUTHOR'S NOTE: I am indebted to the women in this study. This piece would not have been possible without the time, honesty, and vulnerability of the women who spoke with me. I also want to thank Sheena Malhotra, Daniel Gross, Takis Poulokis, Patricia Washington, and Heal for their careful and impassioned readings of this manuscript. Thank you, also, to Mary Jane Collier and the *Annual*'s reviewers and editorial staff for pushing me to be clear.

The transformative possibilities that reside within bridgework are no less salient today than they were 20 years ago with regard to productively working across lines of difference in ways that reconfigure those lines, as well as the political and affective investments of those who would be bound by them. In her recent autobiography, Becky Thompson, a white lesbian mother of a black son, writes of her experience with transgressing racial borders and her son's reaching out through his blackness to understand her lesbianism as forms of "bridgework." She describes it as "how knowing about one oppression can, in some situations, lead people to want to learn about other oppressions" (Thompson, 2000, p. 129). Allen (2000) provides a portrait of an alliance and an intimate, empathic, and affective context for understanding homophobia in a way that runs deeper than did the abstract conception of the struggles gays face that she held prior to knowing Anna, her ally in authenticity. Out of their intimate relationship, each has become an ally and an advocate for the "other." Allen tells us how homophobia has become her struggle, something that she sees as directly relating to her life, because of her personal and political investments in Anna's daily struggles as a lesbian.

On the other hand, transracial feminist alliance formation comes at a dear price and carries a heavy burden that is unequally distributed across differently racialized backs. What really can be gained, after all, through a series of movements in the direction of each other? Centuries of pain, anger, betrayal, injustice, guilt, and shame leave the sociopolitical terrain scarred, war torn, and hardly livable. Who wants to go there? When academic women speak—at conferences, in corridors, in e-mail conversations, and in coffeehouses—these are the words that emerge between the lines: "So many pitfalls, so much pain. Don't want to step onto a landmine buried in some other woman's body, or my own, or in the space in-between us. Worlds travel in a glance. Step aside. Prove your solidarity. Forgive me . . . . I can't forgive you the history that has made us. Forgive yourself. I can't, I'm bleeding, I'm dying, I want something solid. The fissures of difference run deep. Step out onto that bridge and you might just fall through the cracks."

Feminists of color have consistently published poetry, prose, and theory agitating for a heartfelt white feminist grappling with racism and race-based privilege (Alexander & Mohanty, 1997; Anzaldúa, 1990; Bannerji, 1995; Combahee River Collective, 1983; Córdova, 1998; Guy-Sheftall, 1995; hooks, 1992, 1995; Hurtado, 1996; Hurtado & Stewart, 1997; Johnson Reagon, 1998; Mohanty, 1991; Moraga & Anzaldúa, 1981; Moya, 1997). These authors point to the work white women must do in order to

become viable allies, in order to step onto the bridge and co-occupy that slippery terrain with racialized sisters. Many of these texts implore white feminists to share the burden of being "bridges" (Moraga & Anzaldúa, 1981) across cultural, racial, gender, national, and class lines—for this burden falls disproportionately on the backs of women of color.[2]

While the voices of women of color have audibly expressed discontent with feminism's whiteness for the past two decades, relatively few white women have seriously wrestled with the implications of these critiques as laying the groundwork for a "more possible" (Lorde, 1984, p. 103) feminism.[3] And yet, for those who have taken up this challenge to become bridge people through their written work and lived practices, their lives (their identities, their relationships to whiteness, their affective investments in relations of domination and resistance) have been altered (Bulkin, Pratt, & Smith, 1984; Frankenberg, 1993, 1996, 1997; Harris, 2000; Moon, 1999; Russo, 1991; Segrest, 1994; Thompson, 1996, 2000). The presence of transracial alliances often anchors a process of transformation that goes beyond intellectual understandings of power and privilege and moves into the realm of embodied knowing. Russo (1991) recounts that "for many years as an active feminist I thought issues of race and class were important to deal with in the women's movement, yet until I began to work and hang out with women of color, I did not fully understand the enormous ramifications of multiracial groups of women developing feminist theory and working together for social change" (p. 297). Frankenberg (1996) echoes Russo's account when she writes:

> What I do know is that, by going where Estée went, meeting who she met, part of the time living with whom she lived with and, I might add, raising all manner of questions from those around us—were we lovers? Was I brainwashed? What *were* we to each other?—my worldview, my sense of self and other, of history, identity, race, class, culture, were remade. (p. 12)

The discursive fields of intercultural communication and feminism stand to be transformed when academic feminists dwell in bridge spaces through the formation of transracial feminist alliances. But institutional structures and modes of relationality are racially encoded in ways that circumscribe social relations, often foreclosing the emergence of affective bonds that span racial boundaries. Racial difference remains a stubborn tripwire that makes the bridge inaccessible to many, if not most, of the folks who need to step out (Alexander & Mohanty, 1997; Anzaldúa, 1990; Bannerji, 1995; Combahee River Collective, 1983; Córdova, 1998; Guy-Sheftall, 1995;

hooks, 1992, 1995; Hurtado, 1996; Hurtado & Stewart, 1997; Johnson Reagon, 1998; Mohanty, 1991; Moraga & Anzaldúa, 1981; Moya, 1997). This chapter tracks such failed moments in an effort to unearth the logics at work and the affective investments at play that keep feminists bounded on differently racialized shores, divided by an abyss that is our colonial legacy, and poised to reproduce it. My hope is that ever more thorough and impassioned wranglings with these logics and investments that naturalize feminist separation can move us to the edge and help us to leap out into the abyss.

Bridgework happens as we cultivate vulnerable communication practices in order to know each other. As Albrecht and Brewer (1990) write in their introduction to *Bridges of Power: Women's Multicultural Alliances*, "We believe that the boundaries of doubt, pain, and fear can be overcome. If we are to successfully mediate these boundaries, it is critical that we listen and respect each other, learn about our differences, and make ourselves vulnerable" (p. 6).

My conversations with a number of differently situated academic feminists—my initial "reading" of them, and now my reflections on these various moments of ethnographic practice in their "vulnerability" (Behar, 1996)—provide the context to wrangle with transracial alliance formation in this chapter. The ensuing section is my effort—as ethnographer, cultural critic, and spiritual seeker—to attune my reader to the nature of the ethnographic inquiry in which I am engaged, which strives toward a bridge methodology. It is a set of practices in an ongoing process in which I strive to dwell on/as a bridge, take stock, reflect, write—all with a sense of awe at the prospect that structuring patterns may be disrupted, even dislodged. From the positionality of striving-toward-bridge I turn toward some moments that arose within several conversations in which possibilities for transracial alliance formation are foreclosed. Here disruption and dislodging remain at the level of prospects of potential in-between—not yet realized. I seek to render visible the roadblocks that prevent transracial alliance formations from taking hold; I focus on a textured engagement with pieces of the wall that stand between shores and become obstacles to the bridges.

DWELLING IN THOSE VULNERABLE SPACES IN-BETWEEN: TOWARD A BRIDGE METHODOLOGY

Is it possible to forge convergences between the theoretico-political aims of transracial feminist alliance formation and the research practices that frame

that inquiry? I seek here for a moment that might be signified as "vulnerability."[4] By vulnerability I mean placing myself within the text as an embodied, complicated, and invested author in ways that seek to displace and mark traditional authorizing functions. The aim is not just to challenge canonical forms of ethnographic inquiry through positioning myself as "researcher," but to place my-self within the kind of critical inquiry that strives to manifest the very subject of inquiry within the text: transracial feminist alliance formation. In other words, "Vulnerability doesn't mean that anything personal goes. The exposure of the self who is also a spectator has to take us somewhere we couldn't otherwise get to" (Behar, 1996, p. 14). The "somewhere" that I seek to evoke in these pages is a space of connection that spans racial boundaries and registers moments of lost opportunity to do so. The difficulty in such traversing involves recognizing, naming, and locating strategies to rectify power imbalances. Vulnerability provides a mechanism that redefines power as "a process in which people transform themselves personally and collectively" by rendering visible the linkages between the personal and the political, by mapping the "self" as author as "vitally connected to others" (Albrecht & Brewer, 1990, p. 5). My aim is to conduct and evaluate conversations with differently situated feminists from a positionality *in-process* that strives-toward-bridge and from here read glimpses of bridge potential and defeat. In other words, I strive to dwell in a space of connection in ways that reveal moments of such striving in others and to make stark the predominant moments of disconnect.

Approaching and reapproaching this work vulnerably means reveling in the limits of my own "uni-versity"[5] education, my cultural training in white bonding, my assimilated Mexican American heritage scripted as "Spanish," and my enculturation as woman. Navigating boundaries constitutes and troubles my author-ity.[6] My motivation for theorizing transracial feminist alliance formation is guided by both a radicalizing gesture within intercultural and feminist modes of inquiry and a selfish desire to map a locality in which I can res(is)t[7] among all of my conflicted positionalities. "Home" is an uneasy locale for people like me. Queer by association and the forms of my intimate affiliations, but not clearly marked as lesbian other, my "lesbian-ness" is contingent: (un)marked by those with whom I affiliate. White by cultural, familial, and chromatic productions of assimilation and privilege but Chicana according to maternal genealogy and politics, my racial identity moves and slides in ways over which I am not always in control. As Cherríe Moraga (1996) writes in her reflections on her own shifting and mixed-race positionality, "We light-skinned breeds are like chameleons, those *lagartijas* with the capacity to change the color of their

skins. We change not for lack of conviction, but lack of definitive shade and shape" (p. 232). Living in the spaces in between identity categories, I feel like I am constantly in flux. Lacking a concrete identity from which to move into politicized communities, meanings of "I" shift between contexts and communities. The mobility I acquire as privilege to navigate as insider within hegemonic sociopolitical and institutional structures often feels at cross-purposes with my politics, so that I seek modes of resistance; I erupt in such settings through discursive and affiliative gestures that "other" me. At other times, I hold my tongue and retain covert status, seeking information and access in ways that I hope will be used for ulterior purposes.

In the face of these forces I seek courage to say something that doesn't quite fit within traditional or even critical feminist or intercultural epistemologies, and that allows the space for something beyond, or to the side of, analysis and reified knowledge to emerge. I write in the wake of Visweswaran's (1994) move to blur the distinction between ethnography and fiction. If my project "sets out to build a believable world," then it, "like fiction, no matter its pretense to present a self-contained narrative or cultural whole, remains incomplete and detached from the realism to which it points" (p. 1). Even if something called vulnerability functions as a discourse of fetishized affective interpellation, I wish to draw upon this space for courage to build bridges toward a new fiction of feminist ethnography of cultural difference that operates at the limit of social science to begin to think the unthinkable question.[8] I seek to create a text that might be a "companion" to my readers across racial lines.

> Since we are not looking for a perfect analysis, but we are looking for the mark of vulnerability which makes a great text not an authority generating a perfect narrative, but our own companion, as it were, so we can share our own vulnerabilities with those texts and move. (Spivak, 1990, p. 27)

My readings of the "data"[9] in the following sections are motivated, not neutral. I write "myself" here at least as much as I write the women with whom I spoke for this study. Indeed, what I write here is to mark a moment in an ongoing set of relations among women of various positionalities as we work them out with each other. My mixed-race identity status motivates me, in part, to differentiate myself from the "white women" I describe and produce below in an effort to establish my own racialized authenticity—as one who sees and thus marks *their* whiteness. And in doing so, I also seek to disrupt the force of white bonding that constitutes whiteness. As Hurtado writes of "solidarity" among white folks:

Although whiteness, to them, is natural and although few can articulate the privilege that whiteness brings, most can detect when whiteness is being questioned and its privilege potentially dismantled. Therefore, solidarity on the basis of whiteness will have to be fully understood and dismantled for the deconstruction of race privilege to continue. (Hurtado, 1996, p. 149)

A work in process, as I re-face this manuscript I am compelled to examine my totalizing critiques of white women. This work entails (at least) two gestures: (re)reading the interviews with more nuance (and love) and examining my own desire to produce them as monolithically problematic. This opportunity to reflect has pushed me to recognize how my anger at the injustices of whiteness, and my desire to distance myself from the practices and privileges that accompany whiteness and to repudiate the white woman who I am and am not, are the forces that constitute my reading. I say this not to discount or undermine the legitimacy of my critique, or to trivialize the affective responses that drive it, but to situate the reading in context, to own my-self as active agent, and to mark this investigation *as process*—a striving to dwell in bridge spaces, failing, reflecting, trying again. I am already not the "I" who initially wrote this piece in 2000 but emerge as refracted through the writing-review-reflection-rewriting itself. A white lesbian Southerner colleague, Blanche Boyd, used to ask me in response to my research, "What did you do with your anger?" I could not answer her question when she posed it in 2000. Now I see what she must have seen all along: that my anger was manifest as the totalized "white women" that my own text reified and that the "data" for me to do so came from their words. Does the anger with which my reading was inflected discredit the analysis that arose? Is the dispassionate eye a necessary component of crafting a rhetorically effective criticism? I want to push for a space to the left of dispassion, a legitimate critical space *even as,* or *especially because,* it comes from an invested and impassioned space—a critique that invites dialogue because it is situated within the rhythms of my own anger.

Scene

In 1999 I conducted 28 face-to-face interviews with academic "feminists" from colleges and universities all over the United States. These women self-selected their participation by responding to an e-mail seeking interviews with "academic feminists" who are interested in how race relates to feminist alliance formation (see Appendix A). The letter called for "interviewees for my study of how academic feminists form alliances,

particularly within the academy," emphasizing that "my work draws on that by scholars who seek to understand the dynamics of how race, national origin, ethnicity, and class function in feminist alliance formation." I sent the e-mail to friends, colleagues, and listservs. The letter chained out as individuals and groups forwarded the letter to others, so it is difficult to know, ultimately, how widely received the e-mail was. But I do know that it produced an enthusiastic response from a number of academic women from a variety of racial, class, sexual, and institutional backgrounds, who e-mailed me stating their interest in interviewing with me and/or to raise concerns about my study. No men responded to my e-mail, and I did not seek out any specific cultural group.

I asked each woman the same questions (see Appendix B) in order to create spaces to discuss her understandings of her own practices with regard to four primary themes: career history, alliances, feminism, and identity. The first line of questioning moved from her current academic rank to stories of her career trajectory; next we transitioned to "alliances" in relation to her institutional mobility, then more broadly to how each woman conceptualized alliances and with whom she allied herself. We then moved to a discussion of "feminism," what it meant to her in academic contexts, and how it informed her alliance formation; finally, we discussed her interpretations of their identities as well as mine.

Although I used my interview questions to broadly structure my interviews, I also strayed from the text to follow up on interesting comments, to disclose something of myself, or at times to disagree with my conversation partner. In other words, I tried to have a conversation with the women, not merely ask them a series of questions. I did this as much to put myself at ease as for them. I was not comfortable with a dry, "objective" interview style. But my ability to interact, joke, follow up, and merely connect with the women I met varied according to the overlaps and gaps in our generation, personality, race and antiracist politics, and intellectual interests. I agree with Bloom (1998) when she writes that "subjectivity is also thought to be nonunitary or active and continually in the *process* of production within historical, social and cultural boundaries. . . . It is produced both *collectively* and *relationally* (pp. 4-5, emphasis added). Because my positionality emerged in relation to the women with whom I spoke, I was never "the same" from interview to interview. I was continually produced by the "micropolitics of the research interactions and the macropolitics of societal inequality" (Lal, 1996, p. 197) within each interview context, by each woman's response to "me," who she knew that I knew, and the questions I raised.

I transcribed the interviews with the assistance of three undergraduates from the Department of Women Studies at the University of Washington. I read and reread the transcripts in an effort to detect recursive themes. I then cut and pasted quotes that illustrated such themes into a separate set of documents under a variety of headings (such as "women of color disenchantment," "sexual attractiveness," "reading me," "multicultural allies"). Recursive themes were clustered in a way that enabled me to examine the relationships among different women's articulations of a theme. Then I wrote sets of theoretical frameworks to provide some coherence to the "data."

Vital Statistics[10]

All of the interview subjects are women. I asked them to describe how they identify in terms of race, class, ethnicity, national origin, and sexual orientation (Appendix B). According to their own identifications, eighteen women are white, one is white Jewish; five are black; two are Chicana; one is Filipina; one is Cherokee; and one is Asian. Of the white women, six identified as coming from working-class or lower middle-class backgrounds, four from upper middle-class backgrounds, the remainder from the middle class; three identified as lesbians, one as bisexual, four as "straight" in terms of dating partners but a bit queer or fluid in their approach to and/or experience of sexuality (these women often had queer friends, passed as lesbians, and/or thought that sexuality could not be easily captured within categories such as "lesbian" or "straight"), and the rest as heterosexual; one identified as an "antiracist white woman." Four of the black women said they are from working-class families, one said she was from a middle-class background; two identified as lesbians, the others as heterosexual. Both Chicanas identified as heterosexual; one described her socioeconomic background as working class (her mother was a domestic worker), the other described hers as middle class (her father was an attorney). The Filipina described herself as straight and from a middle-class, "assimilated" family. The Cherokee woman said she had reclaimed her racial identity but was not raised in an "Indian" tradition. The Asian woman identified as bisexual and described her family as upper middle class.

The academic positionings of these women vary a great deal, although they fall somewhat predictably along racial lines. Of the eighteen white women, nine hold currently or had held administrative positions, six are full professors, two assistant professors, and three graduate students. The white women who hold or held administrative positions are from a variety of class positions, but most are from a similar generation (they received their

doctoral degrees in the 60s and 70s), which suggests that class does not necessarily bar white women from securing institutional status. With the exception of one African American woman, who is the chair of her department, none of the women of color hold, held, or even hoped to hold positions of institutional authority. Of the black women, three are assistant professors, two are full professors; the Chicanas are both full professors; the Filipina, an assistant professor; the Cherokee, a full professor; the Asian, an assistant professor.

I cannot emphasize enough the huge disparity in meanings, institutional positionings, and lived experiences that these rigid categories of race, class, gender, sexuality, and institutional status ignore, thus rendering such categories practically useless. For instance, the respondent from a middle-class Chicana family has little in common—spiritually, socially, relationally—with the white women from the same class. Living in the United States as a racialized woman almost renders irrelevant the class connections that she and her white middle-class counterparts might be said to share. Rather, her connections to the world remain predominantly articulated around race, often in the form of political, spiritual, and intellectual endeavors. Nonetheless, her class positioning has enabled her ability to speak as an "articulate other" in white academia, although she says that this is not who she "really" is and that white academics are always surprised, or awestruck, when she speaks Spanish or finds other ways to break white cultural codes of conduct. This is to say that any "sameness" that may connect women of similar categorical positionings is swamped by the complexity of "differentness" that overdetermines each woman's identity. Nonetheless, these vital statistics frame the life experiences, varied career mobilities, and alliances that these women form, even if the complexity of each woman's story and struggles cannot be adequately captured by any of these identity categories. These categories, however clunky and potentially reifying, do reveal certain patterns among groups and thus provide a point of entry to understand the relational gestures that unify and divide them.

COLLISION COURSE: MAPPING
THE POLITICS OF (UN)KNOWING

I looked for moments in which white women and women of color talk about each other in search of bridge possibilities and blockades. My sense is that bridges are opened up when lines of communication that provide information, critique, and reflection are forged.

It is essential that radical feminists confront their fear of and resistance to each other, because without this, there *will* be no bread on the table. . . . The real power, as you and I know, is collective. I can't afford to be afraid of you, nor you of me. If it takes head-on collisions, let's do it; this polite timidity is killing us. (Moraga & Anzaldúa, 1981, p. 34)

I am taking the risk "head-on" here, of "speaking for others" (Alcoff, 1995) and interpreting their words, in ways that aim to render visible the issues that I believe keep the women with whom I met divided from those with whom they would build bridges. Some of the excerpts cited below provide glimpses of bridge potential—an alternative route here, a newly paved road there—that point in the direction of the in-between. And yet the preponderance mark moments of foreclosure of possibilities of transracial feminist alliance formation—the roadblocks, detours, and dead-ends that arose among differently situated women.[11]

Power imbalances make the terrain on various shores difficult to bridge. It would, perhaps, be less complicated to forge such connections among cultural groups who shared equal access to institutional power. However, there tended to be an institutional disparity between the white women and the women of color with whom I met. For this reading, this unevenness means that it is inadequate to merely place the voices of white women and women of color up against each other to map points of convergence and divergence, although that is part of my effort here. Rather, it means attending to the complex ways in which power inflects every conversation, and every evocation of another.

Above I established the notion that the distinction of the public and private spheres is a stumbling block to bridgework. I suggested that redefining power—not as "power over," but as power as "power with"—is central to bridgework (Albrecht & Brewer, 1990). The kind of power that I saw operating across racial lines was often swamped by "power over" structural forces and modes of relationality because this is the nature of the institutional power that separates these women. Thus if white women tend to hold more of it than women of color in academia, the uneven relations that emerge in such contexts remain a roadblock to bridgework.

What my reading of the conversations reveals is the tension that arises between these two forms of power. On the one hand, there are moments that reveal potential connections and practices that supercede institutional power. On the other hand, there are moments in which institutional power provides a distancing mechanism that maintains white women's "power over" women of color. The latter is the "fall back" mode, one that keeps

white women at an arm's distance from women of color, so that they do not *feel* the anger, pain, and disappointment that arise from racialized struggles in academia. In my conversations there was a certain kind of "(un)knowing" that went on, based in disavowal and contradiction, that (re)produces and relies upon certain stereotypic ways of knowing that are part and parcel of public (as opposed to intimate) productions of racialized identities. This interplay creates a cycle of imbalance that is contingent upon a "power over" form of power and that can become destabilized only through the enactment of "power with" forms of power.

If white women, by and large, hold more institutional power than women of color, then this dynamic shapes the conditions under which alliances form, or fail to do so, on uneven terrain. It positions these white women as a gateway through which some women of color must pass in order to secure institutional access. This dynamic functions as white female "power over" women of color, so that women of color must capitulate to it in order to gain institutional access. It provides a context for recognizing why the burden of bridgework falls predominantly on the backs of women of color, as noted above. I draw on the voices of several women here to trace moments of this cycle.

For instance, Cheryl, an African American feminist who is a chair of her department, faced challenges in her struggles to forge alliances with white feminists, who in this case held institutional power over the publication of her work. She says that in order to get her work published, she of necessity

> *became* a part of that [white women's] network. I would say that before actually making that effort, it was very difficult, I was having a difficult time. I came out of a Ph.D. program where I was nurtured and where my ideas were appreciated. . . . And I was validated in my Ph.D. program and so I thought, "this is what women do for each other." Then I came out and submitted a piece of my dissertation to [a particular journal] . . . but people were looking through white women's eyes and white women's experiences . . . and I got some fairly nasty reviews back from feminists.

Her successful negotiation through the "white women's network" points to some potential spaces for transracial alliance formation: This negotiation resulted in making her life less "difficult." In this excerpt her emphasis on her agency, that she "*became* a part of that network," illustrates that sheer determination to affiliate with this network can open up spaces of connection. In other words, if she carries the burden of bridgework on her back, she may forge connections with this network. Yet she juxtaposed this network with her graduate school experience, which she described as one in

which she was "nurtured" and "where her ideas were appreciated." The institutional power held by the white women to whom she refers (as journal editors and reviewers) provides the political frame in which "power over" seems to overshadow the affiliative possibilities for intimate and more "nurturing" connections to emerge.

Such incidents, in which relations based on sharing "power with" are foreclosed by relations overdetermined by "power over," can create a situation in which stereotypic knowledge emerges. Maya, an Asian woman of "immigrant" status and currently an assistant professor, describes a situation in which her noncitizen status became the grounds for her feeling like a "criminal" in her interactions with her white feminist department chair. She explains that "there's just this certain way it has an ability to reduce me. No rights, no nothing. . . . If I can work, I can take care of myself. But if you don't let me, I am dependent and I become criminal." While Maya feels that the bureaucratic entanglements surrounding her effort to work outside of the bounds of her contract could have been avoided if the chair had not gone entirely "by the book," she felt like "the scum of the earth" for asking her chair to "take a risk" for her. "There I am, the scum of the earth, because I'm basically putting at risk, however minimally, or asking more . . . [than] the next person who walked through the door would have had to ask [voice rising, holding back tears]."

In this example, the chair's gestures toward building a bridge (she *does* work *with* Maya to find alternative summer employment) are undermined by her failure to act in this situation in ways that are based in a deep understanding of the unevenness of the playing field. The chair, according to Maya, fails to recognize this unevenness because of her investment in an undifferentiated notion of equality: "She was unable to see that my not being a citizen positioned me differently than everyone else and she wanted to treat everyone the same, which disadvantaged me in comparison with others." This ideology, then, *positions* Maya to *have to* "ask more than the next person who walked in the door"; sometimes treating people "equally" perpetuates inequality. The uneven power relations between Maya and her chair position Maya as dependent upon her chair in ways that leave her feeling dehumanized by the stereotypic logic ("alien = criminal") through which she feels her noncitizen body and practices are being decoded (Anzaldúa, 1987; Bannerji, 1995; Bhattacharjee, 1997; Carrillo Rowe, 1999; Ó Tuathail, 1996; Saldívar, 1997). Her institutional disempowerment, at both the university and national levels, contributes to a context in which she is forced to "ask more than the next person who walked through the door would have to ask." Her chair did not seem to recognize at an affective

level the shame and struggle that Maya faces as "noncitizen" in this situation. Rather, her actions seem to reflect an imaginary that remains bound within the institutionalized logic of "the book" that adjudicates justice on terms that assume undifferentiated citizenship.

Stereotypic knowledge is both a default position, enabled by the lack of intimate knowledge of one another between white women and women of color, and a mechanism for the active subordination of women of color. In the case of the latter, bridge possibilities are foreclosed. For instance, Michele (a black, lesbian, assistant professor from a working-class background) describes the way in which her black body is read as threatening to some white women, including her students and her chair. In addition to dealing with the stereotypes of black women as either desexed "mammy" or overly sexualized "Jezebel," black women must also confront the general stereotype of the violent black (see Collins, 1990). This depiction is often associated with black masculinity and has been used to justify violence against black men, including lynching, for their uncontrollably animal sexual appetites for white women (Bederman, 1995). The image of the "matriarch" also depicts her as sexually aggressive, but only vis-à-vis her own people; her rage is not depicted as directed at whites.

Consider an incident Michele describes:

> When I'm angry, I talk very slow and very direct. The words come out syllable by syllable. But my voice does not go up. It just doesn't. . . . So there are things in my evaluation like, "She yelled at a student' or "She screamed at us." I just, it just doesn't add up. Even when I'm angry I don't yell. It's ludicrous.

She goes on to describe how some of her students (whom she later reveals to be white women) went to her chair, also a white woman, to complain about Michele's frightening and aggressive personae. Michele's chair did not support her, siding "with the students, although she'd never been in my classroom. Never." So Michele decided to videotape herself teaching so that she could protect herself from the charges in an effort to provide "objective" evidence of her interactions with students. But her chair (after a second complaint by the students) prohibited her from doing so. Why couldn't Michele tape her own class? Would the "objective" evidence of video footage, which could be a "legitimate" challenge within institutional registers, threaten to dismantle a comfort zone of white solidarity based in stereotypic knowledge?

This example renders visible the violence through which the black female body emerges within the white imaginary as frightening, as well as the

uneven institutional positionings that frame and are produced by this imaginary, enabling a solidarity of whiteness that circumvents the potential alliance between Michele and her chair. Instead, the chair sides with the students *against* Michele around the theme of the threatening black female body. Michele foregrounds the importance of recognizing the violence through which her body is being decoded when she states, "You have to get people to admit they're scared of the stereotype. A black woman hitting them or something. . . . 'Excuse me, I haven't hit anybody lately!' [laughs] . . . What are they scared I'm gonna do? There's nothing they can name that is actually scaring them." Michele's comment foregrounds the fact that there is no legitimate basis for their fear of her, but that they are "scared of a stereotype." Yet the investment in this fear is so powerful that evidence which would challenge the stereotype of dangerous black femininity is literally excluded from the realm of discourse.

This theme recurs in the discussions of several women of color, particularly black women, and it constitutes the problematic and uneven ground upon which bridgework must take place. Donna shared a series of stories that echo Michele's. She recounts a situation in which she and another black woman encountered similar stereotypic treatment in spite of the fact that they are very different individuals. She describes this black woman as very different from her: She [softly] depicts herself as "kind of loud," short, heavy-set, laid back; while she depicts the other woman as "tall and very slim . . . [with a] calm, or soft-voiced kind of demeanor." In spite of the differences in their personalities, they "got the same thing . . . students were really afraid of [them] and it really upset her." She concludes this discussion with much puzzlement: "I don't know what it's about, this fear. I certainly sense it with white women. . . . There's always a fear that the black woman will overtake them. That we're rather vicious. There's a part of me that just doesn't know, in the academy, I don't know what it is." It is difficult to ascertain "what it is." These narratives are certainly overdetermined with traces of stereotypes about blackness and black femininity, but they also raise questions around white guilt, white anxiety, and white centrality (she entertains the possibility that white women "fear that the black woman will overtake them").

This anxiety, then, becomes the burden of women of color to dissipate, which, as the above illustrations depict, is in most cases an impossible burden. It also frames the struggle that Cheryl faced when she "*became* part of that network" as an African American woman. It is difficult to assert a relationship of "power with" when those relations are so thoroughly inscribed in structural and relational modes of "power over." Much of the

work to move beyond stereotypic knowledge must come from white women with a full awareness of the propensity toward fixing women of color within these modes of knowing, and of the uneven institutional power relations that give them "power over" women of color. Subservience by women of color must not be a precondition for transracial alliance formation, and yet such performances may feel most comfortable to white women in a culture that functions largely through a "power over" mode of interactions with stereotyped others. Consider the following excerpt from Emily, a middle-class white woman who is a full professor, which depicts the kind of black woman with whom she wants to develop a relationship.

> I get e-mails all the time from [an African American woman], she's just that kind of person. I don't know, I'll see her at conferences and she just hugs me and gives me a kiss on the cheek and I don't really know her that well, but I just feel that she exudes this positive spirit that I just love. I would LOVE to get to know her better. But it's. . . . I like that, I like that a lot! [Laughing] I wish more people were like her!

Emily articulates an important gesture toward transracial alliance formation: an enthusiastic *desire* to "get to know" her African American colleague. She reports that while she has no allies of color, she wants to open up her life to women of color so that she can "learn from their experiences." My sense is that she *wants to* experience the transformative possibilities of transracial alliance formation, like those of Frankenberg (1996) and Russo (1991), in which they were transformed by their affective ties to women of color. And yet she does not seem to recognize that she is imposing particular modes of relating and conditions for bridge possibilities in ways that may *preclude* the kind of intimate connections she seeks. In this excerpt she depicts herself as comfortable with this woman because she e-mails her and "hugs [her] and gives [her] a kiss on the cheek" when they see each other. The relationship she evokes resonates with that of a white woman and a "mammy," in which the "mammy" is always happy to see the white woman; she is concerned with the white woman's emotional well-being and never her own; the white woman is safe because the "mammy" "knows her place" (Collins, 1990). As long as her comfort level with transracial alliance formation is contingent upon even subtle forms of subordination of "women of color," the social order of "power over" cannot be challenged.

My sense is that this imaginary for transracial connection, then, cannot move into the realm of intimate connection and "power with" modes of relating. It keeps women of color in the position of carrying the burden of

bridging on their backs. Further, the woman in this story *has* taken on Emily's burden of comfort for relational affiliation, and yet the alliance has not yet emerged. While she would "LOVE to get to know her better," Emily drops this impulse with a sudden, disjunctive, "But it's. . . ." perhaps signifying a moment of recognition of the disjuncture of desire and repudiation that runs through the heart of her narrative.

This is just one example of the form of "(un)knowing" that I allude to above, here the nonrecognition of the stereotypic knowledge that would form the implausible basis of transracial alliance formation. Below I trace a few excerpts from conversations with white women in which "(un)knowing" emerges as contingent upon the submersion of their own "knowing." In other words, these excerpts reveal a simultaneous knowing and unknowing, or disavowal of the full contents of that knowing. For instance, I asked the white women with whom I met if their career advancement was "more smooth or relatively difficult compared to what they know of the stories of women of color." Several responded that they did not know about the experiences of women of color. And yet, later in the interview many either shared a story of the struggles of women of color or expressed amazement that women of color could survive in academia at all. As Emily states:

> You know, I really don't know because I don't have anybody's story. You know, a lot of people don't tell you their story unless something really crappy happens that they'll just come out. You know, I don't know people's story. I mean I don't know a group of men's stories; I don't know a group of women's stories. So I mean it's not a matter of not knowing women of color's stories, I don't know people's stories. It's . . . I find that the stories of injustice unless you're right there and its in your yard, its in your house, that [pause], you don't find out about it.

Here, in a gesture of disavowal, she moves the discussion *away* from the topic of the intersection between racial and gender subordination in a way that levels the playing field of "crappy" things when she says, "I don't know people's stories." She also raises the issue of intimate ways of knowing when she states that "unless you're right there and it's in your yard, it's in your house that [pause] you don't find out about it." That is exactly the issue: This disavowal is contingent upon her capacity to keep women of color at an arm's distance, or to maintain any relationships she shares with women of color as "professional" or public, as opposed to personal. If one's department is not one's "yard," then what is? The maintenance of this distinction, then, enables her to see herself and her own struggles as separate from and unrelated to women of color and their struggles.

Does this excerpt contain a moment of possible intervention? I want to call attention to the pause: It arises at the (dis)juncture between "your yard," representing the intimate sphere, and "you don't find out about it," representing (un)knowing. The pause signifies a flickering of recognition that something is not right in the separation that it seeks to span.

As it turns out, Emily *does* know "somebody's story." She shares an incident in which a woman of color in her department was involved in a tenure struggle. Her narration leaves unclear if, how, and in what capacity she may have acted as an ally to this woman in the department's decisions in that case. However, it does suggest that the relationship has become strained in its wake, over which she seems to experience a sense of *loss,* but she does not seem to know what to do to repair the relationship. Thus the distancing gesture that enables (un)knowing leaves Emily *not* knowing what to do to (re)connect with her colleague, and the cycle of foreclosed bridges turns over again.

This theme also arises in Deborah's discussion, in which early on she claims that she doesn't know stories of women of color, that there aren't "enough data" about women of color stories.

> There have just been so few women of color at *any* of the institutions that I have been involved with. We just now have, in our department, we have two assistant professors who are, um, African American women, so um, it's just so little experience, um, I mean I know a few people at other institutions but always, you know part, only know part of those studies, so you know, I just don't have enough data.

First, like Emily, she disavows knowledge of the struggles of women of color when she says, "there have just been so few women of color at *any* of the institutions that I have been involved with." A bit later in our conversation she shares a story that contradicts this disavowal and reveals her knowing:

> This is gonna be grossly stereotyped, but the African American women that I live with, in the department that, ahh, I don't know how they make it from day to day, and I don't know how to deal with that other than the little ways that I do help with that. I mean you know, the whole society has to change [laughs] and so you do that little thing and this little thing, but you can't solve the big problems.

Why would Deborah first suggest that she lacks "experience" with women of color because "there have just been so few" of them at "*any* of the institutions" that she's worked at, and then go on to say that there are African American women who are struggling in her own department? This

disjuncture points to some kind of dissonance between knowing and disavowal. As with Emily's story, in which she claims a lack of intimate knowledge because no women of color are in her "yard," Deborah seems to struggle with how to speak about the proximity of the struggles of the African American women in her own department. They are simultaneously there and not there, visible and invisible.

Her fear of "stereotyping" African American women becomes a mechanism for maintaining a distance from them and negating her knowledge of their struggles. She ultimately admits that she does not know "how they make it from day to day," stating that she does not "know how to deal with that other than the little ways" that she can "help." She concludes with the observation that the "whole society has to change." Her final comments seem to reflect her own perceived powerlessness to affect, or unwillingness to join in, struggles for racial justice. If "the whole society has to change," and the best she can do is to "help" in "little ways"—then perhaps her disavowal of knowledge of the struggles of women of color arises out of a broader paralysis in the face of dismantling racism.

And why does she frame her knowledge as "grossly stereotyped," while she shares her lack of "data" without comment? Is the risk of knowing in ways that evoke stereotypes of members of marginalized groups greater than that of disavowing knowledge of their struggles? What is at stake for transracial feminist alliances in this (un)knowing? My sense is that this contradiction in Deborah's talk reveals a deep paradox that constitutes transracial relations and makes bridgework so daunting. Because full knowing, for white women, entails coming face to face with the unnamed normalcy of stereotypic knowing, it seems (as in Deborah's example) that knowing and stereotypic knowing become one and the same. Thus to deny knowing is the only way to avoid admitting that one knows stereotypically. Yet if the bodies of women of color are decoded within hegemonic settings through stereotypic tropes, as in the "controlling images" outlined above—white women must acknowledge that they are not outside of the white racist imaginary, but rather, that they are continually disciplined into the folds of white solidarity. As Michele exclaims above, "You have to get people to admit they're scared of the stereotype." Reading women of color through such stereotypic ways of knowing is one of many mechanisms through which self and other are defined. And yet stereotypic knowing relies upon disavowal, or *un*knowing, which means that what may be required in order to begin the work of dismantling stereotypic (un)knowing is for white women to admit that they are "scared of the stereotype." In other words, to admit that they do not really know women of color in an intimate way. To

own their (un)knowledge may be the first step in forming new and more intimate forms of knowledge.

If part of the work of building bridges is coming to terms with the relationship between the "self" and its vital connection to others, then full knowing for white women, such as Deborah, entails an examination of *their* relationship to their own sense of powerlessness in the face of a "whole society" that "must change." Unacknowledged, the paradox of (un)knowing becomes a mechanism of deferral, foreclosing the work of tackling injustice "head on." It enables a cycle in which stereotypic knowledge and disavowal replace full knowing, which, in turn, (re)produces distanced relations among feminists across racial lines. As in the cases of Emily and Deborah, such distancing may enable white women to remain detached from the struggles of women of color, which frees them from an obligation to assume responsibility for contributing to or committing to resolving those struggles.

One moment in which this detachment occurs with the white women with whom I spoke is through the normative production of white space: It is the spaces they occupy, not the choices they make, that preclude their intimate knowledge of women of color. For instance, Jean, the chair of a department, responds to the question of the cultural make-up of her alliances by admitting, with some apparent reticence, that all of her allies are white. She then explains this phenomenon by reporting that she lives and works in a "white space" (as an alibi for inaction):

Culturally, I mean one thing you can say about [the place where she works] is that it's incredibly white. So that is, that's an issue. So there's not a lot of [laughs] cultural feeling you can get, but, um, there have been occasional women of color here and, um, I have been friends with them but most of them leave, I mean it's such a white institution. Um, so try, I don't try hard enough, part of it is energy right now, I keep thinking I should call up this person who's head of multicultural student services and you know we keep making noises about having lunch with each other and I should, um, do that more. . . . [She continues, providing a series of parallel examples of her efforts to connect with people of color] . . . and so I consciously, I'm very, I huh [short laugh], the thing about when you're in an all-white environment you value *anything* like that so much, and so I made efforts to do that, but again, in this white environment it's not a good test. I think if I'd stayed in [a place that she depicts as more racially diverse], I would have really been involved in Chicanas, which would have been different, but here culturally there's not so much difference, which is too bad, something we all complain and worry about a lot.

As a glimpse at a bridge gesture, the disjunctures between Jean's verbal and nonverbal communication intimate some anxiety about, and perhaps an impulse to change, the all-white makeup of her allies (it is something "we all complain and worry about"). However, she jumps around from topic to topic trying to locate some evidence that she has actively worked to remedy the "white space" that she occupies and finds no adequate account for this failure. She changes the topic, seems to contradict herself, and uncomfortably laughs and pauses. Yet the outreach efforts to remedy the white space that she recounts all sound benign and ineffectual. The impulse seems to arise out of a sense of obligation (she feels she "should um do that more"), as opposed to a genuine desire to know the women of color employed in an institution in which she seems to wield some power. The default explanation to which she ultimately resorts is that the space is normatively white, that "culturally there's not so much difference," and while they all "complain and worry about it a lot," she assumes no responsibility for its production.

Massey (1994) cautions against such efforts to naturalize the meanings that become attributed to space, arguing that space must be understood as an ongoing production:

> All attempts to institute horizons, to establish boundaries, to secure the identity of places, can in this sense therefore be seen to be *attempts to stabilize the meaning of particular envelopes of space-time.* . . . For such attempts at the stabilization of meaning are constantly the site of social contest, battles over the power to label space-time, to impose the meaning to be attributed to a space, for however long or short a span of time. (p. 5)

By referring to the spaces that she occupies as normatively "white," a condition that she has no power to alter, Jean fixes the meaning of these exclusionary spaces and forecloses the "battle over the power to label space-time." Jean is not the only white woman to intimate this theme. As Sandra puts it, "so I would say that we are living . . . we're still living in an incredibly white, middle-class academic world and the [university where she works, the state in which she lives] in general is extraordinarily white."

Later in our discussion, Jean shares a disturbing story, which illustrates some racialized and gendered power mechanisms through which this white space is maintained that, in my mind, contradict the normativity of the white space in her earlier account. A woman of color is being sexually harassed by a man of color in their university. Jean notes that the woman is probably "going to leave" because of this incident, but she feels like there is

very little she can say or do to improve the situation and to intervene in the situation. As the conversation continues, it becomes apparent that she has no intimate connection to this woman's struggle. She explains,

J: I can think of a woman of color who's going to leave because of her relationship to someone else in her department and I don't think I'll have very much I can say or do about that. I'll feel terrible about losing her, but I don't have the power [pause] if there's any aid to be given. . . . There's a woman who's in a position to help her, if that's what's called for and would if that's what's called for, [pause] mmm, and she could call on others of us if that is what should happen, but I don't think that's what's gonna happen. I mean she could call on others, but it's so personal and so confidential.

A: I'm just wondering if there's a support network in place for her or is there anything informal where people. . . .

J: Yeah, yeah, but I don't think it'll be enough. You know, if people don't deal with things like sexual harassment on an institutional level, there's very little you can do.

A: Yeah, I was just wondering if she's got people to talk to.

J: She's got that.

A: She's got that?

J: Yeah, yeah for sure.

A: Are you involved with that?

J: No, I heard it through, I mean, I know her, I like her, and I will be more involved with her this year because we're gonna be on the same committee.

In this case, it appears that Jean is not personally invested in providing this woman with any institutional or *personal* support during her struggle. How might Jean discuss this situation if this woman were her friend, her ally, or someone who somehow really mattered to her? Here racial difference appears to have become a stumbling block, which enables Jean to hold this woman at an arm's distance in a context (sexual harassment) that feminists often take seriously. Is Jean, as a white feminist, unwilling to become more involved because the sexual harasser is a man of color? How might this situation be different if the victim were white? Through which cultural myths would the narrative be read? Jean's account raises many more questions than it answers, but it does seem clear that her story represents the kind of betrayal that precludes meaningful, or mutually fulfilling, relationships from forming between white women and women of color.

CONCLUSION: ENDING AND BEGINNING

As with the strange intensity of an intimate encounter with the unknown, I am left at the end with a sense of excitement about possibilities for what the future may hold and a sense of dread that I have made a huge mistake. Did I expose too much of my-self? Did I focus too much on stories of bridges damaged and unbuilt? Have I treated everyone with care and respect? Do I depict white women as too heartless, women of color as too powerless? Does the work offer something to white women in a way that they can hear and may find useful? And what, if anything, does it offer to women of color? The stories are painful, there are lots of pitfalls, and the terrain is treacherous. The history of abuse runs long and deep; its manifestations are always almost unbearable. It seems we should have learned by now, but the patterns of unequal exchange are deeply sedimented, as if in stone.

But they are *not* stone, just sedimented patterns. Patterns are just patterns, not "truth," not "reality," neither unchanging nor unchangeable. Patterns of unknowing, distancing, and disavowal that keep women divided can and must be broken. Lorde argues that transracial feminist alliances hold radical potential for challenging hegemonic norms and institutional systems, but that women must examine their investments in such power structures. She notes, "Mainstream communication does not want women, particularly white women, responding to racism" (1981, p. 103). To do so risks positioning white women outside of the affiliative boundaries that define whiteness and may, in certain contexts, undermine their access to white privilege. White women responding to racism break the pattern, destabilize the sedimentation, and begin the long process of fusing the fissures of racial difference. White women responding to racism entails naming the forces, such as stereotypic knowledge and fear of women of color, that keep us divided. It entails taking the risk of being wrong, of not knowing how to do it, of making mistakes, of letting someone else take the lead, and of becoming a bridge for others.

Where is the motivation here to step out onto the bridge? All of these women tell us. I see them wanting to lean toward each other. There is a whole world out there to know that requires unlearning the world we thought we knew. There is a *desire* to know, to heal, to grow, but not enough knowledge of the slippery terrain to feel safe out there. Perhaps the voices in this piece provide a clue, a phone number in a matchbook, a note scribbled to self and tucked away, then rediscovered, years later, as a new remembering. Perhaps it provides some validation for the alienation, isolation, or fear you thought you alone were experiencing, but no, lots of

women are experiencing for a whole host of historical, political, institutional, social, and relational reasons. Perhaps there is an enticement, a challenge, a new reading of someone you thought you knew—she, you, me, we? Perhaps it will just have to be enough that it does not have to feel safe in order to do this work, but that the stakes are too high to continue to stand on the shore in our own dreary mourning. The raw materials to build bridges, to become bridges, are our hands for *holding*, our hearts for *feeling*, our eyes for *seeing*, our minds for *knowing*, and our souls for *reaching beyond*. With these materials we can forge a new and more livable space in which the struggle for social justice supercedes the complacent desire to feel at ease. And those who travel that road less traveled as bridge people will not be the same for the journey.

NOTES

1. I use this term, in lieu of the term *multicultural* (see Albrecht & Brewer, 1990; for critique of the term see McLaren, 1997) in an effort to mark the points of departure from this former term. First, I wish to retain the root *racial* in order to call attention to the power imbalances and historical and material inequities that constitute relations between white women and women of color. Second, I use the prefix *trans* to mark not only the spatial and cultural movement across racial boundaries that such alliances entail but also the transformative potential that such relations potentially carry. Finally, I wish to evoke the critique of global power relations in the wake of colonial occupation associated with the term *transnational* (Alexander & Mohanty, 1997; Grewal & Kaplan, 1994).

2. Many of the contributors to *This Bridge Called My Back: Writing By Radical Women of Color* (1981) echo Rushin's sentiment that as women of color and feminists, they are positioned as translators of experience, meaning, and histories among a variety of cultural groups. This critique suggests that women of color are not the *only* group who are or should be responsible for this work, but that their intimate understandings of a variety of sociocultural contexts, which arise out of their own "bridge crossing," position them as inside informants across lines of difference. In other words, the burden of border crossing has been disproportionately placed upon the bodies of women of color, but white women could and should take on the work of building bridges and functioning as bridge people.

3. "Feminism" is a formation continually in process. Its production as an inclusive space is contingent upon the imaginary of those involved in struggles under its name. When feminists become blocked around issues of power, it is in large part a question of a blocking of the feminist imaginary—perhaps being too stuck in the head, too invested in hegemonic forms of power, or a lack of literacy in the realms of the heart. In the poetics of Lorde (1984):

We have chosen each other
And the edge of each others battles
The war is the same
If we lose
Someday women's blood will congeal upon a dead planet
If we win
There is no telling
We seek beyond history
For a new and more possible meeting (p. 103)

4. I advocate for "vulnerability" in context and always with an eye toward power relations, not universally. In other words, I do not advocate moving to spaces of vulnerability for all feminists as a gesture to enable racial mending because some are more in charge of their vulnerability than others. For those who are made vulnerable by institutional structures, the move to vulnerability is placed upon their bodies, yet for those who hold institutional power, a move toward vulnerability can destabilize relations of subordination. As Behar (1996) puts it, to write vulnerably evokes vulnerability in others.

5. "One verse," or "one way of saying things" for González (1999, p. 12).

6. By "author-ity" I mean the authority that accompanies the "author function" in the production of knowledge. It is a function of power that seeks to minimize competing discourses by limiting the number of authors who may be authorized to speak (see Foucault, 1984).

7. By "res(is)t" I mean to name the struggle between finding a home in which I can rest and forging a resistive identity that works in opposition to hegemonic categories and forms, and yet is not defined merely in opposition to them. As Anzaldúa (1987) writes:

A counterstance locks one into a duel of oppressor and oppressed; locked in mortal combat, like the cop and the criminal, both are reduced to a common denominator of violence. . . . At some point, on our way to a new consciousness, we will have to leave the opposite bank, the split between the two mortal combatants somehow healed so that we are on both shores at once and, at once, see through serpent and eagle eyes. (pp. 100-101)

8. The gift offered by deconstruction is the insistence on prioritizing the question over the answer. Indeed, the assumed correctness of the latter often negates the possibility of the emergence of the former (see Elam, 1994).

9. I place this term and other terms in quotation marks in an effort to dislodge the social scientific logic that constitutes the history of ethnographic inquiry into which I insert myself. I do not think of the conversations I had with these women as providing "data," although I recognize that they do function as such. I prefer to think of these "data" as snippets of conversations in which glimmers of

transracial connection emerge alongside of the many potholes of difference-as-distance.

10. Because these are academic women, I have taken extreme caution to conceal their identities. All of the names that appear here are pseudonyms; institutional affiliations, specific identifying markers, and geographical regions are left out; and in some cases, information has been mildly altered to retain anonymity, particularly the academic status of women with well-known tenure incidents.

11. The space here is so limited that I am forced to choose certain excerpts. We do not hear the voices of all of the women with whom I met, I selected excerpts from those we do hear from, and I imposed my own reading on the women whose voices we hear. The choices I make here are motivated by an effort to expose breakdowns with as much care for my conversation partners as possible.

REFERENCES

Albrecht, L. B., & Brewer, R. M. (1990). Bridges of power: Women's multicultural alliances for social change. In L. B. Albrecht & R. Brewer (Eds.), *Bridges of power: Women's multicultural alliances* (pp. 2-22). Philadelphia: New Society.

Alcoff, L. (1995). The problem of speaking for others. In J. Roof & R. Wiegman (Eds.), *Who can speak? Authority and critical identity.* Urbana: University of Illinois.

Alexander, M. J., & Mohanty, C. T. (1997). Introduction: Genealogies, legacies, movements. In *Feminist genealogies, colonial legacies, democratic futures* (pp. xiii-xlii). New York: Routledge.

Allen, B. J. (2000). Sapphire and Sappho: Allies in authenticity. In A. Gonzalez, M. Houston, & V. Chen (Eds.), *Our voices: Essays in culture, ethnicity, and communication* (3rd ed., pp. 179-183). Los Angeles: Roxbury.

Anzaldúa, G. (1987). *Borderlands/La frontera: The new mestiza.* San Francisco: Aunt Lute.

Anzaldúa, G. (1990). En rapport, in opposition: *Cobrando cuentas a las nuestras.* In G. Anzaldúa (Ed.), *Making face, making soul/Haciendo caras: Creative and critical perspectives by feminist women of color* (pp. 142-148). San Francisco: Aunt Lute.

Bannerji, H. (1995). *Thinking through: Essays on feminism, Marxism and anti-racism.* Toronto: Women's Press.

Bederman, G. (1995). *Manliness and civilization: A cultural history of gender and race in the United States, 1880-1917.* Chicago: University of Chicago Press.

Behar, R. (1996). *The vulnerable observer: Anthropology that breaks your heart.* Boston: Beacon.

Bhattacharjee, A. (1997). The public/private mirage: Mapping homes and undomesticating violence work in the South Asian Immigrant Community. In

M. J. Alexander & C. T. Mohanty (Eds.), *Feminist genealogies, colonial legacies, democratic futures.* New York: Routledge.

Bloom, L. R. (1998). *Under the sign of hope: Feminist methodology and narrative interpretation.* New York: State University of New York.

Bulkin, E., Pratt, M. B., & Smith, B. (1984). *Yours in struggle: Three feminist perspectives on anti-Semitism and racism.* Ithaca, NY: Firebrand.

Carrillo Rowe, A. (1999). *Fortifying borders: Spatializing whiteness.* Paper presented at the National Communication Association, Chicago.

Collins, P. H. (1990). *Black feminist thought: Knowledge, consciousness, and the politics of empowerment.* New York: Routledge.

Combahee River Collective. (1983). The Combahee River Collective Statement. In B. Smith (Ed.), *Home girls: A black feminist anthology* (pp. 272-282). Latham, NY: Kitchen Table.

Córdova, T. (1998). Power and knowledge: Colonialism in the academy. In C. Trujillo (Ed.), *Living Chicana theory* (pp. 17-45). Berkeley, CA: Third Woman Press.

Elam, D. (1994). *Feminism and deconstruction: Ms. en abyme.* London: Routledge.

Foucault, M. (1984). What is an author? In P. Rabinow (Ed.), *The Foucault reader* (pp. 101-120). New York: Pantheon.

Frankenberg, R. (1993). *White women, race matters: The social construction of whiteness.* Minneapolis: University of Minnesota Press.

Frankenberg, R. (1996). When we are capable of stopping, we begin to see: Being white, seeing whiteness. In B. Thompson & S. Tyagi (Eds.), *Names we call home: Autobiography on racial identity.* New York: Routledge.

Frankenberg, R. (1997). Introduction: Local whiteness, localizing whiteness. In R. Frankenberg (Ed.), *Displacing whiteness: Essays in social and cultural criticism* (pp. 1-33). Durham, NC: Duke University Press.

González, C. M. (1999). *Ethnography as spiritual practice: A change in the taken for granted.* Paper presented at the National Communication Association, Chicago.

Grewal, I., & Kaplan, C. (1994). *Scattered hegemonies: Postmodernity and transnational feminist practices.* Minneapolis: University of Minnesota Press.

Guy-Sheftall, B. (1995). *Words of fire: An anthology of African-American feminist thought.* New York: The New Press.

Harris, H. (2000). Failing "white woman": Interrogating the performance of respectability. *Theatre Journal, 52,* 183-209.

hooks, b. (1992). Eating the other. In *Black looks: Race and representation.* Boston: South End.

hooks, b. (1995). *Killing rage: Ending racism.* New York: Henry Holt.

Hurtado, A. (1996). *The color of privilege: Three blasphemies on race and feminism.* Ann Arbor: University of Michigan Press.

Hurtado, A., & Stewart, A. J. (1997). Through the looking glass: Implications of studying whiteness for feminist methods. In M. Fine, L. Weis, L. C. Powell, &

L. M. Wong (Eds.), *Off white: Readings on race, power, and society.* New York: Routledge.

Johnson Reagon, B. (1998). Coalition politics: Turning the century. In M. Anderson & P. H. Collins (Eds.), *Race, class and gender: An anthology* (pp. 517-523). Belmont, CA: Wadsworth.

Lal, J. (1996). Situating locations: The politics of self, identity, and "other" in living and writing the text. In D. L. Wolf (Ed.), *Feminist dilemmas in fieldwork* (pp. 185-214). Boulder, CO: Westview.

Lorde, A. (1981). An open letter to Mary Daly. In C. Moraga & G. Anzaldúa (Eds.), *This bridge called my back: Writings by radical women of color* (pp. 94-97). Latham, NY: Kitchen Table.

Lorde, A. (1984). *Sister outsider: Essays and speeches.* Trumansburg, NY: Crossing Press.

Massey, D. (1994). *Space, place, and gender.* Minneapolis: University of Minnesota Press.

McLaren, P. (1997). *Revolutionary multiculturalism: Pedagogies of dissent for the new millennium.* Boulder, CO: Westview.

Mohanty, C. T. (1991). Under Western eyes: Feminist scholarship and colonial discourses. In C. T. Mohanty, A. Russo, & L. Torres (Eds.), *Third World women and the politics of feminism.* Bloomington: Indiana University Press.

Moon, D. (1999). White enculturation and bourgeois ideology: The discursive production of "good (white) girls." In T. Nakayama & J. Martin (Eds.), *Whiteness: The communication of social identity* (pp. 177-197). Thousand Oaks, CA: Sage.

Moraga, C. (1996). The breakdown of the bicultural mind. In B. Thompson & S. Tyagi (Eds.), *Names we call home: Autobiography on racial identity* (pp. 230-239). New York: Routledge.

Moraga, C., & Anzaldúa, G. (1981). *This bridge called my back: Writings by radical women of color.* Latham, NY: Kitchen Table.

Moya, P. M. L. (1997). Postmodernism, "realism," and the politics of identity: Cherríe Moraga and Chicana feminism. In M. J. Alexander & C. T. Mohanty (Eds.), *Feminist genealogies, colonial legacies, democratic futures.* New York: Routledge.

Ó Tuathail, G. (1996). *Critical geopolitics: The politics of writings global space.* Minneapolis: University of Minnesota Press.

Rushin, D. K. (1981). The bridge poem. In C. Moraga & G. Anzaldúa (Eds.), *This bridge called my back: Writings by radical women of color* (pp. xxi-xxii). Latham, NY: Kitchen Table.

Russo, A. (1991). "We cannot live without our lives": White women, antiracism, and feminism. In C. T. Mohanty, A. Russo, & L. Torres (Eds.), *Third World women and the politics of feminism* (pp. 297-313). Bloomington: Indiana University Press.

Saldívar, J. D. (1997). *Border matters: Remapping American cultural studies.* Berkeley: University of California Press.

Scott, J. W. (1998). Experience. In S. Smith & J. Watson (Eds.), *Women, auto biography, theory: A reader* (pp. 57-71). Madison: University of Wisconsin Press.

Segrest, M. (1994). *Memoir of a race traitor.* Boston: South End.

Spivak, G. (1990). *The post-colonial critic: Interviews, strategies, dialogues.* New York: Routledge.

Thompson, B. (1996). Time traveling and border crossing: Reflections on white identity. In B. Thompson & S. Tyagi (Eds.), *Names we call home: Autobiography on racial identity.* New York: Routledge.

Thompson, B. (2000). *Mothering without a compass: White mother's love, black son's courage.* Minneapolis: University of Minnesota Press.

Visweswaran, K. (1994). *Fictions of feminist ethnography.* Minneapolis: University of Minnesota Press.

APPENDIX A

Solicitation Letter

[Name and Address of Author]
August 23, 1999
Dear Friends, Acquaintances, Allies, and Colleagues:

I am a doctoral candidate in Speech Communication at the University of Washington. I am writing to solicit your help in locating potential interviewees for my study of how academic feminists form alliances, particularly within the academy. My work draws on that by scholars who seek to understand the dynamics of how race, national origin, ethnicity, and class function in feminist alliance formation. The specific focus of my study is power balance or imbalance among feminist academics.

I hope to interview at least 20 self-proclaimed academic feminists. The interviews will be done in person. They will take about an hour and, with your consent, will be tape recorded, transcribed, and analyzed by me. Audiotapes will be destroyed within 30 days. Names and other identifying information will be kept separate from interview data and destroyed within one year. No real names will be used when writing my dissertation without explicit permission from interviewees. My dissertation may become a book; chapters may become journal articles.

Here are some of my research questions: (1) How do academic feminists negotiate power and subordination in their work? (2) With whom, and under what conditions, do feminists ally themselves within academic contexts? (3) How do academic feminists position themselves along axes of race, national origin, class, sexual orientation, religion, and other personal identity markers? (4) What do feminist alliances mean to those who

describe them? My hope is that my research will lead to further understandings about how academic feminists arrange their collaborative practices both within and outside of the workplace (the academy).

Will you participate in my study? Would you direct me to others who might be willing to be interviewed? If your answer is yes to either or both of these questions, please call or e-mail me. Participation in this study is voluntary. Interview participants may choose to stop the interview at any time and may select to decline response to any questions they do not feel comfortable answering.

Thank you for your time.

[Signature and name of author]

APPENDIX B

Interview Questions

I. CAREER HISTORY

1. What is your current academic rank or title?

2. Could you provide a brief history of your academic career?

3. Would you describe your career advancement as relatively challenging, or has it been smooth, compared to what you know of the experiences of your white male counterparts? Compared to what you know of the experiences of other feminists (especially those who are culturally different from you)?

4. Would you provide a description or story of the circumstances of your successes and/or failures?

5. What aspects of your own identity do you think may contribute to your ability or difficulties in rising through the academic ranks? (If necessary, ask: for example, your race/whiteness, your gender, your sexual orientation, your class positioning?)

II. ALLIANCES

1. Would you consider the people who facilitated your advancement during critical times of this process to be your allies?

2. What does the term *alliances* mean to you?

3. Have your allies changed over time and in relation to your career advancement?

4. Can you think of a circumstance in which you have disappointed, betrayed, or lost an ally (in this process, especially with regard to your securing more institutional power)?

5. Are there any instances in which you have felt disappointed, betrayed, or lost an ally (in this process, especially with regard to your securing more institutional power)?

6. Could you describe a situation in which someone has considered you an ally and you may not have thought of that person as an ally, or vice versa?

7. In what respects are your allies similar and/or different from you, especially culturally? Institutionally? In terms of their feminist politics?

8. Could you describe an alliance you have with an academic who holds more institutional power than you, especially any challenges that have arisen in this case?

9. How do cultural differences and/or similarities come into play in this alliance?

10. What do you hope to get out of and/or contribute to this alliance?

11. Could you describe an alliance you have with an academic who holds less institutional power than you, especially any challenges that have arisen in this case?

12. How do cultural differences and/or similarities come into play in this alliance?

13. What do you hope to get out of and/or contribute to this alliance?

III. FEMINIST POLITICS

1. Participants in this study are academics who have self-identified as "feminists." Could you describe what this term means to you, especially in the context and under the constraints of academia?

2. Can you recall any experience in which your feminist ethics or politics seemed to be at odds with some aspect of retaining or enhancing your institutional status?

3. Can you describe an instance in which you have used your own institutional power to enhance the status of a junior academic feminist? (If so, discuss cultural differences and/or similarities in this context.)

4. Could you describe any circumstances in which you felt your feminist politics have been compromised within academic settings, especially an instance that relates to your efforts to enhance or protect your own academic status (separate?) or someone else's, or that of a group on campus?

5. To whom, if anyone, did you turn as allies in this case?

6. Whom, if anyone, did you disappoint or betray in this case?

7. How successfully do you feel that you are able to secure power and respect within an academic setting that is not necessarily "feminist" or that you consider to be patriarchal?

(If interviewees foreground "failures," I follow up by asking whom they turn to as allies in such instances, then ask what this term means to them. If they foreground "successes," I pursue questions around how they use their institutional power, particularly with regard to feminists in subordinate positions.)

IV. IDENTITY

1. How would you describe your identity in terms of race, class, ethnicity, national origin, and sexual orientation?

2. Could you describe how you have come to identify as such, especially any changes that you have experienced with regard to your identity?

3. Do you feel that your identity remains relatively stable across academic contexts, or do you feel you foreground different aspects of your identity in different academic contexts?

4

Deconstructing Whiteness Ideology as a Set of Rhetorical Fantasy Themes

Implications for Interracial Alliance Building in the United States

SEAN TIERNEY • Howard University
RONALD L. JACKSON II • Pennsylvania State University

Whiteness ideology in the United States can be construed as a set of fantasy themes, discursively formed, politically charged, and socially constituted within everyday interaction with cultural others. Fantasies are shared rhetorical visions, which are chained out through discourse and framed using the apparatus of culture. Culture, by its very nature, ensures that people will have shared patterns of social cognition; hence, they will use their culture to understand themselves and the norms of the world around them; moreover, ideologies facilitate how these norms are shaped. Intercultural conflict emerges, as Kim (1991) suggests, when the incompatibility of ideologies, as expressed via goals, interests, and values, is compounded by a lack of understanding and/or concern about the other cultural interactant's worldview. Thus interracial alliance building begins with reduced conflict, which presumes compatibility of goals, interests, and values complemented by an understanding of one another's worldview.

An understanding of intercultural communication is dependent upon an operational definition of culture. Grossberg (1997) calls culture "the struggle over meaning. . . . Culture is never merely a set of practices, technologies or messages, objects whose meaning and identity can be guaranteed by their origin or their essences" (p. 157). If culture is the systematic means by which groups make sense of and interact with the world, it becomes clear why intercultural communication can be so problematic. The problem is not so much the differences of the cultures as it is the conflict over

meanings that those differences engender. Cultures survive by providing meaning, and when those meanings are called into question, there is an impulsive need to establish the primacy of one meaning as right and others as wrong:

> Culture is the site of the struggle to define how life is lived and experienced, a struggle carried out in the discursive forms available to us. Cultural practices articulate the meanings of particular social practices and events; they define the ways we make sense of them, how they are experienced and lived. (Grossberg, 1997, p. 157)

So, as Kim (1991) suggests, intercultural conflict is the location of the struggle over meaning, of deciding what is appropriate and inappropriate and who is competent and/or incompetent. What is perceived to be at stake is cultural solidity, often articulated as "our way of life." Too often, however, members of certain cultures have a very limited or distorted understanding of how to relate within and between cultures, and this is only exacerbated when race becomes a marked facet of intercultural discourse. Effective and successful intercultural and interracial relationships require compatibility. Central to this chapter is a definition of culture that elucidates the importance of values, norms, and practices that are instilled via ideologies and reified through rhetoric. It is important to note that the exploration of race that is embedded in culture complicates the discursive equation. Race occupies a precarious space as an inhibitive mechanism that is socially constructed. Rarely, in the large body of literature on race, is it discussed positively. It is neutral at best. Race is not permitted to be an ameliorative construct in the United States, because its social form evokes polarity between Blacks and Whites.

The intercultural communication scholar bears a responsibility to examine the dynamics that not only constitute but also affect intercultural and interracial communication. It would be unfortunate and ill advised to discount the role of dominance in either area of communication inquiry. It would further be cowardly not to place and name that dominance. In the United States, and, increasingly on a global level, the dominant cultural voice in intercultural and interracial communication is what many now call whiteness (Jackson, 1999b; Jackson, Shin, & Wilson, 2000; Nakayama & Krizek, 1999; Nakayama & Martin, 1999).

Having named the dominant voice, it becomes important to construct an understanding of how the particularity of this voice affects the communication in which it participates. The central argument of this chapter is that it

is through the deconstruction of whiteness ideology, as communicated structurally via rhetorical visions and fantasy themes, productive citizens are able to begin the transformative process of alliance building in the United States. The clearest, most direct statement that can be made here about whiteness ideology is that it represents a socialized set of discursive formations. These formations are designed to accent a naturalized way of being that is equivalent to what it means to be White while openly refusing to acknowledge that this ideology exists. When whiteness ideology is ignored, dismissed, or disavowed, it continues, and one major consequence of this is that interracial alliance building is potentially surrendered. It is the position of this chapter that the ideology in use by the dominant segment of North American society is structurally validated and perpetuated. This ideology contains many assumptions, unconscious prejudices, and logical flaws that necessitate analysis prior to the commencement of intercultural and interracial alliance building.

Intercultural communication takes place with increasing frequency in the United States; consequently, it would seem that interracial alliance building would be more common and uninhibited. While it may be endearing to see intercultural communication as a commingling of equal voices, it is also naive, because many U.S. institutions continue to reify whiteness ideology (Gresson, 1995; West, 1994). The "Millennium Breach" (1998), which was recently released by the Milton S. Eisenhower Foundation for the Prevention of Violence as a follow-up to the 1968 Kerner Commission Report, supports this conclusion and states that the United States is still moving toward two societies, one non-White and one White, with the relationship between them separate, hostile, and unequal. Although it is ordinary to find discussions of culture diffused by discussions of race, the link between the two is inextricable due to how "White"-ness is defined. In the United States, one cannot speak fully of culture without attending to the repressive effects of dominance implicit in the social construction of race.

In recent scholarship, many studies have begun the task of trying to put form to something that had for centuries been elusive, due to both concealment and inattention: whiteness. The emerging field of whiteness studies seeks to bring definition and understanding to what has been a determining factor in global history and continues to deeply impact North American society. The focus of this chapter is an examination of a number of rhetorical fantasy themes found in common social, racial and cultural constructions of whiteness ideology that have an impact on interracial alliance building. By using the fantasy theme approach, we show how whiteness is communicated, as well as how its assumptions and position impact

intercultural communication, and, by implication, interracial alliance building.

WHITENESS: TOWARD A DEFINITION

One of the continuing struggles for "whiteness" scholars is to find an acceptable definition for the term itself. It is clear that one of the contributing factors in this search is the intentionally enigmatic nature of the concept. Nonetheless, for the purposes of this work, *whiteness* is defined as the ideological framework of the dominant segment of North American society. This segment of society is White, but as Frankenberg (1997) reminds us, "While it is true that, by and large, those in power in the United States are White, it is also true that not all those who are White are in power" (p. 203). In this sense, whiteness is a matter not simply of race but also of class. Whiteness is not simply physical. It is sociopolitical and is characterized by very real and concrete racial dynamics. Whiteness, regardless of class orientation, encompasses some measure of privilege, status, and power, both social and discursive. It is structurally reinforced via institutions such as education, government, and business (Ani, 1994; Frankenburg, 1997; Gresson, 1995). Rather than concentrating on class here, we accent other structural dynamics that contribute to the deracialization of whiteness.

There is an ongoing debate among social scientists about *essentialism*, which refers to the idea that race is an authentic essence that can be observed and held constant (Hall, 1982). When viewing an essence, one knows all that something is. It is contained, understood, predictable, and controllable. So, to say that whiteness is constant and homogeneous is to commit an intellectually grievous act of generalization formulated as an essentialist argument. It is to suggest that there is an authenticity to whiteness that is understandable and predictable and has little to no deviation. Although anti-essentialists argue that variations of whiteness do exist and are structurally situated, it is very difficult to support their claims that whiteness is agentless, unaware, and without racial relevance. If race is an essentialist construct, anti-essentialists are imposing a regime of truth that reassigns the essence of whiteness as being without a center, elusive, and beyond reproach (Hall, 1997). The fact is that race is an essence that is designed to be authentic (Jackson & Heckman, in press). It is categorical, it is nominal, and it permeates every level of academic and social discourse concerning intercultural communication in the United States. It is one

among several rhetorical visions discussed here and serves as an adjectival signifier of whiteness.

Defining Fantasy Chains and Rhetorical Visions

The deconstruction of whiteness in this chapter is grounded in Symbolic Convergence Theory. Using Bormann's fantasy theme analysis, it is possible to uncover rhetorical visions that both explain and motivate the dynamics that influence social practices of domination between Whites and Blacks during intercultural communication. Although we do realize that some of the same dynamics exist between Whites and non-Whites other than Blacks, here we speak directly only of Black-White relationships.

Bormann's fantasy theme analysis is grounded in social psychology and small group communication research, which found that people will create unified and unifying stories, or fantasies, around which they structure their social beliefs (Hart, 1997). According to Bormann, "some, but not all of the communication coded as 'dramatizations' would chain out through the group" (Bormann, 1972, p. 397). Fantasy chains are a series of fantasized ideas linked together like a movie, and therefore, have all the constitutive parts, such as scripts, heroes, villains, scenes, plot, action, and climaxes. Each chain represents a fantasized set of shared symbols that are mutually understood. Fantasy chains facilitate the movement, growth, and maintenance of a coherent rhetorical vision. These fantasies have a collectivizing function:

> When a number of people within a communication subsystem come to share a group of fantasies and fantasy types they may integrate them into a coherent *rhetorical vision* of some aspect of their social reality. A rhetorical vision is a unified putting-together of the various shared scripts that give the participants a broader view of things. (Golden, Berquist, & Coleman, 1992, p. 368)

These chains are not limited to small group interaction; they can filter or expand out into large social networks. Bales (1970) found that these chains of fantasy were capable of spreading quickly:

> A fantasy, whether formed by an individual, or in a process of interaction in a small group, or by a process of more attenuated communication through large population groups, may "fit" a widespread motivational need for an appropriate image so well that it is widely adopted forthwith. (cited in Mohrmann, 1982, p. 115)

It is possible, then, for a fantasy chain to spread widely, especially if its content allows people to make sense of a situation they find problematic, such as is the case with race and culture. The psychological reward aspect of fantasy chains will be addressed at a later point; for the moment, let us continue to follow the growth of fantasy.

Fantasy themes that chain outward and gain acceptance often interlock, forming a web of fantasy known as a *rhetorical vision* (Littlejohn, 1999, p. 167). Rhetorical visions, then, are what give people a blueprint with which to interact with the world around them. Rhetorical visions are entwined with institutionally sanctioned social norms that indicate wrong and right, good and bad, and more important, how things are done. Human beings tend to want to understand the motivation for why events and behaviors occur; rhetorical visions, and the fantasy chains that comprise them, serve that function, often covertly. That is, given the reinforcement of existing structures and dominant ideologies at work, it is reasonable to assert that interactants often can and do unknowingly adopt the perspective of the information-givers and treat this information as "natural" or "the way things are." Thus the information recipients see the rhetorical vision as the truth, as a reality whose veracity is taken for granted. In this way, rhetorical visions can and do reach differing levels of prominence; the more people who adopt them, the more often and more widely they are communicated and the more institutions recycle them. This is how rhetorical visions grow, and those visions that reach prominence will begin to cement themselves into dominance. Potter (1996) maintains that these rhetorical visions are neither neutral nor objective but intentional acts of inculcation. He may be correct, insofar as social norms are created via dominant ideologies and contained in rhetorical visions. Typically, rhetorical visions are not abstract truisms as much as they are tools of control and influence (Bowers, Ochs, & Jensen, 1993).

Over time, rhetorical visions that remain unchallenged or unchanged slowly mutate into truisms accepted as immutably correct, applicable, or viable (Potter, 1996). In the case of whiteness in North America, this happened when a specific culture reached a level of dominance, which lasted for at least several generations. One troublesome aspect of under-investigated rhetorical visions is the assumed neutrality that they achieve by nature of their adherents' rise to cultural dominance. As Potter (1996) notes, in

> the domain of culture, the struggle is for meaning, where the dominant classes attempt to neutralize the meanings that serve their interests into the "common

sense" of the society as a whole, whereas the subordinate classes resist this process by attempting to construct meanings to serve their interests. (p. 145)

As the dominant class achieves prominence, it begins to silence "meanings" that contravene structural intentions. If the competing meanings can be eradicated or sufficiently silenced, the dominant meaning will be authenticated, becoming not only "true" but also extremely difficult to challenge. Likewise, as Potter suggests, marginalized groups instinctively seek centrality as a response to dominance.

At this level of analysis, it becomes necessary to acknowledge the connections and similarities between dominant rhetorical visions and ideologies. An examination of the concepts will allow the reader to more fully understand these connections as well as the implications thereof.

RHETORICAL VISION AND IDEOLOGY

Rhetorical visions and ideology are not the same, but they are compatible. Rhetoricians and social psychologists often speak of rhetorical visions or fantasy themes as ephemeral or situational without realizing that, if left alone, they become concretized over time. If it is true that, as Bormann suggests, "the sharing of fantasies within a group or community establishes the assumptive system" (1982, p. 292) and leads to the emplacement of the fantasy within the social sphere, then it is only logical that fantasies found within rhetorical visions become commensurate with ideologies. In principle, ideologies are not only proximate to but also continuant of rhetorical visions. With that in mind, it is clear that solidified rhetorical visions no longer can be considered temporary fantasy chains for a public or a community but must transcend this into a more permanent set of ideologies. Ideology theory suggests that meaning is socially propagandized to enforce a set of logics about the way the world works and has some historical basis for its relevancy (Makus, 1990, p. 495). Both rhetorical vision and ideology are institutionally reflected; however, ideology is constituted and reinforced via rhetorical visions, so fantasy themes originate within rhetorical visions and have the potential to move outward to established ideologies if chained out in large publics and broader communities.

Ideologies have been defined as "taken-for-granted frameworks that naturalize our descriptions of the way the world is, including its current power structures" (Crenshaw, 1997, p. 257). Ideology serves the self-preservation function of culture by defining and communicating the

structures by which the environment of that culture is made sensible. According to Hall (1995), ideology is composed in part by the

> premises, which provide the frameworks through which we represent, interpret, understand, and "make sense" of some aspect of social existence. . . . Ideologies "work" by constructing for their subjects (individual and collective) positions of identification and knowledge, which allow them to "utter" ideological truths as if they were their authentic authors. This is not because they emanate from our innermost, authentic and unified experience, but because we find ourselves mirrored in the positions at the centre of the discourses from which the statements we formulate "make sense." (pp. 18-19)

Ideology provides a means through which one may acquire and maintain a sense of social reality, of how and why the world is the way it is. Structurally, ideology does so whether individuals want it to or not. As Grossberg posits, "it is not reality that is represented (and constructed); it is rather our relation to it, the ways we live and experience reality" (1997, p. 159).

Hall (1982) suggests that the power of ideology is in its proselytizing move toward a universal validity and legitimacy, which involves acceptance from the rhetorical community. In other words, ideology is "the struggle to articulate certain codes into a position of dominance, to legitimate their claim" (Grossberg, 1997, p. 158). In this way, a specific ideology becomes the "right" way; it also becomes the dominant explanation of how and why the world is as it is. When that dominance is established, it becomes underinterrogated, "naturalized," and taken for granted in terms of its innate correctness.

The pressure to accept and adhere to a rhetorical vision or ideology is no more natural than is the ideology itself. It is the product of a specific segment of a society or culture, one that has the social power or dominance to exert that pressure: "The process of legitimation allows the dominant class . . . to lead by winning the consent of the dominated" (Makus, 1990, p. 502). Thus, legitimation is not concerned with truth as much as it is with power. It allows for the solidification of a particular set of ideas into a seldom-questioned bedrock of assumptions. What were once the favored practices and prejudices of one group become the overarching, dominant guidelines and influences.

One consequence of this dominance is its effect on language. Ideology is communicated through language just as language is influenced by ideology; the two concepts are deeply interrelated:

Language is not a synonym for ideology because the same terms can be used in very different ideological discourses. However, language is the principle medium of ideologies, and *ideologies are sets or chains of meaning* located in language. . . . These chains of meaning are not the products of individual intention even though they are statements made by individuals. Instead, intentions are formed within pre-existing ideologies because individuals are born into them. Ideologies live within what we take-for-granted. They exist in our assumptions and descriptive statements about how the world is. (Crenshaw, 1997, p. 256; italics added)

The symbiotic relationship between language and ideology seems to ensure that communication must be influenced by ideology; "language, broadly conceived, is by definition the principal medium in which we find different ideological discourses elaborated" (Hall, 1995, p. 18). In this way, language, and by extension communication, is subject to if not the servant of ideology.

Ideology is communicated through language in a systematic fashion, through a framework. Crenshaw defines ideologies as "sets or chains of meaning located in language" (1997, p. 256), much like fantasy themes. Understanding this parallel between ideology and fantasy themes, and the rhetorical visions they create, is crucial to understanding the problematic nature of the impact of whiteness on interracial alliance building. Ideology is a codified set of epistemes or language structures that offer meaning to particular social phenomena (Makus, 1990, p. 499).

The study of rhetorical visions allows us to understand the structure of language; by examining the language-driven aspect of ideology, and the presence of ideological influence on communication, the knowledge that language and power are often if not always interconnected follows. Also, like a rhetorical vision, ideologies perpetuate ideas via a rhetorical community that envisions this idea to be operable. This understanding is necessary for critical scholarship to demonstrate "the silent and often non-deliberate ways in which rhetoric conceals as much as it reveals through its relationship with power/knowledge" (McKerrow, 1999, p. 442).

The similarity between ideology and rhetorical vision is important for communication scholars in general and intercultural communication scholars in particular. Given the avowed purpose of critical scholarship, examination of the parallel allows communications scholars to be cognizant of discourses that lead to "social, cognitive, political processes and outcomes" (Potter, 1996, p. 138). It is crucial to understand whiteness as a power structure, and one way of doing so is by examining the influence and exercise of

power in communication. Through critical investigation of the fantasy themes related to the ideology of whiteness, the communication scholar can discover the ways in which rhetorical visions contribute to the creation and maintenance of social power and control (Crenshaw, 1997, p. 253).

The preceding explication of the similarities and parallels between rhetorical vision and ideology provides the necessary theoretical basis from which to examine the major thrust of this essay: that the dominant ideology or the U.S. fantasy with whiteness will be problematic for those seeking to construct meaningful intercultural alliances. The problem is located in historical nominalism and the counterproductive nature of cultural and social imparity.

COMMON FANTASY THEMES
OF WHITENESS IDEOLOGY AND THEIR IMPLICATIONS

Our examination of the rhetorical vision of whiteness is grounded in Bormann's fantasy theme analysis. This theory was selected for a number of reasons. First, because communication is the vehicle for ideology, it allows us to examine the communicative mechanisms. Second, an ideological analysis would focus on the ideas that power serves; our interest lies in how those ideas are communicated, spread, and maintained. Third, because these three ideas will be shown to be false and manufactured, and not natural or innate, it is only appropriate to examine them as fantasies.

The following section is divided into three common fantasy themes. They are common, publicly understood, socially manufactured constructs that are sustained by a shared set of ideas affirming their existence. These fantasy themes interrelate, creating a web of meaning, a rhetorical vision, which allows its subscribers to make sense of their world and the things that happen in it. Each emerges out of a social history of racial hierarchy and unequal power reinforced via institutions and social norms. They have been selected because they saturate public discourse and are highly problematic for all parties involved. These themes were selected after a literature review of whiteness; these three visions appeared most frequently in the literature (which is cited throughout the chapter), were usually vigorously defended, and are also often heard in popular discourse. It is the systematic and daily reification of these fantasy themes that has indelible and disabling effects upon interracial alliance building in the United States. Following the discussion of each fantasy theme, we provide several implications and effects these fantasy themes have on interracial alliance building.

First Fantasy Theme: Whiteness Equals Humanity

"For those in power in the West, as long as whiteness is felt to be the human condition, then it alone both defines normality and fully inhabits it" (Dyer, 1997, p. 9). The first fantasy theme is: To be White is to be essentially human. It emerges, as all of the fantasy themes here do, out of a very inequitable and oppressive social structure. It is indicative of the belief in an essential humanism independent of race, culture, or ethnicity. A brief examination shows that humanism, whether popular or "classical," speaks of a thought process that is circular at best. In seeking to discover a universal humanity, White "scientists" and "thinkers," through racial purity hypotheses, looked only to themselves. They felt themselves, and reasoned themselves, to be the apotheosis of humanity, one that reflected their whiteness. Therefore, because they were self-designated as most human, they could offer their own definition of humanity. Of course, as Davies (1997) points out, "the most powerful ideas in any epoch are the ideas of the powerful, and it requires no particular ingenuity to demonstrate that the essential human being tends in any period to bear a striking resemblance to the dominant group of that time and place" (p. 59).

In order to create and adopt humanism, Whites had to learn to see themselves not just as human but as *quintessentially* human (Jackson, 1999a). This self-indulgence is evidenced in the popularly celebrated North American baseball event labeled the "World Series," a contest in which no one else in the world is invited to play. Canada was given an invitation to play only a few years after the contest was designated the "World Series." The implication is that North Americans are the world.

Humanism is a White, Eurocentric construct that seeks to speak for all humanity as a foregone conclusive universality (Ani, 1994). Yet, no truly universal definition has ever emerged. Theoretically, the only possible way for a consensual definition of humanity to be achieved would be to give all humans the opportunity to contribute to the definition (West, 1994). Humanism is often traced to the Enlightenment, a sociophilosophical movement in Europe in the 18th century. Its acknowledged leading thinker was Voltaire, whom Victor Hugo compared to Christ, and who, Hugo believed, represented "Man" (Blackham, 1976). A biographer later said of Voltaire that he possessed the "ablest intellect and the finest character" (Blackham, 1976, p. 120). Voltaire stands as one of the "great minds" of Western thought, possessed of knowledge and acumen beyond the pale or understanding of most thinkers. Less well known is his investment in the trans-Atlantic slave trade as well as the open racism and anti-Semitism in

his writings (Poliakov, 1982). Immanuel Kant, another Enlightenment figure, shared Voltaire's racism and anti-Semitism (Lloyd, 1992).

This appropriation of an essential, objective humanity, as well as the unstated subtext of White intellectual superiority, causes what Frankenberg (1993) calls "epistemic violence." This means that whiteness' construction of intellectual engagement, which appears "natural" to Whites, is a product of a sense of entitlement or epistemic freedom. This structural legitimation of intellectual imperialism is an outgrowth of ideology that has permeated the educational system in the United States (Dyer, 1997).

The lack of self-awareness and of self-reflexivity so prevalent in whiteness ideology is a function and example of the strengthened efficacy to be found when fantasies and rhetorical visions transcend their origins and become race- and culture-centered ideologies embedded in everyday life.

Membership in the dominant segment of a culture does not guarantee freedom from ideological influence. In fact, if an ideology provides a framework for nondominant members' reactive pursuit of centrality and inclusion, it also shapes the very process by which the dominant segment creates and maintains the ideological structure. Makus (1990) claims that "in the reciprocal relationship between structure and practice, structure is actively produced and reproduced through practice just as practice is constrained by structure. The combination of structure and practice invites certain meanings and practices and discourages others" (p. 500).

The dominant member of society is in many ways as constrained and influenced by ideology as the nondominant member. The dominant ideology, by virtue of its assumed truthfulness or reliability, becomes an invisible influence on the thoughts and actions of those members it ostensibly benefits. It emplaces a different set of constraints and pressures.

In the case of whiteness, there is an internal contradiction between the ideology and those who are influenced by it (Nakayama & Krizek, 1999). One of the problems with a humanistic ideology is that it innately imbues adherents with a sense of being separate from the very ideology that *allows for that presupposition*. Individualist thinking prejudices people against seeing themselves as not only part of but also subject to ideology; they loathe to admit its existence, much less that they might be influenced or controlled by it. Humanism posits that a person is an individual human being, not merely a member of a group, be it racial, political, or social. The sense of individualism that humanism fosters also motivates objection to being grouped, labeled, or placed. Thus, it is not surprising that Whites often see themselves (and, from their position of social privilege, insist on being seen) as individuals, both ethnically and ideologically. Neither is it

surprising that their sense of individualism is so vociferously defended (Jackson, 1999b). Yet this freedom to be an individual is not and never has been available to all U.S. citizens; it is available only to those who have the social power and privilege to preserve and enforce that freedom—Whites.

One very important implication of this belief in the inviolable human essence, as well as both the ignorance of its limited application and the virulent nature of its defense by Whites, is that it may not be seen by those outside whiteness as particularly credible, laudable, or viable: "At the very least, obliviousness of one's privileged state can make a person or group irritating to be with" (McIntosh, 1992, p. 72). Indeed, it may be seen not as the "best" way to conceive of oneself and others; it may be seen as a continued exercise of privilege, ignorance, and power. In addition, the agency of marginalized groups is often arrested by the dominant group. Although the power to define one's sociopolitical condition is enviable, it may lead to either being oblivious to its social harm or being willing to maintain its hegemonic emplacement despite its potentially injurious nature.

Whiteness is primarily understood by persons of color as a functional political entity that preserves the markings of centrality and periphery among dominant and marginalized groups, respectively. Clearly, whiteness has come to signify, for many Blacks, elitism, normativity, appropriateness, privilege, and superiority (Jackson et al., 2000). For those who embrace whiteness ideology, whiteness does and must have a much different definition; it must be considered another way to characterize one's humanity. Every race or culture is considered to have equal access to having their humanity valued, celebrated, and acknowledged. This is characteristic of the disavowal of privilege that accompanies fantasies and rhetorical visions of whiteness as humanity.

Second Fantasy Theme: Color-blindness Is Beneficial . . . for the Group in Power

The discursive repertoire of color-blindness intersects in several ways with liberal humanism as a philosophical discourse. First, it proposes an essential human sameness to which race is added as a secondary characteristic. This assertion of a distinction between selfhood and racialness makes it possible for White people to claim that they do not see the color, or race, of those with whom they interact, but rather see "under the skin" to the "real" person underneath (Frankenberg, 1997, p. 148).

The second fantasy theme is the idea that color-blindness, or a color-blind approach to intercultural or interracial communication, is functional

and ideal. Color-blindness is an obvious extension of the humanist fantasy. Like that fantasy, it is also used and applied in a less-than-objective manner (Gresson, 1995). The color-blind paradigm has gained a disheartening cachet in popular usage, because this concept, in which the communicant does not "see" color, supposedly provides a progressive and laudable method for racial reconciliation and equanimity (Davies, 1997). Yet a number of unsettling issues that suffuse the color-blind paradigm must necessarily be examined.

First, it is important to note that color-blindness is a conceptual technique designed to diffuse notions of structural inequality. But to claim to not see an intractable aspect of another human being, and to claim "blindness" as a laudable act, is to commit a number of grievous errors. The supposed rejection of racial specificity is often proffered as a progressive color-blindness that will accelerate the process of dismantling racism and building intercultural alliances. Frankenberg (1993) insightfully captures the tone of the "Color-blindness Is Beneficial . . . for the Group in Power" fantasy theme:

> The sharp cutting edge of color-blindness is revealed here: within this discursive repertoire, people of color are "good" only insofar as their "coloredness" can be bracketed and ignored, and this bracketing is contingent on the ability or the decision—in fact, the virtue—of a "noncolored"- or White-self. Color-blindness, despite the best intention of its adherents, in this sense perseveres the power structure inherent in essential racism. (Frankenberg, 1993, p. 147)

In essence, the claim to discount part of a person implies "I don't see the bad and problematic part of you," because seeing color is somehow felt to be wrong. Thus, the person and the color itself must, on some level, be wrong. On the other hand, this act can be interpreted internally as a very generous and caring thing to do. It could seem that marginalized groups would readily embrace such a perspective in an effort to alleviate their socially and structurally disadvantaged position. However, it is often seen by those who are victims of both objectification and reductionism as insulting, degrading, and grossly insensitive (Gresson, 1995). This attitude presupposes the correctness of the institution that espouses it. Moreover, it denies marginalized groups their choice as to whether or not their color is salient to their identity.

The second important dynamic of the color-blind paradigm as a fantasy theme is this: If persons are not to be judged by color, by what criteria

are they to be evaluated? We could say they will be judged by their achievements, but then how do we define achievement or success, if not by the standards of whiteness ideology? Too often, members of the dominant culture assume, and understandably so, that their criteria will be used (Alcoff, 1996). This is because the privilege of membership in the dominant White culture assures them that their methods are superior, objective, neutral, or based on purely "human" considerations. Indeed, to behave in concert with whiteness is to be exemplarily competent. By contrast, counteracting whiteness is often deemed structurally inappropriate, deviant, and abnormal (Jackson et al., 2000). Alcoff (1996) suggests that color-blindness is a concealment strategy and defense mechanism (i.e., "I will promise not to see your otherness and you promise not to see my whiteness") underlying which the politics of identity remain. With this approach, the power and politics of whiteness do not magically disappear. The only difference is that the dominant group agrees not to hold nonwhiteness against the other interactant. At the same time, the criteria of judgment remain steeped in whiteness.

A powerful reality of whiteness, as a structural ideology, is that it gets to center itself, and then make itself invisible (Frankenberg, 1997; Jackson, 1999b; Jackson et al., 2000). The invisible centrality of whiteness transcends privilege into epistemic power. Once whiteness has consolidated its control, it begins a process by which customs, beliefs, and behaviors may move past their specificity, their identity. White racial identity is no longer important to define. Over time, whiteness ideology becomes merely *the way* things are (Alcoff, 1996; Dyer, 1997; Jackson & Heckman, in press; Nakayama & Martin, 1999; West, 1994). That is, due to continued White dominance, and the power consequent to that dominance, one way of doing things became a neutralized universal. Consequently, "the experiences and communication patterns of Whites are taken as the norm from which Others are marked" (Nakayama & Krizek, 1999, p. 91).

By marking *what is* as *what is White*, the artifact or idea can no longer claim its universal position and propose its dismissal in the form of the color-blind paradigm. Deconstructing whiteness means understanding that the United States, and the conditions in which U.S. citizens live, are no longer the *way it is*, but rather the *way that whiteness has made it*. Social understandings of many concepts have been unevenly shaped if not created by a very specific group or culture, and those understandings often function as mechanisms of power and control. One such mechanism is the paradoxical understanding and application of the idea of race.

Third Fantasy Theme: Race Is Used
by the Group in Power to Recycle Notions of Otherness

According to Robert Stebbins (1992), "Strictly speaking, from the standpoint of biological science, 'races' do not exist. There is no biological basis for the concept of race . . . the common sense idea of race is based on inherited physical similarities" (p. 22). Yet, popular and historical thinking dictates that race is a subdivision of Homo sapiens, who are physically differentiated. Stebbins's (1992) primary contention that "races" do not exist is supported by sociologists, and by biologists who claim that phylocentric differences are widely varied within and among races; the tremendous disparity among scientists regarding the existence, number, and types of races also supports this claim.

Webster (1992), author of *The Racialization of America*, complains that race is too often equated with culture. He clarifies race as being the product of a classification scheme in which anatomical differences are tantamount and social meaning is ignored. As the ideology of whiteness propagates humanism and color-blindness, it also seeks to manipulate definitions of race to correspond with the sociopolitical milieu. Evolving from a history of social hierarchy, particularly advanced with the advent of 17th- and 18th-century eugenicist ideologies that reinforced biological and innate inferiority of non-Whites, the present sociopolitical construction of race benefits Whites most. The current whiteness ideology counters the argument that race is real and that race is an actual obstruction; yet, race is still one of the most real, socially manufactured constructs in existence. This is evidenced by the continued presence of racial and linguistic profiling (Baugh, 2000; Wallace, 2001). This does not mean that Blacks are always victims; it does mean that a very real consequence of marginalization is the decentering of the cultural worldviews of those who are marginalized. The actual condition of marginalization is predicated upon the stability of race as a discriminatory force (Appiah & Gutmann, 1996). Such a fantasy theme is most effective when it is internalized by the rhetorical community and recycled among its members (McWhorter, 2000). When race as a fantasy theme begins to affect life possibilities and self-efficacy, it is effectual. When those effects are felt by a small, politically disempowered minority and not by the dominant segment of the society, it is understandable that the fantasy of race continues.

To say that this fantasy has no effect on Whites would be wrong. However, it is important to understand how the fantasy of race does in fact affect Whites, the dominant group. As Crenshaw (1997) suggests, whiteness

elusively functions as an ideology when it is employed as a framework to categorize people and understand their social positionality. Both Helms (1994) and Jackson (2000) contend that many Whites simply feel protected, authorized, empowered, and entitled to privilege in every domain of public life, even when they are temporarily removed from positions of power, such as in the classroom (Jackson, Morrison, & Dangerfield, 2002). Although some Whites may not see race as theoretically real, institutional structures complicitous with whiteness ideology verify the operation of race as a protective mechanism by not acknowledging its presence (Jackson, 1999b; McPhail, 1994).

In her purview of White-Black racial relations in the United States, hooks (1995, 1997) explicitly describes a fantasy of whiteness in the Black imagination. Initially, it seemed odd to have a Black feminist intellectual assert that whiteness is a fantasy, which signifies something not real, a hallucination, dream, or reverie. Nonetheless, it is quite appropriate to identify race as a fantasy when it has been proven nonscientific, nonbiological, and substantiated by nothing other than a socially designed understanding of White and non-White relations. The fantasy of whiteness is based on color. Nakayama and Krizek (1999) agree with this, and assert their interpretation of an interview participant's self-definition of his White identity as "not Black, Brown, Yellow or Red":

> the use of colors here is important in understanding the workings of the assemblage. White is seen as a noncolor . . . the unstated, silenced implication, given its meaning and power from historical usage, is that White means not having any other "blood lines" to make it impure. Unlike other categories, one can only be White by not being anything else. This negative definition may be related to the invisibility of whiteness as a category or a position from which one speaks. (p. 97)

Identifying people as colors or colored facilitates the enactment of race and positioning of whiteness as superior, because it is *not* identified in this color schemata and hence seems nonexistent; this speaks to the assumption of "naturalness" that characterizes dominant ideology.

Arguably, this White and non-White chasm includes the Browns, Yellows, and Reds, but even as other non-White colors or races are named, it sounds foreign to the average person. No one says, "I have a Brown friend I want you to meet." They just say that their friend is Latino, Asian, or some other ethnicity. This is important to note, because whiteness parasitically feeds off of the dynamic of a Black-White polarity, with other

non-White groups situated along the bipolar continuum. The Browns, Yellows, and Reds have always been "segregated from mainstream [North] American society" (Delgado, 2000, p. 389), but have not been expected to carry the burden of racial difference as have Blacks. Jackson (2000) clarifies this point well:

"Race," as the progenitor of racism, occupies a peculiar position in the lives of African Americans, for truly, we are the reason why racism as a social disease still has utility in the United States of America. It is not because we have created it, but that we are the primary canvas upon which the racist's insecurities, fears and anxieties get projected. (p. 50)

This is not to necessarily suggest that one culture is better or worse off than another, but it does suggest that the color caste system in the United States has been so unfortunately effective that those who more closely resemble Whites tend to enjoy greater prosperity (Jackson, 1999b). Consequently, the power of whiteness is heightened perceptually by the physiognomic polarity, then sustained by a constant social polarity and unequal distribution of resources as demonstrated by the Milton S. Eisenhower Foundation for the Prevention of Violence report and countless other reports on race. So, perhaps hooks (1995) was right in her naming of whiteness as a fantasy. Whiteness is an imagined construct with no validity (Jackson et al., 2000; Stebbins, 1992) except the social relevance it still enjoys as a seemingly insurmountable racial enigma. Therefore, the ideology of whiteness can suggest "race is real to you, but not to me," which projects and countertransfers the burden of race onto marginalized groups while freeing up the dominant group from being problematized by race. The dual function of this disingenuous ideological transposition is that marginalized persons begin to rethink whether race really is real and from whence it emerges.

There is fantasia implicit in the correspondence between the chromatic polarity among Whites and Blacks and their manufactured social polarity. Social difference is accented physiognomically, because Whites enjoy the privileged position of social dominance in this society. They have the discursive power to render themselves invisible, unraced. Unless they choose to racially self-identify, race remains someone else's problem. Among the consequences of this concept is the idea that, as Richard Dyer (1997) states, "Having no content, we can't see that we have anything that accounts for our position of privilege and power. This is itself crucial to the security with which we occupy that position" (p. 9). Whiteness ideology facilitates a level of unawareness that leads to a number of serious assumptions:

White people have power and believe that they think, feel and act for all people; White people, unable to see their particularity, cannot take account of other people's; White people create the dominant images of the world and don't quite see that they thus construct the world in their own image; White people set standards of humanity by which they are bound to succeed and others to fail. (Dyer, 1997, p. 9)

One of the tragic implications that has so much bearing on building intercultural alliances is that the social reality of race overutilizes myths while underutilizing the human impulse to deny the illusory nature of race. Racial differences are not scientifically real, but they are socially real because the hierarchical system allows one group in power to make them seem real through ideological discourse, pseudoscience, and the media (Dixon & Linz, 2000; Entman & Rojecki, 2000). Hence, the unraveling of race and potential for alliance building is predicated upon demythologizing race. The alternative, to do and say nothing except in compliance with the illusion, contributes to the present conditions of race relations and intercultural communication in the United States.

Another important illusion around race is that if race is constructed, then it has no reality or consequences. Yet this constructed fantasy can and does transcend its origins into "truth" via inferential racism. Hall (1995) explains,

By *inferential* racism I mean those apparently naturalised representations of events and situations relating to race, whether "factual" or "fictional," which have racist premises and propositions inscribed in them as a set of *unquestioned assumptions*. These enable racist statements to be formulated without ever bringing into awareness the racist predicates on which the statements are grounded. (p. 20)

The impulse to deny the idea of race may stem from the reality that those in a position of social dominance have the privilege to deny it. Whites in the United States can afford to ignore the (constructed) realities of race because whiteness is normal and Whites are not forced to live with the same realities as Blacks, much less the consequences of those realities. If U.S. constitutional rights and the pillar of U.S. democracy rhetorically ensure full access to humanity and to equal treatment under the law, then it would be antithetic to whiteness ideology's themes of humanism and color-blindness to suddenly acknowledge racial disadvantages. In other words, it is consistent for whiteness to remain resolute about the nonexistence of race as a real barrier to human progress. With this is mind, it is difficult for whiteness to

be the pervading ideology and still suggest that because one is Black, one is less likely to succeed due to structural constraints that preserve the centrality of whiteness.

Distinct yet incorrect definitions of (color)-ness are plentiful in U.S. society (Dixon & Linz, 2000; Entman & Rojecki, 2000). Radio, TV, film, and print media constructions of Blacks, Latinos, and Asians are similar. In essence, what is being mediated is a White definition of what it means to be (color or ethnicity), no matter how flawed. Yet no similar definition of whiteness exists. This is possible because Whites wield the power and are not subject to it (Jackson, in press).

One example of definition by color is the image of OJ Simpson on the cover of *Time* magazine. After being accused of stabbing his (White) ex-wife and her companion, his face was darkened by the magazine. This is a literal instance of race amplification, of a Black man *being raced*.

IMPLICATIONS

Fantasy themes of whiteness are constructed and communicated individually, ideologically, socially, and racially. This rhetorical vision also affects interracial and interracial alliance building or cultural contracts. When Blacks and Whites enter into "cultural contracts" (Jackson, in press; Jackson et al., 2002), they bring with them a set of assumptions and convictions. Cultural contracts are implicit agreements about whether to coordinate a relationship with cultural others. It is an identity negotiation paradigm, which suggests that cultural interactants exchange codes of personhood as they come into contact with one another.

Authorial Perspective

I, the first author of this chapter, am a White male, and I have been taught as a white to assume my way is the right way. Whiteness ideology, which is pervasive in the United States, solidifies White entitlement. As Crenshaw (1997) states, "If one pretends one's own privileged social location has no impact on her ability to make epistemic claims, the result may very well be the continuation or (re)production of oppression" (p. 268).

Race is interesting to me, the second author of this chapter, as a Black male because it is about an attempt to seize one's humanity. My disenchantment with extant interracial alliance strategies is that they often appear and function as vacuous, self-serving political maneuvers toward satisfying

political action mandates or hidden agendas of dominant institutions rather than as genuine efforts. This unfortunately leads to poor outcomes, ones that inhibit progress toward unifying with the intended community(ies). Racial resolution strategies are much more compelling when they lead to personal growth, institutional change, or social reform. They are practical when they get beyond views of cultural diversity, which only seek to acknowledge the presence of difference without fully valuing it. Multiculturalism, on the other hand, is about full valuation. That is where interracial alliance building must begin.

We believe that the concept of humanism has always been selectively applied. Therefore, to use it as a foundation for alliance building may not, in the view of non-Whites, be an effective strategy. Humanism as a concept is not necessarily flawed; its history, however, is. Those who might believe in the universal applicability of humanism would do well to acknowledge the concept's tarnished history.

Color-blindness may also be problematic in interracial and intercultural alliance building when those who can afford to deny their own coloredness problematize color. This does little to aid alliance building. By making color something to be avoided, to be overlooked, ignored, or written off, the assumption of White as a noncolor continues, thus preserving its centrality and superiority. Conversely, it places the burden of wrongness, in the form of color, on people of color. Whiteness ideology preserves its centrality and the implicit assumption that Whites are already ahead in the debate by virtue of their "transcendence" of color into "humanity." This reifies people of color as wrong, ideologically underdeveloped, and in need of philosophical assistance so that they too might achieve the heights of "humanity." Whiteness' schizophrenic ideas about color and race, therefore, lead to difficulty in alliance building. Whites' refusal to see race except in persons of color helps to camouflage their position and that position's particularity.

Whiteness' rejection of race explains the popular resistance to hate-speech codes; if race is not real, then criminalizing "racist" speech seems pointless (Jackson & Heckman, in press). Yet the premise behind hate-speech codes is the disquieting reality that the real-life consequences of race are felt primarily by non-Whites.

When a denial of race is operationalized in interracial alliance building, another set of problems arises. First, to deny the realities of race is to refuse to acknowledge a large segment of the lived realities of people of color. Critical understandings of racial profiling, the inequalities in the justice system (especially in the use of the death penalty), and real estate redlining (in which African Americans are shown and sold houses based on the

surrounding neighborhood's ethnicity rather than their income; Frankenberg, 1993, p. 47) hinge on the knowledge that the socially constructed realities and consequences of race are far from mythical. Thus, when one half of an alliance asserts the illusory nature of what for the other half is a lived reality, the alliance is doomed.

Perhaps the most important implication whiteness carries for interracial alliance building has to do with unconsciously equating what is natural or "human" with what it means to be White. Further, membership in the dominant segment of society provides a cementing of the rhetorical vision because there exists no equal (in terms of social power), opposing framework.

Our intention in this chapter is to contribute to scholarship that seeks not only to define whiteness but also to show where it is placed. For too long whiteness has occupied an unwarranted and invisible position at the center. It is especially important to understand that due to the ideology of whiteness, conceptions of reality, ideas of how things ought to be (and ought to be done), are seen as White. Whiteness tells Whites that they are acting as humans, as objective beings; the reality is quite different. What is dangerous is the assumption of the innate rightness or superiority of these methods and beliefs: By strenuously reserving their right to their "humanity," by demanding to be seen and/or treated as individuals, and assuming the rightness of their perspective, Whites are perpetuating and preserving rhetorical and ideological dominance. This assumption of rightness is especially harmful when non-Whites are intellectually or philosophically discounted or dismissed for seeking to highlight the placement of Whites and whiteness at and as the center.

RECOMMENDATIONS FOR FURTHER RESEARCH

There are a number of concepts related to social definition based on difference that would be very rewarding avenues of research. This chapter does not intensively examine the class or gender dynamics of whiteness. However, we know that many would argue that class and race are inextricably linked and that a solely race-based analysis is impossible. In this chapter, we have attempted to offer examples of dominance, which in a capitalist economy clearly signify issues of class. We have not focused on economic forecasting or foregrounding, though we would encourage future research in that area of inquiry.

Frankenberg's (1997) assertion that to be White is not necessarily to be powerful is a class argument in support of whiteness ideology and needs to

be addressed in future studies. Recent postcolonial whiteness literature has touched on this aspect, but more is needed. The effect of gender on whiteness, as well as the inverse relationship, is also an important area in need of further research. Likewise, there are clear intersections between sexuality, gender, race, religion, and identity. Future studies must explore rhetorical visions and ideologies concerning these topics. Disability is yet another important issue; there is great potential in conducting investigations of rhetorical visions to interrogate assumptions while elucidating the presumptive claims of normality and competence.

Frameworks like Jackson's "cultural contracts theory" (Jackson, in press; Jackson et al., 2002) or McPhail's (1994) "complicity theory" may be useful paradigms for further exploring how White identities and ideologies are socially constructed. McPhail's (1994) complicity theory explores the means by which two or more parties engage one another and move toward "coherence," or genuine connectedness. The tragedy, McPhail contends, emerges when communities and individuals comply with illusions about race and difference without seeking to understand and value one another first.

The deconstructive nature of this exploration has served as one critical approach to the study of whiteness. There will be many more added to the growing body of whiteness research. The central concern of this chapter is that it is through the deconstruction of whiteness ideology as communicated in rhetorical visions and fantasy themes that we begin the transformative process of alliance building in the United States. Alliance building may best begin via honest and open dialogue between dominant and marginalized group members. There is no natural way to be, so there must be a coalition between persons and ideas that consciously progresses toward positive, unified social transformation.

REFERENCES

Alcoff, L. (1996). What should White people do? *Hypatia, 13*(3), 6-26.

Ani, M. (1994). *Yurugu.* Trenton, NJ: Africa World Press.

Appiah, K., & Gutmann, A. (1996). *Color conscious.* Princeton, NJ: Princeton University Press.

Bales, R. F. (1970). *Personality and interpersonal behavior.* New York: Holt, Rinehart & Winston.

Baugh, J. (2000). Racial identification by speech. *American Speech, 75*(4), 362-364.

Blackham, H. J. (1976) *Humanism.* New York: Penguin.

Bormann, E. G. (1972). Fantasy and rhetorical vision: The rhetorical criticism of social reality. *Quarterly Journal of Speech, 58*, 396-407.

Bormann, E. G. (1982). Colloquy: Fantasy and rhetorical vision: Ten years later. *Quarterly Journal of Speech, 68*, 288-305.

Bormann, E. G., Cragan, J. F., & Shields, D. C. (1994). In defense of symbolic convergence theory: A look at the theory and its criticisms after two decades. *Communication Theory, 4*, 259-294.

Bowers, J., Ochs, D., & Jensen, R. (1993). *The rhetoric of agitation and control.* Prospect Heights, IL: Waveland.

Crenshaw, C. (1997). Resisting whiteness' rhetorical silence. *Western Journal of Communication, 61*(3), 253-279.

Davies, T. (1997). *Humanism.* New York: Routledge.

Delgado, F. (2000). All along the border: Kid Frost and the performance of brown masculinity. *Critical Studies in Media Communication, 20*(4), 388-401.

Dixon, T., & Linz, D. (2000). Overrepresentation and underrepresentation of African Americans and Latinos as lawbreakers on television news. *Journal of Communication, 50*(2), 131-154.

Dyer, R. (1997). *White.* New York: Routledge.

Ellison, R. (1947). *Invisible man.* New York: Random House.

Entman, R., & Rojecki, A. (2000). *The black image in the white mind.* Chicago: University of Chicago Press.

Frankenberg, R. (1993). *White women, race matters: The social construction of whiteness.* Minneapolis: University of Minnesota Press.

Frankenberg, R. (1997). (Ed.). *Displacing whiteness: Essays in social and cultural criticism.* Durham, NC: Duke University Press.

Golden, J. L., Berquist, G. F., & Coleman, W.E. (1992). *The rhetoric of Western thought.* Dubuque, IA: Kendall Hunt.

Gresson, A. (1995). *The recovery of race in America.* Minneapolis: University of Minnesota Press.

Grossberg, L. (1997). History, politics and postmodernism. In D. Morley, K. Chen, & S. Hall (Eds.), *Critical dialogues in cultural studies.* New York: Routledge

Hall, S. (1982). The rediscovery of "Ideology": Return of the repressed in media studies. In M. Gurevitch, J. Woollacott, T. Bennett, & J. Curran (Eds.), *Culture, society and the media.* New York: Routledge.

Hall, S. (1995). The whites of their eyes. In G. Dines & J. M. Humez (Eds.), *Gender, race and class: A media reader.* Thousand Oaks, CA: Sage.

Hall, S. (1997). *Representation.* London: Sage.

Hart, R. (1997). *Modern rhetorical criticism.* Boston: Allyn & Bacon.

Helms, J. E. (1994). A race is a nice thing to have: A guide to being a white person. Topeka, KS: Content Communications.

hooks, b. (1995). *Killing rage: Ending racism.* New York: Henry Holt.

hooks, b. (1997). Representing whiteness in the black imagination. In R. Frankenberg (Ed.), *Displacing whiteness: Essays in social and cultural criticism.* Durham, NC: Duke University Press.

Jackson, R. L. (1999b). White space, white privilege: Mapping discursive inquiry into the self. *Quarterly Journal of Speech, 85*(4), 1-17.

Jackson, R. L. (1999a). *Negotiation of cultural identity*. Westport, CT: Greenwood.

Jackson, R. L. (2000). So real illusions of Black intellectualism: Exploring race, roles, and gender in the academy. *Communication Theory, 10*(1), 48-63.

Jackson, R. L. (2002). Exploring African American identity negotiation in the academy: Toward a transformative vision of African American communication scholarship. *Howard Journal of Communication, 12*(4), 45-50.

Jackson, R. L. (in press). Cultural contracts theory: Toward an identity negotiation paradigm. In P. Sullivan & D. Goldzwig (Eds.), *Communities, creations, and contradictions: New approaches to rhetoric for the twenty-first century*. East Lansing: Michigan State University Press.

Jackson, R. L., & Heckman, S. (2002). Perceptions of White identity and White liability: An analysis of White student responses to a college campus racial hate crime. *Journal of Communication, 52*(2), 434-450.

Jackson, R. L., Morrison, C. D., & Dangerfield, C. (2002). Exploring cultural contracts in the classroom and curriculum: Implications of identity negotiation and effects in communication curricula. In J. Trent (Ed.), *Included in communication: Learning climates that cultivate racial and ethnic diversity* (pp. 123-136). Washington, DC: National Communication Association & American Association of Higher Education.

Jackson, R. L., Shin, C. I., & Wilson, K. B. (2000). The meaning of whiteness: Critical implications of communicating and negotiating race. *World Communication, 29*(1), 69-86.

Kim, Y. Y. (1991). Intercultural communication competence: A systems-theoretic view. In S. Ting-Toomey & F. Korzenny (Eds.), *Cross-cultural interpersonal communication*. Newbury Park, CA: Sage.

Littlejohn, S. W. (1999). *Theories of human communication*. Belmont, CA: Wadsworth.

Lloyd, D. (1990). Race under representation. *Oxford Literary Review, 12*, 62-93.

Makus, A. (1990). Stuart Hall's theory of ideology: A frame for rhetorical criticism. *Western Journal of Speech Communication, 54*, 494-514.

McIntosh, P. (1992). White privilege and male privilege: A personal account of coming to see correspondences through work in women's studies. In M. Anderson & P. Hill-Collins (Eds.), *Race, class, and gender: An anthology* (pp. 70-81). Belmont, CA: Wadsworth.

McKerrow, R. E. (1999). Critical rhetoric: Theory and praxis. In J. L. Lucaites, C. M. Condit, & S. Caudill (Eds.), *Contemporary rhetorical theory: A reader*. New York: Guilford.

McPhail, M. (1994). The politics of complicity: Second thoughts about the social construction of racial equality. *Quarterly Journal of Speech, 80*, 343-357.

McWhorter, J. (2000). *Losing the race: Self-sabotage in Black America*. New York: Free Press.

Milton S. Eisenhower Foundation. (1998). *Millennium breach, the American dilemma, richer and poorer: In commemoration of the thirtieth anniversary of the National Advisory Commission on Civil Disorders.* Washington, DC: Milton S. Eisenhower Foundation.

Mohrmann, G. P. (1982). An essay on fantasy theme criticism. *Quarterly Journal of Speech, 68,* 109-132.

Nakayama, T., & Krizek, R. (1999). Whiteness as a strategic rhetoric. In T. Nakayama & J. Martin (Eds.), *Whiteness: The communication of social identity.* Thousand Oaks, CA: Sage.

Nakayama, T., & Martin, J. (Eds.). (1999). *Whiteness: The communication of social identity.* Thousand Oaks, CA: Sage.

Poliakov, L. (1982). Racism from the enlightenment to the age of imperialism. In R. Ross (Ed.), *Racism and colonialism: Essays on ideology and social structure.* The Hague, The Netherlands: Martinus Nijhoff.

Potter, W. J. (1996). *An analysis of thinking and research about qualitative methods.* Mahwah, NJ: Lawrence Erlbaum.

Shipler, D. K. (1997). *A country of strangers: Blacks and Whites in America.* New York: Random House.

Stebbins, R. (1992). *Sociology: The study of society.* New York: Harper & Row.

Thompson, H. S. (1997). *The proud highway: Saga of a desperate Southern gentleman.* New York: Random House.

Twine, F. W. (1997). Brown skinned White girls: Class, culture, and the construction of White identity in suburban communities. In R. Delgado & J. Stefancic (Eds.), *Critical white studies: Looking behind the mirror.* Philadelphia: Temple University Press.

Wallace, L. (2001). *Are Black shoppers treated unfairly? An expensive new reason to care.* Retrieved June 8, 2001, from http:www.diversityinc.com/insidearticlepg.cfm?submenuID

Warmoth, A. (1996). *Humanistic psychology and humanistic social science.* Retrieved June 8, 2001, from www.sonoma.edu/classes/psych490/fall96/writings/arthurw/humsoc.html

Webster, Y. (1992). *The racialization of America.* New York: St. Martin's.

West, C. (1994). *Race matters.* New York: Random House.

5

The Two Nations Talk

An Analysis of Rapprochement and Alienation in Two South African National Radio Talk Shows

MELISSA E. STEYN   •   *University of Cape Town*

> The constitution provides a historic bridge between the past of a deeply divided society characterized by strife, conflict, untold suffering and injustice, and a future founded on the recognition of human rights, democracy, peaceful coexistence, and development opportunities for all South Africans, irrespective of colour, race, class, creed or sex. The pursuit of national unity, the well being of all South African citizens and peace require reconciliation between the people of South Africa and the reconstruction of society.
>
> The adoption of this constitution lays the foundation for the people of South Africa to transcend the divisions and strife of the past, which generated gross violations of human rights, the transgression of humanitarian principles in violent conflicts and a legacy of hatred, fear, guilt and revenge.
>
> Epilogue of the Interim Constitution of South Africa (Act 200 of 1993)

Reconciliation was the task to which South African society nervously set itself as the 1994 elections ushered in the nation's first experience of full democracy, headed by President Nelson Mandela. From an intercultural communication perspective, the magnitude of the task of South African reconciliation cannot be underestimated. South Africa had been a pathologically divided society, structured by systems of racial inequality and endemic violence (Foster, 2000; Marais, 1985; Schutte, 1995; Wilson, 2000; Zegeye, 2001b). The vision for the new social order was to bridge chasms brought about by three centuries of colonial rule and 40 years of legally institutionalized segregation, and to create a national culture that

would "decrease the barriers between different identities, language groups and cultures" (Zegeye, 2001a, p. 337). In reality, alliance across racial and ethnic divides, inspired by a vision of a united society, was far from new— it was imbedded within the previously subjugated liberation struggle movement both as an ideal and a practice (Gerwel, 2000; Zegeye, 2001b). Drawing diverse activists into a common identification, the movement saw itself as "an exercise in nation-building at the same time as it represented an opposition to a racially based system" (Gerwel, 2000, p. 227). Now that several years have passed since the end of the struggle era and the change to majority rule, commentators and analysts increasingly reflect on the extent to which this ethos has infused the nation and on whether the South African groupings within the general populace have taken on the challenge to ally themselves across the historical divides and reconstruct themselves as the reconciled nation envisaged by those who wrote the constitution (Bell, 2001; Chabedi, 2001).

This chapter attempts to capture something of the ongoing intercultural negotiation process under way in this context where social identities and group allegiances have been unsettled (Bekker, 1996; Dolby, 2001; Morrell, 2001; Steyn, 2001; Zegeye 2001a). I suggest that although many South Africans are working tirelessly to bridge the divides, there is resistance within the country to the processes of dismantling the boundaries of "us" and "them," and that, in fact, at the level of ordinary citizens, considerable effort is being put into extending past alignments into the present where it is perceived to be in some group interests to do so. To illustrate this, the first section of this chapter summarizes current commentary and research on intercultural and interracial relations in South Africa, pointing to the enduring existence of separate life-worlds. Lotman's (1991) concept of the semiosphere is drawn on as an explanatory framework.

The second section presents a close analysis of the discourses used by callers participating in two radio talk shows. The shows were broadcast on the national radio station, SAFM, which serves the English-speaking community in South Africa. Its listenership has been predominantly white in the past but is increasingly more diverse. The mix of programs is similar to that of National Public Radio in the United States, and its motto is "the station for the well-informed." The two talk shows chosen for analysis were *Microphone-in* and *The Tim Modise Show*. Until recently the former was broadcast weekly in the evening, and the latter still is broadcast every weekday in the morning.

Two key questions that are the source of ongoing debates and that have bearing on issues of reconciliation between white and black South Africans[1]

and on nation building were chosen for analysis, namely: Can white South Africans be regarded as Africans? and Do white South Africans owe black South Africans financial restitution? These themes, variously formulated, reach back into the colonial past of the country, and have been recurrently revisited within the political, public, and academic domains in South Africa, helping to shape both the liberation struggle and the dominant white position.[2] As such, the still active debates in the society around these themes are part of the ongoing struggle for reconciliation.

Using critical discourse analysis, the comments were analyzed according to a conceptual framework suggested by Baumann (1997). Baumann argues that the two discursive competencies employed in cross-cultural alliance building are dominant and demotic discourses. Dominant discourses attempt to hold extant boundaries intact; demotic discourses provide transgressive opportunities that disrupt dominant cultural closures. This chapter concludes with some suggestions of what the analysis shows about intercultural alliance building.

THE "RAINBOW NATION"?

The debate on just how well the nation is achieving the goal of reconciliation is charged with contestation. Under the presidency of the Nobel Peace Prize recipient and internationally acclaimed icon of reconciliation, Nelson Mandela, South African society readily adopted the self-label of the "Rainbow Nation." The term was used by Archbishop Desmond Tutu, at the first session of the Truth and Reconciliation Commission, when he spoke of "we, this rainbow people of God" (Chabedi, 2001). It signified bringing together the many distinct groupings within the country into an inclusive whole through the promise of reconciliation; a multicultural people allied to a common destiny, belonging to a common home, and sharing a common nationhood.

The "rainbow" characterization played such a prominent role in structuring the cultural politics of the 1990s (Nuttall & Michael, 2000a) that the "rainbow nation" became synonymous with South Africa itself (Gqola, 2001). But the metaphor has been vigorously criticized for obscuring too much (Chabedi, 2001; Gqola, 2001; Ramphele, 2000) and for being "about polite proximities, about containment" (Nuttal & Michael, 2000a, p. 6).

One stream of objection to the "rainbow nation" symbol can be traced back to the negotiated settlement that laid the foundations of national reconciliation. The political process that forged the provisional constitution

had come about as a result of the recognition that a military stalemate had been reached in a context where there was no clear victor (De Lange, 2000), leaving a sense of an incomplete resolution of the power struggle and an unfinished process of decolonization. Masrui[3] has characterized this kind of compromise as the division of labor between black political power and white economic privilege: "The white man said to the black man: 'You take the crown, and I will keep the jewels.'" By this analysis, the rainbow metaphor may mask the realities of the inequities that still eat away at the heart of the society.

The Truth and Reconciliation Commission was charged with the task of laying the foundations for an inclusive future (Asmal, Asmal, & Roberts, 1997; Chabedi, 2001; James & van de Vijver, 2000; Nuttall & Coetzee, 1998; Villa-Vicencio & Verwoerd, 2000). The commission was to deal with the past in such a way that an honest footing could be established on which the nation could stand as it stepped into the future. This purpose necessitated that the reality of the suffering and victimization of the black majority be acknowledged. It also required that the gross violations of human rights that had occurred during the Apartheid years, and the people who had performed these deeds, be "outed" and shamed publicly (De Lange, 2000). The task of the commission could also be seen as creating common frameworks of understandings and shared discourses through which white and black realities could be drawn closer together. "The exercise of facing the South African past, no mere horror story or exercise in historical voyeurism, is rather, in multiple ways . . . the cornerstone of reconstruction" (Asmal et al., p. 11). Its work has been generally regarded as groundbreaking, and is often seen as helping to avoid a civil war in South Africa (Hayner, 2000; Shea, 2000).

A body of criticism within the country, however, maintains that the commission focused too much on reconciliation and not enough on the righting of wrongs; that it was, in fact, a perpetrator-friendly process that short-changed victims and neglected the deeper structural injury inflicted by Colonialism and Apartheid, to the advantage of the beneficiaries (Bell, 2001; Biko, 2000; Bundy, 2000; Henry, 2000; Mamdani, 2000; Mandaza, 1999). In this view, black people were once again doing the emotional work required for reconciliation and freely extending forgiveness, whereas white South Africans were not being honest enough about their complicity with the past system, and were not approaching the process with sufficient humility or even interest[4] (Biko, 2000; Henry, 2000). More radical critics believe that in taking an excessively "gentle" approach toward the

Apartheid past, the process has actually exacerbated divisions across racial lines in South Africa (Gibson & Macdonald, 2001). Future generations, in this view, have been endowed with "a poison chalice" in the form of unfinished business, which will inevitably resurface at a later stage in the country's history (Bell, 2001).

Several studies have attempted to ascertain the extent to which the groupings within the country have in reality drawn closer together. While the society has made progress toward developing a sense of nationhood, marked differences persist in the ways in which white and black South Africans react to key issues in the life of the nation. A survey conducted in 1999 by the Independent Newspaper Group and the Henry J. Kaiser Family Foundation, "Reality Check: South Africans' Views of the New South Africa" (Brodie, Altman, & Sinclair, 1999), found notable differences between the perceptions of the New South Africa of white and black South Africans. The reporters found that the black population, while overwhelmingly poor, believed that the future would be better and were appreciative of the changes that had taken place. The white population, by contrast, who more logically could be regarded as the "winners" in the process of reconciliation, were disgruntled, and seemed to view everything through a veil of negativity (Brodie et al., 1999; MacGregor, 1999). The coloured and Indian groups positioned themselves between these two poles.[5]

Other significant research conducted by independent civic institutes notes similar attitudinal faultlines persisting into the New South Africa. The Institute for Justice and Reconciliation (2001), established as an internationally-funded, nongovernmental organization that seeks to continue the work of the TRC (Truth and Reconciliation Commission) (Shea, 2000), published a report titled "Truth—Yes, Reconciliation—Maybe: South Africans Judge the Truth and Reconciliation Process" (Gibson & Macdonald, 2001). The report found the evidence of reconciliation mixed and concluded that "South Africa is far from being a contented 'Rainbow Nation,' but it is also a country in which many seem to reject the intense racial animosity of the past" (p. 19).[6] The researchers commented:

> The survey results are not surprising but rather disappointing. . . . White South Africans appear negative and unwilling to contribute to the process of national reconciliation. This is in stark contrast to black and coloured attitudes. Perhaps this is the reason why South Africa was able to undergo peaceful political transition, as black South Africans seem far more willing to embrace the notion and responsibility of reconciliation than white South Africans. (p. 4)

Finally, national leaders have raised pointed questions about the commitment of all South Africans to forming alliances across racial barriers. In his final report as the leader of the African National Congress, thenpresident Nelson Mandela chastised white South Africans for exploiting national reconciliation in such a way that the goal of social transformation was obscured (Mandela, 1997). A year later, in an even more outspoken, and highly contentious, speech, the then deputy-president, Thabo Mbeki (1998), spoke against the "rainbow" grain by arguing that the material conditions of the society resulted in the persisting division of the country into two nations: one rich, and predominantly white, and one poor, and predominantly black. He maintained that South Africans had not created a sense of common destiny:

> The longer this situation persists, in spite of the gift of hope delivered to the people by the birth of democracy, the more entrenched will be the conviction that the concept of nation building is a mere mirage and that no basis exists, or will ever exist, to enable national reconciliation to take place. (p. 188)

His words contained a clear statement of disappointment in, and an implied reprimand of, white South Africans for a lack of integrity regarding the process of reconciliation and nation building. As he put it: "Those who were responsible for, or were the beneficiaries of, the past, absolve themselves from any obligation to help do away with an unacceptable legacy" (p. 192).

In pointing to the different experiences occasioned by the unequal material conditions of sections of the population, and the marked divergence in understanding of these inequalities, Mbeki was insisting that the continuing existence of unreconciled interpretive communities in relation to the process of societal reconciliation and reconstruction be acknowledged. And in linking the projects of nation building and democratization to social justice, to dismantling gross inequity, and to deracializing the nation, he was indicating his sensitivity to the voices of the African majority. While heavily criticized, the view has nonetheless been supported by some prominent South African academics (Bundy, 2000; Lever & James, 2000; Wilson, 2000).

TWO NATIONS?

The Apartheid ideology that the new order seeks to transcend was premised upon notions of culture as static and exclusive and was based at heart on a

belief in the "fundamental irreconcilability of peoples" (Asmal et al., 1997, p. 51). Maintaining culturally distinct and constructed communities was also part of the "project of gaining political hegemony" (Zegeye & Liebenberg, 2001, p. 316). People were taught to fear those who were not part of "their" social entity and to reject the cultural manifestations of the "other." As Zegeye and Liebenberg put it: "Although Apartheid failed to create viable self-sufficient nations for the majority of people in society, it did create the cultural ethos associated with defending those nationals and groups" (p. 317). Starkly opposed to this view of culture, cultural theorists now generally acknowledge that all cultures are hybrid (Nuttal & Michael, 2000a, 2000b; Werbner & Modood, 1997). "Culture . . . exists only in its variations and transitions. Culture in itself, then, is the result of past, present, and future processes of creolisation" (Wicker, 1997, p. 38). Conceptions of culture as a coherent, homogenous, reified "thing" that people "have" are increasingly regarded as extensions of racist conceptualizing and as simply inaccurate, especially in the age of globalization (Friedman, 1997).

The same kind of debate has emphasized de-essentialized notions of identity. Current conceptions theorize identity as complex, fluid, multiple, palimpsestic, and hybrid, and as constructed by drawing on available symbolic systems within the social realm. Melucci (1997), for example, sees identity as a *field* defined by sets of relations and suggests that we should think of it in terms of *identitisation*, a term that communicates the dynamic processes by which individuals construct their identities (p. 64).

The more interesting question, then, as Werbner (1997a) points out, is not why creolization occurs but why actors in a "negotiated field of meaning constantly attempt to deny and defy these processes of hybridisation" (p. 8). Indeed, the current flux in the social and political organization within South Africa accentuates the fluidity inherent in the nature of social processes. The context necessitates that individuals and collectives undertake a certain amount of self-redefinition (Bekker, 1996; Morrell, 2001; Steyn, 2001; Wicomb, 2001). At the same time, the society offers increased choice and new possibilities for identitisation, offers greater opportunities for breaking down clearly demarcated notions of self and other, and exerts new pressures toward blurring cultural boundaries.

It may be useful to draw on Lotman's (1991) concept of the semiosphere in seeking to understand the tenacious character of the largely incommensurate life-worlds of black and white South Africans implicit in the findings cited above. Lotman sees the semiosphere, "the whole semiotic space of culture," as the cultural equivalent of the biosphere in environmental

theory (p. 125). It is the heterogeneous totality of the "dynamic process of influence, transformation and coexistence within the space of culture" (Papastergiadis, 1997, p. 268).

One could argue that, historically, black South Africans have inhabited a semiosphere infused with suffering and abject poverty, steeped in discourses of struggle, hope, and resistance held in tension with discourses of endurance, despair, and internalized oppression. White South Africans, by contrast, have lived in privileged conditions, largely unaware of, even indifferent to, the world in which black South Africans lived. Their semiosphere has been infused with the centuries-old racist discourses of Eurocentric Colonialism, recycled into the logic of Apartheid (Magubane, 1999; Ndebele, 1998, 2000a; Steyn, 2001; Wicomb, 2001). The blindnesses that accompany whiteness (Dyer, 1997; Frankenberg, 1993; Gabriel, 1998; McIntyre, 1997; Nakayama & Martin, 1999), and the discursive resources that circulate in this life-world, encourage notions of entitlement and provide scant wherewithal for understanding the sense-making that shaped the experience of being black in South Africa. Through its position of privileged power, the "white world" was largely able to subjugate the free expression of the categories, tropes, and definitions emerging from the subordinated majority. Where internal contestation existed within this life-world, it occurred primarily along the deeply entrenched English-Afrikaans ethnic divide, which, while providing different stances toward the Afrikaner nationalist government, was allied in terms of constructing a white identity with the African majority as the "other" (Fredrickson, 1981; Steyn, 1999, 2001; Wicomb, 2001).[7]

A situation of such polarized interpretive communities clearly presents particular difficulties to effective intercultural rapprochement. Lotman (1991) argues that every culture begins by dividing the world into "its own" internal space and "their" external space, which are separated by boundaries that "control, filter and adapt the external into the internal" (p. 140). In the South African context, a great deal of "border work" was done to maintain worlds that were in great measure closed along political as well as social lines. Yet the process by which cultural transformation occurs, according to Lotman, begins at the boundaries between semiospheres, where "creolized semiotic systems come into being" (p. 142). Working back through the cultural space toward the center, a kind of semiotic convection current is set in motion, which works through to the center. The "strangeness" of the "other" is gradually dissolved within the receiving culture, which is transformed in the process (p. 147). A precondition for this process to occur,

however, is that both groups are interested in overcoming the barriers that inevitably arise in this process of dialogue (p. 143).

Applied to the South African context, forging a different, inclusive South African society requires a concerted, dedicated project of culture making at the boundaries of the semiospheres, creating sufficient shared symbolic resources to begin the process of mutual transformation. Received sense-making has to be sufficiently disrupted to allow for revision of past understandings, for discursive practice to draw more individuals across the interpretive borders, enabling a significant measure of cultural creolization. At the same time, sufficient continuity for social groups, with their multiplicity of memories (De Kok, 1998) has to be preserved to prevent complete disintegration of social identities. "Culture-making," in the words of Gerd Baumann (1997), "is not an ex tempore improvisation but a project of social continuity placed within, and contending with, moments of social change" (p. 214). At the level of social identity formation, it requires the creation of much more complex selves, selves based less on simple dichotomies that dehumanize the other and trade on enemy images. Simply put, both the culture-making and identity-forming dimensions of generating new meanings of, and for, the nation depend on transgressive acts to blur the borders of the semiospheres and open up possibilities of alliance building across hitherto entrenched divides. Such realignments may take multiple forms: recognition of existing sites of disruption; complex processes of making connections; developing commonly shared, hybridized, multiple identities; synergistic, third culture building, and movement toward greater social integration (Nuttall & Michael, 2000b; Steyn & Motshabi, 1996; Kriger & Zegeye, 2001).

"THE DAILY PLEBISCITE OF MANY NATIONAL VOICES"

Discursive work at the boundary of the two semiopheres outlined above plays a major constitutive role in shaping social identity. Foster (1999) explains: "Categories are not given, but are debated and argued over: they are constantly reconstructed in everyday discursive patterns.... Social positionings are due to active arguments, rhetorical positions, and discursive construction of categories" (p. 342). All of these are constantly being reworked through "the quotidian daily plebiscite of many national voices" (Werbner, 1997a, p. 14). Two popular talk shows on the national English radio station, SAFM—*Microphone-in* and *The Tim Modise Show*—are sites

that provide occasions during which "the nation talks with the nation," where discursive jockeying can be caught "in the act." These radio programs provide the material that is analyzed below. Two themes have been chosen for analysis: (1) the issue of whether white South Africans can legitimately call themselves "African," and (2) whether they owe black South Africans financial restitution. The themes are hotly contested precisely because they affect the boundaries between the two semiospheres: the retention of current alignments and identifications, the separation of interests, and the differentiation of realities.

The programs were recorded and transcribed during 1998 and 1999. A note was made of whether the caller was male or female and whether the caller's "race" was identifiable on the basis of accent, language of family name, or self-identification. Given the historical segregation of groups in South Africa, such distinctions can be made with a great deal of accuracy, and generally, callers did self-identify wherever there was any doubt, given the racially charged topics under discussion. Working within the general framework of discourse analysis, each caller's comments were closely analyzed to identify how each comment fit in with the broader culturally shared interpretive frames of reference (Wetherell & Potter, 1998). The analysis focused on what the comment did as opposed to merely what it said. Attempting to situate comments within a broad social context in this manner is part of the task of discourse analysis (Billig, 1988).

After the first phase of analysis, the comments were further analyzed using the conceptual framework suggested by Baumann (1997), who argues that in working cultural terrain in order to (deconstruct or re)construct boundaries of collective identification, people draw on at least two discursive competences: dominant discourses that attempt to hold reified boundaries intact and demotic discourses that attempt to dislocate community and culture, and thereby provide transgressive opportunities that may change identification.

The sample obviously is, in a sense, self-selected in that it consists of people who have voluntarily contributed their opinions to a public forum. Although it cannot be assumed that these voices necessarily articulate a generalizable "mass" opinion (if there is such a thing), it can safely be assumed that these voices are representative to some degree of various strains of sense-making among the population. The callers are identified in terms of gender for the reader's interest, but no attempt has been made to infer generalizations on gender from the data in this sample.

DOMINANT AND DEMOTIC DISCOURSES IN THE THEME: CAN WHITES BE REGARDED AS AFRICANS?

The majority of black Africans who commented on this topic used dominant discourses, evincing a sense of ownership of the identification of African through an emotional and historical claim. They clearly felt that they should be the ones to determine who belongs to this category, and who does not. Callers communicated the belief that there is some kind of "real," authentic, essential African quality, trait, or heritage by which Africanness can be identified.

> You are an African if you have only one ancestry. This is what we have always called ourselves. A European person remains European. Whites are at best European-African, but only one out of ten would qualify for that. The rest are simply European. [female]

> Their [white people's] ancestors are from Europe. [male]

There is an undertone of distancing, even rejection, that runs through the above quotations, and it seems to be driven by skepticism about the "good faith" in which whites are now claiming to be African. The fact that whites have based their identities and behavior on a sense of European superiority to black South Africans is illustrated in the comments below:

> Some whites take umbrage at being called African. They see it as an insult. [male]

> The people from Europe see themselves as having a common destiny. [male]

A question mark hangs over the motives of those who previously benefited from the exploitation of the black majority, largely indifferent to their suffering, now claiming to be one of them. For the callers below, there is a suggestion that whites don't want to pay the costs bequeathed to the New South Africa by the system they previously supported, and that they again want to appropriate the most advantageous subject position.

> Whites are looking for justification now. [male]

> Now that it suits whites they want to be African. They didn't want to before 1990. [male]

Yet for some black callers, it appears to be less the fact of white pigmentation that militates against inclusion of whites as Africans than the whiteness ideology to which they subscribe. Comments pointed to chauvinism, participation in the denigration of the continent, and superficiality of engagement with the issues of the continent. Attitudes of mind such as these disqualify white South Africans from being accepted as Africans.

They don't know Africa. If they go on holiday it's to Europe or America. They've never traveled north of the Limpopo river. They even talk about South Africa as if it's separate from Africa. [male]

They always make as if it is only African countries that fight wars. [male]

Making a pointed jibe at this perceived lack of integrity, the question was asked by the next caller whether whites would share not only the new recognition of black Africans' legitimacy which has come with democracy, but also the insults that have been inflicted on them historically:

If Europeans can be Africans, can there be European kaffirs?[8] [male]

Conditionality therefore enters the discourse of some of these callers. Being African is something that whites will have to earn through a change of heart and by dint of commitment.

Few whites feel that they are genuinely African. Being African has to do with where your heart lies, where your loyalties are. It is something which whites will have to earn. Some are now becoming African. [male]

One can judge whether whites are African by their actions. [male]

The above quotation shows that while most callers who identified as black African used dominant discourses, some callers to this program were prepared to use discourses that can be described as conditionally demotic: the boundary that defends Africanness can be redrawn, but only if there is convincing evidence of an authentic will to be allied with black South Africans in working toward a better life for all the people of the country.

In summary, the responses of black African callers to the question of whether whites can be African tended to be resistant, emphasizing the contradictions in the position of white South Africans who claim Africanness. The arguments lie along a continuum from outright rejection, through

skepticism, to conditional acceptance based on perceived authenticity and genuine solidarity on the part of whites.

By contrast with the dominant discourses employed by black African callers on this topic, the whites who commented on the topic used only demotic discourses—they expressed a strong desire to see the boundaries that have been used to draw the distinction between "us" and "them," regarding the basis for being accepted as African, dismantled. The arguments presented provide the very broadest, unconditional definition of "African":

All those people who are born in Africa should be regarded as African. [female]

The term African should be applied to all the people of this continent. It is a continental name, which they are entitled to by birth. [male]

It's where you live that matters. For people anywhere it's the state they live in that matters. [male]

White callers challenged the "ownership" of Africanness that black South Africans callers seemed to feel, some claiming that it is inherently racist to use an ethnic term of identification that could be understood to exclude whites. Often these objections drew on power-evasive discourses of color-blindness:

The only way one can decide on the issue is through looking at history. It is not only black people who have been called African in earlier times. [male]

Only in racial terms does European or African mean something. It means nothing to me. [male]

Alternatively, callers defused the controversy by deflecting the question onto other inclusive terms that can provide common identification, but to which white South Africans have stronger historical claim:

Europeans don't identify themselves that way. Albanians don't think of themselves as Europeans, but as Albanians. Continental identification is not important. The important thing is *our South Africanness.* [male]

Most of the arguments from white callers depended on formal definitions of the term *African.* A few, however, made their claim to Africanness on the basis of the emotional bond they feel with the continent:

I've been to the village in Europe where my people come from. It means nothing to me. [male]

I get upset when people exclude white-skinned Africans like myself. I cheer for African soccer teams, and miss hearing African languages when I am overseas. [male]

In sum, then, white callers stressed their historical, legal, and emotional claim on the continent to counter exclusionary uses of the term *African* by black South Africans. The use of demotic discourses indicates the desire to be included, but the use of formal, minimalistic definitions of *African* indicates they want this inclusion as a matter of entitlement rather than because they identify with the issues facing those who have inherited the enduring legacies of conquest, slave trade, colonialism, and exploitation of the continent.

DOMINANT AND DEMOTIC DISCOURSES IN THE THEME: DO WHITES OWE BLACKS EXTRA FINANCIAL RESTITUTION?

The arguments that black South Africans put forward on this topic were all unequivocally demotic, in that they presented an unambivalent case for dismantling the historically inherited economic support base for the different life-worlds of whites and blacks in South Africa.

The black callers drew attention to a pervasive white denial. Their discourse indicated that they were looking for acknowledgment of past injustice, of inequity, of suffering, and of the enduring effects of dispossession in the present.

You are not looking at how you benefited from the Apartheid. [male]

You are missing the point. The majority of young people are not graduating at all—they have no funds to complete their studies. We need to put money into things like providing equal education. [male]

There is an urgent need for land redistribution. [male]

This challenge to white denial was accompanied by a strong call for recognition of the moral dimensions of the issue. The callers seemed to be

prompting a sense of social responsibility toward those disadvantaged by the past, and appealing to a sense of fair play:

This is a colonial debt, it's a legacy of colonialism and its exploitative system. [male]

We need to level the playing fields. [male]

The black South African callers characterized the white response to the question of reparations with an implicit reproach for the white callers' self-serving attitudes, self-indulgently negative attitude to the possibilities of the future, and one-sided emphasis on the worst aspects of the present. In the examples below, there appears to be an implied imputation of a lack of generosity in their compatriots, who seem to be withholding the benefit of their expertise, education, and technical advantage.

Instead of looking at how they can assist, they are talking of running away to other countries. [male]

You are not looking for ways to reduce the crime, poverty, and the problems you are always worrying about. [male]

In the past you were the ones who used to sing *Ons sal lewe ons sal sterwe, ons vir jou Suid Afrika.*[9] Now you are not saying "We will build together, we will work hand in glove." [male]

The appeal is to fairness, to an honest acknowledgment of how the odds are still stacked and of the difficulties with which the black community is grappling. The black Africans who called in on this topic were demanding respect and confidence in their ability to take their rightful place as contributing members of the society:

This sort of tax is not giving handouts; it will enable people to get tractors; it will assist them to move forward. [male]

The demotic nature of these comments emerges strongly in the appeals to a commitment to a spirit of community, to a cooperative approach to the problems facing the country, as is evident in the comment below.

If we put our heads together, we will be in a position to find ways to deal with our problems. [female]

Also important, the callers emphasized that reconstructing the society was a long-term undertaking that would require a great deal of effort, and that the structural, systemic, and institutional factors that need to be addressed cannot merely be glossed over. For this to happen, the arguments suggest, the boundary between those who have and those who are in want needs to be rendered less secure. Callers argued that people need to reach across the separation, emotionally as well as in deed, and align themselves against the issues that divided them in the past:

We're not yet a society; we need to build a society through our actions. [male]

In contrast to these demotic arguments, the rhetorical force of arguments offered by white South Africans were dominant in tenor, fighting for the status quo, though not always openly. Callers presented a catalogue of the dire consequences that would flow from the attempt to tax wealth acquired during the Apartheid era. The withdrawal of white skills and capital, seen as inevitably following from restitutive measures, was repeatedly mentioned as a threat to the economy.

Money goes where the profit flows. . . . In our global world, where the barriers that prevented movement in the past are falling, we'll see a huge financial drain out of the country. [male]

The people whom we need will leave, we'll chase away those that produce. [male]

Young people can get jobs anywhere in the world. We have to make the choice to stay in South Africa attractive to them. [male]

The increased flow of capital into the country will create inflation. [male]

Some comments suggested that restitution not only was foolish but actually couldn't be done, either because the idea is inherently unworkable or because the new government cannot be trusted to administer it effectively.

Such a tax has not been efficient anywhere in the world. [male]

How practically would it be redistributed to the deserving poor? [male]

With so much corruption in the government, who would administer it? How can it be done? Money just gets frittered away. [male]

Whites, in the overall discourse, present themselves as having no obligation beyond the simple legal requirements of citizenship. They are, it is argued by these callers, morally in the clear. The impact of the unequal past on the present is minimized, and the current contribution of white business, in particular, and the white population in general, is regarded as sufficient, even generous:

> We already pay tax. The minister of finance assesses the priorities and pays out for education, crime, housing, etc. [male]

> We are already overtaxed. This would be the final nail in the coffin. We are taxed like no other nation on earth. [male]

> We have the most socially responsible business sector anywhere in the world. [male]

> The so-called underprivileged get their slice of the budget through welfare, hospital services, and so on. They can't say they don't receive benefits. [male]

Denial of the depth of the inequity of the past manifests itself in many ways. The attempt to introduce racial cognizance into the argument is simply equated with racism. Africa is seen to be intrinsically prone to poverty; Africans are the cause of their own misery:

> The government is just bringing in the race card again, just like in the Apartheid days. [female]

> Is all the poverty of black people the result of white people's actions? Go to the rest of Africa, and see the poverty there. When Jan van Riebeeck [the founder of Cape Town] first arrived here, there was abject poverty. [male]

> Talk about exploitation! In the old South Africa we couldn't keep all the blacks who were streaming into the country out. [male]

> There is no such thing as human equality. Poverty is a measure of individual productivity. [male]

A tax on wealth accumulated during Apartheid is construed as punishment. Whites are seen to have become wealthy through their own moral endeavor, which renders wealth an entitlement, and using it to benefit anyone but oneself purely a matter of individual altruism. The interrelationship

between white wealth and black poverty is unacknowledged, and therefore restorative measures are uncalled for.

This is a punishment to the individual for having accumulated wealth through hard endeavor. [male]

You cannot punish people who have sacrificed for having invested wisely. [male]

What about all those of us who worked hard to put together something for our retirement, only to find that now most of it goes to the poor? [female]

People worked for their money; they should be allowed to pass it on to their children. [male]

Individual companies should have the right to decide where they want to pay extra towards social welfare. [male]

Where participation in the Apartheid racial economy is acknowledged, it is minimized or individualized, and declared no longer relevant. The focus is transferred to the future.

Those who participated in Apartheid have already apologized. We must look forward, and train a new generation of employees. [male]

Business is now colorless. We want to make the economy succeed. [male]

Apartheid was unequal, but now that is all over. [male]

The hypothetical cases that callers cited to emphasize the unfairness of the concept evoked marginal or the most vulnerable situations, or referred to the more exceptional situation of people who are wealthy but not white. These tactics divert attention away from the economic center—white, middle-class South Africa—to the least representative scenarios.

What about a widow with six children? [male]

What about an immigrant who arrived just before 1994? [male]

What about those who became wealthy after 1994? [female]

Alternatively, the definition of the problem was shifted:

Our real problem is unemployment. The devil finds work for idle hands. [male]

In all of the above arguments, as well as those that the limitation of space does not permit me to analyze here, the effect is to minimize the obligation of the historically privileged group toward the less privileged and to keep the economic boundaries watertight enough to prevent unwanted seepage into the coffers of all who are "not-us."

White callers who supported the proposal represented lone voices in the face of such powerful expressions of dominant discourse. In the mode of demotic discourse, they advocated reaching out to their black compatriots. Some, however, added qualifiers and hedges.

Surely we all benefited, and we should all make amends. This is about reconciliation. We should show our willingness and be prepared to share. [female]

There are people in this country who have obscene wealth. There should be a wealth tax, but it should not be racially based. [female]

On the issue of restitution, therefore, it is clear that black callers were working to dismantle extant borders. They tended (1) to focus on the local, (2) to use appeals to conscience, (3) to raise social and/or moral issues, (4) to insist on taking history seriously, (5) to regard questions of group accountability a natural corollary to historical group victimization, and (6) to show a marked skepticism about the prospects of the capitalist, free market system changing economic disparities. The pervasive sentiment that seemed to permeate this cultural terrain was a feeling of disappoinment.

By contrast, white callers, who phoned in prolifically, tended to construe the proposal as punishment. They based arguments to maintain the status quo on entitlement to private wealth and notions of individual worth, retaining a sacrosanct status for the private capital system. They weighted their participation in the welfare of the nation by maximizing their part in contributing to change, and minimizing their collusion in the historical processes where gain was based on group positioning; they also individualized the issues. The sheer amount of discourse defending this boundary indicates its emotional salience to white South Africa.

CONCLUSION: SOME IMPLICATIONS

The above analysis shows high levels of discursive activity at the boundaries between the two semiopheres, where the cultural work for transformation is taking place. The analysis also goes some way toward explaining

how the continuing phenomenon of "two nations" maintains itself. On both of the contentious issues chosen for analysis, white and black callers tended to push in opposite directions: the one group wants to dismantle the boundaries that the other defends. The conclusion has to be drawn that the borders of the respective groups are being carefully patrolled to protect perceived group interests. White callers use whatever discursive means are available to them to deflect attention away from the continuities of their privilege, choosing "rainbowism" whenever it serves this purpose. Black South Africans argue vigorously to expose such strategies, but they also protect their own "cultural capital." The analysis shows unaligned interpretive worlds coexisting parallel to each other—a still uneasy alliance in the interests of national reconciliation. This conclusion accords with that of Ansell (2001), who analyzed the written submissions leading up to the National Conference on Racism in 2000. She concludes:

> Although the submissions reveal a variety of perspectives on racism within each self-identified group, a significant racial dimension—even bifurcation—is clearly manifest. Black and white South Africans approach the questions that were the topic of the National Conference on Racism in meaningfully different ways, suggesting the existence of "two nations of discourse." (p. 1)

For genuine alliance to develop, the question "What constitutes alliance for you?" needs to be addressed. The answer to this question has to do with deep-seated interests that shape the respective worlds. As can be seen from the above analysis, a crucial disparity permeating the "cultural territories of race" (Lamont, 1999) in South Africa concerns the appropriate relationship to the past, and how it should inform present attitudes and shape solutions for and in the future. For black African callers, alliance requires that the past be acknowledged, and its legacy actively factored into the nation's ideologies, policies, and actions. Privileged white callers (and increasingly, the semiprivileged groups that are allying themselves with this discursive world), on the other hand, are working hard to deflect attention away from cleavages in the society resulting from the past. The Truth and Reconciliation process has itself become a site where the two worlds wrestle over the meaning of the past (Zegeye, 2001b).

At a theoretical level, the South African example analyzed above does provide some insights. First, it is clear that intercultural alliance building does not take place in a uniform manner, but rather, tends to be patchy, tends to progress unevenly, and may be issue specific. In this case, the willingness to reach out on one theme through demotic discourses did not

imply a willingness to ally on another. Tortoiselike, groups may reach out on one issue and then pull back on the next. Alliances probably are achieved by complex cross-stitching, with many a slipped stitch.

Second, the strategic nature of discursive practices requires that the demotic and dominant discourses in any given context need to be carefully scrutinized. In the South African case, the fact that both groups desire to break down some boundaries, while simultaneously entrenching others, indicates complex motivations. Some nifty footwork is taking place here as layers of discourse run counter to each other and perform different functions in the overall objective of maximizing the group's perceived interests. For example, one can read the white South African callers' demotic discourses on the issue of "Africanness" as essentially positive self-presentation, serving to ameliorate, even obfuscate, an intransigence demonstrated in the discourses relating to economic matters. Similarly, further scrutiny of the strategic deployment of discourses in a particular context may uncover how apparent demotic discourses may not, in fact, indicate an intention to build intercultural alliance. They may, for example, serve to effect co-option or containment. An analysis in terms of Baumann's dominant discourses and demotic discourses is strengthened when the strategic use of these discourses in relation to desires, expedience, and interests of the group is taken into account.

Third, it follows from the above that whether discourses actually do lead to closer alliance may ultimately depend on what underlying relational meaning is communicated. To encapsulate this element of alliance building, we may add the notions of *discourses of rapprochement* and *discourses of alienation* to Baumann's framework. The crucial element here is not just whether boundaries are being dismantled or defended, but how the intention in doing so is perceived by the other party. For example, demotic discourses, if experienced as strategically self-serving, superficial, or insincere, may in fact constitute discourses of alienation and form a barrier to alliance building. Discourses of rapprochement would signal a kind of emotional work that affirms the other's experience and communicates integrity. The analysis in this chapter shows that for the black African callers demotic discourses that do not signal relational rapprochement run the risk of being perceived as "a desire for cheap and painless reconciliation amounting in fact to an acceptance of the past as normal rather than a renunciation of it." (Asmal et al., 1997, p. 48).

Finally, a question that needs to be raised in the context of alliance building between social groups involves the relative moral onus that rests on the interested parties. Although this chapter clearly cannot pursue the topic in

any detail, alliance building may be an imperative unequally apportioned to different groups[10] (De Gruchy, 2000; Ndebele, 2000a). The South African example shows that in a context of profound injury committed by one group upon the other "reconciliation cannot be a symmetrical process of mutual absolution" (Asmal et al., 1997, p. 49). In the words of Desmond Tutu (1985): "It is the victims, not the perpetrators, who must say whether things are better or not. When you are throttling me you can't really tell me that things are better, that you are not choking me quite so badly" (cited in Asmal et al., 1997, p. 49). The analysis in this chapter shows that discourses of rapprochement would demonstrate sensitivity to these moral dimensions of alliance building.

Social identities and groupings are very much in flux in the New South Africa. The analysis of these talk shows represents a snapshot at a particular moment in a highly dynamic context. Although many individual South Africans of all groups are reaching out to each other, separate realities persist, and too many South Africans are still "choking badly." The call for a nation allied against the legacy of racial divides still sounds: "We search for the New South Africans, neither white nor black, democratic by inclination, capable of transcending the divides of culture, language and geography" (Lever & James, 2000, p. 200). We should add "and the legacy of racial inequity."

NOTES

1. The concept of "race" as well as actual "racial" groups are socially constructed, and this applies to ethnic and cultural groups as well. To facilitate reading, however, I am not using quotation marks time I use such a group label for any of the four "racial" groups that have been historically constructed within the country, namely, "coloureds," "Indians," "whites," and "blacks." I acknowledge that we cannot yet dispense with these categories as units of analysis because the major faultlines in the society still run along these "racial" divides, particularly as the racial economy of the past has had such a profound effect on the expression of other markers of difference. The task of reconciliation requires that South Africans continue to examine the dynamics that impede or facilitate the development of social movements that transcend and deconstruct this divide at the level of lived experience. The fact that scholars recognize "race" as the reified, essentializing construct of an earlier global European social movement should not be allowed to mask its ongoing and long-term continuities in shaping the society.

2. The following quotation from the Manifesto of the ANC (African National Congress) Youth League, issued in March 1994, shows how the issues of the

relationship of white people to the continent, and the material compensation on which reconciliation would be built, are part of the discourse of struggle:

Africa was, has been and still is the Black man's Continent. The Europeans, who have carved up and divided Africa among themselves, dispossessed, by force of arms, the rightful owners of the land—the children of the soil. . . . Although conquered and subjugated, the Africans have not given up, and they will never give up their claim and title to Africa. The fact that their land has been taken and their rights whittled down, does not take away their right to the land of their forefathers. They will suffer white oppression, and tolerate European domination, only as long as they have not got the material force to overthrow it. There is, however, a possibility of a compromise, by which the Africans could admit the Europeans to a share of the fruits of Africa, and this is inter alia:

that the Europeans completely abandon their domination of Africa;

that they agree to an equitable and proportionate re-division of land;

that they assist in establishing a free people's democracy in South Africa in particular and Africa in general.

We . . . realise that the different racial groups have come to stay. But we insist that a condition for inter-racial peace and progress is the abandonment of white domination, and such a change in the basic structure of South African society that those relations which breed exploitation and human misery will disappear. (Mandela, 1994, p. 25)

3. Quoted in Mandaza (1999, p. 81).

4. Some of the comments are worth quoting in full. Nkosinathi Biko (2000) comments on the pain of the Biko family:

Bluntly put, white South Africa, by virtue of acts of commission or omission, prolonged the existence of discrimination in general and Apartheid in particular. In this context, the single most painful aspect concerning transition has been the obvious disinterest of many white South Africans in the TRC [Truth and Reconciliation Commission] hearings. Apart from those applying for amnesty, few chose to attend the hearings. For many whites the victim hearings were a non-event. Under Apartheid some possibly "did not know", but when the occasion presented itself for the nation to face the truth in order to effect reconciliation, few were prepared to do so. The question is whether the process was about truth and reconciliation at all. For some it was about amnesty—as a basis for ensuring that those directly implicated in the atrocities of the past were able to join the ranks of the indifferent. (p. 196)

5. I have not attempted to analyze in detail how the coloured and Indian groups position themselves in the New South Africa. However, data gathered in KwaZulu-Natal in 1999 showed the coloured and Indian communities moving closer to the Afrikaans and English white communities, respectively. Their attitudes toward black South Africans had deteriorated. Among white South Africans, English-speaking South Africans, particularly, showed a more negative attitude toward black South Africans (Mynhardt, 1999). Similarly, Finchilescu and Dawes (1999) found coloured adolescents and Indian adolescents moving closer to white adolescents in terms of their ideological constructions of the future. It seems that an alliance of whites and a growing number of coloureds and Indians has been forming, in contradistinction from the majority black African population (Lever & James, 2000). This process of reconfiguring its boundaries to draw in previously excluded groups in order to secure privilege has been documented as a strategy of whiteness in other contexts (Ignatiev, 1995; Jacobson, 1998; Warren & Twine, 1997). What this research points to, then, is that the old divides have not been bridged so much as realigned. Gans (1999) predicts a similar dynamic in racial alignments in the United States, where a polarization seems to be developing in which all nonblacks could be increasingly categorized as whites, pitted against blacks, who remain the stigmatized group.

6. The Institute for Justice and Reconciliation (Gibson & Macdonald, 2001) found that disparities in attitudes toward and perceptions of the TRC, in particular, and of the process of reconciliation, in general, were deep, and coincident with the racial divide. Some of the findings included: Only 50% of white South Africans feel some responsibility to contribute to the process of national reconciliation, compared with 77% of black South Africans. Only 29% of white South Africans believe that the TRC was necessary to build a united South Africa, compared with 77% of black South Africans. Only 20% of white South Africans feel that material compensation is a necessary part of national reconciliation, compared with 70% of black South Africans.

7. To argue that these two predominating, disparate symbolic systems continue to exist in large measure is not to argue for an essentialist reading of the South African intercultural context. These life-worlds have never been homogenous, nor did coherent meaning systems arise endogenously from within the social groups. Rather, both interpretive communities were a consequence of, and material for, the continual and interlocking processes of culture making and social identity formation, which took place within the broad contours of the political, economic, cultural, and historical domains operating within the country. These semiospheres each contained diverse, and shifting, subject positionalities, influenced by such factors as historical events, ethnic affiliations, gender, class, and language. Moreover, the semiopheres were deeply implicated in each other, being largely constructed in relation and/or reaction to each other through processes of alterity (Wicomb, 2001).

8. The word *kaffir* is a derogatory term used to refer to black Africans. It has the same emotional resonance in South Africa as the term *nigger* has in the United

States. Derived from an Arabic term for "nonbeliever," it was imported along with the slave trade from East Africa.
  9. These words are from the national anthem of the "old" South Africa. The English version was: "At thy will to live or perish, oh, South Africa, dear land!"
  10. Ndebele (2000a) spells the argument out more fully:

> On balance, though, white South Africa will be called upon to make greater adjustments to black needs than the other way round . . . "whiteness" has a responsibility to demonstrate its bona fides in this regard. Where is the primary locus of responsibility for white capital, built over centuries with black labour and unjust laws? A failure to come to terms with the morality of this question ensures the continuation of the culture of insensitivity and debilitating guilt. (p. 52)

REFERENCES

Anderson, B. (1983). *Imagined communities*. London: Verso.

Ansell, A. (2001, July). *Two nations of discourse: Mapping racial attitudes in post-Apartheid South Africa*. Paper presented at the conference "The burden of race? 'Whiteness' and 'blackness' in modern South Africa," University of the Witwatersrand, Johannesburg.

Asmal, K., Asmal, L., & Roberts, R. S. (1997). *Reconciliation through truth: A reckoning of Apartheid's criminal governance* (2nd ed.). Cape Town: David Philip.

Baumann, G. (1997). Dominant and demotic discourses of culture: Their relevance to multi-ethnic alliances. In P. Werbner & T. Modood (Eds.), *Debating cultural hybridity: Multi-cultural identities and the politics of anti-racism* (pp. 209-225). London: Zed.

Bekker, S. (1996). Conflict, ethnicity and democratisation in contemporary South Africa. In S. Bekker & D. Carlton (Eds.), *Racism, xenophobia and ethnic conflict*. Durban, South Africa: Indicator.

Bell, T. (2001). *Unfinished business: South Africa, Apartheid and truth*. Cape Town: RedWorks.

Biko, N. (2000). Amnesty and denial. In C. Villa-Vicencio & W. Verwoerd (Eds.), *Looking back reaching forward: Reflections on the Truth and Reconciliation Commission of South Africa* (pp. 193-198). London: Zed.

Billig, M. (1988). Methodology and scholarship in understanding ideological explanation. In C. Antaki (Ed.), *Analysing everyday explanation: A casebook of methods*. London: Sage.

Boraine, A. (2000). *A country unmasked: Inside South Africa's Truth and Reconciliation Commission*. Oxford, UK: Oxford University Press.

Brodie, M., Altman, D., & Sinclair, M. (1999). *Reality check: South Africans' views of the New South Africa. A report on a national survey of the South African*

People, 1999. Menlo Park, CA: Henry J. Kaiser Family Foundation and Independent Newspapers.

Bundy, C. (2000). The beast of the past: History and the TRC. In W. James & L. van der Vijver (Eds.), *After the TRC: Reflections on truth and reconciliation in South Africa.* Cape Town: David Philip.

Chabedi, M. (2001, July). *Whither the rainbow nation?: The ANC, the black middle class, and chaining perceptions of "blackness" in the post-Apartheid South Africa.* Paper presented at the conference "The burden of race? 'Whiteness' and 'blackness' in modern South Africa," University of the Witwatersrand, Johannesburg.

Constitution of the Republic of South Africa. Act 200 of 1993. (1993). Retrieved August 13, 2002, from http://www.gov.za/constitution/1993/1993cons.htm

De Gruchy, J. (2000). The TRC and the building of a moral culture. In W. James & L. van der Vijver (Eds.), *After the TRC: Reflections on truth and reconciliation in South Africa.* Cape Town: David Philip.

De Kok, I. (1998). Cracked heirlooms: Memory on exhibition. In S. Nuttall & C. Coetzee (Eds.), *Negotiating the past: The making of memory in South Africa* (pp. 57-74). Oxford, UK: Oxford University Press.

De Lange, J. (2000). The historical context, legal origins and philosophical foundation of the South African Truth and Reconciliation Commission. In C. Villa-Vicencio & W. Verwoerd (Eds.), *Looking back reaching forward: Reflections on the Truth and Reconciliation Commission of South Africa* (pp. 14-31). London: Zed.

Dolby, N. E. (2001). *Constructing race: Youth, identity, and popular culture in South Africa.* Albany: State University of New York Press.

Dyer, R. (1997). *White.* London: Routledge.

Finchilescu, G., & Dawes, A. (1999). Adolescents' future ideologies through four decades of South African history. *Social Dynamics, 25*(2), 98-118.

Foster, D. (1999). Racism, Marxism, psychology. *Theory and Psychology, 9*(3), 331-352.

Foster, D. (2000). What makes a perpetrator? An attempt to understand. In C. Villa-Vicencio & W. Verwoerd (Eds.), *Looking back reaching forward: Reflections on the Truth and Reconciliation Commission of South Africa* (pp. 219-229). London: Zed.

Frankenberg, R. (1993). *White women, race matters: The social construction of whiteness.* Minneapolis: University of Minneapolis Press.

Fredrickson, G. M. (1981). *White supremacy: A comparative study in American and South African history.* Oxford, UK: Oxford University Press.

Friedman, J. (1997). Global crises, the struggle for cultural identity and intellectual porkbarrelling: Cosmopolitans versus locals, ethnics and nationals in an era of de-hegemonisation. In P. Werbner & T. Modood (Eds.), *Debating cultural hybridity: Multi-cultural identities and the politics of anti-racism* (pp. 226-254). London: Zed.

Gabriel, J. (1998). *Whitewash: Racialized politics and the media.* London: Routledge.

Gans, H. J. (1999). The possibility of a new racial hierarchy in the twenty-first-century United States. In M. Lamont (Ed.), *The cultural territories of race: Black and white boundaries* (pp. 371-390). Chicago: Chicago University Press.

Gerwel, J. (2000). National reconciliation: Holy grail or secular pact? In C. Villa-Vicencio & W. Verwoerd (Eds.), *Looking back reaching forward: Reflections on the Truth and Reconciliation Commission of South Africa.* London: Zed.

Gibson, J. L., & Macdonald, H. (2001). *Truth—yes, reconciliation—maybe: South Africans judge the truth and reconciliation process.* Research report, Institute for Justice and Reconciliation. Rondebosch, South Africa: Institute for Justice and Reconciliation. Retrieved August 13, 2002, from http://www.ijr.org.za/papers.html

Gqola, P. D. (2001, July). *Defining people: Power, language, and metaphors of the New South Africa.* Paper presented at the conference "The burden of race? 'Whiteness' and 'blackness' in modern South Africa," University of the Witwatersrand, Johannesburg.

Hadland, A., & Rantoa, J. (1999). *The life and times of Thabo Mbeki.* Rivonia, South Africa: Zebra.

Hayner, P. (2000). Same species, different animal: How South Africa compares to Truth Commission worldwide. In C. Villa-Vicencio & W. Verwoerd (Eds.), *Looking back reaching forward: Reflections on the Truth and Reconciliation Commission of South Africa.* London: Zed.

Henry, Y. (2000). Where healing begins. In C. Villa-Vicencio & W. Verwoerd (Eds.), *Looking back reaching forward: Reflections on the Truth and Reconciliation Commission of South Africa* (pp. 166-173). London: Zed.

Ignatiev, N. (1995). *How the Irish became white.* New York: Routledge.

Institute for Justice and Reconciliation, and Graduate School of Humanities, University of Cape Town. (2000, October). *Reparation & memorialisation: The unfinished business of the TRC.* Supplement circulated by the Independent Newspapers.

Jacobson, M. F. (1998). *Whiteness of a different color: European immigrants and the alchemy of race.* Cambridge, MA: Harvard University Press.

James, W., & van de Vijver, L. (2000). *After the TRC: Reflections on truth and reconciliation in South Africa.* Cape Town: David Philip.

Kriger, R., & Zegeye, A. (Eds.).(2001). *After Apartheid: Vol. 2. Culture in the New South Africa.* Cape Town: Kwela.

Krog, A. (1998). *Country of my skull.* Johannesburg: Random House.

Lever, J., & James, W. (2000). The second republic. In W. James & L. van der Vijver (Eds.), *After the TRC: Reflections on truth and reconciliation in South Africa.* Cape Town: David Philip.

Lamont, M. (1999). *The cultural territories of race: Black and white boundaries.* Chicago: University of Chicago Press.

Lotman, J. M. (1991). *The universe of mind* (A. Shukman, Trans.). London: I. B. Tauris.

MacGregor, K. (1999, April 20). Surprising facts about the winners and losers in the new SA. *Cape Times*, p. 11.

Magubane, B. M. (1999). The African Renaissance in historical perspective. In M.W. Makgoba (Ed.), *The African Renaissance: The new struggle.* Cape Town: Tafelberg.

Mamdani, M. (2000). A diminshed truth. In W. James & L. van der Vijver (Eds.), *After the TRC: Reflections on truth and reconciliation in South Africa.* Cape Town: David Philip.

Mandaza, I. (1999). Reconciliation and social justice in Southern Africa: The Zimbabwean experience. In M.W. Makgoba (Ed.), *The African Renaissance: The new struggle* (pp. 77-90). Cape Town: Tafelberg.

Mandela, N. (1994). *Nelson Mandela: The struggle is my life.* Bellville, South Africa: Mayibuye Books, University of Western Cape.

Mandela, N. (1997, December 16). Report by the president of the ANC to the 50th national conference of the African National Congress.

Marais, H. C. (1985). On communication in a divided society. *Communicare, 4*(2), 38-43.

Mbeki, T. (1998). South Africa: Two nations [Statement of Deputy President Thabo Mbeki at the opening of the debate in the National Assembly on reconciliation and nation building in Cape Town on May 29, 1998]. In A. Hadland & J. Rantoa, *The life and times of Thabo Mbeki.* Rivonia., South Africa: Zebra.

McIntyre, A. (1997). *Making meaning of whiteness: Exploring racial identity with white teachers.* Albany: State University of New York Press.

Melucci, A. (1997). Identity and difference in a globalized world. In P. Werbner & T. Modood (Eds.), *Debating cultural hybridity: Multi-cultural identities and the politics of anti-racism* (pp. 58-69). London: Zed.

Morrell, R. (2001). *Changing men in southern Africa.* London: Zed.

Mynhardt, J. C. (1999, October). *A social psychological approach to managing diversity.* Paper presented at the conference "The productive management of diversity" at the National Productivity Institute, Johannesburg.

Nakayama, T. K., & Martin, J. N. (1999). *Whiteness: The communication of social identity.* Thousand Oaks, CA: Sage.

Ndebele, N. (1998). Memory, metaphor, and the triumph of narrative. In S. Nuttall & C. Coetzee (Eds.), *Negotiating the past: The making of memory in South Africa.* Oxford, UK: Oxford University Press.

Ndebele, N. (2000a). *Iph Indlela?* Finding our way into the future—The first Steve Biko Memorial Lecture. *Social Dynamics, 26*(1), 43-55.

Ndebele, N. (2000b). Of lions and rabbits: Thoughts on democracy and reconciliation. In W. James & L. van der Vijver (Eds.), *After the TRC: Reflections on truth and reconciliation in South Africa.* Cape Town: David Philip.

Nuttall, S., & Coetzee, C. (Eds.). (1998). *Negotiating the past: The making of memory in South Africa.* Oxford, UK: Oxford University Press.

Nuttall, S., & Michael, C-A. (2000a). Introduction: Imagining the present. In S. Nuttall & C-A. Michael (Eds.), *Senses of culture: South African culture studies.* Oxford, UK: Oxford University Press.

Nuttall, S., & Michael, C-A. (Eds.). (2000b). *Senses of culture: South African culture studies.* Oxford, UK: Oxford University Press.

Nyatsumba, K. (2000). Neither dull nor tiresome. In W. James & L. van der Vijver (Eds.), *After the TRC: Reflections on truth and reconciliation in South Africa.* Cape Town: David Philip.

Papastergiadis, N. (1997). Racing hybridity in theory. In P. Werbner & T. Modood (Eds.), *Debating cultural hybridity: Multi-cultural identities and the politics of anti-racism* (pp. 257-281). London: Zed.

Ramphele, M. (2000). Law, corruption and morality. In W. James & L. van der Vijver (Eds.), *After the TRC: Reflections on truth and reconciliation in South Africa.* Cape Town: David Philip.

Schutte, G. (1995). *What racists believe: Race relations in South Africa and the United States.* Thousand Oaks, CA: Sage.

Shea, D. (2000). *The South African truth commission: The politics of reconciliation.* Washington, DC: United States Institute of Peace Press.

Steyn, M. E. (1999). White identity in context: A personal narrative. In T. K. Nakayama & J. N. Martin (Eds.), *Whiteness: The communication of social identity.* Thousand Oaks, CA: Sage.

Steyn, M. E. (2001). *Whiteness just isn't what it used to be: White identity in a changing South Africa.* Albany: State University of New York Press.

Steyn, M. E., & Motshabi, K. B. (1996). *Cultural synergy in South Africa: Weaving strands of Africa and Europe.* Randburg, South Africa: Knowledge Resources.

Thornton, R. (1996). The potential of boundaries in South Africa: Steps towards a theory of the social edge. In R. Werbner & T. Ranger (Eds.), *Postcolonial identities in Africa* (pp. 136-161). London: Zed.

Villa-Vicencio, C., & Verwoerd, W. (Eds.). (2000). *Looking back reaching forward: Reflections on the Truth and Reconciliation Commission of South Africa.* London: Zed.

Warren, J. W., & Twine, F. W. (1997). White Americans: The new minority? Non-blacks and the everexpanding boundaries of whiteness. *Journal of Black Studies, 28*(2), 200-218.

Werbner, P. (1997a). Introduction: The dialectics of cultural hybridity. In P. Werbner & T. Modood (Eds.), *Debating cultural hybridity: Multi-cultural identities and the politics of anti-racism* (pp. 226-254). London: Zed.

Werbner, P. (1997b). Essentialising essentialism, Essentialising silence: Ambivalence and multiplicity in the constructions of racism and ethnicity. In P. Werbner & T. Modood (Eds.), *Debating cultural hybridity: Multi-cultural identities and the politics of anti-racism* (pp. 226-254). London: Zed.

Werbner, P., & Modood, T. (Eds.). (1997). *Debating cultural hybridity: Multicultural identities and the politics of anti-racism.* London: Zed.

Wetherell, M., & Potter, J. (1988). Discourse analysis and interpretive repertoires. In C. Antaki (Ed.), *Analysing everyday explanation: A casebook of methods.* London: Sage.

Wicker, H. (1997). From complex culture to cultural complexity. In P. Werbner & T. Modood (Eds.), *Debating cultural hybridity: Multi-cultural identities and the politics of anti-racism* (pp. 29-45). London: Zed.

Wicomb, Z. (2001). Five Afrikaner texts and the rehabilitation of whiteness. In R. Kriger & A. Zegeye (Eds.), *After Apartheid: Vol. 2. Culture in the New South Africa.* Cape Town: Kwela.

Wilson, F. (2000). Addressing poverty and inequality. In W. James & L. van der Vijver (Eds.), *After the TRC: Reflections on truth and reconciliation in South Africa.* Cape Town: David Philip.

Zegeye, A. (2001a). Imposed ethnicity. In A. Zegeye (Ed.), *After Apartheid: Vol. 2. Social identities in the New South Africa.* Cape Town: Kwela.

Zegeye, A. (2001b). Depoliticising ethnicity in South Africa. In A. Zegeye (Ed.), *After Apartheid: Vol. 1. Social identities in the New South Africa.* Cape Town: Kwela.

Zegeye, A., & Liebenberg, I. (2001). The burden of the present. In R. Kriger & A. Zegeye (Eds.), *After Apartheid: Vol. 2. Culture in the New South Africa.* Cape Town: Kwela.

6

The (In)Visible Whiteness of Being

Stories of Selves in Sojourn

LEDA COOKS • University of Massachusetts, Amherst
ELIZABETH FULLON • University of Massachusetts,
Amherst

Accounts of the self in sojourn[1] are always tied to the complexities of experiencing identification and difference. We intricately negotiate these positionings, depending on the ways in which we are (always?) already raced and gendered (as well as being labeled with other identifiers) in the society and the flexibility we have in creating a different story about our selves. This chapter looks at the accounts of two female scholars (one Anglo American, one Filipino American) living in countries where they both constituted themselves and were constituted as different. We undertake this effort as an attempt to narrate and explicate moments of intercultural interaction as well as to read *across* each other's stories toward an articulation of whiteness[2] that builds cultural understanding. The first narrative is taken from the fieldnotes and journals of a white woman living in Panama (Leda); the other narrative is from the fieldnotes, interviews, and lectures of a Filipino American woman living in Iceland (Elizabeth). Although our research projects and experiences in each country were different, no attempt is made here to place a value on or to compare the two experiences. Rather, this chapter focuses on the experience of self-as-foreigner (as tied to gender, race, and ethnicity)—the coming to consciousness of the cultural marking of identities, visibility, and difference.[3] Our hope is that, in situating our performances of differences in our own stories, we can begin to understand how the *experience* of difference, as raced, gendered, and classed, is variously positioned. For both of us, skin color was highlighted in the construction of our outsider position in social and cultural contexts in contrasting ways. In each story, the experience is that of confrontation with an overt discourse of privilege based on skin color and ethnic orientation,

yet the value placed on that difference recognized and reified *nativeness* and *foreignness* differently.

The negotiations of cultural and social boundaries, combined with the ways in which cultural notions of self are constructed, are the focus of this chapter, as are the stories that we tell about our movement through contexts that have shaped our notions of cultural and personal boundaries. At the center of this analysis are the complex ways in which identities are intricately woven around stories of skin color, ethnicity, gender, and other differences, and the location of those differences in cultural politics. Although it could be argued that the experience and negotiation of otherness is not new to intercultural encounters, only recently has intercultural communication research begun to consider the politics of position within these interactions (e.g., Martin, Nakayama, & Flores, 1998; Tanno & Jandt, 1998). This chapter looks at the situatedness of such encounters, using social constructionist theory and autoethnography against the backdrop of prevailing discourses of self as constructed in social performance.[4]

The purpose of this chapter is fourfold: (1) to look at the ways bodies (as white or nonwhite, male, female, or other) are positioned and privileged through narratives of sojourn; (2) to tell these stories in two different voices and from two embodied viewpoints; (3) to examine the complexities of intercultural negotiations of raced and gendered performance; and (4) to use critical autoethnography, to provide an analysis of the stories told. We do so in the hope of simplifying sojourn narratives, by examining the representation of whiteness that give them significance, as well as complicating them, by identifying the unevenness through which identity, difference, power, and privilege are rendered (in)visible in interaction.

In the following sections, we first establish the links between cultural and intercultural communication studies of whiteness, of (in)visibility, of sojourn, and of critical ethnographic analysis. Next, we turn to the sojourn stories, to specific scenes and episodes where constructions of nativeness and foreignness, of whiteness and femaleness, and of researcher and researched marked the boundaries of the interaction, even as the meaning of those boundaries was under negotiation. In the concluding sections, we move back and forth between the details of interaction (through ethnographic analysis) and the social and cultural premises that make them meaningful (critical analysis). These tropes necessarily frame any analysis of cultural and social differences of sojourn, as well as those spaces between traveler and traveled to.

WHITENESS AND THE DIALECTICS OF EMBODIMENT

Increasingly, communication scholars in areas such as postcolonial, cultural, and intercultural studies have turned to the representation of whiteness as foundational to the understanding and interpretation of Western discourses on race, ethnicity, and difference. Nakayama and Martin (1999) argue that communication as a discipline is central to understanding whiteness because of the socially constructed nature of the phenomenon. They note that "as a social construction, whiteness gains its meaning from its encounters with nonwhiteness" (p. vii). Following from this reasoning, some recent studies of whiteness in intercultural and international contexts have attempted to center and locate whiteness as it is communicated within specific and localized interactions (e.g., Frankenberg, 1993; Moon, 1999, Steyn, 1999). Locating and positioning whiteness, however, demands attention to its historical and discursive construction within particular sites of power. White is invisible and ubiquitous to most white people (Martin, Krizek, Nakayama, & Bradford, 1999; Nakayama & Krizek, 1999) precisely because of its historically vested interest in dominance and control over bodies and spaces. Although whiteness maintains cultural specificity and visibility in majority-minority relations (where whites are outnumbered, or some whites—due to gender, class, religion, and so on—are on the lower end of unequal relations of power), it both structures and puts into operation forms of discursive power. Such power can be manifest in different meanings ascribed in intercultural interactions to terms such as *diversity, development, multiculturalism,* and *ethnicity,* among many others. Steyn (1999) notably argues that there is not one whiteness but several whitenesses that position white people culturally and nationally in relation to others.

Intercultural communication scholarship has focused on communication as both process and product of interpreting the (cultural) meanings of whiteness. Johnson (1999) observes that "understanding these larger social discourses means that the challenge of whiteness studies lies not in any individual trying to change his or her communication patterns; rather we need to understand the ways that communication about whiteness is embedded in our social fabric" (p. 5). The representation and dissemination of white ideologies as universal principles for living and being have been studied as historical narratives sanctioned through policies and politics in the imperial West (King, 2000; Omi & Winant, 1994) as they inform white identity and cultural practices that lead to invisible privileges and the

oppression of those not identified as white (Nakayama & Martin, 1999). Because white is assumed to be beyond culture, beyond representation, it is precisely the cultural practices that make whiteness appear normal and natural that white studies seeks to define and make visible. A primary place to locate such practices has been in the representation of bodies and embodiment in imperialist struggles over land and nation building (Hulme, 1986; McClintock, 1992).

Dyer (1997) writes of embodiment as it informs whiteness, and his categorizing themes are also useful for examining spaces of sojourn. Dyer notes the expression of embodiment in three areas that frame his analysis: Christianity, race, and enterprise/imperialism. In situating the body thus, Dyer attempts to locate embodiment as a process that incorporates and integrates spiritual, physical, and political and/or ideological activity. While all three of Dyer's frames for embodiment are important to our analysis, here it is important to add to our discussion the contributions of Christianity. Dyer (1997) remarks that whiteness involves "something that is in but not of the body" (p. 14). Christianity is based in the body of Christ but is founded and relies on the notion of incarnation as its spiritual basis. Dyer states that:

> For all the emphasis on the body in Christianity, the point is the spirit that is "in" the body. What has made Christianity compelling and fascinating is precisely the mystery that it posits, that somehow there is in the body something that is not of the body which may be variously termed spirit, mind, soul or God (p. 16).

Christianity, then, relates the symbolism of spirit-in-the-body through the figures of Mary and Christ. Where Christ provides a model for men of the conflict between mind and body and "suffering as the supreme expression of both spiritual and physical striving," Mary provides for women a model of "passivity, expectancy, receptivity, a kind of sacred readiness and motherhood as the supreme fulfillment of one's nature" (p. 17). Dyer thus relates the material location of Christianity in the figures of Christ and Mary to both the split between mind and body that typifies representations of whiteness and the gender ideologies that are intimately connected to the dualistic split.

Where Dyer (1997) focuses on the representational frameworks that privilege whiteness and make it the invisible location for the exercise of power, our research focuses on the ways these themes inform analyses of the body in sojourn. Keeping in mind his three themes of Christianity, race, and enterprise/imperialism, we turn now to studies of these ideas in the context of travel and sojourn experiences.

The Embodiment of the Traveler:
Representing the (White, Male, Educated) Self in Sojourn

In her examination of ethnographic fieldnotes and research, Pratt (1986) found little to distinguish these "reports" from early travelogues, in which the traveling subject became the invisible viewer or voyeur through which the object (bodies, spaces) could be constructed. Much like the travelogues that emerged from British elite in the 1800s (McClintock, 1992), the ethnographies of the early 20th century presented the reader with culture-as-object, thus establishing and solidifying understandings of culture as experienced only outside the reader or traveler's own bodily and spatial boundaries (of race, nation, gender, etc.). Travel, then, was experienced as unidirectional movement across an objectified (and fetishized) space. Accounts of the self in sojourn were thus necessarily framed through a subject-object relationship, in which the subject remained the invisible backdrop against which scenes of cultural (in)difference could be played out and interpreted. The distance implied by the colonial relationship also encouraged a universal colonial voice, a voice that needed no explicit authority to assume its location as other-wise. It is from this location of pure power that subjectivity can be read and interpreted as objectivity—the neutral coloring of perception. Indeed, the dualism of colonial relationships implies a colonial subjectivity and a colonized objectivity that somehow exist in "pure" form, untainted by travel and cultural exchange.

Analysis of stories of sojourn experience provides a way of seeing relationships, of seeing intercultural contact and cultural imperialism. It implies contact and collision as well as assimilation and coherence of views about the meaning of everyday experience. Travel as a metaphor for cultural research and social science implies a relationship that can never be completely pure or objective, never be open to convenient categorization, never be free from bias. It will always be tainted by that which makes us all human: communication. Travel implies the imperialism of the traditional ethnographic relationship of travel to distant lands that defines colonial relationships for exploitation by the mother country. Travel, Clifford (1992) argues, is essential to understanding cultural and national identity.

Sojourn narratives have traditionally been the voice of modern displacement, of the angst and coming to consciousness of those who have opted to leave their homeland. While sojourn narratives are often assumed to tell a story about one's home culture as well as the culture traveled to, it is significant to note that sojourn narratives differ in important ways from narratives of exile, of immigration, and of diaspora. Sojourners choose to leave and

can choose to go home; the (often solitary) exile is forced for political reasons from her or his homeland. Expatriates are sometimes positioned as either true or false exiles. None of these categories are purely constructed; positioning the privilege and power of the sojourner or expatriate against the powerlessness of the exile or immigrant blurs the ways in which narratives may be both and/or none of these constructions. Still, as Kaplan (1996) observes:

> Euro-American poststructuralist and postmodern critical practices have been slow to acknowledge this transnational material context. The subject position of the critic (or the multiplicity of subject positions available to the critic) has not received significant attention, either dismissed as vulgar and essentialist "identity politics" or erased through the Eurocentric rhetoric of universality. (p. 103)

The question that connects these ideas to the particular analysis at hand is how the metaphors of colonialism, whiteness, culture, and sojourn *work* in particular kinds of cultural narratives—and toward what ends.

In attempting both to highlight the (in)visibility of whiteness, gender, and culture and to demonstrate the complex layering of our performances, we multiply position ourselves, as academics who choose to go and live in other countries, as sojourners with privilege but also with memories of immigration, as intellectuals who are also positioned by skin color and as women, as writers whose home is located in the "First World" and not in the "Third World." Yet, it is important not to let these categories define the stories we tell; perhaps the best criticism of critical and postcolonial scholarship is that it rarely engages the lives it positions on the global stages. Likewise, the binaries constructed in categories such as sojourn/exile or sojourn/immigrant, or even location in First or Third World, do not speak to the complexities of traveling stories.

NARRATING CULTURAL (IN)VISIBILITY

Auto- and Critical Ethnography

By acting and speaking in certain ways, we perform ourselves, thereby contributing to the reification and naturalization of cultural forms, such as gender or race. Frankenberg (1993) talks about the importance of analyzing performances of whiteness, as structural advantage, as a place from which white people look at themselves and as a set of cultural practices. Whites perform their structural advantage through the options they have and the

choices they can make; yet, at the same time, within whiteness we find structurally different positions, based on gender, class, language and dialect, and cultural differences. For our purposes, whiteness is the structural backdrop, the invisible and unnoticed setting through which complexities of power and cultural differences are played out. While white figures in important ways as skin color, discursive forms of power, image, and ideology in this chapter, whiteness alone does not and cannot determine the complexities that position our selves as sojourners in the scenes we describe.

The narratives that we construct as we re-present our journal and fieldnotes from time spent in Panama and Iceland are not based on native or informants' descriptions of cultural phenomena. Rather, we approach our analysis from the standpoints of critical autoethnography. Critical ethnographic work attempts to connect the details of social and cultural practices with frameworks that make such practices comfortable or uncomfortable, sanctioned or punished, and visible or invisible (among other relations of power). While critical ethnographic research is often grounded in the views and observations of both researcher and researched, it focuses on the larger frameworks that constitute social interaction, rather than on the details that comprise social scenes. Autoethnographic work is similarly located in the junctures among cultural, structural, and ideological practices, but is more often grounded in the self-reflexive analysis of the researcher, and in the details of interaction that lead to specific interpretations in the research report. Our motivation in using both of these methods is to move toward critical engagement with ourselves as researchers located *other-wise* in a particular cultural scene, in an effort toward what Lukacs (1971) calls "critical realism." Critical realism penetrates to the deeper levels of meaning that lie beneath the surface. Extending this idea, Thomas (1993) observes that "bodies of ideas, norms and ideologies, create meanings for constructing social subjects and concepts like 'gender,' 'race,' [sojourner]. These and other roles and identities typify the invisible realm of meanings that stratify people and distribute power and resources in subtle ways" (p. 34).

Corey (1998) describes autoethnography as the blending of the autobiography and the study of a people. In our case, we blend our own stories with the cultural texts and/or performances of Filipino, Panamanian, U.S. American, Icelandic, and female identities, among others. Autoethnography serves as a method for organizing the pieces of our selves as we recall them into awareness and tell them into narratives of identities.

Autoethnography is perhaps best characterized as a methodology that situates meaning and interpretation as local knowledge, indeterminate and fragmented to both the researcher and explorer and the "natives." Within a

specific speaking community, the ways in which ideas about identity and difference are communicated construct ideas about culture, community, and nation. This type of ethnography often contradicts and contrasts with the modernist notions of the self that have traditionally characterized ethnographic texts. Clifford's work (1988, 1992) on the politics of location and others' more recent work in autoethnography (Alexander, 1999; Corey, 1998; Crawford, 1996; Kaplan, 1996; Nicotera, 1999) are examples of the displacement of narrative, of the traveler and the place, that is important to this study of the experience of sojourn. These stories are, after all, academic stories of both researcher and researched, and the ways in which these two can be one and the same. The meanings assigned to them as they occurred, in writing them in journals, in rereading them for this chapter, in writing them down, and in telling them to the reader have of course been altered, changed through reflection, editing, memory, and presentation. What remains important is in the telling, in what is told, what is said, what is not said, and what happens in between.

Given this framework, we use our own and each other's accounts as a point of entry for critical reflection—making visible the ideological seams that naturalize whiteness as it structures interactions as foreign/self and native/other or foreign/other and native/self. In the following sections, each of us presents incidents taken from our fieldnotes and observations.

Although many narratives could be used in our analysis, we focused specifically on moments that called the meanings that we had for ourselves, for others, and for what was going on in the interaction, sharply into question. Of primary concern to us in culling narratives from the journals we had collected was the ways the (in)visibility of gender and whiteness became meaningful and relevant in interacting across cultures. As well, we used Lincoln and Guba's (1985) technique of constant comparison of our data through unitizing and categorizing the experiences about which we had written. Rather than choosing a representative sample of the data, we selectively sampled and included themes based on the degree to which they demonstrated the marking of difference across cultural encounters.

NARRATIVES OF SOJOURN

Performing Self, Performing Sojourn: Leda Cooks

My story begins in Panama, in 1997. I had received a Fulbright scholarship to conduct research and to teach in the country. Although this was not

my first time in Panama, and I had traveled throughout Central America, it was my first time living and working in the country on my own. This is significant in that my interactions as a tourist in Latin America had been relatively brief and catered to my needs as a traveler. In Panama this time as a sojourner, I had to build a place for myself in a community and culture with which I had little familiarity. Therefore, in this analysis, I focus on myself as both the subject and object of ethnography, highlighting the contexts (cultural readings of spaces and places) in which the (socially constructed) meanings I held about myself pushed up against those of people around me. Scrutiny of the contexts and of the process through which one is defined and held accountable for certain meanings of the self is important to understanding the history, present, and future of cultural and intercultural interpretation.

In the following paragraphs I tell three stories, based on my journal entries from 1997 to 1998, about the ways my identities (raced, gendered, and classed) came to hold meaning in various scenes in Panama. These stories illustrate the ways in which these identities were constructed in performance, and coded in specific ways through the cultural contexts of which we (the participants) were a part. These codes, as I call them, may not have been shared, nor might we have ever reached mutual agreement as to the meaning of the episodes. Nonetheless, the ways in which the episodes were negotiated identified me as white and female, sometimes privileged, sometimes unusual or strange, but always an outsider, even as the meaning I assigned to that position apparently differed dramatically from the meaning assigned to it by those around me.

My research project in Panama was to be based on national identity, or the meanings constructed by Panamanians about their nation and citizenship. On the broader national level, I was interested in how Panama was negotiating the break with the United States and the withdrawal of U.S. troops, and, some would say, of U.S. money from the country. Panama was launching a national campaign called Panama 2000. Through the efforts of national and local governments the plan was/is to redefine national identity and begin a new era of Panamanian business relationships defined on their (sovereign) terms. Negotiations (since fallen apart) were under way with the United States for the construction of a multilateral drug task force center in Panama, to ensure a continued U.S. presence in the Canal Zone. The Panamanian government was struggling with decreasing interest, from other parts of the world, in the country or its canal. In effect, Panama had just gained their sovereignty in a global era when sovereignty no longer meant much of anything. Panama was struggling as a country to set itself

apart from other Central American countries, doing business with South America (Chile and Peru), and conducting limited trade with Europe and Asia, at a time when block trading and free trade agreements were becoming important in the world economy.

Ambiguity on the national level set the context for the reactions I found among the Panamanian people I interviewed. Most did not want to talk about themselves as Panamanians, or perhaps didn't want to talk to me as a researcher on the topic. Although many did talk to me off the record, I soon abandoned my plans for the project and went to work full time for several women's, indigenous, and community nongovernmental organizations (NGOs). It was my work in this context that provided the first episode that I wish to discuss. In my capacity as a foreign teacher and trainer in community development, I often worked with NGOs to set up training programs, lectures, and workshops. I very much enjoyed the training sessions, mostly because the women were extremely eager to participate and were very grateful for the programs. I soon realized, however, that the enthusiastic responses I was receiving were due in part to the fact that I was a foreigner, different from the women in the community and from the women leaders in the NGOs. The NGOs, well aware of this fact, had used me in this capacity because of my whiteness and my position as an academic, and not in spite of it. The credibility I gained here seemed to function to ensure the attention of the women, but I was unsure about the sustainability of the program and worried that the women were responding in ways that they assumed would please me—giving me the answers that they thought I wanted.

The Focus Groups

Journal Entry: May 4, 1997

Today Ana[5] and I went to San Miguelito, to the house of a woman who was an organizer for the neighborhood. Although Mercedes doesn't officially have her own NGO, she basically serves as the intermediary for any NGO involvement in this area. We conducted the first of several focus groups with women on the topic of health and healing. Our purpose is to compile these narratives in the hope of submitting a report to the Board of Health in Panama City so that they might better serve this population. Of course, the women were bitter about the hospital that had recently been built in their neighborhood. They neither have the skills to work there nor the money to utilize the facility. Indeed, I am not sure that all of the women even care to use a modern medical facility at all. For the time being, anyway, the women seem to rely on herbs and *brujas* (witches) for healing and on

the local community health center for those ailments not deemed curable through local medicine.

I found a stark mix of healing methods among the women, some of whom relied on myth and native wisdom for everything from determining pregnancy and giving birth to healing the common cold. On the other hand, in the midst of a discussion of herbal medicine, Mercedes called us in to view a commercial on her television for Panadol. "This," she exclaimed, "is the Panamanian national medicine!" Whether in seriousness or in jest, it was clear that the women were influenced by a mix of native and modern approaches to medicine, even as these choices were circumscribed by their locations as (until recently) rural, primarily indigenous, single mothers without access to health care. The women often interrupted our agenda of talking about healing to discuss the conditions of their lives that helped to determine the health choices that they felt they had. All of the women (with the notable exception of Mercedes) were without a man in their lives. They mentioned that they did not believe in marrying the fathers of their children because the men never stayed around. "Better to be an unmarried, single mother," one woman said, "than to be known as another wife whose husband left her." Another woman remarked that most of the men in the neighborhood were unemployed and addicted to alcohol or drugs.

In light of the political, economic, social, and cultural barriers facing these women, my own privileges became glaringly obvious. I was leading focus groups and training sessions in neighborhoods I could enter and leave at will. My visibility as a white woman was heightened in these spaces by measure of the contrast between my skin color and lifestyle and that of those with whom I was working. It is a measure of the invisibility of such power that I was nonetheless interpreted as the "expert" educator and trainer possessed with the skills that would somehow empower these women to change the circumstances of their neighborhood and provide them with access to the local hospital. While such changes were certainly my goal, they could only be accomplished through my invisibility as an intermediary player between the neighborhood women, the NGOs, and the board of health. This position is detailed further in the following narrative.

The Trainer and the Trained

Journal Entry: June 5, 1998

Enrique [a worker with one of the NGO's sponsoring the training program] drove us out to the site in San Miguelito today. It's a cement block bunker-type building

with no windows and a tin roof. There is absolutely no source of ventilation, as we soon found out. There was only one light bulb hanging from the ceiling, not nearly enough to light the whole place. We were training in the dark, with children running all over and around us and stopping every five minutes because the torrential rains drown out any other sound. Trying to set up video equipment and filming the women's stories was perhaps the biggest challenge; there wasn't enough light and not enough cameras to capture the action. Nonetheless, despite the tremendous heat and humidity of the rainy season and the lack of continuity in our training, the women seemed to love the process. They were so thrilled with watching themselves on tape that I almost forgot all the things that went wrong between my intentions for the session and what actually happened.

I believed in the mission of the women's NGO groups I worked with and thought that I had resources that might help them achieve their goal of assisting women in making informed choices in their lives. I was willing to devote my time and energy to the effort if it meant some degree of change for these women; I was hoping for less resistance or more motivation to continue the work. However, my idea of what resources I could provide (i.e., past experience training and creating programs) was rather different from the resources the groups saw me providing. To them, my expertise as a trainer in conflict, mediation, and media literacy was less important than my image and the credibility they gained through my affiliation with their program. Although I believed that I was "working from within," challenging the women (participants) to create their own meanings for the work we were doing, I am not sure now that such a goal could be accomplished without first deconstructing the images we had of each other and then deciding if we could still work toward the same ends.

In other sessions on the topic of media literacy, we were able to look at the various constructions and interpretations of women and men in tele-novelas (Latin American soap operas, usually with a strong moral message), news, commercials, and music videos. Here I found that deconstructing the images was important, in pointing to women's own interpretations of difference, as well as to the meaning they assigned to my image. Interestingly, it was the sole man in one group who turned the conversation (on the privileging of whiteness, of thinness, and other ideals of beauty) back on me: "But look at you, a white woman wearing makeup [I was not wearing makeup at the time], how can you tell us this?" I responded that I was not wearing makeup, but that it was my choice as to whether I wanted to or not. I discussed the implications of women making choices. Although the women did not question my response, I understood later that most of them had little experience with the ideas of choices and of consequences. Most of the

women in this neighborhood described religion or God as dictating their lives; others spoke of poverty performing the same function.

In this setting, the construction and performance of being female meant having limited options. My presence as an educator and trainer who had made choices, and was offering a means for understanding representation, choice, and consequences, was complicated by my difference (as a white foreigner). The negotiation of this difference was complicated further by the fact that the NGO leaders were utilizing the same meaning constructions in using me to train women on the topic. Because these meanings were negotiated, they did not entirely oppress the women, nor did they offer a pure space for empowerment. The women themselves had a very different cultural interpretation of freedom from the one I hold. Freedom to make choices about appearance or who they wanted to represent them was as foreign to the women in this cultural scene as I was as a white woman critiquing the representation of white women on Panamanian television.

The story told above is complicated further by the fact that women were organizing for social justice, and that they were using me, among other people, to help them toward their goals of practical education for the betterment of their lives. To the extent that they networked with each other and other NGOs, created new (and their own) stories about themselves and their possibilities, and planned for future events, my position helped them move toward meeting those objectives. Nonetheless, as Kapoor (1999) notes, "the introduction of the project of development in the Third World is a system of valuation and not an objective system, which demonstrates how things *ought* to be different. It not only shows another way of doing things but also poses this modern "alternative" lifestyle as better, opening up the scope for a range of concomitant value judgments" (p. 250). As both a critic of and a participant in training and development in the "Third World," I felt keenly the contradiction between wanting to help women who were obviously impoverished (and seeking help for them from NGOs for a variety of reasons—abusive personal relationships, abusive relationships in the workplace, literacy needs, etc.) and understanding that the kind of "help" I could offer perpetuated colonial relations of power by diminishing the power of those in need of "development."

The women in these training sessions never hesitated to share their stories with me. Although the women did not interpret the program as a research project (as in *gathering data* from *research objects*), I could not easily say that we were coparticipants in an equal process of sharing. Nonetheless, we were all enthusiastic about the process and in our hope for change on a personal and interpersonal level. I am less clear that we had a

common vision of what structural changes might be accomplished through these training sessions. The differences and meanings that we had constructed for gender, relationships, education, justice, skin color were never to be resolved; we could only hope for a reasonable level of coordination toward the larger goal of movement and positive change in the conditions of everyday living.

Dating and Relationships

The next journal entry was written the day after I went to a party hosted by a woman I worked with at a prominent women's NGO in Panama City. The journal reflects my discomfort and confusion about the cultural (and gender, race, and class) rules that were in place and about the latitude that I might have in breaking those rules and still maintaining important relationships.

Journal Entry: April 25, 1997

Last night we all went to the party in Chorrera [a town near Panama City] at the home of Betsaida's boyfriend [Betsaida was a friend who worked with a women's NGO]. Several incidents there brought my gringa sensibilities sharply into question. First off, Betsy had told us that this was a pool party and indeed the pool was the prominent feature. However, it was dark green and I was a little scared to go into the water. Meanwhile, it's HOT out and everyone is wondering why I won't come swimming. After I started to worry that I was offending the host, I dove into the murky water. . . ugh.

Throughout the day I had been noticing that Betsy and her friends kept trying to set me up with her cousin, Jose. He kept trying to show off, playing in the pool, playing baseball, etc. We started talking later on and were immediately surrounded by what seemed like 25 of his friends, all joking with him (for trying to get with the gringa) and calling him "Negrito." Each time this happened I noticed he would get increasingly embarrassed. Finally I asked him why they were doing this. He said that they always called him that, but that now they were doing it to embarrass him in front of me.

Race, per se, is not an issue for discussion in Panama. Although more than 87% of the population is mestiza/mestizo, or the result of a racial mixture, the tendency is to mark differentiation among peoples based on skin color (black, white, brown, yellow). It is fairly common for one Pan-African to call or differentiate another (affectionately or otherwise) using

the term *negrita/negrito*, although to an outsider the skin color of both might appear to be same shade of brown. Such was often the case with the man mentioned above, who seemed to my foreign eyes to have the same skin color as many of his friends; nonetheless, they often used that term to hail him. This embarrassed him when I was around, mostly because the term highlighted his darkness, which contained cultural codes for attractiveness, African (rather than Latina/Latino), and native or indigenous heritage, and was generally construed negatively in mainstream Panamanian culture.

This phenomenon is not unique to Panama, although in Panama the terms *negra/negro* and *blanca/blanco* hold several contradictory and paradoxical meanings. While light skinned people are often coded as more attractive and better educated (having clearer ties to Hispanic or colonial origin), Panamanians frequently poke fun at the cultural elite or *rabiblancos*. *Rabiblancos* are lighter skinned, generally middle- to upper-class Panamanians who are chided for wanting to be gringas/gringos. They are often educated in the United States or Europe, but they were born in Panama and return there to live. The term is used to mark someone as snobbish or elitist, one who discounts Latina/Latino culture and designates as superior all things from the United States, Canada, or Western Europe. However, there are aspects of *rabiblancoism* that pervade relationships among men and women from Panama and those from outside the country (particularly the United States). For darker skinned men or women who have a light partner, an underlying assumption is that the person has gained some kind of cultural capital (status and reputation); however, the reverse is often true as well—that is, men and women with lighter skinned partners are sometimes perceived as sell-outs or traitors to their people (pueblo).

I encountered these various interpretations of my friendships and romantic relationships with Panamanians. The negative value that I placed on objectifying women (and myself in particular) did not translate easily to the Latin (Panamanian) context. In Panama the body and, moreover, the meanings assigned to bodies in public places are understood and interpreted differently from meanings assigned in mainstream U.S. culture. The female body is displayed for public consumption in Panama and other Latin American countries and is valued (commodified) as such. While my male friends and I worked to coordinate each other's meanings for what it meant to perform dating in Panama, I am reasonably sure that they never quite understood how I could be angry at their responses to me and to other women.

In the telling of these stories, I wish to emphasize that I have expressed only a few out of multiple possibilities for representing the negotiations of identities. I know that even as I write about these journal entries, my consciousness of myself (my selves) as invisible, as white, as gringa, as female, has changed through my interactions with the people and in the situations described above. Yet, my investment in and awareness of my own privilege as a white woman remains somewhat hidden to me as I exercise choices about when and where to be (in)visible. No story is ever completely told, and certainly men and women in Panama and other parts of the world have the agency to create different and varying meanings for relationships, cultural space, and justice. I have attempted to reexamine the place of sojourn as a term with multiple relationships to (my)self, other, explorer, native, researcher, and researched. In doing so, I have highlighted some aspects of these negotiations and perhaps neglected others. Nonetheless, it is hoped that this reading adds some complexity to notions and narratives of sojourn and self.

Reflexivity and (In)Visibility: Elizabeth Fullon

As a Filipino American researcher, I had been gathering narratives about Filipino immigrant life in Iceland, but I came back with as many narratives of my own experience as of others' experiences. While the proposal for my one-year dissertation research mandated that I travel through Iceland to gather stories, I found myself telling many of my own stories in many unexpected venues. I was assigned by the Fulbright Commission to use the Social Sciences Department at the University of Iceland as a base for my research. As word about my presence and my work got around, I began to be viewed as a resource by organizations and government agencies involved in welfare and services to minority groups. It was in and about this "world constructed through everyday interactions" with Icelanders that the stories I write about in this chapter were told.

As a "native" among the over 300 Filipino immigrants in Iceland who mostly work in fish factories and as domestics, I was considered "privileged" because of my academic affiliation. At the University, I was an *utlendinga* (a "foreigner") who would occasionally be mistaken as a cleaning woman or a "woman who was bought" (an Icelandic term for a mail-order bride) by those who did not know me. And to those who knew why I was in Iceland, I nevertheless was "privileged" because it was assumed that my ethnic background would automatically make me an "insider" who had access to a prime research site—the Asian immigrant community.

The data presented here are culled from various materials I brought back with me from Iceland. They include a journal entry, a memoir, a newspaper clipping, an e-mail message, and text from a lecture and presentation. These have been arranged chronologically to span the 10-month duration of my stay in Iceland. Although the overall format of this chapter is that of a standard academic presentation, this section on data presentation is set up documentary style and organized as a narrative in itself.

E-racing Filipino Identities

Journal Entry: November, 1997

I must have first read PG's work more than ten years ago when I took a course on Icelandic sagas at Harvard. He is a distinguished social scientist and a respected scholar who despite his prominence is friendly, accommodating, and maintains an open-door policy at the department. He promptly responded to a letter of inquiry I sent him when I was applying for the Fulbright fellowship. He also took the time to comment on my research proposal. I made it a habit to drop by his office regularly to chat about research procedures or interesting data. The first time one of my Filipino respondents told me about receiving hate mail, I became so apprehensive that I decided to share the information with PG immediately.

It was by chance that my Filipino friend told me about hate mail. We were sitting in the kitchen of her second floor apartment when we started hearing a violent argument between the couple living downstairs. "Doesn't that bother you?" I asked. "That's nothing compared to what that guy[her downstairs neighbor] does," she said. She told me about how he sometimes makes obscene gestures when she and her friends pass by and then went on to say that she suspected that it was he who wrote "that letter." "What letter?" I asked. She described it as a white sheet of bond paper with Icelandic writing in crayons saying, "Iceland for Icelanders" on top, "Asians go home" at the bottom and a swastika in the middle. "I was terrified," she said, "so I gave it to my lawyer. He said it was nothing (*bale wala*)."

I asked other Icelanders about some racial incidents I had heard about and I was invariably told that these are "isolated incidents" with the perpetrators dismissed as "a bunch of crazies." I was hoping PG would not dismiss the incident the way my friend's lawyer had dismissed it (the lawyer had also "misplaced" the note in the meantime). After I finished telling him the story, he answered, "So, do all Filipinos think all Icelanders are racists?" I was so stumped by his response that I changed the topic and left.

As we had established our roles and relationship as professor and student or expert and novice, I was expecting an explication or an interpretation of the hate-mail incident I had just narrated. The expressive means I used in telling the story, that of apprehension, might have betrayed my need for succorance or sympathy. But I interpreted his response as a dismissal or an erasure. The ground rule in this interaction was to keep within the bounds of professionalism and academic discourse. I wondered if, being a Filipino myself, I had exhibited my own fears for my safety and if that helped shift the frame of my storytelling from data sharing to agonistic discourse.

Yet another possibility is that within the bounds of academic discourse, he had shifted to the role of advocate by asking "Do all Filipinos think all Icelanders are racists?" as a rhetorical question, thus positioning me in the role of an interlocutor, a respondent, and an informant. The focus of the question in that instance was not on my identity as Filipino and his as Icelander, but on the word "all" whereby he questioned the generalizability of the conclusions I was making on the basis of information drawn from the narrated event.

The conclusion that can be readily drawn from a review of this narrative event is that a multiplicity of identities functioning within a single narrative interaction could bring about as many interpretations depending on where either narrator or narratee—or both—positioned the self and the other.

Emotioning in My Fieldwork: Close Encounters

Fieldwork Update for Academic Committee: March 20, 1998

Personal Note: Talking about racial prejudice in Iceland is like reporting UFO sightings. People don't want to hear about it. And victims are hesitant to talk about it. . . . As I wrote those lines at the crowded computer room yesterday, a young man who had been waiting for his turn to get on a computer walked across the room past five rows of Icelandic students and came up [to] where I sat, the farthest from the aisle next to the windows, and said in a loud voice, "Are you just playing on the Internet or are you writing something?" I looked around the room. Other people were on the Internet. The woman sitting next to me had just returned from a 15-minute coffee break during which she left her files open and her things around the computer. A group of three students in the next row had a group project on their screen but were chatting and showing each other photographs. He had approached the only person whom he thought did not belong. How could an Asian woman in Iceland possibly be doing serious academic work like these bright young Icelandic students? I would not have asked myself "Why me?" if not for the fact that this was not the first instance of racial prejudice I've

put up with since I got here. . . . When I speak to my Filipino friends about this, they either change the topic or offer some lame consoling words ("don't mind it" or "it doesn't mean anything"). . . . I was so shaken by the computer room incident that I did not feel like going out of my dorm room this morning. . . . I am accumulating deep emotional wounds from this fieldwork. It is very debilitating. I have to get out of here as soon as I can.

This account is part of one of the longer fieldwork updates that I e-mailed to my academic committee every 2 or 3 months. This section was marked "personal note" and was clearly separated from the rest of the research report, signaling a shift in genre—from description or exposition to narrative, specifically to personal narrative and self-disclosure. This might have been a breach of the advisor-advisee relationship, but my emotions were so powerful that I decided to include the narrative in the report that I was typing at that time. Steier (1995) notes that "emotioning" in research reveals what we value and makes narratives "real."

The event itself was a defining moment for me, the proverbial last straw. Unlike the other negative experiences I'd had in Iceland in the past, this was blatant, confrontational, and worst of all, public. To my mind, the young man, whom I later found out was a sophomore law student, had in this encounter obviously positioned himself in a role connoting authority, superiority, and privilege. I could only imagine his assumptions when he decided to pick on me for eviction. I felt defiled and shamed. I was afraid of going out of my dorm room the next morning for fear that the whole world now knew about this humiliating episode.

On the other hand, the fact that this confrontation was situated in a public space signaled the opening of the floodgates. The local practice of denial and accommodation that I had all along respected, albeit with great discomfort, had been breached. The line that separated me as a "privileged" academic from "other" Filipino women in Iceland had been completely withdrawn. This narrative was so powerful that it became my emblem, which I shared with others to gain support and succorance and to elicit responses such as stories of their own. I shared this story immediately with two other graduate students who were Icelandic and with whom I shared an office. Although the story was discomforting, they responded with affirmations of friendship and sympathy. And it did break down the walls around a topic that was taboo. We could now discuss the gray areas around racism, discrimination, segregation, and exclusion. A new euphemism emerged from these discussions. I would on occasion be greeted in jest with: "Any close encounters recently?"

Intervention: Speaking the Unspeakable

Icelandic Human Rights Center Address: July 1, 1998

I would like to thank the Icelandic Human Rights Center for giving me the opportunity to address you this afternoon, and also the Fulbright Commission, which sponsored the research I conducted during the past academic year.

I was born in the Philippines, immigrated to the United States. I have lived in Israel, wrote my undergraduate thesis on international media, my master's thesis on representations in Israeli literature, and am currently conducting research on one of the many ethnic minority groups in Iceland. My job here has been mostly to gather stories told by and told about the Philippine-born residents of Iceland.

One of the most frequently asked questions during the course of my research here is whether there is racism in Iceland. I have brought this question back to audiences in past lectures only because I think a native-born Icelander should be a better judge of this than a researcher who is here only for a year. So, how many of you think there is racism in Iceland? How many think there is no racism in Iceland? Now, let me ask a couple more questions which are just as important as the one I am always asked: How many of you discuss racism in Iceland openly with your family, colleagues, and friends? If you have a friend who confides in you about being a victim of racism, how many of you know where to go for help? I hope that by the end of this meeting we can respond positively to these questions.

The invitation to speak at the Icelandic Human Rights Center came at the recommendation of the director of the Immigrants' Center where I had previously addressed a gathering of social workers, Icelandic language teachers, and immigration lawyers and workers. The forum was held at a restaurant in downtown Reykjavik but was publicized in the newspaper as open to the public. Among the audience members, I recognized officials from the Ministries of Justice, Education, and Social Welfare, from the Red Cross, and from Amnesty International, as well as members of the Society of New Icelanders, a contingent from the university, and some of my Filipino friends.

I was introduced by the chairman of the board of directors of the center who first reported on the recent accomplishments of the center in terms of human rights legislation in Iceland and participation in international forums. I delivered the address as a formal performance on a podium in front of the microphone next to the overhead projector, passing around press clippings that depicted the representation of Asians in the Icelandic

press, and encouraging feedback from the audience at various parts of the presentation.

The narrative strategy of the performance may be simplified into two parts. The first part answered the question "Who am I?"; the second part answered the question "Why am I here?" It was clear that I had been afforded the role of researcher and authority by being invited to deliver this presentation. But I was aware that the forum was open to the public and had in fact been well publicized. The prospect of facing an "Icelandic public" that did not know me made it necessary to stress my background and my credentials. There was also a very real fear that members of extremist groups (which are not illegal in Iceland, most of which exist under the banner of "Icelandic nationalism") would be in the audience. Under these circumstances, it was necessary to justify why I was "here" in Iceland, as well as "here" in this forum.

As it was a formal gathering, the interactional ground rules were clear. I presented the evidence and provided tools and a vocabulary for discussion, but I left it for the audience to judge if racism in fact exists in Iceland. I included no personal narratives, but I did present my personal experience in the third person in one of the case studies. I had from the very beginning sought a strategy for bringing back my research findings to the Filipino community and thereby receiving some sort of validation. When I agreed to deliver the address, I was afraid that the presentation would be a breach of the silence about racism in Iceland.

There was coverage of the event in the evening news that day. All night and for the rest of the following week, my telephone rang with calls from friends and strangers, as well as immigrants from other countries who wanted to meet me because they had to tell me their story. With only 3 weeks left to stay in Iceland, it felt like my research had just begun.

EXAMINING OUR (IN)VISIBILITY ACROSS NARRATIVES

In this chapter, we have used cultural and communication studies of sojourn and whiteness to inform our analysis of the scenes through which self is created or interpreted in interaction. Rather than focusing on whiteness as a blanketing discourse, through which all other forms of identification are covered, we chose instead to focus on the dynamics of cultural scenes and the unevenness through which gender, sexuality, class, and whiteness (among other things) were made visible or invisible. The focus on language as creative places action and context at the center of analysis, thus adding

variety and complexity to the study of *intercultural* as well as *interpersonal* communication. Yet, underlying the relations of power that both create and reduce cultural and creative vitality, we see an organizational theme that frames the sojourn narratives constructed here—that of embodiment. This trope is offered not as a reduction of the narrative but as part of the dialogical process of working from the discourse to narrative structure to the dialectics of (in)visibility that inform these cultural scenes.

Across the stories we tell, the common focus is on the (in)visibility of cultural values (of whiteness, gender, relationships, and class position, among other things) in our various encounters. In Leda's journal entries, whiteness is positioned in diverse ways: as desirable, as visible, as uncomfortable, and as "other," albeit often as a privileged and exotic other. While the desirability and visibility of whiteness in Leda's narratives connote the privilege of being other in a primarily mestiza/mestizo culture, racial privilege intertwined with gender and class considerations (among others) raises more complex issues of power that can be traced back to the various ways bodies and embodiment have been marked through colonial and religious discourse. She writes of the ways her privilege as a white woman was complicated by both her (dis)avowal of that privilege and the cultural contexts in which that privilege was enabled or constrained. In Elizabeth's stories, whiteness is invisible, comfortable, and everywhere, which in turn positions her as a Filipino in her interactions as occasionally exotic, visible, and (under)privileged, depending on context and audience. Specifically, Elizabeth's discomfort, anxiety, and even terror at being a "target" of racist acts because of her visibility as a Filipino researcher cannot be separated from the invisibility of whiteness in the Icelandic cultural scene. Her attempts to speak out against the racism she and others encountered as nonwhite minorities in Iceland were attempts to mark the invisibility of whiteness and white privilege.

In the following section we return to the theme of embodiment as it took two shapes in the episodes we have described in this chapter. The particular positions of our selves in sojourn that we chose to highlight here are those that resonated across both of our experiences, albeit in quite different ways. We emphasize these aspects of our positions as they inform and are informed both by cultural understandings of the scenes in which they occur and through the theoretical frameworks for acknowledging the positions we occupied in those scenes.

Embodiment: The Positioning of the Scholar in Sojourn

Leda: Although I interpreted my work in Panama as codeveloping programs that were intended to improve the quality of life for women on their terms, the various NGOs framed the training sessions as part of a larger program of economic and social development. Kapoor (1999) observes that, "the focus of development is economic and that is where it seems to stop. Concerns for the education for women and reduction of 'family' size are reduced to economic concerns" (p. 252). Program content that I viewed as dealing with symbolic or representational issues of valuing the self and empowerment for women was translated by the NGOs as self-improvement for economic purposes. It is important to note as well that while Kapoor (1999) states that this is a modernizing motive and motif of Western programs designed for "Third World development," many of the nongovernmental organizations for which I worked had designed their programs with such a motive in mind. In this venue, working both with the NGOs and with their constituencies as a "scholar" from the United States meant that I was valued as an asset for the skills that I could teach others. Where my goal had been to learn collaboratively with the women about issues that affected their lives, the women who ran the NGOs were interested in the efficient delivery of programs with measurable results. The knowledge that I possessed (although perhaps culturally misaligned) was all the more valued because I was a white foreigner.

Elizabeth: My position as a scholar in Iceland was almost nonsensical to white Icelandic students and some faculty. There was no discursive or symbolic vocabulary in which I could be represented or understood as a foreign Filipino American scholar; therefore, I was an aberrant vision. Although I was visually marked as a native or Filipino, I was a foreigner from the United States. I was a scholar but I was not white; therefore, as a scholar, I could not be a credible source for anything more than my Filipinoness. Of course, there had to be some room for agency here, for me to assert myself as a scholar and as an ally for Filipino women in Iceland, or I would not have been invited. Development education, if it was called that at all, occurred not in the context of economic development

but in the First World context of tolerance and diversity. As a sojourning scholar I found myself attempting to represent and open up the spaces for performance of Filipino identity in Iceland. The positions available for nonwhites in Iceland (both symbolically and occupationally) were limited and inflexible. My struggle was both to be seen as representing my ethnic (gendered, classed) identity and to be able to have a legitimate role as a sojourning scholar within (and despite) that representation.

Embodiment: The Movement From Objectivity to Subjectivity

Leda: My involvement for many years in conflict and diversity training allowed me to move in and out of my position as white with relative comfort. I could trace white as a discourse in opposition to difference and as a discourse that silenced diversity. I could be antiracist, in other words, without necessarily having to confront the specific details of my privilege as it played out in my everyday life.[6] Steyn (1999) notes that the particular configuration of historical relations of conquest in the United States "created a psychological map in which the 'white' center has been so stable and so confident that the 'others' [Native Americans, Africans made into slaves in America, Latinas/Latinos, Asians, etc.] . . . could be rendered psychologically 'far' even while yet constitutive of the center" (p. 267). This particular form of whiteness, informed by my cultural and national history, made my objective antiracist stance seem viable. Just as Steyn (1999) observes that she felt differently "white" while sojourning in the United States than she had at home in South Africa, so too did my experience of my whiteness change while living in Panama. Steyn suggests that the degree to which whiteness is marked is indicated by the closeness of the subjective experience in its colonial framing. I would add to this the relative positioning of white in terms of minority-majority relations, as well as that of native (nonwhite) and foreigner (white). During my sojourn in Panama, I felt that I became visible in ways that were uncomfortably *foreign* to me, yet intimately connected to the privileges of white skin experienced around the "Third World." Whiteness was/is the invisible, ideological backdrop against

	which development, enterprise, skin color, and interpersonal relationships, among other things, were/are marked.
Elizabeth:	For me the movement from objectivity to subjectivity was perhaps less stark but difficult nonetheless. Living as a journalist and reporter in the Philippines and in Israel, I had sought to maintain objectivity—as a stance from which to report the news, as well as for my reputation as an educated professional. On the other hand, in my role as a jet mechanic in the Air Force reserves I had a good deal of visibility, but this visibility was primarily as a woman doing a man's job in a "color- and class-blind" military. As a student, an educator, and a professional living in Boston, I aligned myself more closely with the issues (and thus) visibility of immigrant population; however, we were one of several visible Asian immigrant communities in Boston and thus our visibility allowed for certain flexibilities of image not available to me in the Icelandic context. In Iceland, the categories of educator and scholar, sojourner, Filipino American, and woman, representing selves that had always been multiply positioned and arranged in the various locales and roles I played, seemed to collapse into each other. In Iceland, I could be an educator in an educational context, but my function was only to educate white people about my nativeness. Offstage in my role as a scholar, and outside the university, I was both visible as a racialized woman and invisible through my assumed class status (maid, cleaning woman).

The movement to subjectivity was, for me, movement in which I could no longer deny my closeness to an identity that was deeply mired in classist, racist, and misogynist cultural discourses. Yet, at the same time, this movement gave me an awareness of my privileges relative to my position as a foreign scholar. I had mobility where my friends had little or none. I had access to the university and an audience for my voice. Most of the Filipino women I knew in Iceland had yet to be heard. In short, the movement to subjectivity was movement that simultaneously exposed as false the privileges that I thought I had (of distance and objectivity) and gave me insight into those privileges afforded by my position as a sojourner in Iceland that made me a visible and viable presence.

POSITIONING THE SOJOURN
NARRATIVE: CONCLUSIONS

Reflecting on the recording and rewriting of our stories, we have discussed the frustration, shame, anger, joy, connection, and sadness we have experienced in attempting to negotiate our identities as sojourners. We read each other's stories with an eye toward the complexities of whiteness and of visibility in intercultural encounters out of our own very different positions within these encounters. Our goal in this chapter has been not to seek certain "truths" about whiteness or about culture but, rather, to examine the contradictions and complexities inherent in different sojourner positions.

For these reasons, our hope is that the stories we have told are read first and foremost as performances of the (in)visibility of our sojourn experiences across cultural contexts. The narratives raise questions and blur categories of race, class, ethnicity, privilege, oppression, gender, and so on, rather than providing easy closure to these positions. Our stories exhibit the potential for multiple identifications and multiple possibilities for reading. Moreover, the stories we tell demonstrate that intercultural communication scholars are themselves situated in and can learn from their cross-cultural encounters; alliances can be built through reflection and reflexivity both within and across intercultural encounters.

NOTES

1. The term *sojourn* refers to voluntary travel to a new cultural context for a limited period of time, usually between 4 months and a year, for work or for study.

2. *Whiteness* is used throughout this chapter to signify a form of racial identification that shifts and changes in different social and cultural contexts. Omi and Winant (1994) note that race "signifies and symbolizes social conflicts and interests by referring to different types of human bodies" (p. 55). While whiteness as a racial identifier confers privilege across many contexts, race itself is not a natural, fixed phenomenon. Therefore, race interacts with other forms of identification, with history and politics, to assign meaning to bodies and performances of identity.

3. For our purposes, *culture* is used throughout this chapter to describe a lens or map through which social relations are organized and actions are understood. Cultural markers can be referenced by nation, race, class, gender, sexuality, and occupation and are created and contested in interaction with others.

4. Although it is beyond the scope of this chapter to elaborate a critique of the discourse on the ways identity is performed and managed in intercultural,

interpersonal, performance studies, we hope to provide an alternative approach to report the ways selves are embodied as well as negotiated in performances of (social and/or cultural) difference.

5. All names (other than those of the authors) have been changed.

6. Consciousness of race and forms of racism is not an either-or distinction, but rather, one that exists on a continuum. In my case, I have been conscious of my race and location since I was a child, always feeling not quite "white" as a Jew, with primarily Cuban and Vietnamese friends who taught me their language and about their homelands.

REFERENCES

Alexander, B. (1999). Performing culture in the classroom: An instructional (auto)ethnography. *Text and Performance Quarterly, 19,* 307-331.

Brennan, T. (1989). Cosmopolitans and celebrities. *Race and Class, 31*(1), 1-20.

Chow, R. (1994). Where have all the Natives gone? In A. Bammer (Ed.), *Displacements* (pp. 125-151). Bloomington: Indiana University Press.

Clifford, J. (1988). *Predicament of culture.* Cambridge, MA: Harvard University Press.

Clifford, J. (1992). Travelling cultures. In L. Grossberg, C. Nelson, & P. Treichler (Eds.), *Cultural studies* (pp. 96-111). New York: Routledge.

Corey, F. C. (1998). Crossing an Irish border. In J. N. Martin, T. K. Nakayama, & L. Flores (Eds.), *Readings in intercultural contexts* (pp. 121-126). Mountain View, CA: Mayfield.

Crawford, L. (1996). Personal ethnography. *Communication Monographs, 63,* 158-170.

Dijk, Teun A. van (1993). Stories and racism. In D. K. Mumby (Ed.), *Narrative and social control* (pp. 110-121). Newbury Park, CA: Sage.

Dyer, R. (1997). *White.* London: Routledge.

Ellsworth. E. (1997). *Teaching positions: Difference, pedagogy and the power of address.* New York: Teachers College Press.

Frankenberg, R. (1993). *White women, race matters: The social construction of whiteness.* Minneapolis: University of Minnesota Press.

Hoonaard, W. C. van den (1996, May 28-31). *A "new ethnography" in an old field setting: Iceland.* Paper presented at the XIII Qualitative Analysis Conference, McMaster University, Ontario, Canada.

Hulme, P. (1986). *Colonial encounters: Europe and the Native Caribbean, 1492-1797.* London: Methuen.

Johnson, P. C. (1999). Reflections on critical whiteness studies. In T. K. Nakayama & J. N. Martin (Eds.), *Whiteness: The communication of social identity* (pp. 1-12). Thousand Oaks, CA: Sage.

Kaplan, C. (1996). *Questions of travel.* Durham, NC: Duke University Press.

Kapoor, P. (1999). Provincializing whiteness: Deconstructing discourses on national process. In T. K. Nakayama & J. N. Martin (Eds.), *Whiteness: The communication of social identity* (pp. 249-263). Thousand Oaks, CA: Sage.

King, D. (2000). *Making Americans: Immigration, race, and the origins of the diverse democracy.* Cambridge, MA: Harvard University Press.

Lincoln, Y. Y., & Guba, E. G. (1985). *Naturalistic inquiry.* Beverly Hills, CA: Sage.

Lukacs, G. (1971). *Realism in our time: Studies of Marxist dialectics.* London: Merlin.

MacCannell, D. (1976). *The tourist: A new theory of the leisure class.* New York: Schocken.

Martin, J. N., & Davis, O. I. (2001). Conceptual foundations for teaching about whiteness in intercultural communication courses. *Communication Education, 50*(4), 298-313.

Martin, J. N., Krizek, R. L., Nakayama, T. N., & Bradford, L. (1999). What do white people want to be called? A study of self-labels for white Americans. In T. K. Nakayama & J. N. Martin (Eds.), *Whiteness: The communication of social identity* (pp. 27-50). Thousand Oaks, CA: Sage.

Martin, J., Nakayama, T., & Flores, L. (1998). A dialectical approach to intercultural communication. In J. Martin, T. Nakayama, & L. Flores (Eds.), *Readings in cultural contexts* (pp. 5-15). Mountain View, CA: Mayfield.

McClintock, A. (1992). The angel of progress: Pitfalls in the term "postcolonialism." *Social Text, 31/32,* 84-98.

Moon, D. (1999). White enculturation and bourgeois ideology. In T. K. Nakayama & J. N. Martin (Eds.), *Whiteness: The communication of social identity* (pp. 177-197). Thousand Oaks, CA: Sage.

Nakayama, T., & Krizek, R. L. (1999). Whiteness as strategic rhetoric. In T. K. Nakayama & J. N. Martin (Eds.), *Whiteness: The communication of social identity* (pp. 87-106). Thousand Oaks, CA: Sage.

Nakayama, T., & Martin, J. (1999). Introduction: Whiteness as the communication of social identity. In T. K. Nakayama & J. N. Martin (Eds.), *Whiteness: The communication of social identity* (pp. vii-xiv). Thousand Oaks, CA: Sage.

Nicotera, A. M. (1999). The woman academic as subject/object/self: Dismantling the illusion of duality. *Communication Theory, 9,* 430-464.

Omi, M., & Winant, H. (1994). *Racial formation in the United States: From the 1960's to the 1990's.* New York: Routledge.

Paul, R. (1996, May 9-12). Iceland's invisible immigrants. In *Kriminalitet, konstruktioner og virkelighed* (pp. 117-121). Report from the 38th seminar of the Nordisk Samarbejdsrad for Kriminologi, Iceland.

Pratt, M. L. (1986). Fieldwork in common places. In J. Clifford & G. Marcus (Eds.), *Writing culture: The poetics and politics of ethnography* (pp. 27-50). Berkeley: University of California Press.

Shome, R. (1999). Whiteness and the politics of location: Postcolonial reflections. In T. K. Nakayama & J. N. Martin (Eds.), *Whiteness: The communication of social identity* (pp. 107-128). Thousand Oaks, CA: Sage.

Steier, F. (1995). Reflexivity, interpersonal communication, and interpersonal communication research. In W. Leeds-Hurwitz (Ed.), *Social approaches to communication* (pp. 63-87). New York: Guilford.

Steyn, M. (1999). White identity in context: A personal narrative. In T. K. Nakayama & J. N. Martin (Eds.), *Whiteness: The communication of social identity* (pp. 264-278). Thousand Oaks, CA: Sage.

Tanno, D., & Jandt, F. (1998). Redefining the "other" in multicultural research. In J. Martin, T. Nakayama, & L. Flores (Eds.), *Readings in cultural contexts* (pp. 477-485). Mountain View, CA: Mayfield.

Tedlock, B. (1991). From participant observation to the observation of participation: The emergence of narrative ethnography. *Journal of Anthropological Research, 47,* 69-94.

Thomas, J. (1993). *Doing critical ethnography.* Newbury Park, CA: Sage.

7

Interrogating Identities

Composing Other Cyberspaces

RADHIKA GAJJALA • *Bowling Green State University*

> What is it that will give me "identity"? A lot of it is how I am perceived by someone else. Today I seem to have given away this power to people who have a vested interest in seeing me as one thing or the other. . . . I am constantly in the position of negotiating for more space. . . . Do I get more people to negotiate on my side, do I decide that I and only I will decide my identity . . . in a "RL" [real life] world where my identity is already threatened by my own ignorance. . . . Will not the net just be one more place where I am "ignorant"?
>
> —personal e-mail exchange with someone from the "Third World"

> Today, with globalization in full swing, telecommunicative informatics taps the Native Informant directly in the name of indigenous knowledge and advances biopiracy.
>
> —Spivak (1999, p. ix)

This chapter is part of a larger discussion of how South Asian diaspora is manifested in the "Intercultural Global Village" (Ess & Sudweeks, 2001, p. 1) in cyberspace (Bahri, 2001; Gajjala, 1998; Lal, 1999b; Mallapragada, 2001; Mitra, 1997; Rai, 1995; Sudha, 1993). In an attempt to illustrate the contradictory discourses that emerge online, while discussing the possibilities and impossibilities for opening up counterspheres in cyberspace for alternate collaborative ways of forming communities, I focus on a specific exchange on the sa-cyborgs list. In order to contextualize this exchange, I provide a history of how and why the list was formed.

AUTHOR'S NOTE: I wish to thank my research assistant Robert Ochieng for his help in proofreading the manuscript. In addition, I wish to thank the anonymous reviewers and Dr. Mary Jane Collier for their helpful and constructive feedback on previous drafts of this chapter.

As we rediscovered with deadly clarity in the month of September 2001, globalization, information communication technologies, nationalisms, and religious diasporas are inextricably linked with a need for intercultural understanding. The world becoming "smaller" is enabled through a variety of technologies, and the clashing of various cultural, religious, and political discourses and extremisms has material consequences. While the rest of the world has experienced these consequences several times these past few decades, the United States experienced the material effects on September 11, 2001, in a way it has never before. Because of the political and economic power and influence that the United States and its actions and reactions have over the daily life of people all over the rest of the world, there is now a sense of urgency and immediacy to the need to understand one another's cultural practices and belief systems.

Cyberspace is just one of many sites for possible intercultural encounters and dialogue. During the past decade, Internet communication and online cultures and subcultures have taken on great importance for transnational economic and cultural flows; these have considerable impact on intercultural and international relations and communication. Intercultural communication scholars have studied Internet communication from a variety of perspectives (see, for example, Chen & Starosta, 2000; Ess & Sudweeks, 2001; and Lengel, 2000). My chapter contributes to this body of knowledge while insisting that the study of intercultural communication via the Internet needs to take into account historical, economic, political, and cultural processes of globalization. My examination of intercultural communication online is founded on a basic questioning of the ability of new technologies to further equality. Underlying my analysis is the unavoidable recognition of the fact that the context of intercultural communication in cyberspace is driven through an agenda of commercialization that is implicitly and explicitly digitally Darwinistic, emphasizing the survival of the fastest, as well as the consumption of brand names.

As Susan Herring (2001) states: "The globalization of the Internet raises intellectual and social challenges concerning cultural bias in CMC, mechanisms of technology diffusion, and barriers to equitable access" (p. x). Furthermore, Ess and Sudweeks (2001) argue for: "an interdisciplinary effort to explore the role culture plays in forming our fundamental beliefs and values—not only with regard to communication and technology, but still more fundamentally towards such basic values as those that cluster about our preferences for democratic polity, individual autonomy, etc." (p. 3). They call for: "a distinctive conjunction of theory and praxis—one that articulates interdisciplinary foundations and practical models for

designing and using CMC technologies in ways that avoid the Manichean dualism of Jihad or McWorld, and mark out instead a trajectory toward a genuinely intercultural global village" (p. 4).

While I question the epistemological, political, economic, and cultural premises on which this vision of a "genuinely intercultural global village" implicitly relies, I agree with Ess and Sudweeks regarding the importance of emphasizing the theory and practice of designing, producing, consuming, and interacting in cyberspace. However, I do not agree with what appears to be a positioning of "Jihad" and "McWorld" as two opposites in a Manichean dualism—they are in fact not opposed but products of the same logic of capital and consumption that produces our present postmodern, transnational world. In fact, as Barber suggests, "McWorld cannot do without Jihad . . . neither can Jihad do without McWorld" (Barber, 1995, p. 155). The processes of production and cultural activities surrounding these processes are both products of an economic globalization and transnationalization that rest on the need for self-contained identity formations (consumer demographics) and a performance of multicultural difference. "Jihad" and other religious fundamentalisms and nationalisms (including modern day "crusades") are examples of "concepts of belonging" and ways of imagining community that are "currently being mobilized in the service of the larger political and economic demands associated with globalization" (Sadowski-Smith, 1999, p. 8).

As is the case with the processes of rebordering and the recent surge of ethnonationalisms in Eastern Europe and elsewhere, different fundamentalisms based in ethnic and religious identity formations are linked to emerging "global reconfigurations" that help the imagining of ethnic and religious communities transnationally while providing selective class-based access to global capital. Thus new hierarchies emerge that feed into "the logic of uneven global development." Sadowski-Smith (1999) further states, "It is essential to realize that . . . concepts of belonging are currently being mobilized in the service of larger political and economic demands associated with globalization" (p. 8).

Situated within such a real world context, what kind of migratory subjects emerge in digital diaspora,[1] at the intersection of the local and the global? What "regulatory fictions" and theoretical frames discipline (in a Foucauldian sense) manifestations of identity formations and communities online? Is communicating as digital diaspora, across contexts, necessarily "empowering"? In this chapter, I examine the (im)possibilities for the emergence of countersubjectivities and counterspheres online[2] with a specific focus on South Asian digital diasporic formations. The emergence of

counterspheres and alternate subjectivities (underprivileged or not) requires the opening up of discursive categories (including academic and political reworkings and disruptions of available frameworks). These discursive countercategories allow the imagining of community in different ways (Anderson, 1991). By looking at split and conflicted subject positions and the epistemological contradictions and disruptions that emerge through their voicings, scholars might be able to understand how individuals design and produce collaborative counterspheres in cyberspace and elsewhere.

In discussing Chicano as a nationalism, communication scholars Flores and Hasian (1997) argue that nationalism is maintained through a sharing of beliefs and symbolic constructs as much as through geographical alliances and communal identities. Adapting Anderson's (1991) notion of imagined communities, they propose a view of nationalism that is constructed through political rhetorics. Flores and Hasian (1997) write that nationhood:

> is more than a static monolithic concept . . . [and is] a multilayered description of a form that provides us with an "imagined" discursive unit of analysis for studying particular symbol systems. . . . As Anderson once astutely observed, people may believe themselves to be a part of a nation even though they "will never know most of their fellow-members, meet them, or even hear them" . . . . These political ties that bind are thus culturally constructed and coproduced by rhetors and their audiences who live in imagined communal relationships. . . . Nationhood can thus be viewed as a rhetorical achievement that may transcend the boundaries of geographic space and historical time. (pp. 189-190)

Such manifestations of imagined nationhood are visible online as diasporic communities come together through virtual meeting spaces such as listservs, bulletin boards, and so on. Digital diasporas of real people form online imagined communities. In this chapter I focus on South Asian digital diasporas with an emphasis on the imaginings of nationhood that implicitly and explicitly occur along religious frameworks. Thus, several South Asian communities online are framed not along nationalisms based on present geographical boundaries and demographics but on imaginations centered around reproductions of religious discourse in the form of religious diasporas. It is within such an overall imagined context that the imagining of nationhood in diaspora is framed through various religious fundamentalisms while, at the same time, it is also framed through the discourses of accessing and participating in the transnational corporate world. As Bahri (2001) puts it: "Second and third generation South Asians can now connect with those of their own age newly arrived from South Asia (and, of course,

with the small but growing number of postcolonies who have access to the internet) to negotiate each other's sense of self " (p. 224).

SOUTH ASIANS ONLINE

While there is a growing body of mainstream literature on topics related to South Asians and IT (information technology), South Asians in cyberspace, and the digital divide, most of the articles are celebratory with regard to the potential of informational technologies for the various populations of the world. Much of this literature relates to business applications, software production and design for businesses worldwide, and programming, labor, and jobs for South Asians in the rest of the world, or it relates to issues of access of South Asia to the global commercial centers of the world. None of these adequately address the discursive sociocultural spaces that Internet spaces enable, or how the design of information technologies shapes the possibilities and impossibilities of the emergence of marginalized subjectivities. Perhaps this is so because the discussion in these areas (whether online or offline) does not explicitly engage the sociocultural aspects of technology production, reproduction, and use. Online contributors as well as many scholars of published literature regarding these issues tend to maintain an illusion of secularism and universality and do not confront the basic epistemological problems related to science, technology, and knowledge production being situated within unequal cultural and material power relations.

Other bodies of literature related to South Asia and the IT phenomena do, however, exist. Scholars here examine sociocultural aspects of online activity and discursive formations online in relation to subjectivities that emerge online and to issues such as "voice and voicelessness," "subaltern counterspheres," and so on addressed by cultural studies, postcolonial theory, and feminist theory. Literature examining the sociocultural and communicative aspects of South Asian digital diasporas has been largely done by scholars from a variety of disciplines focusing on the study of South Asia and post-colonialism. My work draws from this body of literature and connects it with the themes and topics within the field of intercultural communication.

Some issues of concern for this latter set of scholars are gender, sexuality, nation and community, construction of South Asian identities in diaspora, subaltern speech, representation of South Asians in Western and global media, and so on. Rai (1995) and Lal (1999b) for instance, examine the "Hindu diaspora" and the discourses surrounding Hindu fundamentalist

instigated events in Ayodhya, India, in 1992. As Lal (1999b) points out in relation to the Indian and South Asian digital diaspora:

We speak with unreflective ease of the "information revolution," and in this clichéd expression there is the most unambiguous assertion of confidence in the benign telos of history. . . . It is the agenda of the "Internet elites," if they may be so termed, that dictates the modernization and liberalization of the Indian economy, and it is their interests and ambitions that have led to the emergence of the cell phone culture while the greater part of the country remains without reliable ordinary telephone service. The development of an internationally renowned software industry even while nearly 50% of the Indian population remains mired in poverty is yet another of the anomalies engendered by the culture of the Internet elites. Their mobility in cyberspace furnishes them with opportunities to work within the world of international finance and business; like the elites of the First World, they are beginning to live in time, and space poses no barriers for them. . . . The time-space compression that cyberspace typifies only works to the advantage of these elites. (pp. 137-140)

Others, such as Mallapragada (2001), focus on the gendered nature of these online religious diasporas with their implicit and explicit objectification of the Hindu woman as an icon of pure Hindu culture. Mallapragada (2001) argues:

The articulation of "Indianness" which is prolific on diasporic websites is problematic for many reasons—chiefly for its idealization of a traditionally upper-caste, middle class male Hindu (oftentimes North Indian Hindu) version of cultural tradition and practices. In the Indian national context, this middle class version of culture achieved and continues to do so, with varying degrees of success, a hegemonic status as Indian culture. This particular dynamic of class, caste, gender, religion and language continues to be pertinent in diasporic spaces. (p. 9)

This idealization of a specific type of masculinity relies on the objectification of an Indian and Hindu femininity. Rai (1995), for instance, addresses the gendered nature of these online diasporas by pointing out how these discourses engage the history of the Indian nationalist resolution of the "Woman's Question," which objectified the woman as an icon of cultural purity, the maintainer of the cultural essence of home. An image of the "New Hindu woman" was produced in such nationalistic discourses. This woman was the "other" of the common woman, who was "coarse, vulgar, loud, quarrelsome, devoid of superior moral sense, and sexually promiscuous" (Chatterjee, 1989, pp. 238-239). The construction of such a woman

in nationalist discourses carried into the diasporic means that South Asian women in diaspora face a double bind in relation to the Western feminism and resistance to colonial discourses sometimes implicit in liberal feminist attempts to "save" the "oppressed" Third World woman. Western feminist narratives regarding Third World women seem to echo colonial discourses (only in this case, instead of the white man attempting to rescue the brown woman from the brown man, it is a case of the white woman trying to "enlighten" the "politically immature" brown woman).

Indian and other South Asian feminists are faced with a problem in relation to their national identities. Feminism is equated with "Westernization," and femininity is equated with the traditional and objectified female in nationalist discourse. Online, therefore, the South Asian woman is faced with negotiating the gendered nature of South Asian digital diasporas and the implicit class based, colonial hierarchies and rules and "regulatory fictions" (Butler, cited in Rai, 1995, p. 33) that police online interaction (such as "netiquette").

Rai (1995) examines the style in which online diasporic communities are imagined and notes that imagined communities of South Asians in digital diaspora are shaped through the "regulatory fictions" produced by officers of the British Empire. For instance, it is such classificatory grids (such as the census categories and definitions of gender identity, caste, and religion based on the British social understandings and framings of "Indian" social structures), categories produced under British rule, that became "the antagonisms that constituted what came to be known as 'representative' communal politics under the British Raj" (Rai, 1995, p. 37). These classificatory grids continue to shape and frame discourse even within online spaces populated mostly by Western-educated elite populations. Thus, the effect of the circulation of such grids continues to result in the reproduction of the same tensions and ideologies that are visible within diasporic communities not online (the communities in real life). Rai, therefore, does not see such online spaces as "oppositional" formations in the sense suggested by those that talk about the radical democratizing potential of cyberspace. It is thus through the "totalizing classificatory grid[s]" (Anderson, 1991, p. 184) produced in British colonial times that South Asian identities—in the form of communal and religious diasporas—are performed online. These classificatory grids have been further extended to work within a multicultural global(ized) village. The performance of diasporic identities in these online communities is thus regulated and mediated through historic, political, and religious discourses associated with colonial and postcolonial geographic territories and nationalisms.

Furthermore, the South Asian digital diaspora exists between the notions of "being home" and "being away." Even while many from actual Third World geographical (home) locations are connected and online, the discourse is framed by notions of "being home" and "being away"; not having left home yet (or at all) and having arrived (i.e., made it) in the Western world.[3] These discourses are situated in themes of nostalgia and reconstructions of South Asian immigrant identities invoked in contexts of diaspora and travel shaped by transnational capital and labor flow. Thus they are continually negotiating "model minority" performances and essentialized cultural performances based on fetishized, mummified notions of "home" traditions and cultural practices. These multicultural cyborgs, visible in digital diasporic contexts, therefore exist in an ethos of continual reconfiguration and shifting of narratives in relation to "being home" and "being away," while simultaneously they are also about "not having left home yet" and "having arrived." These various reconfigurations do not occur "through the heroic act of an individual (the migrant), but through the forming of [virtual] communities that create multiple identifications through collective acts of remembering in the absence of a shared knowledge or a familiar terrain" (Ahmed, 1999, p. 329). They occur through collective acts of storytelling and sharing of knowledge and experience of the "unfamiliar" and "new" terrains.

Some of these self-narratives by model native informants, who have moved "away" from home, yet fetishized "home" while celebrating their moving away and arriving as progressive (social upward mobility), perform the dual and simultaneous function of "modernization" and "exoticization" of the postcolonial (underdeveloped) subject.[4]

It is against such a South Asian technospatial imaginary that sa-cyborgs was started. Sa-cyborgs[5] is an e-mail list, born out of my dilemmas in relation to the above, started with the idea of trying to experiment against, examine, and negotiate such frameworks within the ethos of cyberspace.

Sa-cyborgs

In an attempt to illustrate the contradictory discourses that emerge online, I focus on an exchange between M, G, T, and R[6] on the sa-cyborgs list. In order to contextualize this exchange, I provide a history of how and why the list was formed. Note, however, that neither the interaction nor the e-mail discussion list should be considered "representative" in any sense.

My experience within a women-only South Asian e-mail discussion list (SAWnet) during the summer of 1995 (see Gajjala, 1998, 2002) led me to

ask questions regarding the design and production aspect of interactive Internet spaces such as e-mail discussion lists. In an effort to understand the technical and applied process of founding and maintaining a discussion list focused on women and creative expression, I started e-mail discussion lists (specifically the Third World women list, women writing culture list, and sa-cyborgs, which originated as "seminar-13") with the help of the Spoon Collective.[7] Prior to starting these lists, I gained experience moderating e-mail lists by being one of several moderators for the discussion list SAWnet and comoderating the postcolonial list as a member of the Spoon Collective. Over the years, the sa-cyborgs policies and list description have been changed periodically based on the problems encountered and conflicts that have occurred. These changes can be viewed in the public Web archives of the list from http://lists.village.virginia.edu/~spoons. The latest information sheet describes the list as follows:

> This list focuses on interactive, experimental creative writing with an implicit focus on gender, race, class, caste, sexuality, age, geographical location . . . identity/political/economic/spacio-temporal/geographic . . . issues pertaining to voice and voicelessness, silence and resistance, Self and Other narratives . . . "women" produce "writerly texts" (writerly texts—see Barthes—interrupt conventions of reading/writing and require readers to participate in meaning making—online this can happen visibly only if you participate on-list . . . "readerly texts," on the other hand, are those which fulfill our expectations of conventions that allow readers to be passive consumers . . . this is not the goal of this "list"). Participation is thus necessary and invited.

Note that the focus is on "wo-men's" subjectivities and creative "self" writing. Also note that there are implicit rules for list users that are not articulated in the info sheet. There are a variety of theoretical and practical reasons for these implicit rules, as well as for the explicit rules (see the archives at http://lists.village.virginia.edu/~spoons for more on these rules[8]). The information sheet continues:

> Rude, sexist, racist, classist and so on interruptions will not be tolerated. join with an open adventurous mind. Don't expect to understand it all. There are no organized dictionaries for the unsaid, yet-to-be-said, the silences and refusals of counter-hegemonic narratives . . . nor should there be.

In framing and reframing the sa-cyborgs list, I have not only confronted the limitations of the available populations of cyberspace but also faced the limitations of Westernized academic categories for analysis based on the

assumptions implicit in available categories such as gender, race, subaltern, and so on. Just as the classificatory grids from the British Raj time continue to be reproduced within and constrain bourgeois online diasporic spaces (Rai, 1995), classificatory grids situated within Western academic discourse have imposed limitations that affect how I open up online spaces for discussion. Thus, even labels, definitions, and categories such as gender, race, and class are shaped through discussions and articulations from within a Westernized academy and are situated in contexts that are culturally, economically, and historically specific to only certain populations around the world. They therefore impose ways of seeing that close off options for speaking by the people living within the contexts that the academics and policy makers are describing. This means that the populations that seek a voice are allowed a voice only within hegemonically available categories and labels. Discourse (however well intentioned and democratic the rhetoric and ideals contained within it) becomes limiting to the ability to produce counterspheres. These struggles for articulation are visible in the archives of sa-cyborgs.

Performing Diaspora Identity Locations[9]

Based on their posts to the list, M and G have been members of the list since 1996. Lacking face-to-face contact with either of these people, I cannot claim to know that either of these women is definitely South Asian or even that they are indeed women. In the case of one of them, however, I have talked with her by telephone, exchanged personal e-mails, as well as engaged with her on other e-mail discussion lists; I am quite sure that she is a South Asian woman who has lived in the United States for a considerable number of years. In the case of the other individual, I have guessed that she has some connection to "South Asianness" based on her posts to the lists. I have also seen her name appear on conference panels. Both women have contributed creative work to the sa-cyborgs list, and their writing has sometimes been centered on identity negotiations based in postcolonial female subjectivities. I have no real information on who T is, except that she is at a university in New York. I have been active since the list was started. My own multiply mediated sociocultural locations are variously visible through http://www.cyberdiva.org. While posts by T and R are used in my analyses in this chapter, below I focus on the exchange between G and M.

A complex, layered history is apparent in G's subject position, as expressed by her in the following piece of writing posted to the list in October 1996[10]:

Afrindianativeamaboriginalausinuitquechuafilmmaking
I screen/teach
and I read   white
ethnograppleanthroapologetical
white/black breasted nation algeographic
gazeye knowledgeablepower
and the whiteaustralianboy drugged out sleeps on the leather tutorial seat
saying I didn't get up today because nothing came up about
whiteheterosexualmales
faces that read
whileIgoonandonaboutracegenderandclassandthebolivianswhoweresteri
    lizedbythebadassedpeacecorpsortheamericanswhohelpedmassacrepe
    asantsinsouthamerica
my skin
oncetheylearnedaboutheuniversalityoftheirartandtheirknowledgeandthe
    irmight
brown   a sign
whichstillradiateslikeawhitehotspearthroughthefleshofthosethatliveandd
    ieinthis
theageofneocolonialgrandeur
that I speak
butnowtheytireoflearningaboutculturaldifferenceandminorityoppressedg
    roups
toomuchworktheysayandwhydowehavetolearnhistoriesofdarknessandstr
    uggle
but will not be heard
abovetheroarof theirmy word
"Those epistemologicaterminal terms dammit"—Ruth Forman

The present discussion will be based on one specific interaction between
G and M, about M's writing. This piece of writing authored by M was
posted to the list by me in October 1999, with M's permission from the
South Asian Women's Forum Web site, and it is available in full at
http://www.sawf.org/newedit/edit101899/index.asp.

ABHIMAAN
Yesterday's India,
I remember you.
Inexplicable, daunting exile
clutches at culture not mine.

Inner flashes grope for meaning:
Three blind men define Elephant.
The edges of my mind
flanked by Hindu myths
grasp life-shaping images.
Devout Prahlad cannot save an Unbeliever
devoured by a raging, ravaging Lion
God's alter ego fastens its teeth
tearing at flesh.
The Unbeliever is Prahlad's father.
The disciple cobra refuses to even hiss
and bleedingly succumbs to stones and rocks
and his guru's musing
"Yes, remain nonviolent, but surely
you can stand up for your rights?"
Hinduism molds me.
I question what I see,
hasten after what I cannot.
I defer to greatness reduced to ashes.
Desperate pounding rhythms
distanced from days filled
with anguished cries caught
between reality and dreams
give no succor to the heart.
Heart beats rival
perilous rhythms,
desolate measures
of silent depths.

As we can see, both these creative pieces are expressions of negotiations of gendered diasporic subjectivities. Each of the authors in her own way was struggling with available categories and labels and to identify and disidentify with available categories of belonging and owning and disowning of several histories based on the displacements and dislocations experienced by each. Each of these pieces, in its own way, performs an "outside the sentence[ness]" (Bhabha, 1994, p. 180).[11]

Exchanges on the list create problematic spaces of the sort described by Barthes (1975) and Bhabha (1994, pp. 180-182) in relation to various South Asian diasporic imaginings of community available online and carry

the possibility to open up "narrative strateg[ies] for the emergence and negotiation of those agencies of the marginal, minority, subaltern, or diasporic that incite us to think through—and beyond—theory" (Bhabha, 1994, p. 181).

While G's form in writing seems to indicate a problematization of the very structure and form of meaning making available to her, as her words and sentences run into each other and emotions and thoughts leak in and out of given categories, M's form in writing suggests a more conventional (but "conventional" only in comparison to G's writing) negotiation of available structures for self-expression. Yet neither is writing traditional English poetry in any sense. It is obvious that in writing they both seek tactics for disrupting available frameworks that do not allow for the emergence of complex, contradictory subjectivities with multiple, layered histories of travel and continually mutating cultural practices. G's entry reflects a struggle with layers of regulatory fictions shaped by colonial placements of race, patriarchal positioning of gender, teleological narratives of progress and the universalizing of Westernized epistemologies, as they regulate her students' ability to hear her voice as she speaks.

M writes apparently from within, yet problematizes, British colonial regulatory fictions of the "Hindu" imaginary. She slips outside of these frames; in her retelling of mythology and stories from the Upanishads and Panchatantras, and the invoking of Shiva's ashes (all unified under the term "Hindu"), she fleetingly, if hesitantly, dares to touch on the unbeliever's view, she refuses the homogeneity imposed on so-called Hinduism by British colonial and Indian nationalistic regulatory frames. For instance, she apparently aligns her view with that in colonial descriptions of the Indian woman by writing "Hinduism molds me," but she quickly switches from an implicit tone of cultural and religious piety to a tone that goes against the grain of the perception of non-Christian religions that colonial descriptions encourage with the next sentence, "I question what I see/ hasten after what I cannot," thus defiantly characterizing Hinduism as a culture that encourages the questioning of authority. The exchanges that happened between October 18, 1999 and October 22, 1999 on the sa-cyborgs list[12] construct a problematic, discursive social space. There is something in M's self-explanation of the writing of this poem (placed next to the poem at http://www.sawf.org/newedit/edit101899/index.asp) that appears to invoke conventionally available imagining of Indianness through regulatory frameworks situated in a colonial discourse that constructs "America" as new. The following section of the explanation, for instance, seems to romanticize

a past through a colonial and/or modernist imaginary that juxtaposes the "ancient" of India with the "new" of America:

G (to M]):   While your poem is perhaps intense for you, it really breaks my heart to see how our (Indian immigrant) poeticizing (if I can coin that word) re-installs a colonial repetitiveness in the affirmation of the U.S. as "new world."
Turtle Island, one of the U.S.'s many names was only new to those who came from Europe. There are never "new worlds" or frontiers, not even in space.

M and G on Poetries and Histories
I refer mainly to the thread entitled "poetries and histories" next. In this exchange, the continuity of emotion (in this case, nostalgia for an imagined or remembered homeland and coming to terms with a certain self-identity as an immigrant Indian) invoked in the poem by M and the commentary that follows, is disrupted (discontinued) by G's apparently sudden question, which displaces the perhaps intended (expected, anticipated) narrative logic of the poet. In this exchange, G insists on disidentifying herself from the "weness" implicit in M's narrative, while noting "how our (Indian immigrant) poeticizing reinstalls a colonial repetitiveness in the affirmation of the U.S. as "new world."
In addition—after some more list exchanges—G clarifies that it was not the poem itself that was the sole cause of her reaction:

G: Perhaps there are other things we need to ask ourselves here. Why is it that we "feel" like foreigners? Isn't it because the systems of racism and colonization that resulted in the dispossession of Native Americans continue to extend to other groups even if they are "born" in this land. I mean just think of the absurdity of people who belong to this land having to struggle to survive emotionally, psychically, politically, physiologically, let alone survive economically.
In this sense, I'm not attacking you, I just think we need to understand these histories and the connections between them in a way that is anti-colonial, otherwise we are dictated by the very language we communicate in even as we feel the conditions of exile in whatever manifestation it may be.

Even as M's moving poem invokes affective identification points for many immigrant Indians, and suggests a metaphoric representation of

Indian immigrants' feeling "othered" yet at home in the United States, the comments inserted in the discussion contrast with a unitary reading of the exchange within the technospatial South Asian imaginary.

While the exchange itself does not lead to a dialogue or a "resolution" of conflict, it holds the possibility of leading to associations "based on contiguity and context" (Jarratt, 1998, p. 59). As M points out, the way the poem was read was not how she intended it to be read. The decoding (meaning-making) processes surrounding the reading of the poem did not result in the meaning she intended to encode. In the following posts, she explains her intention, which in fact turns out not to be opposed to G's critique. G and M, it appears, were using different experiential and theoretical lenses.

M: By "new world," I mean it can never have a rich history. If I'm politicizing, then I'm politicizing the fact that as a citizen of this nation, I still have felt an exile, thanks to 10 job losses within 3 decades. America does not, still, welcome "foreigners." We are second-class citizens. Thus, my feeling like an "exile." It *is*[13] political, regardless of the academic and philosophic argument we could have over semantics. If I cannot survive economically, then what is America but "new" to me. And I actually grew up here, had all my schooling [here] since [I was] a child of seven.

I am not politicizing anything, but have been politicized by a country I thought I belonged in from childhood, but as an adult realized I do not, and felt the pangs of an "exile," forgotten by the country of my birth.

Why is America "new" to me . . . again, it is an experiment in living on land and space belonging . . . to others. It is Eurocentric, perhaps the worst example of that, and its institutions do not take to criticism well, if at all.

G: These comments are not meant to be harsh, please take it in the spirit of dialogue. My heart didn't break because of your poem, it breaks when I realize how much "we" still need to decolonize ourselves. I never said you were politicizing, I said you were poeticizing and, in doing that, affirming a colonial narration of the U.S. Perhaps that is a productive misreading.

M: I agree with you. My essay is a glimpse what America has been for me politically, economically, and emotionally . . . a total drain on my energy.

I'm aware that Massachusetts has its own Native Americans who are searching for their identity and their land, and have been rewarded

with casinos. By "new world" I meant that America is "new" because it is the history of Europe extended to North America, displacing indigenous peoples. And still an experiment, one that seems to have failed every other people except those of European descent. And how can it have been otherwise? With our Eurocentric educations, generations of us have fallen into the expected and predictable grooves.

I also agree with you about language. As long as we communicate using the language of colonizers, we won't reach an "anti-colonial" solution. Also, I don't feel that being "anti-" anything can help us. We have to revive who we are. The parables in my poem are a definition of who I really am. As for the histories of all of us and our connections, that's existing knowledge; in fact, that's knowledge that has existed for millennia, but the U.S., especially, has left our roots behind in the dust. Those of us who value those roots can revive them but that revival has no ground to stand on. We either conform per expectation, as stereotypes, or we die. An exile's longing for those roots never dies. Perhaps it's time to find a language in which to communicate.

G: See, I'm still not sure we're in on the same forcefield (if I can put it that way). Any "we" is always defined in relation to the other "we" are defining against. In this case, the "we" is getting defined against an America that is identified with Europe as you say. As we know, America in terms of populations and identities is not another Europe. There are specific reasons for displacements and migrations for the different group identities.

Also, maybe it is time to take into account the whole plant, not just roots. The becoming that iswaswillbe which will not either conform to stereotypes or die.

I say this also because I question the weness, the oneness of words like India, statehoods which in themselves like the naming of America or U.S. become grounds for erasures of histories, poetries in other ways.

M: "We" can go round and round with this and nothing will ever change. India was never a nation. Understood. Neither was America. Understood. I wrote a poem about my feeling like an exile in a country that is supposed to be my home. Let's just leave it that. I fairly tire of academic debates which lead nowhere. If you and R want to do a semantic analysis, please go ahead, without me! :) We all know all of the things you and R mention. The point is, everyday people still field the arrows of stereotype regardless of how the argument is phrased

academically regarding "we" and "nationhood," post-colonial fallout notwithstanding.

Contrary to the assumptions that brought some of us to the United States, we may thus find ourselves forced to contend with our places of departure, asked to function as native informants from "elsewhere." From what position of authority would we speak? The very attempt to become such cultural representatives, the falterings of our memory, must, then, lead to a different realization: the need for an examination of the historical, institutional, and social relations that have, in fact, produced subjects so quite unlike "the native informant" of old (John, 1996, p. 26).

Posts on Intentionality and Reading—Intersecting Threads

R: What we perceive as "my" meaning "my intentions" often work with existing narrations and discourses to reproduce hierarchies—even unintentionally—what you term "mis/interpretation mis/representation" happen based on varied con/texts of reading and varied (multiple) con/texts of writing and meaning thus not even the "original author" has absolute control (authority) over her/his meaning—there is always a surplus that gets picked up.

M: Every writer has ownership over intent. If that intent gets changed through whatever other action, then it is no longer the original writer's "words" nor is the original writer the owner of that changed meaning. What happened on this list, I feel, is a politicization of my writing which was not my intent. My intent was and is self awareness and re-definition out of any hierarchy. Academic language shrouds reality like no other use of language can! If we want to emerge from power structures and hierarchies, perhaps we should begin by shunning the language of those entities. However, as academics, I find we merely serve to recycle the same through generations.

M: I have no issue with the "borrowing, re-using, spitting out and circulating," etc. I have an issue with jumping to erroneous conclusions never intended by the writer and then interminable rhetoric over such presumptions. Of course words travel ... whatever their form ... This has been true from the first recorded word(s), but does not in any way exonerate misrepresentation, misinterpretation, lack of understanding (vs. misunderstanding).

T: Thissuddenrushedswirloftangledintentsstruckmeassalientthe firsttimearoundbutcaughtinthelensoftranslationinthetransitsof

interpretationthemessagechangessometimes.sometimesforthe
betterandsometimesforworseandsometimesjustchangestha-
tonethingissure.doesanyonehearderridatalkinthedistanceofthis
conversation?derridatalksofmorphologyofgrammatologyso
faccentsandglyphs.derridasaysnotmuchnewnothingthatthoseonthis-
listhavenotalreadysaid.hetalksofthewaysthat"meanings"
travelthroughtimeandtraverse.transitthroughtimeandthroughspace-
meansanticipatethemultiplewaysinwhichothersuntieones"own"sense-
andmakenew.alwaysanticipatesandwiches:thesinewylayersofnostalgi
aamnesiadistortionrepressionandpersonalmemorythatreaderswill-
bringto"ones"texts.alwaysanticipateghosts.intentionisnotso
methingstableorfixedbutratherasnakeinthegrassaspringajackin
theboxan"abracadabra"anewsongnewsoundsofullofdistortion,
yetthere.anoldsonganoldsoundandoldhold, stillthere.

agreedisagreeagreedisagreedisagreeagreemymindisnowinaswirl
ofbinaryframingididnotintendbutwhathasagreedisagreegottodowith-
theissuesathandiwonderwhatmyintentreally isdoyouknowperhaps?

CONCLUSION

These writers struggle with layers of regulatory fictions and personal
histories, as well as identifications and disidentifications that might enable
an exchange to produce a community that allows an imagining outside of
these frames. In this chapter, I have attempted to explore these issues,
through a focus on a set of interpersonal exchanges that occurred in a public
space (a publicly archived e-mail discussion list). Such interpersonal
exchanges are obviously not unique to "the Internet" spaces—such debates
and conversations occur often in everyday life. Nor are they totally enabled
by the technology. However, cyberspace is relevant to this exchange
because it is situated in a South Asian digital diaspora enabled by the
Internet. These spaces have become sites for the emergence of South Asian
diasporic connections, and it is important to examine how they are being
framed and how they permit certain voicings.

Furthermore, as Gurak (1997) points out:

It is important to move away from generalizations about life in cyberspace and
begin to analyze specific instances of computer-mediated-communication, not
only as a way of understanding patterns of current discourse but also as a method
of building theory so we can design communication systems that encourage new

social spaces that are appropriate, functional, accessible, and, perhaps even democratic. (p. ix)

In addition to being cautious and aware of the celebratory technospatial imaginary and mainstream discourses regarding information technologies and the Internet as great equalizers, it is important for us to reexamine our assumptions and look for possibilities for alternate uses of this medium, rather than totally discounting them in dystopic reaction. It is important to examine the populations using this medium and discourses they build together.

NOTES

1. The word *diaspora* can be traced back to the notion of the Jewish diaspora and suggests the idea of dispersal and fragmentation; and in much of the literature there is a presumed relationship between the diasporic community and the land which they left and to which the possibility of return always subsists, or what we are apt to term "motherland" or "home." The conditions that make for diasporic community are admittedly complex, but this presumed link between the diasporic community and the motherland is easily questioned, nor is there any reason why we must be held hostage to any form of linguistic and epistemological tyranny. No substantive issue can be decided on the issue of "origins." It thus appears perfectly reasonable to speak of an Indian Diaspora, as it does of the Chinese Diaspora, the African Diaspora, the Palestinian Diaspora, and of course, the Jewish Diaspora. (Lal, 1999a, p. 42). By "digital diaspora" I simply mean various traveling transnational subjectivities that inhabit online spaces.

2. I use the terms to mark oppositional, marginalized, and alternative subjectivities (countersubjectivities) and the social spaces composed through the interaction of such subjectivities (counterspheres) drawing from Nancy Fraser's critique and rearticulation of the Habermasian public sphere, where she maps a topology of opposition and fractures the paradigm of the public sphere. Fraser argues that instead of "the" public sphere, we must speak of numerous counterspheres (i.e., many social spaces of discussion embedded within circuits of unequal power). She asserts that "public life in egalitarian, multicultural societies cannot consist exclusively in a single, overarching lens" (Fraser, 1990, p. 59). Countersubjectivities therefore are subjectivities that if performed would fracture the apparent homogeneity of "the" public opinion in any social space.

3. See, for instance, online spaces such as www.rediff.com

4. Such discourses and self-narratives can be viewed over the Internet—look especially in recent discussions concerning the Hijab and Muslim women. See http://newsvote.bbc.co.uk/hi/English/talking_point/debates/south_asian/newsid_1530000/1530266.stm, where some posts fall into this category.

5. See http://lists.village.virginia.edu/~spoons

6. M, G, and T gave me permission to cite from their online interactions on the list. R is myself. It should also be noted that sa-cyborgs is a publicly archived list.

7. The Spoon Collective is a group of individuals who run a few discussion lists via a server at http://lists.village.virginia.edu and operated through The Institute for Advanced Technology in the Humanities at the University of Virginia. According to the Web site, "The Spoon Collective is dedicated to promoting discussion of philosophical and political issues."

8. These rules are based on my experiences online since 1994, which I can cite. Feel free to discuss these with me "off-list" sometime.

9. M and G are published poets and scholars and their work is available in public spaces. Their full names are available in the archives of sa-cyborgs and elsewhere on the Internet. T has remained anonymous.

10. To get a better idea of the form that G used in her post, please refer to this URL: http://lists.village.virginia.edu/~spoons and search the archives for the posts in October 1996 under the thread "poetry and histories."

11. "Outside the sentence[ness]," as I use it, is articulated in Homi Bhabha's essay, "The Postcolonial and the Postmodern" (Bhabha, 1994, pp. 171-197), where he also uses the phrase "beyond theory." In an effort to evoke the notion of "a liminal form of signification that creates space for the contingent," which he refers to as being "beyond theory," he draws from Roland Barthes's "exploration of the cultural space 'outside the sentence'" (Bhabha, 1994, p. 179).

12. This chapter contains a very small portion of the whole exchange, which can be found in the archives of sa-cyborgs at http://lists.village.virginia.edu/~spoons

13. Placing an * on either side of a word, phrase, or sentence is an e-mail convention used (like italics) to show emphasis.

REFERENCES

Ahmed, S. (1999). Home and away: Narratives of migration and estrangement. *International Journal of Cultural Studies, 2-3,* 329-347.

Anderson, B. (1991). *Imagined communities.* London: Verso.

Bahri, D. (2001). The digital diaspora: South Asians in the new pax electronica. In M. Paranjpe (Ed.), *In diaspora: Theories, histories, texts* (pp. 222-232). New Delhi: Indialog.

Barber, B. (1995). *Jihad vs. McWorld.* New York: Times Books.

Barthes, R. (1975). The pleasure of text (R. Miller, Trans.). New York: Hill.

Bhabha, H. (1994). *The location of culture.* London & New York: Routledge.

Chatterjee, P. (1989). The nationalist resolution of the women's question. In K. Sangari & S. Vaid (Eds.), *Recasting women* (pp. 232-253). New Delhi: Kali for Women.

Chen, G., & Starosta, W. J. (2000). *Communication and global society.* New York: Lang.

Delgado, F. P. (1998). When the silenced speak: The textualization and complications of Latina/o identity. *Western Journal of Communication, 62*(4), 420-438.

Ess, C., & Sudweeks, F. (2001). *Culture, technology, and communication: Towards an intercultural global village.* New York: State University of New York Press.

Flores, L.A., & Hasian, M.A. (1997). Returning to Aztlan and la raza: Political communication and the vernacular construction of Chicano/a nationalism. In A. Gonzalez and D. V. Tanno (Eds.), *Politics, communication, and culture.* Thousand Oaks, CA: Sage.

Fraser, N. (1990). Rethinking the public sphere: A contribution to the critique of actually existing democracy. *Social Text, 8-9,* 56-80.

Gajjala, R. (1998). The SAWnet refusal: An interrupted cyberethnography (Doctoral dissertation, University of Pittsburgh, 1998). *Dissertation Abstracts International* (UMI No. 9900131).

Gajjala, R. (2002). An interrupted postcolonial/feminist cyberethnography: Complicity and resistance in the "cyberfield." *Feminist Media Studies, 2*(2).

Gurak, L. J. (1997). *Persuasion and privacy in cyberspace: The online protests over Lotus MarketPlace and the Clipper chip.* New Haven, CT: Yale University Press.

Herring, S. (2001). Foreword. In C. Ess & F. Sudweeks (Eds.), *Culture, technology, and communication: Towards an intercultural global village* (pp. vii-x). New York: State University of New York Press.

Jarratt, S. (1998). Beside ourselves: The rhetoric of postcolonial feminism. *Journal of Advanced Composition, 18*(1), 57-75.

John, M. (1996). *Discrepant dislocations: Feminism, theory and postcolonial histories.* Berkeley: University of California Press.

Lal, V. (1999a). Establishing roots, engendering awareness: A political history of Asian Indians in the United States. In L. Prasad (Ed.), *Live like the banyan tree: Images of the Indian American experience* (pp. 42-48). Philadelphia: Balch Institute for Ethnic Studies.

Lal, V. (1999b). The politics of history on the Internet: Cyber-diasporic Hinduism and the North American Hindu diaspora. *Diaspora, 8*(2), 137-172.

Lengel, L. (2000). *Culture and technology in the new Europe: Civic discourse in transformation in post-Communist nations.* Norwood, NJ: Ablex.

Mallapragada, M. (2001, April 6-7). *Indian women in the U.S. diaspora and the "Curry Brigade": The politics of nation, gender and sexuality on the Web.* Paper presented at the conference "Constructing cyberculture(s): Performance, pedagogy, and politics in online spaces," University of Maryland, College Park.

Mitra, A. (1997). Virtual commonality: Looking for India on the Internet. In S. Jones (Ed.), *Virtual culture: Identity and communication in cybersociety* (pp. 55-79). London: Sage.

Rai, A. S. (1995). India on-line: Electronic bulletin boards and the construction of a diasporic Hindu identity. *Diaspora, 4*(1), 31-57.

Sadowski-Smith, C. (1999). U.S. border theory, globalization, and ethnonationalisms in post-Wall Eastern Europe. *Diaspora, 8*(1), 3-22.

Spivak, G. C. (1999). *A critique of postcolonial reason: Toward a history of the vanishing present.* Cambridge, MA: Harvard University Press.

Sudha, S. (1993). Compu-Devata: Electronic bulletin boards and political debates. *SAMAR: South Asian Magazine for Action and Reflection, 2,* 4-10.

8

Collective Memory, Media Representations, and Barriers to Intercultural Dialogue

JOLANTA A. DRZEWIECKA   •   *Washington State University*

Collective memory is a fertile and yet treacherous terrain where histories of different groups intertwine in the production of group identities, differences, and connections. Collective memory is a highly contested sense-making process that shapes the present through a selective appropriation of the past in order to support cultural identities and political goals. Similarly, media images are powerful means of reconstructing events in the past to satisfy needs in the present (Hasian & Carlson, 2000). How these images are read can give us insight into how viewers are embedded in discourses of memory and how they strategically negotiate their positions in different contexts and in relationship to "others." In particular, an examination of how memories are rehashed, circulated, and fragmented, and for what purposes, provides unique insight into relationships between groups, obstacles to dialogue between them, and the potential for alliances. Rhetorical media scholars argue that examinations of what is resisted, and how it is resisted, through oppositional readings as "historically particular acts" can help us understand how to "bring about specific social changes" (Condit, 1989, p. 119; see also Cloud, 1992; Flores, 2000). A conjunctural analysis of media interpretations (Fiske, 1991) can give us insight into complexities and nuances of relations between groups.

Decades after World War II (WWII) and the Holocaust, relations between Polish gentiles and Polish Jews are still strained by divided memories and complexities of history that victimized many groups in ways that were both similar and different. The meanings of past events are being renegotiated since democratization processes in Poland opened borders to international influences. In one significant case, a coalition of international

Jewish organizations is negotiating with the Polish government a removal of all religious symbols from Auschwitz, the former concentration camp and now the museum, to establish its multinational, multireligious, and multigroup character. Simultaneously, a controversial new book by NYU Professor Jan Gross, *Neighbors*, published in Poland and scheduled for publication in the United States, attributes a WWII pogrom of the Jewish population of a small Polish town, Jedwabne, to its gentile Polish neighbors, albeit under Nazi orchestration. These two examples are among many efforts to reexamine Polish-Jewish history and relations. These endeavors are not limited to Poland in its exclusive territory or national belonging, but occur in multiple sites where survivors or their descendants come into contact and/or carry personal and collective memories. Migrations of Polish Jews and Polish gentiles after WWII resulted in fragmentation of discourses about the Holocaust. The complexity of relations between Polish gentiles and Polish Jews during WWII is overwhelming at times, complicated by personal experiences, narratives of suffering and heroism, and nine centuries of history of gentile-Jewish relations in Poland.

A PBS *Frontline* documentary, *Shtetl*, produced by Marian Marzynski (1996), a Holocaust survivor and Polish Jew living in the United States, enters this complex discourse. The documentary elicited very strong responses from Polish Americans and Jewish Americans. In this chapter, I examine the polyvalent and polysemic character of cultural memories and historical narratives by analyzing national and cultural positions activated in the process of reading *Shtetl*. To this end, I analyze responses to the documentary by different viewers that were either sent directly or forwarded from a discussion list to the documentary's photographer and producer, Slawomir Grunberg. Hasian and Carlson (2000) argue that we need to further our understanding of the interested character of historical narratives: "We should subject every such narrative to an exacting analysis, revealing as many facets of a story as possible, thus enlarging the repository of memory from which to construct competing narratives" (p. 60). A critical examination of historical narratives informing the multiple readings of documentaries can also provide insight about barriers to dialogue and persisting divisions. My goal is to understand how cultural and national positions are strategically taken up in polysemic readings of *Shtetl* and how these positions are shaped by cultural memories.

The notions of diaspora and the diasporic subject have been romanticized as enabling subjects to overcome the limitations of a single nation-state and become empowered by the fluidity of the in-betweenness (Ong, 1999). However, diaspora as a social formation is structured in relations of

domination and subordination. The processes of globalization reorganize
these structures, creating new relations and challenging our assumptions
about intergroup relations. The context of globalization compels communication scholars to examine the production, circulation, and consumption of
meaning and "address the differentiated meanings and significance of specific reception patterns in articulating more general cultural negotiations
and contestations" (Ang, 1996, p. 137). As audiences have become frac-
tured and fragmented, we need to attend to readings produced by different
interpretive communities and "conflict-ridden reception" of texts circulated
across national borders (Ang, 1996). Close textual attention to clashes
between different interpretive communities positioned in different systems
throws into question our assumptions about marginalized groups, oppositional readings, and identities.

POLYVALENT AND POLYSEMIC READINGS

Scholars have argued that differences in interpretations of popular culture
texts result from the polysemy of those texts and/or the polyvalence of
interpretations. Fiske (1986, 1991) contends that the polysemic qualities of
mass mediated texts empower audiences to construct their own resistive
readings. A polysemic text is an open text that contains unresolved contradictions enabling "the various subcultures to generate meanings from it that
meet the needs of their subcultural identities" (Fiske, 1986, p. 392). Various
patterns of interpretations of polysemic texts give us insight into the needs
of cultural groups that produce them. Significantly, polysemy is not a free
for all but "a bounded multiplicity" (Ceccarelli, 1998) structured through
relations of domination and subordination because "audience activity is
an engagement in social relations across social inequality" (Fiske, 1991,
p. 471). Although viewers actively produce interpretations, they do so
"from the restricted range of cultural resources which [their] . . . structural
position has allowed them access to" (Morley, 1986, p. 43). The needs driving specific interpretations give us insight into the structures that produced
them and relations between different groups.

While Fiske (1986) argues that oppositional readings are liberating and
pleasurable, Condit (1989) intervenes in the "presumption that marginal
readers of texts are the potential source of liberation" (p. 119). She proposes that readings are often polyvalent, that is, audiences share the denotation of a text but interpret it through their different values producing
different interpretations. It is the connotation and not the denotation that is

unstable (Condit, 1989). Furthermore, "decoding requires *differential* amounts of work for different audience groups" (p. 108), depending on how they are positioned in relationship to the preferred reading in the text. Those who engage in oppositional readings might depart from the text to the larger background in order to support a reading not favored by the text, engage in distortion of truth, become incoherent in their arguments, and get caught up in contradictions (Condit, 1989). Such endeavors are hardly pleasurable, indeed they are produced by and further a sense of marginalization; however, they point to the existence of unmet needs. Social subjectivities and the needs embedded in them are relevant to how viewers interpret mass media texts (Cohen, 1991; Press, 1989; Press & Cole, 1995). Jensen (1990) demonstrates that viewers form interpretive communities on the basis of shared interests in relationship to media. Such communities produce and are produced by the cultural repertoires they use to decode media. Viewers selectively focus on meanings relevant to their social positioning. However, the relevant discourses they employ to affirm their identities and experiences do not necessarily resist interpretations that might be oppressive to them (Cohen, 1991).

Although resistive readings might be liberating, it is necessary to ask, liberating from what and for whom? The presumption seems to be that the dominant in the text represents the dominant outside the text. However, viewers might occupy positions that are dominant in one context (e.g., in Poland) but perceived as marginal in another (e.g., in the United States). When these viewers are confronted with a text that turns their dominant gaze on them in a context in which they conceive themselves as marginal, they might oppose it on grounds that are or are not liberating. As Condit (1989), Cloud (1992), and Ceccarelli (1998) caution, resistive readings should not be universally celebrated as liberating; any group can engage in oppositional interpretations. Thus, it is necessary to not only suggest rhetorical possibilities, although such work is clearly necessary (e.g., Cloud, 1992; Flores, 2000), but also to conduct close readings of audience interpretations in order to decode whose interests an activated polysemic potential serves and what the politics of oppositional codes and polyvalence are (Ceccarelli, 1998; Cohen, 1991, 1994; Condit, 1989).

Many media scholars in particular are concerned with education, furthering participative democracy and developing skills for critical viewing. Analyses that further this goal examine what particular issues are resisted and how that resistance occurs, and explore the relative decoding abilities of audiences and their access to counterrhetorics (Condit, 1989). Specifically, scholars need to interrogate how viewers are embedded in larger

political occasions that create collective experiences. Such examinations will give us greater insight into how specific aspects of viewers' positions inform the cultural repertoires they use to decode media texts.

CULTURAL MEMORY AND HISTORY

Nora conceptualizes a distinction between history and memory:

> Memory is life, borne by living societies founded in its name. It remains in permanent evolution, open to the dialectic of remembering and forgetting, unconscious of its successive deformations, vulnerable to manipulation and appropriation, susceptible to being long dormant and periodically revived. History, on the other hand, is the reconstruction, always problematic and incomplete, of what is no longer. Memory is a perpetually actual phenomenon, a bond tying us to the eternal present; history is a representation of the past (cited in Katriel, 1994, p. 2).

While it is useful to make a conceptual distinction between memory and history, Katriel (1994) demonstrates that "history and memory orientations inter-penetrate in producing multi-layered discourses of the past" (p. 17). The past is invoked through a dialectical tension between history and memory. Katriel argues that when "the authenticating force of memory and the objectifying thrust of history" are merged, the resulting product has a compelling and legitimating power (p. 5). However, this merger is problematic as historical facts are selectively appropriated to support particular representations.

Collective memory, as "a set of ideas, images, feelings about the past," results from a collective process of interpretation of "public offerings" consisting of presences and absences (Irwin-Zarecka, 1994, p. 4). Information that is not available in history books and popular media is just as important to understanding the relationship between cultural identities and collective memories as information that is repeated. In collective memories, the past is selectively made to matter to satisfy particular goals, needs, and emotions in the present (Hasian & Carlson, 2000; Irwin-Zarecka, 1994; Zelizer, 1995). Specifically, the past is keyed to the present by transforming "the meaning of activities understood in terms of one primary framework by comparing them with activities understood in terms of another" (Schwartz, 1996, p. 911). Memories are reconfigurations establishing "social identity, authority, solidarity, political affiliation" (Zelizer, 1995, p. 217). "Bounded

and bonded communities" produce their own collective memories (Irwin-Zarecka, 1994; Zelizer, 1998), but are also produced by them as memories forge individual and collective identities (Bellah, Madsen, Sullivan, Swindler, & Tipton, 1985). Generations, further and further removed from the past, carry particular memories that reinforce group ideologies and their own subjectification. The telling and retelling of the past forms communities of memory with a "shared sense of meaning and relevance" (p. 54) that often outlive the actual sharing of experience. Collective memory is a creative and purposeful process that "allow[s] for the fabrication, rearrangement, elaboration, and omission of details about the past, often pushing aside accuracy and authenticity so as to accommodate broader issues of identity formation, power and authority, and political affiliation" (Zelizer, 1998, p. 3).

The very notion of collective memories presumes "multiple conflicting accounts of the past" (Zelizer, 1995, p. 217), and it is necessary to interrogate the historical context, timing, purposes, and interests served by particular memories. Memories are necessarily partial and incomplete; however, that partiality serves specific interests and "collective memory is always a means to something else" (p. 226). Different communities of memory sharing a past may contest each other's memories and struggle to impose one interpretation on others. Zelizer (1998) observes that "memories become not only the construction of social, historical, and cultural circumstances, but a reflection of why one construction has more staying power than its rivals. The study of collective memories thereby represents a graphing of the past as it is woven into the present and future" (p. 5). Collective memory is a rhetorical bridge built from the present to the past, "an evoking of a past to frame a present but also to conform that past to the present" (Gronbeck, 1998, p. 58).

CONJUNCTURAL ANALYSIS

Conjunctural analysis has been very useful in the politically committed analyses of popular culture texts (Cloud, 1992; Fiske, 1991; Hall, 1985). A conjunctural analysis "seeks to understand the variety of social forces that come together and conflict at any one particular historical moment" (Fiske, 1991, p. 472). Such analysis involves examining specific viewing sites and practices and macro economic and social structures, and moving back and forth between them (Fiske, 1991). Attention to macro- and microstructures is useful to understanding not only the function of popular culture texts but

intercultural communication practices as well (Collier, 2000; Hasian & Carlson, 2000). It is necessary to interrogate how intercultural audiences decode messages, what their countermessages are, and what codes they have access to and rely on. Audience interpretations constitute a discursive formation "structured in dominance." The following analysis focuses on relations of domination and subordination in the interpretations of *Shtetl*, with particular attention paid to issues of collective memory. I situate this analysis within larger discourses of memory of the Holocaust and representations of Poland in the West. I then focus on specific responses to *Shtetl*.

DOCUMENTING POLISH-JEWISH RELATIONS

The Plot

Marian Marzynski, the director and producer of the documentary, is a Polish Jew who survived the Holocaust as a child in a Christian orphanage and subsequently left Poland in the 60s. He travels back to trace Polish-Jewish relations during the war in a small town, Bransk. *Shtetl*, the documentary he produces, concentrates on memories about the events surrounding November 8, 1942, when 2,500 Jews who lived in a shtetl in Bransk were rounded up by the Nazis, who then ordered Polish farmers to transport them to the train station. The Jews died in Treblinka gas chambers within 24 hours. Marzynski travels with Nathan Kaplan, whose father left Bransk for the United States before the war started. This is a personal journey for Marzynski, who explains that he was not able to visit his own birth town because he was overwhelmed by the pain of unexplainable complexities. Marzynski and Kaplan are accompanied by a young gentile, Zbyszek Romaniuk, the town's historian, who has been tracing the Jewish history in Bransk.

Shtetl is about memory as Marzynski, in an investigative reporting fashion, talks to Bransk farmers who lived during the war about their attitudes and actions toward Jews when many who managed to run away from the transport hid either on farms or in the nearby forest. Both groups were dependent on farmers' help for survival. Marzynski wants to find names of those who betrayed Jews to the Nazis or killed them. His questions focus on anti-Semitism and betrayal. In one case, Marzynski confronts, on camera, a man accused of murdering Jews. The accusation turns out to be false—the man's last name is similar to that of the accused killer, but he is not the accused man. Nevertheless, we also learn that some Polish farmers hid Jews

in their homes or farm buildings, some were killed by the Nazis for helping to hide Jews, some would not do it because of the threat of punishment by death. The interviewees are all old men and women. The camera often focuses on their soiled hands or on the men's partially buttoned work pants. Several men are senile. Many have favorable memories of Bransk's Jews; for example, one remembers and breaks into a song he played with Jewish musicians before the war. Many tell horrific stories, such as those describing the bodies of Jews, who had been murdered by the Nazis, floating down the river.

In the second part of *Shtetl*, Marzynski brings Zbyszek Romaniuk to the United States to visit several descendants of Bransk Jews. The scenes are very moving, as all involved recount with tears either their childhood memories or memories passed down to them by their parents of the life in the old country. The memories are positive, focusing on lost traditions and stories from the past. In one crucial scene, a Jewish woman is uncomfortable with Zbyszek, a Christian, investigating Jewish history in Bransk. She questions his motives and doubts him. Interestingly, her young daughter pronounces that Zbyszek is better able to do it than her mother, who is filled with memories and longing. In contrast to scenes in Poland, the homes visited convey that their hosts are affluent.

Next, Marzynski takes Romaniuk to Israel to visit the Yad Vashem museum where one-third of trees planted to honor "The Righteous Among the Nations" who helped Jews during the war are dedicated to Poles. In another significant scene, Marzynski and Romaniuk visit with Israeli High School students. In this emotional scene, the students accuse Poland of not having saved enough Jews while Romaniuk, forced into a defensive position, attempts to explain the conditions. The students see his explanation as a mere justification, and Marzynski clearly takes "their side" in demanding from Romaniuk an admission that Poles are in a large part responsible for the Holocaust. This section of the documentary ends with close-ups of Romaniuk, who is very upset after the students have left. He refuses to give a simple admission of guilt without a complex historical contextualization eschewed by Marzynski. However, rather than as a historian, Romaniuk is portrayed as a Pole loyally defending his nation from unjust accusations.

In the final segment, Marzynski goes back to Bransk accompanied by Jack Rubin. Rubin, as a young man, managed to escape when a separate group of Polish Jews attempting to leave Bransk in the middle of the night was stopped by Nazi soldiers. Rubin's family ran a farm in Bransk, and now he is a businessman living in the United States. He walks around the village

visiting the site of his parent's farm and meeting people who remember his parents. A complex picture emerges as some betray anti-Semitism in their stories about Jewish wealth and cunning while others are brought to tears. In particular, a very old man who worked for Rubin's father cries and embraces Rubin. Jack Rubin hands the man a gift of $20. The documentary ends with celebrations of the anniversary of Bransk that do not include any mention of its Jewish history.

In contrast to the traditional understanding of documentary as "fullness and completion, knowledge and fact," documentary "has come to suggest incompleteness and uncertainty, recollection and impression, image of personal worlds and their subjective construction" (Nichols, 1994, p. 1). From this position, a documentary defies easy identification of dominant readings. All documentaries are necessarily partial; history "is that [to] which all documentaries refer and that which can never be wholly contained by the documentary" (Rabinowitz, 1994, p. 23). The relationship between the documentary and the real is problematic, "a documentary is a negotiation between reality on the one hand and image, interpretation and bias on the other" (Bruzzi, 2000, p. 4). *Shtetl* is polysemic; it enables viewers to detect complexities and produce different interpretations, but it does not explicitly place complexities in its focus. It is difficult to identify the dominant reading in the text. Marzynski makes it clear that his focus is on Polish peasants who persecuted Jews, and he concludes that Poles could have done more to help and save Jews during WWII but did not because of their anti-Semitism. The one dominant reading of anti-Semitism that emerges from *Shtetl* is that it is a property of individuals and communities; specific structural factors are ignored. However, the documentary includes many images and information that present a much more complex picture of Polish gentile-Jewish relations during the war. Complexities emerge in the village scenes as the villagers talk about the war conditions and their relations with Jews before the war. The images seem to contradict some assertions made by Marzynski in the voiceover. The interviewees "take over," and, ignoring the filmmaker's intentions, create a polysemic text (Rabinowitz, 1994). It is possible to conclude after watching *Shtetl* that WWII imposed inhuman conditions; caught in horrific circumstances people responded with good and evil, often falling back on historical and structural anti-Semitism, and sometimes overcoming it.

Shtetl gave Eva Hoffman, a writer, an impetus to travel to Bransk, meet Zbyszek Romaniuk, conduct her own research, and write a book under the same title. Hoffman (1997) attempts to capture the complexities, in part, by describing her own family history:

My parents lived throughout that period in a region of Ukraine that belonged to Poland before the war and became Soviet immediately thereafter. On several occasions they had to escape hostile local peasants who might have given them away to the Nazi authorities. But my parents were also repeatedly helped by people who gave them food and temporary shelter, and by a peasant who hid them for nearly two years, with the full knowledge that he was thereby risking death for himself and his sons. The other awful aspect of my family story was that two relatives died because of an act of betrayal committed by a fellow Jew—a man who, in the hope of ensuring his own survival, led the Germans to a hiding place. (pp. 5-6)

However, it is not Marzynski's *Shtetl*'s simplifications that interest me here. Rather, I am interested in responses from another audience. *Shtetl* was received with outrage by many Polish Americans, who felt that it shifted the blame for the Holocaust from Nazis to Poles and portrayed Poland in an unjustifiably negative light. Zbyszek Romaniuk wrote a letter opposing the way he and the information he provided were used in the film. The Polish Historical Society of Connecticut and Chicago responded with angry and critical statements. These and other statements, including a statement from Polish Canadians, can be found on the PBS *Frontline* Web site. My goal is to examine positions that are revealed in responses to *Shtetl* by some Polish American viewers.

The Data

In this chapter, I analyze responses to *Shtetl* from Poles and Polish Americans, which were included in two compilations of responses posted on the Web site of Log In Productions, a professional film and video production company owned by Slawomir Grunberg (who photographed the documentary). One compilation consists of responses in Polish posted to the "Discussion of Polish Culture List" between April 17 and June 27 of 1996. The compilation (www.logtv.com/shtetl/polish.html), which consists of 111 single-spaced, 11-point-type pages, is an unprecedented collection of unsolicited interpretations and heated discussions over the interpretation of the documentary. Participants often refer to earlier messages in a continuous conversation. It is a very rich data set containing personal information about the participants, quotes from other discussions, posts of articles printed in newspapers in the United States and in Poland, and even a poem. Being bilingual, I served as translator. The other data set (www.logtv.com/Shtetl/comments.html) is a compilation of comments sent to or forwarded

to Grunberg in English, including posts from the "Discussion of Polish Culture List" in English. This compilation consists mostly of single posts and fewer back-and-forth responses. The printout is 49 pages long when formatted as described above. Grunberg, who graduated from a famous Polish film school in Lodz before emigrating to the United States, collected the responses during several months following the date *Shtetl* aired on PBS (Grunberg, personal communication, 2001).

In this chapter, I focus on responses from viewers who contributed to both online discussions, and who identify themselves as gentile Poles or Polish Americans. These respondents constructed an interpretive community that emerged through their responses. They also represent the largest group of viewers (e.g., there were only a few respondents in the second compilation who identified themselves as "Jewish" or of more distant "Polish heritage"). Their identification was evident from comments, references, and descriptions they provided. Most of the participants were born after WWII either in Poland or in the United States. A few were Holocaust survivors or WWII participants, or their descendants. Their responses do not represent all possible responses to *Shtetl*; however, recurring themes and patterns of positions activated by participants constitute interpretive repertoires that informed their interpretations. These viewers demonstrated knowledge of Polish history and a shared, although not unified, cultural memory. Focus on this particular group of responses enables an in-depth examination of the relationship between cultural memory, polysemic readings, and cultural subjectivities (see, e.g., Cohen, 1991; Press & Cole, 1995). I excluded responses from participants who identified themselves as Jewish or Polish Jews or Jewish Poles primarily because their numbers were very low and could not be representatively compared to the gentile Polish or Polish American group. The responses of the latter group give us an indication of the variety of ways in which participants reacted to being turned into an object of the gaze of the "other."

I identified cultural themes and repertoires through open coding. I then excerpted the themes and compared and contrasted them with each other. The excerpts presented in this chapter represent what I see as the most telling and most representative examples. I took care to select excerpts from different participants. In the following analysis, I am concerned with how the relationship between collective memories and history feeds into the polyvalence and polysemy of readings of *Shtetl*. First, I situate *Shtetl* within macrostructures of the Holocaust memory.

Macrostructures

What is the macrocontext of *Shtetl*? Although the documentary aired on U.S. public television, the macrocontext of *Shtetl* is transnational, consisting of several different overlapping historical and national structures. Although, in the United States, Polish immigrant viewers might be a marginal and oppositional audience of *Shtetl*, their readings are informed by dominant codes from Poland. Gentile Poles occupy a dominant position in relationship to Polish Jews in representations of WWII, even though this situation is changing. Historical contextualization is due, although I am painfully aware that "no one can say a word without creating a void consisting of all that is not being said at that moment" (Wander, 1996, p. 408), particularly within journal space constraints. An analysis of the rhetoric of "gentile Polish-Jewish Polish" relations is a step in a precarious territory because it evokes strong emotions, long complicated history, and ideologies of remembering and forgetting. As Hoffman (1997) succinctly puts it,

> Fifty years after the cataclysmic events, there is perhaps no past as powerfully contested as that of the Polish Jews. The Holocaust in Poland, and all of the Polish-Jewish history, continues to be the embattled terrain of three different and sometimes bitterly competing sets of collective memory: Jewish memory, Polish memory, and the memory of the West. In postwar Jewish memory, in the minds of many Holocaust survivors and their descendants, Poland has come to figure as the very heart of darkness, the central symbol of the inferno. (p. 3)

Before WWII, the Polish Jewish population constituted a significant percentage of the Polish population. Jews first began arriving to the religiously tolerant Poland in the 11th century, and over time their community became the largest one in Europe. Their relationship with the gentile population ranged from separation and segregation to incorporation, conversion, and Polonization (Irwin-Zarecka, 1990). The events of WWII turned Poland into a Jewish graveyard, reducing the number of Jews in Poland from 3 million to between 240,000 and 300,000 (Hoffman, 1997), while simultaneously victimizing gentile Poles. Gentile responses to the Holocaust ranged from indifference to active help, although those providing help constituted a small group in the context of Nazis punishing anyone who helped Jews by death. Anti-Semitism was a significant element of every context of gentile-Jewish relations in Poland, including the Holocaust.

After the initial postwar period of honoring Jewish martyrdom, the specificity of Jewish WWII experience was gradually erased by Polish historiography, which reconstructed Polish Jews as "Poles" (Irwin-Zarecka, 1990).

The incomprehensibility of the Holocaust, gentile Poles' own sense of guilt and victimization by WWII, the Communist takeover, and the Communist censorship of political issues aided the repression of memory. Anti-Semitic purges conducted in 1968 by the Communist government, which scapegoated "Jews" to maintain its legitimacy, led to the departure of the majority of those who survived in or returned to Poland after the war, and perpetuated the image of Poland as an anti-Semitic country (Checinski, 1982; Irwin-Zarecka, 1990). The majority of those who stayed were either assimilated or remained under the Aryan identity that helped them survive the war. The majority of gentile Poles grew up in a Poland "without Jews," where nevertheless one could be nominated "a Jew" and Jews functioned as a culturally significant "other" against whom gentile Poles defined themselves (Swida-Ziemba, 2000).

The rebirth of Jewish communities, culture, and identities, and the interest in Polish-Jewish issues in Poland, began to occur only recently, following democratization changes in Poland (Hoffman, 1997; Irwin-Zarecka, 1990). As Poland opened itself to broader contact with the West, dialogue with displaced Polish Jews and/or their descendants became possible. At this historic moment, a coalition led by Miles Lerman, chairman of the U.S. Holocaust Memorial Museum, approached the Polish government in 1996 with a request that all religious symbols be removed from the grounds of the Auschwitz museum, the former death camp (hereafter the Auschwitz request). The coalition, which included the American Jewish Committee, Anti-Defamation League, American Gathering of Holocaust Survivors, World Jewish Congress, Ronald S. Lauder Foundation, and Yad Vashem, successfully negotiated the removal of eight crosses in 1998 from the area known as the Field of Ashes, although talks over other details continue. The Auschwitz request and ongoing negotiations with the Polish government regarding settlements of property claims by displaced Polish Jews are certainly evidence of an emerging new set of relations and possibilities of dialogue, even if opposition and obstacles persist.

The interest in the Holocaust, gentile-Jewish relations, and Polish Jews in general increased dramatically in Poland as the democratization processes shattered old propaganda and censorship (Gutman, 2000; Irwin-Zarecka, 1990). The second volume of *The Jews in Poland* (Kapralski, 1990), published in English in Poland by the Judaica Foundation, and a special issue of the journal *Znak* titled "Shoah. Pamiec zagrozona?" (Is Memory of Shoah in Danger?) (2000) focus on gentile-Jewish relations, examining history, memory, and identity. The question arises why memory of the Holocaust should become important at this particular historical juncture,

over 50 years after WWII, in a country with a very small Jewish population. The crumbling of the Communist regime, whose censorship and suppression of political issues provided an illusion of unity against a common enemy, forces questions about the Polish collective identity. A question being asked is: Who are we now when we are free to decide for ourselves? Polish identity is intricately tied with the history of Polish Jews. The *Znak* issue on Shoah takes stock of issues involved in the contemporary understanding of the Holocaust. *Shoah*, a Hebrew word that means desolation, has come to be the preferred term for the Holocaust by Jewish scholars who feel that *Holocaust* has lost much of its significance through overuse. Articles published in the volume demonstrate that Shoah is a complex terrain in Poland. Popular collective memory is often splintered between "Poles" and "Jews," amounting to two different versions of the Holocaust. A historian finds this unacceptable, arguing that the responsibility of a scholar is to arrive at truth (Gutman, 2000). In the scholarly arena, as some note, there are no differences between the positions taken by Polish and Israeli historians who meet during international conferences (Czajkowski, Friszke, & Krajewski, 2000; Gutman, 2000). Nevertheless, the circulation of different memories held by different groups necessitates an investigation of persisting divisions and different understanding of their relationships. The *Znak* issue on Shoah is clearly concerned with the transnational dimensions of this issue, not just its importance and implications for Jews and gentiles in Poland. The authors of the issue see the dangers in, on the one hand, the lack of historical knowledge and stereotypical representations of gentile Poles as willing Nazi helpers held in the West, and on the other hand, the tendency of Poles to see themselves as innocent witnesses or to emphasize help Poles provided to Jews. There is also a damaging tendency to focus on marginal but flagrant statements made on both sides, which deepens the divide and forces groups and individuals into two sides.

Relations between Polish Jews and gentile Poles are not limited to Poland, as both groups migrated to the United States and other places. Although in the United States both groups are considered "white," they both have a history of marginalization and both fight stereotypes. Although the two groups cooperated during the early years of their migration to the United States, Polish Jews became prominently absent from Polonia organizations, many of which identified themselves as Catholic and often were anti-Jewish (Pula, 1995; Stone, 1996). Relations between gentile Poles and Polish Jews in the United States continue to be fraught with tensions, as evidenced in a variety of statements, publications, films, and other projects.

The well-known documentary, *Shoah*, and a comic book version of WWII Jewish experience in Poland, *Mouse* (Spiegelman, 1991), are only two of the most notable texts that have elicited defensive and hurt responses from Poles and Polish Americans. In the immigrant context, "where Poles and descendants of Polish Jews come into direct contact, visions of the past have a vital impact on the continuing, still highly charged dialogue between the two groups" (Hoffman, 1997, p. 14).

Another part of the context that is important to consider is the image of Eastern Europe and Poland in the United States. Eastern Europe has stood for the "exotic" other (Hoffman, 1993), or more specifically, the other who is gray, sad, monotonous, and marginal squashed by totalitarian Communism. Although Poland attracted attention of the West when it made the heroic effort to overthrow the totalitarian regime, the common knowledge of historical particularities and present complexities is still limited to a few generalizations.

Finally, it is necessary for me to situate myself in a historical context (Collier, 2000). I grew up in Poland as a gentile. I lived in Bedzin, a town whose pre-WWII predominantly Jewish population was almost totally annihilated by the Holocaust. When I look back on stories I heard and on my education, Polish Jews were simultaneously present and absent. I learned that Jews were singled out during WWII and were the primary victims. I did not learn much about Polish anti-Semitism until I watched Lanzmann's (1999) documentary *Shoah* on Polish television and did further reading after I came to the United States 11 years ago. I come to this project as an intercultural scholar interested in understanding how divisions are manifested and how understanding may be reached.

READING SHTETL

Participants negotiated different readings of *Shtetl* as a representation of gentile-Jewish relations and Polish anti-Semitism. While for all participants *Shtetl* was about "Poles" and "Jews," their readings were polysemic. The cultural repertoires participants used to decode *Shtetl* were constructed through several memory sites: memory of national and religious identity, memory of relations between Poland and the Soviet Union, and memory of Polish cultural identity in the United States. These memories were connected through to the present U.S. cultural context to counteract the ambivalent positioning of Polish American identity in the United States.

Cultural Memory and National Ideology

Some participants read *Shtetl* as "the" representation of Polish-Jewish relations, and resisted it on the grounds that it simplifies and thus falsifies these relations. Participants argued that *Shtetl* is anti-Polish because it omits specific historical information that would cast a broader light on gentile-Jewish relations in Poland during WWII. These readers brought in specific historical information in order to back up their interpretation:

> For the average viewer, there was no reference to conditions in wartime Poland, nor any mention of the deaths of 3 million Polish Christians during the war. Lacking this context, the film presents a distorted view of Polish-Jewish relations during the period of the Holocaust. *Shtetl* tells us nothing about the rich 800-year history of Jewish culture in Poland, or about the history of Poland. . . . The film mentions nothing about the occupation by Soviet forces during or after the war. . . . There is no reference to the cynical way both the Soviets and the Germans encouraged ethnic rivalry and hatred among Poles, Jews, Belorussians and Ukrainians. . . . Marzynski's chosen theme is Polish anti-Semitism.

Others added that Poland was the only country under Nazi occupation where hiding a Jew was punishable by death. The viewers also objected to what they perceived as faulty interpretations. For example, objections were raised against defining AK, the Polish underground army, as anti-Semitic because that suggests that it was created to fight with Jews rather than with the Nazis during WWII. These and other details were filled in to create a more complex picture, although these viewers did not deny that anti-Semitism existed and continues to exist in Poland. Some also criticized the documentary for reducing Jewish-gentile relations to the events in one village in 1942. Others attempted to cast a wider contextual net for these relations in order to broaden the understanding and knowledge of Polish-Jewish relations. They attempted to both marginalize and contextualize anti-Semitism as a situated phenomenon that does not describe the Polish society as a whole.

The use of facts is a powerful rhetorical move because facts, sequentially and causally related, naturalize a particular version of the past (Katriel, 1994). Those who presented "facts" labor within an assumption that it is possible to arrive at the final, objective, and complete account of what really happened. However, this is often "a battle over representations, where each side attempts to archive the past in order to disprove the 'false' claims that are being promulgated by the other side" (Hasian, 1998, p. 98). Although there are many facts that were omitted by the documentary, those presented by the

respondents serve the interests of "Poles" as national subjects. In particular, participants stressed that there was insufficient information about Poles helping Jews, or suggested that this information was given only grudgingly. The documentary mentioned in several places that Poles also saved Jews and that their efforts have been recognized at Yad Vashem, although this is clearly not the museum's focus. However, these viewers selectively emphasized points in the documentary in order to support their interpretation. Those who objected to the documentary seemed to want to carry a memory of Poles during the war as those struggling heroically with the Nazis and helping Jews, and they argued that to do otherwise is to damage relations between gentile Poles and Jews. Their perspective emerged from a historically constructed position that became evident in Poland following WWII.

THE SHAPING OF NATIONAL AND RELIGIOUS HISTORY

Official governmental and historical discourse in post-WWII Poland erased Jewish presence in Polish history and, paradoxically, emphasized help provided to Jews (Checinski, 1982; Hoffman, 1997; Irwin-Zarecka, 1990; Steinlauf, 1997). After WWII, the Polish Communist government, failing economically and under pressure from student and intellectual groups, scapegoated "Jews" and began purging Poland of Polish Jewish intellectuals, who headed for the West (Checinski, 1982). During this time, Polish historiography appropriated the Holocaust, "The three million Jews now all became Poles, and when added to the three million Polish victims of the Nazis, made up the total of *six million Poles*—victims of *genocide*" (Irwin-Zarecka, 1989, p. 62). Finally, Jews (first erased, now reconstructed) were portrayed "as singularly ungrateful to Poland, both for its traditional tolerance and for aid extended during World War II" (p. 63). Following the anti-Semitic purges in 1968, government media claimed that "Poland was not and had never been an anti-Semitic country," that this label was just a political tool of Poland's political enemies in the West, and hailed early historical tolerance toward Jews (Irwin-Zarecka, 1989, p. 62). This erasure was part of the processes of legitimization of the Polish Communist government that attempted to construct its "people" as ethnically homogenous. It is from this complex, historically emergent position that viewers claimed that *Shtetl* "promotes hostility and ignorance" and "negative bias against Poles," and that "the Polish view is not presented." The collective identity these viewers activated is a product of national ideologies, and the specific information presented in *Shtetl* activated defensive responses. This

"memory of identity" (Jewsiewicki, 1995), however, was formed long before WWII.

The claim that "Poles saving Jews" more accurately represents Polish-Jewish relations not only is based on the post-WWII nation-making claim but also emerges from a much longer tradition that represented national history as history of martyrdom and heroic struggle. The struggle took place against "others"—Tartar infidels, a Swedish Protestant invasion, and Soviet Communists (among other groups and historical events) (Jewsiewicki, 1995). In myths and stories, these "others" are cast against national and deeply Catholic images that represent "Poland's providential mission to protect Christianity against the barbarians" (Jewsiewicki, 1995, p. 243). Participants who opposed *Shtetl* in the name of defending Poland's image defend a national myth of martyrdom in which Poles can only be victims of WWII, not perpetrators of crimes against Jews. Christianity and Polish nationality are deeply connected; however, in the historical context, Polish identity was marginalized within the context of Christian identity and, consequently, few participants cast their responses from the position of wider Christian identity. Those who did still gave primacy to Polish national identity. For one participant, *Shtetl* had parenthetical implications for Christian identity, "The more publicity *Shtetl* gets, the *worse* for (Christian) Polish-Jewish relations." Another one, an Auschwitz survivor, argued that "To show Polish Catholics beaten, shot, hanged or gassed by the Nazis would naturally pull out the underpinnings from the anti-Polish scenario he [Marzynski] tries to construct." *Shtetl* did specifically focus on Polish gentile-Jewish relations; however, participants made no attempt to recast it in terms of "European" gentile-Jewish relations or Christian-Jewish relations. Significantly, one of the main arguments was that *Shtetl* shifted the blame for the Holocaust from Nazis to Poles, and that others might deduce that "Poles unjustly accuse Germans of murdering Jews since it is the Poles who murdered them." Participants were concerned with how their "Polish" identity was constructed in relationship to historical others in the context of Polish European WWII history. Before I address this point in greater depth, I turn to readings in which viewers accepted *Shtetl*'s invitation to interrogate Polish cultural memories.

Memory and Accepting Shtetl

Some participants eschewed accusations that *Shtetl* was anti-Polish and argued that even though the documentary presented a partial view of Polish-Jewish relations, that view was true. One participant argued that the

documentary is made from the position of loyalty toward "the Jewish nation." He added, "The author confronts the film's viewer, who belongs like the author to the same enlightened and liberated West, with a mentality of a Polish farmer from backwoods of Bialystok [a region in Poland] where the time stood still. He concentrates on the not so glorious for Poles, but after all true, acts of hostility, and even participation in robbery and massacres by some peasants." This viewer did not think that *Shtetl* should be condemned, although he did support "an action to balance the picture by propagating positive points in Polish-Jewish history." Another participant also expressed his surprise at the strong reactions on the list: "This film is about Polish anti-Semitism. I do not understand how you can close your eyes to the facts. How can you change reality with protest? . . . The goal of the film is to ask: What has changed? What would have happened if today the situation was repeated? How would people from Bransk behave? Would they save?" These questions encourage critical self-examination that is rejected by other participants. In his response correcting some interpretations presented by others, this participant wrote, "We all know how it really is." His response is an attempt to break up the ideology of memory of identity from the inside. Similarly, another participant admitted, "I think that we have something to be ashamed of, not the Holocaust, but the smaller and larger misdeeds of which there were many and which are remembered for a long time." A different participant posted a poem about anti-Semitism by a celebrated Polish poet of Jewish background, Jan Tuwim, and provided information that interwar literary critics, Tuwim's contemporaries, did not consider him a Pole. This prompted another participant to react:

> I am not surprised anymore that Jews have a negative opinion about Poles, if such was the atmosphere among literary critics before WWII. Next came Holocaust in occupied Poland and anti-Semitism after the war. It is difficult to have good memories from such a place and remember your neighbors fondly. . . . Anyway, we were taught an idealized version of Polish history in PRL [Polska Republika Ludowa (Polish People's Republic)]. Does anyone know what it is like now?

These participants almost never resorted to facts. The story about Jan Tuwim was an interesting exception that aimed to demonstrate the depth and pervasiveness of Polish anti-Semitism. The Tuwim story strikes at the complexities of "Polish-Jewish" relations because Jan Tuwim was represented as a poet, a Polish poet, after WWII. This story demonstrates that the meaning of Polish identity cannot be taken for granted and that "Poles" and "Jews" are intricately connected, even though they stand separate in collective memories.

"Poles" and "Jews"

Many discussions focused on the relationships between "Poles" and "Jews." The two categories were seen as separate, although some participants challenged that separation. In particular, "Polish" and "Jewish" memories were seen as divided against each other. The following excerpt demonstrates this division.

Would it be possible to collect funds to make a film for an American (world?) viewer about years of German occupation of Poland from our point of view? Not about bandits ready to murder for gold always and anywhere, but about ordinary Poles—living in the inhuman world, powerless while looking at the burning ghetto while the distant world does not want to hear.

What is perhaps most interesting here is that from other exchanges, it is clear that this participant was born about 20 years after WWII. What she knows about "ordinary Polish WWII experience" is a part of a collective memory constructed through historical accounts as well as documentary and fictionalized media representations. These rhetorical and media representations emphasized a "universal Polish" martyrdom and struggle that marginalized Jewish specificity (Irwin-Zarecka, 1990; Steinlauf, 1997). Her desire for a different representation of Polish WWII experience is driven by a need to affirm a constructed collective memory and identity that is separate from "the burning ghetto." In this memory, *gentile* Poles are *ordinary* Poles in spite of the fact that while Polish Jews were a minority in Poland, about equal numbers of Polish Jews and Polish gentiles perished during the war. In this collective memory, "Jews" feature as the perpetual outsider whose experience is excluded from the "Polish" experience. It is also interesting that in her earlier posts she tried to eschew categorization and insisted that one needs to consider that "nobody can foresee how he or she would act in a similar situation. We should realize that, we-Jews and we-Poles, it is only then that we can come closer together" and think "what would happen today, if helping a human being were punishable by death." While she tried to evoke deeper human reflection by casting WWII gentile-Jewish relations outside of the historical group context, she later fell back on "our point of view" accepting the separateness and specificity of her group identity as a basis of WWII experience. The appeal to humanity functions in this context as a discursive device that obscures the deeper understanding of Polish gentile-Jewish relations.

Other participants probed deeply into Polish gentile-Jewish relations. In one case, participants engaged in a discussion about the character of anti-Semitism in Poland, making a distinction between "native" and "biological" anti-Semitism. According to one participant, "Native anti-Semitism is a part of our historical baggage. Similarly, native antipolonism is part of the historical baggage of Polish Jews. Biological anti-Semitism . . . implies that we all as ethnic Poles are, on the basis of some Polish murderous gene, anti-Semites, meaning we were, are, and always will be." This participant acknowledged the historical contingency of anti-Semitism in response to those who made a defensive circular argument that Polish anti-Semitism existed because of Jewish anti-Polonism and there was no hope for dialogue. In response, a different participant listed committees, conferences, and groups, both Polish and Jewish, who were "communicating to increase understanding since, if I am not mistaken, the end of 70s; included is Pope John Paul II, the most famous Pole in the world dedicated to this issue." He added that a conciliatory approach to *Shtetl* would involve a double look, "looking as a gentile Pole [you] and as a Polish Jew [the film's addressee] simultaneously." This response suggests that it is possible to acknowledge anti-Semitism and accept *Shtetl* without threatening Polish identity.

While some participants focused on Jewish membership in the Soviet army as an explanatory factor for Polish violence against Jews, one responded that the focus on Jews "welcoming the Red Army in L'viv, joining the Communist party" ignored "several hundred years of contributions made by Jews to Polish economy, science, law, medicine, math, logic, physics, national uprisings in the 19th century, Pilsudski's Legions, literature, music, art . . . and final liberation from Soviet Communism." Participants like this are against exclusions and divisions; they argue that *Shtetl* can help provide understanding of a "Jewish" perspective. They also are against a very narrow understanding of Polish identity as threatened and opposed to "the Jew." They are able to articulate "a range of subjectivities" that defy categorical oppositions (Cohen, 1994), in part because their collective memories are less unified and include the "other."

For other participants, the categories of "Jews" and "Poles" are irreconcilable in their historical separation. Some argued that Poles also were killed "only because we were Poles" and that the documentary is another attempt to "cover up the atrocities of communist Jews in Poland." The issue of Jewish Communists emerged as an important element in participants' interpretations of *Shtetl*.

"Poles," "Jews," and "Soviets"

The understanding of relations between "Jews and Poles" is mediated by the relationship between Poles and Soviets. One of the most significant issues emerging in participants' responses is the conflict between Poles and Soviets (Stalinists and Communists) when the Soviet Union invaded Poland during WWII. Some Polish Jews, like gentile Poles, joined the Soviet forces for a variety of reasons (Schatz, 1991). Poland has had a very contentious relationship with Russia, and later the Soviet Union, in particular following the partitions of Poland by Russia, Prussia, and Austria starting in 1795. When Poland came under the domination of the Soviet Union, "the Soviet" or "the Communist" came to represent a foreign "other" whose experience was antithetical to that of the Pole. Because this position was also occupied by "the Jew," the two were connected, and "Jews" were identified with and as "Communists" in popular discourses. The incomplete merging of these two others was facilitated by a political context in which "affiliation with the Church became the symbol of opposition to the upper [pro-Soviet] government; whoever was not Roman Catholic was considered a servant of Moscow" (Milosz, 1957, p. 40). Hence, some participants talked about "Jewish communist betrayal" and argued that Jews who were killed in different circumstances by Poles were killed not because they were Jews but because they were in Soviet forces and were killed along with other Poles in Soviet forces.

Some participants departed from *Shtetl* to discuss events in Jedwabne. They argued that "the events in Jedwabne [a pogrom of the Jewish population] were quite typical for the whole of Eastern Poland, the Baltic Republics, and other areas under then Soviet occupation when the U.S.S.R. was attacked by the Germans in June 1941." As Irwin-Zarecka (1994) notes, memories of oppression are particularly potent with the oppressor serving as the "other." Positioning "Poles" in relationship to "the Soviet," and connecting "the Soviet" with "the Jew," enables Poles to escape responsibility for Polish anti-Semitism. It also demonstrates that identities are constructed in relationship to multiple "others" who enter into complex configurations with each other and against each other in and through memory. The Soviet as the significant "other" for Poles casts a shadow on the relationship between the Pole and the Jew. Some gentile Poles privilege the relationship that positions them as victims rather than as oppressors.

This particular interpretation strengthens their bid for a self-marginalized position in the West, as many Poles nurture memories of being "dealt" to the Soviet Union in post-WWII agreements. Yalta in particular is seen as

"the treacherous Western approval of Soviet imperialism" (Jewsiewicki, 1995) feeding Poles' feeling of marginalization in the West.

Cultural Needs: "Pole" in Relationship to "American"

Many participants referred to *Shtetl* as anti-Polish. This negotiated reading of *Shtetl* is driven by a specific cultural need of Polish Americans in the United States. Participants argued that *Shtetl* was produced by and feeds into negative portrayals of Poles in U.S. popular media. These negative portrayals include the "stupid Polack" as well as the "eternal anti-Semite." The following response describes the sensitivity of some viewers:

> Like many Polish Americans, I sat down to watch the film *Shtetl* on PBS (April 17) with a mixture of hope and trepidation. Would this be another *Shoah*? Would Poland be systematically defamed once again on television with no hope of effective response? Or would the complex issue of Polish-Jewish relations be treated in an evenhanded manner? As it turned out, *Shtetl* was both better and worse than I had hoped.

This participant explained that *Shtetl* was worse because it was clearly anti-Polish in simplifying relations between Poles and Jews, and better because the filmmaker was not skilled enough to prove his thesis, thus contradictory information was allowed to emerge.

Many participants responded with great sensitivity to the visual representation of the Polish peasants interviewed in the documentary. For them, the overlap between these images and the wider stereotypical image of "a Polack" is the primary relevant issue. These viewers pointed to very specific media codes, such as the contrast between peasants caught in the midst of their work around their farms, wearing work clothes, their hands dirty, and the "Americans" represented by Marzynski, Kaplan, and the Jews visited in the United States in their clean, suburban, middle-class homes. Many viewers also pointed to the camera angles that brought into focus some of the Polish interviewees' unbuttoned pants. The documentary's use of these stereotypical codes undermined for these viewers any self-reflective impact the documentary might have induced otherwise. As a matter of fact, their oppositional reading centers on this stereotype: How should we fight with stereotypes? This is the main issue . . . Isn't the image of Poland and Poles in Marzynski's movie stereotypical? Toothless, unbuttoned flies, primitive Polish peasants colliding with the wealth of America?

This participant saw this image of Poles as a dominant image of Poland and Poles in the United States. This interpretation is informed by a collective memory of images of Poles in the United States. From my position, negative portrayals of Poles in the United States are extremely limited at present; however, these viewers respond from a collective memory that has become a part of Polish identity in the United States. As one viewer specified, he had "no problem with *Shtetl* per se, but it adds to a very negatively balanced view of Polish culture. . . . We in Polonia have been abused and degraded; *Shtetl* is a Polish witch hunt." Another participant argued that the focus on an unflattering image of Poland presented in *Shtetl* was misguided. He said, "as you know, stereotypes exist in America, Polish jokes since the turn of the century. Polack. Uneducated. Uncivilized. These are stereotypes held not by Jews in particular but [by] 'white adults' about Poles—simpletons."

Responses to *Shtetl* indicate that some Polish Americans have difficulty finding a position in U.S. cultural politics as they attempt to negotiate positions in relationship to many "others" and to their own memories. They fall back on historical stereotypes to claim marginalization as a strategy of escaping the implications of positioning as "whites"—a dominant group. Responses to a statement already discussed earlier provide insight into complexities discussed here:

A: Would it be possible to collect funds to make a film for an American (or world) viewer about the years of German occupation of Poland from our point of view? Not about bandits ready to murder for gold always and anywhere, but about ordinary Poles—living in the inhuman world, powerless while looking at the burning ghetto while the distant world does not want to hear.

The following exchange ensued:

B: Do we also have to organize a "march of ten-million Polish-Americans" for us to be heard?

A: Oh, I would love to participate in such a march!!! It must be a wonderful feeling of power, bonding, and love. Can Poles unify? I would love for us to be able to do it.

C: We could do it but for whom and why? Who will buy it, broadcast it, and most importantly, who will watch it without an appropriate preparation. . . . It is enough to look at the letters to PBS after

the last presentation to realize that nobody is interested in the other side.

This brief exchange demonstrates specific cultural needs driving oppositional responses to *Shtetl*. These participants position themselves not only as separate from "Polish Jews" but also in opposition to "the distant world" that did not "want to hear" in the past and is not interested in their side now. However, they are also troubled by a lack of unity among Poles in the United States. The lack of unity is perhaps caused by a lack of common goals and an ambivalent positioning in the power structure. *Shtetl* provides these participants with a political cause, a focus for their feelings of a lack of power and of marginalization as they assert their memory of identity as heroic victims of WWII and powerless witnesses of the Holocaust.

Participants' responses indicate that they position themselves as a subordinated group that opposes and devalues the representation of Poles as anti-Semites. Their response is complicated by their positioning in the United States. They are not just Poles responding to the documentary in Poland—they are in the United States attempting to protect a national image that provides a reference for their identity. Additionally, historically, Polish identity has been represented in the United States through the images of the "stupid Polack" and Polish jokes.

However, the status of Polish Americans increased with news about Solidarity and Poland's leading role in the demolition of Communism and with the election of the Polish pope, John Paul II. Still, Polish history is not widely known in the United States, and WWII is more widely associated with the Holocaust than with Polish losses. Indeed, for many participants, representations of the Holocaust provide a relevant context for their responses. A participant observed dryly,

All of you who watched *Shtetl*, I want you to realize one thing, you watched "a documentary" that will win a 1997 Oscar in the category of a moving document from the past. This is in agreement with the principles of 1996 Hollywood: "If you want to win an Oscar, make another short document about Holocaust." It was similar with *Schindler's List* (Spielberg, 1993), when after the first screening you could hear: "Were you on Schindler's list? No? How did you survive?"

The participants point out the limits of the politics of representation of WWII in the United States and position themselves as the "other" in the widely circulated representations of WWII.

The bid for marginalization present in participants' responses is problematic. Turning discomfort—caused by circulation of some stereotypes and a lack of knowledge, as well as by the group's ambivalence about its position in U.S. cultural politics—into systemic subordination contributes to a construction of a false binary of domination and subordination. Chow (1993) ties this phenomenon to the larger process of representation of the "other," which by valorizing difference and ignoring class and intellectual hierarchies within "other" cultures, "produces a way of talking in which notions of lack, subalternity, victimization, and so forth are drawn upon indiscriminately, often with the intention of spotlighting the speaker's own sense of alterity and political righteousness" (p. 13). Chow further adds that strategic "self-subalternization . . . has increasingly become the assured means to authority and power" (p. 13). Indeed, groups situated in power positions, such as white males, claim victimization as means of reaffirming their centrality (Kennedy, 1996). In this case, Poles and Polish Americans are grappling for language and subjectivity in a sociocultural context where seemingly one can only be either the oppressor or the oppressed. While power is pervasive in social structures, it is impossible to reduce structural relations to a binary of domination and subordination. For many "Americans," Polish immigrants and Polish Americans represent a white privileged ethnic group. Additionally, relations between Polish Americans and Jewish (Polish) Americans are very complex and are mediated through their relationships with "mainstream America" and Poland. Both groups have a long history of marginalization in the United States, and both are still plagued by continuing stereotypes.

"Americans"

The Poles' and Polish Americans' need to construct a positive cultural identity is expressed in their negotiated readings of *Shtetl* through a construction of "Americans." The participants objected to *Shtetl* on the grounds that it operates on the basis of stereotypes held by "Americans." A particular image of "Americans" emerges in these responses. Americans are described as "gullible," lacking historical knowledge, and simple-minded, unsophisticated viewers who cannot contextualize what they see. One of the participants bitterly explained,

> You have to realize one fundamental fact about this "masterpiece." It was made for the American market, for viewers who do not know history, confuse notions of "German" and "Nazi," for whom the image of war reality was shaped by

Hogan's Heroes, The Dirty Dozen or *Schindler's List.* We, people from the "other" part of Europe, brought up among ruins of Warsaw, with stories from fathers and grandfathers, for whom Oswiecim is not an abstract Auschwitz from black and white movies, watch *Shtetl* from a different position than an average American viewer, especially a Jewish teenager whose grandparents lived in Poland once. . . . For an American viewer it is not clear what really happened in Bransk, who really murdered all the Jews. They only see primitiveness and back-wardness, ignorance and disregard, because that is what Marzynski wanted to show.

Another viewer does not oppose the documentary but wants it specified that it was not "Poles" but only "a handful of Poles, traitors, collaborators, or people who did not like Jews. All Poles should not be held responsible for actions of a few. Unfortunately, Americans think differently, and when you say 'Poles,' they think 'everyone.'" This portrayal of "Americans" allows Polish Americans to assert themselves in a power position not only in relationship to the text but also in relationship to the "dominant" audi-ence. This move constructs an empowered subjectivity asserted against the image of a "Polack."

CONCLUSIONS

An examination of the role played by collective memories in the production of polyvalent and polysemic reading of popular texts can provide insight into cultural identities and relations between groups. Collective memories give us insight into the strategic operations of national and cultural identi-ties in response to divergent perspectives. Participants are interpellated by an intersection between *Shtetl* and memory sites, including memory of national and religious identity, memory of relations between Poland and the Soviet Union, and memory of Polish cultural identity in the United States. These memories are connected to the present U.S. cultural context to coun-teract the ambivalent positioning of Polish American identity in the United States. The responses analyzed in this chapter demonstrate that collective memories generate polysemic readings of *Shtetl*. Collective memories are intersecting, crossed by group identities and loyalties, and not unified. Fractures in a group's collective memories allow for self-reflection and questioning of their intersecting character and enable more complex under-standing. Additionally, memories of Polish identities in the Polish context, as well as Polish and Polish American identities, were understood through

each other in response to *Shtetl*. The memory of the heroic Polish identity fending off oppressors was keyed through the past of Polish American identity to the present context of reading *Shtetl*'s memory in the United States. As Schwartz (1996) observes, keying is never perfect and it produces tensions. In this context, the tension was sustained through a construction of "Americans" as lacking adequate preparation to understand the complexities of WWII, gentile-Jewish relations, or *Shtetl* as a representation of them.

Poles and Polish Americans did not position themselves in a uniform way in relationship to "Jews" or to *Shtetl*'s representation of Polish gentile-Jewish relations. They took up positions in relationship not only to "Jews" but to "Soviets," "Nazis," and "Americans." Their positions in relationship to "Soviets" and/or "Communists" and to "Americans" mediated their relationship to "Jews." The power dynamics change as the participants move back and forth between several relevant contexts, including the history of Polish gentile-Jewish relations, Polish-Soviet history, and the historical position of Poles in the United States. These positions were taken up strategically to "manage" Polish identity in the Polish, Eastern European, and U.S. American contexts. While these viewers diverged in their polysemic readings of Polish gentile-Jewish relations in *Shtetl* (how much information was presented about Poles helping Jews, whether Poles were presented as murdering or betraying Jews, etc), they came together in their agreement that Polish identity is marginalized in the United States. This chapter demonstrates that viewers who to some extent share cultural memories read *Shtetl* differently, indicating that polysemic readings result not only from social positions but also from "differential involvement and positioning in discourse formations" (Morley, 1980, p. 141). Although participants shared memories, they engaged with these memories differently, and their memories were more or less open to other points of view. Careful attention to the strategic mobilization of cultural identities can give us insight into effective strategies for intergroup dialogue.

Media viewers are skilled in interpreting texts (Jensen, 1990); however, they are also constrained by their social positioning and skills. Cohen (1994), who is concerned with intervention in sociocultural processes and facilitating positive social action, argues that viewers empowered to engage in social action recognize the social location of their interpretations, do not oversimplify their social identities, and produce interpretations that interact with others. This chapter demonstrates that understanding how viewers are embedded in and mobilize collective memories can give us insight into the factors that limit as well as enable critical viewing skills. Memories that

facilitate readings that interact with rather than silence others include different stories and points of view. Constructing broader, contingent, and more inclusive collective memories may facilitate understanding others' perspectives and dialogue. The study described in this chapter indicates that viewers are more skilled at reading their own oppression than at responding to the ways they are implicated in domination. This is a serious limitation to dialogue.

The above analysis demonstrates the necessity to further interrogate the role of cultural needs in oppositional discourses that struggle for social power and strategically assume positions that allow them to reap highest benefits. Such interrogations need to problematize the notions of oppositional discourses, liberation, and materiality of experience. Scholars studying intercultural communication between groups positioned in different systems, and sometimes straddling different systems, need to pay attention to how macrostructures and microstructures interact and position groups and individuals.

REFERENCES

Ang, I. (1996). *Living room wars: Rethinking media audiences for a postmodern world.* New York: Routledge.

Bellah, R., Madsen, R., Sullivan, W. M., Swindler, A., & Tipton, S. (1985). *Habits of the heart: Individualism and commitment in American life.* Berkeley: University of California Press.

Bruzzi, S. (2000). *New documentary: A critical introduction.* New York: Routledge.

Ceccarelli, L. (1998). Polysemy: Multiple meanings in rhetorical criticism. *Quarterly Journal of Speech, 84,* 395-415.

Checinski, M. (1982). *Poland: Communism, nationalism, anti-Semitism.* New York: Karz-Cohl.

Chow, R. (1993). *Writing diaspora: Tactics of intervention in contemporary cultural studies.* Bloomington: Indiana University Press.

Cloud, D. (1992). The limits of interpretation: Ambivalence and the stereotype in *Spencer: For Hire. Critical Studies in Mass Communication, 9,* 322-324.

Cohen, J. R. (1991). The "relevance" of cultural identity in audiences' interpretations of mass media. *Critical Studies in Mass Communication, 8,* 442-454.

Cohen, J. R. (1994). Critical viewing and participatory democracy. *Journal of Communication, 44,* 98.

Collier, M. J. (2000). Reconstructing cultural diversity in global relationships: Negotiating the borderlands. In G. M. Chen & W. J. Starosta (Eds.), *Communication and global society* (pp. 215-236). New York: Lang.

Condit, C. M. (1989). The rhetorical limits of polysemy. *Critical Studies in Mass Communication, 6,* 103-122.

Czajkowski, M., Friszke, A., & Krajewski, S. (2000). Dzielic cudzy bol (Sharing others' pain). *Znak, 541,* 67-82.

Fiske, J. (1986). Television: Polysemy and popularity. *Critical Studies in Mass Communication, 3,* 391-408.

Fiske, J. (1991). For cultural interpretation: A study of the culture of homelessness. *Critical Studies in Mass Communication, 8,* 455-474.

Flores, L. A. (2000). Challenging the myth of assimilation: A Chicana feminist response. In M. J. Collier (Ed.), *International and Intercultural Communication Annual: Vol. 23* (pp. 26-46). Thousand Oaks, CA: Sage.

Gronbeck, B. (1998). The rhetorics of the past: History, argument and collective memory. In K. J. Turner (Ed.), *Doing rhetorical history: Concepts and case* (pp. 47-60). Tuscaloosa: University of Alabama Press.

Gutman, I. (2000). *Uczmy sie byc razem* [Let's learn how to live together]. *Znak, 541,* 63-66.

Hall, S. (1985). Signification, representation, ideology: Althusser and the post-structuralist debates. *Critical Studies in Mass Communication, 2,* 91-114.

Hasian, M. A., Jr. (1998). Intercultural histories and mass-mediated identities: The re-imagining of the Arab-Israeli conflict. In J. N. Martin, T. K. Nakayama, & L. A. Flores (Eds.), *Readings in cultural contexts* (pp. 97-103). Mountain View, CA: Mayfield.

Hasian, M. A., Jr., & Carlson, A. C. (2000). Revisionism and collective memory: The struggle for meaning in the *Amistad* affair. *Communication Monographs, 67,* 42-62.

Hoffman, E. (1993). *Exit into history: A journey through new Eastern Europe.* New York: Viking Penguin.

Hoffman, E. (1997). *Shtetl: The life and death of a small town and the world of Polish Jews.* New York: Houghton Mifflin.

Irwin-Zarecka, I. (1990). *Neutralizing memory: The Jew in contemporary Poland.* New Brunswick, NJ: Transaction.

Irwin-Zarecka, I. (1994). *Frames of remembrance: The dynamics of collective memory.* New Brunswick, NJ: Transaction.

Jensen, K. B. (1990). Television futures: A social action methodology for studying interpretive communities. *Critical Studies in Mass Communication, 7,* 129-146.

Jewsiewicki, B. (1995). The identity of memory and the memory of identity in the age of commodification and democratization. *Social Identities, 1,* 227-262.

Kapralski, S. (Ed.). (1990). *The Jews in Poland.* Cracow, Poland: Judaica Foundation.

Katriel, T. (1994). Sites of memory: Discourses of the past in Israeli pioneering settlement museums. *Quarterly Journal of Speech, 80,* 1-20.

Kennedy, L. (1996). Alien nation: White male paranoia and imperial culture in the United States. *Journal of American Studies, 30,* 87-100.

Lanzmann, C. (Director).(1999). *Shoah* [Film]. Les Films Aleph and Historia Films, with the assistance of the French Ministry of Culture. New York: New Yorker Films.

Marzynski, M. (Producer/Director). (1996). *Shtetl* [Film]. A production of Marz Associates in association with *Frontline*. Burlington, VT: WGBH Video.

Milosz, C. (1957). Anti-Semitism in Poland. *Problems of Communism, 3,* 35-40.

Morley, D. (1980). *The nationwide audience: Structure and decoding.* London: British Film Institute.

Morley, D. (1986). *Family television: Cultural power and domestic leisure.* London: Routledge.

Nichols, B. (1994). *Blurred boundaries: Questions of meaning in contemporary culture.* Bloomington: Indiana University Press.

Ong, A. (1999). *Flexible citizenship.* Durham, NC: Duke University Press.

Press, A. L. (1989). Class and gender in the hegemonic process: Class differences in women's perceptions of television realism and identification with television characters. *Media, Culture & Society, 11,* 229-252.

Press, A. L., & Cole, E. R. (1995). Reconciling faith and fact: Pro-life women discuss media, science, and the abortion debate. *Critical Studies in Mass Communication, 12,* 380-402.

Pula, J. S. (1995). *Polish Americans: An ethnic community.* New York: Twayne.

Rabinowitz, P. (1994). *They must be represented: The politics of documentary.* New York: Verso.

Schatz, J. (1991). *The generation: The rise and fall of the Jewish Communists of Poland.* Los Angeles: University of California Press.

Schwartz, B. (1996). Memory as a cultural system: Abraham Lincoln in World War II. *American Sociological Review, 61,* 908-927.

Shoah. Pamiec zagrozona? (Is memory of Shoah in danger?) (2000). *Znak, 541.*

Spiegelman, A. (1991). *Maus: A survivor's tale.* New York: Pantheon Books.

Spielberg, S. (Director/Producer), Molen, G. R., & Lustig, B. (Producers). (1993). *Schindler's List* [Film]. Los Angeles: Universal Studios.

Steinlauf, M. C. (1997). *Bondage to the dead: Poland and the memory of the Holocaust.* Syracuse, NY: Syracuse University Press.

Stone, D. (1996). Jewish emigration from Poland before World War II. In J. J. Bukowczyk (Ed.), *Polish Americans: Community, culture, and politics* (pp. 93-120). Pittsburgh, PA: University of Pittsburgh Press.

Swida-Ziemba, H. (2000). Rozbrajac wlasne mity (Disarming our own myths). *Znak, 541,* 41-48.

Wander, P. (1996). Marxism, post-colonialism, and rhetorical studies. *Quarterly Journal of Speech, 82,* 402-435.

Zelizer, B. (1995). Reading the past against the grain: The shape of memory studies. *Critical Studies in Mass Communication, 12,* 214-239.

Zelizer, B. (1998). *Remembering to forget: Holocaust memory through the camera's eye.* Chicago: University of Chicago Press.

9

Connecting Hawaiians

The Politics of Authenticity in the Hawaiian Diaspora

RONA TAMIKO HALUALANI • *San Jose State University*

In February 2000, in the *Rice v. Cayetano* case, the U.S. Supreme Court ruled that non-Hawaiian residents of Hawai'i could no longer be barred from voting for officers of the Office of Hawaiian Affairs (hereafter OHA), a state organization created to aid and serve Native Hawaiians (TenBruggencate, 2001). The Supreme Court decision asserted that the previous OHA policies that allowed only Hawaiian participation reflected unconstitutional race-based discrimination. In addition, this decision ruled that non-Hawaiians could also run for office in OHA. Such a ruling refused the notion that Hawaiians are indigenous to Hawai'i and thus are entitled to native claims (e.g., land, benefits, assistance). The *Rice v. Cayetano* case therefore represented one of many recent political and legal moves that have complicated the struggle to define who is a "real" Hawaiian. Is a "real Hawaiian" someone who belongs to an ethnic group that claims to historically originate from the islands (or that was on the land "first")? Is a "real Hawaiian" someone who has lived in Hawai'i as a state resident for a set number of years? Or rather, is a member of an ethnic group that emigrated to Hawai'i as plantation labor from the 1800s through the early 1900s a "native" or a "Hawaiian"?

These questions circulate in what is known as a *politics of authenticity*, or a larger set of politicized significations and discursive constructions of cultural membership that intermingle and oppose one another (Anderson, 1998; Hall, 1990). These identity constructions of authenticity are political in that each construction is created and spoken from different positionalities and in

---

AUTHOR'S NOTE: This chapter is an earlier draft of data presented in my book, *In The Name of Hawaiians: Native Identities and Cultural Politics (2002).*

response to past and present discourses of identity. Identity constructions framed as "authentic" also work for different power interests and carry varied political effects. The politics of authenticity have continually shifted for Hawaiians because of the connections and tensions between Hawaiians in Hawai'i (those living in the homeland) and Hawaiians on the mainland (those who identify themselves as diasporic Hawaiians). Given their long history of colonialist dispossession and U.S. neocolonialism, Hawaiians "at home" have always strived to reclaim their identity as "sovereign," indigenous, and predating any Western modern form of governance (see, e.g., Kame'eleihiwa, 1992; Trask, 1993). More explicitly, many Hawaiians have formed sovereignty movement collectives that seek to reestablish Hawaiian sovereignty, or an indigenous people's right to define for themselves the type of governance and society they want (Hawaiian Voices on Sovereignty, 1993; Kame'eleihiwa, 1992; Trask, 1993). Sovereignty movement groups have therefore demanded that the United States recognize Hawai'i as a sovereign nation rather than seeing Hawai'i as a U.S. state. As a result, sovereignty rhetoric has framed Hawai'i as the original home of Hawaiians and as the site of a burgeoning Hawaiian population ready to reestablish and renew a more "native" way of life (Trask, 1993).[1]

The sovereignty debate has become more complicated due to the increasing migration of Hawaiians from Hawai'i to the U.S. continental mainland and the settlement of large Hawaiian communities in Washington, Oregon, California, Texas, and New York, to name a few. According to the 2000 U.S. Census, there are approximately 72,216 Hawaiians on the mainland, and a total of about 215,000 Hawaiians in Hawai'i (U.S. Census, 2000). The dispersal of Hawaiians away from Hawai'i (and resurfacing historical proof that Hawaiians have migrated to the U.S. mainland since as early as the late 1700s) has thus threatened the political viability of a united Hawaiian nation, as well as weakened the rhetorical claim that Hawaiians are original and firmly rooted "natives" of Hawai'i. Sovereignty leaders have even lambasted diasporic Hawaiians for "abandoning" their homeland and assimilating to the white upper-class lifestyle of the mainland.[2] In response, diasporic Hawaiian communities have grappled with the challenge of connecting their identity with that of Hawaiians in Hawai'i in terms of indigeneity and 'aina (land), while also differentiating themselves as uniquely Hawaiian in a new and different way that opposes the binaries of "rootedness" and "displacement" and "indigenous Hawaiian on the land" and "American citizen away from home" (Clifford, 1997).

In this chapter, I focus on the tension-ridden debate between Hawaiians in Hawai'i and Hawaiians on the mainland about what it means to be an "authentic" Hawaiian. The alliance of Hawaiians in the two locales is intracultural and intercultural in that cultural signifiers—such as *'aina* (land), *koko* (blood), and indigeneity—are shared throughout their identity discourses, and yet, in the two communities the functions and uses of such signifiers differ. Here I focus on the alliance between mainland and diasporic Hawaiians from the vantage point of the diasporic Hawaiian community because of its unique position. Diasporic Hawaiian identity discourses are enabled by the potential plurality of identity significations such as *koko* (blood), in that these constructions can be resignified and adapted to fit a positionality away from and yet in memory of a homeland. However, at the same time, such identity discourses are oftentimes constrained by the historical and political limits that surround certain significations "at home." Thus, as with other cultural groups, the diasporic counterparts of a culture experience both enabling and constraining factors in their identity discourses, constructions of authenticity, and connections with their homeland members.

In this chapter, I analyze the identity discourses of diasporic Hawaiians and the politicized discursive struggle over defining their Hawaiianness in connection with and differentiation from Hawaiians "at home." First, I review several works in intercultural communication studies that have examined diasporic identity and cultural authenticity. Second, I explicate the cultural studies method and the theoretical and methodological concept of articulation used to analyze the diasporic Hawaiian discourses of identity and the embedded politics of authenticity. Next, I analyze the identity discourses of a community of diasporic Hawaiians who moved from Hawai'i to the continental U.S. mainland as early as the 1930s. Diasporic movements of Hawaiians are due in large part to the concentration of globalized power and corporate colonialism *back at home* (within the small space of Hawai'i) and the resulting dispossession of Hawaiians. Hawaiian diasporic movement, which itself seems to contradict the notion of indigenous peoples (those who are "rooted" in their ancestral land), is therefore transformed in the context of globalization and colonial power into a culturally authentic act. Finally, I discuss the implications for intercultural communication research in examining the identity discourses and the politics of authenticity within cultural groups and diasporic communities.

A CRITICAL REVIEW:
AUTHENTICITY, DIASPORIC CULTURES,
AND COMMUNICATION PRACTICES OF IDENTITY

Authenticity

Authenticity, which in this context refers to the notion of what it means to be a "true or real" or "native" member of a group, is a theoretical concept (see, e.g., Hall, 1990). Cultural groups participate in the construction of their identities and definitions of authentic membership. These definitions, however, are politically charged in that they are created within specific historical contexts and social conditions and from specific positionalities (Hall, 1990). Thus, what it means to be an authentic Chinese in the United States today is different from what it meant 10 or 15 years ago because of the increase in Chinese immigration from Taiwan, Hong Kong, and China and the political shifts in power between these sites. The challenge then lies in uncovering different identity constructions of authenticity and tracing the political consequences these carry for members of a cultural group. Who is included and/or excluded in terms of generation, age, language, place of birth, and geographic residency? What types of signifiers and speech acts are used to connect cultural members and exclude others?

In communication studies, several scholars have examined the relationship between cultural authenticity and identity politics—see, for example, Katriel, 1997; Weider & Pratt, 1990; and Wong (Lau), 1998. Weider and Pratt (1990) focus on the notion of cultural authenticity in the case of Native Americans by posing the question: How does one know if someone is a "real" member of a cultural group? While they focus on speech acts of identity and the behavioral forms of criteria that define "authenticity," Weider and Pratt do not trace the sociopolitical effects that such speech acts of authenticity carry for Native Americans and how these speech acts may change in both form and function.

Wong (Lau) (1998) links the construction of authenticity with the plurality of meaning in the Asian American community. Wong (Lau) explains that immigrants often preserve certain aspects of their cultural practices in their new site of settlement and construct their identities in memory of practices and histories from the homeland (or practices held in the home country at the time of immigration). In this way, in the United States, Asian immigrant groups with diasporic pasts struggle to define an "authentic" ethnic identity or a larger community centered on their specific social and political needs. Diasporic groups therefore face the pressure of authenticating their

identities, maintaining links with homeland communities or sites, and reconstituting their identities to speak to a new context.

Diasporic Cultures

The politics of authenticity becomes more tangled for diasporic cultures that attempt to reestablish their cultural identity in a new site, maintain connections with their homeland, and yet politically and economically disassociate from the nation-state of their homeland. With regard to issues of authenticity, it is important to think of "diaspora" as a culture. While diaspora is a theoretical concept that gains its meaning from its specific historical and political context, defining diaspora has proved to be no easy task. One often cited definition is presented by Safran (1991), who provides several key parameters for delimiting a diaspora. Of these, three should be highlighted: (1) diasporas are typically "expatriate minority communities" that dispersed from an original center, (2) diasporic groups hold close a "memory, vision, or myth" about their homeland, and (3) diasporic members feel a deep relational tie to the original homeland, hoping to return in the future. From Safran's explication, we gain a traditional perspective of an ideal diaspora as consisting of groups forcibly dispersed from their homeland due to political events (Safran, 1991). In addition, though the diasporic community settles into a new "home," Safran theorizes that diasporic groups always desire to return to the original homeland. Such groups are conceptualized as existing in a liminal space in which they feel isolated and excluded from the community of settlement and still remain loyal to their homeland government (see, e.g., Safran, 1991; Tölölyan, 1996).

Safran's (1991) framing of diaspora may not accurately reflect or speak to the experiences of diasporic groups who have incorporated themselves into new heterogeneous communities while also, simultaneously, turning toward and away from their homelands in the search for their cultural identity in the diaspora (see Panagakos, 1998; for alternative definitions, see, e.g., Conner, 1986; Sheffer, 1986). A more useful theoretical framing of diaspora is one that focuses on those communities that migrate away from a homeland and settle and recreate their identities (and the discourses of authenticity) in a new site (Drzewiecka & Halualani, 2002). In addition, such communities exist in fluid and unstable connection with homeland communities and governments, and do not necessarily desire a return, but rather, seek to practice and recreate their identities differently in a new locale. Thus, diasporic identity should not be theorized as derivative of national or homeland politics. Instead, diasporic identity stands as a flexible

and hybrid set of significations that can be adjusted (in form and function) to fit new circumstances. However, such significations remain inexorably tied to and in articulation with aspects of collective memory and nation-state or homeland politics (see, e.g., Drzewiecka & Halualani, 2002). This notion of a flexible yet bound diasporic culture helps to explain how diasporic identity constructions may intensify the politics of authenticity. Diasporic groups experience the pressure of preserving their cultural ties to the homeland in a way that acknowledges their new circumstances and locale, thereby making "authenticity" a challenge for them to sustain and express. The stakes are high as diasporic groups face potential expulsion and alienation from their homeland community.

More study is needed on diasporic politics within the communication field, and on their influence on identity formation and the discourses and politics of authenticity (see, e.g., Drzewiecka & Halualani, 2002; Kraidy, 1999; Shome, 1996). Examining the construction of diasporic subjectivities away from and in memory of a nationalist homeland, and the political implications of such identities, can yield significant theoretical knowledge about the many cultural groups that frame themselves as "diasporic," as well as about the intercultural and intracultural alliances and discourses between cultural groups in many different home sites (e.g., homeland, multiple settlement sites). The communication discourses on identity in cultural groups therefore reflect enabling and constraining aspects, in that such discourses often feature renewed nationalist sentiments and essentialized constructions of authenticity. Moreover, identity discourses recombine nation-state influences, newly articulated stances against the homeland, and an ambivalent tone with regard to ethnic or national loyalties, belonging, and the positioning of a "new home" in relation to nationalism, sovereignty, and cultural rights. With global concerns and the fluid unpredictability of identity formations, the challenge lies in deeply engaging the multilayered communication discourses of diasporic groups, the embedded political and structural forces, and the dynamic politics of authenticity. Therefore, in this analysis I pose the following research questions: In what ways do diasporic Hawaiians construct their identity claims of authenticity in a complex alliance with their homeland communities? What are the political consequences of such constructions?

CULTURAL STUDIES METHOD AND ARTICULATION

For this analysis, I use a cultural studies ethnography perspective and method (see, e.g., Alasuutari, 1995; Halualani, 2000). Cultural studies is an

interdisciplinary, multinational field of study, consisting of many traditions (e.g., British cultural studies, American cultural studies, Black British studies, Asian American, Pacific, and feminist cultural studies, among others). The main objective of cultural studies is to thoroughly examine the relationship between culture and society. Specifically, cultural studies scholars seek to analyze the formation of culture in relation to the everyday practices of social actors and the invisible social structures of governmental control, media, and economic power (Alasuutari, 1995; Blundell, Shepherd, & Taylor, 1993; Hoggart, 1957; Thompson, 1968; Turner, 1992; Williams, 1958). Thus, when cultural studies scholars explain that "culture is a struggle," they are referring to the dynamic interplay between the lived experiences of people and the larger social forces (Grossberg, 1992, 1993, 1996; Turner, 1992). Therefore, according to cultural studies, experience is not inherently explanatory; it is constituted historically and politically by systems of language, governmental and class ideologies, and concrete social interaction.

With regard to specific research methodology, cultural studies scholars have used a variety of methods to investigate the interrelationship between the structural formation of identity and concrete social interaction (private narratives, experience, and community life): ethnography (i.e., social, material, and historical forms of anthropology), textual analysis, historical studies, and political economy (see, e.g., Alasuutari, 1995; Halualani, 2000; Johnson, 1987). For this analysis, I use a form of cultural studies ethnography in which I analyze the identity discourses of a diasporic Hawaiian community and the structural formations constituting these discourses, especially in terms of the homeland politics in Hawai'i, past representations of Hawaiians via colonialist discourses, and U.S. legal constructions (see, e.g., Halualani, 2002). I do so by conducting fieldwork, including participant observation and qualitative interviews with diasporic Hawaiians. In addition, in my analysis stage, I also examined archival and contemporary historical and legal documents and sovereignty movement publications. Such a focus enabled me to contextualize diasporic Hawaiian identity narratives in terms of the larger social structures and to pinpoint the linkages and conflicts between the diasporic community, Hawaiians in Hawai'i, and those who are members of the Hawaiian sovereignty movement collectives.

In my analysis, I invoked my own positionality as a diasporic Hawaiian who was born and raised away from Hawai'i in California. With this perspective, I connected with the community members of the diaspora, and at the same time, I relied on a close analysis of newspaper and sovereignty documents from Hawai'i in order to capture the dialectical connections and tensions between Hawaiians at "home" and in the diaspora. I later

conducted interviews with Hawaiian communities in Hawai'i to round out the analysis.[3] Specifically for this study, I conducted field observations with three different diasporic Hawaiian communities in the Pacific Northwest by participating in monthly meetings, events, and programs. To date, I have collected approximately 300 hours of fieldwork over a period of 3 years. In addition, I have conducted 90 interviews with diasporic Hawaiians of varied positionalities: those who migrated from Hawai'i in the 1930s, 1940s, or 1950s, as well as those who had spent most of their lives on the mainland and never or rarely been to Hawai'i (as in the case of diasporic youth). The interviews constitute the major focus of my data analysis in this chapter. My interviewee sample also spanned a wide range of ages (18- to 75-year-old females and males) and socioeconomic class positions.

Following Alasuutari (1995), I asked probing questions: What does it mean to be a "true" Hawaiian? How is such an identity performed and enacted? What is the shared set of meanings, symbols, and membership criteria? To analyze the ways in which Hawaiians construct authenticity claims of identity, I also used grand tour "private and oral memory" interviews with questions and/or statements: What does it mean to be Hawaiian? Tell me what it was like growing up as a Hawaiian. How do you know if someone is a Hawaiian? (Spradley, 1979, 1980). These differ from more standard interview formats in allowing respondents great latitude to construct the history of their lives and explain cultural membership. As interviewees narrate their experiences, they reveal what moments and conditions they view as central to the shaping of their lives and the larger Hawaiian culture, and they share how they identify themselves and others as "Hawaiian." At the conclusion of these narratives, I asked a series of follow-up questions on points made earlier and specific demographic data. Interviews varied in length from 2 to 6 hours. I taperecorded, transcribed, and analyzed all of the interviews in terms of themes of identity and the performative or narrative process of how "authentic" Hawaiian identity is articulated and made real. After a preliminary analysis, I presented my findings to my interviewees to solicit feedback and more insights on the authentic constructions of Hawaiianness. To protect the confidentiality of my interviewees, I have changed their names in the analysis that follows.

After my data was collected, I used the theoretical and methodological concept of articulation to analyze my ethnographic observations and interview data. Within cultural studies, articulation is defined as a practice in

which noncorresponding meanings are linked in terms of a variety of relationships: through difference, similarity, contradiction, juxtaposition, and essence (Hall, 1980a; Laclau, 1977; Laclau & Mouffe, 1985). These constructed yet naturalized linkages are attached to particular historical conditions and social structures. Meanings therefore do not naturally and necessarily correspond to one another; rather they are conjoined into complex structures of unity (Hall, 1980a; Slack, 1996). Through articulation, the identity discourses created by and in the name of cultural groups can be traced in order to examine the process through which specific meanings become associated with a cultural group's identity and social structures, as well as the political effects of such meanings (Slack, 1996). Grossberg (1992) explains that articulation is "the production of identity on top of differences, of unities, of fragments, of structures across practices. Articulation links this practice to that effect, this text to that meaning to that reality, these experiences to those politics. And these links are themselves articulated into larger structures" (p. 54). Thus, articulation allows cultural studies scholars to examine a context deeply and to unveil *how* meanings constituting identity constructions are aligned with and against one another in unpredictable, unimaginable articulated combinations, as well as the political operations of such relations for a cultural group.

I traced the identity themes and the associated structures that were articulated in my interviews in terms of the "authentic" construction of "Hawaiianness," and I highlighted the signifiers that recurred in the diasporic community. In addition, I traced these diasporic identity themes in line with or against the identity themes from past newspaper and sovereignty movement documents, as well as those that emerged in my interviews with Hawaiians in Hawai'i. I asked the following: What types of signifiers does the diasporic community use? How are these signifiers used? For which functions? In response to which identity discourses? How similar and/or different are these from the identity, newspaper, and sovereignty discourses in Hawai'i? In what ways? How are these significations practiced? What are the discursive and political effects when certain significations are practiced by Hawaiians at home and then by diasporic Hawaiians? Overall, I examined the constitutive nature, form, and function of these significations, as well as the discursive effects of these significations when spoken from different positionalities. I traced the articulated themes of authentic Hawaiianness and highlighted the recurring, contradictory, and oppositional themes within the larger context of the struggle over native sovereign identity.

THE STRUGGLE OVER
AUTHENTICITY IN THE HAWAIIAN DIASPORA

To ground my analysis, I present a brief historical summary of Hawaiian cultural politics and the Hawaiian diaspora.

Historical Background: Hawaiians as a Diaspora

Hawaiians represent a cultural group rarely considered to be moving between two nations: an American one borne of U.S. colonialism and a sovereign nation—the historically remembered independent Hawaiian kingdom prior to 1893. The diasporic Hawaiian community in the United States is a land-based cultural group that struggles to define itself against the still-present colonial U.S. nation-state. However, identity reconstruction has proven to be difficult for diasporic Hawaiians in that they have had to recreate their identity while also residing on the "American" or "white" continental U.S. mainland and away from the "authenticating" marker of native land.

The year 1778 marked the pivotal moment in which Westernization dramatically altered the Hawaiian culture (I'i, 1959; Kame'eleihiwa, 1992; MacKenzie, 1991; Malo, 1951). Up until then, Hawai'i had been a self-sustaining and organized society and an independent kingdom. Afterward, struggles over political governance, sovereignty, and native and land rights dominated the next few centuries (I'i, 1959; Kame'eleihiwa, 1992; MacKenzie, 1991; Malo, 1951). With the increase of foreign travelers and residents in Hawai'i, native belonging and residency in Hawai'i quickly lost its ethnic distinction and began to liberally include all residents (see Halualani, 1998). Outsiders and external business interests flocked to Hawai'i as U.S. colonialism overthrew the independent Hawaiian Kingdom in 1893. As a result, Hawaiians lost any cultural right to land that they had previously held.

Throughout World War II and afterward, Hawai'i's economy and land base focused on two areas: the tourist industry and military defense. As Hawai'i increasingly became the site of global access, belonging, and consumption, Hawaiians who had limited access to land and economic opportunities left their homeland and settled as far away as Europe, Japan, Mexico, and the United States. Thus, "home" for Hawaiians became a concentrated site of colonial and globalized interests. In response to the colonization of Hawai'i, there were three waves of Hawaiian out-migration that resulted from the lack of jobs at home and the challenges and obstacles put forth by the Department of Hawaiian Home Lands and the Office of

Hawaiian Affairs in securing a Hawaiian homestead (Barman, 1995; Kauanui, 1999; Wright, 1983). For Hawaiians, it seemed economically better to stay away from "home." As of today, there are approximately 72,272 Hawaiians living "off island" on the continental U.S. mainland in comparison to 138,742 Hawaiians living in Hawai'i (Kauanui, 1999; Office of Hawaiian Affairs, 1996). Diasporic Hawaiian communities have settled in British Columbia, Mexico, Europe, and the U.S. mainland (e.g., in Arizona, Northern and Southern California, Colorado, Florida, Illinois, Nevada, New York, Oregon, Texas, Utah, Virginia, and Washington) (Office of Hawaiian Affairs, 1996).

Interview Themes

Theme 1: The Search For "Home":
Diasporic Identity as "Traditional" or "Hawaiian"

Throughout the interviews, diasporic Hawaiians refused the popular notion that to be Hawaiian or native is to be rooted to the land (in terms of residency). Instead, community members framed the mainland as the extension of their "home" in the face of, as one interviewee described, "a Hawai'i that is colonized and commercialized beyond repair." When asked about their identities, mainland Hawaiians incorporated their diasporic movement into their historical memory, framing it as both a pressure externally induced by colonialism and global capitalism and a necessary cultural adjustment for survival as "Hawaiians." For example, one interviewee, "Mary," a Hawaiian woman who moved to San Francisco in 1950, framed her "traditional" background as a little girl raised "in the day when Hawaiian was spoken and there was Hawaiian land for Hawaiians." She explained, "All of that changed. I left for the mainland. If I stayed in [Hawai'i], we'd get no benefits, no home. So I lived here like a Hawaiian, with *'ohana* (family) and it was home all over." Mary, who was born in the early 1920s, shared her lived experience in Hawai'i, a reality marked by significant changes: the eradication of spoken Hawaiian in communities, the loss of traditional all-Hawaiian communities, economic and business development, and increasing militarization.

Another member, "John," explained that "being Hawaiian for many of us meant leaving. There was so much change . . . the haole ways set in and you couldn't make it. My parents told me to leave for the mainland. I could carry the traditions there."[4] John also frames the notion of Hawaiianness with diasporic migration, and even links the word "traditional" with his movement away from Hawai'i.

In their speaking practices, diasporic Hawaiians like Mary and John therefore describe themselves as "traditional" counterparts of their community and their mainland positionalities as distinctively Hawaiian. In the context of colonial and globalizing effects at home, including the appropriation of land, the shortage of jobs, and the increasing presence of outsiders, a "traditional" standpoint suddenly changes. "Tradition" dialectically shifts as "home" becomes the center of modern business development and foreign control. Clearly, a traditional life is no longer possible at home. Mary and John therefore associate "home" in Hawai'i as being newly foreign while out-migration and resettlement in this context are resignified as practices that connote true Hawaiian identity, meaning practices that provide a self-sufficient and family-oriented living.

Similarly, "Hale," a diasporic interviewee, described her resettlement in Las Vegas, Nevada, as a "cultural adjustment." She explained the nature of her diasporic identity:

> It was clear for me that I couldn't live like my grandparents—on their homestead. Or the old way. I applied for homestead land. Nothing came of it. OHA and DHHL have been bad for us as a group. I would have eroded here. The mainland was an adjustment. Moving, I mean. It's a Hawaiian adjustment. You could live here on your own terms. Your own. To me, Hawai'i just wasn't for Hawaiians anymore.

In her interview, Hale focused on her move from an economically strapped and restrictive Hawai'i. The statement "Hawai'i just wasn't for Hawaiians anymore" revealed her view that the combined forces of colonialism and globalization had dissolved an original cultural site. For Hale, in the context of the threat of globalization, the diasporic movement represented a means to preserve a cultural spirit that was being suppressed at home. In addition, given the illegal overthrow of the Hawaiian kingdom in 1893 and the dispossession of Hawaiian land, which is now administered by the Department of Hawaiian Home Lands (DHHL), Hawaiian identity, which has always been tied to 'aina (land), is now signified in tension with Hawaiian land because most Hawaiians cannot gain access to their native land. The movement away from Hawai'i therefore becomes for some a necessary adjustment to a seemingly indiscriminate capital market and the unjust withholding of Hawaiian homestead land from Hawaiians. Hale saw her actions as being "Hawaiian" (and not "American" or "haole") and in contradistinction from the contemporary and "foreign" shifts at home. Also, Hale refers to the state agencies, the Office of Hawaiian Affairs

and the Department of Hawaiian Home Lands, as "bad" and unfair. Given the struggle between Hawaiians and these state agencies, diasporic movement away from Hawai'i can also be considered a political act of identity and a means to separate oneself from unjust and "real non-Hawaiian" interests.

In most of my interviews, when asked about the nature of Hawaiian identity and experience, Hawaiians emphasized the topic of out-migration and characterized it as a "Hawaiian" act. Such an act is "Hawaiian" in a very different way from past identity claims that highlight rootedness and indigeneity. At the very moment contemporary colonial and globalizing structures took hold of Hawai'i, culture transformed into a larger dialectic of indigenous memories, modernized Hawaiian cultural practices, and modern forms of governance, labor, and living. This dialectic holds new points of meaning as traditional Hawaiian life takes on two different forms: living on a homestead and, if this is not possible, moving away to new spaces with one's family members and memories. Globalization thus changes the conditions of culture and the means (the forms) through which culture is enacted.

In Hawaiian community meetings in Northern California and Las Vegas, Nevada, I frequently listened to several adult community members narrate a tale of Hawaiian history to children of the diaspora, most of whom had never been to Hawai'i. The narrative included three main themes: (1) a discussion of the early Hawaiian kingdom with "sovereign rulers" like King Kamehameha and Queen Lili'uokalani; (2) a tracing of the U.S. overthrow of Hawai'i in 1893, which revolves around the story of Hawai'i's last monarch, Queen Lili'uokalani; and (3) the "search" for another "home." Rather than focusing on the replacement of their homeland, community members emphasized how they are newly creating and extending it in different contexts. "Home" stands as a relational discourse stretched across an interregional network of Hawaiians. It involves remembering the past and discursively incorporating and making sense of the presence of diasporic Hawaiians. A member explained to an audience of children how their community originated in Las Vegas, Nevada:

Many came to Hawai'i from all over. There were so many people and not enough space or land to go around, especially to Hawaiians. A new government came into existence that had no sovereign rulers like the ones before it had. And so it happened that Hawaiians—our relatives—traveled to every port and town and took with them what they knew. There they looked for new jobs and somewhere new to live, to create a home, to create a community for us.

In the description of diasporic movement as an act of community, it is not characterized as a form of exile or temporary refuge. In fact, most of these Hawaiians do not return home to live and many do not desire to do so. Diasporic movement is framed, then, as a direct result of the foreign changes and colonialism in the islands, as well as a cultural adjustment. For example, "Jon," an 18-year-old Hawaiian male who was born and raised in Las Vegas, Nevada, and has never been to Hawai'i, explains that

> In hula practice, my teacher told of our past. That for centuries we lived in an ordered society, ruled by *Ali'i* and then it changed as more and more outsiders came. The sovereign period had ended with the overthrow of the kingdom of 1893. Which is how I am here today. The Hawaiian people left home when their home changed . . . to Oregon, Washington, California, New York, and Nevada.

Similarly, another diasporic youth, "Lane," a 22-year-old woman who was born and raised in Oregon and has only been to Hawai'i twice, shares the following:

> My life here is directly linked to the period of the overthrow. If that did not happen, I wouldn't be here. No mainland Hawaiian would be here if that did not happen. The time had changed so much . . . that Hawaiian survival depended on going to the mainland. Spreading our seeds. You could see that here, California, lots there, Washington, all over. The community spread cuz they had to.

What is most interesting about the interview excerpts above is the identity articulation of Hawaiians who have not been raised in or been to Hawai'i. Instead, Hawaiians like Jon and Lane are enculturated into a diasporic Hawaiian memory that *remembers* mainland settlement as both a result of colonialism and globalization (with the overthrow directly creating a mainland Hawaiian community) and a survival tactic of Hawaiians to preserve and recreate community. In their narrations, Jon and Lane share how diasporic movement became a way to preserve a Hawaiian identity; this same theme re-emerged in several other interviews, such as the interview with a young woman who claimed that she hails from "Hawai'i by way of Las Vegas." Diasporic Hawaiians of all ages have fused together historical events, foreign influences, and their settlement on the mainland. The children of diaspora therefore symbolize how cultural memory and identity are dynamically constructed beyond and yet in remembrance of Hawai'i.

As a displaced nation, the diasporic Hawaiian community stands between a Hawaiian nationalist discourse and a racialized hierarchy of identity

positions of the United States. Kehaulani Kauanui (1999) states that diasporic Hawaiians "are off-island, but not exactly immigrants; in America but not 'of' America and many Hawaiians refuse an American identity. Hawaiians both on- and off-island hold U.S. citizenship, complicating the binaries between core and periphery, immigrant and indigenous" (p. 685). There exists the primary tension that Hawaiian diasporic movement contradicts the notion that indigenous peoples (those who are "rooted" in their ancestral land) are more authentic. Clifford (1997) explains that

> Tribal or Fourth world assertions of sovereignty and "first nationhood" do not feature histories of travel and settlement, though these may be part of the indigenous historical experience. They stress continuity of habitation, aboriginality, and often a 'natural' connection to the land. (p. 252)

Sovereignty groups in the past were invested in upholding the fixed geographic residency definition of Hawaiians (that Hawaiians live in Hawai'i) and have marginalized diasporic members as being "Americanized" or "haole-ified" (Whitened). For example, as Kauanui explains, in 1993, Lilikala Kame'eleihiwa, a Ka Lahui Hawai'i sovereignty group member, said, "If they [off-island Hawaiians] want to have a vote (to decide what kind of sovereign government to work towards), they have to come home and eat it with the rest of us" (cited in Fernandez, 1993, p. A6). Moreover, indicative of the criticisms circulating at the time by Hawaiians in Hawai'i, Kame'eleihiwa also said, "One understands why they move away. They are only there to live and feed their families, to live a life of luxury and own a house. . . . I couldn't do that; I would rather die here" (cited in Fernandez, 1993, p. A6).

Thus, the identity narratives that frame diasporic movement as "Hawaiian" exist in relation to and in tension with the continual marginalization of their identities away from Hawai'i in newspaper and sovereignty discourses in Hawai'i. Such a contested discourse around the meaning of "native belonging" and the different positionality of diasporic Hawaiians illustrates the difficulty in connecting Hawaiians around sovereign causes and politics that are tied to geographic residency, Hawaiian resident population counts, and the strength of a unified Hawaiian nation rooted to the land.

Theme 2: Practicing Pi'ikoi

Within new contexts, diasporic Hawaiians continually negotiate the oppositional construction of "on-island" authenticity and "off-island"

assimilation (Kauanui, 1998). These Hawaiians reimagine their unique relation to the homeland and to one another as Hawaiians. Throughout the interviews, I encountered how diasporic members reimagine and authenticate their Hawaiian identity by engaging in *pi'ikoi*. According to Pukui and Elbert (1986), *pi'ikoi* refers to the practice of "claiming to be of higher rank than one is," of claiming to be something one is not. Within Hawaiian culture, to engage in *pi'ikoi* used to be considered a negative act; relatives would say, "No make *pi'ikoi*. Tell them who you are. Be true." or "No make high nose or *pi'ikoi*." As Pukui and Elbert (1986) note further, Hawaiians were typically told not to act or talk out of their own cultural place and location; one was to speak one's true status and name.

The enactment of *pi'ikoi* enables diasporic Hawaiians to disavow popular and sovereignty criticism of their "pseudo-Hawaiian" identity. By way of these speech practices of *pi'ikoi*, they discursively connect themselves to sovereign Hawaiian royalty, which authenticates their identity and speaking authority as "real" Hawaiians. For example, in her description of Hawaiian identity, one interviewee shared with me a large set of books and genealogical documents and professed her linkage to Hawaiian royalty, to the Great King Kamehameha I. She claimed, "I am his relative through a relative in the 1800s. Can you believe it? Our family holds this legacy in pride." As another example, "Richard," a diasporic Hawaiian in his 80s, proudly shared the story of how his family realized they were related to King Kalakaua. For close to 3 hours, I was given a narrative tour of his ancestral linkages to this royal monarch and of the unified nature of his family to date. In fact, throughout most of my interviews, diasporic community members shared stories of their familial connections to Hawaiian royalty, particularly to King Kamehameha and Queen Lili'uokalani, two of the most beloved figures of Hawaiian royalty in the history of Hawai'i. At first, as the researcher, I overlooked such long narratives and tried to place the interviewees back on "track" by posing more questions about what being Hawaiian means to them. The interviewees would always come back to discussing their Hawaiian lineage. I finally realized that these enactments of *pi'ikoi* represented a symbolic means of reauthenticating their identity as Hawaiians in the face of the contested struggle over Hawaiianness with regard to the sovereignty movement and blood quantum mandates of the state.

A female interviewee, Moana, narrated her family line. She said, "Yes, King Kamehameha I. The king. He is one of us. In my family. I tell my children all the time the relations that prove we are his descendants. It is true." She shared every genealogical table and faded photo she could find to

talk about her family and their royal blood. Moana had no "concrete" proof that King Kamehameha I was her descendant. In fact, the dates of the designated server in Kamehameha I's court failed to coincide with the estimated time of Kamehameha I's existence. It did not matter because her practicing of *pi'ikoi* represented a significant identity encoding for her as a diasporic Hawaiian. Through historical retellings, Moana authenticated and sanctified both her personal experience and her individual voice as a "Hawaiian" on the mainland. Forced to move to the mainland with her son when her homestead loan fell through, she longed for a time when, as she put it, "being Hawaiian was a real high honor—the time when Hawaiians were acknowledged."

Perhaps *pi'ikoi* is spread throughout diasporic Hawaiian communities as a practice in response to both a historical memory threatened and dispossessed by colonialism and neocolonial globalization *and* the marginalizing perception of "off-island" Hawaiians as "absentee" or less Hawaiian cultural members. Mainland Hawaiians remember and redraw their family lines to sovereign monarchs who represent the authentic Hawaiian traditions and spirit. In this practice, Hawaiians continually refer to the historical past of Hawai'i as their origin, but they also use it as a dynamic link that exceeds specific genealogical lines, bloodlines, and geographic place. Speaking of the past, which is always a resignified construction, fulfills a cultural function in response to the present. Linking one's identity to that of the sovereign monarchs enables diasporic Hawaiians to authenticate their identity claim as Hawaiian. In this way, mainland Hawaiians can remake their identities in order to claim a political power diminished by globalizing forces, state agencies, and foreign control of Hawai'i.

Pi'ikoi thus operates in a way that reestablishes the political prestige and power stripped away by Western colonialism. Within the diasporic community, it worked not just to enhance just an individual's name and reputation—but also to narratively recreate an entire Hawaiian *Lahui* (a sovereign or independent nation) and an era in which their subjectivity was preserved and protected. It also created a means by which Hawaiians could authenticate their mainland positionalities via relations to historical figures. Moana highlights the glossing over of the Hawaiian hegemony of Kamehameha I's time. She describes her descendant as a royal servant under the king, which wouldn't make him a blood relative (royal lines presided over court servants and commoners). This then becomes an interesting narrative strategy that speaks to the current political and diasporic conditions of Hawaiians. So, as Hawaiians struggled for a space in which to exist at all, Hawaiian royalty was politically transformed into cultural heroes and brave

warriors fighting for all Hawaiians. It is in this vein that Moana identifies her descendant as Kamehameha's server. His descendancy is not a matter of blood or genealogy, rather, it refers to his historical placing and situatedness. Moana's great, great, great grandfather is signified as a relative to Kamehameha by virtue of historical moment; she could connect him to his time and his sovereign monarchy. Through this, she has authenticated her family line and magnified her cultural voice as descendant of Kamehameha's time. It was a time when "Hawaiianness" was assumed to be an honor and when it already held cultural capital. It was also a historical time when a sovereign Hawaiian identity would never be denied. Significantly, these *pi'koi* appeals, these verbal attempts of Hawaiians to connect themselves to a royal bloodline, refuse a geographic specificity of Hawaiianness in that the genealogical and blood connections provide mainland Hawaiians with a sense of cultural permanency. Connecting to a sovereign ruler in terms of genealogy naturalizes individuals' Hawaiian identity in new spaces.

In the diasporic context, "Hawaiianness" carries a heavy burden of proof for Hawaiians. One man shared that "My name is part of the Kamehameha dynasty. Everyone told we crazy. That it couldn't be. But it here and we know we part of that line." Another interviewee narrated how her family line was linked to a royal monarch in Maui through another royal line in which an ancestor was adopted. Thus, by linking themselves to family lines, historical moments, and traditions, diasporic members authenticate their "Hawaiianness" in new locales. One part-Hawaiian interviewee even commented that "Hey, I no look like one [Hawaiian]. You look through my line, no doubt." *Pi'ikoi* therefore also symbolizes a means to refuse the concept of authenticity as *both* racial purity and native residency. Again, diasporic Hawaiians on the mainland engage in *pi'ikoi* in order to authenticate their mainland identities and experiences and to remember a historical past and sovereign period that traverses geographic boundaries and racial purity in identifying who they are. Through collective memory, mainland Hawaiians claim their authenticity through a modernist identity discourse of blood.

Theme 3: Performing Blood Authority

The signifier of blood (*koko*) has been contentious within the Hawaiian community. This is due to the historical context of the 1900s when "blood amount" or "blood quantum" was used by the U.S. government to racialize and identify specific cultural groups (e.g., African Americans, Native

Americans, Hawaiians; Goldberg, 1993, 1997). Blood became a form of "scientific" classification used by governmental agencies to determine a person's race (Goldberg, 1993, 1997). In the case of Hawaiians, in the early 1900s the U.S. government ruled that a person must prove that she or he has at least 50% Hawaiian blood (or blood quantum) in order to be recognized as a "Hawaiian" (see Halualani, 1998, 2002). Ultimately, it became almost impossible for individuals to prove they had the necessary blood amount because federal and state agencies required complete documentation—in the form of birth, death, and marriage certificates on which all the names had to match. In Hawai'i, document recorders and census enumerators often did not record accurate information, thus many Hawaiians have not been able to secure any homestead land because their blood amount could not be proven. Even more tragic is the reality that to this day many Hawaiians are still not recognized as "Hawaiian" in terms of proven blood quantum (see Halualani, 2002).

Blood as Real The discourse around authenticity grows more complex as diasporic Hawaiians reproduce the scientific discourse of ethnicity as "blood percentage" (Halualani, 1998). Such a discourse involves three elements. First, many interviewees claim that indeed "blood amount" is an accurate indicator of their Hawaiianness. For example, "Harry," a Chinese-Hawaiian in Northern California, claims that "It's in the blood. Being Hawaiian is about a blood tie." In addition, "Elia," a Hawaiian woman from Kauai who is now living in the Southwest, attests to the veracity of blood in marking Hawaiian identity. She says, "It (blood quanta) is accurate. It makes us who we are. I agree with it. You see, the pure ones, the old-timers, they live Hawaiian style—speak ol' Hawaiian, fishing village, go to Hawaiian church. But the mixed ones are more Americanized, parents married all kinds."

Diasporic Hawaiian community members practice blood talk in their daily lives by invoking blood as real and here and now. They refer to blood as coming first and as being *a priori*. Lei, a mixed-blood Hawaiian woman, reinforces the importance of blood:

> Percentage tells you that pure bloods are having more difficulties than mixed-bloods. I personally agree.... Pure bloods ... have a hard time fitting in a Western lifestyle. They need the land more than us. They should get *'aina* before any of us. No one wants to admit that, but that is the truth.

As illustrated above, *koko* (blood) is embedded in diasporic identity discourses in sophisticated and creative ways. I was stunned at how deep a

blooded communication practice identified and reimagined the Hawaiian voice. At first, I rationalized the blood references as dominant metaphors, thus revealing how the state once again overdetermined the Hawaiian community. After doing a series of ethnographic interviews and oral histories, I knew it was more; blood talk carried a resonating force within Hawaiians' everyday practices. Using articulation, I situated blood in relation to the specific context that historically and legally framed "Hawaiianness." As I uncovered a blood signifier in diasporic identity discourses, I also began analyzing influential government documents, such as the Hawaiian Homes Commission Act (HHCA) of 1920, for how "blood" was discursively framed in them. The Hawaiian Homes Commission Act formalized policy mechanisms of identification for "Native Hawaiian" that required at least 50% Hawaiian blood. Rigid definitions of "Hawaiian" identity centered on the scientific verifiability of blood and its unquestioned nature, in addition to the state's supposedly neutral procedures in proving, presenting, and certifying an individual's blood quantum and thus his or her "Hawaiianness." However, as diasporic Hawaiians claim "blood" as an accurate reflector of their identity, the "blood" signifier and discourse is remade and resignified to authenticate their identity and speaking authority.

Throughout variously situated positions, Hawaiians, through their speech, frame blood as real to their lives. The above examples reproduce a sequence in which blood is deemed via communicative signification as a reflector of material conditions and resources, material and cultural experiences, and losses. Blood is presupposed as always coming first and long before their act of talking about it. Through talk, then, blood is naturalized and reified into existence, a naturalization afforded by communication practice. Indeed, the repeated performativity of blood as always "coming before" is enabled and made more powerful through the naturalized language and imagery discursively created around blood (through formal policy, identity certification for health care, and the rhetoric of science). Consequently, the performative speech of blood allows for its verifiability and symbolically makes it real among Hawaiians.

According to Butler (1990), identity and discourse are embedded within performativity. The performative act of a blooded "Hawaiianness" "brings into being or enacts that which it names, and so marks the constitutive or productive power of discourse" (p. 134). Simultaneously, though, somewhere within the moving performativity of discourse, through its necessary repetitive nature and coding, there lies the possibility of resignifying dominant forms and identity positions.

Inaccurate State Processes of Blood Verification The second element in the blood discourse of diasporic Hawaiians is emphasized in the arbitrary nature of verification. Mainland Hawaiians individually shared the difficulties in proving quantum and challenging the widely interpreted public records, documents, and census reports. For example, like many Hawaiians, Bob's performance of proof was ill-fated.

> Hawaiians are the real, first settlers in the islands. Descendants of descendants of the originals. Me? No more. Not really. Not one written record exists for my parents, their families, my cousins like that. Believe me . . . it's a long story. A big mess, really. We tried to match a name of ours—"Lahua"—with my name— "Keoni." On so many forms like this, with lots of families, the names are all misspelled or missing.

Many other interviewees shared their difficulties in proving their blood quantum because of missing documents on the part of the state agencies or inaccurate information that is recorded on the documents. One interviewee pointed out that "most of the errors are in the hands of the agencies that hold our records. We get the documents from them and if they are inaccurate, then your blood quantum is thrown up in the air." One of the persistent themes throughout my interviews was the critique by diasporic Hawaiians of the state agencies that require 50% blood quantum and oversee the blood quantum verification process. These diasporic Hawaiians exposed the state identification process as skewed and the census records as wholly inaccurate. Bob and others bemoaned the state of blood quantum policy and strongly critiqued formalized blood technology (via administration and procedurality) as not being verifiably accurate.

Resignifying Blood as True Authenticity In the third element of the blood discourse, with *koko* deemed real and yet its accurate recording clearly flawed, Hawaiians themselves by way of their blood emerge as the only true authorities or cultural experts in recognizing "Hawaiianness." Diasporic Hawaiians thus claim that only the Hawaiians themselves and their blood amounts speak to the true authenticity of Hawaiians. Diasporic Hawaiians narratively and performatively emerge as the sole cultural authorities as to who they are. As one woman put it, "The state got it right— Hawaiian is about the blood. The procedures are wrong. Only we—us—we are the living proof of Hawaiians."

Another interviewee established the true criteria for "Hawaiianness":

> You can point to *Kanaka*, you know who is, where they are from, how much they are, how they grew up. We knew plenty da kine pure. You knew, by their last names, where they wen grow up. Like which side of the street they wen live. ou know how traditional the family was. At parties, you knew who danced, who sang ol kine, wen prepare Hawaiian style *imu* (underground oven).

Other Hawaiians said: "It's all the old timers who '*make*' (died) by now. Today is real different, too much blending of local and Hawaiian style, not real old style, not like the pure kine *Kanaka*"; "*Koko* can't be seen or made. . . . It's who you are"; "[It's] how you carry the culture."

In the interview excerpts above, Hawaiians themselves are deemed as the experts in recognizing those who are truly "Hawaiian." The notion that Hawaiians are the "living proof" as opposed to the state requirements of blood quantum reveal how a blood signifier can be remade and resignified from a dominant discourse to a cultural group's resistive stance in reclaiming their authenticity. The quote "*Koko* can't be seen or made. . . . It's who you are" reflects how blood, unseen and unproven yet spoken and performed, makes the difference; it makes Hawaiians naturally "Hawaiian." Thus, reclaiming "blood" as naturalized authority establishes Hawaiians' indigenous rights to an identity historically and legally written over (e.g., as U.S. citizens, wards of the state, and the people of *Aloha*) and authenticates an identity created in a new site.

As Butler theorizes, the performativity of discourse houses its own becoming and un-doing, its own actions-in-process (Butler, 1995). Such is the case for Hawaiians whose subjectivity is *layered* with a resiliently dangerous dominant framework of blood authority and a community's deployment of blood as a means to write themselves back into indigenous authority through the scientific reification of blood (and its undisputed, naturalized circulation today). John explains what a Hawaiian is not:

> You cannot just be from Hawai'i. Living there for years. Living on state land. But . . . it is about originally being Hawaiian and how much you are. Myself. I am half Hawaiian, half haole. The Hawaiian blood part distinguishes you, what you can genealogically trace as living proof. I see too many . . . they say they *Kanaka* cuz live there. And that is just not true. At one point, can tel' by home. Or by Church . . . the religion one went to. After years, so many missionaries and visitors stayed here and we let them. Now, today, the only way you can know if da guy next to you is Hawaiian, is by blood amount . . . you know, the *koko*. . . . You know, everyone goin' know their blood amount. You have to these days. Hawaiians about what is here (pounds on chest). Anyone can act like one *Kanaka*

(Hawaiian)—right, you could fish like one, weave, dance the most difficult hula, know the *'olelo* (language). plenty haole, guys from Hawai'i, act like *Kanaka*, but no more the blood. So cannot truly be. But it is our way to still share what we can.

Here John argues that blood amount differentiates the true Hawaiians from the false ones (the state residents and locals who claim to be "Hawaiian."). He specifies how the historical recognition of "Hawaiianness" changed as a result of foreign contact, Western religion, and tourism. In the end, then, only blood amount stands out as the real identifying factor. Although blood amount is associated with names, certificates, and racial (physical) essence, John implicitly delimits these as belonging to a particular group— Hawaiians. A group that he claims is not enacted; it just "is." Acting like a "Hawaiian" (dancing, speaking the language) does not necessarily make a person a "Hawaiian." Rather, John suggests that acting like a "Hawaiian" is easily taken up and learned. Thus, cultural enactment can be deceptive. Identity actions can indeed deceive us, but "Hawaiianness" *takes more than performance.* From John's earlier comments, it is clear that it takes the naturalized authority of blood, which he brings about through speech and is strengthened through the scientific image and rhetorical leverage of blood. He uses state-originated blood quanta to redefine who is not "Hawaiian" against a public sentiment of claiming everyone is.

The diasporic identity discourse reveals a performativity of identity that uses the scientific realism of a blood representation politically. Kondo (1996) explains that

> "realism" itself must be problematized and opened to the play of historically and culturally specific power relations. The speaker's position, the intended audience, the stakes, and the larger discursive fields of history and power through which meanings are constituted are not mere "contexts" that nuance an essentialized meaning; rather, these are essential in determining the political weight of any narrative strategy. (p. 109)

Thus, as the sociopolitical context reproduces and widely distributes a "Hawaiian" identity claim for state residents and to visiting tourists, the Hawaiian identity discourse described here relies on a scientific classification for its presumed authority and discursive leverage to make real a more exclusive and privatized Hawaiian identity, authentic cultural voice, and authority. In this way, Hawaiians will ensure that they continue to authorize their names, experiences, and identities in relation to the signifying power of blood. Resituating blood quantum as a layered performativity, filled with

dominant encodings and challenging reconstitutions, suggests that a Hawaiian social subject can indeed be remade.

IMPLICATIONS

In the alliance with Hawaiians at home, diasporic Hawaiians work hard to authenticate their identity via the resignification of "home," "tradition," and "blood." They have created identity discourses that speak to the politics of authenticity within the struggle over defining "native" or "sovereign" Hawaiian identity. Mainland Hawaiians have contested the notion that they must be living on the land to be Hawaiian (a central claim made by the sovereignty movement) and that being Hawaiian away from Hawai'i is culturally empty (or assimilated). Consequently, their identity discourses reveal how signifiers can be remade to speak to new circumstances and changing politics. For diasporic Hawaiians, authenticity therefore becomes a relational discourse between a collective memory of what it means to be Hawaiian; the politicized debates over native belonging, residency, and blood amount; and a strong connection with cultural and historical memories of Hawai'i.

This analysis of diasporic identity and the politics of authenticity carries several implications for intercultural communication studies. First, intercultural scholars can benefit from attention to the unique subjectivity of diasporic cultures as groups that live in between collective memories, homeland politics, and the politics of their new locales. In fact, the discourses between homeland cultures and their diasporic counterparts can be analyzed for the types of connections and differences created within the larger cultural group but within different contexts and needs. Thus, diasporic cultures can deepen our understanding of specific cultural groups, such as Europeans in the United States, African Americans, Latinos, Asians, and Asian Americans, and the changing nature of their identities both in the homeland and in the diaspora due to complex homeland-diaspora relationships.

Second, the politics of authenticity may be examined in terms of cultural identity discourses and with regard to the unique contexts of diasporic subjectivities. The field's interest in cultural identity and the communication practices of identity can be enriched by analyzing how identity discourses and the politics of authenticity grow more complicated in light of increasing migrations and settlements of diasporic groups. The questions now revolve around: Who is a member of the group? How is membership defined? By whom? In what circumstances and context of the cultural

group? The latter questions indicate that our focus on identity should consider the contextual changes and migration patterns of culture and how this significantly restructures the process of identity formation and expression.

Finally, analyzing the alliances between homeland and diasporic cultures in terms of the politics of authenticity will also enable scholars to explore how identity signifiers from dominant discourses can be remade by cultural groups, and especially diasporic groups, to speak to new conditions and changing political moments. Diasporic groups may creatively recombine and reshape (within limits) dominant meanings to speak to the unique nature of their identities. Thus, a focus on the intercultural and/or intracultural alliances and tensions created between homeland and diasporic cultures can shed light on the relationship between cultural identity, context, politics, and communication discourses of identity and authenticity.

NOTES

1. See Halualani (1997) for an analysis of Hawaiian sovereignty rhetoric.
2. See Fernandez (1993) on sovereignty.
3. See Halualani (in press).
4. *Haole* is a Hawaiian term originally meaning "foreigner." Through vernacular discourse, it has come to mean a "white," "Caucasian," American, or English person (Pukui & Elbert, 1986). The term *haole* is also significantly different from a *local* identity position (see Okamura, 1994; Yamamoto, 1979).

REFERENCES

Alasuutari, P. (1995). *Researching culture: Qualitative method and cultural studies.* London: Sage.

Anderson, B. (1998). Nationalism, identity, and the world-in-motion: On the logics of seriality. In P. Cheah & B. Robbins (Eds.), *Cosmopolitics: Thinking and feeling beyond the nation* (pp. 117-133). Minneapolis: University of Minnesota Press.

Barman, J. (1995). New land, new lives: Hawaiian settlement in British Columbia. *Hawaiian Journal of History, 29,* 1-32.

Blundell, V., Shepherd, J., & Taylor, I. (1993). *Relocating cultural studies: Developments in theory and research.* London: Routledge.

Butler, J. (1990). *Gender trouble: Feminism and the subversion of identity.* New York: Routledge.

Butler, J. (1995). For a careful reading. In S. Benhabib, J. Butler, D. Cornell, & N. Fraser (Eds.), *Feminist contentions* (pp. 127-144). New York: Routledge.

Clifford, J. (1997). Diasporas. In J. C. Clifford (Ed.), *Routes: Travel and translation in the late twentieth century* (pp. 244-278). Cambridge, MA: Harvard University Press.

Conner, W. (1986). The impact of homelands upon diasporas. In G. Sheffer (Ed.), *Modern diasporas in international politics* (pp. 16-46). London: Croom Helm.

Drzewiecka, J. A., & Halualani, R. T. (2002). The structural-cultural dialectic of diasporic politics. *Communication Theory, 12* (3).

Fernandez, Y. (1993, August 29). Mainland Hawaiians: Out of sight and out of rights. *The Honolulu Advertiser,* pp. A1, A6.

Giddens, A. (1990). *The consequences of modernity.* Cambridge, UK: Polity.

Goldberg, D. T. (1993). *Racist culture: Philosophy and the politics of meaning.* Oxford, UK: Blackwell.

Goldberg, D. T. (1997). Taking stock: Counting by race. In D. T. Goldberg (Ed.), *Racial subjects: Writing on race in America* (pp. 27-58). New York: Routledge.

Grossberg, L. (1992). *We gotta get out of this place: Popular conservatism and post-modern culture.* New York: Routledge.

Grossberg, L. (1993). Cultural studies and/in new worlds. *Critical Studies in Mass Communication, 10,* 1-22.

Grossberg, L. (1996). History, politics and postmodernism: Stuart Hall and cultural studies. In D. Morley & K. Chen (Eds.), *Stuart Hall: Critical dialogues in cultural studies* (pp. 151-173). London: Routledge.

Grossberg, L. (1997). *Bringing it all back home: Essays on cultural studies.* Durham, NC: Duke University Press.

Hall, S. (1980a). Cultural studies: Two paradigms. *Media, Culture & Society 2*(1), 57-72.

Hall, S. (1980b). Encoding, decoding. In S. Hall, D. Hobson, A. Lowe, & P. Willis (Eds.), *Culture, media, language* (pp. 128-139). London: Hutchinson.

Hall, S. (1990). Cultural identity and diaspora. In J. Rutherford (Ed.), *Identity: Community, culture, difference* (pp. 222-237). London: Lawrence & Wishart.

Halualani, R. T. (1997). A sovereign nation's functional mythic discourses. In A. Gonzalez & D. V. Tanno (Eds.), *Intercultural and International Communication Annual: Vol. 20. Political Communication Across Cultures* (pp. 89-121). Thousand Oaks, CA: Sage.

Halualani, R. T. (1998). *Communicatively signifying identity positions by, for, and in the name of Hawaiians: A cultural studies project.* Unpublished doctoral dissertation. Arizona State University.

Halualani, R. T. (2000). Rethinking "ethnicity" as structural-cultural project(s): Notes on the interface between cultural studies and intercultural communication. *International Journal of Intercultural Relations, 24,* 579-602.

Halualani, R. T. (2002). *In the name of Hawaiians: Native identities and cultural politics.* Minneapolis: University of Minnesota Press.

Hawaiian Voices on Sovereignty. (1993). He Alo A He Alo: *Face to face.* Honolulu: The Hawaii Area Office of the American Friends Service Committee.

Hitch, T. (1991). *Islands in transition: The past, present, and future of Hawai'i's economy.* Honolulu: First Hawaiian Bank.

Hoggart, R. (1957). *The uses of literacy.* Harmondsworth, UK: Penguin.

'I'i, J. P. (1959). *Fragments of Hawaiian history* (Mary Kawena Pukui, Trans.). Honolulu: Bishop Museum Press.

Johnson, R. (1987). What is cultural studies anyway? *Social Text, 16,* 38-80.

Kame'eleihiwa, L. (1992). *Native land and foreign desires: Pehea La E Pono Ai?* Honolulu: Bishop Museum Press.

Katriel, T. (1997). *Performing the past: A study of Israeli settlement museums.* Mahwah, NJ: Lawrence Erlbaum.

Kauanui, J. K. (1999). Off-Island Hawaiians "Making" ourselves at "Home": A [gendered] contradiction in terms? *Women's Studies International Forum, 21*(6), 681-693.

Kim, Y. (1977). Communication patterns of foreign immigrants in the process of acculturation. *Human Communication Research, 4*(1), 66-77.

Kim, Y. (1979). Toward an interactive theory of communication-acculturation. In B. Ruben(Ed.), *Communication yearbook 3* (pp. 435-453). New Brunswick, NJ: Transaction.

Kim, Y., & Gudykunst, W. (Eds.). (1988). *Cross-cultural adaptation: Current theory and research.* Newbury Park, CA: Sage.

Kondo, D. (1996). The narrative production of "home": Community, and political identity in Asian American theater." In S. Lavie & T. Swedenburg (Eds.), Displacement, diaspora, and geographies of identity (pp. 97-117). Durham, NC: Duke University Press.

Kraidy, M. M. (1999). The global, the local, the hybrid: A native ethnography of globalization. *Critical Studies in Mass Communication, 16,* 456-476.

Laclau, E. (1977). *Politics and ideology in Marxist theory.* London: New Left.

Laclau, E., & Mouffe, C. (1985). *Hegemony and socialist strategy: Towards a radical democratic politics* (W. Moore & P. Cammack, Trans.). London: Verso.

Lavie, S., & Swedenburg, T. (1996). Introduction: Displacement, diaspora, and geographies of identity. In S. Lavie & T. Swedenburg (Eds.), *Displacement, diaspora, and geographies of identity* (pp 1-25). Durham, NC: Duke University Press.

MacKenzie, M. A. (1991). *Native Hawaiian rights handbook.* Honolulu: Native Hawaiian Legal Corporation and Office of Hawaiian Affairs.

Malo, D. (1951). *Hawaiian antiquities* (N. B. Emerson, Trans.) in 1898. Honolulu: Bishop Museum Press.

Office of Hawaiian Affairs. (1996). *Native Hawaiian data book.* Honolulu: Office of Hawaiian Affairs Research Study.

Okamura, J. Y. (1994). Why there are no Asian Americans in Hawai'i: The continuing significance of local identity. *Social Process in Hawaii, 35,* 161-178.

Panagakos, A. N. (1998). Citizens of the trans-nation: Political mobilization, multiculturalism, and nationalism in the Greek diaspora. *Diaspora, 7,* 53-73.

Pukui, M. K., & Elbert, S. H. (1986). *Hawaiian dictionary.* Honolulu: University of Hawaii Press.

Safran, W. (1991). Diasporas in modern societies: Myths of homeland and return. *Diaspora, 1*(1), 83-99.

Sheffer, G. (1986). New field of study: Modern diasporas in international politics. In G. Sheffer (Eds.), *Modern diasporas in international politics* (pp. 1-15). London: Croom Helm.

Shome, R. (1996). Postcolonial interventions in the rhetorical canon: An "other" view. *Communication Theory, 6*(1), 40-59.

Slack, J. D. (1996). The theory and method of articulation in cultural studies. In D. Morley & K. H. Chen (Eds.), *Stuart Hall: Critical dialogues in cultural studies* (pp. 112-127). London: Routledge.

Spradley, J. P. (1979). *The ethnographic interview.* Fort Worth, TX: Harcourt Brace Jovanovich.

Spradley, J. P. (1980). *Participant observation.* New York: Holt, Rinehart & Winston.

TenBruggencate, J. (2001, January 7). "The state of the Hawaiian." *The Honolulu Advertiser,* pp. 1-2.

Thompson, E. P. (1968). *The making of the English working class.* Harmondsworth, UK: Penguin.

Tölölyan, K. (1996). Rethinking diaspora(s): Stateless power in the transnational moment. *Diaspora, 5*(1), 3-36.

Trask, H. K. (1993). *From a Native daughter: Colonialism and sovereignty in Hawai'i.* Monroe, ME: Common Courage.

Turner, G. (1992). *British cultural studies: An introduction.* New York: Routledge.

U.S. Census. (2000). *Population documents for Native Hawaiians alone.* Washington, DC: Census Publications.

Weider, D. L., & Pratt, S. (1990). On being a recognizable Indian among Indians. In D. Carbaugh (Ed.), *Cultural communication and intercultural contact* (pp. 45-64). Hillsdale, NJ: Lawrence Erlbaum.

Williams, R. (1958). *Culture and society: 1780-1950.* Harmondsworth, UK: Penguin.

Wong (Lau), K. (1998). Migration across generations: Whose identity is authentic? In J. N. Martin, T. K. Nakayama, & L. A. Flores (Eds.), *Readings in cultural contexts* (pp. 127-134). Mountain View, CA: Mayfield.

Wright, P. (1983). Ethnic difference in the outmigration of local born residents from Hawaii. *Social Process in Hawaii, 30,* 731-750.

Yamamoto, E. (1979). The significance of "local." *Social Process in Hawaii, 27,* 101-115.

10

Bridging Theory and Cultural Politics

Revisiting the Indigenization-Poststructuralism Debates in Filipino and Filipino American Struggles for Identity

S. LILY MENDOZA • *University of Denver*

The rise of deconstructive and poststructuralist theorizing in the West, along with its transnational export to other academies around the world, presents an interesting challenge for intercultural communication scholars. Within the field, the turn toward "post" theorizing is hailed as the likely wave of the future in intercultural theorizing (see Martin & Nakayama, 1999). In this regard, a number of critical scholars (Collier, 1998; Drzewiecka, 2000; Drzewiecka & Nakayama, 1998; Drzewiecka & Wong (Lau),1999; Halualani, 2002; Mendoza, 2001a, 2001b, 2002; and Nakayama & Martin, 1999, among others) recognize its strategic importance in terms of offering the opportunity to examine critically the politics undergirding our theorizing practices in intercultural communication. As Nakayama (cited in Collier, Hegde, Lee, Nakayama, & Yep, 2001) proposes:

> We should be attentive to the ways in which intercultural communication has, in some ways, served the interests of white U.S. Americans. . . . If we do not bring this sensitivity to the project of intercultural communication, then we risk serving a more traditional strand in (social) scientific research that—unwittingly or not—services the needs of imperialism, colonialism, and sometimes white racial politics. (p. 223)

Toward this end (of undoing or avoiding the unwitting complicity of theory with exploitative politics), Nakayama sounds the call for

self-reflexivity by encouraging scholars in the field to "take a postcolonial turn" in their theorizing of intercultural communication (p. 223). Indeed, one of the acknowledged contributions of the "post" theory discourses, notably, postmodernism, postcolonialism, and poststructuralism, is their serving as an important critique of the oppressiveness of Western logocentrism and its foundationalist metaphysics. These discourses reject the assumptions of a transcendental, autonomous Cartesian subject; the stability of meaning; and the unity, coherence, and determinacy of knowledge. As such, they open up possibilities of other ways of knowing previously consigned to the margins or denied legitimacy altogether (see Butler, 1990; Harvey, 1989; Jameson, 1991; Lyotard, 1993; Sarup, 1989, 1996; Schwarz & Ray, 2000; Young, 2001).

At the same time, however, such a turn to "post" theorizing has not been without its critics among scholars working within and outside the field of intercultural communication (see Dirlik, 1997; Mendoza, 2001b, 2002; Parry, 1987; Shohat, 1996; Thiong'o, 1986; and Warren, 1998, among others). Hartsock (1987), for example, sounds a common concern:

> Somehow it seems highly suspicious that it is at this moment in history, when so many groups are engaged in [reclaiming their past and remaking their future in their own terms] . . . that doubt arises in the academy about the nature of the "subject," about the possibilities for a general theory which can describe the world, about historical "progress." Why is it, exactly at the moment when so many of us who have been silenced begin to demand the right to name ourselves, to act as subjects rather than objects of history, that just then the concept of subjecthood becomes "problematic"? Just when we are forming our own theories about the world, uncertainty emerges about whether the world can be adequately theorized. (p. 196)

Such complaint as voiced by Hartsock suggests the link being made between theorizing and the enabling or constraining of agency, that is, the potential implications that the turn to deconstructive theorizing might have for those who might be differently positioned vis-à-vis the debates. At the same time, the phenomena of ethnic resurgence and ethnic absolutisms, along with the rise of cultural nationalisms witnessed in the latter half of the last century, raise concern as to the dangers of essentialist identity politics (deemed inherent in all such movements). Indeed, the problematic of the purchase of essentialist versus anti-essentialist cultural politics, often framed as a strict binarism, is one that has vigorously exercised scholars in various fields (see, e.g., Butler, 1990, 1995; Fuss, 1989; Gilroy, 1997; Goldberg, 2000; Hall, 1996a, 1996b; Spivak, 1996; Weaver, 2000; Werbner &

Modood, 1997; Woodward, 1997), with the more thoughtful of them invariably ending up arguing for a more complex and nonreductive framing of the debates. In this chapter, I offer my own take on this problematic from a communication perspective. What I hope to do is a "bridging work"—one that avoids an *a priori* valorizing of one position over the other in a kind of generic, generalized way and instead proposes a careful examining of the politics fueling each form of identity invocation. My goal is to help keep the dynamic of such movements open and open to critical (self-)interrogation. In performing this bridging work, I seek to engage the debates on two levels: (1) on the level of theory, between the camps of scholars on either side of the debates; and (2) on the level of practical cultural politics, right where theory meets politics on the ground. For a concrete context for this study, I look at the ongoing transnational debates surrounding the construction of national "identity" between and among Filipinos in the homeland and Filipino Americans in the North American diaspora. More specifically, I propose to examine the theoretical tensions between the discourse of indigenization, on the one hand, and that of deconstructive and poststructuralist theorizing, on the other. Mainly, I will seek to argue, by way of proposing an alternative approach to the polarization of the debates, for a communicative reframing of these two theoretical positions not as inherent epistemological incommensurabilities but as a communication problem, one requiring dynamic translation and adequate contextualization. Toward this end, I propose to underscore: (1) the contingent nature of theories and the need for radical contextualization in their invocation across cultures, contexts, and locations; (2) the context of power as indispensable to the project of theorizing cultural politics; and (3) the relevance of translation in the overall task of theorizing across cultures and contexts.

My own position in the debates, to engage in necessary self-reflexivity here, is one that I acknowledge I owe equally to both theoretical traditions. To the indigenization movement in the University of the Philippines,[1] I owe my initiation into critical theorizing previously unknown to me, having been schooled mostly in the received knowledge coming out of a largely Western liberal system of education that was a legacy of the American colonial experiment in the Philippines at the turn of the 20th century. On the other hand, coming to graduate school in the United States as a Filipino international student in 1995, I received my first introduction to continental philosophy. This initial encounter with Eurocentric critical theory was exhilarating at first, but proved somewhat problematic later. It was exhilarating because I saw it as providing allies in my process of undoing

the colonial gaze at that point in my journey in the way that deconstructive theorizing effectively imploded the Enlightenment master narratives for me. These narratives were enshrined in the rhetorical trilogy of the "White Man's Burden," "Manifest Destiny," and "Benevolent Assimilation" (see Horsman, 1981; Jordan, 1974; and Miller, 1982) and were bought into by both Filipino and U.S. publics. Together, they effectively formed the basis of U.S. expansionist policy at the turn of the 20th century.

When I began subsequently to articulate a reconstructive cultural history of my own based on the indigenization counternarrative from the homeland, I found myself suddenly, unwittingly, on the other side of the fence from those I had previously thought to be my poststructuralist allies. As it turned out, I would face charges of "nativism," of trafficking in "romanticist illusions" (about an impossible return to mythic origins and imagined roots), and of falling prey to strict "binarisms," and "essentialist politics" that were deemed inherent in all identitarian and communitarian projects (i.e., in the "longing to belong").[2] The oppositional challenge was to have a salutary effect, however, in the way it helped propel and shape the direction of my subsequent work (Mendoza, 2001b, 2002), thus proving the productivity of dialectical challenge in the building of theory. My way out of the split, out of the seeming contradictory and incommensurable demands of reconstructive theorizing in indigenization on the one hand, and of deconstructive theorizing in poststructuralist criticism on the other, is through reframing the tensions—not as substantive epistemological contradictions but as problems of communication. For this, I found helpful the mediation of dynamic translation and radical contextualization as a way of nuancing the application of Eurocentric critical theory across differing contexts and locations.

In what follows, I wish to provide a background to the debates as I engage them here by situating this study's key problematic within a concrete historical context.

THEORIZING FILIPINO AND FILIPINO AMERICAN IDENTITIES: THE ELUSIVE SEARCH FOR SCHOLARLY LEGITIMATION[3]

This is perhaps almost too trite an observation to make, but if there is one theme that has obsessed Filipino and Filipino American scholars alike for decades, it is the quest for recognition, beginning, aptly, with collective self-recognition. A nation of 7,100 islands peopled by an estimated

80 ethnolinguistic communities, the Philippines (as is the case with any other social order that has undergone the violence of colonization[4]) appears to have had difficulty emerging out of the psychological wreckage and trauma of protracted colonization by Spain (for more than 350 years) and by the United States (for nearly half a century; as a neocolony, for much longer). Filipinos and Filipino Americans alike have been dubbed in various literatures with all kinds of unflattering identity ascriptions. In the Philippines, Filipinos have been called *ang Pilipinong nawawala sa sarili* (the Filipino lost to herself) (Maggay, 1993, Preface), a "country without a soul" (Iyer, 1988, p. 174), and a "damaged culture" (Fallows, 1987). Filipinos have also been accused of suffering from all sorts of cultural malaise (such as an "identity crisis" and "regionalism"[5]). In the United States, Filipino Americans are the "forgotten Asian Americans" (Cordova, 1983), "the New Empire's forgetful and forgotten citizens" (Campomanes, 1995), subject to all kinds of institutional invisibility (Campomanes, 1994), a diasporic mass "in need of a cartography and a geopolitical project" (San Juan, 1997, p. 13). Interestingly enough, these ascriptions are not wholly external but are experienced psychically, daily and collectively, by Filipino Americans in their common lot as a thrice-marginalized ethnic community. First, they are marginalized vis-à-vis the mainstream white majority; second, they are marginalized vis-à-vis the larger Asian community; and third, they are marginalized (still) vis-à-vis their own (internalized) racist ideological reckoning of themselves in the aftermath of U.S. neocolonialism in the Philippines (see Bonus, 2000; Strobel, 1996, 2001).

In a national life where the *doxa* is that of a racialized colonial ideology, assimilation becomes the only logical mode of survival (or so it seems). Whether in the case of Filipinos in the Philippines growing up dreaming of "snow," "a white Christmas," and someday being able to "go to Disneyland or live forever in the land flowing with milk and honey,"[6] or of Filipino Americans frantically erasing traces of their otherness by unlearning their native accents, erasing their past, denying their ethnic background, or simply acting white, internalized racism, for many centuries, served as the naturalized defining condition of the Filipino. A curious psychological state, I refer to it elsewhere as a form of "reverse ethnocentrism" ([Mendoza]-Silva, 1995)—a phenomenon akin to W.E. B. Du Bois's (1901/1961) notion of "double consciousness," "this sense of always looking at one's self through the eyes of others, of measuring one's soul by the tape of a world that looks on in amused contempt and pity" (p. 16).

On June 12, 1998, the Philippines celebrated its first centennial of independence. It was on the same date in 1898 that a Filipino revolutionary

government inaugurated what was to be the first-ever republic to be established in Asia—this, upon defeating the Spanish forces in a nationwide uprising that finally ended close to four centuries of Spanish colonial rule in the Philippines. Although the fledgling republic was not to enjoy substantive independence until half a century later (the United States at that point having decided to take over Spain's role as the Philippines' new colonial master), nationalist leaders insisted on marking June 12, 1898 as the Philippines' official date of independence. This act was politically strategic. In rejecting July 4, 1946—the date of the U.S. official "grant" of independence to the islands—as its date of independence, the Philippine government aimed to underscore the point that when the United States invaded the Philippines at the turn of the 20th century, it was in effect invading a sovereign nation. This is because, except for a few remaining Spanish strangleholds in the city of Manila, the Filipino revolutionaries, by the time the United States came onto the scene, had all but virtually routed the Spanish army.

I make this historical reference here to make the point that by the time the United States mounted its most brutal attack on Filipinos,[7] the *doxa* of European racist assimilation had already been effectively exploded by a countrywide revolution that wrested Filipinos' freedom from centuries of Spanish domination. Thus, when the United States, which at first had masqueraded as champion and ally of all oppressed peoples of the world, turned around and invaded the Philippines and claimed it for its territorial possession—against the abject wishes of its native population—it was only logical that Filipinos deemed it the most dastardly act of betrayal. Determined to keep their hard-won freedom, Filipinos fought a protracted suicidal war against the occupying army that lasted about a decade into U.S. colonial rule. However, by the arrival of what Elliot (cited in Constantino, 1977) referred to as the United States' "second army of occupation" (p. 126), that is, the army of U.S. civilian administrators, Thomasites,[8] Protestant missionaries, and Peace Corps volunteers, the campaign strategically shifted onto the ideological terrain. Saturating the fabric of the nation's educational system with white racial ideology, racist assimilation once again resumed its hegemonic hold in the islands. So effective and total was the ideological triumph of alleged white American racial superiority and its "benevolent civilizing mission" that for subsequent decades, the brutal memory of the Filipino-American war was all but virtually wiped out from the national memory."[9] Textbooks, written mostly from the victor's perspective, installed in its place the glowing myth of a "special relationship" between the United States and the Philippines. As Francisco (1976) would note, "One price of victory is that the winners get to write the

history books" (p. 1). A discourse deployed in the popular imagination through various means of colonial propaganda, it effectively reconstructed the image of the United States from that of a villain, foe, and ruthless conqueror to that of a "faithful friend," "ally," and virtual "savior" (see Constantino, 1977; Ileto, 1998). Brief as the U.S. occupation may have been compared to Spain's protracted regime, because of its systematic ideological inscription in the educational system via the very instruments of knowing, U.S. American colonialism in the end seems to have marked the Filipino psyche in far more lasting ways, if not more insidiously. Thus, for decades to come, the undoing of this colonial "romance" with the United States was to become an all-consuming nationalist project.[10] Colonial domination having been effectively secured through the installation of a colonial system of education, the academy became the logical site for critical contestation and intervention by Filipino nationalist intellectuals.

An important tradition that arose out of this decolonization imperative is the indigenization movement in the Philippine academy. Its purported goal is to seek to form a national(ist) discourse on civilization separate from the West. A collaborative endeavor spanning decades and various disciplines, it has endeavored to undertake what Fanon (1963) refers to as "a passionate search for national culture" (p. 209). Comprised of several strands of interdisciplinary narratives, this project envisions the work of nationhood as of necessity beginning with the revision of theory as the very instrument of knowing. At the core of the movement's anticolonialist thrust is an attempt to deconstruct centuries of colonial Western epistemological legacy. This it has aimed to accomplish through a rejection of the premises of the West and a rethinking of theorizing practices in the academic disciplines. Meant to be a massive cultural reclamation project, it is designed to recover (read: uncover) "indigenous" ways of knowing and being. This project began with the early works of Filipino anthropologists reconstructing Philippine prehistory and culture and positing an "organic" nation; the works of Filipino linguistic philosophers asserting a distinct indigenous Filipino philosophy; those of Filipino psychologists retheorizing "the" Filipino "personality" and challenging the universalist assumptions of a Western-oriented psychology; and the perspectives of Filipino historians that undertook a complete rewriting of Philippine history. More contemporary developments in Philippine studies include the programmatic trilogy of *Sikolohiyang Pilipino* (liberation psychology), *Pantayong Pananaw* (proposing a new ethnocentered framework for Philippine historiography), and *Pilipinolohiya* (a newly emergent discourse on civilization intended to serve as an indigenously conceived academic discipline).

An important strand in this multiple discourse on indigenization (i.e., *Sikolohiyang Pilipino*) found its way into the Filipino American scholarly community in the early 1990s through the work of one of its movement pioneers, University of the Philippines professor Virgilio Enriquez, who came to Northern California on a stint as a visiting professor at University of California, Berkeley. Although social activist movements were not unknown within the Filipino American community prior to that point, the new discourse on indigenization provided a language with which many Filipino American student groups could now articulate their newfound sense of connection to a (forgotten) native land. Thus began what was later dubbed the "Born-Again Filipino" movement, which adopted "the" Filipino indigenous experience as the new interpretive principle in its worldview and practice of everyday life, and launched careers in the academy by inspiring Filipino American students to enter graduate school where, before, this was virtually unheard of (Strobel, 1996). The transforming impact of that first-time cultural encounter with a lost past through the power of discourse gave a tremendous boost to second, third, and fourth generation American-born Filipino Americans whose prior assimilationist orientation had earned for the community the unflattering title, "the invisible minority" (Campomanes, 1995).

This budding movement, however, was not to be accorded validation among the more established and prominent Filipino American postcolonial scholars.[11] The latter's criticism of what they considered the movement's "dubious methodology" and "spurious theorizing" premised on "essentialist" assumptions about Filipino "culture" and "identity"[12] kept them from taking it seriously as a legitimate intellectual tradition. This lack of engagement with the more mature U.S.-based Filipino scholars, who were steeped in the discourses of Eurocentric critical cultural theory, appears to have stymied the theoretical project of indigenization in the United States, owing to the movement's consequent failure to cast the discourse in a theoretical language compatible with the current "post" theory trajectory of the debates in U.S. academe and thereby gain scholarly legitimation. This is in contrast to its activist dimension, which to this day, continues to win converts among the young.[13] Meanwhile, its parent counterpart movement in the Philippines, along with the other strands of the indigenization narrative, appears to thrive. Currently moving in new directions, it seems to have gained a tremendous influence on Filipino popular culture, as evidenced by reported demands from industry, business, media, and advertising companies for *Sikolohiyang Pilipino* knowledge and expertise (see Mendoza, 2002).

Today, however, it appears that developments elsewhere in the world have once again overtaken the national(ist) agenda. Barely making it onto the national scene in belated celebration of nationhood, Filipinos, at the end of the 20th century, found foisted on them a claim of an impending global postnational scenario.[14] Here, once again, one finds obscured the uneven processes of political development in what some regard as mostly a Western-led, Western-centered deployment of globalization discourses. With the decreasing importance of the "nation-state" and its growing displacement as the traditional linchpin of earlier forms of globalization, the "nation" as an identity category is said to be fast losing its currency and naturalness as its borders undergo redefinition, challenge, and redrawing (see Hall, 1997a, 1997b). Scholars such as Gilroy (1997), Goldberg (2000), and Hall (1996a, 1996c) claim that, as a result, hybridization is now the norm without exception for all national communities.

In view of these acknowledged significant global developments, Filipino scholars in the homeland and in the diaspora—such as Diokno (1997), Pertierra (1995), and Tolentino (2001), among others—have become keenly aware of the inadequacy of old theoretical models for theorizing the global moment. Indeed, they are becoming increasingly persuaded that traditional models of decolonization that turn on projects of indigenization are no longer tenable for theorizing contemporary national realities. Criticisms range from finding such models "vulgar" and counting on an impossible return to illusory nativist beginnings to charges of anachronism, essentialism, ethnic chauvinism, and imposing false homogeneity on what in fact have always been multiethnic populations (Mendoza, 2002). Convinced of the productivity of the discourses of Eurocentric critical theory, notably postmodernism, poststructuralism, and postcolonialism, this new breed of Filipino and Filipino American scholars adopts and advocates instead a normative deconstructive mode in their theorizing.

In the United States, this deconstructive theoretical trajectory has proven productive for the struggles of Filipino Americans in many respects. For example, it has succeeded in surfacing the submerged history of U.S. imperialism heretofore denied in mainstream historiography, which previously admitted only to a U.S. "diplomatic" history (Campomanes, 1994). Likewise, the renarrativization of Philippine and Filipino American histories from a deconstructive perspective has succeeded in unmasking racist U.S. policies directed against Filipinos and Filipino Americans, such as those inscribed in the legal discourses of antimiscegenation laws and the manipulation of Filipino immigrant quotas in the early 1900s (Cordova, 1983; Melendy, 1967). Such oppositional narratives, to name only a few, are today giving

Filipino Americans a basis for reevaluating their former colonial and assimilationist loyalties. What is approached with a certain ambivalence, however, is the matter of how to *constructively* theorize the expressive forms of culture in the attempt to put substance to the performativity of identity, "history-making, counter-memory, and nationalist- and community-form[ation]" (Gonzalves, 1998, p. 36). Having rejected essentialism, scholars such as Gonzalves admit to the complexities of knowing how to read, for example,

re-invented traditions of "indigenous" martial arts, the study of languages and pre-European syllabaries, the consumption of history and literary texts, the extrinsic marking of cultural authenticity through sartorial signification (woven bags, backpacks, amulets, etc.), and the theatricalization of Philippine dance and popular narrative. (p. 36)

Gonzaves is quick to offer a disclaimer (almost admitting to a certain embarrassment) saying, "The possibility that such strategies are prone to essentializing Philippine and Filipina/o American cultures has not escaped me" (p. 36), which is clearly indicative of the influence of the canonical discourse of deconstructionism that demands that all cultural readings and interpretations answer to its scrutiny. Likewise, San Juan (1998b), reflecting on the fact that what he calls "revisions of orthodoxy" have yet to impact on the sedimented ethnographic and historical descriptions of "the" Filipino in U.S. "Filipinology," notes in this regard, "Shying away from fixities, generalizations, and stereotypes, we end up ironically with a conundrum, perhaps a postmodern riddle" (p. 3). Then, quoting Gochenour's wry observation of "a general sense of [Filipinos] being neither this nor that, of sharing something of the Pacific Islands, of being heavily influenced by Spanish and American cultures, and of perceiving only a remote historical relationship with the major civilizations of Asia," he underscores the enormity of the task: "As simple as it may seem, this business of identifying and validating 'ourselves' is a formidable challenge" (p. 3).

Gonzalves (1997) discusses this conundrum within the tradition of the "Pilipino Cultural Night" (PCN)[15] and shows the difficult challenge of making (nonessentialist) cultural representations. In the piece, Gonzalves interrogates the PCN as a performance genre, noting its use as "part of the labor to recover parts of ourselves" through the constitution, through song, dance, and narration of "insurrectionist knowledges" (pp. 166-167). It is also a "historiographical intervention [involving an active editing] tak[ing] place amid thousands of learned academic writings that have constructed images,

paradigms, and notions about Filipinos and Filipino Americans as lazy natives, little brown brothers, fawning tutees of American democracy, and so on" (p. 166), as well as a strategic "rhetorical device for denoting a decentered notion of 'America' . . . decentered from Europe as its sole author" (pp. 170-171). Finally, PNC is read as a strategically essentialized, problematic, commodified production of entertainment, yet "with contingency, transgression, [and] testimony" and, from another notion of entertainment, as "*reception*—welcoming and harboring . . . [and doing] more than simply keep one busy . . . [but allowing] some time for laughter, tragedy, surprise, and wonder—for entertaining ourselves" (pp. 180-181).

It is from such a complex, conflicted history that there arises the need to theorize anew, and in more adequate and compelling ways, the attempts at cultural self-reclamation of such historically marginalized communities. And the challenge is to do so in ways that capture the difficult dynamics of the process across transnational and cultural lines and contexts.

PUTTING ESSENTIALISM INTO MOTION: A POSTSTRUCTURALIST PROJECT

Scholars with some sympathy for the cause of indigenization (including this author) have not all been remiss in taking cognizance of the danger of essentialism as a potential pitfall in all such cultural reclamation movements (e.g., Dirlik, 1997; Hall, 1996a; Parry, 1987; Shohat, 1996; Thiong'o, 1986; Warren, 1998; and Weaver, 2000). To the extent that the formation of a reconstructed group or communal identity becomes more a matter of boundary keeping and less a matter of survival, it is in danger of devolving into another exclusionary and repressive regime (Mendoza, 2002, pp. 3-7). Indeed, this kind of exclusionary politics is evident in all attempts to search for a putatively "authentic," "purified" identity, such as can be found in the dynamic of ethnic cleansings, exclusions, and fratricidal wars currently raging in various parts of the world, including the United States.[16]

However, to thus automatically assume a continuous logic between the imperative of cultural reclamation projects such as the movement for indigenization, on the one hand, and such extreme forms of ethnic exclusions and absolutisms, on the other, is to be guilty of flattening out diversely complex phenomena into a singular reductive logic. My own proposal is for a careful nuancing of theory and a calibrating of its application across contexts, or, to borrow Rosaldo's (1989/1992) phrase, to find a way of "putting

into motion" (p. 91) our reading of cultural politics. The goal is to intervene, through theorizing, in the momentum of such processes of identity formation to keep them from foreclosing. As such, it behooves would-be critical intercultural theorists to gain a better sense of such groups' inner dynamic, beyond the automatic ascribing of "nativism," "reverse stereotyping," or "bankrupt essentialist politics" at the first sight or sign of their outward, surface politics, the latter practice being what Hall (1981) refers to as "intellectual terrorism" (p. 380). This imperative is all the more crucial given that essentialism remains, concededly, the default mode of the popular imagination.[17] How to engage essentialist logic differently to perchance move it toward a more open-ended form of politics is the challenge I see in this striving for a different way of theorizing cultural politics.

TRANSLATION AND THE READING OF CULTURAL POLITICS

A few theoretical insights from linguistic translation and communication studies that I wish to propose in this regard have to do with making some needed theoretical moves, notably, recognizing (1) the primacy of process over static categorical descriptions, (2) the nondeterminate relationship between signifier and signified and between structure and agency or consciousness, (3) context (in particular, the context of power) as the primary determinant of meaning versus the mere formalistic correspondence of forms in cultural and political strategies, and (4) freedom and resistance (as well as the drive toward either coherence/stability or change) as defined always in dialectical tension and relation to whatever is the dominating element in any ideological and/or social formation. I derived these principles from my synthesis of a number of perspectives from linguistic and communication studies, and I discuss them briefly in what follows.

One perspective that informs my reading of cultural politics is the "dynamic equivalence model" of translation. This model departs from the more static conception of linguistic translation known as the "formal correspondence model" (Nida & Taber, 1969). The latter assumes a static conception of languages as merely alternative codes made up of different sets of labels but expressive of the same unchanging reality, a relic of the nominalist, Platonic and Aristotelian view of languages (Steinfatt, 1989). The dynamic equivalence model, on the other hand, offers a more dynamic view of language. Drawing inspiration from the Sapir-Whorf linguistic relativity hypothesis and consistent with Saussurean semiotics (Sapir, 1929; Whorf,

1940), it proposes that linguistic codes are not merely expressive, but *actually constitutive,* of conceptual understandings and meanings in different cultures. As such, they are not mechanically or unproblematically interchangeable between languages, given that "people of different cultures, speaking different languages, are not simply attaching different linguistic labels to elements of the same real world but are actually operating in terms of *different* [linguistic] *realities*" (Kraft, 1979, p. 288).

In the case of dynamic equivalence, exact formalistic correspondence is deemed less the goal of translation than is the striving for approximate equivalence of *functions* and *meanings.* Such is considered desirable even if it is bought at the price of formalistic verisimilitude that is, in any case, seen as an impossible ideal. Thus to translate (or to read) across contexts or cultures requires the mediation of context-sensitive analysis and comprehension of how formal codes are actually functioning within their use in specific epistemic contexts. This is an important element in the translation process since it may very well be that the same signifiers carry entirely different signifieds when employed in different contexts.

As applied to theorizing—and to the theorizing of cultural politics in particular—what the dynamic equivalence model implies is that it is not enough to stop at the surface rhetoric of a movement or its formalistic expressions (e.g., its cultural strategies). Rather, given, for example, a group's outwardly essentialist articulations of identity, one must go on to historicize and identify what functions are being served within the group's overall political agenda—recall Spivak's (1990) notion of "strategic essentialism" (p. 51) and Butler's (1995) "contingent foundations." In other words, rather than assuming automatic correspondence of meanings given the same formalistic codes, one must ask how each code is actually operating or functioning (i.e., signifying) within the context of its particular use. As Hall (1996b) argues, for example, it could very well be that seemingly essentialist invocations are

about questions of using the resources of history, language and culture in the process of becoming rather than being: not "who we are" or "where we came from," so much as what we might become, how we have been represented and how that bears on how we might represent ourselves. (p. 4)

Such caveats come from the recognition that individual codes come in systems and take on meaning only within the signifying system to which they belong.[18] Therefore, extracting them from their source contexts and reading or assessing them from the standpoint of a generalized criterion or a

framework imbues them with other meanings or connotations that may not have been intended in their originary context. For example, concluding that, theoretically speaking, the ethnic cleansing occurring in Bosnia possesses the same dynamics as the indigenization movement in the Philippines, simply because both operate on the same assertion or valuing of (essential) ethnic indigeneity, is a case of such a problematic framing. Ironically, it is possible to apply the discourse of anti-essentialism in an essentialist manner and thereby presume or expect the same end-result of such groups' political momentum: the senseless violence of a fratricidal war. What is missing in this essentializing analysis is a "radical historicization" (or in communication or translation parlance, "radical contextualization") of each phenomenon (Hall, 1996b, p. 4) so that each is understood on its own terms prior to cross-contextual comparison. This alone is what allows for a more dynamic (processual) and less deterministic theoretical linking of the two nationalizing imperatives. Furthermore, using the framework of dynamic equivalence transculturation, we may want to ask: What conditions might be fueling the two movements and are accounting for the persistent invocation of essentialist self-definitions in each particular context? Hall (1996b) proposes that a productive question to ask in this regard might be, "In relation to what set of problems [by way of assessing the function served by the invocation of identity politics within each historicized context] does the *irreducibility* of the concept, identity, emerge?" (p. 2). In other words, what does the invoking of essential identities do for the respective movements and how does it articulate to the movements' emancipatory agenda?

To go back to the example of the indigenization narrative in both Filipino and Filipino American communities, one might, based on this reading, choose to read the deliberate, conscious, and systematic production of reconstructed "histories," "cultures," and "identities" as turning on a range of strategic functions, notably: (1) the effecting of a discursive reversal from a bastardized, degraded, and degrading narrative of subjectivity to one capable of materializing an alternative legitimate human community, or from that of a colonial *object* acted upon to an acting, initiating *subject* of history; (2) the first-time securing of a much-needed separation (albeit in the symbolic realm) from the dominating psychic and epistemic element so that agency can be released from its fixation as "other" or as "othered" self; (3) a first-time coming to representation, through self-naming and self-centering, from historic erasure, invisibility, and marginalization; and (4) communal solidarity as a base for launching effective collective political action (see Mendoza, 2002). The irony of ascribing the label "essentialism" to such a project is that active invention and reimagination,

not "'rediscovery" or literal "recovery," appear to be the norm in its construction.[19] Furthermore, evidence suggests that such cultural constructions and/or reconstructions, at least within the Filipino indigenization narrative, are not deemed given once for all. Although neither totally up for grabs, they appear to be wide open in their process and dynamic to contestation and critical interrogation.[20] Read within the framework of dynamic equivalence, the indigenization narrative, as enacted within Filipino and Filipino American cultural politics, may then be seen as carrying within it possibilities of its own continuing critique through eschewing any form of discursive closure, which is otherwise known to characterize most essentialist politics.[21]

A corollary model to dynamic equivalence translation that I find helpful for the nuancing of the application of deconstructive theory to the reading of cultural politics is what Kraft (1979) calls the "starting-point-plus-process" model of communication (pp. 239-257). Kraft contrasts this model with the "static positioning" model. Inspired by the mathematical distinctions between "(fixed) sets" and "fuzzy sets," Kraft explains:

> What I call here a *positional* basis, or model, corresponds roughly with a mathematical "set," or "fixed set," where positioning within certain borders is determinative for categorizing. What I call a *directional* basis, or model, corresponds roughly with what Zadeh calls a "fuzzy set," where the direction of movement with respect to a given goal is determinative for categorizing. (p. 240)

Conceived specifically with reference to communicating for social advocacy, it is an approach that makes evaluative and/or interpretive judgments on the basis not of where someone or something is *positionally* located at any given point in time but of whether one is moving toward or away from an identified target or objective. In other words, in terms of a starting point, distance from the goal is considered not nearly as important as in *which direction* the movement is ultimately heading.

I think of this model with specific reference to the ways in which identity processes, particularly those within de/colonizing contexts, such as those of Filipinos and Filipino Americans, may be differently read or understood. A vision I have of the politics of (minority) identity (trans)formation in such power-dominated contexts is one that takes essentialism, binarism—"the search for that one 'great refusal,' the singular transformation that somehow must precede and guide all others," "the urge to unity enforced by epistemological closure" (Soja, 1996, pp. 93, 94)—not as a final fixed point but as an often needed psychological starting point for agency. Within

indigenization as an anticolonial reaction, narcissism or the self-obsession that comes from having one's brain "empt[ied] of all form and content" and one's past "distort[ed], disfigure[d] and destroy[ed]" (Fanon, 1963, p. 210) becomes the inevitable effect of colonialism and, in terms of healing it, there seems to be no heroic way around it but to give it what it wants (Moore, 1992).[22] To demand otherwise would be presumptuous, what Tournier (1968) calls a demand for "premature renunciation" or "premature [self-]abdication" (pp. 112-138) that is of the order of formalistic compliance with the requirements of deconstruction without accounting fully for differing contextual needs. Such an approach (to colonial narcissism) is unlikely to lead to any movement toward resolution. It is for this reason that I tend to see such postmodernist notions as "placeless imaginings of identity" (Gilroy, 1997, p. 317), the abandonment of essential categories in favor of a politics of criticism (Hall, 1996c), and the celebration of hybridity and shifting, playful subjectivities as places of privilege—spaces of agency for those who already have secured a measure of place and belonging, but spaces of threat and further disenfranchisement for those still in the phase of narcissistic self-reclamation. Yet one must note that the value of this narcissistic phase is not so much that it would ultimately fulfill the want(ing); quite the contrary, such a relentless pursuit carried to its logical end is bound to prove totally inadequate. Yet it is precisely the reaching of this limit that then prepares one for entry into that difficult place of another kind of politics: the politics of criticism and difference.

Dollimore (cited in Parry, 1987) argues on a slightly different note:

A crucial stage in [the] deconstruction [of binary oppositions] involves an overturning, an inversion. . . . The political effect of ignoring this stage, of trying to jump beyond the hierarchy into a world quite free of it, is simply to leave it intact in the only world we have. Both the reversal of the authentic/inauthentic opposition . . . and the subversion of authenticity itself . . . are different aspects of overturning in Derrida's sense. Moreover, they are stages in a *process* of resistance. (p. 30)

Likewise, Hall (1996c) contends in this regard:

The effect of a theoretical encounter between . . . cultural politics and the discourses of a Eurocentric, largely white, critical cultural theory . . . is always an extremely difficult, if not dangerous, encounter. . . . Once you abandon essential categories, there is no place to go apart from the politics of criticism and to enter the politics of criticism in [any] culture is to grow up, to leave the age of critical innocence. (pp. 443, 448)

One sees this as a pattern of conceptual transformation, as in the case of Black Power movement leader Malcolm X (Diamond, 1994), as well as in the experience of first-generation Filipino writer, labor leader, and pioneer in America, Carlos Bulosan (1946). In both cases, one finds the movement leaders starting from essentialized conceptions of race and racism but then being forced to open up those categories once the signifiers "white" and "colored" started failing to deliver automatically the same signifieds (expected attitudinal or behavioral correlates) every time (e.g., not all the whites encountered were acting like the "enemy" and some of the "colored" people were thinking and behaving "white" rather than identifying with their own kind; De Castro, 1994, pp. 308-311).

This, however, is not to suggest an automatism in the movement from narcissism and essentialism to a politics of difference and criticism. Indeed, what seems evident is that a change in the form of consciousness is a necessary mediating process. Otherwise, without such a conceptual transformation, a denaturalization of essentialized appearances of the contingent and the historical is not all that likely to happen. It is here, in the need to facilitate those agentic interventions in the popular consciousness, that I find important the ability to learn how to "read" (i.e., theorize) with nuanced sensitivity those identity articulations so that one might, where needed, prod them toward a different kind of political engagement.

What is intimated in this way of reading is the need to adopt shifting hermeneutical lenses when looking at identity articulations coming from below rather than coming from above (i.e., ones emanating from a disenfranchised group as compared to ones from the ruling power).[23] In other words, one must learn to read not only dynamically but also dialectically. This is because the form of resistance cannot be essentialized into one normative formalistic expression but always must be defined in dialectical opposition to whatever is the reigning element in the social or ideological formation when considering the relation between the context of power and the politics of identity.

Tabios (in Mendoza, 2002) provides a stark example of this dialectical principle:

It seems as if in the Philippines (where the canon is the western text), incorporating indigenous or ethnic references is part of this attempt not to be colonial . . . versus . . . in the U.S. where in recent decades' history of Asian American poetry, you had Asian American poets like Garrett Hongo, David Mura, etc. arguing for the right of Asian Americans (or any writers of color) to write poems that do not incorporate ethnic references. Kinda like an opposite

position from that in the Philippines because to be in the U.S. means that people of color are "others" and that such other-ness needs to be defined by their cultural roots. . . . Why should a Pinoy poet—especially one who specifically DOES NOT want to have the colonialist mentality—allow his/her poetry to be further victimized by history? (p. 190)

READING DIALECTICALLY: TWO MOVEMENTS, TWO IMPERATIVES

Tournier (1968) speaks of the need for a place of belonging as a vital human need. He remarks, "To exist is to occupy a particular living-space to which one has a right" (p. 25). Thus, he issues the call to give a place to those who have none. And yet, in almost the same breath, he hastens to add, "That is the very rhythm of life. Every place we find must in the end be relinquished, if it is not to become our prison" (p. 147). In seeking productive dialogue between the discourse of indigenization and that of deconstructionism, I suggest that we recognize two dialectical movements. Taking the cue from Tournier, we might think of the first movement as consisting of the will to coherence and stability (i.e., a marking or fixing of one's place in the world). It is a movement borne of the thrust toward securing a certain measure of self-determination. Historically, for instance, to place this discussion within a larger framework, one might see in the discourse of modernity (at least within its originary impetus), the legitimate human desire to wrest agency from external determination and the prison walls of necessity (e.g., science and reason being made to serve as modern Man's[24] weapons against his determination by Nature, Fates, God, etc.). The other is the will to movement or change (deconstruction, decentering, giving up of place). Where coherence, normative identity, and rationality—having reached their limits and exhausted their emancipatory possibilities—would have rigidified into another normative prison, the call is now for the challenge of contrary thought (i.e., the negative prong of the dialectic); this, if only to expose, fracture, and loosen such conceptual rigidities' totalizing hold on the social order and on individual and collective subjectivities.

It is in this regard, if I may now affirm the deconstructive challenge, that I find the antifoundationalist stance of the "post" theory discourses helpful. I submit, however, that precisely because even originally oppositional movements can devolve into reactionary and repressive regimes once articulated to power, one must not preclude the possibility of such deconstructive critiques themselves being turned (essentialized?) unwittingly into

dominating discourses once articulated to power and invoked indiscriminately without regard to context. This is a dangerous and unfortunate pitfall since it is so contrary to such critiques' originary spirit that disavows precisely all grand(iose), totalizing, knowledge claims.

For me, then, within the Western discursive context, the antifoundationalist, anti-essentialist critique of poststructuralism, at this point in the "game," is a serious call to the second movement. And rightfully so. This is in much the same way that, at another point in history, early modernism was compelled to revolt against what had coalesced into a repressive, monopolistic discourse of ecclesiastical and imperial authority over the course of the Middle Ages. Where late modernist rationality now takes its turn at needing to be at the deconstructive "guillotine" is at the point of its articulation to power, in its having become the instrument of racial slaughter and the ideological justification for the imperial project as well as the colonial and neocolonial exploitation of its "others."[25] This is the moment of its centering and arrogation upon itself of all material and symbolic power (i.e., the power of definition, the prerogative of the capture of the "sign," to the marginalization of all others; Mouffe, 1988). Interestingly enough, in the career of any social (or discursive) order, it is that very moment of ideological triumph that also constitutes the moment of peril (Boyarin, 1994; Gerlach & Hine, 1970; Mendoza, 2002).

But while the call for decentering and "giving up of place" might be the fitting call for much of the West, I contend that the same may not be true in the case of marginalized players in the global arena (e.g., the Philippines and other newly decolonizing countries in Africa and elsewhere in much of the so-called Third World). In the uneven distribution of the spoils of ideological and economic triumph, what the marginalized may well need, if only as a take-off point and not a point of arrival, is precisely the call to self-centering, the assertion of their rightful prerogative to a place and space in the world denied them historically. And for this, such historically marginalized peoples certainly need the centering of their own cultures, their own interests, and their own subjectivities.

I submit that it is to this first movement that the project of indigenization belongs.

CONCLUSION

In revisiting the indigenization-poststructuralism debates within Filipino and Filipino American cultural politics in this chapter, I have shown that

context is the single most important consideration in the adequate exercise of cultural criticism. In particular, the context of *power* is shown to be constitutive of meaning in the act of making sense of what appear to be the incommensurable theoretical positions of indigenization and poststructuralism. In the reading of cultural politics, I argue that the same tools, the same materials, the same discursive strategies, and the same political weapons may be understood as not necessarily having the same signifieds; rather, they attain differing legitimacies and valences depending on who is wielding them at any given moment (i.e., whether invoked or employed by the weak and disempowered to defend themselves or by the strong, to perpetuate their power). Boyarin (1994) strikes a similar pose when he notes, for example, the differing outcomes of Israel's practice of cultural separatism as a survivalist strategy in the diaspora, on the one hand, and as an instrument to dominate others within its new position as an established, powerful nation-state, on the other.

In the case of Filipino and Filipino American cultural politics, then, I maintain that insofar as the indigenization project is a way of getting at the radical roots of "identity" (i.e., the very terms people use to make sense of and define who they are), I find it crucial as a scholar to account carefully for what people mean when, for example, they embrace the traditions of the homeland they had chosen to leave behind, or when deracinated peoples seek to retrace their roots and ground themselves in renewed communities of ethnic belonging. Rather than immediately presuming "pathology," "dangerous politics," or "crass functionalism," I want to ask: What are these indigenization moves doing in this particular context? What is the relevant project here? What is the source of domination that this reactive discourse is a rabid response to? And perhaps where the discourse (of indigenization) would have converted into a mere *doxa*, a mantra, invoked as an automatic nativist guarantee ensuring delivery of "correct" politics every time, I ask: Where are the openings for critique and deconstruction where a questioning of the *doxa* might be a timely insertion? Where are the cracks in the discourse ideology, the tired strategies that no longer excite or energize but, for lack of viable functional substitutes, continue to be relied on? For this, I take Dirlik's (1997) helpful caveat:

> What renders indigenous ideology significant . . . is not what it has to reveal about postmodern/postcolonial criticism. Its intellectual and political significance rests elsewhere; in its claims to a different historicity that challenges not just postcolonial denials of collective identity, but the structure of power that contains it. To criticize indigenous ideology for its reification of culture is to give it at best an

incomplete reading. It also disguises the complexity of what indigenous authors have to say about the relationship between culture and history, which is considerably more radical ideologically than is suggested by its apparent culturalism. (p. 228)

In conclusion, in the dispute between the project of indigenization and that of deconstructive critical cultural theory, I find it productive to frame the debates as two dialectical movements. If indigenization is about rootedness, about finding one's grounding in a *pook* ("place" in Filipino) or location, about a return to a place called "home," and about the healing of colonial narcissism and cultural alienation, this I count as the first necessary movement in any cultural struggle. As such, it must be seen only as an entry point, or at best, a point of departure rather than as an endpoint in one's process of subject formation. With its attainment must immediately begin the second movement, that of decentering, of oppositional challenge, and the difficult entry into what Hall (1996c) calls, "the politics of criticism" (p. 448).

NOTES

1. The University of the Philippines was my home institution for many years prior to coming to the United States to pursue a doctoral degree in intercultural communication.
2. These charges arose in remarks made to me in public presentations, in the context of classroom discussions, and in private conversations with classmates, professors, and colleagues.
3. A version of this historical contextualization appears in Mendoza (2002, pp. 9-14).
4. Pratt (1994) describes the colonized condition thus: "Under conquest social and cultural formations enter long-term, often permanent states of crisis that cannot be resolved by either conqueror or conquered" (p. 26).
5. These are prevalent ascriptions in both Filipino and Filipino American popular discourse.
6. These are common notions of the "American Dream" in Philippine popular discourse. See also Canieso-Doronila's (1989) documentation of an alarming trend that "as [Filipino] students progress through the grades, their preference for their own nationality decreases" (p. 72).
7. Recent historiography now asserts that the Philippines was in fact the United States' "first Vietnam," with an estimated half a million Filipinos massacred in the Philippine-American war (see Francisco, 1976).
8. The Thomasites were the army of 540 American teachers and their families who sailed from the wharf of San Francisco to the Philippines aboard the U.S. Army

Transport Thomas to take part in the mission of "civilizing" the newly acquired U.S. colony.

9. As recently as the 1998 centennial, for instance, when I participated in two community celebrations (one in Phoenix and another in San Francisco), I was struck by how, in dramatized reenactments of Philippine history in song and dance, there was virtually no account of the Philippine-American War. Rather, what was made much of was U.S. General Douglas MacArthur's return and the much-touted U.S. "liberation" of the country from 3 years of Japanese occupation between 1942 and 1945.

10. See Mendoza (2002) for an in-depth historical discussion of this project.

11. Examples include noted postcolonial scholars Campomanes (1992, 1994, 1995), Rafael (1988, 1995, 2000), and San Juan (1990, 1994, 1997, 1998a, 1998b, 2000). Although with varying degrees of empathy for, and knowledge of, the project of *Sikolohiyang Pilipino* (or more generally, indigenization), these Filipino and Filipino American scholars had serious misgivings as to the theoretical soundness or long-term purchase of the value of such a cultural project.

12. Criticism was reportedly circulated as oral commentary among members of *Sikolohiyang Pilipino* and was recounted to me in a number of interviews that I document elsewhere (see Mendoza, 2002). Attempt at a more public debate was made at a forum organized in San Francisco by a group called the Institute of Filipino Studies (IFS) in 2000, but it failed to prosper for lack of adequate representation from *Sikolohiyang Pilipino* (see an account of this event in Mendoza, 2002, Chapter 6).

13. Enthusiastic adoption of the discourse has been reported among service and mental health providers and educators in California (e.g., at the Pilipino Mental Health Resource Group, the San Francisco Mental Health Services/Consultation, Education and Information Unit, Cross Currents, the Philippine Resource Center, Filipinos for Affirmative Action, etc.; Mendoza, 2002, p. 128).

14. See the problematization of such a claim in Hall (1997a) and Kapur (1999). Both authors, among others, note the need for a careful calibrating of our theoretical lenses in mapping out the differing valences or legitimacy of the nation-state within particular historicities and contexts. As Kapur (1999) notes:

From where I speak there is still ground for debate about the nation-state. With all the calumny it has earned, it may be the only political structure that can protect the people of the third world from the totalitarian system that oligopolies establish—ironically, through the massive state power of the advanced nations. Whether the nation-states of the third world can become, yet again, the site of opposition is now a particularly vexed issue; nor is this the place to go into the possibilities of survival, of national economies and national cultures. (p. 193)

15. The letter *P* in PCN comes from the old Tagalog-based spelling of the term *Pilipino*. Tagalog is one of the major Philippine regional languages and does not

have the letter *F* in its alphabet. *Filipino*, on the other hand, signals the expansion of the Tagalog-based alphabet to include letters present in the other Philippine regional languages, *F* being one of them. The rationale behind such a linguistic move is to constitute a more encompassing basis for the construction of a Filipino national language.

16. One example of this is in the fanatical backlash to multiculturalism by white supremacist groups.

17. As Geertz (1973) notes,

The tendency to desire some sort of factual basis for one's commitments seems practically universal; mere conventionalism satisfies few people in any culture . . . In sacred rituals and myths, values are portrayed not as subjective human preferences but as the imposed conditions for life implicit in a world with a particular structure. (p. 126)

18. Individual codes are defined in the larger sense of elements, parts, and/or aspects of any signifying system, "social text," or episteme.

19. Campomanes calls this "strategic parochialism" (personal e-mail communication, 2000).

20. See also Alejo (2000) and the corpus of new historiographic work by various Filipino scholars examined in Chapter 5 of Mendoza (2002).

21. See both internal and external critics of Philippine indigenization by Azurin (1993), Diokno (1997), Guillermo (2000), and Sta. Maria (1996).

22. "The healing of narcissism, the fulfilment of its symptomatic hunger, is achieved by giving the ego what it needs, the pleasure in accomplishment, acceptance and some degree of recognition" (Moore, 1992, p. 73).

23. See Cornel West's (1995) distinction between what he calls "identity from above" and "identity from below" (pp. 17-18).

24. Gendering is intended.

25. This is not to deny or diminish the achievements of modernist rationality in the realm of medicine and other humanitarian endeavors.

REFERENCES

Alejo, A. E. (2000). *Generating energies in Mount Apo: Cultural politics in a contested environment.* Quezon City, The Philippines: Ateneo de Manila University Press.

Azurin, A. M. (1993). *Reinventing the Filipino sense of being and becoming.* Quezon City, The Philippines: CSSP Publications & University of the Philippines Press.

Bonus, R. (2000). *Locating Filipino Americans: Ethnicity and the cultural politics of space.* Philadelphia: Temple University Press.

272 • INTERCULTURAL ALLIANCES

Boyarin, D. (1994). *A radical Jew: Paul and the politics of identity.* Berkeley: University of California Press.

Bulosan, C. (1946). *America is in the heart: A personal history.* New York: Harcourt, Brace.

Butler, J. (1990). *Gender trouble: Feminism and the subversion of identity.* New York: Routledge.

Butler, J. (1995). Contingent foundations. In S. Benhabib, J. Butler, D. Cornell, & N. Fraser, *Feminist contentions: A philosophical exchange* (pp. 35-57). New York: Routledge.

Campomanes, O. V. (1992). Filipinos in the United States and their literature of exile. In S. G. Lim & A. Ling (Eds.), *Reading the literatures of Asian America* (pp. 49-76). Philadelphia: Temple University Press.

Campomanes, O. V. (1994). The institutional invisibility of American imperialism, the Philippines, and Filipino Americans. *Maganda Six, 7-9,* 60-62.

Campomanes, O. V. (1995, Spring). The new empire's forgetful and forgotten citizens: Unrepresentability and unassimilability in Filipino-American post-colonialities. *Critical Mass, 2*(2), 145-200.

Canieso-Doronila, M. L. (1989). *The limits of educational change: National identity formation in a Philippine elementary school.* Quezon City: University of the Philippines Press.

Collier, M. J. (1998). Researching cultural identity: Reconciling interpretive and postcolonial perspectives. In D. V. Tanno & A. Gonzalez (Eds.), *Communication and identity across cultures* (pp. 122-147). Thousand Oaks, CA: Sage.

Collier, M. J., Hegde, R. S., Lee, W. S., Nakayama, T. K., & Yep, G. A. (2001). Dialogue on the edges: Ferment in communication and culture. In M. J. Collier (Ed.), *Transforming communication about culture: Critical new directions* (pp. 219-280). Thousand Oaks, CA: Sage.

Constantino, R. (1977). The miseducation of the Filipino. In C. N. Lumbera & T. Gimenez-Maceda (Eds.), *Rediscovery: Essays in Philippine life and culture* (pp. 125-145). Quezon City, The Philippines: Department of English, Ateneo de Manila and National Book Store.

Cordova, F. (1983). *Filipinos: Forgotten Asian Americans.* Seattle, WA: Demonstration Project for Asian Americans.

De Castro, S. (1994). Identity in action: A Filipino American's perspective. In K. Aguilar-San Juan (Ed.), *The state of Asian America* (pp. 295-320). Boston: South End.

Diamond, A. (1994). *Malcolm X: A voice for black America.* Hillside, NJ: Enslow.

Diokno, M. S. I. (1997). Philippine nationalist historiography and the challenge of new paradigms. *Diliman Review, 45*(2-3), 8-13.

Dirlik, A. (1997). *The postcolonial aura: Third World criticism in the age of global capitalism.* Boulder, CO: Westview.

Drzewiecka, J. A. (2000) Discursive construction of differences: Ethnic immigrant identities and distinctions. In M. J. Collier (Ed.), *Intercultural and*

International Communication Annual: Vol. 23 (pp. 241-270). Thousand Oaks, CA: Sage.

Drzewiecka, J. A., & Nakayama, T. K. (1998). City sites: Postmodern urban space and the communication of identity. *Southern Journal of Communication, 64,* 20-31.

Drzewiecka, J. A., & Wong(Lau), K. (1999). White ethnicity born in performance. In T. K. Nakayama and J. Martin (Eds.), *Whiteness: The social communication of identity* (pp. 198-216). Thousand Oaks, CA: Sage.

Du Bois, W. E. B. (1961). *The souls of black folk.* New York: Fawcett. (Original edition published 1901).

Enriquez, V. G. (1992). *From colonial to liberation psychology: The Philippine experience.* Dilliman, Quezon City: University of the Philippines Press.

Fallows, J. (1987, November). A damaged culture: A new Philippines? *Atlantic Monthly, 49-54,* 56-58.

Fanon, F. (1963). *The wretched of the earth.* New York: Grove.

Francisco, L. (1976). The first Vietnam: The Philippine-American War of 1899-1902. In *Letters in Exile: An introductory reader on the history of Filipinos in America* (pp. 1-22). Los Angeles: The Regents of the University of California.

Fuss, D. (1989). *Essentially speaking.* New York: Routledge.

Geertz, C. (1973). *The interpretation of cultures.* New York: Basic Books.

Gerlach, L. P., & V. H. Hine (1970). *People, power, change: Movements of social transformation.* Indianapolis, IN: Bobbs-Merrill.

Gilroy, P. (1997). Diaspora and the detours of identity. In K. Woodward (Ed.), *Identity and difference* (pp. 299-343). London: Sage.

Goldberg, D. T. (2000). Heterogeneity and hybridity: Colonial legacy, postcolonial heresy. In H. Schwarz & S. Ray (Eds.), *A companion to postcolonial studies* (pp. 72-86). Malden, MA: Blackwell.

Gonzalves, T. S. (1997). The day the dancers stayed: On Pilipino cultural nights. In M. P. P. Root (Ed.), *Filipino Americans: Transformation and identity* (pp. 163-182). Thousand Oaks, CA: Sage.

Gonzalves, T. S. (1998). When the walls speak a nation: Contemporary murals and the narration of Filipina/o America. *Journal of Asian American Studies, 1*(1), 31-63.

Guillermo, R. (2000). *Pook at paninindigan sa pagpapakahulugan: Mga ugat ng talastasang sosyalista sa rebolusyong Pilipino.* Quezon, The Philippines: Limbagang Potopot at Amado V. Hernandez Resource Center.

Hall, S. (1981). In defence of theory. In R. Samuel (Ed.), *People's history and socialist theory* (pp. 378-385). London: Routledge.

Hall, S. (1996a). Cultural identity and diaspora. In P. Mongia (Ed.), *Contemporary postcolonial theory: A reader* (pp. 110-121). London: Arnold.

Hall, S. (1996b). Introduction: Who needs "identity"? In S. Hall & P. Du Gay (Eds.), *Questions of cultural identity* (pp. 1-17). London: Sage.

Hall, S. (1996c). New ethnicities. In S. Hall, D. Morley, & K-S. Chen (Eds.), *Critical dialogues in cultural studies* (pp. 441-449). London: Routledge.

Hall, S. (1997a). The local and the global: globalization and ethnicity. In A. D. King (Ed.), *Culture, globalization and the world-system: Contemporary conditions for the representation of identity* (pp. 19-39). Minneapolis: University of Minnesota Press.

Hall, S. (1997b). Old and new identities, old and new ethnicities. In A. D. King (Ed.), *Culture, globalization and the world-system: Contemporary conditions for the representation of identity* (pp. 41-68). Minneapolis: University of Minnesota Press.

Halualani, R. T. (2002). *In the name of Hawaiians: Native identities and cultural politics.* Minneapolis: University of Minnesota Press.

Hartsock, N. (1987). Rethinking modernism: Minority vs. minority theories. *Cultural Critique, 7,*187-206.

Harvey, D. (1989). *The condition of postmodernity.* Cambridge, MA: Blackwell.

Horsman, R. (1981). *Race and manifest destiny: Origins of American racial Anglo-Saxonism.* Cambridge, MA: Harvard University Press.

Ileto, R. C. (1998). *Filipinos and their revolution: Event, discourse, and historiography.* Quezon City, The Philippines: Ateneo de Manila University Press.

Iyer, P. (1988). *Video night in Kathmandu and other reports from the not-so-far-East.* New York: Knopf.

Jameson, F. (1991). *Postmodernism or, the cultural logic of late capitalism.* Durham, NC: Duke University Press.

Jameson, F. (1999). Notes on globalization as a philosophical issue. In F. Jameson & M. Miyoshi (Eds.), *The cultures of globalization* (pp. 54-77). Durham, NC: Duke University Press.

Jordan, W. D. (1974). *The white man's burden: Historical origins of racism in the United States.* New York: Oxford University Press.

Kapur, G. (1999). Globalization and culture: Navigating the void. In F. Jameson & M. Miyoshi (Eds.), *Cultures of globalization* (pp. 191-217). Durham, NC: Duke University Press.

Kraft, C. (1979). *Christianity in culture: A study in dynamic biblical theologizing in cross-cultural perspective.* Maryknoll, NY: Orbis.

Lyotard, J-F. (1993). *The postmodern condition: A report on knowledge* (G. Bennington & B. Massumi, Trans.). Minneapolis: University of Minnesota Press.

Maggay, M. P. (1993). *Pagbabalik-loob: A second look at the moral recovery program.* Quezon City, The Philippines: Akademya ng Kultura at Sikolohiyang Pilipino.

Martin, J. N., & Nakayama, T. K. (1999). Thinking dialectically about culture and communication. *Communication Theory, 9* (1), 1-25.

Melendy, H. B. (1967). California's discrimination against Filipinos 1927-1935. In J. M. Saniel (Ed.), *The Filipino exclusion movement, 1927-1935* (pp. 3-10). Occasional Papers No. 1. Quezon City: Institute of Asian Studies, University of the Philippines.

Mendoza, S. L. (2001a, November). *Bridging paradigms: How not to throw out the baby of collective representation with the functionalist bathwater in critical intercultural communication.* Paper presented to the Intercultural/International Division, National Communication Association Annual Convention, Atlanta, GA.

Mendoza, S. L. (2001b). Nuancing anti-essentialism: A critical genealogy of Philippine experiments in national identity formation. In L. C. Bower, D. T. Goldberg, & M. Musheno (Eds.), *Between law and culture: Relocating legal studies* (pp. 224-245). Minneapolis: University of Minnesota Press.

Mendoza, S. L. (2002). *Between the homeland and the diaspora: The politics of theorizing Filipino and Filipino American identities.* New York: Routledge.

[Mendoza-] Silva, S. L. (1995). *The intercultural perspective and its relevance to teaching.* Manila: Information, Publication and Public Affairs Office, University of the Philippines, Manila.

Miller, S. C. (1982). *"Benevolent assimilation": The American conquest of the Philippines, 1899-1903.* New Haven, CT: Yale University Press.

Moore, T. (1992). *Care of the soul.* New York: HarperCollins.

Mouffe, C. (1988). Radical democracy: modern or postmodern? In A. Ross (Ed.), *Universal abandon? The politics of postmodernism* (pp. 31-45). Minneapolis: University of Minnesota Press.

Nakayama, T. K., & Martin, J. N. (1999). Whiteness as the communication of social identity. In T. K. Nakayama & J. N. Martin (Eds.), *Whiteness: The communication of social identity.* Thousand Oaks, CA: Sage.

Nida, E., & C. R. Taber (1969). *The theory and practice of translation.* Leiden, The Netherlands: Brill.

Parry, B. (1987). Problems in current theories of colonial discourse. *Oxford Literary Review, 9,* 27-58.

Pertierra, R. (1995). Anthropology and the crisis of representation. *Diliman Review, 43* (2), 3-14.

Pratt, M. L. (1994). Transculturation and autoethnography: Peru 1615/1980. In F. Barker, P. Hulme, & M. Iversen, *Colonial discourse/postcolonial theory.* Manchester, UK: Manchester University Press.

Rafael, V. L. (1988). *Contracting colonialism : Translation and Christian conversion in Tagalog society under early Spanish rule.* Ithaca, NY: Cornell University Press.

Rafael, V. L. (1995). Introduction: Writing outside: on the question of location. In V. L. Rafael (Ed.), *Discrepant histories : Translocal essays on Filipino cultures* (pp. xiii-xxviii). Manila, The Philippines: Anvil.

Rafael, V. L. (2000). *White love and other events in Filipino history.* Durham, NC: Duke University Press.

Rosaldo, R. (1989/1992). *Culture and truth: The remaking of social analysis.* Boston: Beacon.

San Juan, E. (1990). *From people to nation: Essays in cultural politics.* Manila, The Philippines: Asian Social Institute.

San Juan, E. (1994). *Allegories of resistance : The Philippines at the threshold of the twenty-first century.* Diliman, Quezon City: University of the Philippines Press.

San Juan, E. (1997). Fragments from a Filipino exile's journal. *Amerasia Journal, 2,* 1-25.

San Juan, E. (1998a). *Beyond postcolonial theory.* New York : St. Martin's.

San Juan, E. (1998b). *From exile to diaspora: Versions of the Filipino experience in the United States.* Boulder, CO: Westview.

San Juan, E. (2000). *After postcolonialism: Remapping Philippines-United States confrontations.* Lanham, MD: Rowman & Littlefield.

Sapir, E. (1929). The status of linguistics as a science. *Language, 5,* 207-214.

Sarup, M. (1989). *An introductory guide to post-structuralism and postmodernism.* Athens: University of Georgia Press.

Sarup, M. (1996). *Identity, culture and the postmodern world.* Athens: University of Georgia Press.

Schwarz, H,. & Ray, S. (Eds.). (2000). *A companion to postcolonial studies.* Malden, MA: Blackwell.

Shohat, E. (1996). Notes on the "post-colonial." In P. Mongia (Ed.), *Contemporary postcolonial theory: A reader* (pp. 321-334). London: Arnold.

Singh, A., & Schmidt, P. (Eds.). (2000). *Postcolonial theory and the United States: Race, ethnicity, and literature.* Jackson: University Press of Mississippi.

Soja, E. W. (1996). *Thirdspace: Journeys to Los Angeles and other real-and-imagined places.* Cambridge, MA: Blackwell.

Spivak, G. C. (1990). *The post-colonial critic: Interviews, strategies, dialogues* (S. Harasym, Ed.). New York: Routledge.

Spivak, G. C. (1996). Subaltern studies: Deconstructing historiography. In D. Landry & G. MacLean (Eds.), *The Spivak reader: Selected works of Gayatri Chakravorty Spivak* (pp. 203-235). New York: Routledge.

Sta. Maria, M. (1996). Is the indigenization crisis in Philippine social sciences resolved in Sikolohiyang Pilipino? *Layag, 1*(1), 101-120.

Steinfatt, T. M. (1989). Linguistic relativity: Toward a broader view. In S. Ting-Toomey & F. Korzenny (Eds.), *Language, communication, and culture: Current directions* (pp. 35-75). Newbury Park, CA: Sage.

Strobel, E. M. (1996). "Born-Again Filipino": Filipino American identity and Asian panethnicity. *Amerasia Journal, 22*(2), 31-53.

Strobel, L. M. (2001). *Coming full circle: The process of decolonization among post-1965 Filipino Americans.* Manila, The Philippines: Giraffe.

Thiong'o, N. (1986). *Decolonising the mind: The politics of language in African literature.* Portsmouth, NH: Heinemann.

Tolentino, R. (2001). "It's a crazy planet." *Diliman Review, 49*(1-2), 97-101.

Tournier, P. (1968). *A place for you: Psychology and religion.* New York: Harper & Row.

Warren, K. B. (1998). *Indigenous movements and their critics: Pan-Maya activism in Guatemala.* Princeton, NJ: Princeton University Press.

Weaver, J. (2000). Indigenousness and indigeneity. In H. Schwarz & S. Ray (Eds.), *A companion to postcolonial studies* (pp. 221-235). Malden, MA: Blackwell.

Werbner, P., & Modood, T. (Eds.). (1997). *Debating cultural hybridity: Multicultural identities and the politics of anti-racism.* London: Zed.

West, C. (1995). A matter of life and death. In J. Rajchman (Ed.), *The identity in question* (pp. 15-19). New York: Routledge.

Whorf, B. L. (1940). Science and linguistics. *Technological Review, 42,* 229-241, 247-248.

Woodward, K. (Ed.). (1997). *Identity and difference.* London: Sage.

Young, R. J. C. (2001). *Postcolonialism: An historical introduction.* Oxford, UK: Blackwell.

11

Intercultural Alliances

A Cyberdialogue
Among Scholar-Practitioners

BRENDA J. ALLEN

BENJAMIN J. BROOME

TRICIA S. JONES

VICTORIA CHEN

MARY JANE COLLIER

Mary Jane Collier

Introduction to the Cyberdialogue

As a white European American female editor of this volume, with race, ethnic, and class identifications, among others, that grant me privilege; and as one whose itineraries of study include interpretive as well as critical perspectives, I find that dialogue with those who have different identifications and experiences helps me see what I may be taking for granted and have overlooked in the past. Dialogue among scholars-practitioners about intergroup and interpersonal intercultural alliances creates an opportunity to acknowledge constraints, wrestle with critical issues, and recognize the transformative potential of such relationships.

My goal for this chapter, therefore, is to provide a new kind of forum, a cyberdialogue, in which scholar-practitioners listen to, reflect on, and engage each other's views rather than reporting a set of findings, justifying conclusions, or advocating for a particular paradigm. I envision this kind of dialogic collaboration as enabling scholars to talk together, providing time for reflection and thought about alternative perspectives, and offering the opportunity to ask questions and follow up with additional information. This cyberdialogue is an alternative form to the more conventional position paper or article heard at conferences and read in journals.

I invited four scholar-practitioners, whose work I know and respect, to participate in this cyberdialogue. Brenda J. Allen, Benjamin J. Broome, Tricia S. Jones, and Victoria Chen each have a commitment to studying, facilitating, and developing intercultural alliances. Each brings knowledge and experience from various contexts and backgrounds to this chapter. Each writes about, studies, teaches, and/or facilitates groups that are involved with culture and communication and alliance building. Each one of us brings a different set of embodied and constructed cultural identities and histories to our writing/teaching/practice, which is invaluable in this kind of unfolding conversation.

Because Victoria has experience facilitating community dialogues and has been working with the Public Dialogue Consortium, I invited her to be a cofacilitator of our dialogue. As we began, Victoria described our goals as using dialogue as a means to engage and connect with one another's ideas and experiences, to listen to one another with critical intelligence, and as a vehicle to generate new possibilities to transform difficulties in communication.

The dialogue consisted of e-mail messages sent to the group from the end of November 2001 through the middle of March 2002. Because including a chronologically ordered sequence of actual postings would be difficult for readers to follow, the posted messages are roughly reorganized according to topic and related issues. Similar to spoken dialogues, some messages are longer and some are shorter, and at times some individuals offer more points than others. Although participants did have the opportunity to edit their comments in the final version of the cyberdialogue, minimal changes were made to the initial messages posted.

To begin the dialogue, we asked each of the three scholar-practitioners to begin by describing one or two personal experiences with intercultural alliances in whatever context they wished: research, facilitation, or personal relationship experiences. We wanted each scholar to share his or her experiences of intercultural alliances so that we could start with some situated examples (in an almost autoethnographic sense) and get an idea of the sound, look, and feel of the intercultural alliances being described.

In order to provide a structure for the rest of the cyberdialogue, we decided to use an adaptation of a facilitation model—concerns, visions, actions (CVA)—that is often used by the Public Dialogue Consortium. This three-step format not only worked well in a scholar-editor dialogue session at the National Communication Association conference in 2001 but also is one that Victoria has experience with and is working to adapt to different types of communities and groups.

More specifically, the CVA model we used to guide this cyberdialogue involved a reflexive three-step process. After the scholar-practitioners shared detailed descriptions of situations in which they facilitated or experienced intercultural alliances, we asked them to look for and describe the conceptualizations of and/or conditions for intercultural alliances that were emerging. In this way we moved toward identifying *visions* of intercultural alliances that seemed to be inherent in the situated examples. As a second step, we asked the scholars to address *concerns* that they had related to accomplishing the visions of intercultural alliances. In the last step we asked for descriptions of *action* steps that encouraged individuals and groups to go beyond "mere talk." We solicited examples of concrete actions that could be taken to accomplish the visions and address the concerns and challenges identified.

In summary, this chapter contains not only an important form of dialogue about intercultural alliances but also a demonstration that the process of dialogue is messy, challenging, at times seemingly unwieldy, and yet worth the effort. As editor of this volume, I am grateful to all four scholar-practitioners, who were willing to openly share their experiences and ruminations and who coconstructed such a thought-provoking text.

Mary Jane Collier

Here is a request to get the dialogue started. Describe an interaction, situation, and/or relationship in which you have experienced or observed others developing intercultural alliances. (If you have *not* experienced or observed intercultural alliances, according to the way you define them, then describe an experience that comes close to being an intercultural alliance.) Be as specific as you can about the context, people present, messages, conduct, and so on—whatever you think is relevant to help us understand your example.

Brenda J. Allen

As I thought about the question regarding intercultural alliances, two relationships immediately came to mind. Both of them originated within a department where I was a faculty member. One person was a faculty colleague; the other was a graduate student. I characterize my relationship with each as an intercultural alliance because of ways that each person and I differ. My faculty colleague is a middle-aged, white lesbian; the graduate student (who now is an assistant professor) is a young, white, heterosexual woman. So, I'm defining "intercultural" using the following aspects of

social identity: race, sexual orientation, and age. Since I am not an intercultural communication scholar per se, I realize that my definition might not correspond with how those of you who study intercultural communication conceptualize it.

Also key to my choices is my connotation and the dictionary's denotation of *alliance*. To me, an ally is someone with whom I share a bond, someone with whom I work to achieve a goal. An alliance, then, is a relationship based upon working together to accomplish a goal. Webster's Collegiate Dictionary defines *alliance* as: "an association to further the common interests of the members," which corresponds nicely with my sentiments. In my alliance with each person, we address(ed) issues related to acknowledging, affirming, and valuing differences, in a variety of contexts. Anna was my colleague. She and I have since taken other jobs, so we no longer work together. However, we are friends for life and we remain in touch. She currently is employed as an EEO (equal employment opportunity) officer for the federal government, and she recently gave me a stack of information about race designations to inform a writing project I'm completing. So, our alliance continues! I've already written about my relationship with her in a chapter in *Our Voices* entitled "Sapphire and Sappho: Allies in Authenticity" (Allen, 2000). Anna was instrumental in helping me to understand some of the challenges that gays and lesbians routinely face, as well as how heteronormativity imbues our society. We became allies because we both were concerned about how our curriculum and our colleagues dealt with diversity issues.

Karen was a graduate student who wanted to study feminism in a program that had no feminist scholar. I agreed to direct her independent study on feminism and communication, and I am glad that I did. As a result of reading and discussing her review of related literature, my consciousness was raised, and I eventually began to self-identify as a scholar who applies feminist perspectives to research and teaching. We became allies in conducting research and developing curricula that addresses issues of power, domination, complicity, and resistance. We recently wrote and presented a paper at the National Communication Association conference titled "The Racial Foundation of Organizational Communication," which critiques "our field's participation in preserving the normative power of organized whiteness," and offers "specific suggestions for revising the racial subtext of our scholarship." We have submitted the manuscript for consideration for publication.

I've known both of these women for at least a decade. I can elaborate on either or both of these relationships, but I'll close for now with an

observation. One reason that my alliances with Anna and Karen have been rewarding and enduring stems from our similarities (for instance, as women, or, for Anna and me, as Baby Boomers) as well as our differences. A second reason why I believe those alliances have succeeded and endured is that, in addition to accomplishing various goals, each relationship has allowed me to grow and to learn. I'm confident (but humble—smile) enough to say that Anna and Karen would say the same for their alliance with me.

Benjamin Broome

The most powerful case of intercultural alliance building in which I have been personally involved centers around the work of Greek Cypriot and Turkish Cypriot peace builders in the small eastern Mediterranean island of Cyprus. Members of the two ethnic communities, who have been physically separated for decades, speak different native languages (Greek and Turkish), follow different religious traditions (Christian Orthodox and Muslim), hold drastically different views of history, and are schooled from an early age to view the other community as the enemy. Ethnic division began to occur following skirmishes in 1963, when the Turkish Cypriots withdrew into enclaves. In 1974 a full-scale war broke out, resulting in the ethnic division of the island, creating hundreds of thousands of refugees and resulting in the loss of homes and businesses by nearly one-third of the population. Today there stands between the two communities a buffer zone guarded by United Nations peacekeeping forces separating heavily armed Turkish and Turkish-Cypriot forces in the north and Greek-Cypriot forces in the south. Since the cease-fire that was arranged in 1974, political negotiations have made little progress toward resolving the conflict.

In the late 1980s, members of the two communities made contact, primarily through workshops they attended abroad, and started working toward ways to promote peace in Cyprus. Because it was very difficult for them to communicate directly with one another (there are no telephone or mail links between the two sides of the buffer zone), and because authorities would not grant them permission to hold bi-communal meetings, progress was slow and there were many frustrations. In the early 1990s, a U.S.-based third party, Louise Diamond of the Institute for Multi-Track Diplomacy (IMTD), based in Washington, D.C., began visiting the island periodically and working separately with members of each community, offering training in conflict resolution. Based on the success of their work, the participants approached the Cyprus Fulbright Commission about

bringing a conflict resolution specialist from the United States to work with them on a full-time basis. In September 1994 I took up this newly created position as Senior Fulbright Scholar in Cyprus.

My primary task in Cyprus centered on helping the existing group develop ways to work together productively across the physical, historical, cultural, and conflict divide that separated them. As I was to discover, there were nearly as many intragroup differences as intergroup differences. During the first 9 months, I met on a regular basis (weekly) with 15 Greek Cypriots and 15 Turkish Cypriots. Each group consisted of men and women from various sectors of society (education, business, politics, NGOs), a range of ages (approximately 25 to 55), and across the political spectrum (left-leaning to right of center). Participants spoke English as their second language, and although the group sometimes used Turkish or Greek in the monocommunal meetings, English was used in the joint meetings. We progressed through several "phases" of work, including an in-depth examination of the barriers facing the group in their efforts to develop a citizen-based peace movement in Cyprus, their goals for these efforts, and the design of specific activities that would help make their vision a reality (see Broome, 1997, for an overview of these activities).

In the beginning, most of our meetings were held in separate communal groups, because we could not obtain permission from the authorities to meet jointly. Later, we were able to come together on a regular basis over several months in bicommunal meetings. Discussions (in both the mono-communal and bicommunal settings) were often intense and emotional, at times inspiring and at other times extremely frustrating for everyone. The group nearly broke apart on several occasions, but the commitment and dedication of participants kept us together. The group bonded in a special way through these meetings, and they became the core group of peace builders in Cyprus, forming the nucleus around which most of the developing intercommunal activities were centered.

Over the 4-year period following the series of meetings described above, more than 2000 people became involved in bicommunal activities organized by this core group. By that point, the size of the group had become threatening to those who wanted to maintain the division on the island, and the Turkish Cypriot authorities stopped giving permission to individuals in the north to cross into the buffer zone to meet with their counterparts in the south, resulting in a "ban" on bi-communal meetings that is still in effect today. Fortunately, Internet access was just being established in Cyprus when the ban was first put in place, and many projects have gone forward with electronic communication providing the primary means for people to

maintain contact and work together. In addition, a number of meetings have been held abroad, and on a limited basis, in a small, remote village located within a British-controlled military area. Thus, the work has continued to this day, although it has had to take different forms.

My stay in Cyprus lasted approximately 2½ years. After the initial 9-month series of meetings with the core group, I continued my Fulbright assignment and assisted with several projects, helping to form other, more specialized groups, consisting of young business leaders, young political leaders, women activists, and university students. Since my return to the United States in 1997, I have traveled back to Cyprus numerous times, and I have organized several workshops, seminars, and other meetings outside Cyprus. The members of the core group remain my most trusted colleagues, as well as good friends. We help each other keep the faith, even during difficult times.

Victoria Chen

Ben, as I read through your case, I was wondering what you would consider the essential "conditions" that make the intercultural alliances between the Greek and Turkish Cypriot possible. What was the nature of their dialogue in the process? How did the construction of their intercultural alliance evolve over time? And would it be helpful for us to know something about how your facilitation helped make this intercultural alliance possible? I understand that it might take more time for you to reflect on your role in the two groups, but I'm curious how you presented or identified yourself as a U.S. American, and how they related to you while you were trying to make a difference by creating this intercultural alliance. So anything you'd like to share would be great.

Brenda J. Allen

As I reflected further, I identified two points that might inform our sense of how and why people might form alliances. First, I recognize the important role of physical proximity to the formation of the alliances I described. Not only were we all in the same academic department, but Anna and I initially sat side by side in an open office area; after our department moved, we were located next door to one another and shared an adjoining small reception area. Karen had been a student in a course I taught (I believe during her first semester), and she happened to live in the same building of the apartment complex where I stayed.

I also realized that I became engaged in both alliances rather serendipitously. That is, I did not actively seek them. The alliances emerged in response or reaction to situations that somehow challenged and/or troubled all parties. Already I can conclude that I would like to become more proactive in initiating alliances, even as I am pleased that I responded to those opportunities.

Tricia S. Jones

Let me start by talking about the project that comes most to my mind when I think about intercultural alliances. About 5 years ago, right after Mandela was elected to the presidency in South Africa, I got a United States Information Agency (USIA) grant to work with a team of South African Educators and U.S. American educators to put into place "Community Peace and Safety Networks" in the Johannesburg region. These networks were based on a model used in Philadelphia that linked community mediation and school mediation programs. The project lasted over a 2-year period and involved a team of South Africans and a team of U.S. Americans.

The South African team was multicultural in and of itself. It was composed of two educators from each of the four school communities involved and two members of the South African NGO. One school community was a very affluent Afrikaner community and the team members were white Afrikaner women, neither of whom had ever interacted with Black South Africans as colleagues of equal status in a project. Another school community was Thokoza, a very large Black South African township. The team members were two young black South African men. A third school community was Soweto, another Black South African township. The team members from Soweto were middle-aged male and female South Africans. The fourth school community was a private Catholic girls school in the Rosebanks area, which was largely British and quite affluent. The team members from this school were two women, a middle-aged, white teacher and a middle-aged, white nun and teacher. The two members of the South African NGO were young, Black South African men.

When the project started, none of the South African members knew the members from other schools. Moreover, most of them, given the background of the country, had never worked with colleagues from the other cultural groups before this project. And they had fairly if not very stereotypical views of each other.

The South Africans also had very little to no contact with U.S. Americans and certainly had had none with the intercultural U.S. team that had been

developed. The U.S. team had nine core people—four African American women, one gay male Caucasian, and four Caucasian women. I give you these details just to give you a flavor of the multiplicity of ways that these folks, in various groupings, can be understood to be intercultural and/or multicultural.

Over the course of the 2 years of this project, working with and across teams, and working with and across communities, I had several "insights" (and more questions) about intercultural alliances. So, for the rest of this message I'll just recount some of those initial thoughts. Many of these thoughts overlap so I apologize in advance for the stream of consciousness you are about to read.

As I begin, let me confess that I am a fond admirer of dialectical theory and specifically of Smith and Berg's work (1987) on paradoxes in group interaction. With that said, one of the realities of our project and, I suspect, all intercultural alliances is that to ally with one is to "distance" from another. Whether this distance is one that results in simple detachment and lessened interdependence or whether it is one that results in increased suspicion and hostility is an open question. But it is clear that movement toward is also always movement away and/or against in some larger social context. I believe it is often the case that we have a fairly unrefined idea of why we are moving "toward" in the beginning, and we have even less of an idea of how we are distancing from others at the same time. In our project I know that this was true. We began with a very naive motivation to "collaborate" and made many assumptions about what that could and should be. Frankly, we chose to deny the tension toward distance until it became too explicit to deny. If this tension exists in all alliances, what is the additional complexity of intercultural alliances?

In addition, there are many ways that culture impacted our alliances and tension in the project. I'll just mention the most obvious. First, our cultures certainly had a great influence on what our perceptions of our "interests" were. As others have mentioned, an alliance is a political move to promote or secure self-interest. But, how one sees "self-interest," or whether one sees interest in terms of "self" or from a more collective frame, is another question. Looking back, now I believe that the Black South Africans had a much more collective sense of interest that the Afrikaners, British, or Americans. As the project unfolded, several of their actions really emphasized this collective view. Frankly, I think that the Americans were the most truly "self"-interested of all. Second, our cultural frames also had a profound impact on what "alliance" meant to us. For some it was a fairly utilitarian, immediate, and convenient notion of shared resources. Also, it was clearly

project bound, as in, let's "work together well" during this project so we can be a "success" for the funders. For others, alliance meant truly forging lasting relationships that could weather a lot of social pressure and the reality of great inequity. So, for some, alliance was only understandable in relation to some other outside force or antagonism; while for others, alliance was an internal state that did not need an external threat to make it manifest.

Third, our cultures made it very difficult to really understand these frames on interest and alliance until we were quite far into the process. This was the most frustrating aspect of the project for me personally. I didn't realize what I should have been able to find out until it was almost too late to do anything about it. So many times I have gone back to the initial meetings of the teams—many days spent together, so many words exchanged, and so little meaning conveyed or understood. In our best efforts we all tried to be polite, open, appropriate. But, we simply didn't understand each other and how we viewed "the team" until 16 months in to the project. Perhaps if we were all multilingual and could have switched back and forth in languages it would have helped. But that probably wouldn't have overcome the basic propensity of the South Africans to be very indirect in their conversation. Certainly we should have known more about the other "general culture"—but that too is easier said than done. As we all learned, reading about one another's culture and experiencing it firsthand are quite different.

Fourth, the various power relations between cultural groups made it very difficult for us to surface our uncertainties and concerns. If "alliance" is seen as "power over" by one group and "power with" by another, communicating about the action of alliance becomes fraught with difficulty. And, for some groups, the act of allying is seen as a profound betrayal of their larger culture.

Fifth, our cultures provided us with very different rules for how one enacts alliance. By this I mean the variety of communication rules that we used to "be allies" and "communicate our alliance relations." This sounds pretty vague, but I am trying to capture the whole set of rules of behavior that are invoked when one is framed as an ally versus enemy of the other. There seemed to be times when members of the different teams were assuming the same meaning for "alliance" but then stepped on each other's toes by using communication patterns that were foreign or off-putting to others.

Victoria Chen

Trish, as I read through your fascinating case, it struck me that one of the challenges for intercultural alliance building is to develop and cocreate a shared context in which identifying shared interests should be a primary agenda. When you wrote "so many words exchanged, and so little meaning conveyed or understood," it reminded me once again of the inadequacy of emphasizing people's intention and motivation in understanding how the process of communication works. It seems that the group needed to develop some kind of shared language (linguistically and culturally) in order to begin building intercultural alliances. And this seems to be particularly important when power is a critical issue in the group and assumptions are unchallenged. Maybe this is something on which you can elaborate in moving toward a vision of intercultural alliances.

Brenda J. Allen

Trish, your example is fascinating. I look forward to hearing more. Please elaborate on your observation that "to ally with one is to 'distance' from another," perhaps in the context of your example. The idea intrigues me, but I'm not sure I follow it. Thank you.

Victoria Chen

Hi Brenda. I thoroughly enjoyed what you wrote on intercultural alliances, and maybe it's even better that you are not one of the "intercultural scholars"! I am familiar with your essay in *Our Voices* and was glad to learn about your experience with Karen. It strikes me that the way you described these two experiences seems to suggest that there would have to be some similar, shared, overlapping interests, concerns, or "problems" to motivate people to develop intercultural alliances. In other words, if two people don't really have to deal with each other's different experiences and there is no situation to "force" them to interact, it would be unlikely for them to develop this kind of bond. Would you comment on this?

Also, can you say a bit more about the notion of "authenticity" as you described it? For anyone in the group, please feel free to pose any questions or response to what Brenda and Ben wrote. Thanks.

Brenda J. Allen

Yes, Victoria, I believe that we develop intercultural alliances based upon "similar, shared, overlapping interests, concerns, or 'problems'" that somehow incite us to forge a bond. It seems that people will form alliances when they discern a need to work together *for* something, and therefore also *against* something else. In addition, the problem or need may seem pressing to all parties, which might provoke them to act in concert sooner rather than later.

Also, interested parties might voluntarily initiate an alliance, or a person (or people) in power might force them, which might affect the nature and quality of the alliance.

Cybercollaborators, what do y'all think?

Brenda J. Allen

Victoria, I used the word authenticity in the title of the chapter about Anna and me to refer to our quest to develop and sustain an organizational culture (in our department and our classes as well as throughout the university) that allowed individuals to feel comfortable being and expressing who they are, to be their authentic selves, to be free to exhibit any of their multiple facets. The need for such a quest arose from our mutual sense that members of dominant cultures constrained such expression. That quest eventually expanded to include the discipline of communication and other venues (e.g., for Anna, religious groups). Is this a helpful elaboration?

Victoria Chen

Brenda, yes, it's helpful, and thanks for the clarification. I like it that you used "authenticity" in the context of creating a self with multiple facets. I didn't think you meant "authenticity" in an essentialist sense and that interaction takes a back seat in constructing the self. If true intercultural alliances foster authenticity in the process of communication, then that authenticity is one attribute that characterizes intercultural alliances? All the features of "authenticity" that you listed might be a way to move into discussing a vision of intercultural alliances.

Brenda J. Allen

Victoria, I agree that true intercultural alliances should foster authenticity in the process of communication. Aspects of authenticity could include

feeling free to express oneself according to one's social identity group's (or groups') norms (e.g., through communication styles, language, nonverbal behaviors, and dress). Being authentic also could mean that members of the alliance should identify and discuss their own "isms" and stereotyping tendencies, especially as related to the cultures with which they are allying.

What do y'all think? (I just revised my original spelling of "you all" to "y'all" because I'm comfortable with y'all!)

P.S. I think that language and communication styles are an important element of authenticity because being or feeling obliged to use a "second" language can constrain one's expression. For instance, participants in workshops that I have conducted often express frustration that they cannot "be themselves" in predominantly white work settings. They feel stifled, silenced, and controlled. A woman who spoke English as a second language told me about a white female supervisor who constantly "corrected" her when she rolled her *r*'s. Even when she told her supervisor that her pronunciation was correct in her native language, and that she had difficulty *not* rolling the *r* in certain words, the supervisor continued to reprimand her, often in front of others.

Tricia S. Jones

I agree with Brenda that we develop intercultural alliances based on overlapping or similar concerns or problems. One of the least studied and understood facets of alliances in the conflict literature is how the nature of the alliance actually changes the perceived "common" interests over time and the iterative nature of that.

In most of the reading that I have done, alliances are really studied and conceptualized in very short time frames if the focus is on the more microdynamics of the alliance. Also, more historical and long-term treatments of alliances seem to have more emphasis on the external social-political factors rather than on cultural and communicative sources of influence.

As I began to mention in my last message, it takes more time for members of intercultural alliances to get to know each other; that is, I think the relational development patterns of intercultural alliances are probably quite different from the relational development patterns of alliances between culturally similar members.

I also would like to mention that another interesting (and in our project, important) factor in the development and maintenance of the intercultural alliance was the response and support of the cultural constituencies. Again, conflict theory has a fair amount to say about how constituencies impact

conflict dynamics, but it has relatively little to say about the role of culture as a primary or critical factor in such dynamics.

Brenda J. Allen

Oh, yeah, Trish, you're on to something in this comment: "I think the relational development patterns of intercultural alliances are probably quite different from the relational development patterns of alliances between culturally similar members."

As I contrast the development of my relationship with Anna with that of relationships with women whom I would characterize as more similar to me (i.e., black and straight), I can identify differences that might be significant to our dialogue. For instance, Anna and I self-consciously interrogated (ugh, I don't like that word, but I'll stick with it to keep my flow) one another to learn about our cultural differences. I think we were committed (without any agreement beforehand) to learning about each other as individuals and as "representatives" of social identity groups. However, we were careful not to assume that we represented those groups, if that makes any sense. Because we trusted one another, we became increasingly comfortable asking and responding to questions that we probably would not tolerate from other "others," because, for instance, we might have viewed them as stereotyping or voyeuristic. Karen and I enact similar behaviors, even to the point of an ongoing tongue-in-cheek practice of saying, "In my culture, we. . . ." Does anyone else have any thoughts about either of these issues?

Mary Jane Collier

I am learning so much by reading each posting. I wonder if we can continue to move toward identifying the characteristics and features that are similar and different for each of your intercultural alliances. Part of the visioning process is to think about how you have each created these alliances and to see what we might point to that is similar.

For example, I'm fascinated by this idea of tension between enmity and alliance that Brenda and Trish have brought up. Is it like a tension between closeness and distance, or connection and autonomy? An ally relationship, then, has a tension, and alliances may ebb and flow over time. Trish, you are pointing us to a broader context in which an alliance with one person also affects relationships with others in that context. This is bringing more of a systems perspective to the description of alliances, which seems quite

important! Family communication scholars of course would say that an alliance between two family members strongly affects the relationships of the other members of the family. Your experience showed that this was the case in South Africa too. Brenda and Ben, do you have any other examples of this tension or its effect on other relationships?

Could we say that authenticity is another characteristic of intercultural allies, or is it necessary only in particular ones? I'd like to hear more about the concept of authenticity. Brenda, as I think I am understanding this feature of alliances, authenticity is the freedom that allies feel to "express who they are." How does this fit with ideas of individual agency I wonder? Your examples made me think that dominance and hierarchy make the safety needed for authenticity more difficult where there is a climate of dominance and submissiveness and "power over" as the norm. What do you think?

Tricia S. Jones

Brenda, I'm also quite taken by your discussion of authenticity. How did you and Anna broach the topic of authenticity in the larger department? Did you have open dialogue about this? If so, how? If you did not have an ally who was also "nondominant," how would (or did) you handle this same issue? This certainly raises the idea that one of the possible benefits of an intercultural alliance between members of nondominant groups is to request or demand safe space in which to be authentic.

Benjamin Broome

The concept of authenticity, introduced into our discussion by Brenda, is also applicable in the context of the Cyprus work. For both Turkish Cypriots and Greek Cypriots, there was a feeling that they could explore genuinely their own thoughts and feelings, instead of presenting and defending the "national cause." Participants were able to move beyond the typical political positioning that characterizes most encounters between Greek Cypriots and Turkish Cypriots. This was a liberating feeling for most of them. In addition, for the Turkish Cypriots, who had long been treated as a minority in most settings where they had contact with Greek Cypriots, the opportunity to discuss issues and be heard by the Greek Cypriots was a very confirming experience.

In general, traditional Cypriot norms view intense argumentation as an appropriate form of communication, especially when discussing topics related to the Cyprus conflict. This is true in both communities, although in

my experience, the Greek Cypriots were more emotional and more expressive than the Turkish Cypriots. This means that in most discussions about the conflict, the focus usually is more on presenting arguments than listening to the other person. In the workshops and seminars that we organized, we were able to introduce norms that promoted more productive communication patterns. The intercultural alliance the Turkish Cypriots and Greek Cypriots formed in these meetings was made possible in part because they were able to listen to one another and learn about each other's perspective. They listened to the pain felt by the other and they came to appreciate the suffering that others had experienced. They no longer felt that "their side" was the only one that suffered in the past. Most important, they acknowledged that their own community had contributed to the suffering of the other, whereas previously their focus had been on how the other community has caused *them* to suffer. Thus, I believe that authenticity was based not only on their being able to express themselves more genuinely but also on their being able to really listen to and learn from the other.

Tricia S. Jones

The tension of alliance and distance (I'll use "distance" rather than "enmity," although I guess enmity would actually be the other end of that tension) is a tough one to describe in other than abstract terms. (This is one of the reasons that the dialectical theorists are so wonderful but dialectical analysis and research is so rare.) I'll give one example from the very beginning of the project and focus on the South African team rather than the U.S.-South African interaction.

In the beginning of the project, none of the four school subteams knew each other, but they all knew the South African NGO members (to some extent). One school, the British school, actually had very close relations with the head of the NGO. The two Black South African teams felt more closely aligned with each other than did the Afrikaner or British teams, for obvious reasons. In the initial parts of the project we encouraged a great deal of interaction and socializing among all team members, to begin to lay the foundation for building relationships. In one 2-week trip to the United States, the team members spend 4 to 5 days in Washington, D. C., doing some work, but mainly sightseeing and just getting to know each other. In that 2 weeks it began to be apparent that the Thokozans and the Afrikaners were actually having a pretty great time together. They were probably more shocked than anyone, but they were actually seeking one another out for walks to the monuments, and so on. It seemed that the more social and

communicative they became, the more the British and the South African NGO felt excluded, and the more the Sowetans felt they were being shunned (just a little) by the Thokozans. And, in some ways they weren't being actively excluded, but they were being treated with more distance. As project "leader," I found myself wanting to encourage the closeness that was developing but concerned about the sense of distance that might be part and parcel of increased closeness. Frankly, it reminded me a little of high school friendships and how the group dynamics shift when a new friend comes in to the picture. It's easy to talk about "everybody" being friends, but it's another thing when it looks and feels like some folks are being better friends than others. Much, much later in the project we all talked about this first trip to the United States and the distances and new closenesses that they were feeling. While hindsight is suspect, they clearly saw all moves toward some members of the team as also moves away (in time or space) from others.

Brenda J. Allen

Thanks, Trish. Your example clarifies the tension of alliance and distance. It's easy to see how it occurred in an alliance team. Now I'm trying to see if and how that tension operates in my dyadic alliances with Anna and Karen.

Victoria Chen

Thanks for all the ideas so far. I'm learning much from what you've written and am looking forward to move along in our dialogue. I think, based on what has been exchanged, that we have some rich ideas and visions about intercultural alliances in various contexts and examples. At this point, I would like to invite everyone to address anything else about the visions of intercultural alliances that has not yet been shared. If not, can we move along to talk about concerns.

The question is, given the visions of intercultural alliances that we have come up with, what are some concerns that you have in the process of trying to accomplish and/or practice these visions? Are there issues that you think might be "problematic" or difficult, or that we need to pay attention to? For example, we have mentioned critical issues such as power, equality, authenticity, trust, various voices, collaboration, and so on. These might be (but don't have to be) some beginning points for addressing concerns with regard to practicing intercultural alliances. I remember Trish stated earlier

something about the dimension of culture being somehow curiously missing from mediation and conflict theory. Would this be a concern in forming intercultural alliances when engaging in mediation?

Benjamin Broome

One of the "concerns" with practicing intercultural alliances in divided societies is differences between the conflict groups in their *perceptions of history*. In Cyprus, the Turkish Cypriots and the Greek Cypriots have completely different readings of the past, especially about the period during which they lived together on the island. Although human settlements in Cyprus date from 6000 BCE or earlier, Greek Cypriots tend to focus on the period since 1500 BCE, when the first Greek settlers established a presence on the island. Turkish language and culture in Cyprus dates from the late 1500s CE, with the Ottoman conquest of the island. From the perspective of the Greek Cypriots, the Turkish Cypriots have been around "only" 400 years, making them relative "newcomers" and creating a sense they don't belong there. This perception of Cyprus as a "Greek island" brought about many of the troubles that characterize the conflict, and it still exists on a subconscious level today, affecting relationships between the two communities. The Turkish Cypriots see Cyprus as an island that has been host to many cultural groups over the centuries, and while they don't claim a presence before 1571, they feel very closely tied to the land. While the Greek Cypriots tend to trace the heritage of Cyprus primarily in terms of the Greek influence, the Turkish Cypriots emphasize the Phoenician, Roman, Arab, Lusigian, Venetian, British, and other influences. For them, the Greek influence is just one of many contributions over the centuries that have shaped the current character of the land and people.

In terms of recent history, the Greek Cypriots place the start of the conflict in 1974, when Turkish troops invaded and forced them from their homes, lands, and businesses in the north part of the island. For the Turkish Cypriots, the conflict started well before that, at least in the 1950s, when the Greek Cypriots were fighting a guerrilla war against the British colonizers in order to force union with Greece. For the Turkish Cypriots, this was an attempt to officially Hellenize the island and force the Turkish Cypriots to leave. In the view of the Turkish Cypriots, the 1974 intervention by the Turkish motherland was the result of a long chain of persecutions by the Greek Cypriots, leaving Turkey with no choice but to step in and "rescue" the Turkish Cypriots from annihilation.

These are but two examples of dozens of ways that perceptions of history create and fuel the conflict between the two groups. In order for an alliance to be formed, the parties have to work through these perceptions and develop an understanding and appreciation of each other's point of view. Furthermore, they must work to form a shared vision of the island's future, so that in spite of the differences in their interpretations of the past, they can move beyond these opposing views to create a place where both communities can live in peace and work toward common goals.

Although the situation is probably different when intercultural alliances are formed in less conflictual circumstances, I have the feeling that perceptions of history still play a major role. For example, the images of the other that have been presented to us during our education process significantly influences our perceptions of the other in most of our relationships, and particularly when the other is from a different ethnic group, social class, sexual orientation, religious background, etc.. I believe that overcoming these perceptions is a major concern in developing any kind of intercultural alliance.

Another concern about establishing intercultural alliances that occurred in the Cyprus group had to do with a mismatch in orientation to action. The Greek Cypriots were more proactive, risk-taking initiators than the Turkish Cypriots, who took a more reactive, careful, wait-and-see attitude to events and activities. Thus, the Turkish Cypriots tended to view the Greek Cypriots as impulsive and controlling, while the Greek Cypriots saw the Turkish Cypriots as docile and unwilling to take a chance in order to move things forward. In addition, the Greek Cypriots were more willing to work actively to define the future, while the Turkish Cypriots seemed (to the Greek Cypriots) to dwell on the past. (It is interesting to note that by "U.S. American norms," both groups would appear to emphasize the past entirely too much.)

This mismatch in approach to "doing" presented a significant barrier to the formation of an intercultural alliance between the two groups. The Greek Cypriots said they were continuously frustrated by what they perceived as the unwillingness of the Turkish Cypriots to join them on projects they had conceptualized, and the Turkish Cypriots said that they were constantly offended by the Greek Cypriots push for action. The Turkish Cypriots didn't trust the Greek Cypriots, who they saw as always taking steps without their participation. The Greek Cypriots couldn't understand why the Turkish Cypriots would complain about their initiatives, since the Turkish Cypriots wouldn't take initiative themselves. In addition, the Greek Cypriots felt that everything they did was with the best interests of the

Turkish Cypriots in mind. The situation was worse when the two groups couldn't meet, because then neither could listen directly to the concerns of the other, but even when they could meet and discuss the issues there was tension centered around when and how to take appropriate action, and what the form of this action should be.

My guess is that while the particular type of "mismatch" I have described in Cyprus may be different in interpersonal situations, the same dynamic might be at work there as well. To develop a successful intercultural alliance, it is likely that the two parties must find a way to reconcile, live with, or otherwise deal with the differences in style that are almost always present.

Brenda J. Allen

Ben's comments above imply that those who intend to build intercultural alliances should be mindful of a variety of cultural issues that members probably will display through communication styles. To deal with these, facilitators as well as members will somehow need to identify potential differences and then decide on how to address them. Otherwise, ethnocentrism might impede progress because each group believes that their "way" is the right and best one.

Tricia S. Jones

I'll comment a little on Brenda's and Ben's thoughts here. Trust building is key. Figuring out what builds trust is a cultural excursion in itself. I remember that the turning point in our relationship with the Black South Africans was when we were willing to visit the townships and go to their homes and meet their families and neighbors. It was the act of walking to the corner "store" in Thokoza to get a soda with some of the Black South Africans. I thought nothing of it. For them it was the turning point in their perception of me.

I would like to see more conversation about what trust means in general in these cultures that are allying, and how trust can be shown and lost. Such conversation wouldn't have to be between members of that alliance, it could be between an alliance member and someone from the general culture.

Benjamin Broome

The larger Greek Cypriot and Turkish Cypriot communities, who tended to see participants in our design sessions as "collaborating with the enemy,"

did not view positively the friendships and working relationships that were being formed by their compatriots. This can be examined in terms of Trish's earlier suggestion about "closeness and distance," as well as Mary Jane's observation about how intercultural alliances are embedded in larger systems. In order for any of the individuals even to meet with someone from the other side of the buffer zone, they had to endure criticism from their fellow citizens. As they collaborated more closely on joint projects, they were branded as traitors. They were attacked in the media, they received threatening phone calls, they sometimes lost job opportunities (a few even lost their jobs), and in some cases they had family members turn against them. On one occasion a participant was told that she was no longer welcome at a restaurant where she and her family had been eating for years. In a tragic case, someone who was the brother-in-law of one of our group members, who had been writing newspaper articles that were critical of the officials, was assassinated by a gunman who many assumed to be part of a government sanctioned group.

For the most part, these "attacks" made the formation of the alliances more difficult, increasing the tension within the group and making it easy for people to "give up" and withdraw from active participation. In several cases, the group lost members who decided it was not worth the danger it brought to their careers and families. And it was very difficult for many people to sustain commitment in the face of difficulties, because there was so little support for the group's work. Although the effect on the group of these "attacks" was mostly negative, the resistance participants experienced from the larger society also helped strengthen their intercultural alliance. The shared persecution served a bonding function within the group, providing a very tangible shared reality.

In many ways, I suppose that such pressures face most intercultural alliances. Becoming friends or working partners with someone outside one's cultural group often leads to criticism by one's own cultural group members, and sometimes it leads to rejection by family members, friends, or coworkers. Thus, to use Trish's notion, in order to become close in an intercultural alliance it may be necessary to create distance from one's friends, family members, or colleagues. Intercultural alliances seldom happen without a cost.

Brenda J. Allen

Ben, thank you for sharing your paper (Broome, 2001) and your in-depth comments. As I read your paper, I jotted down several notes. Like you, I

believe that allies must consider in-group responses or reactions to their involvement with "others." As you observe, they might encounter any number of sanctions, including being viewed as and/or called a traitor, or a (fill in the blank with any derogatory label)-lover, or much worse.

I recall an unexpected and jolting interaction after Matthew Shepard was murdered. A black male acquaintance of mine used harsh words to express his opinion that "their" (meaning gays) issues were not comparable to "ours" (meaning blacks). Because I had always viewed this person as compassionate and concerned about social justice, I was floored. And, I am ashamed to confess, I was too concerned about how he might respond to me to refute or otherwise challenge his comments. I felt like I'd been punched in the stomach, and that I had to act as if I hadn't. Although I didn't agree with him, he surely took my silence to symbolize agreement.

Tricia S. Jones

Hello everyone. Yes, here I am, back in the conversation. Since I have so much to catch up on I thought I'd do it this way, starting from the most recent e-mails from Ben and working back.

On Perceptions of History: In reading Ben's comments about the Turkish and Greek Cypriots, I certainly resonated when he talked about their different perceptions of history. I saw some of the same thing (although not in as much clarity or detail) in the South Africa project where the British and Afrikaners wanted to mark the "history of South Africa" starting with their immigration and conquest (although they wouldn't have used the term "conquest"), and the Black South Africans of course wanted to go centuries, even millennia, back in their history of occupation of the land. This punctuation problem translated into different blame frames and different assumptions about needs for change. I don't think that there needs to be a common framing of history in order for intercultural alliances to proceed; but, I do think there needs to be a common understanding of where the frames differ. It's a certain form of perspective-taking that seems to be very important in understanding the other's motivation and action.

On Imaging a Future: I also started thinking about a related condition that I think must be present for intercultural alliance and that is an ability to conceive of a certain kind of future where alliance is a reality. This overlaps a little with the visioning ideas of others, but let me give an example. At the end of the USIA project we had a full day "conference" with all the adult and student members of the project as well as members of their communities who had not yet been directly involved. During the afternoon of the

conference we facilitated a visioning workshop as a means of having them talk about very long-term goals for continued action (we asked them to imagine the South Africa of 2050 and to talk about what it would be like in their ideal and what it would take to get there). At the request of the students we had two groups—an adult group and a high school student group. Both groups were very multicultural. And, in both groups the majority of members had not worked together before.

At the end of the afternoon, each group was going to present their "visions" and "action lines" to the other group. Two hours passed and the adult group had not progressed at all. They were complaining that this was impossible, that there were too many pragmatics to consider, and so on and so forth. They actually started talking about how to help the students face this disappointment (of course assuming that the students were as blocked as they were). The students came in and asked whether we were ready to see what they had come up with. They proceeded to unfurl a huge banner on which they had developed a 50-year timeline of action leading to a well-articulated future reality. Literally, in 2 hours, they had created a future that they could articulate, critique, modify, and bond together about. The adults were stunned, truly speechless, in genuine awe (I was one of them). That moment has stayed with me as much more than a "Nike moment" ("see it and you can be it"). These students weren't "playing at" alliance. They were planning for and engaging in alliance because they allowed themselves to perceive a future so radically different from the present. I don't know where that ability comes from or how you can engender it in one who does not possess it. I wish I did. But I am convinced that it is an absolutely critical part of getting people from diverse backgrounds to work together.

On Mismatch of Styles: I think Ben is right on target with his comments about how mismatches in style can undermine an intercultural alliance. They don't necessarily ruin it, but they can certainly slow things down and create unnecessary conflict. In the USIA project one of the biggest problems was a difference in preference for direct communication (à la Tannen, 1986). The Black South Africans were very indirect in their language. So much so that there were times when I would have paid for a direct answer. But, as we learned later, the directness that the U.S. Americans sought (and that the British and Afrikaners were comfortable giving) was extremely uncomfortable for the Black South Africans. The more we pushed, the less comfortable they felt telling us what we thought we needed to know in the way we needed to hear it. This style preference could easily have contributed to a perception of factionalization and bias in the team. In fact, initially my sense was that because the U.S.

Americans were so much more comfortable being direct with the British and Afrikaners, there was a good chance that the Black South Africans would feel left out, sided against.

When there is this difference of styles there is also the question of "who changes to suit whom?" Brenda's comments about authenticity in her e-mails and in her Sapphire and Sappho piece (thanks by the way, I loved reading that) really point out that one aspect of being authentic is to be able to communicate and act in the way you prefer rather than in the way that accommodates someone else's need or perception of you. When we asked the Black South Africans to be more direct in their speech by more clearly stating preferences or more clearly articulating interests and demands, we thought we were simply trying to move forward in a collaborative process. What we were also doing, unfortunately, was indicating implicitly that in order for us to collaborate "well" with them, they had to become more like us. The parallel of a "doer" asking a more passive "be-er" to change applies as well.

So where does this leave us in terms of articulating conditions for intercultural alliances? I think it suggests some basic ones. The first is that members of the alliance should at least be open to, cognizant of, the potential for communication and behavioral style differences (while that seems simple, it is more than just seeing differences—it is a willingness to see differences as dissimilarities rather than disabilities). Second, it suggests an ability or willingness to metacommunicate about these differences in order to make them explicit and/or change them. And third, it suggests a willingness to embrace the explicit differences (a *vive la différence* approach) or work together to negotiate new behavioral and communication patterns that are novel for both to some extent.

More on Authenticity: This is a really complex issue, as others' comments have already indicated. I want to pick up on one exchange between Brenda and Ben that caused me to think. In responding to Brenda's comments about the ability to be authentic in terms of "being yourself," Ben mentioned, regarding the Cypriot conflict, the ability of participants to present themselves rather than defend the "national cause."

An important accomplishment is the ability to distance yourself from the cultural group in which you are perceived to be a member, even to the point of feeling comfortable critiquing yourself as well as others. While this ability is rarely a condition for beginning intercultural alliance, I think it is a product of effective intercultural alliances. In fact, it may be one of the most explicit signs of the development of trust in an intercultural alliance. This is similar to feeling comfortable enough with a friend to air some family

troubles. There are probably lots of routes to the general "end," but one is clearly being willing to start this process and hope that others reciprocate. If the focus of the alliance is to mend some previous conflict, Ben's point about accepting responsibility for part of the conflict becomes even more important.

One other thought about authenticity is that one needs to be willing to support someone who does not want to change, even if that means she or he is obstructing some other "forward" progress of the alliance. And, of course, this is tricky because of the potential consequences. The more usual behavior when faced with "authentic obstinance" (as one might term it) is to delimit interaction with the other rather than try to find different ways to work with his or her authenticity. Allow me another little ramble down memory lane on the South Africa project.

About halfway through the project, it became clear that there was an ongoing conflict between the British and the rest of the team (including me and the U.S. Americans). From my perspective (this was shared by others but I'll own it), the British were fine with the project as long as they were seen as "better" than the others. By "better" I mean, that their decisions were recognized as better than the others, that their information was seen as better, and that their general "wisdom" about how to handle things was seen as better. (I know that this sounds really nasty, but I'm being authentic— this is what I really thought). I believe that the British were being very authentic in their presentation. I also believe they could have been much "nicer" and much less authentic in order to "get along." But they chose not to. The response of the rest of the team was to subtly but consistently marginalize them. Communication practices, meeting places, decision-making structures, and so on were all altered in order to diminish the British influence as much as to handle tasks of the project. At the time, I believe that most of us felt it was the only way to move the project forward, and maybe it was a case where a complete intercultural alliance with all parties was not realistic or feasible. But, after the smoke settled, I often thought that there were ways to negotiate with the British team members differently—ways that would have allowed them their "superiority" in the service of the alliance rather than as an obstacle to alliance.

Of course, this raises the very thorny issue of true equality and acceptance. Do you really have to equally value and respect people in order to work with them? If we do, then I think we're in a world of hurt when it comes to forging alliances. Because I believe that for some people (groups, cultures, etc.), perceived superiority is an absolute cornerstone of their identity. I could go on at great length about this, but I won't. Suffice it to

say, there are those folks who will never see the other as equal, or see the other as even close to equal. They may move more in the desired direction, but they'll never get there. What are we to do with them? If we ostracize them, delimit them, dispose of them, we are limiting our own ability to forge alliance. It seems more strategic and beneficial to try and understand ways of allying with those who will never truly accept us.

On the Presence of the Other: I know we've talked about the importance of the broader community and I want to reinforce how critical it is in terms of a condition for effective intercultural alliance. So let me use a metaphor from *In Search of Excellence* (Peters & Waterman, 1982). There's a story in that book about the guys at 3M who invented Post-it® notes. The inventor explains that they needed to hit a "midpoint" in "adhesiveness." Too little stickiness and the note just falls off. Too much stickiness and the note tears the paper. I think the external community has to be in a "midpoint of readiness" for an intercultural alliance. If there is no conflict or tension in the broader community, there is no real motivation for an alliance to occur. It's just too easy to do nothing. However, if there is too much resistance to the alliance it can be torn asunder. Where the midpoint is and how large the midpoint range is for any conflict varies with the situation. But as a general rule, I'd argue that having reached this midpoint is a critical condition for effective intercultural alliance.

This contextual support can be created and managed. It needs to be monitored and managed as the alliance changes. Perhaps one of the true contributions of dialogue processes is in monitoring and maintaining this midpoint that allows for smaller groups with more targeted action to create alliances and induce change.

Brief Thoughts About Victoria's Questions (to Ben): Victoria asked what conditions make possible intercultural alliances. I just wanted to say that I really like Ben's ideas. In the South African case I would also add a general expectation by the broader society of the success of intercultural alliances. The fact that so many people and institutions throughout the world wanted to see these kinds of changes in South Africa was not a minor factor. It came up in our conversations frequently. It gave us hope, and gave others a sense of responsibility.

Victoria asked "What was the nature of their dialogue in the process?" At the end of the project it was clear to me that one of the very best things that happened in the project was the informal conversations that began between members of the teams and that were able to take place outside of the whole team gatherings. It reminded me that first and foremost people relate to

other people, not to groups. By allowing, providing, and/or reinforcing opportunities for that kind of interpersonal dialogue to happen, we inadvertently strengthened the group alliance.

Victoria asked how the construction of the intercultural alliances evolved over time. A critical process that receives little attention is how the new participants in the alliance are brought in, oriented, and engaged in the dialogue. The "admittance" of individuals and groups should be given more thought than it often gets.

Finally, Victoria asked to hear more about the facilitation. Although the USIA project was successful, it was probably successful as much in spite of me as because of me. In hindsight, I would have done a great deal differently. But, the one thing I believe I did (as did others) in our facilitation of the process was to try and keep the purpose of the project (ultimately serving the children of these communities) at the forefront. It was our touchstone and allowed us to overcome the more tension-ridden moments of the process. I'm sure there's some great mythic metaphor that I can't remember—one that tells of the voice that continues to lead the way through the storm (not that I see myself as that mythic figure, just that there is the need for someone to serve that purpose). This is kind of like the "lighthouse" idea. As long as there is someone to bring up the vision and help people to keep seeing it, you can rally. It really is bigger than "us." (If you're humming "As Time Goes By" and seeing Bogie tell Bergman "We don't amount to a hill of beans," then you've got my general drift.)

Brenda J. Allen

Thank you, Trish, for your insightful and provocative comments. You've got me thinking about several things, but I'll focus on just a few of them for now. You said, "It reminded me that first and foremost people relate to other people, not to groups." I totally agree with this sentiment. It seems that we need to strike a balance between recognizing that people are individuals and seeing them as members (and sometimes representatives) of various social identity groups.

When talking about the conditions that make possible intercultural alliances, Trish, you said, "I really like Ben's ideas. . . . In the South African case I would also add a general expectation by the broader society of the success of intercultural alliances." This point, as well as Ben's descriptions, elicited two related conditions that I think might facilitate intercultural alliances: buy-in by appropriate stakeholders at the local level and higher and

availability of a variety of resources (e.g., communication media and techniques, meeting locations that all parties can and will access). What other resources might be helpful?

As for the question, "Do you really have to equally value and respect people in order to work with them?" Now that's a tough one. I guess it depends on what you're trying to accomplish, as well as the extent to which participants will have to interact with one another. For instance, if the goal is to develop policy and then to disband, perhaps valuing and respecting one another is not as crucial as getting the job done. On the other hand, if the parties must somehow interact and work together for an extended period of time, I can't see how they could succeed, especially if they were aware of the dynamics. But maybe the groups or individuals others do not value or respect can transcend the situation (a) for the sake of the goal, and/or (b) because they do not "need" the others to respect or value them.

Trish, you note that "A critical process that receives little attention is how the new participants in the alliance are brought in, oriented, and engaged in the dialogue. The 'admittance' of individuals and groups should be given more thought than it often gets." Good point. Adding members can disrupt a group's cohesiveness. Alliance participants probably should discuss and agree upon procedures for admitting, and even orienting, new members.

Brenda J. Allen

Ben, do you think that your role as facilitator, as well as your education and experience, helped you to recognize and respond to the differences in orientation to action? Also, do you think that participants would have effectively dealt with the mismatch without you or someone like you?

Benjamin Broome

I am quite sure that my education and experience helped me recognize and respond to the differences in orientation to action. I give credit especially to my experience studying, researching, and teaching intercultural communication.

It is difficult to say how the participants would have dealt with the mismatch (that I discussed earlier) without an experienced facilitator. It is likely that they would have had more problems dealing with these differences. However, with their level of commitment to peace in Cyprus, I am sure they would have managed to keep moving forward, in spite of the obstacles. Probably more than anything I did, their level of commitment to

a shared goal—or at least their realization that the goal they held could not be reached without the other—is what leads to their progress.

Brenda J. Allen

A related concern implied by your comments and your paper is a need to train or otherwise orient alliance members to communicate with one another. Listening certainly is key, as is "relational empathy" (Ben, did you coin that term, and how does it contrast with "dialogue"?).

Benjamin Broome

Relational empathy, a concept I wrote about in the early 90s (see Broome, 1993), undergirds most of my research and practice in intercultural communication. Basically, I use the term to mean the process of creating shared meaning and joint action between individuals or within a group. Traditional conceptualizations of empathy, usually viewed as a psychological construct that involves one person empathizing with another, have real limitations in intercultural encounters. To become useful, especially in conflict situations, I believe it is necessary to treat empathy as a relational process that involves individuals and groups working together to build a collective interpretation of the situation they face and to develop a consensus for performing joint action. For me, relational empathy lies at the heart of forming intercultural alliances. Without it, people might be able to get along on a superficial level, and society might be able to function over a period of time without major disruptions, but only through the practice of relational empathy can meaningful alliances be formed and maintained between parties that start out with division, mistrust, misconceptions, and the other obstacles that invariably accompany intercultural situations. As a third-party facilitator, I see it as one my responsibilities to develop and apply consensus-building methodologies that promote relational empathy. This is the essence of the work in which I have been involved with other groups (see Broome, 1995; Broome & Christakis, 1988).

Brenda J. Allen

A few other concerns described in Ben's postings include the need to build and maintain trust among alliance members and to clarify goals. For the latter, I can see the value of applying group techniques. However, I realize that some of the techniques that I teach in the United States (e.g., a

sequenced problem-solving model) might not be appropriate or well received in other countries. As I type this, I realize that some of them might not even be appropriate for groups in the United States!

Benjamin Broome

I agree completely! I agonized long and hard in Cyprus about the cultural appropriateness of the methodologies I used. Although I did not change significantly the basic structure of the process that I often employ with groups in the United States, I did adapt the implementation of the process in many ways to the culture of Cyprus. One of my biggest complaints about some of my conflict resolution colleagues who worked from time to time in Cyprus is that they did not seriously consider how the methods they implemented were culture bound.

Tricia S. Jones

It may be that the best alliances are those where people feel connections on an interpersonal level completely apart from whatever the task or goal of the alliance is. It seems to me that Brenda's questions to Ben earlier about his abilities and background as a facilitator may also be very relevant here. As is his notion of relational empathy. Ben, have you consciously used an interpersonal relational building focus to encourage relational empathy in some of your work? Could you talk a little more about that?

Brenda, you wrote about "two related conditions that might facilitate intercultural alliances: buy-in by appropriate stakeholders at the local level and higher and availability of a variety of resources (e.g., communication media and techniques, meeting locations that all parties can and will access)." Brenda, do you have a sense of the kinds of stakeholders who are absolutely critical to have buy-in from? I know this is very context related, but in a somewhat cynical way it seems to me that if you don't have buy-in from the government authorities that control access to the kinds of resources you mention, you are pushing the rock up the hill from the beginning. For long-distance alliances, I think a serious look at communication technology is very important. I know that technology had a very important impact on the USIA project. Some team members automatically became gatekeepers simply because they were the only ones with access to the communication technology.

I would also add that an important resource, but one difficult to define in all cases, is the support of the people or element of society that many feel

have the higher ground. For example, having the support of the clergy and/or church in South Africa was very important. If they expressed support for the project's efforts, then there was a certain credibility conferred that didn't have to be singularly earned.

Brenda, I think you made a very good point about the long-term and relational goals of the alliance. It is hard to want to stick it out in a relationship with someone who sees you and yours as illegitimate, as in the South African project. One of the strangely freeing aspects for the black South Africans was that they came into the project assuming they would not be respected by the Afrikaners and British. I don't think they had any idea of obtaining respect as a goal in the project. As a result, I think they did gain the respect they did not seek.

Benjamin Broome

I believe that we are discussing a nice complementary mix of alliances in this dialogue. Brenda is writing about a dyadic alliance at the interpersonal level. Trish is writing about a work-group alliance. I am writing about an intergroup alliance in which I was playing the role of third-party facilitator. It's great to see common themes emerging that run across these three types of alliances. Now I'd like to offer a few short responses to questions that were raised earlier.

Brenda, I like the two conditions you articulated. The "buy-in" at the local level and higher has not occurred yet in Cyprus, although conditions have improved somewhat, at least on the Greek Cypriot side, from the days when members of the group were viciously attacked in the media. Although these early attacks made it difficult for the group, causing a few of them to drop out, in some ways their out-group status was one of the bonding factors that brought the two different community groups closer together. Both were experiencing persecution and this was something each side could understand about the other. Taken too far, however, and existing for too long, this negative pressure wears down people and can help bring such movements to an end. The second condition you mentioned, availability of resources, was a continual struggle for the group. Two of the factors that allowed the peace movement to grow in Cyprus were (a) the availability of better meeting space (which became irrelevant when permission was no longer granted for bicommunal meetings) and (b) widespread access to the Internet (which occurred about the same time as the permissions stopped). Most of the early bicommunal meetings were held in a former hotel in the buffer zone that had been caught in the cross-fire of the 1974 war. It was

used by the U.N. forces to house their troops, so it had been repaired and was in a functioning state. However, it was a depressing place to meet, with paint flaking off the walls, drapes that were not working, a very dirty red carpet on the floor, broken chairs, very little heat (and very noisy heaters), dim light, no working toilets, no access to food, and bullet holes to remind all of us of the war. When the bicommunal activities started flourishing in 1996, the Fulbright office in Cyprus obtained funds to build a meeting space in the buffer zone, where groups could convene in better conditions. Just the fact that such attention was given to the group helped buoy everyone's feelings, and the well-lighted room with comfortable chairs and tables, and so on made a great difference (although the photos of U.S. Ambassadors, State Department personnel, the U.S. American President, etc. didn't help!). Unfortunately, after only about 6 months of using the meeting space, the Turkish Cypriot authorities closed the checkpoint and further meetings could not take place. The building has been used by the Greek Cypriots, who have access to it from the south, but very few bicommunal events have been held there in recent years. Fortunately, the availability of Internet access, which came along about the same time, allowed those individuals who already knew each other to continue their communication, and it led to quite a few projects.

Brenda, I'd like to add one more comment to the very important point you raised earlier. As I discussed before, I have seen it happen many times that U.S.-American trainers bring in their U.S.-developed techniques and try to apply them without sufficient given to the cultural appropriateness of these techniques in the new cultural setting. At the same time, however, it has been my experience that some of the methodologies that have been developed in the United States can, if implemented with the appropriate degree of cultural sensitivity, make a positive difference. Cultures can be enriched by appropriate "imports," although they can be destroyed by selfish and arrogant imposition of outside products. So for me the important principle is mindful application of conflict resolution techniques and principles. (I have discussed this in more detail in Broome, 1997.)

Thanks Trish, for picking up on the point about relationship building and relational empathy. I think these two processes lie at the core of intercultural alliances. I know that working relationships can be established between persons or groups without a strong sense of interpersonal connection, but I've never seen that happen in Mediterranean cultures. Everything seems to revolve around the interpersonal relationship, including the effectiveness of an outside facilitator. And once a strong interpersonal relationship is established, then it can "withstand" a lot of disagreement and

argument. When the interpersonal relationship isn't there, then disagreement about issues stands in the way of the interpersonal relationship. In Cyprus, I spent much more time at dinners in people's homes, going on excursions with friends, and other social activities than I did in formal meetings. And group work of every sort—workshops, seminars, and trainings—almost always included a social component. Even when a social event was not planned as part of a meeting, we sometimes spent more time in pre-meeting social talk and long breaks than we did in content discussions. It was almost impossible, in fact, to hold a meeting without food and drink. To a group I took to Brussels, for a week of meetings at the European Commission, I said (after a particularly difficult day together) that they spent most of their day saying things to destroy the group and then most of the evening at dinner (and well into the night) repairing (though jokes, songs, storytelling, and sometimes dances) everything they had broken during the day! I've speculated that one of the biggest drawbacks to the Green Line that separates the two communities is that they still have plenty of time to create conflict, but because they can't eat together in the evenings they have no opportunity to resolve conflict.

Nevertheless, social activities are not enough by themselves to lead to a resolution of the Cyprus conflict. Relational empathy requires dialogue, and the structured sets of activities we implemented with the groups were designed to help participants create new understandings and new frameworks for viewing the situation. Neither side can adopt the point of view of the other as their own, but together the two sides can build a collective vision and joint framework for action.

Mary Jane Collier

Thank you, Ben, for your detailed account of the actions you took as a facilitator in Cyprus. Brenda, I'm wondering about the specific actions that you and Anna took in your department. How did you talk about the need for attention to lesbian and/or gay issues among the faculty, and did you work with Anna to decide how to raise awareness? Which actions would you say were particularly successful?

Brenda J. Allen

Anna and I had more of an informal alliance than those that Ben and Trish described. We also worked together rather than helping others to work together. Basically, we supported, informed, and encouraged one another in

our quest for social justice. When we worked together in a university department, we were advocates for addressing "issues related to oppression and domination in its many guises" (Allen, 2000, p. 181). Without formally agreeing to do so, we became allies within our department.

Formally, we were members of the diversity committee. We convened meetings with faculty and graduate students to discuss curricular issues related to diversity. As I recall, those meetings were not particularly successful. Attendance, which was voluntary, was relatively sparse, which could have been due to a variety of factors. I can't recall much about those meetings except feeling frustrated. I don't even remember our agreeing on what we meant by "diversity," and it seems that we concentrated more on race than on any other aspect of social identity.

Anna specifically introduced the topic of sexual orientation at an off-site faculty retreat. She had invited a gay student to write a memo to faculty to express his sense of invisibility based on his experiences in a particular course, as well as generally within the program. Anna disseminated copies of the memo and invited faculty to talk with her or to discuss how we might address the student's concerns. Except for me, no one ever said anything to Anna about the memo. I confirmed this with Anna last night, just to be sure. Some time later, Anna placed a copy of the memo in everyone's mailbox, again with an invitation to discuss it. Again, no one responded.

As coordinator of the introductory course in organizational communication, I began to require teaching assistants to assign Anna's article, "The Price of 'Passing'" (Spradlin, 1998). This was extremely effective. Some of the teaching assistants came to Anna for guidance on how to address sexual orientation not only in the organizational communication course but also as they developed as teachers. Anna recalls these as in-depth, often passionate discussions. At that time, Anna was the director of teaching assistants who taught public speaking, and she was the lead teacher for multiple sections of public speaking. Numerous students who were or had been in the public speaking course who read her article in the organizational communication class came to talk with her. Some of them were gay or lesbian. They were relieved to know that someone like them was on the faculty. Some confided in Anna and asked for her advice. Others were not gay or lesbian, but they wanted to talk with Anna about other issues. For instance, they knew that she is Christian, and they wanted to discuss religion and sexual orientation. Some of them outright challenged her. Both gay and straight students asked her why she hadn't told them (their classes) about her sexual orientation. Although responses varied, the bottom line is that we "outed" the topic in our department, and that was wonderful.

Another way that our alliance succeeded stems from the publication of Anna's essay, "The Price of 'Passing'" (Spradlin, 1998), and my essay, "Sapphire and Sappho" (Allen, 2000). Both of these are products of our alliance. Anna told me last night that she never would have written the essay had it not been for our relationship and my encouragement and support.

Similarly, if not for our relationship I never would have written my essay, which has been well received. Moreover, Anna often uses her essay when she conducts workshops for a variety of groups. I believe that many others are using these publications in diverse teaching and training situations. That's gratifying.

Victoria Chen

Thank you so much for the wonderful exchanges in the past few weeks. Mary Jane and I thought perhaps we should begin wrapping up the dialogue, and we would like to ask you for a final round of response on actions. All of you, in responding to one another's writing earlier, have in many ways elaborated on the notion of intercultural alliances and raised concerns about the process of accomplishing this idea. In some postings you've also begun to indicate a general direction for what needs to take place in order to address various issues.

At this point, Mary Jane and I would like you to respond more specifically with some action plans that might lead us to the visions of intercultural alliances that we have identified, and also with ideas for actions that would critically address the various concerns you've raised. Perhaps all of you could be so kind as to write one more round, to add to anything that has been said in our dialogue.

Let me just state some of the concerns and proposed actions that I have read in your postings. All of you mentioned the importance of trust in building intercultural alliances, and Ben specifically talked about two parties sharing (painful) history and experience and building a more similar perception of history. How do we do that? What do we do when (which is all too often) mutual understanding and respect have been built, but fundamental disagreement and tension still persist? What do we do about the mismatched action orientation that Ben pointed out? What about the issue of the tension between building an alliance with the outside group and needing to maintain "allegiance" to one's own cultural group, which all of you have mentioned in describing your projects?

These are complex, intriguing, and challenging issues. I don't mean that we need to generate specific "solutions," but I think that some kind of specific action plans that might address these concerns would be helpful. What are some actions or practices that can build relational empathy? What can be done if colleagues in Brenda's department consistently refused to respond to Anna's invitation for a discussion on matters that are important to Brenda and Anna, and that should be important to everyone? I certainly think that having students and/or colleagues read your published articles is a great action to take in making changes and building intercultural alliances.

Regarding the cultural appropriateness of methodologies, you have raised some very fine points and highlighted the challenge of doing intercultural alliances, whether as a facilitator or a participant. Are there any specific actions that we can take to engage with this issue in addition to the discussion that we've had?

I think the buy-in process that Brenda emphasized is significant. Are there any more specific suggestions on how to do this in a specific context? I like Trish's point that we relate to people, not groups, and her example of building trust via a simple action such as walking together to the corner store. Are there any other actions that we can take to build trust?

All of you mentioned the importance of building and/or enhancing support and resources in accomplishing visions of intercultural alliances. For Trish's project, connecting with the clergy and church is important; in Brenda's case, departmental and university participation and genuine support are necessary; and for Ben's project, local government and communities play a critical role in making changes possible. What else?

Thank you all for your ongoing participation in this dialogue. You've enriched my understanding and broadened the scope of my thinking.

Brenda J. Allen

As I reflected on what actions one should take, I realized that prior to taking action, one must be motivated. So, I thought about how to motivate oneself and others to form and engage in intercultural alliances. People might ask, Why bother? What's in it for me? My responses offer a testimony that might contribute to the dialogue. Intercultural alliances have facilitated my personal growth and development. I am more empathic, open-minded, and mature. I have a more diverse group of friends and acquaintances, and my quality of life is enhanced. I think it's easy and

expected for us to limit ourselves, to stay within certain circles. But now that I have a taste of how wonderful difference can be, I'm hooked for life! Experiences in intercultural alliances have also informed and advanced my teaching. I have acquired information that enriches the content of my teaching, and I have become more sensitive to students' needs. The gay student who wrote the memo to my department helped me to better understand how someone might feel excluded. I had dealt with this idea as it relates to race and gender, but I had not actively considered sexual orientation. Now I have expanded this notion to include class, religion, and ability. I strive to somehow acknowledge social identity differences throughout my teaching (e.g., in content, examples, anecdotes, etc.), regardless of the subject matter, and not simply as a special topic or afterthought.

My research program also has benefited. As I mentioned earlier, I became interested in studying gender and feminism as a result of an intercultural alliance with Karen Ashcraft, a white graduate student who needed a professor to direct an independent study on feminism. At around the same time, I was working on a project on socialization of faculty and graduate students of color. This project was outside of my formal specialty of computer-mediated communication. Those two endeavors moved me to change my focus to gender and race. Then, my experiences with Anna prompted me to include sexual orientation. A series of other occurrences led me to this moment of being engaged in this dialogue on intercultural alliances at the same time that I am teaching a course on it and writing a book titled *Difference Matters: Communicating Social Identity in Organizations*. Fascinating!

The reasons cited above lead me to a final reason for becoming involved in intercultural alliances: I believe that I am helping and have helped in my small way to heighten awareness of what I consider to be important societal issues, to promote social justice, and by being an agent of change. Thus, intercultural alliances can be rewarding, gratifying, and enjoyable. Although they also can be extremely challenging, the effort for me has always been worthwhile.

Actions: Be proactive. Most of my experiences, including this dialogue, have been serendipitous, or at least initiated by someone else. I plan now to ponder ways that I might originate new alliances, or cultivate existing ones. Various types of intercultural alliances are possible. Figure out what kind you might create (or are already engaged in) and go for it!

Persist. Organize. Record experiences. Keep track of progress. Identify needs. Enlist support from a variety of sources. Communicate. Disclose

positive and negative feelings. Express concerns. Share experiences. Provide information. Listen to content and emotion. Clarify for yourself and for alliance members why you're involved. Seek a variety of venues for disseminating information and insight. Collect materials (training techniques, exercises, books, articles, videotapes, Web sites, etc.) that might be useful for anyone who is building or working in intercultural alliances.

Acknowledge and celebrate victories, however small they may be. Identify and interact with others who have experience with intercultural alliances. Engaging in this cyberdialogue has enlightened, affirmed, and motivated me. If key entities do not buy in, or do not offer adequate support, strategize as to how you and your allies can move ahead anyway. I realize that by telling my story I took action rather than waiting for others to do so. I exercised the power I had as course coordinator to place sexual orientation into at least one segment of the curriculum, and to educate and enlighten some of the teaching assistants. However, I don't recall making a conscientious decision, that is, saying, "Well, if they won't act, then I will." In hindsight, I wish that I had enlisted Anna's assistance to develop a plan of action. Anna recently told me that she decided to relent because she felt tired of initiating the conversation, and she didn't want to seem pushy. She also was frustrated because she knew that even if our colleagues agreed to do something, they would expect her (and probably me) to offer guidance. As I write this, I see that I might have been more empathic with Anna during that time. So another lesson is that we should practice relational empathy with our alliance team members as well as with others with whom we might be working.

Finally, there is something that we have not addressed: I think one should know when to pull up stakes and move on. The good and bad news is that there's always work to be done. Therefore, if you don't feel that you're making sufficient progress in one situation, and/or if the challenges seem insurmountable, you should look for (or create) another opportunity that seems more desirable and amenable.

Benjamin Broome

I think that Brenda has done a thorough and inspiring job of discussing action that one can take to make intercultural alliances "work." For the moment, I want to add one thought. In addition to Brenda's excellent note about personal motivation, I wanted to mention something about personal maintenance, especially during periods of intense facilitation of intercultural alliances. In order to remain effective as a facilitator, I had to "escape"

periodically for isolation and reflection. Fortunately, Cyprus afforded many places where I could enjoy a hike in the forest or along the sea. I found several places where I could retreat and gain strength from the beauty of nature. Sitting by the sea, watching the sunset or sunrise, spending the night listening to the sound of the waves on the rocks, or just gazing at the stars—all these "getaways" helped me keep the work of the groups in perspective, reminding me that these natural forces have been around much longer than any of the difficulties we were experiencing. This helped give me strength to face the pressures and burdens of the work. For others in different circumstances, I can imagine that different outlets would work better, but perhaps those who find themselves in the role of promoting third-party alliances could benefit by keeping in mind the renewing power of personal retreats.

A few more thoughts about actions: Brenda offered some very wise advice: Recognize when it's not working and be willing to move on. Although Brenda was talking about intercultural alliances in which you are one of the partners, I think the same applies to third parties who are facilitating intercultural alliances. Sometimes the parties themselves are not ready to move forward, or the third party is not an appropriate fit—in either case it is not helpful to force the issue. Sometimes there is another reason to "move on." When you have "played out your role" as a third party, and when staying in that role hinders the growth of the intercultural alliance, then it is time to back away. It is not easy to judge when this is the case, and because the third party is so closely tied to the situation, she or he usually is not in a good position to know that it is time to step back. On the other hand, it might be hard for someone else to give helpful advice on this issue, because the person may not know the situation very well.

I don't know which is worse, to exit the stage too early, leaving the group in a "lost" state, or to stick around too long, promoting an unhealthy dependency. However, "moving on" should not mean to "abandon" the group. They will need support, encouragement, advice, and other forms of involvement "for the duration." And the third party, who has made a tremendous investment in the group, needs to feel a part of their progress and needs to maintain a sense of connection to the group.

For me, one of the most important aspects of appropriate third-party involvement in conflict situations is commitment. Before I accepted the Cyprus project, I had already adopted a posture that the "parachute in" mentality prevalent among U.S.-American conflict resolution practitioners doing work abroad was inappropriate in most cases and often counterproductive. I was concerned that the standard 9-month Fulbright term would be insufficient time for my work to have a meaningful impact, but I was

unsuccessful at the outset in persuading Fulbright to extend my stay. I discussed my concerns with Cypriots from both communities during the initial contacts and received confirming responses. My intense feeling for this position, and our persistence over many months, led eventually to two extensions of the Fulbright grant, which provided an added message of international support for local efforts. It is difficult to know how the work would have progressed without the continuous presence of a third party, but by remaining in Cyprus over a long period, I was able to play a meaningful role in expanding the work and in helping those involved move through several difficult situations that could have significantly hampered or even stopped the work for long periods of time. Over the years, I have continued to visit Cyprus regularly to work with an expanding group of peace builders on their joint projects, and I maintain regular contact with colleagues through telephone and e-mail. I am no longer living in Cyprus, working on a daily basis with my colleagues, but I remain involved and available when needed. Without a personal commitment, my work would have been "finished" a long time ago.

Victoria Chen and Mary Jane Collier

Conclusion

Working on this cyberdialogue has been an exciting and challenging process for us. We began in November 2001 with an initial conceptualization of this project, accompanied by many uncertainties and hesitations. Now, upon completion of this chapter, we feel enriched and motivated to continue the conversation. As the facilitators, we are very grateful to Brenda, Tricia, and Ben. Their initial excitement, commitment of time and energy, and willingness to engage each other's ideas is exemplary. Their involvement made the need for any facilitation at times quite unnecessary, and at other times a pleasure. Their openness to working with each other's ideas and collaborating in building visions, concerns, and actions for intercultural alliances offers us an alternative model of intellectual engagement.

This has been a learning process, as well as rewarding, for us to work together as cofacilitators. We have learned from each other and cherish our many conversations along the way. We hope this project provides a rich view of varied intercultural alliances that inspires readers. We invite you to participate in the continuation of this cyberdialogue with us, with each other, and with others; we hope that many will embrace the challenge

and rich potential of using critical dialogue as a means of transforming intercultural relationships.

REFERENCES

Allen, B. (2000). Sapphire and Sappho: Allies in authenticity. In A. Gonzalez, M. Houston, & V. Chen (Eds.), *Our voices: Essays in culture, ethnicity, and communication* (3rd ed., pp. 179-183). Los Angeles: Roxbury.

Broome, B. J. (1995). Collective design of the future: Structural analysis of tribal vision statements. *American Indian Quarterly, 19*(2), 205-228.

Broome, B. J. (1993). Managing differences in conflict resolution. In D. J. Sandole & H. van der Merwe (Eds.), *Conflict resolution theory and practice: Integration and application* (pp. 95-111). Manchester, UK: University of Manchester Press.

Broome, B. J. (1997). Designing a collective approach to peace: Interactive design and problem-solving workshops with Greek-Cypriot and Turkish-Cypriot communities in Cyprus. *International Negotiation, 2,* 381-407.

Broome, B. J. (2001, November). *Reaching across the dividing line: Building a collective vision for peace in Cyprus.* Paper presented at the annual meeting of the National Communication Association, Atlanta, GA.

Broome, B. J., & Christakis, A. N. (1988). A culturally-sensitive approach to tribal governance issue management. *International Journal of Intercultural Relations, 12,* 107-123.

Peters, T., & Waterman, R. (1982). *In search of excellence: Lessons from America's best run companies.* New York: Harper & Row.

Smith, K. K., & Berg, D. N. (1987). *Paradoxes of group life: Understanding conflict, paralysis, and movement in group dynamics.* San Francisco: Jossey-Bass.

Spradlin, A. L. (1998). The price of "passing" : A lesbian perspective on authenticity in organizations. *Management Communication Quarterly, 11,* 598-605.

Tannen, D. (1986). *That's not what I meant!: How conversational style makes or breaks relationships.* New York: Ballantine.

Author Index

Subject Index

Agency, 13, 14-15, 39-40
Alliances. *See* Intercultural alliances
Alternative dialogic modes, 3, 14
Anti-Semitism. *See Shtetl*
Apartheid. *See* South Africa
Appropriation dynamics, 21, 22,
    23, 29-31, 41
Artisans, 4, 11
    agency and, 13, 39-40
    appropriation dynamics and, 29-31, 41
    colonization and, 18-24
    commodification and, 19-22
    consumer expectations and, 12, 20,
        22, 27, 28, 33, 35
    contemporary work, 32-33,
        36-39, 43-44
    cultural representation and,
        17-18, 22-24
    hybridized creative forms and, 27
    identity, negotiation of, 35-41, 36
        (figure), 38 (figure), 40-41, 42
    primitivist tradition, 21-22
    representation, negotiation of, 27-31, 28
        (figure), 30 (figure), 41-42
    traditions, negotiation of, 31-35, 34
        (figure), 42, 43
See also Critical theoretical research
Asian diaspora. *See* Internet technology
Assimilationist trends, 19
Authenticity, 12-13, 17
    appropriation dynamics and, 29-31
    blood authority, 238-244

commodifying market pressures and,
    42-43
essentialism and, 84-85
politics of, 221-224, 226
primitivist tradition and, 21-22
racial purity, 19
See also Diasporic identity; Embodied
    negotiation
Autoethnography, 142-144

Born-Again Filipino movement, 256
Boundary work, 114-115, 138
Bridge methodology, 15, 49-50, 251
    demographic information, 57-58
    fictional ethnography, development of,
        54-55
    interview questions, 56-57, 78-80
        (appendix)
    participant solicitation, 77-78
        (appendix)
    setting, 55-57
    vulnerability and, 53-54

Classification systems, 23
    blood authority, 238-244
    categorical positionings and, 58
    race, definitions of, 96, 97, 98
Collective memory, 5-6, 189-190,
    215-216
    conjunctural analysis and, 194-195
    cultural memory, history and, 193-194
    diaspora, structuring of, 190-191

critical realism and, 143
fantasy chains and, 85-86
identitisation and, 113
race, polarity and, 82, 96-98
social subjectivities and, 192
whiteness phenomenon, 139
See also Collective memory; Fantasy
themes; South Africa
Sojourn experience. *See* Self-as-foreigner
South Africa, 4-5, 10-11, 107
alliance-building in, 126-128
authentic Africanness in, 117-120
black emotional work in, 110-111
cultural hybridization and, 112-113
cultural transformation, border work
and, 114-115
discursive patterns, multicultural
plebiscite, 115-116, 127
financial restitution issue, 120-125
rainbow nation metaphor, 109-110, 126
reconciliation/majority-rule and,
107-108, 110-111
semiosphere framework and, 108,
113-115
Truth and Reconciliation Commission,
role of, 109, 110-112, 126
white population in, 111-112,
114, 117-120
South Asian diaspora. *See* Internet
technology
Sovereignty movement, 222, 235
Starting-point-plus-process of
communication, 263-265
Status quo. *See* Power structures
Stereotyping, 17, 21
racialized identities, 60, 61, 62
representational practices and, 23, 41
stereotypic knowledge, 62-65
Symbolic convergence theory, 85

Tourism industry. *See* Artisans
Traditions. *See* Artisans; Embodied
negotiation
Translation process, 260-266
Transracial feminist alliances, 4
agency and, 13

allies in, 50-51
bridgework in, 49-50, 52-58, 77-80
(appendixes)
categorical positionings and, 58
cultural difference, fictional
ethnography of, 54-55
institutional structures, relationality and,
51-52
power imbalances and, 58-61, 63-64
stereotypic knowledge and, 62-65
unknowing and, 64-68, 71
vulnerability and, 53-54
white solidarity and, 55, 63
white space, normative production of,
68-70
See also Feminism; Interracial alliances
Trust, 9, 298, 302-303, 307
Truth and Reconciliation Commission, 109,
110-112

Westernization, 7, 10
feminist ideals and, 173
humanism, definition of, 91-92
orientalism and, 23
Whiteness ideology, 4, 81
embodiment and, 140
essentialist argument, 84-85
fantasy chains and, 85-86
hate-speech codes, 101-102
ideology and, 87-89, 92-93, 95
individualist thinking and, 92-93
inferential racism and, 99-100
intercultural communication and,
81-83, 139-140
interracial alliance building
and, 100-102
invisible centrality of, 95, 97, 98,
139, 142-143
pervasiveness of, 11
research trends, 102-103
rhetorical vision and, 85, 86-90
self-reflexivity and, 92, 93, 98-99
solidarity and, 54-55
whiteness, definition of, 84-85
See also Fantasy themes; Iceland; Panama;
South Africa

About the Editor

Mary Jane Collier (Ph.D., University of Southern California) is a Professor in the Human Communication Studies Department in the School of Communication at the University of Denver. Her research program focuses on the social construction and structural constraints affecting the enactment of interrelated cultural identifications and the negotiation of intercultural relationships. Her work appears in international and national journals. She is editor of Volumes 23 to 25 of *the International and Intercultural Communication Annual*. She has been a visiting scholar at the University of Cape Town and University of London. Her current research involves investigating dialogue and conflict and alliance relationships, as well as the intersections in discourse of race, ethnicity, gender, and class.

About the Contributors

Brenda J. Allen (Ph.D., Howard University, 1989) is an Associate Professor in the Department of Communication at the University of Colorado at Denver. Her scholarship focuses on organizational communication and social identity (e.g., gender, race, class, age, sexuality, and ability). She is completing a book titled *Difference Matters: Communicating Social Identity in Organizations.*

Benjamin J. Broome (Ph.D., University of Kansas, 1980) is a Professor in the Hugh Downs School of Human Communication at Arizona State University. His teaching and scholarship focuses on intercultural communication, conflict resolution, and group facilitation. His central concern is developing and applying culturally appropriate processes that allow groups in conflict to develop relational empathy and build consensus for collective action. He regularly facilitates workshops and seminars with a variety of groups and organizations in the United States, Mexico, Europe, and the eastern Mediterranean.

Aimee M. Carrillo Rowe (Ph.D., University of Washington, 2000) is an Assistant Professor of Rhetoric at the University of Iowa, where she also teaches in the Department of Women's Studies. She is working on a book on transracial feminist alliances. Her work has also appeared in the journal *Communication Theory* and the book *Our Voices: Essays in Culture, Ethnicity, and Communication* (Roxbury, 2000).

Victoria Chen (Ph.D., University of Massachusetts, 1988) is an Associate Professor in the Speech & Communication Studies Department at San Francisco State University. She teaches courses in culture and communication, systemic inquiry, and dialogue facilitation. She has published in

journals and is the author of several book chapters. She is also the coeditor of the book *Our Voices: Essays in Culture, Ethnicity, and Communication* (Roxbury, 2000). Her research interests include communication theory, with a focus on gender and cultural identity issues; the theory of coordinated management of meaning (CMM); and critical dialogue in systemic inquiry. She is a member of the Public Dialogue Consortium.

Leda Cooks (Ph.D., Ohio University, 1993) is an Associate Professor at the University of Massachusetts. Professor Cooks's research focuses primarily on power, identity, and culture. She has taught, trained, published, and presented research in the areas of interpersonal, intercultural, and organizational communication, communication/information technologies, and critical pedagogy. Her work has appeared in journals such as *Communication Theory, Communication Education, Electronic Journal of Communication, Communication Quarterly, Howard Journal of Communication, Western Journal Of Communication, Women's Studies in Communication, Feminist Media Studies, Mediation Quarterly, Negotiation Journal, World Communication Journal,* among others, and in edited books in the communication field. She is currently writing a book on museums, collective memory, and national identity and working on several research projects that focus on the power of place in constructing identities.

Jolanta A. Drzewiecka (Ph.D., Arizona State University, 1999) is an Assistant Professor in the E.R. Murrow School of Communication at Washington State University. Her research explores constructions of cultural and transnational identities, diaspora formations, and intergroup relations. Her work has been published in such journals as *Communication Theory, Communication Quarterly,* and *The Southern Communication Journal,* and in the *International and Intercultural Communication Annual.*

Elizabeth Fullon (MA, Harvard University, 1993) is a Ph.D. candidate at the University of Massachusetts, Amherst. Her research and teaching focus on cultural communication and qualitative methods of research.

Radhika Gajjala (Ph.D., University of Pittsburgh, 1998) is an Assistant Professor in Interpersonal Communication/Communication Studies at Bowling Green State University. She teaches courses on cyberculture, humanistic research methods, and feminist research methods in communication. Her research interests include new media technologies, critical theory, feminist theory, transnational communication, and postcolonial theory. She is a member of the Spoon Collective and runs a few online lists

related to gender and postcolonial theory. Her work has appeared in journals such as *Gender and Development, Feminist Media Studies,* and *Works and Days* and in books such as *Technospaces: Inside the New Media* (Continuum, 2001) and *Bolo! Bolo! A Collection of Writings by Second Generation South Asians Living in North America* (SAPNA, 2000).

Rona Tamiko Halualani (Ph.D., Arizona State University, 1998) is an Assistant Professor of language, intercultural communication, and cultural studies in the Department of Communication Studies at San Jose State University. Her main research interests focus on culture, identity, intercultural contact and race relations, globalization, diaspora, and transnationalism, especially in terms of Asian Pacific American groups and immigrant groups in the Silicon Valley. She has written a book titled *In the Name of Hawaiians: Identities and Articulations* (University of Minnesota Press, 2002).

Ronald L. Jackson II (Ph.D., Howard University, 1996) is an Assistant Professor of culture and communication theory in the Department of Communication Arts & Sciences at Pennsylvania State University. He is author of *The Negotiation of Cultural Identity* (Praeger, 1999), and of two dozen articles found in several peer-reviewed outlets in addition to five books in press. His theory work includes the development of two paradigms coined "cultural contracts theory" and "black masculine identity theory."

Tricia S. Jones (Ph.D., Ohio State University, 1985) is a Professor in the Department of Psychological Studies at Temple University in Philadelphia. Her teaching and research interests are in conflict processes, conflict resolution education, and developing emotional and conflict competence in children. Her research has been funded by the William and Flora Hewlett Foundation, the Packard Foundation, the Surdna Foundation, the United States Information Institute, and the State Justice Institute. She has coedited three books and over 40 articles on conflict. She is currently editor of *Conflict Resolution Quarterly.*

S. Lily Mendoza (Ph.D., Arizona State University, 2000) is an Assistant Professor in Culture and Communication at the University of Denver. She is the author of *Between the Homeland and the Diaspora: The Politics of Theorizing Filipino and Filipino American Identities* (Routledge, 2002). Her research interests include identity and cultural politics, cultural translation, nationhood, indigenization, transnationalism, and the politics and dynamics of cross-cultural theorizing.

Kathryn Sorrells (Ph.D., University of New Mexico, 1999) is an Assistant Professor in the Department of Communication Studies at California State University, Northridge. She is also a faculty member at the Summer Institute for Intercultural Communication in Portland, Oregon. She is currently working on a book titled *Women Creating New Mexico* that explores how artistic forms of expression are sites where intercultural communication issues such as cultural representation, identity, adaptation, and transformation are negotiated. As a professional potter and artist with a critical perspective on sociocultural interactions, Kathryn's personal and research interests include the politics and poetics of intercultural relations. She is particularly committed to engaged scholarship and is currently directing a community-based action research project addressing racial tensions in a Los Angeles area high school.

Melissa E. Steyn (M.A., Arizona State University, 1996) is the Director of the Institute for Intercultural and Diversity Studies of Southern Africa, University of Cape Town. A Fulbright scholar, Melissa has published on various aspects of diversity, including race, culture, gender, and sexuality. Her books include *Whiteness Just Isn't What It Used to Be: White Identity in a Changing South Africa* (State University of New York Press, 2001) and the coedited collection, *Cultural Synergy in South Africa: Weaving Strands of Africa and Europe* (Knowledge Resources, 1996). She is currently working on *The Prize and the Price: Shaping Sexualities in the New South Africa*.

Sean Tierney (M.A., Howard University, 2000) is a lecturer and doctoral student at Howard University in the Department of Communication and Culture.